INTRODUCTION TO CATALOGING AND CLASSIFICATION

Library Science Text Series

Audiovisual Technology Primer. By Albert J. Casciero and Raymond G. Roney.

The Collection Program in High Schools: Concepts, Practices, and Information Sources. By Phyllis J. Van Orden.

The Collection Program in Schools: Concepts, Practices, and Information Sources. By Phyllis J. Van Orden.

Developing Library and Information Center Collections. 2d ed. By G. Edward Evans.

The Humanities: A Selective Guide to Information Sources. 3d ed. By Ron Blazek and Elizabeth Aversa

Immroth's Guide to the Library of Congress Classification. 3d ed. By Lois Mai Chan.

Information Sources in Science and Technology. By C. D. Hurt.

Introduction to Cataloging and Classification. By Bohdan S. Wynar. 8th edition by Arlene G. Taylor.

Introduction to Library Automation. By James Rice.

Introduction to Library Public Services. 5th ed. By G. Edward Evans, Anthony J. Amodeo, and Thomas L. Carter.

Introduction to Library Science: Basic Elements of Library Service. By Jesse H. Shera.

Introduction to Library Services for Library Technicians. By Barbara E. Chernik.

Introduction to Technical Services for Library Technicians. 5th ed. By Marty Bloomberg and G. Edward Evans.

Introduction to United States Public Documents. 3d ed. By Joe Morehead.

The Library in Society. By A. Robert Rogers and Kathryn McChesney.

Library Instruction for Librarians. 2d rev. ed. By Anne F. Roberts and Susan G. Blandy.

Library Management. 3d ed. By Robert D. Stueart and Barbara B. Moran.

Micrographics. 2d ed. By William Saffady.

Online Reference and Information Retrieval. 2d ed. By Roger C. Palmer.

Problems in Library Management. By A. J. Anderson.

Reference and Information Services: An Introduction. Richard E. Bopp and Linda C. Smith, General Editors.

The School Librarian as Educator. 2d ed. By Lillian Biermann Wehmeyer.

The School Library Media Center. 4th ed. By Emanuel T. Prostano and Joyce S. Prostano.

The Social Sciences: A Cross-Disciplinary Guide to Selected Sources. Nancy L. Herron, General Editor.

BOHDAN S. WYNAR

INTRODUCTION TO CATALOGING AND CLASSIFICATION

eighth edition

ARLENE G. TAYLOR

1992
LIBRARIES UNLIMITED, INC.
Englewood, Colorado

LIBRARIES UNLIMITED, INC.
P.O. Box 6633
Englewood, CO 80155-6633

Library of Congress Cataloging-in-Publication Data

Taylor, Arlene G., 1941-
    Introduction to cataloging and classification / Bohdan S. Wynar. -
- 8th ed. / by Arlene G. Taylor.
    xvii, 633p. 17x25 cm. -- (Library science text series)
    Includes bibliographical references and index.
    ISBN 0-87287-811-2 (cloth) -- ISBN 0-87287-967-4 (paper)
    1. Cataloging. 2. Classification--Books. 3. Anglo-American
cataloguing rules. I. Wynar, Bohdan S. Introduction to cataloging
and classification. II. Title. III. Series.
Z693.W94 1991
025.3--dc20   91-24851
                                    CIP

Z
693
.W94
1992

Contents

Part IV
AUTHORITY CONTROL

25 – AUTHORITY CONTROL

Part V
ORGANIZATION

Preface to the Eighth Edition

Since the publication of the seventh edition of this text in 1985 there have been changes in virtually every area of bibliographic control. As a result the task of writing and revising in order to create this eighth edition has been formidable. Nevertheless, I have attempted to create the most current text for beginning and intermediate catalogers possible given the necessity of meeting publication deadlines.

There are a number of changes in this edition in addition to updating. Chapter 1, "Cataloging in Context," is new to this text. It is an introduction to the whole area of bibliographic control, instead of the introduction to descriptive cataloging found in chapter 1 of previous editions. Chapter 2, "Development of Cataloging Codes," has been expanded to show the continuity in development of cataloging rules from the time of Panizzi and to include developments leading to the publication of the *Anglo-American Cataloguing Rules, Second Edition, 1988 Revision (AACR2R)*.

Part II, "Description and Access," continues to be a discussion of descriptive cataloging using *AACR2R*. An introduction to descriptive cataloging precedes the discussion of rules. New rules and new Library of Congress (LC) rule interpretations have been incorporated, and most of the examples are new to this text. Discussion of some of the less-used rules has been eliminated from this edition in an effort to concentrate on the fact that this text is intended to be, as titled, an introduction.

A major revision in part III, "Subject Analysis," is the addition in chapter 15, "Subject Arrangement of Library Materials," of material discussing the process of determining what an item is about. In addition the publication of the 20th edition of the Dewey Decimal Classification prompted the complete reorganization and rewriting of chapter 17, "Decimal Classification." Discussion of LC Classification in chapter 18 has been thoroughly updated to reflect the numerous new editions of LC class schedules that have been published.

The major conceptual shift of LC Subject Headings from being a published list to being a constantly changing and growing entity, along with its being available online to many users, is reflected in the reorganization and rewriting of chapter 22. Many examples and explanations of MARC-formatted LC subject authority records have been added. In like manner the publication of the 14th edition of *Sears List of Subject Headings* prompted numerous revisions to chapter 23.

In addition to routine updating of material in the discussion of "Other Types of Verbal Analysis" in chapter 24, the section on PRECIS was completely rewritten, first to assist readers in understanding PRECIS strings in older MARC records from the British Library, and second, to reflect the changes in the subject analysis system now being used by the British Library.

Part IV, "Authority Control," is completely new to this edition. A new chapter on the subject has been added, pulling together aspects of the whole concept, regardless of its application to names, titles, or subjects. Examples from online catalogs, as well as examples of all types of MARC-formatted authority records, are used to illustrate the discussion.

Two appendixes are new to this edition. The first is an introduction to the USMARC format, and it includes examples of the same bibliographic record as it is displayed in four different systems. The second appendix gives instructions for typing catalog cards and includes a detailed analysis of the punctuation and spacing to be used when conforming to the International Standard Bibliographic Description (ISBD). In addition the glossary and bibliography have been completely reworked.

Examples of MARC records used in this edition are shown in the format that is displayed in OCLC's PRISM system. I am grateful to OCLC for permission to use their format in this book.

There are a number of people whose assistance I wish to acknowledge. First, I would like to acknowledge again the assistance of Hans H. Wellisch and the work he did for the subject analysis section of the previous edition. Although rapid change has dated some of his material, some of it is still in use in this edition.

I would like to acknowledge the assistance and moral support of my colleague, Richard P. Smiraglia, Assistant Professor, School of Library Service, Columbia University. He spent many hours talking with me about new ideas presented in this edition, and he read and commented upon several parts of the manuscript. In addition he did most of the work of revising the glossary for this edition, and the original outline for the appendix on the MARC format was his.

The major work of rewriting chapters 26 and 27 was completed by Barbara B. Tillett, Head, Catalog Department, University Library, University of California, San Diego. I am very grateful for her assistance.

Sherry L. Vellucci also deserves special thanks. While a doctoral student at the School of Library Service, Columbia University, she spent many hours looking for new examples to use in this edition and checking LC rule interpretations to determine how they would affect the text.

I am also grateful to four other people who gave their time in consultation on specific parts of the manuscript. Ann Case, Associate Director of Indexing Services, and Martha T. Mooney, Editor of the *Sears* List, both at the H. W. Wilson Company, gave valuable hours of their time reading the manuscript of chapter 23 and assisting me with updating it to agree with the 14th edition of *Sears*. Edward Swanson, Principal Cataloger, Minnesota State Historical Society, read the manuscript versions of chapter 3 and appendix B and made numerous helpful comments about the examples. Patricia M. Thomas, Head, Cataloging Department, Stockton-San Joaquin (California) County Public Library, provided many current examples from new cataloging and also examples of displays from the online catalog.

As for the previous edition, some current users of the text were invited to make suggestions for this edition, and again, there were many responses. All suggestions were seriously considered, and many were taken. Those who wrote and whose comments are greatly appreciated are James D. Anderson, Associate Dean and Professor, School of Communication, Information and Library Studies, Rutgers, The State University of New Jersey; Lawrence W. S. Auld, Chair, Department of Library and Information Studies, East Carolina University; Esther G. Bierbaum, Associate Professor, School of Library and Information Science, University of Iowa; William D. Boyd, Jr., Associate Professor, School of Library Science, University of Southern Mississippi; Lois Buttlar, Assistant Professor, School of Library Science, Kent State University; Florence E. DeHart,

Professor, School of Library and Information Management, Emporia State University; John O. Everette, Lecturer, School of Library and Information Science, Catholic University of America; John B. Hall, Associate Dean and Associate Professor, College of Information Studies, Drexel University; Joe A. Hewitt, Associate University Librarian for Technical Services, University of North Carolina at Chapel Hill; Sheila S. Intner, Professor, Graduate School of Library and Information Science, Simmons College; Patricia E. Jensen, Associate Professor, Graduate School of Library and Information Studies, University of Rhode Island; Tanja Lorkovic, Curator, Slavic Collection, Sterling Memorial Library, Yale University; S. Michael Malinconico, Ebsco Professor, School of Library and Information Studies, University of Alabama; Margaret F. Maxwell, Professor, Graduate Library School, University of Arizona; Leslie R. Morris, Director of Libraries, Niagara University Library; Nancy B. Olson, Professor, Memorial Library, Mankato State University; Larry N. Osborne, Associate Professor, School of Library and Information Studies, University of Hawaii at Manoa; Joseph W. Palmer, Associate Professor, School of Information and Library Studies, State University of New York, Buffalo; Kenneth C. Pengelly, Associate Professor, Library Media Education Program, Mankato State University; Kathleen Reed, Assistant Professor, College of Information Studies, Drexel University; Paule Rolland-Thomas, Professor, Ecole de bibliotheconomie et des sciences de l'information, Universite de Montreal; Theodore Samore, Professor Emeritus, School of Library and Information Science, University of Wisconsin—Milwaukee; Jerry D. Saye, Assistant Dean and Associate Professor, School of Information and Library Science, University of North Carolina at Chapel Hill; Lee Shiflett, Associate Professor, School of Library and Information Science, Louisiana State University; Ellen Soper, Assistant Professor, Graduate School of Library and Information Science, University of Washington; Lois N. Upham, Lecturer, College of Library and Information Science, University of South Carolina; Arnold S. Wajenberg, Principal Cataloguer, University Library, University of Illinois at Urbana-Champaign; and Francis J. Witty, Professor Emeritus, School of Library and Information Science, Catholic University of America.

I am particularly grateful to my husband, A. Wayne Benson, for his never-flagging patience, encouragement, and willingness to listen. He is the only one who truly understands how totally this project has consumed my life.

I continue to be grateful to Dr. Bohdan S. Wynar for the opportunity to publish this work he so ably initiated. I wish to thank the editorial and production staffs of Libraries Unlimited for their assistance—David Loertscher served as content editor, Louis Ruybal as managing editor, Anna Huff as copyeditor, and Judy Gay Matthews handled production, design, and typesetting. Rosanna O'Neil, Head, Catalog Department, University of Pennsylvania Library, created the index.

—Arlene G. Taylor

Part I

INTRODUCTION

Cataloging in Context

1

INTRODUCTION

The purposes of this chapter are to set the context in which cataloging takes place and to introduce the basic concepts of cataloging. The discussion begins with an introduction to the whole realm of bibliographic control and where catalogs fit into that realm. Catalogs are then discussed, with attention given to their functions, their forms, arrangements of their entries, and their component parts. An overview of the entire process of cataloging is then given — descriptive cataloging, subject analysis, and authority control — followed by a look at cooperative and copy cataloging that makes original cataloging of all materials for every collection unnecessary. Finally, there is an introduction to the formats of bibliographic records in catalogs.

BIBLIOGRAPHIC CONTROL

Definitions

Cataloging is a subset of the larger field that is sometimes called bibliographic control, and it is helpful to view it in that context. Bibliographic control has been defined by Svenonius as "the skill or art ... of organizing knowledge (information) for retrieval."[1] Smiraglia defines it as "encompassing the creation, storage, manipulation, and retrieval of bibliographic data."[2] Anyone who has attempted to maintain a file of references to articles, books, and other types of materials containing information on a particular subject, or perhaps by a particular artist or author, has practiced bibliographic control over a very small part of the universe of information/knowledge. For such a project to succeed it is necessary to decide what pieces of data to record about each article, book, or other container of information/knowledge. It may be decided to record author(s), title, keywords, abstract, and location of the item. These become the bibliographic data to be created, stored, manipulated, and retrieved. As the file grows, storing, manipulating, and retrieving become more and more complex. Then, art and skill become necessary for successful maintenance and use of the file.

In the universe of all knowledge (including knowledge that cannot necessarily be expressed verbally — e.g., music, art) there is a certain amount of that knowledge that has been recorded in some way — e.g., written down, printed, digitized, taped, painted. This subset is often referred to as the bibliographic universe. Only the bibliographic universe can be controlled. Such control is performed by means of bibliographic tools in which each discrete item of knowledge is represented by a bibliographic record (also sometimes called an entry). Bibliographic tools include bibliographies, indexes (both printed and online), catalogs, and bibliographic databases. We are told by futurists that someday when all recorded information/knowledge is digitized and available online, it will be possible to gain access to needed information directly online without the intermediate step of using bibliographic tools. While this is difficult to imagine, it may happen; but it will not happen without some kind of control. There is simply too much knowledge to make it even desirable to request, for example, every use of Shakespeare's name ever recorded.

Component Parts of Bibliographic Control

Librarians and library users have traditionally been taught that bibliographies, indexes, catalogs, and bibliographic databases are quite different tools. In fact they are all parts of the same realm of bibliographic control, but they have developed separately and in somewhat different formats for various reasons. Economic factors have been pervasive in the development of catalogs in libraries. Because libraries are generally not-for-profit agencies, there have seldom been enough resources to allow library catalogs to provide access deeper than what might be called "macrolevel indexing"—i.e., access to a whole book, entire serial, etc. Other agencies have stepped in to create indexes with what might be called "microlevel indexing"—i.e., access to articles in serials, poetry in collections, chapters in books, etc. These are sold for profit, while access to library catalogs generally has not been sold. (There are also indexes that analyze the contents of a single item—e.g., "back-of-the-book" indexes—but these are usually published at the same time as the item rather than being prepared later for the purposes of bibliographic control.) Economic constraints have also dictated generally that library catalogs could index only materials owned and housed in that particular library, and in this sense each one has been a microcosm of the entire bibliographic universe. On the other hand, periodical indexes have covered items owned and not owned by the library, or a larger portion of the bibliographic universe. Bibliographies typically cover much smaller parts of the universe than either catalogs or indexes. That is, each bibliography usually has one subject or theme—e.g., works of an author, works on a particular subject, items published during a particular time or in a particular place. (Subsets of this category include discographies and art catalogs.) Because of their limited scope, bibliographies can easily include entries at both macro- and microlevels.

In the recent past technology has enabled bibliographic databases to be developed without the earlier economic constraints that limited the level of indexing. Many online bibliographic databases are enhanced indexes. That is, they provide microlevel indexing of bibliographic entities and provide more bibliographic data for each item indexed—e.g., more keywords, abstracts. There are also a number of bibliographic databases that provide primarily macrolevel indexing and function as extended catalogs.

An important feature of catalogs is that they typically have some kind of authority control, while the other tools typically have little or no such control over names and titles, although they often have some control over subject terms used. Authority control is, in part, the process of maintaining consistency in the form of the headings in a bibliographic tool. A heading is the character string provided at the beginning of an entry in a bibliographic tool and provides the means for finding that entry. In some printed tools and in most computer systems the heading is provided at the top of a column, page, or screen on which several entries for the heading may appear. In a tool with authority control the heading is given in the "official" form representing a name, title, or subject. Authority control is defined and discussed in more detail later in this chapter.

One difficulty with the fragmentation of bibliographic control into different bibliographic tools is that users are expected to know about the existence of all of them and to be able to use them effectively. This is a somewhat unreasonable expectation since the tools overlap in their coverage of the bibliographic universe but provide their coverage in different ways. Approaches to searching the tools differ, as do the vocabularies used for searching. Once desired entries are found, conventions for displaying bibliographic data differ. In tools where there is no authority control, one cannot know whether all possible forms of a name, title, or term have been found. In an ideal bibliographic control environment a user could start with any tool and be led to other tools as needed without having to know ahead of time which tool would be appropriate.

Functions of Bibliographic Tools

Bibliographic tools have three basic functions. The first is the identifying or finding function. All tools aim at allowing a user, who has a citation or has a particular bibliographic item in mind, to match that known item with an entry in the tool – limited, of course, by the scope of the tool. The scope of a library catalog, for example, is usually the items owned by the institution; therefore, the user should be able to match or identify or find an entry for a known item that the library owns, but not for one that the library does not own.

The second function is the collocating or gathering function. Collocation is a means for bringing together in one place in a bibliographic tool all entries for like and closely related materials; for example, items about dinosaurs are grouped together. And in many cases a particular work is shown in its relationship to a larger group of works – e.g., the bibliographic record for a play based upon *Huckleberry Finn* should be found with records for editions of *Huckleberry Finn*, which are in turn found with records for other works of Mark Twain. One of the best ways of accomplishing collocation is through the process of authority control. If entries for *Huckleberry Finn* are sometimes found in the H's and sometimes in the A's under *Adventures of Huckleberry Finn* with no connecting references, collocation has not been accomplished.

The third function of bibliographic tools is the evaluating or selecting function. This function allows a user to choose from among many records or entries the one that best seems to represent the knowledge/information or specific physical item desired. For example, a user looking for a particular edition of *Huckleberry Finn* should be able to select it from among several, if it is one of those listed in the tool; or, given a choice between a spoken recording on tape or disc, a user could choose the one appropriate for the equipment available. It can be seen that the three functions are somewhat interdependent.

Uses of Bibliographic Control

Catalogers, indexers, abstractors, bibliographers, and information scientists establish bibliographic control over portions of the bibliographic universe. Reference librarians, readers' advisers, and information specialists create a bridge between the user and the many bibliographic tools available. The institutional library is a major focus of these activities, but not the only one. Individual free-lance efforts and commercial enterprises also play a role.[3]

The bibliographic tool *created* in the institutional library is the catalog, although extensive *use* is made of all the bibliographic tools in that setting. *Groups* of libraries work together to create some of the online databases—those that are essentially extended catalogs for the holdings of more than one library. The remainder of this book concentrates on the processes involved in creating, maintaining, and providing access to catalogs and catalog-like databases.

CATALOGS

Definition and Functions

A catalog is an organized set of bibliographic records that represent the holdings of a particular collection. A collection may consist of any of several types of materials—e.g., books, periodicals, maps, coins, sound recordings, paintings, musical scores, to name a few. Traditionally the collection represented by a catalog has been located in one place or at least in different parts of the same institution. Increasingly, however, catalogs represent the holdings of more than one library, as libraries form consortiums and otherwise link their catalogs for the purposes of interlibrary sharing. (Such catalogs are sometimes called union catalogs.)

Why prepare catalogs? Catalogs are necessary whenever a collection grows too large to be remembered item for item. A small private library or a classroom library has little need for a formal catalog; the user can recall each book, sound recording, map, or other such item by author, title, subject, the item's shape, its color, or its position on a particular shelf. When such a collection becomes a little larger, an informal arrangement, such as grouping the items by subject categories, provides access to them. But when a collection becomes too large for such a simple approach, a formal record is necessary. There are two major reasons to make such a formal record in larger collections: for retrieval and for inventory purposes. In addition to being unable to remember what is in a large collection for access purposes, it also becomes impossible for the collector to remember what has been acquired, lost, replaced, etc. A catalog can serve as a record of what is owned.

The functions of bibliographic control identified earlier—identifying, collocating, evaluating—are functions of every bibliographic tool, including catalogs. These functions for catalogs were first stated by Charles A. Cutter in his *Rules for a Dictionary Catalog* in 1904. His statement serves as the basis for today's understanding of the functions of a catalog although in modern practice the statement is somewhat incomplete:

Objects

1) To enable a person to find a book when one of the following is known:
   a) The author
   b) The title
   c) The subject

2) To show what the library has
   d) By a given author
   e) On a given subject
   f) In a given kind of literature

3) To assist in the choice of a book
   g) As to the edition (bibliographically)
   h) As to its character (literary or topical).

Means

1) Author entry with the necessary references (for a and d)
2) Title entry or title reference (for b)
3) Subject entry, cross references, and classed subject table (for c and e)
4) Form entry and language entry (for f)
5) Edition and imprint, with notes when necessary (for g)
6) Notes (for h)[4]

To conform to modern practice, the first objective needs to be rephrased as follows: To enable a person to find any intellectual creation whether issued in a print or nonprint format. Cutter's first object is inadequate even for printed materials inasmuch as "book" does not unambiguously encompass "periodical," "serial," or "pamphlet."

Cutter's object "e" also does not go far enough for our current understanding. Rephrased, it should read "on given and related subjects." It is clearly a prime function of a catalog to guide patrons in using the system of subject headings that any particular library may have adopted. Cutter's apparent assumption that the user always has a clearly formulated "given" subject in mind is contrary to all observation of catalog users.

Cutter's objectives remained the primary statement of catalog principles until 1961, when the International Federation of Library Associations (IFLA) at the Paris Conference approved a statement about the purpose of an author/title catalog. It stated that the catalog should be an efficient instrument for ascertaining:

1) whether the library contains a particular book specified by:
   a) its author and title, *or*
   b) if no author is named in the book, its title alone, *or*
   c) if author and title are inappropriate or insufficient for identification, a suitable substitute for the title,

and 2) a) which works by a particular author *and*
   b) which editions of a particular work are in the library.[5]

These principles, often called the "Paris Principles," were purposely restricted to an author/title catalog, and so no mention is made of subject access; but they, as well as Cutter's rules, bring out the three functions already mentioned of identifying (1.a-c), collocating (2.a-b), and evaluating (2.b). In both Cutter's statement and the Paris Principles, the evaluating function is limited to choice of edition and to Cutter's "choice of a book ... as to its character." With time and the advent of multiple ways of presenting the same work, both intellectually and physically, it has become more important to make certain that the catalog can assist in making choices. This continues a long history of evolution of functions of the catalog.

A fourth function served by a catalog is that of locating, a function not often served by other bibliographic tools. One can tell from a library catalog whether the library contains a certain item and, if so, where that item is physically located. This is true even of expanded interlibrary union catalogs in the sense that the catalog identifies which libraries house particular items, although one may need more detail to know where in a particular library to find an item.

Forms of Catalogs

Presently, the library catalog exists in one of several physical formats: book catalog, card catalog, microform catalog, or online computer catalog. The printed book catalog is the oldest type known in the United States; it was used by many American libraries as the most common form of catalog until the late 1800s. The report of the Bureau of Education in 1876 gives a list of 1,010 printed book catalogs, 382 of them published from 1870 to 1876. Because the book catalogs were rather expensive to produce and quickly became outdated, they were gradually replaced by card catalogs. In a survey of 58 typical American libraries undertaken in 1893, 43 libraries had complete card catalogs and 13 had printed book catalogs with card supplements.[6] Thus, for many years book catalogs were out of favor in American libraries. It was only with more modern, cheaper methods of printing and with the advent of automation for quicker cumulation that book catalogs again became popular with certain types of libraries. An example of a book catalog produced by more modern production techniques is the Library of Congress *Catalog of Books Represented by Library of Congress Printed Cards*, known since 1956 as the *National Union Catalog*. This catalog was published monthly, with quarterly, semiannual, annual, and quinquennial cumulations through 1982. It is now published only in microform. The *National Union Catalog* for many years was produced by photographic reduction of pre-existing catalog cards; hence, it was a by-product of a card catalog. A similar technique is used by a number of commercial publishers (e.g., G. K. Hall), which reproduce card catalogs of certain libraries in a book catalog format.

Beginning in the 1950s, a new type of book catalog appeared, based on the use of computers. These computer-produced catalogs, using machine-readable cataloging records, vary widely in format, typography, extent of bibliographic detail, and pattern of updating. The Library of Congress (LC) began publishing its book catalog series via computer in the 1970s.

The card catalog is the library catalog most often found in the United States. Each entry is prepared on a standard 7.5x12.5 cm card (roughly 3x5 inches), although the size was not always standard. In the first card catalogs a variety of sizes was used from library to library, including 1½x5 inches, 1½x10 inches, and

4x6 inches. Prepared cards are filed, usually in alphabetical order, in trays. Entries on cards were at first hand-written; later the typewriter came into standard use. Typeset cards were available from the LC beginning in 1901. Later, cards were often prepared by photo-reproduction of a printed or typed original. However, they are now most often computer-produced from machine-readable catalog records.

Microform catalogs became much more popular with the development of computer-output microform (COM). COM catalogs are produced in either microfilm or microfiche. It is feasible with this form of catalog to provide a completely integrated new catalog every three months or so, rather than providing supplements to be used with a main catalog. Many libraries now have COM catalogs, and there is a voluminous amount of literature on the subject.

The online computer catalog, often referred to as an online public access catalog (or OPAC), is rapidly becoming the catalog of choice. Bibliographic records stored in the computer memory or on compact disks (often called CD-ROM, standing for compact disk — read only memory) are displayed on a video screen in response to a request from a user. Entries may comprise the full bibliographic record or only parts of it, depending on the system and/or the desires of the user. Until recently such systems were costly, and only very large libraries were able to afford them. Now systems have been developed for use on every size computer from mainframes to personal computers and have become quite affordable. However, there are so many choices of systems with operations and retrievals configured so differently that many librarians are finding it difficult to choose among them. Our current era resembles the time before the standardization of the card catalog, when sizes of cards and order of elements of bibliographic data differed from library to library. As we learn what works best, OPACs will eventually become standardized as did card catalogs.

An effective catalog in any format should possess certain qualities that will allow it to be easily consulted and maintained. If it is too difficult, too cumbersome, or too expensive, it is virtually useless. Hence the following comparative criteria exist for judging a catalog:

1) A catalog should be flexible and up-to-date. A library's collection is constantly changing. Since the catalog is a record of what is available in that library, entries should be added or removed as items are added to or discarded from the collection. The card catalog and the OPAC are totally flexible. Records can be easily added to or removed from the files whenever necessary. However, backlogs of records to be entered can develop, especially with card catalogs. Book, COM, and CD-ROM catalogs are inflexible in that once they have been printed, they cannot admit additions or deletions except in supplements or new editions of the catalog. On the other hand, because they are computer-produced, they can provide flexibility in making changes in existing entries. For example, a single command can change many entries, while with a card catalog, each change must be made individually. Thus, OPACS can be considered the most flexible and current of all catalog formats if bibliographic records are stored on read/write disks quickly accessible to the memory. Additions, deletions, and changes can be made at any time, and the results are often instantly available to the user, or at least are available by the next day. Undoubtedly compact disk technology will

soon overcome the "read-only" limitation, and then CD catalogs will be as flexible as other online catalogs.

2) A catalog should be constructed so that all entries can be quickly and easily found. This is a matter of labeling, filing, and, in the case of online catalogs, simple and clear screen instructions. So far as the card catalog is concerned, the contents of each tray must be identified to the extent that a patron who wants to locate, for example, the works of Charles Dickens can find the Dickens entries easily. The patron must know exactly what part of the alphabet each tray contains. Within the trays themselves, arrangement of entries must be such that items are not overlooked because the filing is not alphabetical, and guide cards should be sufficiently plentiful to identify coverage. Book catalogs are usually labeled on the spine, like encyclopedias. Often they have guides at the top of each page, indicating what entries are covered there. Microfilm catalogs typically are stored in readers that are equipped with alphabetic index strips designed to get the user to the desired part of the alphabet. Microfiche catalogs have at the top of each sheet of fiche eye-readable labels that indicate the part of the alphabet covered. Typically, each sheet of fiche has a microimage index in one corner that tells in which cross section of the fiche particular parts of the alphabet are found. Such systems are time-consuming to use, and reading the magnified fiche is often difficult. Many patrons will do almost anything to avoid using a microfiche catalog. Filing arrangement in computer-produced catalogs is not the same as in traditionally filed card catalogs because of the difficulty of programming computers to arrange according to traditional library filing rules. As a result, traditional rules have been re-evaluated, and new filing rules closely resemble computer filing rules; but few card catalogs have been refiled according to the new rules.

Entries are located in online catalogs in a variety of ways. In some the computer must be told whether an author, title, or subject search is desired. Some systems also require the user to construct "search keys" made up of combinations of letters and/or words. For example, a title search key may consist of the first three letters of the first word that is not an article plus the first letter of each of the next three words. In other systems one can enter as much of the title, author, or subject as seems useful, starting at the left of the entry as it would appear in a card catalog. Still other systems allow users to input only the words they remember in any order, and the system searches for all records containing all the words input. These methods all have disadvantages, and it will take more time and experience before we know the best means of providing access to online catalogs.

Responses to searches in online catalogs also vary by system. In some systems, display of multiple responses (e.g., a listing of works by Charles Dickens) is in the order of "last in, first out"—the last record cataloged or worked on in some way is the first one displayed—and there is no alphabetical collocation. Many systems alphabetize such displays, but strictly by title-page title. Thus, records with the titles *Life and Adventures of Nicholas Nickleby* and *Nicholas Nickleby* are not collocated and may appear on different screen displays. It can be seen that this situation does not meet the criterion for quick and easy access.

3) A catalog should be economically prepared and maintained. The catalog that can be prepared most inexpensively and with greatest attention to currency has obvious advantages.

4) A catalog should be compact. It should not only take up the least possible amount of space, but it should also be easily removable for consultation and prolonged study if possible. The catalog most closely fitting this description is the microfiche catalog, although its use requires a reader. With the development of small, portable microfiche readers, such catalogs could conceivably be taken to individual homes or offices. Microfilm catalogs take up little space, but readers are not portable. Because only one person at a time can use a microfilm catalog, multiple copies (including multiple readers) are usually required. Book catalogs are compact and can be removed for private study, but again, multiple copies may be required in a single location. An online catalog is as compact as the terminal used to gain access to it and can be accessible from any location having terminal access to the memory bank containing the catalog. It is becoming increasingly common for a library user to gain access to online catalogs via dial access from office or home using a personal computer and a modem. The card catalog is the least compact, and it cannot be removed for private consultation.

In summary, the following observations can be made about the major types of catalog:

Cards for the card catalog are easy to prepare and relatively inexpensive. The chief virtue of the card catalog is its flexibility. Although it is not compact and trays cannot ordinarily be removed for long intensive study, it should be remembered that many people can use it at the same time, as long as they do not need the same drawer.

The book catalog is expensive to prepare unless numerous copies of the catalog are required; library systems that need multiple copies will find the book catalog less costly than the card catalog. Entries can be found quickly in the book catalog, and it is compact, easy to store, and easy to handle. However, it lacks flexibility.

The microform catalog is much less expensive than the book catalog, and there is evidence that its maintenance is less expensive than for the card catalog, although the initial investment in catalog conversion to machine-readable form is high. It is compact and easy to store. It can be flexible if the library can afford to run new cumulations often. However, many patrons find the microfiche versions particularly unpleasant to use.

The online catalog, with the exception of that using CD-ROM technology, is the most flexible and current. Online catalogs, including the CD-ROM versions, are compact and entries can be found quickly. Searching methods and retrieval displays, however, are not standardized, and collocation is not as reliable as in other types of catalogs.

Arrangement of Entries in a Catalog

A printed catalog (unlike an online catalog) requires multiple copies of each bibliographic record so that the record can be found under any of several access points. Traditionally there is an access point for each author and any other person or corporate body associated with the work and deemed important enough that someone might search for them. There are also access points for titles, variant titles, and subject headings assigned to the record. A copy of the bibliographic record appears under each access point. In some book and microform catalogs a full copy of the record appears only at the "main" access point (a concept discussed in more detail later in this chapter and in chapter 9), and abbreviated versions appear at all other access points. In all printed catalogs each access point with its associated version of the bibliographic record is called an entry.

Online catalogs do not have "entries" in the same sense. One master copy of each bibliographic record is stored by the system. Indexes are made that link each name, title, subject heading, or other entity decided upon as an access point to any associated bibliographic record. In response to a search request, selected data elements from each relevant bibliographic record are copied to the user's screen in the display format chosen for that system.

A printed catalog (unlike an online catalog) must be arranged according to some definite plan. Depending on the subject and scope of the collection, many arrangements are possible. But no matter which one is used, it should cover the contents of the collection and guide the person who consults it to these contents.

Printed public access catalogs are ordinarily arranged according to one of two systems: classified or alphabetical. The differences between them lie in the arrangement and filing of the entries.

Classified Catalogs

The classified catalog has the longest history. Many American libraries used this form before they changed to the more popular alphabetical form. It is based upon some special system of classification. The shelflist, a record of the holdings of a library arranged by classification number, is a classified catalog of a kind. But in a true classified catalog, a bibliographic record may be entered under as many classification numbers as apply to its contents, not under just one number as in a shelflist. In addition, the shelflist lacks an alphabetical subject index, which a true classified catalog has. The major advantage of a classified catalog is that because it uses symbols or numbers it can keep up with changing terminology and thus be up-to-date. It is also useful for in-depth study of a subject. Closely related classes are brought together in sequence – often hierarchically. This is good for scanning or for moving from general to specific. In addition this arrangement permits easy compilation of subject bibliographies. Perhaps its greatest disadvantage is that it is constructed on a particular classification scheme (even though this was an advantage as noted above). Since many patrons are not familiar with classification numbers, they would need special assistance when consulting the classified catalog. However, some fields – particularly the sciences – can make good use of such a catalog, inasmuch as science changes so rapidly, since the classified catalog is flexible and can be easily updated – e.g., only the index entries would have to be changed when terminology for a concept changes, rather than having to revise all records using the concept.

Classified catalogs are also of value in locations where the patrons may speak one or two or more languages. In such a case, an alphabetical subject index may be made in each language. In Quebec, for example, where both English and French are spoken, there would be one major classified catalog with French and English indexes. There are only a few classified catalogs in use in the United States today. They are more widely used in Europe, Canada, and a few other countries. There are some predictions that increasing international cooperation will encourage the use of classification for subject exchange, since classification symbols transcend language.

Classified catalogs are actually only the subject part of a divided catalog (see discussion below). They must be accompanied by a name/title catalog. Fig. 1.1 (see page 14) shows a complete set of cards for a classified catalog.

Alphabetical Catalogs

Alphabetical catalogs came into use because of their ease of arrangement and use. The alphabet is commonly understood. A user is likely to find information under direct terms—those consulted first by choice. Verbal headings are more easily understood than classification symbols. On the other hand, some terminology is quickly dated, and many terms have multiple meanings. In very large catalogs alphabetic arrangement becomes quite complex. There are two basic arrangements of alphabetical catalogs: dictionary and divided.

Dictionary Catalogs

In the dictionary arrangement of entries, widely used in American libraries, all the entries—name, title, and subject—are combined, word by word, into one alphabetical file. This arrangement is said to be simple; undoubtedly it is, in the sense that only one file need be consulted. As the library grows, however, the dictionary arrangement becomes cumbersome and complex because all entries are interfiled. The problem becomes partly one of filing (are books by Charles Dickens, for example, filed before those about him?) and partly one of dispersion. The subject of "industrial relations" has many aspects. How can all these aspects be located if they are entered under headings from "A" for "arbitration" to "W" for "wages"? Two primary justifications are offered in favor of the dictionary arrangement: most patrons seek material on one aspect of a subject rather than upon the broad subject itself, and patrons are provided with ample *see* and *see also* references, which direct them to other aspects of their subjects. Fig. 1.2 (see page 15) shows a complete set of cards for a dictionary catalog.

(Text continues on page 16.)

Fig. 1.1. Card set for a classified catalog.

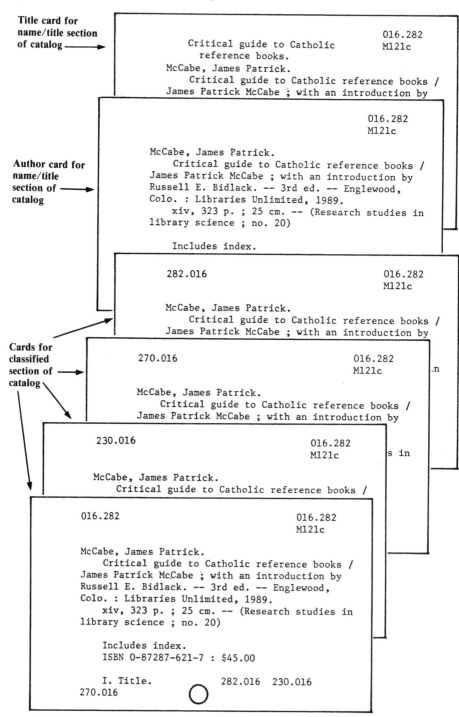

Title card for
name/title section
of catalog ⟶

    Critical guide to Catholic   016.282
       reference books.   M121c
    McCabe, James Patrick.
       Critical guide to Catholic reference books /
    James Patrick McCabe ; with an introduction by

                                          016.282
                                          M121c

    McCabe, James Patrick.
       Critical guide to Catholic reference books /
    James Patrick McCabe ; with an introduction by
    Russell E. Bidlack. -- 3rd ed. -- Englewood,
    Colo. : Libraries Unlimited, 1989.
       xiv, 323 p. ; 25 cm. -- (Research studies in
    library science ; no. 20)

       Includes index.

Author card for
name/title
section of ⟶
catalog

       282.016   016.282
                                          M121c

    McCabe, James Patrick.
       Critical guide to Catholic reference books /
    James Patrick McCabe ; with an introduction by

       270.016   016.282
                                          M121c   .n

    McCabe, James Patrick.
       Critical guide to Catholic reference books /
    James Patrick McCabe ; with an introduction by

       230.016   016.282
                                          M121c   s in

    McCabe, James Patrick.
       Critical guide to Catholic reference books /

Cards for
classified
section of ⟶
catalog

       016.282   016.282
                                          M121c

    McCabe, James Patrick.
       Critical guide to Catholic reference books /
    James Patrick McCabe ; with an introduction by
    Russell E. Bidlack. -- 3rd ed. -- Englewood,
    Colo. : Libraries Unlimited, 1989.
       xiv, 323 p. ; 25 cm. -- (Research studies in
    library science ; no. 20)

       Includes index.
       ISBN 0-87287-621-7 : $45.00

       I. Title.   282.016   230.016
    270.016

Fig. 1.2. Card set for an alphabetical catalog.

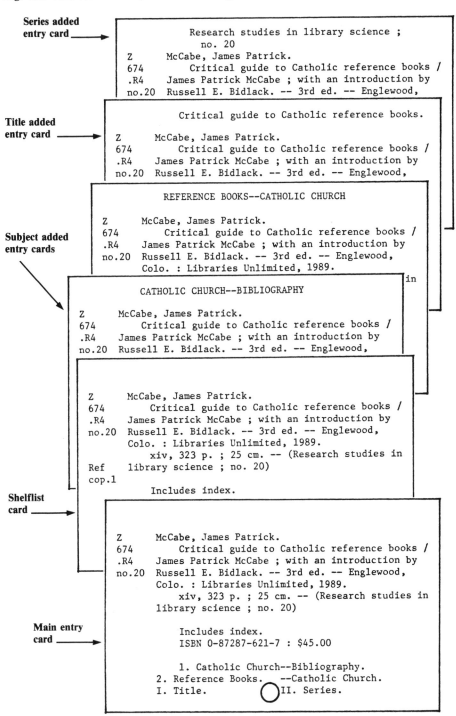

Series added
entry card →

        Research studies in library science ;
           no. 20
Z   McCabe, James Patrick.
674   Critical guide to Catholic reference books /
.R4   James Patrick McCabe ; with an introduction by
no.20 Russell E. Bidlack. -- 3rd ed. -- Englewood,

Title added
entry card →

        Critical guide to Catholic reference books.

Z   McCabe, James Patrick.
674   Critical guide to Catholic reference books /
.R4   James Patrick McCabe ; with an introduction by
no.20 Russell E. Bidlack. -- 3rd ed. -- Englewood,

       REFERENCE BOOKS--CATHOLIC CHURCH

Z   McCabe, James Patrick.
674   Critical guide to Catholic reference books /
.R4   James Patrick McCabe ; with an introduction by
no.20 Russell E. Bidlack. -- 3rd ed. -- Englewood,
      Colo. : Libraries Unlimited, 1989.

Subject added
entry cards

      CATHOLIC CHURCH--BIBLIOGRAPHY

Z   McCabe, James Patrick.
674   Critical guide to Catholic reference books /
.R4   James Patrick McCabe ; with an introduction by
no.20 Russell E. Bidlack. -- 3rd ed. -- Englewood,

Z   McCabe, James Patrick.
674   Critical guide to Catholic reference books /
.R4   James Patrick McCabe ; with an introduction by
no.20 Russell E. Bidlack. -- 3rd ed. -- Englewood,
      Colo. : Libraries Unlimited, 1989.
        xiv, 323 p. ; 25 cm. -- (Research studies in
Ref   library science ; no. 20)
cop.1
      Includes index.

Shelflist
card →

Z   McCabe, James Patrick.
674   Critical guide to Catholic reference books /
.R4   James Patrick McCabe ; with an introduction by
no.20 Russell E. Bidlack. -- 3rd ed. -- Englewood,
      Colo. : Libraries Unlimited, 1989.
        xiv, 323 p. ; 25 cm. -- (Research studies in
      library science ; no. 20)

Main entry
card →

      Includes index.
      ISBN 0-87287-621-7 : $45.00

      1. Catholic Church--Bibliography.
   2. Reference Books. --Catholic Church.
   I. Title.   II. Series.

Divided Catalogs

In the 1930s the realization that dictionary catalogs were becoming more and more complex led to a modification of the dictionary arrangement. The result was the divided catalog, which, in its most common form, is in reality two catalogs: one for entries other than subject; the other for subject entries only. The divided catalog permits a simpler filing scheme than does the dictionary catalog. Thus it is easier to consult, although the problem of scattered subjects still exists. There is a further complication implicit in this arrangement. The patron must determine whether an author or title entry or a subject entry is wanted before knowing which part of the catalog must be checked. When this divided approach is used, books about Dickens and books by Dickens are not filed together in the catalog. Patrons need some guidance and education in this matter.

There are a few libraries that use other types of divided catalogs, such as the three-way divided catalog consisting of separate sections for author, title, and subject entries. Although this system may simplify the filing of cards, it can be even more confusing for a patron than the two-way divided catalog. In this arrangement, entries for books by Dickens are filed under Dickens' name in the author catalog, the titles of his individual novels are filed in the title catalog, and books about Dickens are filed in the subject catalog.

Another type of two-way divided catalog is a name/title catalog and a topical subject catalog. In such a divided catalog, names and titles that are used even as subject headings are filed in the name/title section. This type of divided catalog allows all the material by and about an author or a title to be filed together. Thus, to continue our previous example, books by and books about Dickens would be filed together in the same catalog. This system is potentially less confusing to the patron than any other form of divided catalog.

Arrangements of Online Catalogs

Because entries do not have to be arranged in a linear fashion, online catalogs cannot be placed in the earlier mentioned categories. The internal arrangements of records in the computer vary greatly from system to system and make little difference to a user. What does matter to the user is the way in which entries are displayed in response to a search request. Most online catalogs are in effect divided catalogs because a user must choose to search through one of the indexes: author, title, subject, and sometimes classification and other numbers. In this kind of system, a name as subject is almost always searched through the subject index, separating any records about a person from those representing works by that person. A few systems allow searching of two indexes at once using the words *and, or,* and *not* or their equivalents (a form of what is called Boolean searching). These systems do, of course, allow a sophisticated user to find works by and about a person in a single search, but experience has shown that few library patrons are this capable of manipulating the system. Many systems also allow for keyword searching of almost any words in any record. In such a system, a keyword search for a name brings together for display all records for works by and about the person, but the display is not collocated in any logical fashion.

In online catalogs that provide for searching by classification number, there is a semblance of a classified catalog except that in United States cataloging practice each work is limited to one place in a classification scheme. In this respect it is more like a shelflist (see discussion below). Research has been done on using the classification to enhance subject retrieval in online catalogs.[7] In time there may be ways to gain access to bibliographic records through the hierarchy of the classification scheme used to classify the works they represent.

The Parts of the Catalog

Basically there are three parts making up a whole catalog: a public access catalog, a shelflist, and an authority file or files. The preceding sections on form and arrangements of catalogs have, for the most part, covered public access catalogs. These are the catalogs readily available for the use of library patrons.

A shelflist is a record of the holdings of a library; entries are arranged in the order of the items on the shelf—hence the name "shelflist." With the cataloging of computer files and programs, for which there is often not a physical item to be placed on a shelf, the name is less descriptive. Records of a library's holdings for such entities must be placed in order by classification notation, acquisition number, or some other device. This pattern will increase as libraries provide access to more materials of this sort in the future. The shelflist record usually contains a record of ownership of numbers of copies and/or volumes held, as well as information about locations of copies, especially when a library is made up of several collections.

Shelflists are traditionally kept in an area not accessible to the public. There have been notable exceptions to this, however, especially in situations where the areas in which materials are shelved (called stacks) are not open to the public. In these situations, browsing the shelflist can substitute for browsing in the stacks. Another change in availability of shelflists is occurring with online catalogs. When classification is an access point in the catalog, the results of classification number searches are displayed in shelflist (i.e., classification) order, essentially making the shelflist available to everyone. In addition most online catalogs provide copy and location information at all access points.

Authority files contain records of the forms of names, uniform titles, series, and subject headings that have been chosen as the authorized forms to use as access points in a particular catalog. The authority records also contain lists of references made in the public catalog from unauthorized forms to those used for access points so that users do not have to know authorized forms to use the catalog. Traditionally, these files also have been kept in areas inaccessible to the public. Again, online catalogs are changing this. In some systems authority records serve as an index to the catalog.

Online catalogs contain these three parts, but not always as distinctly separate as they are in printed catalogs. Authority files still are nonexistent in some online catalogs, and in some they are separate files; but increasingly they are being linked to the bibliographic files so that they may serve as the index(es) to the headings used in the system, and in some cases they serve to alert catalogers automatically to inconsistencies in headings. In addition a number of other parts are being added to online catalogs. For example, acquisitions and in-process records are available to the public in many systems, and circulation information—e.g., whether an item is charged out and, if so, when it is due back—has been added to many online catalogs.

CATALOGING

The means by which catalogs are prepared is through the process called cataloging. This process usually begins with descriptive cataloging and continues with subject analysis, and throughout both phases is intertwined the process of authority control.

Descriptive Cataloging

Descriptive cataloging is that phase of the cataloging process that is concerned with the identification and description of an item, the recording of this information in the form of a cataloging record, and the selection and formation of access points—with the exception of subject access points. Descriptive cataloging describes the physical make-up of an item and identifies the responsibility for intellectual contents, without reference to its classification by subject or to the assignment of subject headings, both of which are the province of subject cataloging.

Description

Identification and description are interrelated processes in descriptive cataloging. Identification consists of the choice of conventional elements, guided by a set of rules. When the cataloger has properly identified the conventional elements, they are described in a catalog record in such a fashion that the description is unique and can be applied to no other entity in the collection. In other words each item should be distinguished from everything with which it could be confused. Elements considered essential for this purpose are title, statement of responsibility, edition information, and publication, distribution, or production information. Physical description—extent and size of item—and series data are often essential to this purpose as well. In addition the cataloger gives elements of description that may be helpful to a user in evaluating potential use of the item, such as whether it is illustrated and what equipment may be needed to use it.

Access

After describing an item the cataloger selects access points. Names of persons and corporate bodies associated with a work are chosen according to the cataloging rules used. Title access points also are chosen—in addition to the obvious main title (called title proper) there may be alternative titles, variant titles, series titles, and titles of other works related in some way with the work being cataloged.

In traditional practice one of the access points is chosen as the main one. This is called the main entry, but it should not be confused with the use of the word *entry* as defined earlier, meaning an access point with its associated version of a bibliographic record that appears as a unit in a catalog. The remaining access points are called added entries. Identification of the main entry is usually essential for identification of the work (or intellectual content) that is embodied in an item being cataloged. A combination of main entry and title — uniform title if the work has appeared with variant titles — is the most common way of referring to a work in the realm of cataloging. Of course many works appear only once in one form and are not referred to again, so there is some controversy in the cataloging world about the necessity for choosing a main entry in all cases.

The access points chosen are constructed in a form that will make them readily accessible in the catalog and will enhance collocation. This is done following cataloging rules and through reference to the authority file, thus continuing the process of authority control.

Subject Analysis

Subject analysis involves determining what subject concept or concepts are covered by the intellectual content of a work. Once this has been determined, as many subject headings as are appropriate are chosen from a standard list. Again, an authority file must be consulted if the subject headings are to be properly collocated into the catalog with other works covering the same or related subject concepts.

The final step in the process usually is to choose a classification notation from whatever classification scheme is used by the library. Traditionally in the United States the classification serves both as a means for bringing an item in close proximity with other items on the same or related subjects and as the first element of the call number, a device used to identify and locate a particular item on the shelves. The cataloger therefore must choose only the one best place in the classification scheme for the item.

Authority Control

Authority control is the process of maintaining consistency in the verbal form used to represent an access point and the further process of showing the relationships among names, works, and subjects. It is accomplished through use of rules (in the case of names and titles), use of a subject heading list, and reference to an authority file to create an authorized character string called a heading. An authority file is a grouping of records of the forms of names, titles, or subjects chosen for use in a catalog. Each authority record in an authority file may contain, in addition to the form chosen for use as the heading, a list of variant forms or terms that may be used as references. A very carefully prepared authority record also contains a list of sources consulted in the process of deciding upon the heading and the variant forms to use as references. It is possible to practice authority control by letting the catalog itself serve as the authority file — i.e., by assuming that the form of heading used in the catalog is correct. However, in large files this has proved to be difficult, and it is very difficult to keep track of references made in any size file without an authority file.

It is authority control that makes cataloging more than a process of creating a series of bibliographic records to represent discrete works without apparent relationship to any other. The process of cataloging can be defined as "creation of a catalog using bibliographic records" because authority control allows the cataloger to create headings for names, titles, and subjects that show the relationships among the works cataloged. It means that the heading for the same name in different records is always the same so that bibliographic records for all works by and about the same person or emanating from the same corporate body can be displayed together. The heading for a work (called a uniform title, but often consisting of the name of the author, or other main entry, followed by standardized title, as mentioned earlier) can be consistently presented so that bibliographic records for all editions, translations, sound or video recordings, adaptations, abridgements, or any other kind of manifestation of a work can be displayed together. The heading used to represent the same subject concept in different works can be used always in one form (called controlled vocabulary) so that, to the extent that works are identified as being about the same subject concept, all such works can be displayed together. Authority control of controlled vocabulary also makes it possible to refer users from terms not used to those used and from terms used to other related terms.

Cooperative and Copy Cataloging

The process of cataloging described above is often referred to as original cataloging. Fortunately it is not necessary for every item in every library to be cataloged originally in that library. Because libraries acquire copies of many of the same items, their catalogers can share cataloging by adapting for their own catalogs a copy of the original cataloging created by another library, a process commonly called copy cataloging.[8]

The Library of Congress began to sell its standard printed catalog cards to libraries in 1901. H. W. Wilson entered the field in the 1930s with simplified catalog cards for sale. A number of other companies created and sold catalog cards from the 1950s into the 1970s. In addition the Library of Congress book catalogs were available in large libraries, and methods were devised for photocopying entries from them for adaptation and use in local catalogs.

With the development of the machine-readable cataloging (MARC) format in the late 1960s, cooperative cataloging took a new turn. At first the companies selling cards simply loaded LC's MARC tapes into their computers and printed cards from them. But the beginning of bibliographic networks based on MARC not only changed the availability of cards but also introduced the truly cooperative availability of cataloging data. The first network was OCLC—at first the Ohio College Library Center, but now the Online Computer Library Center. Libraries can become member libraries and then contribute original cataloging to the system. Any member library can use records found in the system contributed by the Library of Congress, several other national libraries, or any other member library.

At first the OCLC network was used only for the production of cards, and cards continue to be a product of the system. Adaptations are easier online than changing photocopies or pre-printed cards. At the network the cards are printed to local specifications after adaptations are made online by the local library, and the cards are then mailed to the library ordering them. Increasingly, however, MARC records are downloaded directly into local libraries' online catalogs. Other major networks in use in the United States include RLIN (Research Libraries Information Network), Utlas International (formerly University of

Toronto Library Automation Systems), and WLN (Western Library Network). Smaller regional and local networks exist in large numbers.

The amount of original cataloging remaining after use of cooperative cataloging depends upon the type and size of library. The more specialized the library, the more original cataloging it has, so specialized collections can require a high percentage of original cataloging, even though they may be quite small. In public, academic, and research libraries the percentage runs from around 5 percent to 35 percent depending upon size—in general, the larger the collection, the higher the percentage.

FORMATS OF BIBLIOGRAPHIC RECORDS IN CATALOGS

The records created in the cataloging process must be displayed in some format. Uniformity of display is very desirable so that patrons can know how to read a record and where to expect to see certain elements of data. In printed catalogs the display of data elements is quite standard. Most libraries and card production sources have followed the Library of Congress pattern, because LC printed cards were so extensively used and because the order of elements devised by LC made a logical presentation of data. That order has been codified by the various versions of the *Anglo-American Cataloguing Rules* (discussed in greater detail in the following chapters).

The elements that have become accepted as standard for bibliographic records are outlined below in the order in which they appear in most records, computer or manual. Not all specific elements are present in every item cataloged, but all elements present should be recorded. (The roman numerals given in the outline identify parts of a bibliographic record and should not be confused with the eight areas of description discussed in chapter 3, "General Rules for Description.")

I.   CALL NUMBER
     A.   Classification number
     B.   Cutter number and workmark, if any

II.   MAIN ENTRY
     A.   Author or other person or corporate body chosen as main entry,
         or
     B.   Title, if (A) cannot be ascribed.

III.   TITLE AND STATEMENT OF RESPONSIBILITY AREA
     A.   Title proper (including alternative title, if any)
     B.   General material designation (GMD)
     C.   Parallel title(s), other title information, if any
     D.   Statement(s) of responsibility

IV.   EDITION AREA
- A.   Edition statement (named, numbered, or a combination of the two)
- B.   Statements of responsibility relating to the edition, but not to all editions

V.   MATERIAL (OR TYPE OF PUBLICATION) SPECIFIC DETAILS AREA
- A.   For cartographic materials, statements of scale and projection
- B.   For music, statement indicating physical presentation of the music
- C.   For computer files, statements of file characteristics
- D.   For serial publications, numeric and/or alphabetic designation (e.g., No. 1-) and/or chronological designation (e.g., 1967-)

VI.   PUBLICATION, DISTRIBUTION, ETC., AREA
- A.   Place of publication, distribution, etc.
- B.   Name of publisher, distributor, etc.
- C.   Statement of function of publisher, distributor, etc. (e.g., production company), when necessary for clarity
- D.   Date of publication, distribution, etc., including copyright date, if necessary
- E.   Place of manufacture, name of manufacturer, date of manufacture, if name of publisher is unknown

VII.   PHYSICAL DESCRIPTION AREA
- A.   Extent of item (e.g., number of pages, volumes, discs, frames, etc.)
- B.   Other physical details (e.g., illustrative material, playing speed, material of which made)
- C.   Dimensions (e.g., height, diameter)
- D.   Accompanying material (e.g., teacher's guide, separate maps)

VIII.   SERIES AREA, if any
- A.   Title proper of series, parallel title(s), other title information
- B.   Statement(s) of responsibility relating to series
- C.   ISSN of series
- D.   Numbering within series
- E.   Subseries
- F.   Second and following series, each in its own set of parentheses

IX.   NOTE AREA. Necessary data that cannot be incorporated in above parts of the record.

X.   STANDARD NUMBER AND TERMS OF AVAILABILITY AREA
- A.   Standard number (e.g., ISBN, ISSN)
- B.   Key-title of a serial
- C.   Terms of availability (e.g., price or for whom available)

XI.   TRACING
A. Subject heading(s)
B. Added entries for joint authors, editors, etc.
C. Title added entry or entries
D. Series added entry or entries

In general, the areas in this outline appear in this order in a MARC (machine-readable cataloging) record, although the elements in the "Material (or type of publication) specific details area" and in the "Standard number and terms of availability area" are found in a different order. There are also a number of additional elements in a MARC record. The standard method for creating a bibliographic record in most libraries today is to create a MARC record, even if the catalog is printed. Most catalog cards and virtually all book and microform catalogs are produced from computer records, usually in a MARC format. An introduction to the MARC formats is given in appendix A.[9] Figure 1.3 (see page 24) illustrates a record in MARC format.

In a printed record the elements are ordinarily formatted in paragraph form. The call number is usually formatted in the upper left corner of a card. It may also appear on the line below the tracing. In a book or microform catalog the call number typically appears on a line below the rest of the entry. The main entry is on the top line. The title through the publication, distribution, etc., areas are given in a single paragraph (often called the body of the entry). The physical description and series areas constitute a second paragraph. If there are notes, each one is a separate paragraph. The standard number area is given in a paragraph following the last note. The tracing (so called because in a card catalog it is used to "trace" the location of all the cards of a set) is in a final paragraph.

Although many bibliographic records are now created in MARC format, some libraries still order pre-printed cards and type their original records, and some of the smaller online systems use non-MARC computer formats for internal storage of records. For those catalogers who find it necessary to type some catalog cards locally, appendix B illustrates a sample method for doing so. Sections in this appendix on spacing, punctuation, capitalization, abbreviations, and numerals are useful in creating original bibliographic records in MARC format as well as in typed format since they identify accepted standards for spacing, punctuation, etc., within areas of the record as well as between any two areas. Figure 1.4 (see page 25) illustrates a record in printed card format.

(Text continues on page 25.)

Fig. 1.3. Identification of information included in a MARC record.

```
OCLC:     15428596        Rec stat:    p
Entered:  19870311        Replaced:    19880627      Used:    19910422
Type: a         Bib lvl: m      Source:              Lang: eng
Repr:           Enc lvl:        Conf pub: 0          Ctry: nyu
Indx: 1         Mod rec:        Govt pub:            Cont: b
Desc: a         Int lvl:        Festschr: 0          Illus: a
                M/F/B:   10     Dat tp:   s          Dates: 1988,
   1 010        87-7510 ◄—20
   2 040        DLC $c DLC  ⟋12
   3 020        0030120195 (pbk.)
   4 043        n------ $a u-at-no
   5 050 0      DU125.T5 $b H37 1988 ◄—18
   6 082 0      306/.0899915 $2 19
   7 090        $b
   8 049        YCLM      19    ⟋1
16—9 100 10     Hart, C. W. M. $q (Charles William Merton), $d 1905-
  10 245 04     The Tiwi of North Australia / $c C.W.M. Hart, Arnold R.
Pilling, Jane C. Goodale.       2      7          3          8
  11 250        3rd ed. ◄—4
  12 260 0      New York : $b Holt, Rinehart and Winston, $c c1988.} 5
17—13 300  6    xvii, 179 p. : $b ill. ; $c 24 cm.} 9
  14 440  0     Case studies in cultural anthropology ◄—10
  15 504        Bibliography: p. 163-176.} 11
  16 500        Includes index.
  17 650 0      Tiwi (Australian people) ◄—14
  18 700 10     Pilling, Arnold R.                          } 13
  19 700 10     Goodale, Jane C. $q (Jane Carter), $d 1926-
                15                              21
```

Key for Fig. 1.3

1. Heading: author's name
2. Title proper
3. Statement of responsibility
4. Edition statement
5. Publication, distribution, etc., area
6. Place of publication
7. Publisher
8. Date of publication
9. Physical description area
10. Series statement
11. Notes
12. Standard number (ISBN)

13. Tracing
14. Subject heading
15. Added entry for personal name
16. MARC indicator that tells computer that title will be added entry
17. MARC tag that indicates that series will be added entry
18. Library of Congress call number
19. Dewey classification number
20. Library of Congress control (card) number
21. MARC subfield code

Fig. 1.4. Identification of information included in a catalog card.

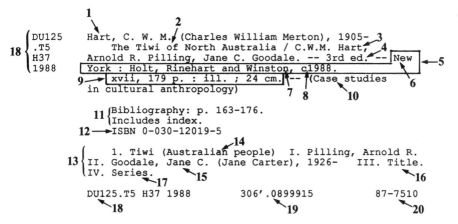

Key for Fig. 1.4

1. Heading: author's name
2. Title proper
3. Statement of responsibility
4. Edition statement
5. Publication, distribution, etc., area
6. Place of publication
7. Publisher
8. Date of publication
9. Physical description area
10. Series statement
11. Notes
12. Standard number (ISBN)
13. Tracing
14. Subject heading
15. Added entry for personal name
16. Title added entry
17. Series added entry
18. Library of Congress call number
19. Dewey classification number
20. Library of Congress card number

Entries displayed to users of online catalogs are taking a variety of forms in experimental efforts to determine what form is most understandable to users. Many so far have chosen to display the records in a form that resembles the form that would be found on a catalog card. Figure 1.5 (see page 26) shows such a display from CLIO, the public catalog module of the Columbia University Libraries' integrated system, based upon NOTIS software. Others have chosen to use a completely different format. Figure 1.6(a.-b.) (see pages 26-27) shows two levels of screen displays as they appear in the public access catalog of the Stockton-San Joaquin (California) Public Library, which uses the integrated system marketed by Data Research Associates.

Fig. 1.5. Sample online catalog display from Columbia University Library's CLIO system (based upon NOTIS software)

```
CLIO SEARCH REQUEST:  A=HART C
BIBLIOGRAPHIC RECORD -- NO. 2 OF 26 ENTRIES FOUND

Hart, C. W. M. (Charles William Merton), 1905-
  The Tiwi of North Australia / C.W.M. Hart, Arnold R. Pilling, Jane
C. Goodale. -- 3rd ed. -- New York : Holt, Rinehart and Winston,
c1988.
  xvii, 179 p. : ill. ; 24 cm. -- (Case studies in cultural
anthropology)
  Bibliography: p. 163-176.
  Includes index.
  SUBJECT HEADINGS (Library of Congress; use s= ):
    Tiwi (Australian people)

LOCATION: LEHMAN
CALL NUMBER:  DU125 .T5 H37 1988 (copy 1)
LIBRARY HAS:
  copies 1


Type m for next record.  Type i for index, g for guide.
Type r to revise, h for help, e for CLIO introduction.
Type your search request and press ENTER==>
```

Fig. 1.6a. Sample online catalog display from Stockton-San Joaquin Public Library's online catalog (from Data Research Associates)

```
AUTHOR: Hart, C. W. M. 1905-
 TITLE: The Tiwi of North Australia

PUBLISHER: Holt, Rinehart and Winston, c1988.

 SUBJECTS: Tiwi (Australian people)


LINE
  #          ---------- CALL NUMBER -------- MATERIAL   LOCATION  STATUS

  1       306.0899915 HAR                               SKTN      AVAILABLE


Press (RETURN) to view holdings at other branches.
Type in a LINE # and press (RETURN) for more information on a copy.
Enter:  P          to display Previous screens of the current search.
        F          to see the Full title record.
        R          to Request the material.
>>
                         You may begin a new search at any time.
```

Fig. 1.6b. Screen showing full title record from Fig. 1.6a.

```
        MATERIAL: Book

          AUTHOR: Hart, C. W. M. (Charles William Merton), 1905-

           TITLE: The Tiwi of North Australia / C.W.M. Hart, Arnold R.
                  Pilling, Jane C. Goodale.

         EDITION: 3rd ed.
       PUBLISHER: New York : Holt, Rinehart and Winston, c1988.
     DESCRIPTION: xvii, 179 p. : ill. ; 24 cm.
           NOTES: Bibliography: p. 163-176.
           NOTES: Includes index.
         SUBJECT: Tiwi (Australian people)
     ADDED ENTRY: Pilling, Arnold R.
     ADDED ENTRY: Goodale, Jane C. (Jane Carter), 1926-


Enter:  B   to Backup.
        F   to redisplay the First screen of the full record.
>>
                    You may enter a ? for HELP or begin a new search.
```

CONCLUSION

This chapter has presented an overview of the entire cataloging process. Greater detail about the content of description is discussed in chapters 3-8. Choice and form of headings are covered in chapters 9-14. Subject analysis is given thorough treatment in part III, with chapters 15-19 devoted to classification and chapters 20-24 devoted to subject headings. Part IV covers authority control, and the final part deals in more detail with networking, computer cataloging, and with cataloging routines and end processes.

NOTES

[1] Elaine Svenonius, "Directions for Research in Indexing, Classification, and Cataloging," *Library Resources & Technical Services* 25 (January/March 1981): 88.

[2] Richard P. Smiraglia, "Bibliographic Control Theory and Nonbook Materials," in *Policy and Practice in Bibliographic Control of Nonbook Media*, ed. by Sheila S. Intner and Richard P. Smiraglia (Chicago, American Library Association, 1987), p. 15.

[3] These ideas are discussed in greater detail by Ronald Hagler in *The Bibliographic Record and Information Technology*, 2nd ed. (Chicago, American Library Association, 1991), pp. 3-4.

[4] Charles A. Cutter, *Rules for a Dictionary Catalog*, 4th ed. (Washington, D.C., GPO, 1904), p. 12.

[5] International Conference on Cataloguing Principles. Paris, 9th-18th October, 1961, *Report* (London, International Federation of Library Associations, 1963), p. 26.

[6]A good discussion of the historical development of cataloging practices is presented in an article written by Charles Martel, "Cataloging: 1876-1926," reprinted in *The Catalog and Cataloging*, ed. by A. R. Rowland (Hamden, Conn., Shoe String Press, 1969), pp. 40-50.

[7]Karen Markey and Anh N. Demeyer, "Findings of the Dewey Decimal Classification Online Project," *International Cataloguing* 15 (April/June 1986): 15-19.

[8]For an in-depth discussion of the decisions and adaptations necessary in the process of copy cataloging see: Arlene G. Taylor, *Cataloging with Copy: A Decision-Maker's Handbook*, 2nd ed., with the assistance of Rosanna M. O'Neil (Englewood, Colo., Libraries Unlimited, 1988).

[9]For a detailed discussion of the MARC formats see: Walt Crawford, *MARC for Library Use: Understanding Integrated USMARC*, 2nd ed. (Boston, G. K. Hall, 1989).

SUGGESTED READING

Byrne, Deborah J. *MARC Manual: Understanding and Using MARC Records*. Englewood, Colo., Libraries Unlimited, 1991.

Carpenter, Michael, and Elaine Svenonius. *Foundations of Cataloging: A Sourcebook*. Littleton, Colo., Libraries Unlimited, 1985.

Crawford, Walt. *MARC for Library Use: Understanding Integrated USMARC*. 2nd ed. Boston, G. K. Hall, 1989.

Dunkin, Paul S. *Cataloging U.S.A.* Chicago, American Library Association, 1969.

Hagler, Ronald. *The Bibliographic Record and Information Technology*. 2nd ed. Chicago, American Library Association, 1991.

Taylor, Arlene G. *Cataloging with Copy: A Decision-Maker's Handbook*, 2nd ed. Englewood, Colo., Libraries Unlimited, 1988.

Development of Cataloging Codes

In current United States cataloging practice there is no comprehensive code of rules that tells a cataloger how to create bibliographic records that provide descriptive cataloging and subject access or how to create a catalog with those records. There is a widely accepted set of rules that covers description and name and title access and addresses authority work to some extent, but provision of subject access, authority control, and creation of catalogs are dependent upon following conventions—to a great extent, those established by the Library of Congress. The rules for description and name and title access, the *Anglo-American Cataloguing Rules*, second edition, 1988 revision (*AACR2R*),[1] is the result of a progression of ideas about how to approach the cataloging process to prepare catalogs that provide the best possible access to library collections. *AACR2R* represents the current agreements that have been reached to standardize descriptive cataloging practice and thereby facilitate cooperation among libraries. It expands on the agreements presented in earlier codes and forms the basis for further agreements that will be added to future codes.

The first cataloging rules were prepared by individuals. Anthony Panizzi, Keeper of the Printed Books at the British Museum, constructed a set of rules for that institution that was published in 1841.[2] This set of rules, often referred to as Panizzi's "91 Rules," was the first major modern statement of principles underlying cataloging rules; as such it has exerted an influence on every Western world code that has been created since its publication. Panizzi believed that anyone looking for a particular work should be able to find it through the catalog, and he wrote rules with that goal in mind—e.g., he insisted on entering pseudonymous works under pseudonym rather than under the author's real name. One characteristic of Panizzi's code was his occasional use of form headings as main entry—e.g., universities and learned societies were entered under the general heading "Academies," and missals, prayer-books, and liturgies were entered under "Liturgies." The concept of subject access as we know it had not yet been separated from that of main entry, and there were no provisions for subject headings as such.

Charles Cutter, Librarian at the Boston Athenaeum, also created an important set of rules. His *Rules for a Dictionary Catalog*,[3] in its fourth edition at his death in 1903, gave voice to the concept that catalogs not only should point the way to an individual publication but also should assemble and organize literary units. These rules were also the first complete set of rules for a dictionary catalog. Cutter's rules were truly comprehensive, incorporating rules for subject access and filing as well as for description and name and title access. From the beginning of the twentieth century codes have been drawn up by committees, but the influence of these early farsighted individuals has been apparent.

As mentioned earlier the rules we have are for description and name and title access. After Cutter's rules for subject headings, two major American lists of subject headings were developed—each containing introductions explaining conventions for use.[4] Haykin enumerated principles for creating subject lists in 1951,[5] and LC issued its *Manual* for applying its headings in 1984 (3rd ed., 1988),[6] but there is no comprehensive code for subject access. Some librarians began calling for such a code in the late 1980s. The history related to subjects is discussed in more detail in chapter 21.

Rules for descriptive cataloging have progressed through a number of different manifestations in the twentieth century: LC's *Rules on Printed Cards* (1899 through the 1930s),[7] American Library Association (ALA) and the (British) Library Association's *Catalog Rules* (1908),[8] *A.L.A. Cataloging Rules* (1941),[9] *A.L.A. Cataloging Rules for Author and Title Entries* (1949),[10] LC's *Rules for Descriptive Cataloging* (1949),[11] *Anglo-American Cataloging Rules* (1967) (*AACR1*),[12] *Anglo-American Cataloguing Rules*, second edition (1978) (*AACR2*),[13] and the present *AACR2R*.

The Anglo-American *Rules* of 1908 were the result of a seven-year study by a committee of ALA and the (British) Library Association. In 1901 the Library of Congress had begun its printed card service, with the result that libraries became interested in ways to use LC cards with their own cards. One of the important responsibilities of the committee was to formulate rules to encourage incorporation of LC printed cards into catalogs of other libraries. The committee attempted to reconcile the cataloging practices of LC with those of other research and scholarly libraries. The use of LC cards increased dramatically between 1908 and 1941; standardization of library catalogs progressed. However, the 1908 *Rules* were not expanded during this 33-year period, drastically curtailing attempts of cataloging practice to stay in touch with cataloging done at the Library of Congress. In 1930 a subcommittee was appointed by ALA to begin work on a revision of cataloging rules, and the problems were outlined. Dissatisfaction with the 1908 code was expressed on the grounds of "omissions"; the basic rules were not in question. Expansion was required to meet the needs of large scholarly libraries or specialized collections:

> The preliminary edition, published in 1941, expanded the rules of 1908 to make more provision for special classes of material: serial publications, government documents, publications of religious bodies, anonymous classics, music and maps; to amplify existing rules to cover specific cases of frequent occurrence.[14]

The revised edition of 1949 states that in the 1949 edition:

> the chief changes from the preliminary edition are a rearrangement of the material to emphasize the basic rules and subordinate their amplifications, and to make the sequence of rules logical as far as possible; reduction of the number of alternate rules; omission of rules for description; rewording to avoid repetition or to make the meaning clearer; and revision, where possible, of rules inconsistent with the general principles.[15]

The 1941 and 1949 rules were sharply criticized for being too elaborate and often arbitrary; emphasis had shifted from clearly defined principles to a collection of rules developed to fit specific cases rather than the conditions that the cases illustrated. Seymour Lubetzky, then a specialist in cataloging policy at the Library of Congress, commented that any logical approach to cataloging problems was blocked by the maze of arbitrary and repetitious rules and exceptions to rules.[16]

Because of the omission of rules for description from the 1949 ALA *Rules*, the Library of Congress published its *Rules for Descriptive Cataloging in the Library of Congress*,[17] also in 1949. This set of rules was much more simplified than had been the rules in Part II of the 1941 ALA preliminary edition. Therefore, these were not criticized, as were the rules for entry and heading, and were incorporated virtually intact into the next edition of rules published by ALA in 1967.

Because the 1949 rules were not satisfactory, ALA invited Lubetzky in 1951 to prepare a critical study of cataloging rules. Early drafts of Lubetzky's principles came out against complete enumeration of "cases" in rules and pointed toward a less complex code based upon well-defined principles. At the International Conference on Cataloging Principles held in Paris in 1961, a draft statement of cataloging principles based upon Lubetzky's *Code of Cataloging Rules* was used as the basis for consideration. The final version of the "Statement of Principles" (often called the "Paris Principles")[18] was adopted and the participants from 53 countries agreed to work in their various countries for revised rules that would be in agreement with the accepted principles.

ANGLO-AMERICAN CATALOGING RULES, 1967 (AACR1)

The Catalog Code Revision Committee that prepared the 1967 *Anglo-American Cataloging Rules* realized that revision must be a complete reexamination of the principles and objectives of cataloging, not merely a revision of specific rules. First, the objectives of the catalog were agreed upon; it was further decided that the Paris Principles should be the basis for rules of entry and heading. This was an important step toward international bibliographic standardization. International standardization was not accepted overnight, however. The British and Americans were attempting to produce a joint code, but American conservatives were worried about the probable costs of full implementation of the Paris Principles. When the code was finally published it was published in two texts—one British and one North American.[19]

AACR1 was oriented toward large research libraries, although in a few instances of obvious conflict, alternate rules were provided for use by non-research libraries. Unlike the 1949 ALA code, which was only for entry and heading, *AACR1* incorporated rules for entry and heading, description, and cataloging of nonbook material. An important shift occurred in the philosophy underlying the rules for entry: "The entry for a work is normally based on the statements that appear on the title page or any part of the work that is used as its substitute."[20] This meant that information appearing only in the preface, introduction, or text was not to be considered unless title page information was vague or incomplete. Another basic shift in point of view was to that of cataloging by types of authorship rather than by types of works and by classes of names rather than by classes of people.

Unlike earlier codes, *AACR1* emphasized that choice of entry was a completely separate activity from construction of the heading used for the entry chosen. General principles became the basis for the rules for choice of entry:

1) Entry should be under author or principal author when one can be determined.

2) Entry should be under title in the case of works whose authorship is diffuse, indeterminate, or unknown.

Application of rules based on these principles continued the practice of choosing a main entry, with other names and/or titles becoming added entries. However, the choice was no longer a result of first determining the type of work involved and then finding the specific rule for that type.

The construction of the headings for names that were to be main or added entries centered on two problems: choice of a particular name, including both choice among different names (e.g., Jacqueline Onassis or Jacqueline Kennedy) and choice among different forms of the same name (e.g., Morris West or Morris L. West), and the form in which that name is presented in the heading (e.g., Seuss, Dr., or Dr. Seuss; Von Braun, Wernher, or Braun, Wernher von). Rules for form of name became based on a general principle of using the form of name used by a person or corporate body rather than the full name or official name as the 1949 ALA *Rules* directed. Thus a person could be entered under an assumed name, nickname, changed name, etc. However, a person who used both his or her real name and an assumed name was still entered under the real name, and a person who used a full form of a forename or used a forename initial, even though rarely, was entered under the fullest form ever used. Another change was to use a firmly established English form of name rather than the vernacular form for many well-known names (e.g., Horace, not Horatius Flaccus, Quintus).

Another important area of change was in the form of entry for corporate bodies. The general rule followed the principle of using the form of name the body itself uses. Entry was usually under that form of name except when the rules provided for entry under a higher body or under the name of the government. However, the North American text gave exceptions exempting specified bodies of an institutional nature from the principle of entry under name; these were to be entered under place as in the old rules. These exceptions were contrary to the Paris Principles and to the British text of *AACR1*, but they had been requested by the Association of Research Libraries, whose member libraries feared being over-burdened with the necessity for changing thousands of entries already in catalogs.

The fear of the research libraries was also eased by the Library of Congress' January 1967 announcement of the policy of superimposition:

> This means that the rules for choice of entry will be applied only to works that are new to the Library and that the rules for headings will be applied only to persons and corporate bodies that are being established for the first time. New editions, etc., of works previously cataloged will be entered in the same way as the earlier editions (except for revised editions in which change of authorship is indicated). New works by previously established authors will appear under the same headings.[21]

This policy continued throughout the duration of the application of *AACR1*. As a result, thousands of headings were made between 1967 and 1981 in a form created under the 1949 ALA *Rules* or earlier rules on bibliographic records that were otherwise *AACR1* records. The abandonment of the policy of superimposition with the implementation of *AACR2* was a major step toward ultimate user convenience in finding entries and improved international cooperation; but for many large libraries, thousands of entries in pre-*AACR* form already in catalogs had to be dealt with after January 1981.

In 1974 the rule in *AACR1* for corporate entry under place was dropped. But because of superimposition, only new corporate bodies were established and entered under their own names. Besides this change, some 40 other rules were changed, and three chapters were totally revised in the years following publication of *AACR1*. Perhaps the most significant change was the application of standards of bibliographic description, based on International Standard Bibliographic Description (ISBD), to descriptive cataloging of monographs, audiovisual media, and special instructional materials. ISBD facilitates the international exchange of bibliographic information by standardizing the elements to be used in the bibliographic description, assigning an order to these elements in the entry, and specifying a system of symbols to be used in punctuating these elements. (These symbols are discussed and illustrated in appendix B of this text.) In addition:

> ISBD requires that a publication be totally identified by the description. It is independent of the provisions for headings, main or added, and of the provisions for the use of uniform titles; these were internationally standardized by the Paris Principles.[22]

ANGLO-AMERICAN CATALOGUING RULES, SECOND EDITION (AACR2) AND THE 1988 REVISION (AACR2R)

The numerous changes to rules in *AACR1* and the progress toward an international standard for description not only of monographs, but also of serials and all media, were two of the reasons for the meeting in 1974 of representatives of the national library associations and national libraries of Canada, the United Kingdom, and the United States to plan for the preparation of *AACR2*. Two other reasons were a proliferation of other rules for nonbook materials that reflected dissatisfaction with *AACR1* treatment of these materials and LC's announcement of intention to abandon the policy of superimposition.[23] The objectives established at that meeting were:

1) to reconcile in a single text the North American and British texts of 1967

2) to incorporate in the single text all amendments and changes already agreed and implemented under the previous mechanisms

3) to consider for inclusion in AACR all proposals for amendment currently under discussion between the American Library Association, the Library Association, the Library of Congress, and the Canadian Library Association; any new proposals put forward by these bodies and the British Library; and any proposals of national committees of other countries in which AACR is in use

4) to provide for international interest in AACR by facilitating its use in countries other than the United States, Canada, and the United Kingdom.[24]

The representatives at the 1974 meeting also agreed to establish a Joint Steering Committee for Revision of *AACR* (JSC) made up of one voting and one nonvoting representative of each author organization. The JSC was to appoint an editor from each side of the Atlantic and was generally to oversee the process of revision through to publication.

The result of the revision process was what the preface to *AACR2* calls a continuation of the first edition: "for, in spite of the changes in presentation and content which it introduces, these are still the *Anglo-American Cataloguing Rules*, having the same principles and underlying objectives as the first edition, and being firmly based on the achievement of those who created the work, first published in 1967."[25] However, *AACR2*, published in late 1978 but not implemented by the major national libraries until January 1981, had some significant differences that are worth noting here.

Before discussing these differences, however, we should note that *AACR2* has undergone a process of continuous revision. Participating countries have committees that work continually on recommendations for revisions. Approved recommendations are passed to the JSC, which then acts to accept or reject the proposals. Before such recommendations can be accepted, they often have to be revised, and differences of opinion must be reconciled among the countries involved. (The countries currently represented on the JSC are Australia, Canada, Great Britain, and the United States.) Approved revisions have been published three times, in 1982, 1984, and 1986.[26] Rather than publish a fourth set of revisions, it was decided to consolidate *AACR2* and all its revisions, including the ones approved since 1986, into a single volume. The result is *AACR2R*. The following discussion applies to *AACR2* and all its revisions unless otherwise noted.

In the process of reconciling the North American and British texts, it was decided to use British spelling of words if the British spelling appears as an alternative in *Webster's Third New International Dictionary of the English Language, Unabridged*. In cases where terminology differs, British usages were chosen in some cases (e.g., *full stop* instead of *period*), while American usages appear in other cases (e.g., *parentheses* instead of the British *brackets*).

One significant change is in the presentation of rules for description: one general chapter presents broad provisions that can be applied in many different situations. This chapter is followed by specific chapters for different types of materials and for different conditions and patterns of publication. The rules for description are deliberately less specific in legislating ways to handle certain phenomena. The cataloger is thereby encouraged to exercise judgment in interpreting the rules in light of the needs of the user being served. One possibility for such interpretation is that *AACR2* provides three "levels" of description with increasing amounts of detail at each level. The cataloger may choose the level that provides the amount of detail relevant to the particular library's users and, at the same time, meet the standards called for in a set of international cataloging rules.

In the rules for choice of access points, it is significant that less emphasis has been placed on "main" entry, although the concept is still present. Many people believe that when multiple access points are readily available, and when the bibliographic description is complete by itself, there is no need to designate one of the access points as the "main" one. The main entry concept, which remained basically unchanged from Panizzi's rules through *AACR1*, was based on the idea that the purpose of the catalog is to identify works and that once the work is identified, sufficient bibliographic detail is added to facilitate finding the item that contains the work. This was based on the assumption that there is a one-to-one correspondence between work and item. This assumption worked fairly well until the latter part of the twentieth century, when the tremendous growth of literatures and formats of all kinds rendered the assumption obsolete. Now, as noted in chapter 1, use of a main entry combined with title or uniform title is the only way we have to identify the same work in several containers. It is also the most common way to identify in a note a work that is related to the work being described by the bibliographic record. As long as this is true the concept of main entry cannot be abandoned.

A significant change in choice of main entry is that a corporate body is no longer considered to be an "author." Instead, there are now specified categories of works that are entered under corporate body. This concept greatly reduces the number of corporate main entries made, although those corporate bodies that would have had main entry under earlier rules are given added entry under *AACR2*, and thus there is not a reduction in number of corporate entries. Another important change in choice of access point is the abandonment of "form subheadings" (e.g., "Laws, statutes, etc.," "Treaties, etc.," "Liturgy and ritual") for legal and religious works. In some of these cases, the function of the form subheadings is now performed by uniform titles, and in other cases it is performed by subject headings.

Rules for form of headings for personal names now emphasize using the form of name most often used by an author (e.g., Benjamin Disraeli instead of Earl of Beaconsfield; Bernard Shaw instead of George Bernard Shaw). If a person, other than one using a pseudonym, uses more than one name, again the predominant one is chosen. Rules for pseudonyms have evolved more than other rules for choice of personal name since *AACR1*, in which only one form—the real name, if used—was chosen to represent a person who used more than one pseudonym or a real name and one or more pseudonyms. In the 1978 *AACR2* a predominant name was chosen; only if there was no predominant name could multiple headings be made for that author. This placed the mathematical works of Charles L. Dodgson under Lewis Carroll. *AACR2R* introduces the concept of "separate bibliographic identities," which allows separate headings in such cases as the Dodgson/Carroll example. It also calls for multiple headings for all contemporary authors who use more than one pseudonym or a real name and one or more pseudonyms.

For corporate names, too, there is more emphasis on using the name as it is used by the body, removing provisions for inverting, amplifying, etc., that appeared in *AACR1* (e.g., W. K. Kellogg Arabian Horse Center instead of Kellogg (W. K.) Arabian Horse Center). Geographic names are treated more internationally (e.g., states of Australia and the U.S.S.R. are treated like states of the United States). In the 1978 *AACR2* counties of England, Scotland, and Wales were also treated like states of the United States, but this has been revised so that places in the British Isles now are qualified by the constituent parts of the British Isles rather than by counties.

At the time of publication of *AACR2* there were some general hopes for advantageous results from use of the new code. First, *AACR2* laid the groundwork for much more international and national cooperative cataloging, which was expected to improve greatly library service of a bibliographic nature and to result in considerable cost savings. Second, by providing the framework for standard description of all library materials, it made possible an integrated, multimedia catalog. Third, it was expected to reduce user search time by providing headings that conform more often to the forms found in works and citations. Fourth, personal name headings were expected to be more stable than formerly, thus reducing catalog maintenance costs.[27] The first two of these expected advantages have been widely accepted as having come to pass. As to the third, Elizabeth Tate demonstrated that headings do indeed conform more often to the forms found in citations.[28] In order to know if the last one has been realized, studies would have to be completed, and this has not been done.

Rule interpretations made by LC in their process of applying *AACR2* are published regularly in *Cataloging Service Bulletin*. Official changes made to the rules are also published there. In an attempt to reduce costs of implementing *AACR2*, LC chose during the first three years of using *AACR2* to allow certain already established names to continue to be used in pre-*AACR2* form when the change was relatively insignificant and did not affect the first entry element of any name and, in some cases, later elements of a famous name. A list of these "compatible" headings was published in *Cataloging Service Bulletin*.[29] Other libraries had to decide whether to follow LC's lead in this implementation. Those libraries that use LC copy found, for the most part, that the cost of *not* following LC would be prohibitive. Even following LC, however, libraries found that there were administrative problems in applying new rules within a catalog based on several earlier sets of rules. A flurry of local *AACR2* studies showed that somewhere between 14 percent and 20 percent of headings dealt with during the first year would be constructed differently under *AACR2*, but only 7 percent to 13 percent of all headings would cause conflict in a catalog (depending upon the size of that catalog).[30] A few libraries decided to close their existing card catalogs and to start new ones with the new rules. Most libraries, however, absorbed the 7 percent to 13 percent conflicting headings into existing card catalogs by interfiling, providing *see also* references, or changing old headings to the new form. Now, of course, libraries are in the process of converting card catalogs to machine-readable form, and in online catalogs all headings can be consolidated under the *AACR2R* form with references from old catalog forms as well as from any variant forms that may appear in the works themselves.

It is hoped that chapters 3 through 14 of this text will prove helpful in illustrating the basic rules. The complete *AACR2R* should be consulted for additional rules covering aspects of problems too detailed for inclusion in this text and for further explanations, definitions, and references.

NOTES

[1]*Anglo-American Cataloguing Rules, Second Edition, 1988 Revision*, prepared by the Joint Steering Committee for Revision of AACR, ed. by Michael Gorman and Paul W. Winkler (Chicago, American Library Association, 1988).

[2]Antonio Panizzi, "Rules for the Compilation of the Catalogue," in British Museum, *The Catalogue of Printed Books in the British Museum* (London, 1841), 1: v-ix.

[3]Charles A. Cutter, *Rules for a Dictionary Catalog*, 4th ed., rewritten (Washington, D.C., GPO, 1904).

[4]Library of Congress, Catalog Division, *Subject Headings Used in the Dictionary Catalogues of the Library of Congress* (Washington, D.C., Library Branch, GPO, 1910-1914); Minnie Earl Sears, *List of Subject Headings for Small Libraries* (New York, H. W. Wilson, 1923).

[5]David Judson Haykin, *Subject Headings: A Practical Guide* (Washington, D.C., GPO, 1951).

[6]Library of Congress, Subject Cataloging Division, *Subject Cataloging Manual: Subject Headings* (Washington, D.C., Library of Congress, 1984).

[7]Library of Congress, *Rules on Printed Cards* (Washington, D.C., Library of Congress, 1899-194?).

[8]*Catalog Rules, Author and Title Entries*, compiled by Committees of the American Library Association and the (British) Library Association, American ed. (Chicago, American Library Association, 1908).

[9]*A.L.A. Cataloging Rules, Author and Title Entries*, prepared by the Catalog Code Revision Committee of the American Library Association, with the collaboration of a Committee of the (British) Library Association, Preliminary American 2nd ed. (Chicago, American Library Association, 1941).

[10]*A.L.A. Cataloging Rules for Author and Title Entries*, prepared by the Division of Cataloging and Classification of the American Library Association, 2nd ed. (Chicago, American Library Association, 1949).

[11]Library of Congress, Descriptive Cataloging Division, *Rules for Descriptive Cataloging in the Library of Congress* (Washington, D.C., Library of Congress, 1949).

[12]*Anglo-American Cataloging Rules, North American Text*, prepared by the American Library Association, the Library of Congress, the (British) Library Association, and the Canadian Library Association (Chicago, American Library Association, 1967).

[13]*Anglo-American Cataloguing Rules*, 2nd ed., prepared by the American Library Association, the British Library, the Canadian Library Committee on Cataloguing, the (British) Library Association, and the Library of Congress, ed. by Michael Gorman and Paul W. Winkler (Chicago, American Library Association, 1978).

[14]*A.L.A. Cataloging Rules*, 1949, p. viii.

[15]*A.L.A. Cataloging Rules*, 1949, p. ix.

[16]Seymour Lubetzky, *Cataloging Rules and Principles: A Critique of the A.L.A. Rules for Entry and a Proposed Design for Their Revision* (Washington, D.C., Processing Dept., Library of Congress, 1953); also by the same author, *Code of Cataloging Rules, Author and Title: An Unfinished Draft ... with an Explanatory Commentary by Paul Dunkin* (Chicago, American Library Association, 1960).

[17]L.C., *Rules for Descriptive Cataloging*, 1949.

[18]International Conference on Cataloging Principles, Paris, 9th-18th October, 1961, *Report* (London, International Federation of Library Associations, 1963).

[19]*Anglo-American Cataloging Rules, North American Text* (Chicago, American Library Association, 1967); *Anglo-American Cataloguing Rules, British Text* (London, Library Association, 1967).

[20]*AACR1, North American Text*, p. 9.

[21]*Cataloging Service*, bulletin 79 (January 1967): 1.

[22]"International Standard Bibliographic Description," *Cataloging Service*, bulletin 105 (November 1972): 2.

[23]"AACR 2: Background and Summary," *Library of Congress Information Bulletin* 37 (October 20, 1978): 640.

[24]*AACR2*, pp. vi-vii.

[25]*AACR2*, p. v.

[26]*Anglo-American Cataloguing Rules, Second Edition, Revisions*, prepared by the Joint Steering Committee for Revision of AACR (Chicago, American Library Association, 1982); *Anglo-American Cataloguing Rules, Second Edition, Revisions 1983*, prepared by the Joint Steering Committee for Revision of AACR (Chicago, American Library Association, 1984); *Anglo-American Cataloguing Rules, Second Edition, Revisions 1985*, prepared by the Joint Steering Committee for Revision of AACR (Chicago, American Library Association, 1986).

[27]"AACR 2: Background and Summary," p. 652.

[28]Elizabeth L. Tate, "Access Points and Citations: A Comparison of Four Cataloging Codes," *Library Research* 1 (Winter 1979): 347-359.

[29]"Implementation of AACR 2 at the Library of Congress," *Cataloging Service Bulletin*, no. 6 (Fall 1979): 5-8.

[30]Arlene Taylor Dowell, *AACR 2 Headings: A Five-Year Projection of Their Impact on Catalogs* (Littleton, Colo., Libraries Unlimited, 1982), pp. 22-35.

SUGGESTED READING

Cutter, Charles Ammi. *Rules for a Dictionary Catalog.* 4th ed., rewritten. Washington, D.C., GPO, 1904.

Dowell, Arlene Taylor. *AACR 2 Headings: A Five-Year Projection of Their Impact on Catalogs.* Littleton, Colo., Libraries Unlimited, 1982.

International Conference on AACR 2, Florida State University, 1979. *The Making of a Code: The Issues Underlying AACR 2.* Chicago, American Library Association, 1980.

Lubetzky, Seymour. *Cataloging Rules and Principles: A Critique of the ALA Rules for Entry and a Proposed Design for Their Revision.* Washington, D.C., Processing Dept., Library of Congress, 1953.

Osborn, Andrew. "The Crisis in Cataloging." *Library Quarterly* 11 (October 1941): 393-411.

Part II

DESCRIPTION AND ACCESS

Description— General 3

INTRODUCTION

Description as a cataloging process was briefly defined in chapter 1. This chapter discusses the process in more detail and then introduces the general rules for description in *AACR2R*.

Description is that part of the cataloging process concerned with identification of an item and with recording information about the item in a bibliographic record in such a way that the item will be identified exactly and cannot be confused with any other item. Many pieces of information about an item contribute to the identification. A title is almost always the first identifying element, followed by the name(s) of a person or persons responsible for the contents of the item. Next, one looks for information identifying an edition: the name of the edition; the name of an editor, a reviser, an illustrator, a translator, a performer, a producer and/or publisher; date of publication; copyright date; or the series of which the edition is a part. Even the size, the type or number of illustrations, or the extent of the item (e.g., number of pages of a book or number of cassettes for a videorecording) may be helpful information for a patron seeking a specific edition of a work. When found, all these elements of information are useful in the description of the item.

TECHNICAL READING OF AN ITEM TO BE CATALOGED

In order to identify conventional elements of an item so that they can be described on a catalog record, it is necessary to know not only what to look for, but also how to look. Technical reading in this manner is scarcely the same as reading for information or for entertainment, when the entire item may be read, seen, or heard. Obviously, the cataloger will have no time for "reading" of this sort, and, therefore, must learn to read technically. Reading technically involves recognizing quickly certain devices peculiar to the particular type of item being cataloged. In this way, the cataloger can quickly determine what the item is about and how it can be described uniquely in such a way that this information can be passed on to the readers. The following discussion contains definitions useful to the cataloger in both descriptive cataloging and subject cataloging.

The first part of an item that the cataloger examines in detail is the chief source of information. This source varies according to the type of material. In books, manuscripts, printed music, and printed serials, it is the title page. In microforms and films it is the title frame(s). For sound recordings, it is the label and sometimes a container that is affixed to the item (e.g., cassette of a tape cassette). For cartographic and graphic materials and for three-dimensional artifacts and realia, the chief source of information is the object itself, including permanently affixed labels or unifying containers. If computer files have title screens, these are used as the chief source; otherwise formally presented evidence or accompanying printed documentation is used. In all these cases, the chief source of information may be absent for some reason, in which case cataloging rules prescribe alternate sources. But usually the chief source of information provides the most complete bibliographic information about the item: the author or other person responsible for the intellectual contents, the fullest form of the title, the name and/or number of the edition, the name of the publisher, distributor, etc., and the place and date of publication, distribution, etc. Figure 3.1 shows half the chief source of information for a sound recording. (The chief source for a sound disc consists of all labels taken together. The side 2 label in this case differs only in the listing of contents on side 2.)

Fig. 3.1. Label from side 1 of a sound disc.

The first element that the cataloger ordinarily notices is the title. The title from the chief source of information, which is generally the item's official title, is called the title proper; as such, it is used in all library records, in trade catalogs, and in bibliographies. It may or may not adequately describe the contents of the item. The book title, *A Short History of the United States*, is self-evident, but the title of the serial, *Toward Freedom*, needs an explanation. A glance through an issue will reveal that the serial discusses the development of new nations; this will be indicated as a subject heading on the catalog record.

In addition to the major part of the title, some items have secondary parts. The alternative title is introduced by *or* and was widely used in books published before the twentieth century. As in Gilbert and Sullivan's *Patience, or, Bunthorne's Bride*, it amplifies the title by telling the reader that "Patience," in this case, is a woman's name rather than the name of a specific virtue. The parallel title is the title proper written in another language or in another script. For instance, a bilingual book on snowmobiles in the Province of Quebec has its title proper in French, *La motoneige au Québec*, and its parallel title in English, *Snowmobiling in Quebec*. Other title information is often used to qualify the title proper. Such qualifications are often called subtitles. For example, the complete title of a tape cassette is *Behavior Control: The Psychologist as Manipulator.* "The Psychologist as Manipulator" is the subtitle. It explains the aspect of behavior control covered in the tape. There is also other title information that is not "subtitle" but does give further explanatory information. In the title, *Barbara Morgan Photography: Trisolini Gallery of Ohio University, Athens, Ohio, January 9-February 3, 1979*, the "other title" information tells where and when the show was held.

The title proper and other titles in the chief source of information, however, are not the only possible ones. Other titles exist, and the cataloger must note those that vary significantly from the title proper. When such titles are noted, the patron who knows a work only by a variant title can be directed to it. For example, Haydn's *Symphony 94 in G Major* is also known as the "Surprise Symphony"; many patrons would look for this popular form of the title instead of the title proper. Books may carry a cover title (i.e., title printed on the cover), binder's title (i.e., title lettered on the original spine of the book), or running title (i.e., title repeated at the top of each page or each alternate page of the book) that differs from the title proper. Sound recordings, motion pictures, or graphic materials may have titles on their containers that differ. Serials may have title variations on the cover or on an added title page.

The series title, however, is not a title variation, but indicates the series, if any, to which the item belongs. A series may be the work of one author or several authors as in Will and Ariel Durant's *The Story of Civilization*, which consists of several uniform volumes. This is called an author's series. A series may also be issued by a publisher who commissions several authors to write one or more volumes on a specified subject. Such is the case with the Rinehart *Rivers of America* series of many volumes. Or perhaps an author is not commissioned but submits a work that happens to fit into a category established by the publisher. Such is the case with Dodd, Mead's *Red Badge* series of mystery novels. Such series are called publishers' series.

The monographic series is a series that is usually issued with some regularity; each title in a monographic series ordinarily is given a number, usually in chronological order. For many patrons, the name of the series and the number of a title in it are the important identifying elements. Patrons often do not remember individual authors and titles but look for these under the series name. Thus, although author and title of an individual item are major identifying elements, the series title in a monographic series assumes a significant role.

The second element to be identified by the cataloger is the statement of responsibility. This is also found in the chief source of information and is usually the author, whose name is usually the main entry. According to *AACR2R*, a personal author is "the person chiefly responsible for the creation of the intellectual or artistic content of a work."[1] In addition to writers of books and composers of music, this includes cartographers, artists, photographers, performers, etc. It may be necessary to locate some information about an unfamiliar author. For example, if the work is imaginative in nature, the author's nationality must be known since most classification schemes use the device of nationality to classify novels, drama, and poetry. This is discussed in the chapters on classification in this text. It is also sometimes necessary to know an author's nationality to know how to form the heading for the name. This is discussed further in the chapter on form of headings for persons. Information about an author may sometimes be found in the chief source of information, in an introduction, or in material accompanying the item, such as the dust jacket of a book or the container of a disc.

However, an author is not the only possibility for inclusion in a statement of responsibility. Any person or persons responsible for intellectual or artistic content or for performance, or any corporate body from which the content is issued, may need to be included in the catalog record.

The edition of the item, if named, is usually found in the chief source of information, but may also be found in other places. In a book, a piece of printed music, or a serial it may appear in the preliminaries (i.e., title page, verso [or back] of the title page, any pages preceding the title page, and the cover), in the preface to the work, or in a colophon (i.e., a statement at the end of the work). In cartographic or graphic material, sound recordings, motion pictures and video-recordings, computer files, and three-dimensional artifacts, the edition may appear in accompanying printed material. For those items with a container, the edition may be found there.

The edition is distinguished from a printing or issue in that a new edition indicates that certain specific changes—additions, deletions, modifications—have been made from earlier versions of the item. On the other hand, a new printing (or reprinting) or issue, means that more copies of the work were manufactured in order to keep up with demand. In the case of books and book-like materials, printings may have minor corrections or revisions, usually incorporated into the original type image. For other materials, a new issue may have slight variations from the original.

Editions may be named (e.g., "revised and enlarged," "abridged," "expurgated") or numbered (e.g., "5th edition"). Any of these edition statements indicates to the cataloger and the patron that some change in content or in form has been made. This information is very important to a scholar. To study the development of a poet, the literary scholar must have early and late editions of the poet's work. A physicist might want only the latest edition of a book on thermodynamics.

Because the name of the publisher or distributor, etc., might indicate the type or quality of a work, this information might be important to the patron who must choose one item from several on a specific subject. If the publisher or distributor, etc., is noted for excellence in a certain area (e.g., Skira in art; McGraw-Hill in technology), publisher/distributor information has some value to the patron. This information, including place and date, is usually found in the chief source of information, but may also be found in the same other locations as the edition statement. If the item is copyrighted, the copyright date and the holders of the copyright must be listed in or on the item. This information is important when the publication date and the copyright date differ. In such a case, both dates are given in the catalog record.

The cataloger must learn to assess quickly the details of physical description. These include the extent of the item (e.g., number of pages or volumes, number of pieces, length of playing time), dimensions (e.g., height), and physical data other than extent or dimensions (e.g., presence of illustrations, playing speed, material of which made).

The cataloger must also be quick to identify other important and useful pieces of information about an item. Such information as variant titles of the same work (e.g., original title of a translation), other related versions of the work, language, edition history, accompanying materials, intended audience, contents of multi-volume items, and presence of bibliographies should often be noted in the catalog record. The standard number (e.g., International Standard Book Number [ISBN] and International Standard Serial Number [ISSN]) is becoming increasingly important as a means of unique international identification. It is often given in the catalog record.

If there is a preface, the cataloger should read it as an aid to determination of the author's plan or objective and as an aid in identifying the edition. It also provides a key to the subject matter of the item. Similar aids are introductions, forewords, accompanying printed materials, and containers. The table of contents, with its listing of topics, is a valuable indication of the scope of a work. An index is a good source for determining subject content and special emphases. Bibliographies may also serve as an aid by indicating an author's point of view.

During the process of the technical reading the cataloger jots down relevant elements of information as they are found so that they can be formed into a coherent description for the bibliographic record that will represent the item in the catalog. Figure 3.2 shows the *AACR2R* description for the sound recording whose partial chief source of information is shown in Fig. 3.1. The description was completed after a technical reading of the item.

Fig. 3.2. Description of the item whose partial chief source of information is shown in Fig. 3.1.*

Jonathan Livingston Seagull [sound recording] / Neil Diamond. — New York, N.Y. : Columbia, p1973.

1 sound disc (43 min.) : analog, 33⅓ rpm, stereo. ; 12 in. + 1 pamphlet ([8] p. : ill. (some col.) ; 31 cm.)

Columbia: KS32550.
Original motion picture sound track.
Instrumental music, and songs sung by the composer.
Contents: Prologue — Be — Flight of the gull — Dear Father — Skybird — Lonely looking sky — The odyssey — Anthem — Be — Skybird — Dear Father — Be.

---

*In the examples of description in chapters 3-7, the choice of main entry is not taken into consideration in the formatting. That is, a "hanging indention" is not used when title would be chosen as main entry. Choice of main entry is discussed in chapter 9 of this text.

If the record is to be entered into an online system, it is usually coded with the tags, indicators, and subfield codes of the MARC format and is formatted with the spacing required by the system into which it will be entered. Figure 3.3 shows the description from Fig. 3.2 with MARC coding, formatted as it would be in the OCLC system.

Fig. 3.3. Description coded according to the MARC format and spaced and formatted as it would be for the OCLC system.

```
028 02  KS32550 $b Columbia
245 10  Jonathan Livingston Seagull $h sound recording / $c Neil
Diamond.
260     New York, N.Y. : $b Columbia, $c p1973.
300     1 sound disc (43 min.) : $b analog, 33 1/3 rpm, stereo. ;
$c 12 in. + $e 1 pamphlet ([8] p. : ill. (some col.) ; 31 cm.).
500     Original motion picture sound track.
511 0   Instrumental music, and songs sung by the composer.
505 0   Prologue -- Be -- Flight of the gull -- Dear Father --
Skybird -- Lonely looking sky -- The odyssey -- Anthem -- Be --
Skybird -- Dear Father -- Be.
```

DESCRIPTION OF MATERIALS
USING *AACR2R*

This section covers in some detail the *AACR2R* rules for descriptive cataloging. Only the more general rules are covered here, however. The reader should carefully examine *AACR2R*, chapter 1, for more complex problems.

AACR2R does not contain instructions for MARC coding. The Library of Congress issues a general outline of the MARC format that includes definitions of all tags, indicators, and subfield codes and dictates the contents of each field and subfield, but does not indicate spacing or layout.[2] Each system that uses the MARC format creates its own spacing and layout, and it issues system documentation demonstrating how MARC records will be formatted in that system. Only *AACR2R* content, spacing, and punctuation are illustrated in the remainder of this chapter, although MARC field numbers and subfield codes are identified beside many of the *AACR2R* rules. For more information about MARC formatting, the reader should consult Appendix A of this text and also the system manual for the system being used.

The first chapter of *AACR2R* covers description in general and is applicable to all types of materials (e.g., print, sound recordings, etc.) in all conditions (e.g., microform) and patterns (e.g., serial) of publication. Chapters 2 through 12 of *AACR2R* cover in detail various types of material and conditions and patterns of publication. These chapters often refer back to chapter 1 for rules that are generally applicable, but they also give specific guidance for situations that are peculiar to the type of material or condition of publication under discussion. Chapters 2 through 12 of *AACR2R* cover:

2 Books, Pamphlets, and Printed Sheets
3 Cartographic Materials
4 Manuscripts (including Manuscript Collections)
5 Music
6 Sound Recordings
7 Motion Pictures and Videorecordings
8 Graphic Materials
9 Computer Files
10 Three-Dimensional Artifacts and Realia
11 Microforms
12 Serials

Chapter 13, rather than dealing with a type of material or condition of publication, covers a special problem in cataloging: analysis. These *AACR2R* chapters are covered in chapters 4 through 8 of this text. There are purposely no chapters numbered 14 through 20 in *AACR2R*. These numbers were left vacant for later construction of rules for new types of material (e.g., holograms) as it becomes necessary to develop rules for cataloging them.

An important concept in using chapters 1 through 12 of *AACR2R* is that the rule numbers are mnemonic. In ISBD, upon which *AACR2R* is based, there are eight "areas" of description as follows:

1) Title and statement of responsibility area
2) Edition area
3) Material (or type of publication) specific details area
4) Publication, distribution, etc., area
5) Physical description area
6) Series area
7) Note area
8) Standard number and terms of availability area

Not all areas are used in describing all library materials, but in chapters 1 to 12 of *AACR2R* all are mentioned, if only to say that the area in question is not used to describe the particular material (e.g., rule 2.3, Material (or Type of Publication) Specific Details Area: "This area is not used for printed monographs."). The rules are numbered in such a way that the number preceding the period is the chapter number and the number following the period is the rule number. Rules 1 through 8 in each chapter represent the eight "areas" named above. Thus, rule 1.2 deals with the edition area in general, while rule 5.2 covers the edition area for music, and rule 8.2 covers the edition area for graphic materials. Further, the rule numbers are subdivided by letters sometimes followed by numerals which are also mnemonic. In the general chapter, rule 1.1D is the rule for parallel titles; for books, the comparable rule is rule 2.1D, and for serials it is rule 12.1D. In addition to the rules for "areas," all the chapters have general rules assigned the numeral "0." Chapters 1-3 and 5-12 also have rules 9, "Supplementary items," and 10, "Items made up of several types of materials." These rules do not all have exactly the same heading, but address the same concept (e.g., rule 10 for serials is entitled "Sections of Serials"). Chapters 1-3, 5, and 8 have a rule 11, "Facsimiles, Photocopies, and Other Reproductions." Chapter 2 has, in addition, rules 12 through 18 that deal specifically with early printed monographs.

Throughout *AACR2R* there are "optional" rules that allow for adding or deleting information in certain instances or that allow alternative methods of handling certain situations. Each cataloging agency must decide whether and how these options will be applied. Because so many libraries rely on the Library of Congress for cataloging data, this text includes, in this chapter and the ones on *AACR2R* that follow, a discussion of LC's decision about application of each option that occurs in the rule sequences discussed in this text.

LC has issued rule interpretations that affect LC's implementation of rules in addition to the decisions about optional rules. LC rule interpretations for *AACR2R* have been published separately and are available from LC's Cataloging Distribution Service.[3] They also have been published in issues of *Cataloging Service Bulletin*.[4] These have been cumulated by individuals outside of LC and are available at modest cost.[5] It is assumed that the version in the *Cataloging Service Bulletin* is available most widely, and so when LC's rule interpretations are referred to in this text, they are cited as *CSB* followed by the issue number and page(s) (e.g., *CSB* 45: 13-15 means *Cataloging Service Bulletin*, number 45, pages 13-15).

SELECTED RULES AND EXAMPLES

RULE 1.0. GENERAL RULES

1.0A. Sources of information
A chief source of information is specified for each type of material or condition or pattern of publication. Information in the chief source is to be preferred to information found elsewhere. Some parts of the description may be taken from "prescribed" sources rather than the chief source. In either case information that is not from the chief source, where required, or from prescribed sources in the other instances, must be enclosed in square brackets.

Lack of a chief source of information may be a problem with such items as locally produced sound recordings. If the item cannot be used as a basis for description, take the information from any available source and give a note explaining the source of the supplied data.

1.0C. Punctuation
Punctuation is covered in detail in Appendix B of this text and so is not discussed here or at the beginning of each "area" of the description. Most areas in most chapters of *AACR2R* have a rule numbered "A1" (1.1A1, 1.2A1, 1.4A1, etc.) in which detailed guidance for punctuation of specific areas of the description is given.

1.0D. Levels of detail in the description
AACR2R provides three recommended levels of description. The minimum requirements for each level are specified in this rule. The rules in chapters 1-12 of *AACR2R* provide guidance for every element of level 3. The examples in this text, for the most part, follow LC practice in cataloging at level 2. Figures 3.4 and 3.5 illustrate the first and second levels for the same item. The third level includes every possible element set out in the rules and is likely to be used only in cataloging such things as rare items.

Fig. 3.4. Rule 1.0D1. First level of description.

Scottish crofters. — Holt, Rinehart and Winston, c1990.
xii, 175 p.

Bibliography: p. 167-169.
Includes index.
ISBN 0-030-03754-6

Note: Cataloging to the first level of description requires use of only rules 1.1B, 1.1F, 1.2B, 1.3, 1.4D, 1.4F, 1.5B, 1.7, and 1.8B.

Fig. 3.5. Rule 1.0D2. Second level of description.

Scottish crofters : a historical ethnography of a Celtic village / Susan Parman. — Fort Worth : Holt, Rinehart and Winston, c1990.
xii, 175 p. : ill. ; 24 cm. — (Case studies in cultural anthropology)

Bibliography: p. 167-169.
Includes index.
ISBN 0-030-30754-6

1.0H. Items with several chief sources of information

Single part items. An item that has more than one chief source of information should generally be described from the first one, with a few major exceptions outlined in this rule. For example, in cataloging sound recordings, two or more chief sources of information (e.g., labels on both sides of a disc) should be treated as a single source. Also, the chief source with the latest date of publication, distribution, etc., should be preferred. In addition, *AACR2R* prescribes preferences to follow by language, if there are different languages in the chief source. (*See AACR2R*, pp. 16-17).

Multipart items. The chief source of information for the first part of a multipart item should be used for the basic description, with variations in later parts shown in notes. If the first part is missing, the first part that is available is used. If there is no "first" part, the part that gives the most information or the unifying container is used.

RULE 1.1. TITLE AND STATEMENT OF RESPONSIBILITY AREA
(MARC field 245)

1.1A2. Sources of information

Title and statement of responsibility information is to be taken from the chief source of information. There is a prescribed order for data, regardless of their order in the chief source. The prescribed order should be followed except when grammatical construction does not allow it.

1.1B.   Title proper (subfield a of MARC field 245)

1.1B1.   The exact wording, order, and spelling of the title proper should be followed in the transcription, but punctuation and capitalization may be changed. *See* Fig. 3.6.

> **Fig. 3.6. Rule 1.1B1. Transcription of title using exact words, but inserting commas and changing capitalization.**
>
> Chief source of information: Feeling Mad
> Feeling Sad
> Feeling Bad
> Feeling Glad
>
> Transcription: Feeling mad, feeling sad, feeling bad, feeling glad.

Three dots or square brackets in the title are replaced by a dash or by parentheses, respectively. Also, if the source of information uses a colon, slash, or equals sign, LC replaces it with other punctuation unless the space may be closed up on both sides. (*CSB* 44: 9-10)

1.1B2.   A statement of responsibility that is connected to the title proper with a grammatical construction (such as a case ending) is transcribed as part of the title proper. *See* Fig. 3.7.

> **Fig. 3.7. Rule 1.1B2. Transcription of title proper including author's name.**
>
> Bill Collins' Book of movies.

1.1B4.   Very long titles may be abridged if this can be done without giving up important information. The first five words may not be abridged, however. The mark of omission (i.e., "...") shows where omissions have been made. *See* Fig. 3.8.

> **Fig. 3.8. Rule 1.1B4. Abridgement of long title proper.**
>
> Hearings before the Subcommittee on the Rules and Organization of the House of the Committee on Rules, House of Representatives, Ninety-fifth Congress, second session ...

1.1B7.   If the chief source of information (or its substitute) lacks a title proper, one may be supplied from some other source, or may be constructed by the cataloger, if none can be found. Square brackets are used in such a case. *See* Fig. 3.9.

> **Fig. 3.9. Rule 1.1B7. Devised title proper enclosed in square brackets.**
>
> [Map of Kerr Lake Recreation Area, North Carolina]

1.1B10.   When a chief source includes a collective title and also the titles of the separate works of the collection, the collective title is transcribed as the title proper. The separate individual titles are given in a contents note. *See* Fig. 3.10. (For transcription of titles when there is no collective title, *see* rule 1.1G.)

Fig. 3.10. Rule 1.1B10. Collective title as title proper with individual titles in a note.

The great stone face & other tales [sound recording] / by Nathaniel Hawthorne. — Charlotte, Md. : Recorded Books, p1986.
2 sound cassettes (120 min.) : analog, mono.

Narrated by Nelson Runger.
"Unabridged."
In container.
Contents: The great stone face — The ambitious guest — The great carbuncle — Sketches from memory.

1.1C. *Optional addition.* **General material designation** (subfield h of MARC field 245)

1.1C1. *AACR2R* gives two lists of general material designations (GMDs). List 1 is for British use and list 2 is for North American and Australian use.

List 1	**List 2**	
braille	art original	microscope slide
cartographic material	art reproduction	model
computer file	braille	motion picture
graphic	chart	music
manuscript	computer file	picture
microform	diorama	realia
motion picture	filmstrip	slide
multimedia	flash card	sound recording
music	game	technical drawing
object	globe	text
sound recording	kit	toy
text	manuscript	transparency
videorecording	map	videorecording
	microform	

Users of list 2 are instructed to add "(large print)" or "(tactile)" to any term in the list when cataloging materials for the visually impaired.

The Library of Congress uses list 2. The examples given in this text will do likewise. The only GMDs currently supplied by LC are:

computer file
filmstrip
kit
microform
motion picture
slide
sound recording
transparency
videorecording (*CSB* 44: 10)

Some of the others would be used if LC were to begin cataloging those kinds of materials. However, the decision was made *not* to use the GMDs for maps, manuscripts, music, and text.

1.1C2. When the GMD is used, it is added to the description in square brackets immediately after the title proper. (It precedes any other title information that may be added using rule 1.1E.) For example:

Scared straight! [motion picture]

Basic concepts of humanistic psychology [sound recording]

The future is information [videorecording] : careers in library and information science

1.1C3. When an item is a reproduction of a work that originally appeared in a different form (e.g., microform of a map, or sound tape of an original sound disc), the GMD for the reproduction, not the original, is given. For example, the videorecording with the following title, although originally issued as a 16mm motion picture, would be entered as:

The Americans, 1776 [videorecording]

The set of slides with the following title, which was originally issued as a filmstrip, would be entered as:

Blood pressure [slide]

1.1C4. Some items consist of parts that fall into more than one category of the list of GMDs chosen. If one of these is predominant in the item, that form is given as the GMD. If none is predominant, the GMD used is "kit." (*See also* rule 1.10.) For example, the following item contains one book, one sound cassette, one poster, two puppets, and an activity guide, and would be entered as:

Why mosquitoes buzz in people's ears [kit]

1.1D. Parallel titles (subfield b of MARC field 245)

1.1D1. Parallel titles are recorded in the order found in the chief source of information. *See* Fig. 3.11.

Fig. 3.11. Rule 1.1D1. Transcription of parallel title.

[1]Sign for
parallel title

[2]Parallel title

La motoneige au Québec = Snowmobiling in
Quebec.

1 / 2 /

1.1E. Other title information (subfield b of MARC field 245)

1.1E1. Other title information is transcribed using the same rules as for the title proper. Other title information includes, but is not limited to, subtitles. *See* Figs. 3.12-3.14.

Fig. 3.12. Rule 1.1E1. Transcription of other title information.

Subtitle

The midnight patrol : the story of a Salvation Army lass who patrolled the dark streets of London's West End on a midnight mission of mercy / by Phyllis Thompson.

Fig. 3.13. Rule 1.1E1. Transcription of two kinds of other title information.

[1]Subtitle

[2]Other title
information

From Poussin to Matisse : the Russian taste for French painting : a loan exhibition from the U.S.S.R.

Fig. 3.14. Rule 1.1E1. Transcription of other title information following GMD.

[1]GMD

[2]Other title
information

The scales of justice [filmstrip] : our court system / Center for Humanities, Inc.

1.1E5. When parallel titles are involved, other title information follows the title proper or the parallel title that it accompanies. *See* Fig. 3.15.

Fig. 3.15. Rule 1.1E5. Transcription of other title information following title proper or parallel title to which it is appropriate.

La nuit : Etüde für Klavier = Night : piano study : op. 31, Nr. 3 / Alexander Glasunow.

1.1E6. In cases where a title proper needs explanation, an explanatory term or phrase is added in brackets as other title information in the same language as the title proper. *See* Fig. 3.16. Such additions are preceded by a colon so as to distinguish them from GMDs.

Fig. 3.16. Rule 1.1E6. Addition of explanatory term as other title information.

Addition to
title

Beginnings : [poems] / by Carol Lynn Pearson ;
illustrated by Trevor Southey

1.1F. Statements of responsibility (subfield c of MARC field 245)

1.1F1. Statements of responsibility that appear prominently in an item are recorded as they appear. Just as for title information, statements of responsibility that do not come from the chief source of information must be enclosed in square brackets. An LC rule interpretation suggests that only statements "that are of bibliographic significance" should be recorded, and guidelines are provided for making such a determination. (*CSB* 13: 4-6). *See* Figs. 3.17-3.19.

Fig. 3.17. Rule 1.1F1. Statements of responsibility recorded as they appear in the chief sources of information.

And then there's always the possibility of disappearing altogether [motion picture] / Pegarty Long.

Fig. 3.18.

Dear Dr. Stopes : sex in the 1920s / edited by Ruth Hall.

Fig. 3.19. Rule 1.1F1. Statement of responsibility taken from outside chief source of information.

Ben Oliel and Seeley / [Dorothy Wood Ewers].

1.1F2. Unlike titles proper, a statement of responsibility is not essential to a description, and if one is not prominent in the item, one is not constructed. *See* Fig. 3.20.

Fig. 3.20. Rule 1.1F2. Item bearing no prominent statement of responsibility.

Blood pressure [slide].

It should be noted that serials and other items often have identical titles proper (e.g., Bulletin). When no statement of responsibility is given, non-distinctive titles become a problem when the title is the main entry and when it is necessary to make an added entry for that title on the record for another work. This problem has been solved with uniform titles. (*See* discussion in chapter 13.)

1.1F5. Often an item names more than three persons or corporate bodies that have all performed the same function or had the same degree of responsibility for the work. If there are three such persons or bodies, all are given in the statement of responsibility. If there are more than three, only the first person or corporate body of each group is listed. The omission of the others is indicated by "... [et al.]" (or the equivalent of "et al." in nonroman scripts). *See* Fig. 3.21.

¹First named
author of a
group of more
than three sub-
sidiary authors

²Mark of
omission and
[et al.]

Fig. 3.21. Rule 1.1F5. Transcription of statement of responsibility with more than three persons performing the same function.

Studies in modality / Nicholas Rescher ; with the collaboration of Ruth Manor ... [et al.].

1.1F6. Multiple statements of responsibility (i.e., for different kinds of responsibility for a work) are transcribed in the order in which they appear in the information source. If the layout is such that the statements are not in an obvious order, the cataloger is instructed to use "the order that makes the most sense." *See* Fig. 3.22.

Fig. 3.22. Rule 1.1F6. Transcription of more than one statement of responsibility.

Persons with
different kinds
of responsi-
bility

Looking backwards / Colette ; translated from the French by David Le Vay ; with an introduction by Maurice Goudeket.

1.1F7. Most titles of address, honor, and distinction; qualifications; dates of founding; etc., are omitted from statements of responsibility. There are four exceptions:

1) when the title is necessary grammatically

2) when only a given name or only a surname is accompanied by a title

3) when a title is necessary for identification

4) when a title of nobility or British title of honor is involved.

See Fig. 3.23.

Fig. 3.23. Rule 1.1F7. Transcription of a title of address in a statement of responsibility.

Title "Mrs."
necessary to
identify author

Suppression of Mutiny, 1857-1858 / Mrs. Henry Duberly.

1.1F8. In instances where the relationship of the person or body in the statement of responsibility to the work is not clear, a word or phrase of explanation may be added in brackets. This does not allow, however, for the former practice of adding "by" and/or "and" in statements of authorship. *See* Figs. 3.24 and 3.25.

Fig. 3.24. Rule 1.1F8. Explanatory phrase added to statement of responsibility for clarity.

Necessary
addition

About interpretation : from Plato to Dilthey : a hermeneutic anthology / [compiled by] Barrie A. Wilson.

Fig. 3.25. Rule 1.1F8. Omission of explanatory words in statement of responsibility.

[by] not added   Potters of Southern Africa / G. Clark, L. Wagner.

[and] not added

1.1F12. Noun phrases sometimes appear between titles and statements of responsibility that are not clearly part of either. One has to decide whether such a noun or noun phrase seems to indicate the nature of the work or the role of the person or body responsible. If it seems to indicate the nature of the work, it is transcribed as other title information. Otherwise it is transcribed as part of the statement of responsibility. Preference is given the latter treatment when in doubt. *See* Figs. 3.26 and 3.27.

Fig. 3.26. Rule 1.1F12. Noun phrase transcribed as other title information.

Noun phrase indicative of nature of the work

Walt Whitman's poetry : a study & a selection / by Edmond Holmes.

Fig. 3.27. Rule 1.1F12. Noun phrase transcribed as part of statement of responsibility.

Noun phrase indicating role of corporate body

Innovative funding : the ABC's of supplementing LMI budgets / a collaborative effort initiated by the ICESA LMI Committee.

1.1F13. The rules for transcription of title information include instructions to give statements of responsibility as part of the title when they are inseparable grammatically. When this has been done, no separate statement of responsibility is given unless there is a separate statement in the chief source of information. *See* Figs. 3.28 and 3.29.

Fig. 3.28. Rule 1.1F13. Person responsible is transcribed as part of the title proper and thus is not repeated as a statement of responsibility.

Horowitz in concert [sound recording] : recorded at his 1966 Carnegie Hall recitals.

Fig. 3.29. Rule 1.1F13. Person responsible is repeated because the chief source of information bears a separate statement of responsibility.

Author's name as part of the title

McGuffey's new third eclectic reader for young learners / by Wm. H. McGuffey.

Separate author statement

1.1G.   Items without a collective title

Items that lack a collective title may or may not have a predominant part. If such a predominant part is present, the title of that part is given as the title proper for the work, and other titles are given in a note. If there is no predominant part, the rule calls for describing the item as a unit, with the option of describing each part separately and linking the separate descriptions with notes for the following materials: cartographic materials, sound recordings, motion pictures and video-recordings, computer files, and microforms. When the item is described as a unit, the titles are transcribed in the order given in the chief source of information (or in the order in which they appear, if there is no chief source). If the parts are all by the same person(s) or body(ies), their titles are separated by semicolons, and the statement of responsibility follows the last one. *See* Figs. 3.30 and 3.31.

Fig. 3.30. Rule 1.1G. Transcription of titles of two sides of a recording by the same person. Each title is taken from a separate label, and there is no linking word.

African politics ; More songs from Kenya [sound recording] / David Nzomo.

Fig. 3.31. Rule 1.1G. Transcription of titles of two works that are published in the same book. The title page gives the linking word *and*.

Fantazias ; and, In nomines / by Henry Purcell ; edited with a foreword by Anthony Ford.

If different persons or bodies were responsible for the various parts, or if it is not known whether all parts were by the same person(s) or body(ies), each title is followed by its other title information, statement of responsibility, and a period. *See* Fig. 3.32.

Fig. 3.32. Rule 1.1G. Transcription of separate titles and statements of responsibility for work that lacks a collective title.

[1]

[1]Separate title and statement of responsibility

The suicide meet / Mary Humphrey Baldridge. Pickle / by Sheila Junor-Moore. The saga of the elk / by Jim Taylor. What it means to me to be a Canadian / compiled from Calgary school children, grades 6 and 7.

[2]Name-title added entries for separate titles

Added entries made for this work:

[2] I. Junor-Moore, Sheila. Pickle. II. Taylor, Jim, 1937-   . The saga of the elk. III. What it means to me to be a Canadian. IV. Title.

RULE 1.2. EDITION AREA (MARC field 250)

1.2B. Edition statement (subfield a of MARC field 250)

1.2B1. If there is an edition statement, it is transcribed as found on the item with the exception that standard abbreviations found in Appendix B of *AACR2R* and numerals as found in Appendix C of *AACR2R* are used in place of the actual words from the source of information. *See* Fig. 3.33.

Fig. 3.33. Rule 1.2B1. Transcription of edition statement.

Export/import traffic management and forwarding /
by Alfred Murr. — 3rd ed., rev. and enl.

1.2C. Statements of responsibility relating to the edition (subfield b of MARC field 250)

1.2C1. A statement of responsibility that applies to the edition in hand, but not to all editions of a work, is given following the edition statement, if there is one. *See* Fig. 3.34.

Fig. 3.34. Rule 1.2C1. Transcription of statement of responsibility relating to this edition but not to all editions.

Statement of authorship in edition area
The Oxford school dictionary / compiled by Dorothy C. Mackenzie. — 3rd ed. / revised by Joan Pusey.

1.2C2. When there is no edition statement, when there is doubt about whether a statement of responsibility applies to all editions, or when one is describing a first edition, all statements of responsibility are transcribed into the title and statement of responsibility area.

RULE 1.3. MATERIAL (OR TYPE OF PUBLICATION) SPECIFIC DETAILS AREA (MARC field 255 for cartographic materials, field 254 for music, field 256 for computer files, and field 362 for serials)

This area, so far, is used only for cartographic materials, music, computer files, and serials. It is also used in describing microforms of cartographic materials, music, and serials. Therefore, the content of this area is discussed in the chapters in *AACR2R* and in this text specifically devoted to the description of these materials.

RULE 1.4. PUBLICATION, DISTRIBUTION, ETC., AREA (MARC field 260)

1.4B. General rule

All details about place(s), name(s), and date(s) of the activities involved in the publishing, distributing, issuing, releasing, and manufacture of items are recorded in this area. When there is more than one place, name, and/or date, they are recorded in an order appropriate to the item in hand. Names of places, persons, or bodies are given as they appear, except that prepositions that are not integral parts of the name are usually omitted, and abbreviations from Appendix B of *AACR2R* are used. Original publication details that are covered by a label giving reproduction details are given in a note (if they can be determined easily), while the information from the label is recorded in the publication, distribution, etc., area. *See* Fig. 3.35.

Fig. 3.35. Rule 1.4B. Publication details from label transcribed in publication, distribution, etc., area with original publication details in a note.

[1]Publisher information relating to reproduction

Human potentialities [sound recording] / Herbert A. Otto. — New York : J. Norton Publishers, [1974?]
1 sound tape reel (27 min.) : analog, 3¾ ips, mono. ; 5 in.

[2]Publication details of original

Publisher information under label reads: New York : McGraw-Hill, 1968.

1.4C. Place of publication, distribution, etc. (subfield a of MARC field 260)

1.4C1. The place of publication (or production, etc.) is recorded as it appears in a prescribed source of information.

1.4C3. The name of the country, state, province, etc., is added to the name when necessary to distinguish between places or if necessary for identification. It is added in brackets if it does not appear in the source of information. *See* Figs. 3.36-3.38.

Fig. 3.36. Rule 1.4C3. Addition of country in brackets where city alone appeared in prescribed source of information.

Name of country added

Vanished fleets : sea stories from old Van Dieman's land / by Alan Villiers. — Cambridge [England] ◄——

LC adds larger jurisdictions that appear with a place name in the source of information even when identification is not needed. When the larger jurisdiction does not appear together with the place name, LC adds it according to the provisions of rule 1.4C3. (*CSB* 44: 12)

Fig. 3.37. Rule 1.4C3. Addition of state to name of city. Name of state appeared in prescribed source of information.

Name of state added

Hans in luck [motion picture]. — Santa Monica, Calif. ◄——

Fig. 3.38. Rule 1.4C3. Name of state not added to city because it was not with the city name on the title page and was not considered necessary to identify the city.

Name of state not added

Troll tales of Tumble Town [filmstrip] / Don Arthur Torgersen. — Chicago ◄——

1.4C5. When more than one place is given in the item for a publisher, distributor, etc., the first named place is transcribed. If another place is typographically prominent, it is also transcribed. In addition, if neither the first named place nor a typographically prominent place are in the home country of the cataloging agency, the first place given that *is* in the home country is also transcribed. *See* Fig. 3.39.

Rule 1.4D5 treats two or more places that relate to two or more publishers, etc.

Fig. 3.39. Rule 1.4C5. Transcription by a U.S. cataloging agency of U.S. city following foreign city.

[1]Foreign city   Educational theory : an introduction / T.W.
               Moore. — London ; Boston
[2]U.S. city
                              1   2

1.4C6. A probable place is given in brackets with a question mark when the place of publication, etc., is uncertain. *See* Fig. 3.40.

Fig. 3.40. Rule 1.4C6. Transcription of probable place of publication with question mark.

Place uncertain   A century in Singapore : 1877-1977 / Hongkong and Shanghai Banking Corporation. — [Singapore?]

If the place is unknown but the country, state, province, etc., is known or probable, the country, state or province, etc., is given in brackets (with a question mark if uncertain).

If no country, etc., or probable country can be given, the abbreviation "s.l." (*sine loco*), or its equivalent in nonroman scripts, is given. *See* Fig. 3.41.

Fig. 3.41. Rule 1.4C6. Transcription of abbreviation "s.l." when no place or probable place is known.

Place unknown   Precious cargo / by Ralph Byrne. — [S.l. : R. Byrne]

Note: Uppercase "S.l." results from its beginning an area of the description.

1.4C7. An option allows transcription in parentheses, after the place name, of the full address of a publisher, distributor, etc. Such an addition should not be made for major trade publishers.

LC has a strict set of provisions for applying this option. The basic ones are that it applies only to monographs published in the U.S., issued in the current year or one of the previous two years, and not bearing ISBNs or ISSNs. (*CSB* 15: 3). *See* Fig. 3.42.

Fig. 3.42. Rule 1.4C7. Addition of address of publisher to the place of publication, etc.

Journey into small groups / William Bangham. — Memphis, Tenn. (1548 Poplar Avenue, Memphis, 38104) : Lay Renewal

1.4C8. Neither place of publication, distribution, etc., nor "s.l." is recorded for unpublished items (e.g., art originals) or for unpublished collections. *See* Figs. 3.55 and 3.56 (pages 66-67).

1.4D. Name of publisher, distributor, etc. (subfield b of MARC field 260)

1.4D1. The name of the publisher, distributor, etc., follows the name of the place to which it relates.

1.4D2. The name of the publisher, distributor, etc., is given in the shortest form it can take to be understood internationally. *See* Fig. 3.43.

> **Fig. 3.43. Rule 1.4D2. Transcription of name of publisher in shortest identifiable form.**
>
> Living with loss : a dramatic new breakthrough in grief therapy / Ronald W. Ramsay, Rene Noorbergen. — New York : W. Morrow ◄——

Note: Publisher statement on title page reads: William Morrow and Company, Inc.

It is important to note the term *internationally*. Because there is now more emphasis on creating bibliographic records for an international audience, the publisher, distributor, etc., area sometimes needs fuller information than was adequate in the past.

LC does not omit parts of a hierarchy for any corporate bodies except commercial publishers. Also, such words as *Inc.* that appear after a serial title being recorded as a publisher are retained. (*CSB* 47: 11)

1.4D3. Two particular parts of names of publishers, distributors, etc., that are to be retained are:

  a) Words that indicate function other than only a publishing function. *See* Figs. 3.44 and 3.45.

> **Fig. 3.44. Rule 1.4D3a. Transcriptions of name of publisher, distributor, etc., including words and phrases indicating functions performed.**
>
> **Published for … by …**
> At the edge of megalopolis : a history of Salem, N.H., 1900-1974 / [Noyes, Turner]. — Canaan, N.H. : Published for the Town of Salem, N.H., by Phoenix Pub. ↘   ↘
>
> **Fig. 3.45.**
>
> **Distributor indicated**
> The National labor relations act : a guidebook for health care facility administrators / Dennis D. Pointer and Norman Metzger. — New York : Spectrum Publications : ——► distributed by Halsted Press

b) Parts of a name that distinguish between publishers, etc. For example:

> Encyclopaedia Britannica Educational Corp.
> Encyclopaedia Britannica, Inc.

(These are separate bodies and cannot be identified simply as Encyclopaedia Britannica.)

1.4D4. A person or corporate body that appears in both the statement of responsibility and the publication area is given in the publication area in a shortened form if the name is in a recognizable form in the title and statement of responsibility area. *See* Fig. 3.46.

Fig. 3.46. Rule 1.4D4. Transcription of shortened form of name that appears in full form in the title and statement of responsibility area.

Shortened
name

> The Dexter Avenue Baptist Church, 1877-1977 / edited by Zelia S. Evans, with J.T. Alexander. — 1st ed. — [Montgomery, Ala.] : The Church◄——

When a person is both author and publisher, the form used in the publisher, etc., area is the initial(s) and surname of the person.

1.4D5. There are four situations in which the transcription of a subsequently named publisher, distributor, etc. (and its place, if different from the first), is to be added after the first named body:

a) when the two bodies are linked in a single statement, e.g.,

> London: Published for the Institute of Mediaeval Studies by Sheed & Ward

b) when a distributor, etc., is named first, while a publisher is named later,

c) When a publisher, distributor, etc., is clearly the principal one (as shown by layout or typography) but is not named first,

d) when the first body is not in the country of the cataloging agency, while a later one is. *See* Fig. 3.47.

Fig. 3.47. Rule 1.4D5. Transcription by a U.S. cataloging agency of U.S. city and publisher following foreign city and publisher.

[1]Foreign city
and publisher
[2]U.S. city and
publisher

> Genetics of forest ecosystems / Klaus Stern, Laurence Roche. — London : Chapman and Hall ; New York : Springer-Verlag

LC, in applying rule 1.4D5, records both entities when two are named. The situations prescribed in the rule, then, are used as guidelines when three or more names are given. (*CSB* 44: 13-16)

1.4D6. An option allows addition of the name (and place if different) of a distributor when the first name is for a publisher. LC is applying this option. (*CSB* 47: 15). *See* Fig. 3.48.

Fig. 3.48. Rule 1.4D6. Transcription of names of both producer and distributor.

> The plow that broke the Plains [videorecording] / United States Resettlement Administration. — Washington, D.C. : National Archives and Records Service : distributed by National Audiovisual Center

1.4D7. When the name of the publisher, etc., is not known, the abbreviation s.n. (*sine nomine*) is given in brackets. *See* Fig. 3.49.

Fig. 3.49. Rule 1.4D7. Transcription of "s.n." to indicate that the name of the publisher is unknown.

Publisher unknown

> The story of Lanark / prepared and written by Elizabeth L. Jamieson. — [S.l. : s.n.]

1.4D9. Neither name of publisher, distributor, etc., nor "s.n." is recorded for unpublished items or for unpublished collections. *See* Figs. 3.55 and 3.56 (pages 66-67).

1.4F. Date of Publication, distribution, etc. (subfield c of MARC field 260)

1.4F1. The date of publication of the edition in hand is the next element of this area.

1.4F2. The date given in the item is used even if it is known to be incorrect, in which case the correct date is added in brackets and an explanation is given in a note if necessary.

1.4F5. An option allows adding the latest copyright date to the publication, distribution, etc., date if it is different. LC has applied this option since the inception of *AACR2*, but late in 1989 announced that the option would no longer be applied to books and printed serials. *See* Fig. 3.50. NOTE: A copyright date is always preceded by a "c," and a phonogram copyright date is preceded by a "p."

Fig. 3.50. Rule 1.4F5. Transcription of copyright date that varies from publication date.

[1]Date of publication
[2]Copyright date

> Attracting birds to your backyard [videorecording] / with Roger Tory Peterson. — Carrboro, N.C. : Nature Science Network, 1990, c1986.

1.4F6. If the date of publication or distribution is not given in the item, the copyright date is used. If there is no copyright date, a manufacturing date, if present, is given. In the latter case, a word such as *printing* or *pressing* is added, e.g., 1989 pressing. *See* Fig. 3.51.

Fig. 3.51. Rule 1.4F6. Use of copyright date when publication date is not given in the item.

Copyright date

> Kept women : confessions from a life of luxury / Leslie McRay with Ted Schwarz. — New York : W. Morrow, c1990.

LC has found it necessary to issue a rule interpretation for when to use copyright date, probable date of publication, and/or date of manufacture. (*CSB* 47: 15-16)

1.4F7. If no date of publication, etc., copyright, or manufacture can be found, the cataloger is instructed to give an approximate date. *See* Fig. 3.52. *See also* examples in *AACR2R*, chapter 1, page 41.

Fig. 3.52. Rule 1.4F7. Transcription of approximate date of publication.

Believed to
be 1987

Carrier Air Wing [videorecording]. — Seattle : Pool & Crew Communications, [1987?]

1.4F8. When a multipart item has been published during more than one year and thus two or more dates are found on different parts, the earliest and latest dates are given. Only the earliest date and a hyphen followed by four spaces is given when a multipart item is incomplete. LC often places the date of a second or later volume that is not the last volume within angle brackets. *See* Fig. 3.53.

Fig. 3.53. Rule 1.4F8. Transcription of earliest date of a multipart item, and showing the practice of placing a subsequent, but not last, volume date in angle brackets.

Date of
last volume
received in
angle brackets

Christ in Christian tradition / Aloys Grillmeier ; translated by John Bowden. — 2nd rev. ed. — London : Mowbrays, 1975-<1987>

An option allows adding the latest or later date when the item is complete. LC follows this option. (*CSB* 45: 12). *See* Fig. 3.54.

Fig. 3.54. Rule 1.4F8. Transcription of earliest and latest dates of a multipart item.

[1]Inclusive
dates

[2]Two volume
work

The narrative unity of Luke-Acts : a literary interpretation / by Robert C. Tannehill. — Philadelphia : Fortress Press, c1986-c1990.◄—1
  2 v. ; 25 cm.
◄—2

1.4F9-1.4F10. No date is given for naturally occurring objects unless they have been packaged for commercial distribution. For the latter and other unpublished items the date of production is given. A date or inclusive dates are given for unpublished collections. *See* Figs. 3.55 and 3.56.

Fig. 3.55. Rule 1.4F9. Transcription of date only for an unpublished item.

[Polar bears] [art original] / Dorothy S. Taylor. — 1985.

Fig. 3.56. Rule 1.4F10. Transcription of inclusive dates for an unpublished collection.

[Photographs of blue ribbon pigs, Iowa State Fair] [picture]. — 1927-1947.

1.4G.   Place of manufacture, name of manufacturer, date of manufacture (subfields e, f, and g of MARC field 260)

1.4G1. If the name of the publisher, distributor, etc., is not known and the place and name of the manufacturer are given in the item, the latter are transcribed into the record after the date. (The date given in the publication date position is often the date of manufacture in this situation; if so, it is not repeated here.) *See* Fig. 3.57.

Fig. 3.57. Rule 1.4G1. Transcription of place and name of manufacturer following date when publisher is unknown.

¹Place of publication unknown

²Name of publisher unknown

2
The offensive side of Lou Holtz / by Lou Holtz. — [S.l. : s.n.], c1978 (Little Rock, Ark. : Parkin Print. Co.)
3

³Manufacturer's imprint

RULE 1.5.   PHYSICAL DESCRIPTION AREA (MARC field 300)

1.5A3. This preliminary rule calls for giving the physical description for the item in hand if the work is available in different formats. Optionally, notes are made to describe the other physical formats in which an item is available.

The part of this rule that calls for describing text on microfilm as microfilm has caused much controversy in the library community. It is believed by many librarians that the importance of text on microfilm is as a version of the text. The fact that the version is in microform rather than regular print is, to these persons, less important than the description of the original in terms of number of pages of text. On the other side, there are those who say that the purpose of bibliographic description is to describe the item in hand. If it is two sheets of microfiche, it is not the same as a 350-page bound volume.

This debate has been resolved for now by LC's decision to catalog microreproductions of certain printed items by transcribing the physical details of the original work in the body of the description while giving the details of the microreproduction in a note. (*CSB* 45: 18-19) This practice has not been adopted as a rule revision because the other countries involved in responsibility for *AACR2R* have not had as much problem about the issue. (*See also* chapter 6 of this text.)

The option of making a note describing other formats is being applied by LC. (*CSB* 8: 9) *See* Fig. 3.58.

Fig. 3.58. Rules 1.5A3 and 1.5B1. Transcription of extent of item in hand with notes of other physical formats in which the work is available.

¹Number of
physical units

²Notes of
other existing
forms of same
item

Macumba, trance, and spirit healing [videorecording] / producer, Madeleine Richeport. — New York, NY : Filmakers Library, 1984.

1——►1 videocassette (43 min.) : sd., col.

2 { Issued as U-matic ¾ in. or Beta ½ in. or VHS ½ in.
Issued also as motion picture.

1.5B. Extent of item (including specific material designation) (subfield a of MARC field 300)

1.5B1. The extent of item consists of the number of physical units in arabic numerals followed by the specific material designation. *See* Fig. 3.58 above. The word *identical* is added before the specific material designation when appropriate (e.g., 10 identical study prints).

How to record the extent of item for different types of materials is covered in detail in each chapter on a type of material. Where appropriate, additions in parentheses are made following the number of physical units (e.g., number of frames on a filmstrip, playing time), and these are explained more fully in the following chapters of this text.

1.5B5. A multipart item that is not yet complete is described with the specific material designation preceded by three spaces. An option allows adding the number of physical units after completion of the item. *See* Fig. 3.59.

Fig. 3.59. Rule 1.5B5. Transcription of designation preceded by three spaces for incomplete item.

Designation for
incomplete
multipart item

Spy. — Oct. 1986-   . — New York, N.Y. : Spy Pub. Partners, c1986-
——► v. : ill. ; 28 cm.

The Library of Congress is applying the option; so if the work in Fig. 3.59 becomes complete in, say, 30 volumes, the physical description area will read:
30 v. : ill. ; 28 cm. (*CSB* 8: 9)

1.5C. Other physical details (subfield b of MARC field 300)

1.5C1. Physical details other than extent of item or dimensions are given following the extent. These vary by type of material. Details are discussed in later chapters of this text. *See* Fig. 3.60.

Fig. 3.60. Rule 1.5C1. Transcription of other physical details following extent of item.

Physical data
about presence
of sound and
color

Ghost stories [videorecording]. — Woodland Hills, Calif. : Celebrity Home Entertainment, 1989.
1 videocassette (60 min.) : sd., col. ; ½ in.

1.5D. Dimensions (subfield c of MARC field 300)
The dimensions of an item serve as an aid in finding it on the library shelves. Dimensions are especially valuable for libraries with separate storage areas for oversized items. They also serve the user who wishes to borrow an item through interlibrary loan.

As is true for other parts of the physical description, instructions for giving dimensions vary by type of material and are discussed in later chapters of this text. *See* Fig. 3.61.

Fig. 3.61. Rule 1.5D. Transcription of dimensions following extent of item, there being no "other" physical details.

Height in
centimeters

Away is a strange place to be / H.M. Hoover. — 1st ed. — New York : Dutton, c1990.
167 p. ; 22 cm.

1.5E. Accompanying material (subfield e of MARC field 300)
Accompanying material includes answer books, teacher's manuals, atlases, portfolios of plates, slides, phonodiscs, booklets explaining audiovisual materials, and other such items. These materials often are placed in pockets inside the cover of the work being cataloged, or they may be loose inside the container. Their description may make up the fourth element of the physical description area. -

1.5E1. Four methods are suggested for handling accompanying material: a) It may be described in a separate entry. b) It may be described in a multilevel description as outlined in chapter 13 of *AACR2R*. c) Details may be given in a note. d) Details may be given as the last element of the physical description area. If the fourth method is used, an option allows addition in parentheses of further physical description of the accompanying material. LC is applying this option on a case-by-case basis, usually to items that are substantial in extent or are significant for some reason. (*CSB* 29: 10) *See* Fig. 3.62.

Fig. 3.62. Rule 1.5E1d. Transcription of physical description for accompanying material.

Accompanying
material with
its physical
description

Evolution of the Arctic-North Atlantic and the Western Tethys : Peter A. Ziegler. — Tulsa, Okla., U.S.A. : American Association of Petroleum Geologists, c1988.
viii, 198 p. : ill. (some col.), maps ; 29 cm. + 1 portfolio (30 plates : col. maps ; 28 cm.).

RULE 1.6.   SERIES AREA (MARC field 4xx)

The first definition of *series* as it appears in the *AACR2R* Glossary is: "A group of separate items related to one another by the fact that each item bears, in addition to its own title proper, a collective title applying to the group as a whole."[6] LC has issued a lengthy rule interpretation that discusses LC practice with regard to sources of information for accepting or rejecting an item as a series, phrases not considered series, multiple series versus subseries versus multipart items, series statements, and series tracings. (*CSB* 47: 17-28)

1.6B.   Title proper of series (subfield a of MARC field 4xx)

1.6B1.   The title proper of a series is transcribed according to the rules for transcribing the title proper of the item. *See* Fig. 3.63.

Fig. 3.63. Rule 1.6B1. Transcription of series title proper in parentheses.

Series title   Vegetable suite : for flute and piano / Graham Powning. – London : Chester Music ; New York : W. Hansen/Chester Music, c1986.
      1 score (6 p.) + 1 part (3 p.) ; 31 cm. – (The Chester woodwind series)

Other title information is seldom recorded for series. It is recorded only if valuable for identifying the series. When other title information or parallel titles for series are recorded, they are transcribed according to the same rules used for the title and statement of responsibility area.

1.6B2.   This rule gives a hierarchy for choice among variant series titles that may appear in an item. A title in the first of the prescribed sources of information for the series is preferred. If the series title does not appear in the first prescribed source, but there are different forms in other parts of the item, the order of preference for sources dictates which form should be used.

1.6E.   Statements of responsibility relating to series (subfield a of MARC field 4xx)

1.6E1.   Statements of responsibility that appear "in conjunction with the series title" are to be recorded if "they are considered to be necessary for identification." LC has issued a rule interpretation stating that this means statements that are in close proximity for titles that are essentially meaningless without such a statement (e.g., Report). (*CSB* 22: 16) *See* Fig. 3.64.

Fig. 3.64. Rule 1.6E1. Transcription of series statement of responsibility following series title.

[1]Generic title   Post-war food and cash crop production in former
[2]Statement of   colonial territories / compiled by B.J. Silk. – [Oxford :
responsibility   Oxford Development Records Project, 1985]
[3]Series number   64 p. ; 30 cm. – (Report / Oxford Development Records Project ; 8)   1   2
      3

1.6F. ISSN of series (subfield x of MARC field 4xx)

The ISSN is the International Standard Series Number, assigned to a serial as an internationally agreed-upon unique identifier. It is useful for identification and ordering purposes. It is recorded in the series area if it appears in the item. *See* Fig. 3.65.

Fig. 3.65. Rule 1.6F. Transcription of ISSN following series title.

¹Series title   Religion, intergroup relations, and social change in South
²ISSN   Africa / G.E. Oosthuizen ... [et al.] ; Human Sciences
³Series number Research Council, Work Committee: Religion. — New
      York ; London : Greenwood, 1988. ⟵1
         xii, 237 p. ; 23 cm. — (Contributions in ethnic studies,
   2⟶ISSN 0196-7088 ; no. 24)⟵3

1.6G. Numbering within series (subfield v of MARC field 4xx)

1.6G1. Numbering given with the series in the item is recorded as part of the series area. Abbreviations as found in Appendix B of *AACR2R* are used and arabic numerals are substituted for nonarabic numerals. *See* Figs. 3.64 and 3.65, above.

LC has found it necessary to issue a lengthy rule interpretation concerning transcription of series numbering. (*CSB* 31: 20-25)

1.6H. Subseries (subfields n and p of MARC field 4xx)

AACR2R defines subseries: "A series within a series (i.e., a series that always appears in conjunction with another, usually more comprehensive, series of which it forms a section). Its title may or may not be dependent on the title of the main series."[7]

Such a subseries, if present, is transcribed after the details of the main series. Parallel titles, other title information, statements of responsibility, ISSN, and numbering are transcribed for subseries in the same way as for series. An LC rule interpretation gives guidelines for judging an item to be part of a subseries and for transcribing subseries into a bibliographic record. (*CSB* 45: 13-15) *See* Fig. 3.66.

Fig. 3.66. Rule 1.6H. Transcription of subseries information following series title.

¹Series title   About interpretation : from Plato to Dilthey ; a
      hermeneutic anthology / [compiled by] Barrie A. Wilson. —
²Subseries title New York : P. Lang, c1989. ⟵1
³ISSN for   xii, 208 p. ; 23 cm. — (American university studies.
subseries   Series V, Philosophy, ISSN 0739-6392 ; v. 30)
⁴Numbering   ⟵2   ⟵3   ⟵4
for subseries

1.6J. More than one series statement

1.6J1. If there is more than one series, each series is recorded in a separate series statement in its own set of parentheses. An LC rule interpretation gives guidelines for application of this rule. (*CSB* 32: 11-12) *See* Fig. 3.67.

Fig. 3.67. Rule 1.6J1. Transcription of two series statements, each in its own set of parentheses.

[1]First series Conducting a successful capital campaign : a compre-
[2]Second series hensive fundraising guide for nonprofit organizations /
Kent E. Dove. — 1st ed. — San Francisco : Jossey-Bass
Publishers, 1988.   ↙1
  xxii, 292 p. : ill. ; 24 cm. — (The Jossey-Bass
management series) (The Jossey-Bass higher education
series)   ↖2

RULE 1.7. NOTE AREA (MARC fields 5xx)

Many works require description beyond that presented formally in the title and statement of responsibility area through the series area. Notes qualify or amplify the formal description. Some notes contribute to identification of a work (e.g., a note giving the original title of a translated work). Some contribute to the intelligibility of the record (e.g., a note explaining the relationship to the work of a person who has been given an added entry). Other notes aid the reader who does not have in hand an exact citation (e.g., a summary or contents note). Still other notes characterize an item (e.g., a thesis note) or give its bibliographic history (e.g., notes giving previous titles).

1.7A. Preliminary rule

1.7A3. Form of notes

This rule gives general guidelines for the formulation of notes.

Order of information. In any one note, data that correspond to data found in descriptive areas preceding the notes area are transcribed in the same order in the note. The prescribed punctuation is used with the exception that a period (full stop), space, dash, space is replaced simply by a period (full stop). *See* Fig. 3.68.

Fig. 3.68. Rule 1.7A3. Transcription of information in the note in the same order it would be transcribed in the preceding areas of the description, but without any period, space, dash, space separating areas.

  Trees and shrubs of the Southeast / Blanche Evans
Dean ; illustrated by Forrest Bonner. — 3rd ed., rev. and
expanded. — Birmingham, Ala. : Birmingham Audubon
Society Press, c1988.
  xx, 264 p. : ill. ; 23 cm.

  Rev. and expanded ed. of: Trees and shrubs in the heart
of Dixie. Rev. ed. Birmingham, Ala. : Southern University
Press, 1968.

Quotations. Quotations in notes are given in quotes followed by an indication of the source, unless the chief source of information is the source of the quotation.

Formal notes. Standard format is used for certain notes because uniformity can assist in recognition of some types of information and because it allows for space economy.

Informal notes. Informal notes should be as brief as they can be without sacrificing clarity, understandability, or good grammar.

1.7A4. Notes citing other editions and works

When notes are made citing other works or other manifestations of the same work, the notes should give enough information to identify the work cited. When giving a note for an original work from which the work in hand is reproduced, all notes relating to the original are combined into one note. An LC rule interpretation gives guidance and examples for applying this rule. (*CSB* 44: 17-18)

1.7B. Notes

A general outline of notes is given here followed by some examples (*see* Figs. 3.69-3.74 on pages 74-76). More specific applications are discussed in the following chapters where notes applicable to the various types of material are discussed in detail.

Notes are to be given in the order listed here, except that a note that has been decided to be of primary importance for a particular type of material should be given first (e.g., publishers' stock numbers for sound recordings). Upon examination, one can determine the logic of the order. First come notes concerning the nature and language of the item. Then come notes that relate to the areas of description from title through series in the order in which they appear in the body of the entry. These are followed by notes that characterize and summarize the item.

(Note: MARC field 500 is used unless otherwise noted.)

1.7B1.   **Nature, scope, or artistic form**

1.7B2.   **Language of the item and/or translation or adaptation** (MARC field 546) (*See also CSB* 44: 18-20)

1.7B3.   **Source of title proper**

1.7B4.   **Variations in title** (*See also CSB* 39: 11-12)

1.7B5.   **Parallel titles and other title information**

1.7B6.   **Statements of responsibility** (MARC fields 500, 508, 511, and 570)

1.7B7.   **Edition and history** (MARC fields 500, 503, 518, and 580)

1.7B8.   **Material (or type of publication) specific details**

1.7B9.   **Publication, distribution, etc.** (MARC field 550)

1.7B10.   **Physical description**

1.7B11.   **Accompanying material and supplements**

1.7B12.   **Series**

1.7B13. **Dissertations** (MARC field 502)

1.7B14. **Audience** (MARC field 521)

1.7B15. **Reference to published descriptions** (MARC field 510)

1.7B16. **Other formats** (MARC field 530)

1.7B17. **Summary** (MARC field 520)

1.7B18. **Contents** (MARC fields 504 and 505)

1.7B19. **Numbers borne by the item (other than those covered in 1.8)** (MARC fields 023-030, 036, 037)

1.7B20. **Copy being described, library's holdings, and restrictions on use** (MARC field 590)

1.7B21. **"With" notes** (MARC field 501) (*See also CSB* 38: 31-32)

1.7B22. **Combined notes relating to the original** (MARC field 534) (*See also* Fig. 3.82, page 79.)

Fig. 3.69. Rule 1.7B. Transcriptions of notes.

[1]Nature, scope, or artistic form (1.7B1)

[2]Language (1.7B2)

[3]Physical description (1.7B10)

[4]Index note (1.7B18)

The poetry of Singapore / editors, Edwin Thumboo ... [et al.] — [Singapore?] : ASEAN Committee on Culture and Information, c1985.

560 p. : col. maps ; 25 cm. — (Anthology of ASEAN literatures ; v. 1)

1→Poems.
2→In Chinese, English, Malay, and Tamil.
3→Maps on lining papers.
4→Includes index.

Fig. 3.70. Rule 1.7B. Transcriptions of notes.

[1]Language (1.7B2)

[2]Source of title proper (1.7B3)

[3]Statements of responsibility (1.7B6)

[4]Edition and history (1.7B7)

[5]Audience (1.7B14)

[6]Other formats (1.7B16)

[7]Summary (1.7B17)

Berlin [motion picture] / Polonius Film Productions ; directors, writers, John Dooley, Tessa Dooley. — Chicago, Ill. : International Film Bureau, 1985.

1 film reel (25 min.) : sd., col. ; 16 mm. + 1 guide.

In German.←1
3 Title from data sheet.←2
Credits: Photographer, Nicholas Struthers ; narrator, Jurgen Schweckendiek.
A foreign film (England) ←4
Junior high school through adults.←5
7 Issued also as videorecording. ←6
Summary: A foreign language teaching program that introduces beginning German students to the history of Berlin and to aspects of contemporary life in the city.

Fig. 3.71. Rule 1.7B. Transcriptions of notes.

[1]Quoted note on nature of item (1.7B1)

[2]Publication information (1.7B9)

[3]Bibliography and index note (1.7B18)

Properties of impurity states in superlattice semiconductors / edited by C.Y. Fong, Inder P. Batra, and S. Ciraci. — New York : Plenum Press, c1988.

xi, 351 p. : ill. ; 26 cm. — (NATO ASI series. Series B, Physics ; v. 183)

[1]↘"Proceedings of a NATO Advanced Research Workshop on the Properties of Impurity States in Superlattice Semiconductors, held September 7-11, 1987, at the University of Essex, Colchester, United Kingdom"—Verso t.p.

[2]→"Published in cooperation with NATO Scientific Affairs Division."

[3]→Includes bibliographies and index.

Fig. 3.72. Rule 1.7B. Transcriptions of notes.

[1]Variations in title (1.7B4)

[2]Statement of responsibility (1.7B6)

[3]Edition and history (1.7B7)

[4]Physical description (1.7B10)

[5]Summary (1.7B17)

[6]Numbers borne by the item (1.7B19)

The alphabet theatre proudly presents The Z was zapped [videorecording] : a play in twenty-six acts / written and directed by Chris Van Allsburg ; produced by King Productions. — New Rochelle, N.Y. : Spoken Arts, 1988.

1 videocassette (9 min.) : sd., col. ; ½ in. + 1 guide.

[1]→Title on container and guide: Spoken Arts presents The Z was zapped.

[1]→Spine title on cassette and container: The Z was zapped.

[2]→Credits: Music by Wayne Abravanel ; performed by the Caslon Players.

[3]→Based on the book of the same title by Chris Van Allsburg.

[4]→VHS.

[5]→Summary: As a player in a play, each letter of the alphabet meets a fate described by a word that begins with that letter.

[6]→"SAV 9010."

Fig. 3.73. Rule 1.7B. Transcriptions of notes.

[1]Accompanying material (1.7B11)

[2]Index note (1.7B18)

The DOS workbook / David Uzzell. — Englewood Cliffs, N.J. : Prentice Hall, c1989.

viii, 77 p. ; 24 cm. + 1 computer disk (5¼ in.)

[1]→System requirements for computer disk: IBM PC, XT, AT, or compatibles; PC-DOS or MS-DOS 2.0 or higher; 1-2 disk drives or hard disk; printer.

[2]→Includes index.

Fig. 3.74. Rule 1.7B. Transcriptions of notes.

[1]Source of
title proper
(1.7B3)

[2]Statement of
responsibility
(1.7B6)

Mother West Wind stories [filmstrip] / Spoken Arts, Inc. ; producers, Arthur Luce Klein and Chris King. — New Rochelle, NY : Spoken Arts, 1986, c1987.

4 filmstrips : col. ; 35 mm. + 4 sound cassettes (45 min. : analog) + 1 teacher's guide.

[3]Physical
description
(1.7B10)

[4]Audience
(1.7B14)

[5]Summary
(1.7B17)

[6]Contents
(1.7B18)

1→Title from data sheet.

2→Credits: Narrators, Frances Sternhagen, Tom Carlin.

3→Sound accompaniment compatible for manual and automatic operation.

4→Kindergarten through primary grades.

5→Summary: Presents adaptations of four children's animal stories by Thornton W. Burgess.

6→Contents: Mrs. Redwing's speckled egg (45 fr., 6 min., 42 sec.) — Why Peter Rabbit's ears are long (71 fr., 13 min., 30 sec.) — Why Bobby Coon washes his food (67 fr., 13 min., 38 sec.) — The most beautiful thing in the world (66 fr., 10 min., 40 sec.)

RULE 1.8. STANDARD NUMBER AND TERMS OF AVAILABILITY AREA (MARC fields 020 and 022)

An LC rule interpretation should be consulted when applying this rule using standards set by LC. (*CSB* 47: 28-29)

1.8B. Standard number (subfield a of MARC field 020 or 022)

1.8B1. An internationally agreed-upon standard number for the item in hand is given in the standard number area following the notes. The numbers usually given here are the International Standard Book Number (ISBN) or the International Standard Serial Number (ISSN). *See* Fig. 3.75.

Fig. 3.75. Rule 1.8B1. Transcription of standard number for the item being described.

Standard
number

The Battle of Britain : the greatest air battle of World War II / Richard Hough and Denis Richards. — 1st American ed. — London : Hodder & Stoughton ; New York : Norton, c1989.

xvii, 413 p., [40] p. of plates : ill. (some col.), maps ; 25 cm.

Includes index.
→ISBN 0-393-02766-X

1.8B2. If there are two or more standard numbers, the one that applies to the item being described should be given. An option allows recording more than one number and adding a qualification (as prescribed in rule 1.8E). LC is applying this option. (*CSB* 8: 9) *See* Fig. 3.76.

Fig. 3.76. Rule 1.8B2, option. Transcription of more than one standard number on a record.

¹Standard
number for
hardback
edition

²Standard
number for
paperback
edition

The American West : a twentieth-century history /
Michael P. Malone & Richard W. Etulain. — Lincoln :
University of Nebraska Press, c1989.
347 p. : ill., maps ; 25 cm. — (The Twentieth-century
American West)

Bibliography: p. 295-330.
1. Includes index.   ²
ISBN 0-8032-3093-1 (alk. paper) — ISBN 0-8032-8167-6
(pbk. : alk. paper)

When ISBNs are inserted into a MARC record, each is input into its own 020 field, and each number is recorded as a block without hyphens.

1.8C. Key-title (MARC field 222)

1.8C1. The key-title of a serial, if found on the item, is added after the ISSN, even if it is the same as the title proper. A key-title is not recorded if there is no ISSN, however. *See* Fig. 3.77.

Fig. 3.77. Rule 1.8C1. Transcription of key-title of a serial following ISSN.

ALCTS newsletter. — Vol. 1, no. 1 (1990)-
— Chicago, IL : Association for Library Collections &
Technical Services, American Library Association, 1990-
v. ; ill. ; 28 cm.

Eight no. a year.
Title from caption.
Continues: RTSD newsletter.
ISSN 1047-949X = ALCTS newsletter

1.8E. Qualification (subfield a of MARC field 020)

1.8E1. A brief qualification is added after the standard number or terms of availability when there are two or more (*see* Fig. 3.76, above).

RULE 1.9. SUPPLEMENTARY ITEMS

Many supplementary items are described as separate entities and are given complete independent bibliographic records. The rule that identifies which supplementary works should be cataloged separately is rule 21.28.

In the cases where a supplementary work is described dependently, one of three methods may be chosen: 1) the supplementary item may be recorded as accompanying material (rule 1.5E1d) (*see* Fig. 3.62, page 69); 2) the item may be described in the note area (rule 1.7B11); 3) multilevel description may be used (rule 13.6).

RULE 1.10. ITEMS MADE UP OF SEVERAL TYPES OF MATERIALS

1.10A. Some items have components that belong to more than one group or type of material (e.g., printed text and slides). This rule deals with their description.

1.10B. If one of the components is so predominant that the item is of no use without that component (e.g., a slide set with an accompanying script that has little value without seeing the slides), the item should be described in terms of the predominant component with details of the other component(s) given as accompanying material or in a note. *See* Fig. 3.78.

Fig. 3.78. Rule 1.10B. Partial description of item made up of three components, one of which is predominant.

[1]Predominant component   Bushy the squirrel [filmstrip] / Cathedral Films, Inc. ; producers, Jim Friedrich ... [et al.] ; writer, John Calvin

[2]Subsidiary components   Reid. — Niles, IL : United Learning, 1987.   2
     1 filmstrip (33 fr.) : col. ; 35 mm. + 1 sound cassette (9 min., 10 sec. : analog) + 1 study guide. — (Parables from nature)   2

1.10C. If there is no predominant component, the item is cataloged as a kit as described below.

1.10C1. General material designation
The instructions in rule 1.1C4 are followed except when an item has no collective title. Then the appropriate GMD is given after each individual title.

1.10C2. Physical description
The cataloger is instructed to choose the most appropriate of three methods of providing the physical description:

    a) listing the extent of each of the individual parts. An option allows adding the name of the container and its dimensions. LC is applying the option on a case-by-case basis. (*CSB* 33: 28) *See* Fig. 3.79.

Fig. 3.79. Rule 1.10C2a. Transcription of parts of a kit as a listing of extent of item of each part.

    Who were the Pilgrims? [kit] / National Geographic Society. — Washington, D.C. : The Society, c1989.
    30 identical booklets, 1 sound cassette, 6 activity sheets (2 copies each), 8 duplicating masters, 1 teacher's guide ; in box 29 x 24 x 5 cm. — (Wonders of learning)

    b) giving separate physical descriptions on separate lines for each type of component. Again, naming the container and giving its dimensions is given as an option. (LC never uses method "b" — *CSB* 11: 12) *See* Fig. 3.80.

Fig. 3.80. Rule 1.10C2b. Transcription of separate lines of physical description for parts of a kit.

Element probe [kit] : an A/V game for teaching the
chemical elements / United Learning, Inc. ; writer,
Richard S. Treptow. — Niles, IL : United Learning, 1988.
100 slides : col.
1 sound cassette (44 min.) : analog, stereo.
10 duplicating masters ; 28 x 22 cm.
1 teacher's guide (28 p.) ; 24 cm.
All in container 30 x 23 x 7 cm.

c) giving a general term with the number of pieces as the extent of item for
items with a large number of different types of materials. The same
option for naming the container and giving its dimensions is allowed,
and LC applies it on a case-by-case basis. *See* Fig. 3.81.

Fig. 3.81. Rule 1.10C2c. Transcription of physical description using a general term for an item with a large number of heterogeneous pieces.

Safety begins with you [kit]. — New York : Children's
Media Productions, c1979.
24 various pieces. — (School craft kits)

RULE 1.11.   FACSIMILES, PHOTOCOPIES, AND OTHER REPRODUCTIONS

Facsimiles, photocopies, or other reproductions of printed texts, maps,
manuscripts, printed music, and graphic items are described in such a way that
the details of the facsimile, etc., are given in all areas except the note area. If the
title of the facsimile, etc., is different, the title of the facsimile, etc., is given as
title proper. The same is true for edition, publication details, or series. In these
cases, the details of the original are given in a single note in the notes area. The
details of the original are given in the same order as they would appear in the
main part of the description. *See* Fig. 3.82.

Fig. 3.82. Rule 1.11. Description of a reproduction with details of the original given in a note.

Frederic Remington / by Ernest Raboff. — 1st Harper
trophy ed. — New York : Harper & Row, 1989.
[31] p. : ill. (some col.) ; 29 cm.

"A Harper trophy book."
Summary: A brief biography of the artist and sculptor
accompanies fifteen color reproductions and critical
interpretations of his works.
Reprint of: Frederic Remington / by Adeline Peter
and Ernest Raboff. Garden City, N.Y. : Doubleday, 1973.
(Art for children)

If the facsimile, etc., is in a form of material different from the original, the chapter relating to the form of the facsimile, etc., is used. For a manuscript reproduced as a book, the chapter on description of books would be used. For maps reproduced on microfilm, the chapter on description of microforms would be used.

NOTES

[1]*AACR2R*, p. 620.

[2]*USMARC Format for Bibliographic Data: Including Guidelines for Content Designation* (Washington, D.C., Cataloging Distribution Service, Library of Congress, 1988-), 3 vols., looseleaf, with updates.

[3]*Library of Congress Rule Interpretations*, 2nd ed. (Washington, D.C., Cataloging Distribution Service, Library of Congress, 1989-), looseleaf, with updates.

[4]*Cataloging Service Bulletin* no. 1- (Washington, D.C., Library of Congress, Processing Services, 1978-).

[5]*Library of Congress Rule Interpretations for AACR 2, 1988 Revision: A Cumulation through Cataloging Service Bulletin* ..., compiled with quarterly looseleaf supplements by Alan Boyd and Elaine Druesedow (Oberlin, Ohio, Oberlin College Library, 1989-).

[6]*AACR2R*, p. 622.

[7]*AACR2R*, p. 623.

SUGGESTED READING

Chan, Lois Mai. *Cataloging and Classification: An Introduction*. New York, McGraw-Hill, 1981. Chapter 3.

Hagler, Ronald. *The Bibliographic Record and Information Technology*. 2nd ed. Chicago, American Library Association, 1991. Chapter 2.

Hunter, Eric J. *An Introduction to AACR 2: A Programmed Guide to the Second Edition of the Anglo-American Cataloguing Rules, 1988 Revision*. Rev. ed. London, Bingley, 1989.

Maxwell, Margaret F. *Handbook for AACR2, 1988 Revision*. Chicago, American Library Association, 1989. Chapter 1.

Description of Books, Pamphlets, and Printed Sheets 4

INTRODUCTION

This chapter and the three following ones in this text each discuss application of the general rules for description to books (and other printed monographic material), nonbook materials, microforms, and serials. Emphasis in each chapter is upon those areas where the description of a type of material must be unique to that type: chief and prescribed sources of information, material specific details, physical description, and notes. For each type of material one or more items has been chosen as an example to demonstrate a bibliographic record for that type of item. For each item, the chief source of information is illustrated, followed by a complete bibliographic record in card format and coded in MARC format. Because no one item can demonstrate every eventuality, other examples of particular instances are also given throughout each chapter.

SELECTED RULES AND EXAMPLES

RULE 2.0. GENERAL RULES

2.0A. Scope
This chapter covers what *AACR2R* calls "printed monographs" — all printed texts except serials, which are covered in *AACR2R* chapter 12 (chapter 7 of this text), and microform reproductions of printed texts, which are covered in *AACR2R* chapter 11 (chapter 6 of this text).

2.0B. Sources of information

2.0B1. Chief source of information
For most printed monographs there is a title page that serves as the chief source of information. If there is no title page, then the part of the item that gives the most complete information is used as a substitute for the title page. In this case, the part used as a substitute is specified in a note, and the information from the substitute is treated as if it were from a title page. That is, brackets are not used for information from a substitute title page. If the item has no part that can substitute, information may be taken from any available source.

If information that would ordinarily appear on a title page is given on facing pages, both pages are treated as "the title page."

2.0B2. Prescribed sources of information
Each area of the description has a prescribed source or sources from which information should be taken. If information in an area is from a non-prescribed source, it should be enclosed in square brackets.

The prescribed sources for printed monographs are:

AREA	PRESCRIBED SOURCES OF INFORMATION
Title and statement of responsibility	Title page
Edition	Title page, other preliminaries, and colophon
Publication, distribution, etc.	Title page, other preliminaries, and colophon
Physical description	The whole publication
Series	Series title page, monograph title page, cover, rest of the publication
Note	Any source
Standard number and terms of availability	Any source

Figures 4.1-4.3 illustrate the title page and "other preliminaries" for the book that is used in this chapter to illustrate building a description. *Preliminaries* is defined in *AACR2R* as "the title page(s) of an item, the verso of the title page(s), any pages preceding the title page(s), and the cover."[1] *Colophon* is defined as "a statement at the end of an item giving information about one or more of the following: the title, author(s), publisher, printer, date of publication or printing...."[2] The book used here has information on the front cover and the spine duplicates that on the title page. It has no colophon. Colophons are not common in English-language books but are found more often in books in other languages.

Fig. 4.1. Title page.

Critical Guide to Catholic Reference Books

Third Edition

James Patrick McCabe

With an Introduction by
Russell E. Bidlack
Dean Emeritus of the School of Library Science
University of Michigan

Libraries Unlimited, Inc. • Englewood, Colorado • 1989

Fig. 4.2. Verso of title page.

Copyright © 1989, 1980, 1971 James Patrick McCabe
All Rights Reserved
Printed in the United States of America

No part of this publication may be reproduced, stored in a retrieval system, or transmitted, in any form or by any means, electronic, mechanical, photo-copying, recording, or otherwise, without the prior written permission of the publisher.

LIBRARIES UNLIMITED, INC.
P.O. Box 3988
Englewood, Colorado 80155-3988

Library of Congress Cataloging-in-Publication Data

McCabe, James Patrick.
    Critical guide to Catholic reference books / James Patrick McCabe;
with an introduction by Russell E. Bidlack. -- 3rd ed.
    xiv, 323 p. 17x25 cm. -- (Research studies in library science ; no. 20)
    Bibliography: p. 263
    Includes indexes.
    ISBN 0-87287-621-7
    1. Catholic Church--Bibliography. 2. Reference books--Catholic
Church. I. Title. II. Series.
Z674.R4 no. 20
[Z7837]
[BX1751.2]
020 s--dc19
[016.282]   89-2835
                                       CIP

Fig. 4.3. Recto of leaf preceding title page (series title page).

RESEARCH STUDIES IN LIBRARY SCIENCE
Bohdan S. Wynar, Editor

No. 1   *Middle Class Attitudes and Public Library Use.* By Charles Evans, with an Intro-duction by Lawrence Allen.

No. 2   *Critical Guide to Catholic Reference Books.* 2d ed. By James Patrick McCabe, with an Introduction by Russell E. Bidlack.

No. 3   *An Analysis of Vocabulary Control in Library of Congress Classification and Subject Headings.* By John Phillip Immroth, with an Introduction by Jay E. Daily.

No. 4.   *Research Methods in Library Science: A Bibliographic Guide.* By Bohdan S. Wynar.

. . .   . . .

No. 19.   *Library of Congress Subject Headings: Principles and Application.* 2d ed. By Lois Mai Chan.

No. 20.   *Critical Guide to Catholic Reference Books.* 3d ed. By James Patrick McCabe.

RULE 2.1. TITLE AND STATEMENT OF RESPONSIBILITY AREA
(MARC field 245)

The title and statement of responsibility area is transcribed as instructed in rule 1.1. As discussed in the general chapter, the GMD "[text]" that is appropriate to the material of this chapter is not displayed in records from the Library of Congress. Its use is not illustrated in this chapter. *See* Fig. 4.4.

Fig. 4.4. Rule 2.1. Transcription of title and statement of responsibility area.

Critical guide to Catholic reference books / James Patrick McCabe ; with an introduction by Russell E. Bidlack

RULE 2.2. EDITION AREA (MARC field 250)

2.2B. Edition statement (MARC subfield a)

AACR2R specifies that if a work contains an edition statement and if the work is different from other editions of the work or the edition in hand is a named reissue of the work, the edition statement is transcribed as instructed in rule 1.2B. In practice editions are not compared during cataloging, and edition statements are taken at face value and transcribed. *See* Fig. 4.5.

AACR2R does not give instructions for transcribing edition statements for multi-part sets when the various parts show different edition statements. An LC rule interpretation addresses this issue. (*CSB* 41: 14)

RULE 2.3. MATERIAL (OR TYPE OF PUBLICATION) SPECIFIC DETAILS AREA

Area 3 is not currently used in the cataloging of printed monographs.

RULE 2.4. PUBLICATION, DISTRIBUTION, ETC., AREA (MARC field 260)

2.4B.-2.4F. Place of publication, name of publisher, date of publication (MARC subfields a, b, and c)

Details of place, publication, distribution, etc., and date(s) are transcribed as instructed in rule 1.4. *See* Fig. 4.5.

Fig. 4.5. Rule 2.4. Addition of edition statement and publication details.

Critical guide to Catholic reference books / James Patrick McCabe ; with an introduction by Russell E. Bidlack. — 3rd ed. — Englewood, Colo. : Libraries Unlimited, 1989.

Note that there are three copyright dates on the verso of the title page (Fig. 4.2). The date that corresponds to the edition statement is the one chosen for transcription.

RULE 2.5. PHYSICAL DESCRIPTION AREA (MARC field 300)

2.5B. Number of volumes and/or pagination (MARC subfield a)

Single volumes

2.5B1. The following terms are used in recording the number of pages or leaves in a publication.

TERM USED	SITUATION
pages (abbreviated "p.")	[volume with leaves printed on both sides]
leaves	[volume with leaves printed on only one side]
columns	[volume with more than one column to a page and numbered in columns]
leaves, pages, and/or columns (in sequence)	[volume that contains sequences of leaves, pages, and/or columns]
broadside	[broadside]
sheet	[folded and other single sheets]
case	[case]
portfolio	[portfolio]

2.5B2. Numbers of pages, leaves, or columns are recorded in accord with the numbered or lettered sequences represented. The number on the last page, leaf, or column of each sequence is recorded, followed in each case by the appropriate term or abbreviation. Examples:

92 p.	[46 leaves printed on both sides]
62 leaves	[62 leaves printed only on one side]
ix, 289 p.	[last numbered page in roman numerals sequence and in arabic numerals sequence]
iv leaves, 224 p.	[last numbered leaf and last numbered page]

See Fig. 4.6 (following discussion of rule 2.5D1).

2.5B3. Unnumbered sequences are disregarded unless the whole item or a substantial part of a publication is unnumbered (*see* rule 2.5B7 and rule 2.5B8). An exception is made when pages in an unnumbered sequence must be referred to in a note, in which case either the estimated number is given preceded by "ca.," or the exact number is given enclosed in square brackets. Examples:

| 79, [1], 64 p. | [unnumbered page referred to in note] |
| Bibliography: p. [80] | [note requiring use of unnumbered page] |

2.5B5. When a single sequence is numbered in more than one way (e.g., when numbering changes from roman to arabic numerals), the first numbering scheme is ignored, and only the last number of the sequence is recorded. Example:

| 252 leaves | [item numbered i-vii followed by leaves 8-252, for a total of 252 leaves – not 7 leaves followed by 252 leaves as would be indicated by: vii, 252 leaves] |

2.5B7. When an entire volume is unnumbered, if it is not too large, the pages are counted and given in square brackets. The number of pages of larger items are estimated and recorded following "ca." Examples:

| [12] p. | [unnumbered pages counted] |
| ca. 200 p. | [unnumbered pages approximated] |

LC does not follow the rule except in the cases of children's literature and rare books. Instead, they record the extent statement as "1 v. (unpaged)." (*CSB* 44: 21)

2.5B8. Three options are given for dealing with complicated or irregular paging:

1) The total number of pages or leaves may be given followed by "in various pagings" or "in various foliations." (Blank pages, advertising matter, and other inessential sequences are excluded from this total.)

2) The number of pages or leaves in major sequences may be recorded followed by the total number of pages or leaves in remaining sequences. This total is given in square brackets.

3) The volume may be described as "1 v. (various pagings)," "1 case," or "1 portfolio."

LC uses only the third option. (*CSB* 44: 21) Examples:

86 p. in various pagings	[total number of pages]
273 leaves in various foliations	[total number of leaves]
128, ix, [48] p.	[two main sequences followed by number of pages in several smaller sequences]
1 v. (various pagings)	[indication of many sequences – perhaps some are numbered, some are not, some may be lettered – too complicated for use of alternatives "1" or "2"]

2.5B10. Leaves or pages of plates

The number of leaves or pages of plates is recorded at the end of the numbers given for paging sequences regardless of whether the plates are placed together or are scattered through the publication. If there is only one plate, it is described as "1 leaf of plates." If plates are unnumbered, follow rule 2.5B7. If paging is complex, follow rule 2.5B8. If there are both leaves and plates, use the term that is predominant. Examples:

vi, 224, [9] p., 26 leaves of plates   [numbered leaves of plates]

176 p., [16] p. of plates   [unnumbered pages of plates]

74 leaves, [33] leaves of plates   [unnumbered leaves of plates]

Publications in more than one volume

2.5B17.-2.5B18. A printed monograph in more than one physical part is described with the number of whichever of the following terms is appropriate:

volumes — each bibliographic unit in its own binding

parts — bibliographic units bound several to a volume

pamphlets — collections of pamphlets bound together or assembled in a portfolio

pieces — items of varying character published, or assembled for cataloging, as a collection

case(s) — box(es) containing bound or unbound material

portfolio(s) — container(s), usually consisting of two covers joined at the back and tied at the front, top, and/or bottom, holding loose papers, illustrative materials, etc.

Examples:

5 v.	[each of five bibliographic units bound separately]
25 pts.	[each part issued separately but specified by the publisher that they should be bound several to a volume when complete]
2 cases	[unbound material held together as a bibliographic unit in two boxes]

2.5B19. When the number of bibliographic volumes is different from the number of physical volumes, the number of bibliographic volumes is given first followed by "in" and the number of physical volumes. Example:

3 v. in 1

2.5B20. When the volumes of a multi-volume set are paged so that the first page numbers of a succeeding volume follow the last page number of the preceding volume (ignoring any preliminary pages in the succeeding volume that may be separately paged), the total number of pages or leaves is given in parentheses after the number of volumes. Example:

> 2 v. (ix, 1438 p., 32 leaves of plates)

2.5B23. Braille or other tactile systems
If appropriate, add to the number of volumes or leaves an appropriate term such as one of the following phrases:

of braille	of press braille
of Moon type	of print and braille [eye-readable
of jumbo braille	print and braille]
of microbraille	of print and press braille

Examples:

> 3 v. of jumbo braille

> 484 leaves of braille

2.5B24. Large print
Items in large print meant for use by the visually impaired should be described by adding "(large print)" to the statement of extent. Example:

> 58 leaves (large print)

2.5C. Illustrative matter (MARC subfield b)

2.5C1-2.5C2. If a monograph has illustrations, the abbreviation "ill." is given in the physical description unless all of the illustrations belong to one of the groups mentioned below. Tables are not treated as illustrations. Illustrated title pages and minor illustrations (e.g., decorations) are ignored.

Illustrations of the following types that are considered to be important are given in the following order:

TERM	ABBREVIATION (IF ALLOWED)
coats of arms	
facsimiles	facsim., facsims.
forms	
genealogical tables	geneal. table(s)
maps	
music	
plans	
portraits (used for both single and group portraits)	port, ports.
samples	

If there are illustrations in addition to these types (including graphs and diagrams), they are described as "ill.," and "ill." precedes the other types in the list. Examples:

47 p. : ill., ports.   [contains illustrations, some of which are portraits]

280 p. : facsims.   [the only illustrations are facsimiles]

176 p., [24] p. of plates : ill., coats of arms, maps, plans   [illustrations include three of the specific types in rule 2.5C2, in addition to other illustrations]

LC uses only "ill." to describe an illustrated printed monograph "unless there are maps present or the publication consists wholly or predominantly of one of the types listed [above]." (*CSB* 47: 30)

2.5C3. If illustrations are in two or more colors, they are described as "col." or "some col." Examples:

48 p. : ill. (some col.)   [some illustrations in color]

216 p. : ill., maps (some col.), col. ports.   [some maps in color, all portraits in color]

xiv, 182 p. : col. ill.   [all illustrations in color]

2.5C4-2.5C7. Treatment of special cases (e.g., number of illustrations known, special locations of illustrations, works consisting of all or nearly all illustrations) is delineated in these rules in *AACR2R*, which should be consulted when such special cases arise.

2.5D. Dimensions (MARC subfield c)

2.5D1. Size of printed monographs is given in terms of the height of volumes in centimeters. The height of the binding (or the height of the item, if unbound) is measured and recorded as the *next* whole centimeter *up* (*not* the *nearest* centimeter). Size of volumes that measure less than 10 centimeters is given in millimeters. *See* Fig. 4.6.

Fig. 4.6. Rule 2.5. Addition of physical description.

Critical guide to Catholic reference books / James Patrick McCabe ; with an introduction by Russell E. Bidlack. — 3rd ed. — Englewood, Colo. : Libraries Unlimited, 1989.
    xiv, 323 p. ; 25 cm.

Note: Book actually measures 24.2 centimeters but is recorded as 25.

2.5D2. Width of a volume is recorded only when it is less than half the height or greater than the height. Examples:

ca. 150 p. : ill. ; 34 x 16 cm.   [width less than half the height]

ii, 97 p. : ill., ports. ; 18 x 21 cm.   [width greater than the height]

2.5D3-2.5D5. These rules in *AACR2R* cover unusual cases and should be consulted when one is cataloging sets with items of varying sizes, or single sheets.

2.5E. Accompanying material (MARC subfield e)

As explained in rule 1.5E, material that is issued with an item and is intended to be used with it may be recorded as the last element of the physical description area. Example:

> 142 p. : ill., maps ; 39 cm. + 1 overlay grid

RULE 2.6. SERIES AREA (MARC field 4xx)

2.6B. Series statements

Each series statement is transcribed as instructed in rule 1.6. *See* Fig. 4.7.

Fig. 4.7. Rule 2.6B. Addition of series statement.

> Critical guide to Catholic reference books : James Patrick McCabe ; with an introduction by Russell E. Bidlack. — 3rd ed. — Englewood, Colo. : Libraries Unlimited, 1989.
> xiv, 323 p. ; 25 cm. — (Research studies in library science ; no. 20)

RULE 2.7. NOTE AREA (MARC field 5xx)

2.7B. Notes (MARC field 500 unless otherwise specified)

As noted in the preceding chapter, notes for all materials are given in the same order. The ones particularly applicable to printed monographs are illustrated here.

2.7B1. Nature, scope, or artistic form

When nature, scope, or artistic form of a work is not apparent from the rest of the description, notes may be made. Example:

> Catalog of an exhibition held Aug. 16-Nov. 2, 1986, at the Fine Arts Museum of San Francisco.

LC generally restricts this type of note for books to those that contain one or more literary works by one personal author *and* fall into one of several categories of languages (e.g., Turkish, Hebrew alphabet, or language indigenous to Africa and in the roman script). LC also makes notes recording the literary forms of belles lettres when their titles are misleading. Fanciful titles are not necessarily considered to be misleading. (*CSB* 43: 30-31)

2.7B2. Language of item and/or translation or adaptation

If the language is not evident from the description or if the fact of translation or adaptation is not apparent, notes may be made. Examples:

> English and French.

> Translation of: Das adoptierte Kind.

2.7B3. Source of title proper
The source of the title proper is noted if the title is not taken from the chief source of information. Example:

> Cover title.

2.7B4. Variations in title
Titles on an item that differ from the title proper should be noted. Example:

> Spine title: 1988 International Display Research
> Conference.

2.7B6. Statements of responsibility
Here is a place for statements of responsibility (e.g., significant persons or bodies connected with previous editions, or persons or bodies not named in the chief source) that were not given in the title and statement of responsibility area. Example:

> Prepared by the Oceanography Course Team.

Note: The statement of responsibility incorporated in the note above did not appear in the chief source of information but was composed by the cataloger from information that appeared elsewhere. Had it appeared in the chief source of information it would have been transcribed in the statement of responsibility area.

2.7B7. Edition and history
Bibliographic history notes and notes relating to the edition in hand are recorded here. A Library of Congress rule interpretation is helpful for constructing notes about reprint editions. (*CSB* 45: 15-18) Examples:

> Reprint. Originally published: New York : Pantheon
> Books, 1986.

> Companion vol. to: The IMF and stabilization. 1984.

2.7B9. Publication, distribution, etc.
Important publication, distribution, etc., details that cannot be given in the publication, distribution, etc., area are recorded in a note. Example:

> Printed at the Tabard Private Press, Oxshott, by Philip
> Kerrigan.

The Library of Congress interprets a date that consists of month and year or month, day, and year, and that appears in a prominent position, to be a date of release or transmittal and records it in a note in quotation marks. It is not considered to be a publication date, although the publication date may be inferred from it and given in brackets. (*CSB* 44: 21-22) Example:

> "March 1990."

2.7B10. Physical description
Important physical details not given in the physical description area may be recorded here. Example:

> Maps on lining papers.

2.7B11. Accompanying material
Notes on the location of accompanying material may be needed. Example:

> Overlay grid in pocket inside back cover.

2.7B12. Series
Series data that cannot appropriately be given in the series area may be recorded in a note. Example:

> Originally issued in series: Research studies in library science.

2.7B13. Dissertations
Dissertations or theses are described with a formal note. The English word *thesis* is followed by the degree for which the author was a candidate (e.g., Ph.D., M.A., Master's), the name of the institution or faculty, and the year the degree was granted (MARC field 502). Example:

> Thesis (Ph.D.)—Texas A & M University, 1988.

Revisions, abridgements, edited editions, and publications lacking formal thesis notes are also noted (MARC field 500). Example:

> Revision of thesis (Ph.D.)—Yale University, 1989.

2.7B14. Audience
If the intended audience is stated in the publication, it may be noted here. Example:

> For adults learning to read.

2.7B16. Other formats
If the content of the item has been issued in a format other than print, it may be noted here. Example:

> Issued also as computer laser optical disk.

2.7B17. Summary (MARC field 520)
Summary notes may be given when the contents of an item are not specified in the rest of the description. Library of Congress practice has generally limited such summary notes on printed monographs to children's books. Since 1984, however, some summary notes created by LC's overseas offices have been included in LC bibliographic records. (*CSB* 44: 22) Example:

> Summary: By falling down a rabbit hole, Alice experiences unusual adventures with a variety of nonsensical characters.

2.7B18. **Contents** (MARC field 500 or 504 or 505)

When parts of an item are titled and would be useful to the user of a bibliographic record, they are brought out in notes. The Library of Congress rule interpretation is lengthy and should be consulted when contents notes seem appropriate. (*CSB* 47: 31-34) LC takes titles from the table of contents rather than from the head of the parts as *AACR2R* directs. *See* Figs. 4.8-4.10.

Fig. 4.8. Rule 2.7B18. Addition of contents note for collection of works of one author.

> Three puzzles for Poirot / Agatha Christie. — 1st omnibus ed. — New York : Putnam, 1989.
>   554 p. ; 25 cm.
>
> ➤Contents: Third girl — Poirot loses a client — Funerals are fatal.
>   ISBN 0-3991-3496-4 : $9.95

Fig. 4.9. Rule 2.7B18. Addition of contents note for collection of works by different authors.

> Paths of resistance : the art and craft of the political novel / Isabel Allende ... [et al.] ; edited by William Zinsser. — Boston : Houghton Mifflin, c1989.
>   167 p. ; 21 cm.
>
> Includes bibliographical references (p. 155-162).
> ➤Contents: Introduction / William Zinsser — We are not excused / Robert Stone — Writing as an act of hope / Isabel Allende — A strip of exposed film / Charles McCarry — Active in time and history / Marge Piercy — The agreed-upon facts / Gore Vidal.
>   ISBN 0-3955-1426-6

Fig. 4.10. Rule 2.7B18. Addition of contents note for multi-volume work.

> The Second World War / Winston S. Churchill. — Boston : Houghton Mifflin, [1985-1986?], c1948-1953.
>   6 v. : ill. ; 20 cm.
>
> Includes bibliographical references and indexes.
> ➤Contents: v. 1. The gathering storm — v. 2. Their finest hour — v. 3. The Grand Alliance — v. 4. The hinge of fate — v. 5. Closing the ring — v. 6. Triumph and tragedy.
>   ISBN 0-3954-1055-X (v. 1)

Two parts of an item that are often titled are "Bibliography" and "Index." By example, they fall under rule 2.7B18 in *AACR2R*. In LC practice formal bibliographies have traditionally been given as "Bibliography:" with the page numbers on which they fall, and other bibliographical references have been given as either "Includes bibliographies" or "Includes bibliographical references." The most recent policy at LC, however, is to use one form of note for bibliographical citations in any form: "Includes bibliographical references." In the case of one formal bibliography, its inclusive page numbers are given in parentheses following the note. "Discography" and "Filmography" are still given as a formal note with page numbers. (*CSB* 47: 32-33) Examples:

> Includes bibliographical references (p. 298-301).
> Discography: p. [109]-111.

While the simplification is welcome, bibliography notes on past LC catalog records are now difficult to interpret. For many years "Includes bibliographical references" meant the book had citations with footnote-type numbering in the order referred to in the text, whether at the bottoms of pages or at the ends of chapters or at the end of the book. Starting in 1984 the note was used only for true footnotes at the bottoms of pages. Then in 1989 it was broadened to be the only form of note used for citations in any form.

Bibliography notes in various forms continue to be shown in this text, because they are allowed by *AACR2R*. Many individual libraries will likely change to LC policy, and in time most current U.S. records will use only "Includes bibliographical references."

2.7B19. Numbers

Numbers found in the item other than ISBNs (which are given in the standard number area) are recorded as notes—often quoted. Example:

> "IEEE catalog number 88CH2542-9."

2.7B20. Copy being described, library's holdings, and restrictions on use
(MARC field 590)

Notes are made about the particular copy in hand, including notes about imperfections or notes giving incomplete holdings of a multipart item. These notes are "copy specific." That is, such a note is applicable only to the copy held by the cataloger who is creating the description. This is fine in an individual library. However, if the library belongs to a network and creates online original cataloging that other libraries eventually use as a basis for their cataloging, this type of note can be a source of difficulty, as is known by libraries that have had to change LC's copy-specific notes to reflect local cataloging. Such notes are tagged 590 in a MARC record and thus are readily identifiable. Examples:

> Library's copy autographed by the author.

> Library lacks v. 3.

This rule also calls for notes about any restrictions there may be on use of the item. Such a note may or may not be copy-specific. Example:

> Restricted use until 2001.

2.7B21. "With" notes (MARC field 501)

For items lacking a collective title and described separately, a note is given beginning "With:" and then listing the other separately titled parts of the item.

The only note required by the book whose title page and other preliminaries are shown in Figs. 4.1-4.3 is the index note. *See* Fig. 4.11 below.

RULE 2.8. STANDARD NUMBER AND TERMS OF AVAILABILITY AREA (MARC field 020)

2.8B. International Standard Book Number (ISBN) (MARC subfield a)
ISBNs are transcribed as instructed in rule 1.8B.

2.8C. *Optional addition.* **Terms of availability** (MARC subfield c)
It is optional to add the price or other terms of availability. The Library of Congress exercises this option for current items. (*CSB* 8: 10) *See* Fig. 4.11.

Fig. 4.11. Rules 2.7-2.8. Addition of note, ISBN, and price.

Critical guide to Catholic reference books / James Patrick McCabe ; with an introduction by Russell E. Bidlack. — 3rd ed. — Englewood, Colo. : Libraries Unlimited, 1989.
xiv, 323 p. ; 25 cm. — (Research studies in library science ; no. 20)

Includes index.
ISBN 0-87287-621-7 : $45.00

The complete bibliographic record in MARC format for the book whose title page and other preliminaries are shown in Figs. 4.1-4.3 is shown in Fig. 4.12.

Fig. 4.12. Complete bibliographic record for the printed monograph in Fig. 4.11 coded according to the MARC format and spaced and formatted for the OCLC system.

```
OCLC:     19124014        Rec stat:    p
Entered:      19890119    Replaced:      19900317    Used:      19910416
Type: a       Bib lvl: m      Source:           Lang:  eng
Repr:         Enc lvl:        Conf pub: 0       Ctry:  cou
Indx: 1       Mod rec:        Govt pub:         Cont:  b
Desc: a       Int lvl:        Festschr: 0       Illus:
              F/B:       0    Dat tp:    s      Dates: 1989,
 1 010     89-2835
 2 040     DLC $c DLC
 3 020     0872876217 : $c $45.00
 4 050  00 Z674 $b .R4 no. 20 $a Z7837 $a BX1751.2
 5 082  00 020 s $a 016.282 $2 19
 6 090     $b
 7 049     YCLM
 8 100  1  McCabe, James Patrick.
 9 245 10  Critical guide to Catholic reference books / $c James
Patrick McCabe ; with an introduction by Russell E. Bidlack.
10 250     3rd ed.
11 260     Englewood, Colo. : $b Libraries Unlimited, $c 1989.
12 300     xiv, 323 p. ; $c 25 cm.
13 440  0  Research studies in library science ; $v no. 20
14 500     Includes index.
15 610 20  Catholic Church $x Bibliography.
16 650  0  Reference books $x Catholic Church.
```

RULES 2.9-2.11.

Supplementary items, items made up of several types of material, facsimiles, photocopies, and other reproductions are described as instructed in the general chapter under rules 1.9-1.11.

NOTES

[1]*AACR2R*, p. 621.

[2]*AACR2R*, p. 616.

SUGGESTED READING

Manual of AACR 2 Examples. Compiled by the Minnesota AACR 2 trainers; edited by Edward Swanson and Marilyn McClaskey. 2nd ed. Lake Crystal, Minn., Soldier Creek Press, 1985.

Maxwell, Margaret F. *Handbook for AACR2 1988 Revision.* Chicago, American Library Association, 1989. Chapter 2.

Saye, Jerry D., and Sherry L. Vellucci. *Notes in the Catalog Record Based on AACR2 and LC Rule Interpretations.* Chicago, American Library Association, 1989.

Description of Nonbook Materials

5

INTRODUCTION

This chapter covers the description of materials that have been variously called "nonbook," "nonprint," "audiovisual," or "media"—the last term often including monographic materials, as in "School Media Center." Often these special materials are not handled in the same way as monographs are handled. An administrative decision within each library determines whether to catalog and/or classify each of these special materials; because of their dimensions, many cannot be shelved with corresponding monographic materials. The dimensions of such materials, then, become quite significant in bibliographic descriptions because this directly influences their location in a given collection, a consideration that often makes classification relatively insignificant and description of greater importance.

If the librarian cannot easily remember the contents of the collection, then cataloging control is needed. If the library has only six maps, for instance, there is little need to catalog them. Sixty maps, however, or even sixteen, may well need to be cataloged. The disadvantage of failing to catalog descriptively any special materials is that the patron must look somewhere other than in the main catalog for the record of the material. It is strongly recommended that as many special materials as possible be cataloged descriptively and thus recorded in the main catalog. Past problems in doing this have been greatly eased by the publication first of *AACR2*, and now *AACR2R*, with its integrated approach to the description of special materials. In *AACR2R* all materials are described according to the same set of principles.

The materials specifically addressed in this chapter are: cartographic materials (covered in chapter 3 of *AACR2R*), manuscripts (*AACR2R*, chapter 4), published music (*AACR2R*, chapter 5), sound recordings (*AACR2R*, chapter 6), motion pictures and videorecordings (*AACR2R*, chapter 7), graphic materials (*AACR2R*, chapter 8), computer files (*AACR2R*, chapter 9), and three-dimensional artifacts and realia (*AACR2R*, chapter 10). Each of these kinds of material presents some interesting challenges to the descriptive cataloger.

Collections of manuscripts can be cataloged at different levels. The collection can be described as a whole (collection-level cataloging), or individual manuscripts can be described separately (item-level cataloging). The challenge of cataloging manuscripts is that each is unique. The manuscript or the manuscript collection does not exist in another library, except perhaps in reproduction. It is not the kind of material for which catalogers can find cataloging copy already in existence. In addition, such materials often do not have any clearly defined chief source of information, and, indeed, they often do not have clearly defined titles. There may be difficulty even reading the handwriting in which a manuscript is written. It may be difficult to know whether one is dealing with an original or with a handwritten copy and, if a copy, the date it was copied and by whom. The manuscript cataloger is often dealing with events and names of persons not recorded elsewhere.

One challenge for cataloging music is that a musical composition in printed form normally appears as a series of staves upon which notes are printed, but occasionally other systems of notation are used. The description of music written for a solo instrument, such as the piano, is relatively straightforward. The description of music written for several instrumental or vocal parts (i.e., scores) presents some special problems, especially in the title and statement of responsibility area, in the physical description area, and in the notes area.

Both classification and description of sound recordings are affected by the fact that extremely disparate materials often appear on a single physical item. This problem is addressed for description in *AACR2R*, rule 6.1G, described below.

Two of the complications encountered in describing motion pictures and videorecordings involve the source of information and the large numbers of people responsible for them. Titles and other information, as they appear in the item itself, in accompanying materials, or on containers, often vary considerably. The large number of people involved presents problems for deciding how many "credits" will provide useful description of an item. Another problem is concerned with the ease with which videorecordings may be made, thus complicating the concepts of "copy" and "edition." These and other problems are addressed in the rules that follow, but ultimately the cataloger must use some judgment based upon general principles.[1]

Graphic materials include: art originals, art prints, art reproductions, charts, filmstrips and filmslips, flash cards, flip charts, photographs, pictures, postcards, posters, radiographs, slides, stereographs, study prints, technical drawings, transparencies, and wall charts. Many of these materials are not cataloged and/or classified in many libraries. An administrative decision within each library determines whether to catalog and/or classify these materials. Because most of them cannot be physically shelved with corresponding monographic materials, a book classification system often is not used. Rather, use is made of a simple accession or serial number to keep them in order. On the other hand, catalog records of the materials can easily be interfiled in the catalog with records for monographic or serial material, because, in *AACR2R*, all materials are described according to the same standard—i.e., ISBD(G). Some libraries provide some identification, such as color coding of catalog records that represent the materials listed above, when they are interfiled in the main catalog. Other libraries provide separate catalogs for special materials.

The cataloging of computer files is a very recent addition to the cataloging field. The need for standards for cataloging these materials was recognized in 1970 when ALA's Cataloging and Classification Section established a subcommittee to develop rules for cataloging computer files (then referred to as "machine-readable data files," or "MRDFs"). Since then, steady progress has been made, but the form in which bibliographic information for computer files can be found varies so greatly that cataloging them is somewhat more of a challenge than for most other materials. The state of the art of production of computer files is comparable to that of books in the early days of printing. A short time ago there was no source of data comparable to a title page. Program files now usually have such a source, with non-standard and varying amounts of information, but data files still usually have no such source. As with videorecordings there is the problem of ease of duplication, complicating the ideas of "copy" and "edition." Microcomputer software developed after the publication of *AACR2* in 1978. As a result it was necessary to develop some supplementary interpretations for the rules in *AACR2*, chapter 9. These guidelines were published as a separate booklet.[2] In 1986, chapter 9 of *AACR2* was completely revised and published as a separate publication.[3] The revision was expanded to include all types of computer files. This revised chapter 9 was incorporated into *AACR2R* with a number of revisions and additions.

Prior to the advent of *AACR2*, three-dimensional artifacts and realia were not cataloged or classified except in a few museum libraries. With a method of description consistent with that of describing other materials, however, we are seeing more cataloging of these materials—especially in media centers where emphasis is no longer on the "book" as the principal means of transmitting information.

A number of manuals have been written that supplement *AACR2* and *AACR2R* in the area of nonbook materials. They are listed in the "Suggested Reading" section at the end of this chapter. They should be consulted for more detailed discussion of the problems of cataloging these materials, for definitions of terms unique to these types, and for in-depth examples of cataloging.

SELECTED RULES AND EXAMPLES

RULE [Chapter #].0.   GENERAL RULES

[Chapter #].0A.   Scope
This rule in each chapter identifies the kinds of materials covered in that chapter. It also sometimes points out certain kinds of items *not* covered or not covered completely and suggests the chapter that should be consulted instead or in addition. For example, rule 4.0A directs that for the cataloging of manuscript cartographic items, one should also consult chapter 3 of *AACR2R*.

[Chapter #].0B   Sources of information

[Chapter #].0B1.   Chief source of information
The following chief sources of information are prescribed in this rule in each chapter:

TYPE OF MATERIAL	CHIEF SOURCE OF INFORMATION
Atlases	Title page (same as for books).
Other cartographic items	a) cartographic item itself, or, if a) is inappropriate, b) container or case, or the cradle and stand of a globe.
Manuscript*	The manuscript itself. If information is scattered the order of preference is: title page if there is one and it was originally part of the manuscript, colophon, caption, heading, text itself. If information cannot be taken from the manuscript, use, in this order: another manuscript copy of the item, a published edition of the item, reference sources, and other sources.
Published music	a) List title page, cover, or caption — whichever furnishes the fullest information. b) If information cannot be taken from "a," use, in this order: caption, cover, colophon, other preliminaries, other sources.

Sound recordings:

Disc	Disc and label	
Tape (open reel-to-reel)	Reel and label	Two or more
Tape cassette	Cassette and label	labels are treated
Tape cartridge	Cartridge and label	as one chief
Roll	Label	source
Sound recording on film	Container and label	

If textual material has a collective title while the chief sources above do not, then the source of the collective title may be treated as a chief source.

If information cannot be taken from a chief source above, use, in this order: accompanying textual material, a container, other sources. Prefer printed data to sound data.

---

*The cataloging manual *Archives, Personal Papers, and Manuscripts* (*APPM*) has been accepted by the Library of Congress, the Research Libraries Group, and OCLC as the standard for cataloging this type of material. One significant difference between this manual and chapter 4 of *AACR2R* is that for manuscript collections *APPM* allows the finding aid to serve as the chief source of information.

Motion pictures and videorecordings	Film itself (e.g., title frames) and, if in a permanent container (e.g., a cartridge), the container and its label. If information cannot be taken from the chief source, use, in this order: accompanying textual material, container that is not an integral part of the piece, other sources.
Graphic materials	Item itself, including permanently affixed labels or containers. For an item consisting of two or more parts (e.g., slide set), use a container that provides a collective title if the items do not. If information cannot be taken from the chief source, use, in this order: non-integral container, accompanying textual material, other sources.
Computer files	Title screen(s). If there is no title screen, other internal sources such as main menus or program statements may be used. If the information cannot be gained from internal sources (either because it is not there or because the cataloger does not have the right equipment), use, in this order: the physical carrier or any permanently attached publisher-produced labels, documentation issued by the publisher or creator with the file, information printed on the container issued by the publisher or distributor. The source with the most complete information is preferred. If the container has a collective title and the sources above do not, the source of the collective title should be treated as the chief source. If information is not available from any of these sources, use, in this order: other published descriptions of the file, other sources.
Three-dimensional artifacts and realia	Object itself along with any accompanying textual material and container issued with the item. Information on the item or permanently affixed to it is preferred.

[Chapter #].0B2. Prescribed sources of information

There are prescribed sources of information for each of the areas of description. These prescribed sources are fairly standard from medium to medium, although there are a few variations. A table of the most common prescribed sources is set out below, with the variations noted.

AREA	PRESCRIBED SOURCES OF INFORMATION
Title and statement of responsibility	Chief source of information*
Edition	Chief source of information, accompanying printed material**
Area 3	Chief source of information***
Publication, distribution, etc.	(Same as for edition area)†
Physical description	Any source
Series	(Same as for edition area)††
Note	Any source
Standard number and terms of availability	Any source†††

Figures 5.1-5.21 show the chief sources of information and some of the prescribed sources for a map, a manuscript, a piece of music, a sound recording, a videotape, a set of stereograph reels, a computer file, and a game. Complete descriptions for these items are given at the end of this chapter.

(Text continues on page 113.)

---

*For manuscripts, published copies of the item may also be used. For computer files, the carrier or its labels, information issued by the publisher or creator, or the container may also be used.

**For those types of materials where the container is not regarded as chief source, the container may be used for this area. For music, the caption, cover, or colophon may also be used.

***Area 3 is used only for cartographic materials, music, and computer files. Accompanying materials may also be used for this area for cartographic materials. Any source may be used for this area for computer files.

†For manuscripts only the date is given in this area and it may be taken from anywhere in the manuscript or from published copies.

††This area is not used for manuscripts. For music, the series title page is used instead of the chief source of information.

†††This area is not used for manuscripts.

Fig. 5.1. Upper right corner of map.

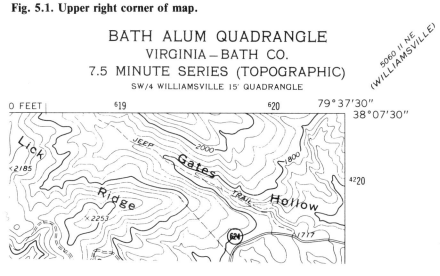

Fig. 5.2. Lower right corner of map.

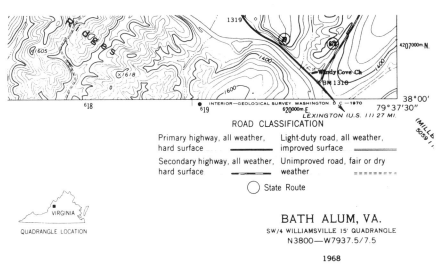

Fig. 5.3. Lower left corner of map.

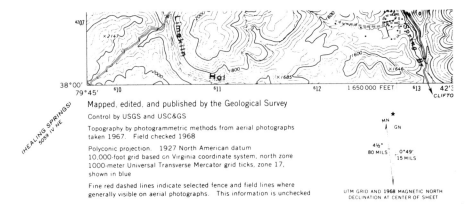

Fig. 5.4. Lower center of map.

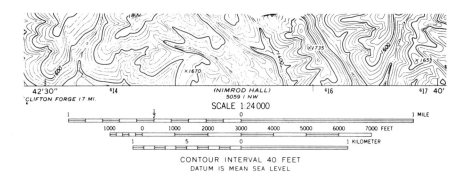

CONTOUR INTERVAL 40 FEET
DATUM IS MEAN SEA LEVEL

THIS MAP COMPLIES WITH NATIONAL MAP ACCURACY STANDARDS
FOR SALE BY U. S. GEOLOGICAL SURVEY, WASHINGTON, D. C. 20242
AND VIRGINIA DIVISION OF MINERAL RESOURCES, CHARLOTTESVILLE, VIRGINIA 22903
A FOLDER DESCRIBING TOPOGRAPHIC MAPS AND SYMBOLS IS AVAILABLE ON REQUEST

Fig. 5.5. Outside of letter shown in Fig. 5.6.

Fig. 5.6. Letter from George III to Henry Dundas.
[Reproduced by permission of the Manuscript Department,
William R. Perkins Library, Duke University.]

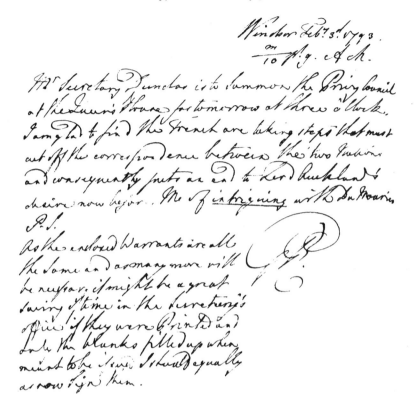

Fig. 5.7. Transcription of letter shown in Fig. 5.6.

[*Windsor, 3 Feb. 1793, 9:10 a.m.*] Mr. Secretary Dundas is to summon the Privy Council at the Queen's House for tomorrow at three o'Clock. I am glad to find the French are taking steps that must cut off the correspondence between the two Nations, and consequently puts an end to Lord Auckland's desire now before Me of intriguing with Du Mourier.

GR.

P.S. As the enclosed Warrants are all the Same and as many more will be necessary it might be a great saving of time in the Secretary's office if they were Printed and only the blanks filled up when meant to be issued I should equally as now Sign them.

Fig. 5.8. Chief source of information for a score.

TOMMASO ALBINONI

TRIOSONATE H-MOLL
für zwei Violinen und Basso continuo

TRIO SONATA IN B MINOR
for two Violins and Basso continuo

op. I/8

Herausgegeben von / Edited by
STEFAN ALTNER

BÄRENREITER KASSEL • BASEL • LONDON • NEW YORK
HORTUS MUSICUS 240

Fig. 5.9. Chief source of information from disc.

Fig. 5.10. Information from accompanying booklet.

INSTRUMENTARIUM

Violin:
Cornelius Kleyman, Amsterdam c. 1680
Bow:
W. Baumann, Amsterdam

Recording Data: 1984-06-07, 09/11 in the Petrus Church, Stock-
   sund, Sweden
Recording Engineer & Digital Editor: Robert von Bahr
Sony PCM F1 Digital Recording Equipment, 4 Neumann U-87
   Microphones, SAM 82 Mixer, Sony Tape
Producer: Robert von Bahr
Cover Text: Stig Jacobsson
English Translation: John Skinner
German Translation: Per Skans
French Translation: Arlètte Chené-Wiklander
Front Cover Picture: Conny Asberg
Back Cover Photos: Robert von Bahr
Album Design: Robert von Bahr
Type Setting: Marianne von Bahr
Lay-Out: William Jewson
Repro: KåPe Grafiska, Stockholm
Print: Offizin Paul Hartung, Hamburg, West Germany 1985

Also available as LP and MC: BIS-LP-275 & BIS-MC-275

© & ℗ : 1984/85, Grammofon AB BIS

This record can be ordered from
Grammofon AB BIS
Väringavägen 6 S-182 63 Djursholm Sweden
Phone: Stockholm (08)*(Int.: +468)* - 755 41 00
Telex: 13880 bis s
or from BIS' agents all over the world

Fig. 5.11. Transcription of title frames at beginning of videotape.

ALA Video

— — —

The Information Age

— — —

The Future is Information:
Careers in Library and Information Science

— — —

Narrated by Raymond Burr

Fig. 5.12. Transcription of credit frames at end of videotape.

Executive Producer
Donna Seaman Kitta

Project Consultant
Margaret Myers

Produced by
Denver Public Library
Cable Television Department

Production Coordinator
Byron West

Producer
Teri Hernandez

Director/Editor
Talliver J. Hare

Script
Rita Lovato

Script Consultant
Raymond Burr

Production Assistant
Lee Mestas

Best Boy
Hugh Jason Wallace

Music Composed and
Performed by
Valentine Productions

Additional Music
Steve Springer

. . .

Copyright 1989
American Library Association
50 E. Huron St.
Chicago, IL 60611

Fig. 5.13. Photocopy of cassette label.

Fig. 5.14. Chief source of information for set of stereograph reels.

Fig. 5.15. Unifying container for stereograph reel set.

Fig. 5.16. First page of accompanying booklet.

Fig. 5.17. Transcription of first screen of information for a computer file.

WordStar Professional Release 5.00 #DAK 085
Copyright (C) 1983, 1988 MicroPro International Corporation.
All rights reserved

IBM PC Compatible
Draft Printer

MailMerge, TelMerge, and MailList copyright (C) 1983, 1988
MicroPro International Corporation. All rights reserved

Thesaurus, speller and hyphenation technology copyright (C)
1986, 1988 Microlytics, UFO Systems, Xerox Corporation.
All rights reserved

Fig. 5.18. Label on storage medium of a computer file.

Fig. 5.19. Top of container of game.

Instructo® ACTIVITY KIT

The
Classification
Game

Fig. 5.20. End panel of game's container.

Instructo® ACTIVITY KIT

The Classification Game

REORDER NO.
1014

Fig. 5.21. Top and bottom of page of accompanying textual material.

INSTRUCTO® TEACHING GUIDE

Instructo educational materials undergo careful testing and evaluation under actual and varying classroom teaching conditions.

No. 1014   THE CLASSIFICATION GAME

© 1969 THE INSTRUCTO CORPORATION • PAOLI. PENNSYLVANIA 19301

RULE [Chapter #].1. TITLE AND STATEMENT OF RESPONSIBILITY AREA (MARC field 245)

[Chapter #].1B. Title proper (MARC subfield a)

[Chapter #].1B1.   This rule in each chapter directs that the title proper be transcribed as instructed in rule 1.1B of the general chapter. Examples:

The four seasons

The future is information

Smithsonian Institution, Washington, D.C.

This rule (rule 5.1B1) in the chapter for music is somewhat more extensive. If a title consists of the name(s) of one or more type(s) of composition with or without the medium of performance, key, date, and/or number, those elements are all treated as the title proper. Examples:

Concerto in B-flat for cembalo and strings

Triosonate H-moll für zwei Violinen und Basso Continuo

If, however, the medium, key, date, and/or number are present with a title other than type of composition, those elements are treated as other title information. Example:

Short meditations : for string trio and harp

An LC rule interpretation for the sound recordings chapter (rule 6.1B1) instructs the cataloger that if the name of an author or performer is given before the titles of individual works and if it is possible that the name was meant to serve as a collective title proper, it should be treated as a title proper, unless the works are musical compositions and the name is the composer of the works, in which case the name would be given as statement of responsibility. (*CSB* 44: 25) An LC rule interpretation for the films chapter (rule 7.1B1) states that credits for performer, director, etc., that precede the title in the chief source are not considered part of the title proper unless they are within the title or represented by a possessive immediately preceding the title. (*CSB* 13: 15) Example:

Chief source:
　　Twentieth Century Fox presents Star Wars

Title proper:
　　Star Wars

This applies only to chapter 7 and thus could not be applied to a title on a sound recording reading, for example, "Armstrong presents Lerner & Loewe's Brigadoon."

[Chapter #].1B2.   Rule .1B2, and sometimes rule .1B3 and following, in each chapter presents special instructions for titles proper for that type of material. For example, in cartographic materials one is instructed to include statement of scale if it is part of the title proper. Example:

Arabian peninsula 1:500,000 / prepared by ...

In most cases rule .1B2 gives instructions for supplying a title when the item lacks one. Examples:

[Letter] 1793 Feb. 3, Windsor [to Henry] Dundas

[Public library advertisement]

[Harris 1967 public opinion survey, no. 1702]

Rule 3.1B3 gives directions to the cataloger on how to choose from more than one title in the chief source for cartographic materials. Choice is made on the basis of language, sequence, or layout, and if these are insufficient, then the most comprehensive title is chosen. Thus the title proper for the map whose chief source is illustrated in Figs. 5.1 to 5.4 would be:

Bath Alum quadrangle, Virginia-Bath Co.

[Chapter #].1C. *Optional addition.* **General material designation** (MARC subfield h)

The Library of Congress is applying GMDs to only some of the materials covered in this chapter. The following table sets out the GMD appropriate to the materials covered and indicates which GMDs are being used by LC. (*CSB* 44: 10)

TYPE OF MATERIAL	APPROPRIATE GMD	GMD USED BY LC
Cartographic	[map] [globe] [text] (for atlases)	none
Manuscripts	[manuscript]	none
Music	[music]	none
Sound recordings	[sound recording]	[sound recording]
Motion pictures and videorecordings	[motion picture] [videorecording]	[motion picture] [videorecording]
Graphics	[art original] [art reproduction] [chart] [filmstrip] [flash card] [picture] [slide] [technical drawing] [transparency]	does not catalog* does not catalog does not catalog [filmstrip] does not catalog does not catalog [slide] does not catalog [transparency]

---

*The Library of Congress would use *chart* and *flash card* if it were to start cataloging such material. If it were to start cataloging art originals, pictures, and technical drawings, it would decide then whether or not to display the GMD. (*CSB* 6: 4-5)

Four special rules appear in a footnote to list 2 in rule 1.1C, and three of them apply to the material covered by the chapter on graphics: "(2) for material treated in chapter 8, use *picture* for any item not subsumed under one of the other terms in list 2; (3) use *technical drawing* for items fitting the definition of this term in the Glossary, appendix D; for architectural renderings, however, use *art original, art reproduction,* or *picture,* not *technical drawing*; (4) use *kit* for any item containing more than one type of material if the relative predominance of components is not easily determinable, and for a single-medium package of textual material (e.g., a 'lab kit,' a set of activity cards)."[4]

TYPE OF MATERIAL	APPROPRIATE GMD	GMD USED BY LC
Computer files	[computer file]	[computer file]
Three-dimensional artifacts and realia	[diorama] [game] [microscope slide] [model] [realia]	does not catalog*
Kits (made up of more than one of the above types of materials, usually in addition to text)	[kit]	[kit]

Examples:

The four seasons [sound recording]

The future is information [videorecording]

Smithsonian Institution, Washington, D.C. [slide]

Perfect writer [computer file]

The classification game [game]

[Chapter #].1D — [Chapter #].1E. (MARC subfield b)
Parallel titles and other title information are recorded as instructed in the general chapter under rules 1.1D-1.1E. Examples:

Triosonate H-moll für zwei Violinen und Basso Continuo = Trio sonata in B minor for two violins and basso continuo

State of California : south half

Teatro del mondo [sound recording] : symphonic rotations in four scenes for large orchestra

American women artists [slide] : the twentieth century

In the case of cartographic materials, manuscripts, and motion pictures, there are specific instructions for additions to be made as other title information. In the case of maps, if the title does not indicate the geographic area, this is added as other title information. Example:

Land use and industry : [in East Germany]

For manuscripts there are extensive directions in rule 4.1B2 for creating supplied titles. If a manuscript item has a title and it lacks information required for a supplied title for that type of document, the information is added as other title information. Example:

The duty of communicating in the Lord's Supper enforced : [sermon]

---

*The Library of Congress has said that for all these types, it would use the GMD if it does start cataloging the material. (*CSB* 6: 4-5)

[Chapter #].1F.   Statements of responsibility (MARC subfield c)

Statements of responsibility are recorded as instructed in rule 1.1F in the general chapter. Examples:

> Bath Alum quadrangle, Virginia—Bath Co. / mapped, edited, and published by the Geological Survey

> Triosonate H-moll für zwei Violinen und Basso Continuo = Trio sonata in B minor for two violins and basso continuo : op. I/8 / Tommaso Albinoni ; herausgegeben von Stefan Altner

> The future is information [videorecording] : careers in library and information science / produced by Denver Public Library Cable Television Department ; producer, Teri Hernandez ; director/writer, Talliver J. Hare

> American movie [motion picture] / [written and produced by] Jan Peterson

Rule 6.1F for recording statements of responsibility for sound recordings is somewhat different from that for other materials. The cataloger must make a decision as to whether the participation of the person(s) or body(ies) involved in the recording goes beyond that of performance, execution, or interpretation of a work. If so, the statement is given as statement of responsibility. If not, the statement is given as a note. Thus, the statement on the chief source of information shown in Fig. 5.9, "Nils-Erik Sparf, The Drottningholm Baroque Ensemble," must be relegated to note position because participation seems to be "confined to performance, execution, or interpretation." However, writers of spoken words, composers of music, and collectors of field material for sound recordings are included in statements of responsibility. Examples:

> Individual differences in susceptibility to hypnosis [sound recording] / E.R. Hilgard
>
> > (This is a lecture given by its author. In the case of a group of poems by E. E. Cummings read by Spencer Tracy, for example, only E. E. Cummings would be given in the statement of responsibility.)

> The new moon [sound recording] / Sigmund Romberg ; [lyrics by] Oscar Hammerstein

An LC rule interpretation for giving statements of responsibility for films (rule 7.1F) and graphics (rule 8.1F) states that names should be given in the statement of responsibility when a person or body has had some degree of overall responsibility. LC usually considers producers, directors, and writers (and, for slides and transparencies, authors, editors, and compilers) to have some degree of overall responsibility. When a person or body has been responsible for only segments or one aspect of a work, the name(s) should be given in the note area. (*CSB* 36: 12)

[Chapter #].1G.   Items without a collective title
As explained in the general chapter, items that lack collective titles generally may be described either as a unit or by making a separate description for each separately titled part. However, *AACR2R* chapters 5 (music), 8 (graphic materials), and 10 (realia) do not have a rule allowing separate descriptions for each separately titled part. For cartographic materials, there is also a rule allowing the cataloger to supply a collective title for an item that consists of a large number of physically separate parts. A collective title may also be supplied for manuscript collections, but is authorized in rule 4.1B2 rather than under rule 4.1G. Examples:

> Rhapsody in blue ; An American in Paris [sound recording] / Gershwin

> [Maps of the United States]

> [Papers] / William Alexander Smith

The Library of Congress has made a decision to describe a sound recording as a unit in all cases. (*CSB* 11: 15)

[Chapter #].2.   EDITION AREA (MARC field 250)
Elements of the edition area are transcribed for nonbook materials in the same manner as instructed in the general chapter. Examples:

> World atlas / Rand McNally. — Imperial ed.

> I will change no wine before my time : [sermon] / A. Wayne Benson. — Prelim. draft

> Brigadoon [sound recording] / book & lyrics by Alan Jay Lerner ; music by Frederick Loewe. — Collector's ed.

> The Braniff Concorde [motion picture] / Braniff Airways, Inc. — Spanish ed.

Two of the materials, music and computer files, have special problems in interpreting whether certain statements are edition statements or not.
A Library of Congress rule interpretation discusses the care that must be taken with music publications to distinguish between edition statements and musical presentation statements. The latter often include the word *edition*, but should not be taken as edition statements. Musical presentation statements indicate the version, arrangement, music format, etc., in which a work is presented. These go in the statement of responsibility when the music itself is meant (i.e., a version, arrangement, or transposition of the music) because an "author" is responsible for changing the original work, even if such a person is not named. When the music format is meant (e.g., edition as a set of parts), the statement is transcribed in Area 3 (see below). (*CSB* 33: 32) Only when edition statements of the book type appear are they transcribed into the edition area. Example:

> Drei Sonaten für Klavier zu vier Händen / Johann Christian Bach ; herausgegeben von Wilhelm Weismann. — Ed. Peters

It may sometimes be difficult to interpret "edition" when cataloging computer files. Changes can be made to a computer file very quickly and easily (e.g., data can be added, changed, or deleted). While published software has fairly standard edition statements (e.g., Version 5.6 or Release 3.0), data files do not. Published data files that are reissued on a regular basis contain a cumulation of all older data plus new data acquired since the previous issue. These are sometimes advertised as being, for example, "a complete new edition each quarter." Most libraries treat these as serials. Rule 9.2B4 instructs the cataloger not to treat as a new edition an issue including such minor changes as corrections of misspelled data, rearrangement of contents, changes in output format or display medium, and changes in physical characteristics (e.g., recording density). If deemed important, such changes may be given in a note. Examples:

> WordStar [computer file]. — Release 5.00

> Science citation index [computer file]. — Compact
> disc ed.

[Chapter #].3   **MATERIAL (OR TYPE OF PUBLICATION) SPECIFIC DETAILS AREA** (MARC fields 255 [cartographic materials], 254 [music], and 256 [computer files])

Three types of material covered by this chapter have special rules in this area: cartographic materials, music, and computer files.

RULE 3.3.   MATHEMATICAL DATA AREA (MARC field 255)

3.3B.   Statement of scale (MARC subfield a)

3.3B1.   The first part of this area is "Statement of scale." Scale is given as a representative fraction expressed as 1:_____ and preceded by the word *scale*. If the statement of scale on the item is not expressed as a representative fraction (e.g., "1 inch to 76 miles"), it is given as a representative fraction in square brackets (e.g., [1:4,815,360]). If any statement of scale is found outside the item, it also is given as a representative fraction in square brackets. If no statement is found, the scale is computed and given preceded by "ca." If it cannot be computed, the statement "scale indeterminable" is used.

3.3B2.   An option allows giving additional scale information found on the item. LC is applying this option. (*CSB* 8: 10) Example:

> West Indies and Central America / compiled and drawn
> in the Cartographic Division of the National Geographic
> Society, for The National geographic magazine. — Scale
> 1:4,815,360. 1 in. to 76 miles.

3.3B3-3.3B8.   Detailed instructions for recording more than one scale value, and for handling other problems, are given in these rules, which should be consulted when one is doing in-depth map cataloging.

3.3C. Statement of projection (MARC subfield b)

If a statement of projection is found on the item or any of the accompanying materials, it is given following the scale, using abbreviations and numerals where appropriate. Example:

> Bath Alum quadrangle, Virginia—Bath Co. / mapped, edited, and published by the Geological Survey. — Scale 1:24,000 ; Polyconic proj.

5.3. *Optional area*. MUSICAL PRESENTATION STATEMENT AREA (MARC field 254)

This area for music was added to *AACR2* in 1984. It calls for recording a statement found in the chief source that indicates the physical presentation of the music. As discussed above under the edition area, it is necessary to distinguish among statements that are true edition statements, those that are statements of responsibility, and those that indicate the physical presentation. LC is applying this optional area. (*CSB* 34: 25) Example:

> Aubade : trio for flute, oboe & clarinet in B^b / DeWailley ; [edited by] Jerry Kirkbride. — Score and parts

9.3 FILE CHARACTERISTICS AREA (MARC field 256)

This area for music was added to *AACR2* in 1984. It calls for recording a recording the type of file [i.e., computer data, computer program(s), or computer data and program(s)] followed by the number or approximate number of files when the latter information is readily available. Other details that may be given include number of records and/or bytes for data, number of statements and/or bytes, or statements/bytes for each part of multipart files. Examples:

> WordStar professional [computer file]. — Release 5.00 — Computer program

> OCLC names project [computer file] / principal investigator, Arlene G. Taylor. — Computer data (3 files: 450, 457, 128 records)

The remaining nonbook materials chapters (except 3, 5, and 9) state that area 3 is not used for the types of material covered by those chapters. The implication is that use of this area is not permitted for the type of material in question. In the chapter on microforms, however, there is instruction in this area to follow the instruction in rule 3.3 for microforms of cartographic materials, rule 5.3 for music in microform, and rule 12.3 for serial microforms. For most types of material, need for this area is rare; but nonbook materials may be produced serially, and occasionally their content is cartographic (e.g., slides of maps). The scope note for the chapter on description of serials says that the rules in that chapter are to be used for serial publications of all kinds in all media. Clearly, then, it is permissible, and certainly desirable, to use area 3 when describing other nonbook materials. For example, videorecordings that are available on a subscription basis so that new parts are added regularly require serial cataloging. Example:

> OCLC report [videorecording]. — No. 1 (Nov. 1986)-

[Chapter #].4. PUBLICATION, DISTRIBUTION, ETC., AREA (MARC field 260)

For the most part the details in this area are recorded in the same manner as discussed in the general chapter under rule 1.4.

This area in the manuscripts chapter is called the "Date Area." It omits details of place and name of publisher (this being unpublished material) and includes only date, and then only if it is not already in the title. The date of a single manuscript is given as a year, optionally followed by the month and day. LC follows the option when the information is readily available.

For a manuscript collection, inclusive years are given. Example:

> [Papers] / William Alexander Smith. — 1765-1949.

In the music chapter there is an instruction to record plate numbers and publishers' numbers in the note area. The sound recordings chapter deals with the issue of trade names, brand names, or subdivision names used by recording companies. In cases where these are used, they are recorded as the name of the publisher. Example:

Label on disc reads:
SUNSET, a product of Liberty Records
A division of Liberty Records, Inc., Los Angeles,
California

Description should read:
Los Angeles, Calif. : Sunset

However, if a trade name seems to be a name of a series, it is recorded as a series rather than as the name of a publisher.

In 1984 ⓟ dates (i.e., dates of "pressing" of sound recordings) were added by example to the ⓒ dates already given as examples, thus authorizing use of these dates that appear on sound recordings. Example:

> The four seasons [sound recording] / Antonio Vivaldi. — Djursholm, Sweden : BIS, p1985.

NOTE: In Fig. 5.9 (see page 107) both the ⓒ and ⓟ dates are 1985. However, in Fig. 5.10 (see page 107) the ⓒ and ⓟ dates are given as 1984/85. Considering that the performance was recorded late in 1984 and the date of "printing" was 1985, the 1985 date is used as the date of first release (publication).

In the motion pictures and videorecordings chapter, "releasing agency," "production agency," and "producer" have been added to "distributor" as names that can optionally be given in this area.

For the materials covered by the films and graphics chapters, LC has chosen not to apply the option allowing one to give the full address of a publisher, distributor, etc. (*CSB* 13: 16) Also for these chapters there is a provision for giving in a note a date of original production that differs from the date in area 4. LC is applying this option when the difference is greater than two years. (*CSB* 33: 37) Example:

> Washington, [D.C.] : Division of Audiovisual Arts : distributed by National Audiovisual Center, 1989.

>> The record on which the above imprint appears would have the following note:

> Made in 1985.

All chapters call for giving only the date for unpublished items. In the realia chapter it is specifically mentioned that this applies to artifacts not intended primarily for communication (e.g., clothing, money, furniture). Example:

> [White treadle sewing machine] [realia]. — 1890.

If the person or body that has manufactured an object is named in the statement of responsibility (as is the case with handmade items such as hand-woven tapestries or handmade pottery), the place and name are not repeated in this area. In such a case, the place, if known, may be part of the cataloger-constructed title proper, or it may be given in a note.

Examples of application of rules for the publication, distribution, etc., area:

> Earth's dynamic crust / produced by the Cartographic Division, National Geographic Society. — Scale 1:78,890,000. 1 cm. = 789 km. or 1 in. = 1,245 miles at the equator ; Van der Grinten proj. — Washington, D.C. : The Society, c1985.

> The future of technical services [sound recording] / (RTSD) American Library Association. — [Chicago] : ALA ; Ballwin, Mo. : [Produced by] ACTS, [1989]

> An introduction to WordPerfect [videorecording] / produced and directed by D.E. Williams. — [Orem, Utah] : Video Projects, Inc. [production company] : Released by WordPerfect Corp., 1987.

> Smithsonian Institution, Washington, D.C. [slide]. — Portland, Ore. : Sawyer's, Inc., [196-?]

>> Note: The date is presumed to be in the 1960s because reference is made in the booklet to a new building projected for completion in 1969.

> The classification game [game]. — Paoli, Pa. : Instructo Corp., c1969.

[Chapter #].5. PHYSICAL DESCRIPTION AREA (MARC field 300)

[Chapter #].5B. Extent of item (including specific material designation) (MARC subfield a)

Each of the chapters for nonbook materials gives a direction to record the number of physical units in arabic numerals followed by a term from the chapter's list of specific material designations. The following lists are provided:

Cartographic materials:

atlas	profile
diagram	relief model
globe	remote-sensing image
map	view
map section	

(Extent is given in number of physical units for atlases and globes, but in number of intellectual units for the other cartographic items in this list.)

Music:

score	vocal score
condensed score	piano score
close score	chorus score
miniature score	part
piano [violin, etc.] conductor part	

Sound recordings:

sound cartridge	sound tape reel
sound cassette	sound track film
sound disc	

Films and videorecordings:

film cartridge	videocartridge
film cassette	videocassette
film loop	videodisc
film reel	videoreel

Graphics: (as distributed by LC among the GMDs appropriate to this chapter. *CSB* 33: 40)

Art original	photograph
art original	picture
Chart	postcard
chart	poster
flip chart	radiograph
wall chart	study print
Filmstrip	Slide
filmslip	slide
filmstrip	stereograph
Flash card	Technical drawing
flash card	technical drawing
Picture	Transparency
art print	transparency
art reproduction	

Computer files:

computer cartridge	computer disk
computer cassette	computer reel

(No physical description is given for a computer file that is available only by remote access.)

Three-dimensional artifacts and realia:

art original	game
art reproduction	microscope slide
braille cassette	mock-up
diorama	model
exhibit	toy

Normally, specific material designations are given to different classes of materials that represent different kinds of physical objects. In the case of published music, specific material designations vary under different circumstances, one of them being whether the music is written for a solo instrument or for several instruments. The physical extent of a piece of music written for a solo instrument is described, as for any monograph, in terms of leaves, pages, or volumes. If the option of using the GMD [music] is not applied, then the term *music* is incorporated in the extent of item statement. Example:

36 p. of music.

A specific material designation using the terms *score(s)* and/or *part(s)* is to be given to a piece of music written for several instrumental or vocal parts. The type of score it is—miniature, piano, vocal, etc.—as well as its pagination and the number of copies of it issued by the publisher are to be recorded. (Definitions of different types of scores are given in the Glossary of *AACR2R*.) If the score is accompanied by parts, the number of these issued by the publisher is to be recorded.

The rules for all nonbook materials covered in this chapter of this text except manuscripts allow the cataloger to use terms other than those listed if needed. Examples:

Music Realia	Realia
choir book	jigsaw puzzle
table book	hand puppet
Sound recordings	quilt
piano roll	tapestry
organ roll	statue
Computer files	sculpture
computer card	bowl (or cup, jar, candle hold-
computer chip cartridge	er, etc.)
computer laser optical disk	dress (or coat, belt, suit, etc.)

The manuscript chapter directs the cataloger to record the extent of single manuscripts as one would for books. The term *bound* is added if the manuscript has been bound. Example:

128 leaves, bound

A collection that occupies one linear foot or less of shelf space is described in terms of the number of items or the number of containers or volumes. LC is applying the option to add the number of items if the collection is described in number of volumes or containers. (*CSB* 8: 10) Examples:

> 1 v. (208 items)
>
> 2 boxes (110 items), 2 v. (68 items)
>
> ca. 600 items

A collection that occupies more than one linear foot of shelf space is described in terms of the number of linear feet occupied. LC is applying the option to add the number of items or containers or volumes. (*CSB* 8: 10)

Various pieces of information may be added in parentheses after the statement of extent of most nonbook materials if easily ascertainable from the item in hand. Numbers of pages are added after statements of extent of atlases and music. Examples:

> 1 atlas (20 leaves)
>
> 1 score (35 p.) + 4 parts

Information about systems intended for the visually impaired may be given for cartographic items, music, and graphic materials. Examples:

> 1 globe (tactile)
>
> 1 score (20 leaves, braille)
>
> 228 p. of music (large print)

Numbers of items may be given for collections of manuscripts, some kinds of graphics, and realia. Examples:

> 2 ft. (ca. 300 items)
>
> 1 transparency (3 overlays)
>
> 3 flip charts (10 sheets each)
>
> 1 game (1 board, 1 timer, 500 word cards, 1 die, 4 markers, 4 category cards, 4 pads of paper, 4 pencils)
>
> 2 dioramas (various pieces)
>
> 1 jigsaw puzzle (ca. 500 pieces)

Running/playing time may be given for sound recordings, films, and video-recordings. Examples:

> 2 sound cassettes (ca. 150 min.)
>
> 1 videocassette (15 min.)

The number of frames may be given for filmstrips, filmslips, stereographs, or videodiscs consisting of still images. Example:

> 4 filmstrips (ca. 40 fr. each)

In a few cases the number of intellectual items may differ from the number of physical items, and this may be specified. Examples:

8 maps on 2 sheets

1 aerial chart in 6 segments

Specific rules in *AACR2R* for any of the above situations should be consulted when cataloging nonbook materials.

[Chapter #].5C. Other physical details (MARC subfield b)
Different kinds of "other physical details" (besides extent of item and dimensions) are given for each of the materials covered in this chapter. The following outlines indicate the kinds of details specified for each type of material. These details are called for only where appropriate. Where there are several kinds of details for one type of material, they are to be given in the order specified in the list.

Cartographic materials:
    number of maps in an atlas
    color
    material
    mounting
    Examples:

        1 atlas (5 v.) : 250 col. maps

        1 relief model : col., plastic

        1 globe : col., plastic, mounted on wooden stand

        1 map : col., mounted on linen

Manuscripts:
    material other than paper for a single manuscript
    illustrations (as instructed in rule 2.5C or rule 8.5C)
    Example:

        42 leaves : parchment, col. ill.

Music:
    illustrations (as instructed in rule 2.5C)
    Example:

        1 score (x, 77 p., [1] leaf of plates) : facsim.

Sound recordings:
    type of recording
    playing speed
    groove characteristic (analog discs)
    track configuration (sound track films)
    number of tracks (tapes)
    number of sound channels

(List continues on page 126.)

Sound recordings: *(continued)*
recording and reproduction characteristics [*optional addition*]
Examples:

1 sound disc (31 min.) : analog, 33⅓ rpm, stereo.

2 sound cassettes (ca. 150 min.) : 1½ ips, mono.

1 sound disc : analog, 78 rpm, microgroove, mono.

1 sound disc (42 min.) : digital, stereo.

Films and videorecordings:
aspect ratio and special projection characteristics (motion pictures)
sound characteristics
color
projection speed (motion pictures)
Examples:

2 film reels (25 min.) : multiprojector, multiscreen, si., col.

1 videocassette (15 min.) : sd., col.

1 videodisc (ca. 35 min.) : sd., b&w

Graphics:
The other physical details required in the description depend upon the kind
of graphic material being cataloged. Some require only an indication of color
(e.g., col., b&w, sepia). These are:

pictures	study prints
postcards	transparencies
posters	wall charts
stereographs	

Others require some description of a characteristic in addition to color.
These are:

art prints – process in general terms (e.g., engraving, lithograph)
or specific terms (e.g., copper engraving) and color

art reproductions – method of reproduction (e.g., photogravure, collotype)
and color

charts and flip charts – indication of double-sided sheets (if applicable) and
color

filmstrips, filmslips, flash cards, and slides – indication of sound if it is integral (if sound is not integral, it is described as accompanying material) and
color

photographs – indication if photograph is a transparency not designed for
projection or if it is a negative print and color. Optionally, the process used
may be given. LC applies this option on a case-by-case basis.

Two kinds of items require description of a characteristic, but no indication of color. These are:

art originals—medium (chalk, oil, pastel, etc.) and base (board, canvas fabric, etc.) are given

technical drawings—method of reproduction if any (blueprint, photocopy, etc.) is given

One kind of graphic item requires no description for other physical details:

radiograph

> Examples:
>
> > 8 study prints : col.
> >
> > 5 filmstrips : sd., col.
> >
> > 1 art original : oil on board

> Computer files:
> encoded sound
> encoded to display in two or more colors

Optional additions, if readily available and considered to be important:

> > number of sides used
> > recording density
> > sectoring
> > Examples:

2 computer cassettes : col.

1 computer disk : sd., col., double sided, high density

> Three-dimensional artifacts and realia:
> material
> color
> Examples:

1 jar : clay, brown and red

1 statue : stone, gray

1 diorama (various pieces) : plastic, col.

[Chapter #].5D. Dimensions (MARC subfield c)
For book-like materials, dimensions are given as instructed in rule 2.5D. This applies to atlases, single manuscripts, and music.
For large, flat items the height x width is given in centimeters; and if the item is stored folded, the dimensions of the folded item follow the dimensions of the extended item. This applies to maps, plans, large manuscripts, technical drawings, and wall charts. Example:

1 map : col. ; 67 x 97 cm. folded to 15 x 22 cm.

Round items are described in terms of the diameter, specified as such. Sound discs and videodiscs are measured in inches, while other items are measured in centimeters. Exception: No measurements are given for stereographs, including stereograph reels, or for computer reels. Examples:

> 1 globe : col., cardboard, mounted on metal stand ; 32 cm.
> in diam.

> 1 computer disk ; 3½ in.

The gauge (width) is given for motion pictures, videotapes, filmstrips, and filmslips. All are given in millimeters except for videotapes, which are given in inches. Examples:

> 1 film cartridge (4 min.) : si., col. ; super 8 mm.

> 1 film reel (12 min.) : sd., col. with b&w sequences ; 16 mm.

> 1 videocassette (15 min.) : sd., col. ; ¾ in.

> 5 filmstrips : col. ; 35 mm.

For a computer cartridge the length of the side that is to be inserted into the machine is given in inches to the next ¼ inch up. Example:

> 1 computer cartridge : sd., col. ; 3¼ in.

Most other items are measured in terms of height x width or height x depth or height x width x depth, and most are recorded in centimeters to the next whole centimeter up. This is true for relief models; manuscript collections when the containers are uniform; sound cartridges and cassettes when the dimensions are other than the standard ones (measured in fractions of inches); all graphic materials (except filmstrips, filmslips, stereographs, and slides whose dimensions are 5 x 5 cm.); computer cassettes (measured in inches to the next ⅛ inch up), computer cards, and other appropriate physical carriers of computer files; three-dimensional artifacts and realia. Examples:

> 1 relief model : col., wood ; 50 x 35 x 4 cm.

> 2 ft. (2 boxes, ca. 300 items) ; 44 x 30 x 15 cm.

> 1 sound cassette (60 min.) : analog, stereo. ; 7¼ x 3½ in.

> 1 art original : oil on canvas ; 31 x 41 cm.

For three-dimensional artifacts and realia it may be necessary to give only one dimension. In such a case the dimension being given is specified. Examples:

> 1 jar : clay, brown and red ; 32 cm. high

> 1 paperweight : glass, col. ; 8 cm. in diam.

Three-dimensional artifacts and realia in containers should have the name of the container and its dimensions given after the dimensions of the object or as the only dimensions. Dimensions of a container are an optional addition for cartographic materials. LC is applying the option. (*CSB* 8: 10) Examples:

1 relief model : col., wood ; 50 x 35 x 4 cm. in box
26 x 19 x 9 cm.

1 jigsaw puzzle (ca. 60 pieces) : cardboard, col. ; 18 cm. in
diam. in box 11 cm. in diam. x 4 cm.

No dimensions are given for stereographs, for sound recordings on rolls, for
sound cartridges or cassettes that are of standard dimensions, for slides that are
of standard dimensions, or for computer reels.

[Chapter #].5E. Accompanying material (MARC subfield e)
Material issued with an item is treated, by both *AACR2R* and LC, as
described in the general chapter in rule 1.5E1. Graphic materials and computer
files are more likely than other materials to have accompanying documentation.
Because no physical description is given for a computer file that is available only
by remote access, the details of any accompanying material for such files are
given in a note. There is no rule for accompanying material in the manuscripts
chapter. Examples:

on side A of 1 sound disc (ca. 22 min.) : analog, 33⅓ rpm, stereo. ;
12 in. + 1 program notes booklet ([8] p. : ill. ; 23 cm.)

1 videocassette (50 min.) : sd., col., ; ½ in. + 1 script booklet

3 stereograph reels (7 pairs of fr. each) : col. + 1 booklet (16 p. :
col. ill. ; 11 cm.)

1 computer reel + 1 machine-readable codebook + 1 codebook
(364 p. ; 25 cm.)

5 filmstrips : col. ; 35 mm. + 5 sound cassettes (60 min. :
2 track, mono.) + 1 teacher's guide (25 p. ; 23 cm.)

[Chapter #].6 SERIES AREA (MARC field 4xx)
Series statements are recorded as instructed in the general chapter in rule 1.6.
This area is not used for manuscripts. Examples:

1 map section : col. ; 58 x 43 cm. — (7.5 minute series :
topographic)

1 score (12 p.) + 3 parts ; 30 cm. — (Hortus Musicus ; 240)

1 sound disc (ca. 57 min.) : digital, stereo. ; 4¾ in. — (CBS
masterworks)

1 videocassette (15 min.) : sd., col. ; ¾ in. — (OCLC ;
no. 6)

3 computer reels + 1 codebook (675 p. ; 24 cm.) — (SRC/CPS
American national election series ; no. 13)

1 game (various pieces) : cardboard, col. ; in box 24 x 28 x 8 cm. +
1 teacher's guide (2 p. ; 28 cm.). — (Instructo activity kit)

[Chapter #].7.   NOTE AREA (MARC field 5xx)

Each chapter gives rules for giving notes for the kind of materials covered by that chapter. The rule numbers are mnemonic, for the most part, from chapter to chapter—that is, rules with the same number are generally for the same kind of note, although the details of what to record in the notes sometimes differ.

[Chapter #].7B1.   Nature and scope of the item (MARC field 500 [520 for manuscripts; 500 and 538 for computer files])

This kind of note is made if the nature, scope, etc., of the item are not apparent from the rest of the description. Examples:

Map:

>Shows locations of important historical events.

Sound recording:

>Organ music to demonstrate the instrument; various organists and organs.

Film:

>Newsreel.

Computer file:

>Data base manager.

This note for manuscripts prescribes terms to be used for originals and copies. The word *signed* is added if appropriate. Examples:

>Typescript, signed.

>Mss. (photocopies)

>Ms., signed (carbon copy)

>Holograph (photocopy)

For collections of manuscripts, the cataloger is instructed to name the types of items that compose the collection and to mention any other characterizing features. Example:

>[Papers] / William Alexander Smith. — 1765-1949. 51 boxes (11,573 items), 101 v. ; 44 x 30 x 9 cm.

>Mss.
>Capitalist and businessman operating mainly in North Carolina from ca. 1866 to 1934. Includes correspondence, reports, financial statements, writings, legal papers, volumes, clippings, genealogy, pictures, bills, receipts, and promissory notes.

In the music chapter, rule 5.7B1 is called "Form of composition and medium of performance." Musical form not apparent from the rest of the description is given briefly. Examples of forms of composition are carol, opera, concerto, and symphony. The medium of performance is given unless it has been given earlier in English or in an easily understood term in a foreign language. Example:

> For harpsichord, 2 violins, viola, and violoncello.

In the computer files chapter, rule 9.7B1 is called "Nature and scope and system requirements." Information on system requirements is given, when readily available, in a note beginning "System requirements:" and followed by information about the make and model of the computer(s) for which the file is designed, the amount of memory required, the name of the operating system, the software requirements, and the kind and characteristics of required or recommended peripherals. Example:

> System requirements: IBM PC XT or 3270; 64K; DOS 1.1 to DOS 2.0.

[Chapter #].7B2.   Language (MARC field 500)
A note about the language is made when the language of the textual content is not apparent from the rest of the description. Examples:

Map:

> Place names in Arabic and English.

Manuscript:

> In French.

Music:

> German and English words.

Sound recording:

> Sung in Latin.

Film:

> In English; also issued in Portuguese and Spanish.

[Chapter #].7B3.   Source of title proper (MARC field 500)
The source of the title proper is always given if it is other than the chief source of information. In addition it is given for sound recordings and graphic materials if it is the container and also is given for sound recordings if it is accompanying textual material. The source of the title proper is *always* given for computer files. Examples:

Sound recording:

> Title from publisher's catalog.

Graphic:

> Title from later reproductions.

Computer file:
> Title from title page of codebook.

Realia:
> Title supplied by cataloger.

[Chapter #].7B4.   Variations in title (MARC field 500)
Examples:

Map:
> Title in lower right hand corner: Bath Alum, Va.

Sound recording:
> Title on container: The last sixteen piano trios.
>> (Label reads: The last sixteen trios.)

Filmstrip:
> Title on container: Saint Pierre of the Cluniac Abbey of Moissac.
>> (Title proper reads: Moissac, the Romanesque abbey church and its sculpture.)

Computer file:
> Title on container: Pro-Cite for the Macintosh.
>> (Title proper reads: Pro-Cite.)

[Chapter #].7B6.   Statement of responsibility (MARC fields 500, 508, and 511)
This note is for persons or bodies that bear some responsibility for the item and are necessary to the description but cannot be named in the title and statement of responsibility area. Examples:

Map:
> Grid and marginal information added by the Army Map Service.

Manuscript:
> Holograph signed note by William Pitt appended to letter.

Music:
> Text based on the drama of the same name by Pushkin.

Sound recordings:
> Hollywood Bowl Pops Orchestra ; Carmen Dragon, arranger-conductor.
>
> Violoncello: Raphael Wallfisch ; piano: Richard Markham.

Barbara Rondelli, soprano ; Nürnberger Symphoniker ; Ljubomir Romansky, conductor.

Films:

Cast: John Howard Davies, Alec Guinness, Robert Newton.

Credits: Editor, Lars Floden ; voices, Hans Conreid, June Forray ; music, Larry Wolff.

Graphic:

Booklet edited by Lowell Thomas.

An LC rule interpretation lists (in prescribed order) the functions for which persons or bodies will be given in a "credits" statement. It also lists the functions that will not be given. (*CSB* 22: 21)

[Chapter #].7B7.   Edition and history (MARC fields 500 and 503)
Examples:

Map:

First published under title: Geographic map of the ... Kingdom of Saudi Arabia.

Manuscript: [note called "Donor, source, etc., and previous owner(s)" in the manuscripts chapter]

Gift of the estate of Mrs. Theodora Cabot, 1955.

Music:

Edited from ms. sources in the National Library of Turin.

Sound recordings:

Recorded in San Francisco in 1971.

Originally issued: New York : McGraw-Hill, 1968. (Sound seminars)

Reissue of: Capitol SW-1804.

Videorecordings:

Originally produced as motion picture in 1960.

Videorecording of play produced at Kathryn Bache Miller Theatre, Columbia University, New York, N.Y., March 10, 1990.

Filmstrip:

Edited from episodes of the television program entitled The undersea world of Jacques Cousteau.

Computer file:

> Data collected Nov., Dec. 1974, and Jan. 1975.

Puzzle:

> Based on a painting by Mather Brown.

[Chapter #].7B8. Material specific details (MARC field 500)
Four of the types of material covered by this chapter have this rule for notes that are specific to the type of material being cataloged: cartographic materials, manuscripts, music, and computer files. The graphic materials chapter originally had this rule, but it has been officially deleted. Examples:

Maps [called "Mathematical and other cartographic data"]:

> "Contour interval 50 feet."

> Relief shown by hachures, shading, spot heights, etc.

Manuscript [called "Place of writing"]:

> At top of letter: Brooklyn.

Music [called "Notation"]:

> Shape-note notation.

Computer files [called "File characteristics"]:

> File size unknown.

> Weighted sample size is 2523.

[Chapter #].7B9. Publication, distribution, etc. (MARC field 500)
Examples:

Map:

> Based on 1972 data.

Manuscript [note called "Published versions"]:

> Published in: Some letters of George III / W.B. Hamilton. p. 416. *In* The South Atlantic quarterly. Vol. 68, no. 3 (Summer 1969).

Film:

> First released in France.

Graphic:

> Issued in 3 parts.

[Chapter #].7B10. Physical description (MARC field 500)
Examples:

Map:

> Maps issued in envelopes bearing copies of inset maps
> of cities.

Manuscript:

> Paper watermarked: 1834.

Music:

> Duration: 13:20.
>
>> [given only if stated in the item; a cataloging decision made in
>> the Music Section, Special Materials Cataloging Division, Library
>> of Congress, indicates that for music and sound recordings, hours,
>> minutes, and seconds are to be expressed in the note area as
>> numerals separated by colons.[5]]
>
> Each copy signed by the composer.

Sound recording:

> Impressed on pliable surface with rectangular edge
> attached to hard paper cover for support.

Videorecordings:

> U standard.
>
> MCA DiscoVision.

Graphic:

> For flannel board.

Computer file:

> Displays in blue, white, and yellow.

Puzzle:

> Vertical sides in straight lines; horizontal sides form
> wavy lines.

Diorama:

> Contains four background scenes and 72 figures of
> animals, people, and plants.

[Chapter #].7B11. Accompanying material (MARC field 500)
Rule 1.5E1 gives four options for treating accompanying material. When
giving details in a note is chosen, the details are recorded here. Examples:

Map:

> Accompanied by: Index to maps of Arabia / issued by
> Army Map Service. 1 sheet ; 25 x 36 cm.

Sound recording:
>
> Program notes by Anthony Hodgson on container.

Film:
>
> With teacher's guide and supplementary material.

Computer file:
>
> Codebook numbered: ISBN 0-89138-111-2.

[Chapter #].7B12. Series (MARC field 500)
Examples:

> Originally issued in series: Musica viva Bohemica.
>
> Part 1 in a series.
>
> Series statement supplied by producer.

[Chapter #].7B14. Audience (MARC field 500 [540 for manuscripts])

Manuscript [note called "Access and literary rights"]:
>
> Information on literary rights available in the repository.

Film:
>
> For dental personnel.

Flash card:
>
> For primary grades.

Slide:
>
> For nurses' training.

[Chapter #].7B15. Reference to published descriptions (MARC field 510 [manuscripts])
This note number appears in only one chapter besides the general chapter. Example:

> Described in: Manuscripts for research / report of the director, 1961-1974, North Country Historical Research Center, Feinberg Library, State University College, Plattsburgh, New York. 1975. p. 31-32.

[Chapter #].7B16. Other formats (MARC field 500)
Examples:

Sound recording:
>
> Issued also on reel (60 min. : 3¾ ips, mono. or stereo. ; 5 in.)

Videorecording:

        Available as cartridge or disc.

Slide:

        Issued also as filmstrip.

Filmstrip:

        Issued also with sound accompaniment on disc.

[Chapter #].7B17.　Summary (MARC field 520)

Summary notes are often given for nonbook materials because of the difficulty of browsing them (as can be done with books) to determine what they contain. Examples:

Sound recording:

        Summary: The author presents an overview and introduction to the area of human potentialities and its implications for humankind.

Film:

        Summary: A sports documentary covering three snowmobile races.

Flash card:

        Summary: Aids young children in developing number and money concepts.

Computer file:

        Summary: Records cover the science and technology of textiles, plus all relevant patent literature in the United Kingdom and the United States dating from 1980 to 1990.

Puzzle:

        Summary: The picture shows a battle scene on the deck of a British war ship during the Revolutionary War. The officers are in full dress uniforms for 1787-1795 period.

[Chapter #].7B18.　Contents (MARC fields 500, 504, and 505)

Examples:

Maps:

        Each sheet includes: "Index to adjoining sheets," glossary, and "Sources of base compilation."

        Inset: Area west of Apalachicola River.

Music:

        Contents: Sonate C dur, op. 15, Nr. 15 — Sonate A dur, op. 18, Nr. 5 — Sonate F dur, op. 18, Nr. 6.

Film:

> Contents: The black league (20 min.) — Doing your own thing (22 min.) — Teamwork against the odds (18 min.) — A new era (15 min.)

Filmstrip:

> Contents: Return to the sea (130 fr.) — To save a living sea (153 fr.) — The liquid sky (120 fr.) — A sea of motion (133 fr.) — Invisible multitudes (147 fr.)

An LC rule interpretation allows addition after the number of frames, slides, etc., of the duration of the accompanying sound. (*CSB* 13: 17) Example:

> Contents: Return to the sea (130 fr., 25 min., 15 sec.) — To save a living sea (153 fr., 30 min., 25 sec.) ...

[Chapter #].7B19. Numbers (other than Standard Numbers) (MARC fields 023-030, 036-037, and 500)

Examples:

Maps:

> Supt. of Docs. no.: I 19.2:V88/4.
>
> Publisher's no.: AMS 5060 II SW-Series V834.

Music:

> Pl. no.: B.S.I. no. 31.
>
> Publisher's no.: Nr. 4516.

Sound recordings:

> Big Sur Recordings: 7110.
>
> Angel: S 37309.

Graphic:

> Packet no. A 792.

Computer file:

> Original study number: CPS study 495441.

Realia:

> "No. 1014."

An LC rule interpretation for the transcription of a label name and number of a sound recording calls for making this note the first one. (*CSB* 14: 17)

[Chapter #].7B20.   Copy being described, library's holdings, and restrictions on use (MARC field 590)

Examples:

Music:

> Library has 2 copies of the score and 1 copy of each part.

Computer files:

> Local data set name: CIPERRS.

> Restrictions: available by lease arrangement. Also available through commercial online vendors.

[Chapter #].7B21.   "With" notes (MARC field 501)

When a separately titled part of an item that lacks a collective title is being described as a separate entity, the other separately titled parts are listed in a note that begins "With:". Examples:

Music:

> With: La plus que lente / Claude Debussy.

Sound recording:

> With: Suite italienne / Igor Stravinskii — Vocalise, op. 34, no. 14 / Sergei Rachmaninoff.

Note: A problem in the "With" note has been noted by music librarians. Because the rules for notes call for referring to another bibliographic item by its title proper and statement of responsibility, musical works that are entered under a uniform title may be "lost" to a user of the "With" note. Such musical works seldom have added entries for title proper, and the filing arrangement under the main entry is by uniform title, not title proper.

[Chapter #].7B22.   (MARC fields 500 and 534)

Two chapters besides the general chapter have a rule "7B22." This rule in the graphic materials chapter is called "Note relating to the original" and calls for description of the original of a reproduced art work. The other chapter that contains this rule is the chapter on microforms and is discussed in chapter 6 of this text.

[Chapter #].7B23.   (MARC field 500)

Two chapters have a rule "7B23." This rule in the manuscripts chapter is called "Ancient, medieval, and Renaissance manuscripts" and gives instructions for more detailed notes for these manuscripts. The other chapter that contains this rule is the chapter on serials and is discussed in chapter 7 of this text.

[Chapter #].8. STANDARD NUMBER AND TERMS OF AVAILABILITY AREA (MARC fields 020 and 022)

Details of this area are recorded as instructed in the general chapter under rule 1.8. Most of the materials covered by this chapter currently are not given international standard numbers, leaving the terms of availability to stand alone.

[Chapter #].9. SUPPLEMENTARY ITEMS

All chapters except that for manuscripts have this rule for describing supplementary items as instructed in the general chapter under rule 1.9.

[Chapter #].10. ITEMS MADE UP OF SEVERAL TYPES OF MATERIAL

All chapters except that for manuscripts have this rule for describing "kits" made up of different types of materials. The reader should take note of the possible ways for describing kits given in chapter 3 under rule 1.10. See the examples given there.

[Chapter #].11. FACSIMILES, PHOTOCOPIES, AND OTHER REPRODUCTIONS

The chapters for cartographic materials, music, and graphics have this rule for describing facsimiles, photocopies, and other reproductions as instructed in rule 1.11.

Figures 5.22 through 5.29 give the *AACR2R* descriptions for the items whose sources of information are shown in Figs. 5.1 through 5.21. Figures 5.30 through 5.37 illustrate the MARC records for the same items.

Fig. 5.22. *AACR2R* description of the map.

Bath Alum quadrangle, Virginia—Bath Co. / mapped, edited, and published by the Geological Survey. — Scale 1:24,000 ; Polyconic proj. — Washington, D.C. : For sale by U.S. Geological Survey, 1968.

1 map section : col. ; 58 x 43 cm. — (7.5 minute series : topographic)

Title in lower right corner: Bath Alum, Va.
"Topography by photogrammetric methods from aerial photographs."
Publisher's no.: AMS 5060 II SW-Series V834.

(Text continues on page 147.)

Fig. 5.23. *AACR2R* **description of the single manuscript.**

[Letter] 1793 Feb. 3, Windsor [to Henry] Dundas /
G.R. [George III].
1 leaf ; 38 x 46 cm. folded to 23 x 19 cm.

Holograph, signed.
Purchase, 1961.
Published in: Some letters of George III / W.B.
Hamilton. p. 416. In The South Atlantic quarterly. Vol. 68,
no. 3 (Summer 1969)

Fig. 5.24. *AACR2R* **description of the score.**

Triosonate H-moll für zwei Violinen und Basso
Continuo = Trio sonata in B minor for two violins and
basso continuo : op. I/8 / Tommaso Albinoni ;
herausgegeben von Stefan Altner. – Kassel ; New
York : Bärenreiter, 1987.
1 score (12 p.) + 3 parts ; 30 cm. – (Hortus Musicus ;
240)

Includes preface in German and English.
Continuo realized in score for keyboard.
Pl. no.: HM 240.

Fig. 5.25. *AACR2R* **description of the sound disc.**

The four seasons [sound recording] / Antonio
Vivaldi. – Djursholm, Sweden : BIS, p1985.
1 sound disc (ca. 40 min.) : digital, stereo. ; 4¾ in.
+ 1 booklet ([10] p. ; 12 cm.)

BIS: CD-275.
Nils Erik Sparf, baroque violin ; Drottningholm
Baroque Ensemble.
Compact disc.
Program notes in Swedish by Stig Jacobson with English,
French, and German translations laid in container.

Fig. 5.26. *AACR2R* **description of the videorecording.**

The future is information [videorecording] : careers in library and information science / produced by Denver Public Library Cable Television Department ; producer, Teri Hernandez ; director/editor, Talliver J. Hare ; script, Rita Lovato. — Chicago, IL : ALA Video, c1989.
   1 videocassette (18 min.) : sd., col. ; ½ in. + 1 flyer.

VHS.
Narrator: Raymond Burr.
Credits: Project consultant, Margaret Myers ; music, Valentine Productions.
Audience: High school students through adults.
Summary: The information field is growing, and the work of librarians, the original information experts, is expanding to keep pace. This video provides an overview of the profession and the great variety of opportunities available.
   ISBN 0-8389-2107-8

Fig. 5.27. *AACR2R* **description of the stereograph reel.**

Smithsonian Institution, Washington, D.C. [slide]. — Portland, Or. : Sawyer's Inc., [196-?]
   3 stereograph reels (7 pairs of fr. each) : col. + 1 booklet (16 p. : col. ill. ; 11 cm.). — (View-master guided picture tour)

Booklet edited by Lowell Thomas.
For use with View-master.
Summary: Shows and describes some of the major exhibits housed in three of the buildings of the Smithsonian.
Contents: Reel 1. Air and space exhibits — Reel 2. Natural history exhibits — Reel 3. History & technology exhibits.
   "Packet no. A 792."
   $2.25

Fig. 5.28. *AACR2R* **description of the computer file.**

WordStar professional [computer file]. — Release 5.00 — Computer program. — San Rafael, Calif. : MicroPro International Corp., c1988.

6 computer disks ; 3½ in. + 1 manual (541 p. : ill. ; 23 cm.) + 1 printer information booklet (18 p. ; 23 cm.) + 1 pocket WordStar (49 p. ; 22 x 10 cm.) + 2 templates + 1 instruction sheet.

System requirements: IBM PC, IBM XT or compatible; 384K; DOS 2.0 or higher; 2 disk drives or hard disk.

Title from disk label.

Summary: Word processor with 87,000 word dictionary, thesaurus, mail merge, indexing, and math calculator. Includes PC-outline.

Fig. 5.29. *AACR2R* **description of the game.**

The classification game [game]. — Paoli, Pa. : Instructo Corp., c1969.

1 game (various pieces) : cardboard, col. ; in box 24 x 28 x 8 cm. + 1 teacher's guide (2 p. ; 28 cm.). — (Instructo activity kit)

Contains 4 store interiors (3 interlocking pieces each), 4 store floors, and 48 picture cards.

For primary grades.

Summary: Helps students improve organizing and classifying skills by learning to place the appropriate items in each of four stores: clothing store, food store, pet store, and toy store.

"No. 1014."

Fig. 5.30. MARC record for the map.

```
Entered:     19790421      Replaced:    19790421        Used:      19910131
Type:    e         Bib lvl: m        Source:   d      Lang:  eng
RecG:    a         Enc lvl: I        Govt pub: f      Ctry:  dcu
Relief: a          Mod rec:          Base:     cp     Form:
Desc: a            Indx:    0        Dat tp:   s      Dates: 1968,
  1 040      IVE $c IVE
  2 034 1    a $b 24000
  3 043      n-us-va
  4 052      3883 $b B3
  5 090      G3883.B3 1968 $b .U5
  6 049      YCLM
  7 245 00   Bath Alum quadrangle, Virginia--Bath Co. / mapped, edited,
and published by the Geological Survey.
  8 255      Scale 1:24,000 ; $b Polyconic proj.
  9 260      Washington, D.C. : $b For sale by U.S. Geological Survey, $c
1968.
 10 300      1 map section : $b col. ; $c 58 x 43 cm.
 11 490 0    7.5 minute series : topographic
 12 500      Title in lower right corner: Bath Alum, Va.
 13 500      "Topography by photogrammetric methods from aerial
photographs."
 14 500      Publisher's no.: AMS 5060 II SW-Series V834.
 15 650      Bath Alum (Va.) $x Maps.
 16 710 20   Geological Survey (U.S.)
```

Fig. 5.31. MARC record for the manuscript.

```
Entered:    19850324      Replaced:    19850324     Used:      19850324
Type: b          Bib lvl: m       Source:    d         Lang:    eng
Repr:            Enc lvl: I                             Ctry:    ncu
Desc: a          Mod rec:         Dat tp:    s         Dates:   1790,
    1 040        IVE $c IVE
    2 045 0      v9v9 $b d17930203
    3 090        DA506.A2 $b 1793
    4 049        YCLM
    5 100 0      George $b III, $c King of Great Britain, $d 1738-1820.
    6 245 00     [Letter] 1793 Feb. 3, Windsor [to Henry] Dundas / $c G.R.
[George III].
    7 300        1 leaf ; $c 38 x 46 cm. folded to 23 x 19 cm.
    8 520        Holograph, signed.
    9 590        Purchase, 1961.
   10 500        Published in: Some letters of George III / W.B. Hamilton.
p. 416.  In The South Atlantic quarterly.  Vol. 68, no. 3 (Summer 1969)
   11 651 0      Great Britain $x History $y George III, 1760-1820.
```

Fig. 5.32. MARC record for the score.

```
OCLC:    17336099        Rec stat:      c
Entered:    19880112      Replaced:    19900606     Used:      19910208
Type:   c        Bib lvl: m       Source: d          Lang:    N/A
Repr:            Enc lvl: I       Format: a          Ctry:    gw
Accomp:          Mod rec:         Comp:   ts         LTxt:    n
Desc:   a        Int lvl:         Dat tp: s          Dates:   1987,
    1 040        FUG $c FUG $d OCL $d RES $d OCL
    2 028 22     HM 240 $b B¨arenreiter
    3 041 0      $g gereng
    4 045        u9u9
    5 048        sa02 $a ke
    6 090        M312.4 $b .A421 op. 1, no. 8, 1987
    7 090        $b
    8 049        YCLM
    9 100 1      Albinoni, Tommaso, $d 1671-1750.
   10 240 10     Trio sonatas, $m violins, continuo, $n op. 1. $n No. 8
   11 245 00     Triosonate H-moll f¨ur zwei Violinen und Basso Continuo =
$b Trio sonata in B minor for two violins and basso continuo : $b op.
I/8 / $c Tommaso Albinoni ; herausgegeben von Stefan Altner.
   12 260        Kassel ; $a New York : $b B¨arenreiter, $c 1987.
   13 300        1 score (12 p.) + 3 parts ; $c 30 cm.
   14 440 0      Hortus Musicus ; $v 240
   15 500        Includes preface in German and English.
   16 500        Continuo realized in score for keyboard.
   17 650 0      Trio-sonatas (Violins (2), continuo) $x Scores and parts.
   18 700 10     Altner, Stefan.
```

Fig. 5.33. MARC record for the sound recording.

```
OCLC:      16474842        Rec stat:      c
Entered:     19870815      Replaced:    19881109      Used:       19910312
Type:    j              Bib lvl: m      Source: d       Lang:   N/A
Repr:                   Enc lvl: K      Format: n       Ctry:   sw
Accomp:                 Mod rec:        Comp:   co      LTxt:
Desc:    a              Int lvl:        Dat tp: s       Dates: 1985,
  1 040      JED $c JED
  2 007      s $b d $d f $e z $f n $g g $h n $i n $m e
  3 020         $c $18.00
  4 028 02   CD-275 $b BIS
  5 090         $b
  6 049      YCLM
  7 100 1    Vivaldi, Antonio, $d 1678-1741. $w cn
  8 240 00   Cimento dell'armonia e dell'inventione. $n N. 1-4
  9 245 14   The four seasons $h sound recording / $c Antonio Vivaldi.
 10 260      Djursholm, Sweden : $b BIS, $c p1985.
 11 300      1 sound disc (ca. 40 min.) : $b digital, stereo. ; $c 4 3/4
in. + $e 1 booklet ([10] p. ; 12 cm.)
 12 511 0    Nils Erik Sparf, baroque violin ; Drottningholm Baroque
Ensemble.
 13 500      Compact disc.
 14 500      Program notes in Swedish by Stig Jacobson with English,
French, and German translations laid in container.
 15 650  0   Concertos (Violin with string orchestra)
 16 650  0   Seasons $x Songs and music.
 17 700 10   Sparf, Nils Erik. $w cn
 18 710 20   Drottningholms barockensemble. $w cn
```

Fig. 5.34. MARC record for the videorecording.

```
OCLC:      19930800        Rec stat:      c
Entered:     19890627      Replaced:    19900829      Used:       19910418
Type:    g              Bib lvl: m      Source:   d     Lang:   eng
Type mat: v             Enc lvl: I      Govt pub:       Ctry:   ilu
Int lvl:  e             Mod rec:        Tech:    l      Leng:   018
Desc:    a              Accomp:  z      Dat tp:  s      Dates: 1989,
  1 040      IEZ $c IEZ $d IBI
  2 007      v $b f $d c $e b $f a $g h $h o
  3 020      0838921078
  4 090      Z682 $b .F8 1989x
  5 090         $b
  6 049      YCLM
  7 245 04   The Future is information $h [videorecording] : $b careers
in library and information science / $c produced by Denver Public
Library Cable Television Department ; producer, Teri Hernandez ;
director/editor, Talliver J. Hare ; script, Rita Lovato.
  8 260      Chicago, IL : $b ALA Video, $c c1989.
  9 300      1 videocassette (18 min.) : $b sd., col. ; $c 1/2 in. + $e 1
flyer.
 10 500      VHS.
 11 511 3    Raymond Burr.
 12 508      Project consultant, Margaret Myers ; music, Valentine
Productions.
 13 521      High school students through adults.
 14 520      The information field is growing, and the work of librarians,
the original information experts, is expanding to keep pace. This video
provides an overview of the profession and the great variety of opportunities
available.
 15 650  0   Library science $x Vocational guidance.
 16 650  0   Information science $x Vocational guidance.
 17 710 21   Denver Public Library. $b Cable Television Department.
 18 710 21   ALA Video.
```

Fig. 5.35. MARC record for the stereograph reel.

```
Entered:    19870612      Replaced:    19870612     Used:      19900309
Type:       g             Bib lvl: m   Source:    d   Lang:    eng
Type mat:   s             Enc lvl: I   Govt pub:      Ctry:    oru
Int lvl:                  Mod rec:     Tech:      n   Leng:    021
Desc: a                   Accomp:    m Dat tp:    q   Dates:   1960,1969
    1 040     IVE $c IVE
    2 007     g $b s $c r $d c $e n $h z
    3 020     $c $2.25
    4 043     n-us-dc
    5 090     Q11.S8 $b S64
    6 049     YCLM
    7 245 00  Smithsonian Institution, Washington, D.C. $h slide
    8 260     Portland, Or. ; $b Sawyer's, Inc., $c [196-?]
    9 300     3 stereograph reels (7 pairs of fr. each) : $b col. + $e 1
booklet (16 p. : col. ill. ; 11 cm.)
   10 440  0  View-master guided picture tour
   11 500     Booklet edited by Lowell Thomas.
   12 500     For use with View-master.
   13 520     Shows and describes some of the major exhibits housed in three
of the buildings of the Smithsonian.
   14 505     Reel 1. Air and space exhibits -- Reel 2. Natural history
exhibits -- Reel 3. History & technology exhibits.
   15 500     "Packet no. A 792."
   16 610 20  Smithsonian Institution.
```

Fig. 5.36. MARC record for the computer file.

```
OCLC:       19650012      Rec stat:      c
Entered:    19890503      Replaced:    19900627     Used:      19891208
Type:       m             Bib lvl: m   Source:    d   Lang:    N/A
File:       b             Enc lvl: I   Govt pub:      Ctry:    cau
Audience:                 Mod rec:     Frequn:    n   Regulr:
Desc:       a                          Dat tp:    s   Dates:   1988,
    1 040     CPO $c CPO
    2 041 0   $g eng
    3 090     Z52.5.W676 $b W675 1988
    4 090     $b
    5 049     YCLM
    6 245 00  WordStar professional $h computer file
    7 250     Release 5.00.
    8 256     Computer program.
    9 260     San Rafael, Calif. : $b MicroPro International Corp., $c
c1988.
   10 265     MicroPro International Corp., 33 San Pablo Ave., San
Rafael, CA 94903
   11 300     6 computer disks ; $c 3 1/2 in. + $e 1 manual (541 p. :
ill. ; 23 cm.) + 1 printer information booklet (18 p. ; 23 cm.) + 1
pocket WordStar (49 p. ; 22 x 10 cm.) + 2 templates + 1 instruction
sheet.
   12 538     System requirements: IBM PC, IBM XT or compatible; 384K;
DOS 2.0 or higher; 2 disk drives or hard disk.
   13 500     Title from disk label.
   14 520     Word processor with 87,000 word dictionary, thesaurus, mail
merge, indexing, and math calculator.  Includes PC-outline.
   15 650  0  Word processing $x Software.
   16 710 20  MicroPro International Corporation.
   17 730 02  PC-outline (Computer program)
   18 753     IBM PC $c DOS 2.0 or higher.
   19 753     IBM XT $c DOS 2.0 or higher.
```

Fig. 5.37. MARC record for the game.

```
Entered:     19870925      Replaced:     19870925     Used:       19900309
Type:      r          Bib lvl: m     Source:    d      Lang:    eng
Type mat: g           Enc lvl: I     Govt pub:         Ctry:    pau
Int lvl:  b           Mod rec:       Tech:      n      Leng:    ---
Desc:     a           Accomp:    r   Dat tp:    s      Dates: 1969,
    1 040      IVE $c IVE
    2 020      $c
    3 090      LB1029.G3 $b C52
    4 049      YCLM
    5 245 04   The Classification game $h game
    6 260      Paoli, Pa. : $b Instructo Corp., $c c1969.
    7 300      1 game (various pieces) : $b cardboard, col. ; $c in box 24 x
28 x 8 cm. + $e 1 teacher's guide (2 p. ; 28 cm.)
    8 490 0    Instructo activity kit
    9 500      Contains 4 store interiors (3 interlocking pieces each), 4
store floors, and 48 picture cards.
   10 521 8    For primary grades.
   11 520      Helps students improve organizing and classifying skills by
learning to place the appropriate items in each of four stores: clothing
store, food store, pet store, and toy store.
   12 500      "No. 1014."
   13 650  0   Educational games.
   14 650  0   Categorization (Psychology)
```

NOTES

[1]A discussion of these problems in relation to *AACR2* may be found in Michael Gorman, "Cataloging and Classification of Film Study Material," in Nancy Allen, *Film Study Collections* (New York, F. Ungar Publishing, 1979), pp. 113-123.

[2]American Library Association, Committee on Cataloging: Description and Access, *Guidelines for Using AACR2 Chapter 9 for Cataloging Microcomputer Software* (Chicago, American Library Association, 1984).

[3]*Anglo-American Cataloguing Rules, Second Edition. Chapter 9, Computer Files*, edited for the Joint Steering Committee for Revision of AACR by Michael Gorman, draft revision (Chicago, American Library Association, 1987).

[4]*AACR2R*, p. 20.

[5]Richard P. Smiraglia, *Cataloging Music: A Manual for Use with AACR2*, 2nd ed. (Lake Crystal, Minn., Soldier Creek Press, 1986), p. 29.

SUGGESTED READING

Cartographic Materials: A Manual of Interpretation for AACR 2. Chicago, American Library Association, 1982.

Dodd, Sue A., and Ann M. Sandberg-Fox. *Cataloging Microcomputer Files: A Manual of Interpretation for AACR2.* Chicago, American Library Association, 1985.

Frost, Carolyn O. *Media Access and Organization: A Cataloging and Reference Sources Guide for Nonbook Materials.* Englewood, Colo., Libraries Unlimited, 1989.

Hensen, Steven L. *Archives, Personal Papers, and Manuscripts: A Cataloging Manual for Archival Repositories, Historical Societies, and Manuscript Libraries.* Chicago, Society of American Archivists, 1989.

Maxwell, Margaret F. *Handbook for AACR2, 1988 Revision.* Chicago, American Library Association, 1989. Chapters 3-9.

Olson, Nancy B. *Cataloging Microcomputer Software: A Manual to Accompany AACR2, Chapter 9, Computer Files.* Englewood, Colo., Libraries Unlimited, 1988.

_____. *Cataloging Motion Pictures and Videorecordings.* Lake Crystal, Minn., Soldier Creek Press, 1991.

_____. *Cataloging of Audiovisual Materials: A Manual Based on AACR2.* 3rd ed., completely rev. and expanded. DeKalb, Ill., Media Marketing Group, 1991.

Policy and Practice in Bibliographic Control of Nonbook Media. Ed. by Sheila S. Intner and Richard P. Smiraglia. Chicago, American Library Association, 1987. pp. 103-181.

Rogers, JoAnn V. *Nonprint Cataloging for Multimedia Collections: A Guide Based on AACR2.* 2nd ed. with Jerry D. Saye. Littleton, Colo., Libraries Unlimited, 1987.

Saye, Jerry D., and Sherry L. Vellucci. *Notes in the Catalog Record Based on AACR2 and LC Rule Interpretations.* Chicago, American Library Association, 1989.

Smiraglia, Richard P. *Cataloging Music: A Manual for Use with AACR2.* 2nd ed. Lake Crystal, Minn., Soldier Creek Press, 1986.

Smiraglia, Richard P. *Music Cataloging: The Bibliographic Control of Printed and Recorded Music in Libraries.* Englewood, Colo., Libraries Unlimited, 1989. Chapters 2 and 3.

Weihs, Jean, with Shirley Lewis. *Nonbook Materials: The Organization of Integrated Collections.* 3rd ed. Ottawa, Canadian Library Association, 1989.

Description of Microforms   6

INTRODUCTION

The cataloging of microforms requires knowledge of a number of different types of material. Books, manuscripts, maps, music, and graphic materials all can be reproduced in microform. In addition, microform can be the original means for publication of some kinds of content—especially data stored in a computer. According to *AACR2R*, all microforms, whether original publications or reproductions, are described in terms of the microform format with details of the original, when applicable, given in a note. As mentioned earlier in this text under discussion of rule 1.5A3, this is a controversial method for handling microforms. Those who oppose it say that the user is misled by being given a modern date in the publication, distribution, etc., area when the intellectual content of the item is much older. They are also concerned about short-entry catalogs in which the notes are not printed. Publishers that specialize in reproducing older printed material in microform say that the purpose of the reproduction is to make older materials available for scholarly study and research, not to create a new edition of it as a printed reprint of the text would do. Earlier rules called for description of the original in the major part of the record with microform details in a note. Those opposed to this method point out that the physical form of the item is important. A user who comes into the library wanting to borrow an item to take elsewhere to read needs to know whether it is in book form or microform. There are also potential problems for the cataloger in determining what the original was and what its physical description should be. A microform of a dissertation, for example, may be a positive copy of a negative master that is a copy of a photocopy of a printout of text originally held in a computer file. Two articles that discuss the issues involved should be read for further information.[1] Americans have tended to prefer the method of describing the original, with details about the microform in a note, but Europeans have espoused describing the original in a note. In 1980 and 1981 ALA's Committee on Cataloging: Description and Access examined this question again and put forth a recommendation; its recommendation was that the original be described in the body of the entry, with details of the microform given in a note. The rules were not revised, but the Library of Congress issued a policy decision to this effect.[2] Both methods are illustrated in this text.

In December 1989 an Airlie House conference sponsored by the Council on Library Resources was held during which a solution was sought to the problem of "multiple versions." "Multiple versions" is the name given to the concept of two or more formats of the same work (e.g., a book, a negative microfilm of the book, and a positive microfilm of it; or, a published research paper and a photocopy of it). At the conference a decision was made to pursue a possible two-tiered hierarchical solution in which the top level of the hierarchy would be a bibliographic record containing a description of the common elements of the various versions of the work, while the next level would contain the elements of description unique to each version. If such a course is followed, the method of cataloging microforms described in this chapter will be changed. The reader should watch for developments on this issue.

SELECTED RULES AND EXAMPLES

RULE 11.0. GENERAL RULES

11.0A. Scope

This chapter covers all kinds of microforms, including those that are themselves original publications, those that are microreproductions of previous publications, and those that are microreproductions of material assembled for the purpose of bringing out an original edition in microform.

11.0B. Sources of information

11.0B1. Chief source of information

The following are the chief sources of information for the different types of microform:

TYPE	CHIEF SOURCE
microfilm	title frame, usually at the beginning of the item giving full title and publication details
aperture cards:	
set of cards	title card
single card	card itself
microfiches and microopaques	title frame

If there is no title frame for a microfiche or a microopaque, the "header" (i.e., eye-readable data at the top of the fiche or opaque) is used unless the title there is in shortened form, while it appears in fuller form on the accompanying eye-readable materials or container. In the latter case the source of the fuller form is used as the chief source of information, and a note is made to indicate the source of the title proper. Information that is usually presented on one title frame or card may be presented on successive frames or cards. In this case, the successive frames or cards are treated as one chief source.

Information not available in the chief source is taken from other sources. The order of preference is:

the remainder of the item
container
accompanying material
other sources

11.0B2. Prescribed sources of information

AREA	PRESCRIBED SOURCES OF INFORMATION
Title and statement of responsibility	Chief source of information
Edition	Chief source of information, rest of the item, container

Special data	[same as edition area]
Publication, distribution, etc.	[same as edition area]
Physical description	Any source
Series	[same as edition area]
Note	Any source
Standard number and terms of availability	Any source

Two items, one in microfilm format and the other in microfiche format, are used in this text to illustrate the building of description for microforms. The item illustrated in Figs. 6.1-6.2 is one that was assembled and filmed specifically for the purpose of bringing out an original edition in microform. The item illustrated in Figs. 6.3-6.5 (see page 152) is a microform of a previously existing work.

Fig. 6.1. Transcription of the first five frames of a microfilm.

Frame 1   WOMEN AND/IN HEALTH
filmed by the
WOMEN'S HISTORY RESEARCH CENTER
JULY 1974

Frame 2   WOMEN'S HISTORY RESEARCH CENTER
2325 Oak Street
Berkeley, California 94707

Frame 3   © Women's History Research Center, Inc. 1974

Reproduction of the material contained herein may not be reproduced in any form except by express permission from Women's History Research Center, Inc. and the Publisher(s).

Frame 4   THIS FILM WAS MADE POSSIBLE BY A REVENUE SHARING GRANT FROM THE ALAMEDA COUNTY BOARD OF SUPERVISORS.

Frame 5   Filmed at a reduction ratio of 15:1

Fig. 6.2. Transcription of label on container of first reel of microfilm.

WOMEN AND HEALTH/MENTAL HEALTH
Reel No. 1   Positive
Section 1
Women's History Research Center

(Text continues on page 153.)

Fig. 6.3. Transcription of title frame of microfiche.

87-15914

BAUM, Christina Diane

THE IMPACT OF FEMINIST THOUGHT ON AMERICAN LIBRARIANSHIP, 1965-1985.

University of Kentucky   Ed.D. 1987

University
  Microfilms
International 300 N. Zeeb Road, Ann Arbor, MI 48106

Copyright 1987
by
BAUM, Christina Diane
All Rights Reserved

Fig. 6.4. Transcription of eye-readable data at top of fiche.

87-15914   c 1987   BAUM, Christina Diane   THE IMPACT OF FEMINIST   1 of 03
          THOUGHT ON AMERICAN LIBRARIANSHIP, 1965-1985

Ann Arbor, Mi.; University Microfilms International 1987

**Fig. 6.5. Copy of title page of original
dissertation (seventh frame of microfiche).**

THE IMPACT OF FEMINIST THOUGHT ON
AMERICAN LIBRARIANSHIP 1965-1985

DISSERTATION

A dissertation submitted in partial fulfillment of the
requirements for the degree of Doctor of Education
at the University of Kentucky

By
Christina D. Baum
Lexington, Kentucky

Director: Dr. Leonard L. Baird, Professor of
Educational Policy Studies

Lexington, Kentucky

1987

RULE 11.1. TITLE AND STATEMENT OF RESPONSIBILITY AREA
(MARC field 245)

11.1B-11.1F.

Titles proper, parallel titles and other title information, and statements of responsibility are transcribed as instructed in the general chapter. The GMD for the material covered in this chapter is "microform." LC decided to add the GMD for microform materials when *AACR2* was implemented, although it was not added in the past. (*CSB* 6: 4-5) *See* Figs. 6.6-6.8.

Fig. 6.6. Rule 11.1. Transcription of title and statement of responsibility area for the microfilm.

Women and/in health [microform] / filmed by the Women's History Research Center

Fig. 6.7. Transcription of title and statement of responsibility area for the microfiche according to *AACR2R*.

The impact of feminist thought on American librarianship, 1965-1985 [microform] / Christina Diane Baum

Fig. 6.8. Transcription of title and statement of responsibility area for the microfiche according to LC policy.

The impact of feminist thought on American librarianship, 1965-1985 [microform] / by Christina D. Baum

11.1G. Items without a collective title

Like other materials, a microform that lacks a collective title can be described either as a unit or by making a separate description for each separately titled part. It is common to find several different serial titles on the same roll of microfilm. These are given separate descriptions in most libraries.

RULE 11.2. EDITION AREA (MARC field 250)

A statement relating to an edition of a microform, rather than the edition of an original that is being reproduced, is called for in this rule. However, for reproduction of previously existing materials under current policy, LC would reverse this rule. *See* Fig. 6.9.

Fig. 6.9. Rule 11.2. Transcription of a statement relating to the edition of a microform, according to *AACR2R*.

Die Kataloge der Frankfurter und Leipziger Buchmessen 1759-1800 [microform] / hrsg. von Bernhard Fabian. — Microfiche-Ed.

RULE 11.3. SPECIAL DATA FOR CARTOGRAPHIC MATERIALS, MUSIC, AND SERIALS (MARC fields 255, 254, or 362)

Material specific details for cartographic materials, music, or serials are recorded as instructed in the chapters for those materials. When reproductions of previously existing works are cataloged, this area contains data relating to the original regardless of the policy being followed. Examples:

> Bulletin of the American Economic Association [microform]. – 4th ser., no. 1 (Mar. 1911)-no. 6 (Dec. 1911)

> Viewpoint [microform]. – Vol. 1 (1976)-

RULE 11.4. PUBLICATION, DISTRIBUTION, ETC., AREA (MARC field 260)

The details of this area are recorded as instructed in the general chapter. Again, if one is following *AACR2R* policy, it should be remembered that the details recorded here are those of the publication of the *microform*, not those of an original being reproduced. *See* Figs. 6.10-6.12.

Fig. 6.10. Rule 11.4. Addition of publication details to descriptions of microfilm and microfiche, according to *AACR2R*.

> Women and/in health [microform] / filmed by the Women's History Research Center. – Berkeley, Calif. : The Center, 1974.

Fig. 6.11.

> The impact of feminist thought on American librarianship, 1965-1985 [microform] / Christina Diane Baum. – Ann Arbor, Mich. : University Microfilms International, 1987.

If one is following LC policy, the details of the original are given here for a microform of a previously existing work. *See* Fig. 6.12.

Fig. 6.12. Rule 11.4. Addition of publication details, according to LC policy.

> The impact of feminist thought on American librarianship, 1965-1985 [microform] / by Christina D. Baum. – 1987.

RULE 11.5. PHYSICAL DESCRIPTION AREA (MARC field 300)

11.5B. Extent of item (including specific material designation) (MARC subfield a)

The number of physical units of a microform item is followed by one of this chapter's specific material designations:

aperture card
microfiche
microfilm
microopaque

LC has chosen not to follow the *AACR2R* option to drop the prefix *micro* when the GMD "microform" is used. The reason for LC's decision is that the resulting bibliographic description will be complete regardless of whether another library chooses to use the GMD.[3]

If the item is described in terms of "microfilm," one of the following terms is added: *cartridge, cassette,* or *reel.* If the item is described in terms of "microfiche," the term *cassette* may be added if appropriate. *See* Fig. 6.13.

If the item is described in terms of "microfiche," the number of frames is added in parentheses if the number can be determined easily. *See* Fig. 6.14.

11.5C. Other physical details (MARC subfield b)

A negative microform is indicated here, followed by a statement of illustrations using instructions in rule 2.5C in the books chapter. If illustrations are in color, the term *col. ill.* is used. If the microform itself is colored, terms used are *col. & ill.* Example:

> 15 microfiches : negative, ill.

11.5D. Dimensions (MARC subfield c)

The dimensions of a microfiche, a microopaque, and an aperture card mount are given as height x width in centimeters to the next whole centimeter up. *See* Fig. 6.14. The width of a microfilm is given in millimeters. *See* Fig. 6.13.

11.5E. Accompanying material (MARC subfield e)

Accompanying material is described as instructed in the general chapter. *See* Fig. 6.13.

> **Fig. 6.13. Rule 11.5. Addition of physical description to description of microfilm.**
>
> Women and/in health [microform] / filmed by the Women's History Research Center. — Berkeley, Calif. : The Center, 1974.
> 13 microfilm reels on 14 ; 35 mm. + 1 guide (88 p. in various pagings ; 28 cm.)

Note: The 14 physical reels are numbered consecutively except that number "3A" falls between "3" and "4." Therefore, the extent of item is given with the number of bibliographic entities preceding the number of physical ones.

> **Fig. 6.14. Rule 11.5. Addition of physical description to description of microfiche, according to *AACR2R*.**
>
> The impact of feminist thought on American librarianship, 1965-1985 [microform] / Christina Diane Baum. — Ann Arbor, Mich. : University Microfilms International, 1987.
> 3 microfiches (276 fr.) ; 11 x 15 cm.

If one is following LC policy, the physical description area for a reproduction of a previously existing work contains details relating to the original. *See* Fig. 6.15 (page 156).

Fig. 6.15. Rule 11.5. Addition of physical description to description of microfiche, according to LC policy.

> The impact of feminist thought on American librarianship, 1965-1985 [microform] / by Christina D. Baum. — 1987.
> x, 255 leaves ; 28 cm.

RULE 11.6.   SERIES AREA (MARC field 4xx)

11.6B.   Series statements

Series statements are recorded as instructed in rule 1.6. When cataloging reproductions a series statement for an original is recorded with other details of the original. If one is following *AACR2R*, this means placing the original series in a note. If one is following LC, the original series is transcribed in the series area. Examples:

> 116 microfilm reels ; 35 mm. — (British publishers' archives on microfilm)

> 7 microfiches ; 11 x 15 cm. — (Columbia University oral history collection ; pt. 2, no. 24)

RULE 11.7.   NOTE AREA (MARC field 5xx)

11.7B.   Notes

Following are some typical notes used for microforms. For further details consult *AACR2R*, pages 269-272.

11.7B1.   Nature, scope or artistic or other form of an item (MARC field 500)
Example:

> Extensive collection of feminist serial literature published 1956 through June, 1974.

11.7B4.   Variations in title (MARC field 500)
See Fig. 6.16 (page 158).

11.7B6.   Statements of responsibility (MARC field 500)
Example:

> Collected by the Women's History Research Center, 1968-1974 ; transferred to the Special Collections Dept., Northwestern University Library, 1974.

11.7B7.   Edition and history (MARC fields 500 and 503)
Example:

> Filmed from the H.G. Wells collection in the Bromley Public Libraries.

11.7B10.   Physical description (MARC field 500)

Reduction ratio. Reduction ratio is given if it is outside the 16X-30X range, using one of the following terms:

Low reduction   *For less than 16X*

High reduction   *For 31X-60X*

Very high reduction   *For 61X-90X*

Ultra high reduction   *For over 90X; for ultra high reduction give also the specific ratio, e.g.,* Ultra high reduction, 150X

Reduction ratio varies
See Fig. 6.16 (page 158).

Reader. If a particular brand of reader is needed for reading a cassette or cartridge, it should be noted.

11.7B11.   Accompanying material (MARC field 500)
Example:

> With companion print index: American public opinion index.

See also Fig. 6.16.

11.7B12.   Series (MARC field 500)
A note is made here only for a microform series of which the item has been part. The rule for a note for any series relating to the original of which the microform is a reproduction is rule 11.7B22. Example:

> Originally issued in series: Archives on microfilm.

11.7B13.   Dissertations (MARC field 502)
See Fig. 6.17 (page 158).

11.7B16.   Other formats (MARC field 500)
Example:

> Library also has volumes in printed form and on microfilm.

11.7B17.   Summary (MARC field 520)
Example:

> Summary: Pamphlets relating to conditions in South Carolina, 1866-1892.

11.7B18.   Contents (MARC fields 504 and 505)
See Figs. 6.16 and 6.17.

11.7B22. Notes relating to original (MARC field 534)
Example:

> Reproduction of original: New York : Teachers College, Columbia University, 1927. xix, 166 p. : ill. ; 24 cm.
> Bibliography: p. 157.

See also Fig. 6.17.

Fig. 6.16. Description of the microfilm.

> Women and/in health [microform] / filmed by the Women's History Research Center. — Berkeley, Calif. : The Center, 1974.
> 13 microfilm reels on 14 ; 35 mm. + 1 guide (88 p. in various pagings ; 28 cm.)

> Collection of microfilmed clippings from newspapers, professional journals, alternative newspapers, academic research papers, theses, and conference speeches. Includes leaflets, poetry and graphic material.
> Title on reel containers: Women and health/mental health.
> Low reduction.
> Guide issued under title: Guide to the microfilm edition of the Women and health collection.
> Contents: Section 1. Physical and mental health of women — Section 2. Physical and mental illnesses of women — Section 3. Biology, women and the life cycle — Section 4. Birth control/ population control — Section 5. Sex and sexuality — Section 6. Black and Third World women–health — Section 7. Special issues of mass periodicals.

Fig. 6.17. Description of the microfiche, according to *AACR2R*.

> The impact of feminist thought on American librarianship, 1965-1985 [microform] / Christina Diane Baum. — Ann Arbor, Mich. : University Microfilms International, 1987.
> 3 microfiches (276 fr.) ; 11 x 15 cm.

> Thesis (Ed.D.)–University of Kentucky, 1987.
> Includes bibliographical references.
> "87-15914."
> Reproduction of original: x, 255 leaves ; 28 cm.
> Typescript. Includes bibliographical references (leaves 245-254).

If one is following LC policy, the description shown in Fig. 6.17 would appear as in Fig. 6.18.

Fig. 6.18. Description of the microfiche, according to LC policy.

The impact of feminist thought on American librarianship, 1965-1985 [microform] / by Christina D. Baum. — 1987.
x, 255 leaves ; 28 cm.

Typescript.
Thesis (Ed.D.) — University of Kentucky, 1987.
Includes bibliographical references (leaves 245-254).
Microfiche. Ann Arbor, Mich. : University Microfilms International, 1987. 3 microfiches (276 fr.) ; 11 x 15 cm.
"87-15914."

The MARC records for the items shown in Figs. 6.16-6.18 are shown in Figs. 6.19-6.21.

Fig. 6.19. MARC record for the microfilm.

Entered:	19860523	Replaced:	19871112	Used:	19900803
Type: a	Bib lvl: m		Source: d	Lang:	eng
Repr: a	Enc lvl: I		Conf pub: 0	Ctry:	cau
Indx: 0	Mod rec:		Govt pub:	Cont:	
Desc: a	Int lvl:		Festschr: 0	Illus:	
	F/B:	0	Dat tp: s	Dates:	1974,

```
 1 040      NYP $c NYP
 2 007      h $b d $d a $e f $f a015 $g b $h u $i c $j u
 3 090      HQ1426 $b .W68 1974
 4 049      YCLM
 5 245 10   Women and/in health $h microform / $c filmed by the Women's
History Research Center.
 6 260      Berkeley, Calif. : $b The Center, $c 1974.
 7 300      13 microfilm reels on 14 ; $c 35 mm. + $e 1 guide (88 p.
in various pagings ; 28 cm.)
 8 500      Collection of microfilmed clippings from newspapers,
professional journals, alternative newspapers, academic research papers,
theses, and conference speeches. Includes leaflets, poetry and graphic
material.
 9 500      Title on reel containers: Women and health/mental health.
10 500      Low reduction.
11 500      Guide issued under title: Guide to the microfilm edition of the
Women and health collection.
12 505 0    Section 1. Physical and mental health of women -- Section 2.
Physical and mental illnesses of women -- Section 3. Biology, women and the
life cycle -- Section 4. Birth control/population control -- Section 5.
Sex and sexuality -- Section 6. Black and Third World women--health --
Section 7. Special issues of mass periodicals.
13 650 0    Women $z United States
14 650 0    Women $x Health and hygiene.
15 650 0    Birth control.
16 650 0    Minority women.
17 650 0    Women $x Psychology.
18 650 0    Women $x Sexual behavior.
19 110 20   Women's History Research Center.
20 740 01   Women and health/mental health.
```

Fig. 6.20. MARC record for the microfiche, according to *AACR2R*.

```
Entered:     19891222      Replaced:     19891222      Used:      19910527
Type: a          Bib lvl: m        Source:      d       Lang:   eng
Repr: b          Enc lvl: I        Conf pub: 0          Ctry:   miu
Indx: 0          Mod rec:          Govt pub:            Cont:   b
Desc: a          Int lvl:          Festschr: 0          Illus:
                 F/B:      0       Dat tp:   r          Dates: 1987,1987
     1 040       NGU $c NGU
     2 007       h $b e $d a $e m $f b--- $g b $h u $i c $j u
     3 037       87-15914
     4 090       Z665 $b .B38 1987
     5 049       YCLM
     6 100 1     Baum, Christina D.
     7 245 14    The impact of feminist thought on American librarianship,
1965-1985 $h microform / $c Christina Diane Baum.
     8 260       Ann Arbor, Mich. : $b University Microfilms International,
$c 1987.
     9 300       3 microfiches (276 fr.) ; $c 11 x 15 cm.
    10 502       Thesis (Ed.D.)--University of Kentucky, 1987.
    11 504       Includes bibliographical references.
    12 500       "87-15914."
    13 534       Reproduction of original: $e x, 255 leaves ; 28 cm. $n
Typescript. $n Includes bibliographical references (leaves 245-254).
    14 650  0    Feminism $z United States.
    15 650  0    Library science $z United States.
```

Fig. 6.21. MARC record for the microfiche, according to LC policy.

```
Entered:     19891222      Replaced:     19891222      Used:      19910527
Type: a          Bib lvl: m        Source:      d       Lang:   eng
Repr: b          Enc lvl: I        Conf pub: 0          Ctry:   xx
Indx: 0          Mod rec:          Govt pub:            Cont:   b
Desc: a          Int lvl:          Festschr: 0          Illus:
                 F/B:      0       Dat tp:   s          Dates: 1987,
     1 040       NGU $c NGU
     2 007       h $b e $d a $e m $f b--- $g b $h u $i c $j u
     3 037       87-15914
     4 090       Z655 $b .B38 1987
     5 049       YCLM
     6 100 1     Baum, Christina D.
     7 245 14    The impact of feminist thought on American librarianship,
1965-1985 $h microform / $c by Christina D. Baum.
     8 260       $c 1987.
     9 300       x, 255 leaves ; $c 28 cm.
    10 500       Typescript.
    11 502       Thesis (Ed.D.)--University of Kentucky, 1987.
    12 504       Includes bibliographical references (leaves 245-254).
    13 533       Microfiche. $b Ann Arbor, Mich. : $c University Microfilms
International, $d 1987. $e 3 microfiches (276 fr.) ; 11 x 15 cm.  "87-
15914."
    14 650  0    Feminism $z United States.
    15 650  0    Library science $z United States.
```

RULE 11.8.   STANDARD NUMBER AND TERMS OF AVAILABILITY
AREA (MARC fields 020 and 022)

This area is treated as described under rule 1.8 in the general chapter. It should be remembered that only a standard number assigned to the *microform* is placed here. A standard number of the original should be included in the note on details of the original.

NOTES

[1] Janet Swan Hill, "Descriptions of Reproductions of Previously Existing Works: Another View," *Microform Review* 11 (Winter 1982): 14-21; and Nancy R. John, "Microforms," *Journal of Library Administration* 3 (Spring 1982): 3-8.

[2] *Cataloging Service Bulletin*, no. 14 (Fall 1981): 56-58; a slightly revised version is in *Cataloging Service Bulletin*, no. 45 (Summer 1989): 18-19.

[3] "AACR 2 Options Proposed by the Library of Congress: Chapters 2-11," *Library of Congress Information Bulletin* 38 (August 10, 1979): 316.

SUGGESTED READING

Frost, Carolyn O. *Media Access and Organization: A Cataloging and Reference Sources Guide for Nonbook Materials.* Englewood, Colo., Libraries Unlimited, 1989. Chapter 8.

Hill, Janet Swan. "Descriptions of Reproductions of Previously Existing Works: Another View," *Microform Review* 11 (Winter 1982): 14-21.

John, Nancy R. "Microforms," *Journal of Library Administration* 3 (Spring 1982): 3-8.

Maxwell, Margaret F. *Handbook for AACR2, 1988 Revision.* Chicago, American Library Association, 1989. Chapter 10.

Rogers, JoAnn V. *Nonprint Cataloging for Multimedia Collections: A Guide Based on AACR2.* 2nd ed. with Jerry D. Saye. Littleton, Colo., Libraries Unlimited, 1987. Chapter 9.

Saye, Jerry D., and Sherry L. Vellucci. *Notes in the Catalog Record Based on AACR2 and LC Rule Interpretations.* Chicago, American Library Association, 1989.

Description of Serials

7

INTRODUCTION

A serial is a publication in any medium issued in successive parts at regular or irregular intervals and intended to continue indefinitely. Serials include both periodicals and non-periodicals. A periodical may be defined as a serial that has a distinctive title and that is issued more frequently than once a year and at regular intervals, with each issue containing articles by several contributors. Non-periodicals are all other forms of serials, such as yearbooks, annuals, memoirs, transactions and proceedings of societies, and any series cataloged together instead of separately.

A clear distinction should be made between serials and monographs. A monograph represents a complete bibliographic unit; it may be issued in successive parts at regular or irregular intervals, but it is *not* intended to continue indefinitely. In most cases, of course, a monographic publication is completed in one volume. However, there are certain types of monographs that are often treated as serials by libraries because they are not complete in one volume. These include continuations of sets, provisional serials, and pseudo-serials. A continuation of a set is a nonserial—i.e., monographic—set in process of publication. The *Oxford History of English Literature* and the *Dictionary of Literary Biography* are examples of continuations of sets. Neither publication is presently complete although many individual volumes have been issued. Such publications require a special order record—i.e., a standing order—for follow-up purposes; if such works are cataloged as sets, this creates problems for maintaining accurate records in the library's holdings record for the set. Provisional sets are those publications that are treated as serials while in the process of publication and as nonserials when complete. The justification for such treatment is often a particularly lengthy period of publication and/or a complicated numbering of individual issues. Either of the two previous examples of continuations of sets could be treated by individual libraries as provisional serials. A pseudo-serial is a frequently reissued and revised publication that is generally treated as a monographic work at first publication but that is often treated as a serial after numerous successive editions have appeared. Serial numbering may be taken from the edition number or from the date of publication. Examples of pseudo-serials are Sir John Bernard Burke's *Genealogical and Heraldic History of the Peerage* (commonly called Burke's *Peerage*) or the *Guide to Reference Books* edited successively by Alice Bertha Kroeger, Isadore Mudge, Constance Winchell, and Eugene P. Sheehy. Monographic treatment of a pseudo-serial requires individual descriptive cataloging for each new edition as well as additional added entries for previous editors or compilers. If a pseudo-serial is treated as a serial, the main entry is made under the title instead of the author and will require only one set of catalog entries.

The principles for cataloging serials are generally the same as those for cataloging monographic publications. On the other hand, certain physical characteristics of serial publications (e.g., numerous changes in bibliographic descriptions, including changes of titles) necessitate some special rules. The aim of these special rules is to prepare an entry that will stand the longest time and will allow necessary changes to be made with a minimum of modification. If the serial is still being published or if the library has only part of the set and hopes to complete it, an open entry is prepared according to the rules that are presented in this chapter.

The descriptive cataloging of serials is generally more complex than that of monographs because of their greatly varied and possibly intricate bibliographic structure. On the other hand, classification and subject headings are likely to be somewhat more general, and therefore simpler. Indeed, in many libraries, periodicals are not classified at all but are shelved alphabetically by main entry. The detail with which serials are described may vary widely from library to library. Some consider a highly analytic description essential, while others reduce serials cataloging to the title and statement of responsibility area and a holdings note, a method most suitable for computer-produced catalogs.

The serials cataloger is likely to be faced with the problem of describing a full set completely although all that may be at hand are a few volumes or current issues. The most important sources of additional information are the *Union List of Serials, New Serial Titles, British Union Catalogue of Periodicals, Standard Periodical Directory, Ulrich's International Periodical Directory* (which now incorporates the formerly separate *Irregular Serials and Annuals: An International Directory*), and *Ulrich's Update.*[1] Other important sources are the Library of Congress catalogs and national and trade bibliographies, as well as publishers' catalogs. *Titles in Series* is useful for its lists of titles in monographic series, especially those published by university presses, and Bowker's *Books in Series in the United States 1966-1975* lists monographs distributed in popular, scholarly, and professional series.[2] In addition, a Library of Congress publication, *Monographic Series*, lists all monographs cataloged by the Library of Congress that appeared as parts of series between 1974 and 1983, as well as all revised records, regardless of the date of publication.[3] Series access has been incorporated in the *National Union Catalog* since 1982. OCLC and other databases would prove sources of additional information, as would published state union lists of serials.

SELECTED RULES AND EXAMPLES

RULE 12.0. GENERAL RULES

12.0A. Scope

The scope of chapter 12 in *AACR2R* is serial publications of all kinds regardless of form. That is, nonbook materials as well as printed text can appear serially. A rule interpretation from LC gives guidelines for distinguishing between monographic and serial publications. (*CSB* 44: 25-28)

12.0B. Sources of information

12.0B1. Printed serials

Chief source of information. The title page (or title page substitute) of the first issue of a serial is used as its chief source of information. If the first issue is not available, the first issue that is available is used. This is a break from pre-*AACR2* practice that called for using the latest issue. While there is some objection to using the first issue because of all the changes that can occur in such areas as the publication area, the pre-*AACR2* practice could not, in fact, be followed because of the physical impossibility of examining every new issue.

If a printed serial lacks a title page, the following substitutes are to be used in this order: analytical title page, cover, caption, masthead, editorial pages, colophon, other pages. LC gives a rule interpretation that makes the following exception: if an item has two or more different titles and the title on the preferred source is known to be less stable than another title, then the source with the stable title is to be used as the title page substitute. (*CSB* 44: 28)

Prescribed sources of information. As it does for other materials, *AACR2R* prescribes sources of information for the various areas of description for printed serials. Information taken from outside these sources is enclosed in square brackets.

AREA	PRESCRIBED SOURCE OF INFORMATION
Title and statement of responsibility	Chief source of information
Edition	Chief source of information, other preliminaries, colophon
Numeric and/or alphabetic, chronological, or other designation	[same as edition area]*
Publication, distribution, etc.	[same as edition area]*
Physical description	The whole publication
Series	The whole publication
Note	Any source
Standard number and terms of availability	Any source

12.0B2. Nonprint serials

The prescribed sources of information for nonprint serials are those called for in the chapter for a particular type of material. The sources for a serial computer file, for example, are named in chapter 9 of *AACR2R* (chapter 5 of this text). In these cases, too, the source in the first issue of the nonprint serial should be used.

The example to be used in this chapter to illustrate the building of the description of a serial is a newsletter whose title has changed. The chief source of information and preliminaries are given for each of the two titles as Figs. 7.1-7.3.

---

*A rule interpretation from LC changes the prescribed source of information for this area to the whole publication. (*CSB* 47: 41)

Fig. 7.1. Masthead of first issue of serial.

 newsletter

RESOURCES AND TECHNICAL SERVICES DIVISION

American Library Association

Volume 1   January 1976
Number 1   ISSN 0360-5906

Fig. 7.2. Masthead of first issue with changed title.

n e w s l e t t e r

Volume 1, Number 1   ISSN 1047-949X
1990   Richard D. Johnson, Interim Editor

Fig. 7.3. Editor's note about title change from
Volume 14, Number 5.

In the recent ALA elections, RTSD members approved the proposal to change the division's name to the Association for Library Collections & Technical Services (ALCTS). The name change was approved by 68 percent of those voting and became effective at the end of the 1989 ALA Annual Conference in Dallas.

The new acronym, ALCTS, is pronounced to rhyme with "collects" or "protects," according to ALCTS President Nancy R. John.

All division materials, such as the membership brochure and stationery, will be revised in the next few months. The name of this newsletter will also be changed. *RTSD Newsletter* will be used through the end of volume 14.

RULE 12.1. TITLE AND STATEMENT OF RESPONSIBILITY AREA
(MARC field 245)

12.1B. Title proper (MARC subfield a)

12.1B1. The title proper is given as instructed in the general chapter. *See* Figs. 7.4 and 7.5.

> **Fig. 7.4. Rule 12.1B1. Transcription of title proper of the original title of the serial.**
>
> RTSD newsletter

> **Fig. 7.5. Rule 12.1B1. Transcription of title proper of the later title of the serial.**
>
> ALCTS newsletter

12.1B2. If a serial title in the chief source of information includes both an acronym or initialism and the words represented by the initials, the full form is recorded as the title proper unless the initials are used alone in other places in the serial. Examples:

Transnational data report
[Chief source and other sources read: TDR Transnational Data Report]

RSR
[Chief source reads: RSR Reference Services Review. Elsewhere the title is given as: RSR]

12.1B3. A corporate body's name is considered to be part of the title proper only when it consistently appears as part of the title in various locations in the serial. LC applies this criterion to any word, phrase, etc., that may or may not be part of the title proper. (*CSB* 44: 29)

12.1B4-12.1B6. These rules cover transcription of titles that are sections of, or supplements to, other serials. In general if the title common to all sections appears with the section or supplement title, both are transcribed as title proper. A lengthy LC rule interpretation should be consulted when using rule 12.1B4. (*CSB* 44: 29-31) Examples:

Solar energy. Cumulative index

Major studies of the Congressional Research Service.
  Supplement

If the common title is not present with the section or supplement title, the section or supplement title is treated as title proper. Example:

Bibliography of Utah geology
  [Note reads:]
  Supplement to: Utah geology.

12.1B7. When the title proper of a serial includes a date or numbering that changes from issue to issue, the date or numbering is omitted. It is replaced by the mark of omission unless it is at the beginning. LC uses the mark of omission at the end of the title proper only if there is a grammatical reason to do so. (*CSB* 44: 31) Examples:

Sport in ...

Proceedings of the ... annual meeting

12.1B8. A change in title proper of a serial (as defined by rule 21.2) means that a new description must be made for the new title.

12.1C. *Optional addition.* **General material designation** (MARC subfield h)
The GMDs appropriate to serials are governed by the type of material being cataloged. As discussed in the general chapter under rule 1.1C, LC will display only some GMDs in its printed records. The reader should consult the discussion in this text of the GMD rule for the medium in which a serial is produced. For example, the discussion of rule 2.1C indicates that "[text]" is not used for printed serials, and the application of rule 9.1C indicates that "[computer file]" should be used for cataloging serial computer files.

12.1D-12.1E. (MARC subfield b)
Parallel titles and other title information are transcribed as instructed in the general chapter. In cases where both an acronym or initialism and the words represented by the initials appear in the chief source of information, the form that was not chosen as the title proper according to rule 12.1B2 is given as other title information. Examples:

Canadian journal of psychiatry = Revue canadienne de
psychiatrie

DNR : daily news record

Transnational Data Report : TDR

Pesticide residues in food : report

Index to Title 40 of the Code of federal regulations : protection
of environment

LC has decided to catalog serials using an augmented first-level description, rather than the second-level description used for other materials. The first-level description is augmented with: GMD (when appropriate); parallel title(s); first statement of responsibility; first place of publication, etc., with first publisher, etc.; other physical details and dimensions; series. Therefore, other title information is usually omitted. However, a rule interpretation gives three instances in which other title information for serials must be given: when the title consists of both an initialism and a full form of the name, when a statement of responsibility is inseparable from the other title information, and when it is needed to explain the title proper as called for in rule 1.1E6. LC catalogers also are permitted to give other title information in other instances where it is judged to be useful. (*CSB* 44: 31)

12.1F. Statements of responsibility (MARC subfield c)

Statements of responsibility are transcribed as instructed in the general chapter. Example:

> Quarterly journal of current acquisitions / The Library of
> Congress

When a title includes a full or abbreviated statement of responsibility as part of the title proper no separate statement is given. *See* Fig. 7.6.

> **Fig. 7.6. Rule 12.1F. Title includes abbreviated form of responsible body; therefore, no "statement of responsibility" preceded by a slash is given.**
>
> ALCTS Newsletter. —

Personal editors are not recorded in statements of responsibility. If considered important they may be given in a note.

RULE 12.2. EDITION AREA (MARC field 250)

12.2B. Edition statement

AACR2R prescribes specific types of edition statements that are to be recorded in the edition area for serials:

a) local edition statements

b) special interest edition statements

c) special format or physical presentation statements

d) language edition statements

e) reprint or reissue statements indicating a reissue or revision of a serial as a whole

Examples:

> Taft Foundation reporter. — Regional ed.
>
> Taft Foundation reporter. — National ed.
>
> Sea. — Eastern ed.

See also examples in *AACR2R*. Edition statements are relatively rare in the cataloging of serials.

RULE 12.3. NUMERIC AND/OR ALPHABETIC, CHRONOLOGICAL, OR OTHER DESIGNATION AREA (MARC field 362)

12.3B. Numeric and/or alphabetic designation (MARC subfield a)

The numeric and/or alphabetic designation of a serial is given as it appears in the first issue of the serial, using standard abbreviations and numerals. The numeric and/or alphabetic designation of the original is used when a facsimile or reprint is in hand. When a serial changes title but continues its previous numbering, the numbering of the first issue with the new title is used. LC comments that numbering recorded in this area should be unique to the issue. If such a designation is exactly the same for more than one issue, it should be given in a note. (*CSB* 23: 19)

Rules 12.3B1-12.3B3 provide for transcription of a numeric and/or alphabetic designation. Rules 12.3C1-12.3C3 treat the transcription of a chronological designation when there is no numeric or alphabetic designation. Rule 12.3C4 covers transcription of both numeric and/or alphabetic designation *and* chronological designation. It would have been clearer if this rule had been accorded a boldface rule heading. There are relatively few instances in which there is a numeric and/or alphabetic designation without also having a chronological designation; however, it is relatively common for serials of the "advances in" and "progress in" type to be dated only with an imprint date (*see* Fig. 7.7). Such a date is recorded as part of the publication area rather than part of the numeric, alphabetic, chronological area (*see* Fig. 7.8). For other examples of numeric designations see the examples under rule 12.3C4.

Fig. 7.7. Title page of serial showing date in imprint only.

ADVANCES IN
CHEMICAL PHYSICS

Edited by I. PRIGOGINE
University of Brussels, Brussels, Belgium

With a Preface by P. DEBYE
Cornell University, Ithaca, New York

VOLUME 1

INTERSCIENCE PUBLISHERS, INC., NEW YORK
INTERSCIENCE PUBLISHERS LTD., LONDON   1958

Fig. 7.8. Rule 12.3B1. Transcription of numeric designation of the first issue of a serial.

Advances in chemical physics. — Vol. 1-   — New York : Interscience Publishers, 1958-

12.3C. Chronological designation (MARC subfield a)

12.3C1. A chronological designation that identifies the first issue of a serial is recorded as it appears, using standard abbreviations and numerals. Examples:

> Index to Title 40 of the Code of federal regulations : protection of environment. — 1978-

> HRA, HSA, CDC, OASH, & ADAMHA public advisory committees : authority, structure, functions, members. — Mar. 1978-

12.3C4. When the first issue of a serial has both numbering and a chronological designation, both are given, with the numbering given first. Examples:

> Developmental medicine and child neurology. — Vol. 4 (1962)-

> Gas turbine electric plant construction cost and annual production expenses. Annual supplement / Office of Energy Data and Interpretation, Energy Information Administration, U.S. Dept. of Energy. — 2nd (1974)-

See also Figs. 7.9 and 7.10.

Fig. 7.9. Rule 12.3C4. Addition of both numbering and chronological designation to the description of the original title.

> RTSD newsletter. — Vol. 1, no. 1 (Jan. 1976)-

Fig. 7.10. Rule 12.3C4. Addition of both numbering and chronological designation to the designation of the later title.

> ALCTS newsletter. — Vol. 1, no. 1 (1990)-

A difficulty with this rule is that it does not refer to the potential confusion caused by a situation in which the numbering sequence is repeated every year so that there is no overall numbering, but only the dates to distinguish issues (e.g., issues published in 1978 are numbered 1 through 4, issues for 1979 are also numbered 1 through 4, etc.). If the numbering is given first, as is called for in the rules, the implication is that the numbering is continuous and a completed serial could appear to have published only a few numbers over a span of many years [e.g., No. 1 (Winter 1940)-no. 4 (Fall 1979)].

An LC rule interpretation says that in such a case the date should be followed by the number as if both were a single numeric designation. Example:

> — 1940, no. 1-1979, no. 4

In such a case a chronological designation would be recorded only when a separate one also appears on the issue. (*CSB* 23: 20)

12.3D. No designation on first issue

When a serial lacks any designation, the cataloger is instructed to record "[No. 1]-" or its equivalent in the language of the title proper, and then if later issues appear with numbering, one is to change to the later form. If an item lacks a numerical designation, but has a date, rule 12.3C1 should be applied.

12.3F. Completed serials

When the serial is completed (e.g., ceases publication, or its title changes) the designation of the last issue is given following the designation of the first. *See* Fig. 7.11.

> **Fig. 7.11. Rule 12.3F. Addition of designation of last issue to the description of the original title.**
>
> RTSD newsletter. — Vol. 1, no. 1 (Jan. 1976)-v. 14, no. 6 (1989)

RULE 12.4. PUBLICATION, DISTRIBUTION, ETC., AREA (MARC field 260)

Details of the publication, distribution, etc., area are transcribed as instructed in the general chapter. If one is following LC policy, this means transcribing only the first place and the first publisher, distributor, etc.

The date of publication is recorded as instructed in rule 1.4F even if it coincides with the date given as the chronological designation in the preceding area. The date of first issue is followed by a hyphen and, if the serial is completed, the date of publication of the last issue. *See* Figs. 7.12 and 7.13.

> **Fig. 7.12. Rule 12.4. Addition of publication, distribution, etc., information to the description of the original title.**
>
> RTSD newsletter. — Vol. 1, no. 1 (Jan. 1976)-v. 14, no. 6 (1989). — Chicago, Ill. : Resources and Technical Services Division, American Library Association, 1976-1989.

> **Fig. 7.13. Rule 12.4. Addition of publication, distribution, etc., information to the description of the later title.**
>
> ALCTS newsletter. — Vol. 1, no. 1 (1990)-   . — Chicago, Ill. : Association for Library Collections & Technical Services, American Library Association, 1990-

RULE 12.5. PHYSICAL DESCRIPTION AREA (MARC field 300)

12.5B. Extent of item (including specific material designation) (MARC subfield a)

12.5B1. A printed serial still in progress is described as *v., no.,* or *pt.* preceded by three spaces. For a serial still in progress that is of a type of material other than print, the specific material designation relevant to that type of material, preceded by three spaces, should be used. *See* Fig. 7.15 (page 172).

12.5B2. When the serial is completed, the specific material designation is preceded by the number of parts in arabic numerals. An LC rule interpretation says that "parts" is to be interpreted as bibliographic units rather than physical units. (*CSB* 42: 33-34) Example:

> The Christian's magazine [microform]. — Vol. 1 (1806)-v. 4
> (1811). — Ann Arbor, Mich. : University Microfilms, 1946-
> 1949.
> 4 v. on 2 microfilm reels ; 35 mm.

See also Fig. 7.14.

12.5C. Other physical details (MARC subfield b)

Other physical details are recorded according to the rule numbered "5C" in the appropriate chapter for the type of material being treated.

The term most often used here for printed serials is *ill.* The first issue may not be totally representative of details that may be found later, but one cannot expect to keep returning to the record with more details. It is better to be more general with this area of a serial. *See* Figs. 7.14 and 7.15.

12.5D. Dimensions (MARC subfield c)

Dimensions are recorded according to the rule numbered "5D" in the appropriate chapter for the type of material being treated. *See* Figs. 7.14 and 7.15.

Fig. 7.14. Rule 12.5. Addition of physical description to the description of the original title.

> RTSD newsletter. — Vol. 1, no. 1 (Jan. 1976)-v. 14, no. 6
> (1989). — Chicago, Ill. : Resources and Technical Services
> Division, American Library Association, 1976-1989.
> 14 v. : ill. ; 28 cm.

Fig. 7.15. Rule 12.5. Addition of physical description to the description of the new title.

> ALCTS newsletter. — Vol. 1, no. 1 (1990)-   . — Chicago,
> Ill. : Association for Library Collections & Technical Services,
> American Library Association, 1990-
> v. : ill. ; 28 cm.

12.5E. Accompanying material (MARC subfield e)

Accompanying material is described only if it is intended to be issued regularly and used with the serial. Its frequency is given in a note. If issued only once or irregularly, such material could be described in a note, ignored, or cataloged separately if it is important enough.

RULE 12.6. SERIES AREA (MARC field 4xx)

12.6B. Series statements (MARC subfield a)

Series statements are transcribed as instructed in the general chapter with the exception that series numberings are not given when each issue has a separate series number. Example:

> Wage chronology : Ford Motor Company / U.S. Bureau of
> Labor Statistics....
> > v. ; 28 cm. — (Bulletin / Bureau of Labor Statistics)

RULE 12.7. NOTE AREA (MARC fields 310, 5xx, and 7xx)

12.7B. Notes

Notes are made as instructed in subrules 12.7B1 to 12.7B23. Many notes (called "linking notes" by LC) refer to another serial. *AACR2R* gives instructions for citing another serial in a note. It suggests using the title or heading-title that is the catalog entry for the serial. If the serial is not in the catalog, or if main entry is not used, the title proper and statement of responsibility are to be cited. An LC rule interpretation changes these instructions to include uniform title of the series when this is appropriate, or to include the edition statement, if needed for identification. Statements of responsibility are not used in LC's linking notes. (*CSB* 46: 23-24)

Following are some typical notes used for serials. For further details consult *AACR2R*, pages 291-296.

12.7B1. Frequency (MARC field 310)

AACR2R prescribes making a frequency note unless frequency is apparent from the title and statement of responsibility area or is unknown. However, an LC rule interpretation calls for a note on the known frequency even if it is apparent from the rest of the item. (*CSB* 21: 16) Examples:

> Eight issues yearly.

> Bimonthly.

> Semiannual.

12.7B2. Language (MARC field 546)

Examples:

> Text and summaries in English or French.

> Text in Afrikaans and English.

> Summaries in English, 1987-Mar./Apr. 1988; summaries in English and Spanish, May/June 1988-

12.7B3. Source of title proper (MARC field 500)

When the source of title proper is not the chief source of information or, in a printed serial, is the title page substitute, a note is to be made. Example:

> Caption title.

12.7B4.   Variations in title (MARC field 500)
Examples:

> Running title: Chemical engineering catalog census.
> [Title proper is: CEC census of buyers in the chemical process industries.]

> Each issue has a distinctive title.

12.7B5.   Parallel titles and other title information (MARC field 500)
Example:

> "An international journal of palaeobotany, palynology and allied sciences."

12.7B6.   Statements of responsibility (MARC fields 500 and 570)
Examples:

> Official journal of: American Academy for Cerebral Palsy and Developmental Medicine.

> Issued by graduate students in the Dept. of French at the Pennsylvania State University.

> Editor: A. C. Strasburger.

12.7B7.   Relationships with other serials
Continuation. When a serial changes title and a new record is created, a note is made for the preceding title whether or not the numbering continues or is different (MARC field 780). Example:

> Continues: Cerebral palsy bulletin.

Continued by. The record for the serial before the title change should have a note added that names the succeeding title (MARC field 785). Optionally, the date of change may also be added. The Library of Congress does not apply the option. (*CSB* 42: 34) Example:

> Continued by: Industrial vegetation, turf and pest management.

Merger. When two or more serials are merged, the names of the previously separate serials are given on the record for the new serial (MARC fields 580 and 787). Example:

> Merger of: Mariah, and: Outside.

Each of the serials that were merged should have a note added to give the title of the new serial and the title(s) with which it has merged (MARC fields 580 and 787). Example:

> Merged with: Outside, to become: Mariah/Outside.

Split. A note is made on the record for a serial that is the result of a split of a serial into two or more parts. The note should name the serial that was split (MARC fields 580 and 787). Example:

> Continues in part: Transportation research.

An option allows also naming the other serial(s) resulting from the split. LC is not applying the option. (*CSB* 8: 12) The serial that was split should have a note added that gives the names of the resulting serials (MARC field 580). Example:

Split into: Transportation research. Part A, General, and: Transportation research. Part B, Methodological.

Absorption. The record for a serial that has absorbed another serial should have added to it a note giving the title of the serial that has been absorbed (MARC fields 580 and 787). An option allows giving also the date of the absorption. LC applies the option when the information is readily available. (*CSB* 44: 32) Example:

Absorbed: American Association of Stratigraphic Palynologists. Proceedings of the annual meeting.

The record for the serial that has been absorbed should have a note added that gives the title of the serial that absorbed it (MARC field 580). Example:

Absorbed by: Palynology.

Supplements (MARC fields 580 and 770). Examples:

Supplement to: Dictionary of literary biography.

Supplements, including laws, ordinances, bills, etc., accompany some numbers.

12.7B8. Numbering and chronological designation (MARC field 515)
Examples:

Report year ends Mar. 31.

Numbering begins each year with no. 1.

12.7B9. Publication, distribution, etc. (MARC field 500 or 550)
Example:

Published: London ; Hillside, N.J. : Published for the Experimental Psychology Society by L. Erlbaum Associates, 1984-

12.7B17. Indexes (MARC field 555)
Example:

Indexes: Vols. 4 (1982)-8 (1986) published separately.

12.7B19. Numbers [other than ISSNs] (MARC fields 023-030, 036, 037, and 500)
Example:

Catalogue 34-217.

12.7B20. **Copy being described, library's holdings, and restrictions on use** (MARC field 506 for restrictions on access pertaining to *all* copies; MARC field 590 for local copy information [in OCLC])
Example:

Library lacks: Nos. 8-10.

12.7B21. **"Issued with" notes** (MARC field 501)
Example:

Filmed with: BYU studies. Vol. 11, no. 1-v. 13.

12.7B23. **Item described** (MARC field 500)
This note is to be used when the description is not based on the first issue.
Example:

Description based on: Vol. 36, no. 1 (Winter 1989).

RULE 12.8. STANDARD NUMBER AND TERMS OF AVAILABILITY AREA (MARC fields 022 and 222)

The ISSN and key-title are recorded as instructed in rule 1.8. *See* Figs. 7.16 and 7.17.

RULE 12.9. SUPPLEMENTS (MARC field 525 or separate record)

Supplements are described as instructed in the general chapter.

RULE 12.10. SECTIONS OF SERIALS

Sections of a serial should be described as separate serials rather than using the "multilevel" structure described in the analysis chapter (chapter 8 of this text). Rules 12.1B4-12.1B6 give instructions for recording separate titles proper for sections of a serial.

Fig. 7.16. Rules 12.7 and 12.8. Addition of notes, standard number, and key-title to the description of the original title.

RTSD newsletter. — Vol. 1, no. 1 (Jan. 1976)-v. 14, no. 6 (1989). — Chicago, Ill. : Resources and Technical Services Division, American Library Association, 1976-1989.
14 v. : ill. ; 28 cm.

Quarterly; 8 no. a year, 1984-1986; 6 no. a year, 1980-1983.
Title from caption.
"Official organ of the Resources and Technical Services Division."
Continued by: ALCTS newsletter.
ISSN 0360-5906 = RTSD newsletter

Fig. 7.17. Rules 12.7 and 12.8. Addition of notes, standard number, and key-title to the description of the later title.

ALCTS newsletter. — Vol. 1, no. 1 (1990)-   . — Chicago, Ill. : Association for Library Collections & Technical Services, American Library Association, 1990-
    v. : ill. ; 28 cm.

Eight no. a year.
Title from caption.
Continues: RTSD newsletter.
ISSN 1047-949X = ALCTS newsletter

MARC records for the items whose descriptions are shown in Figs. 7.16 and 7.17 are shown in Figs. 7.18 and 7.19 (page 178).

Fig. 7.18. MARC record for the original title.

```
OCLC:     1978665         Rec stat:      c
Entered:   19760209        Replaced:    19910219      Used:      19910422
Type:      a     Bib lvl: s     Source:    d     Lang:     eng
Repr:            Enc lvl: I     Govt pub:        Ctry:     ilu
Phys med:        Mod rec:       Conf pub: 0     Cont:     ^^^^
S/L ent:   0     Ser tp:  p     Frequn:    q     Alphabt:  a
Desc:      a                    Regulr:    r     ISDS:     1
                               Pub st:    d     Dates:    1976-1989
 1 010     78-648097//r91 $z sc76-295
 2 040     NSD $c NSD $d COO $d NSD $d DLC $d OCL $d DLC $d NSD $d OCL $d DLC
    m.c. $d NST $d OCL $d AIP $d NSD $d NST $d OCL $d NST $d CRL $d NSD $d NYG
    HUL $d NST $d OCL $d ELM $d WAU $d NST
 3 022 0   0360-5906
 4 043     n-us---
 5 050 00  Z731 $b .A5288a
 6 082     020/.622/73
 7 090     Z673 $b .A5142
 8 049     YCLM
 9 210 0   RTSD newsl.
 0 212 0   Resources and Technical Services Division newsletter
 1 222  0  RTSD newsletter
 2 245 00  RTSD newsletter.
 3 260     Chicago, Ill. : $b Resources and Technical Services Division,
    erican Library Association, $c 1976-1989.
 4 265     50 E. Huron St., Chicago, IL 60611
 5 300     14 v. : $b ill. ; $c 28 cm.
 6 310     Quarterly.
 7 321     8 no. a year, $b 1984-1986
 8 321     Six no. a year, $b 1980-1983
 9 362 0   Vol. 1, no. 1 (Jan. 1976)-v. 14, no. 6 (1989).
 0 500     Title from caption.
 1 500     "Official organ of the Resources and Technical Services Division."
 2 510 1   Library literature $x 0024-2373
 3 610 20  American Library Association. $b Resources and Technical Services
 vision $x Periodicals. $w c
 4 650  0  Processing (Libraries) $x Periodicals.
 5 650  0  Library science literature $x Periodicals.
 6 710 20  American Library Association. $b Resources and Technical Services
 vision. $w cn
 7 785 00  $t ALCTS newsletter $x 1047-949X
```

Fig. 7.19. MARC record for the later title.

```
OCLC:      20820888          Rec stat:     c
Entered:   19891227          Replaced:     19910410      Used:      19910418
Type:      a      Bib lvl: s      Source:    d      Lang:      eng
Repr:             Enc lvl: I      Govt pub:         Ctry:      ilu
Phys med:         Mod rec:        Conf pub: 0      Cont:      ^^^^
S/L ent:  0       Ser tp:  p      Frequn:   b      Alphabt:   a
Desc:      a                      Regulr:   x      ISDS:      1
                                  Pub st:   c      Dates:     1990-9999
  1 010       91-649699 $z sn89-2258
  2 040       NSD $c NSD $d NYG $d CAS $d MYG $d COO $d HUL $d ELM $d WAU $d NS?
$d DLC $d NST $d IUL
  3 022 0     1047-949X
  4 030       ALNWEA
  5 082 10    020/.622/73
  6 090       Z673 $b .A5143
  7 049       YCLM
  8 210 0     ALCTS newsl.
  9 212 0     Association for Library Collections & Technical Services
newsletter
 10 222  0    ALCTS newsletter
 11 245 00    ALCTS newsletter.
 12 260       Chicago, IL : $b Association for Library Collections & Technical
Services, American Library Association, $c 1990-
 13 265       ALCTS, 50 E. Huron St., Chicago, IL 60611
 14 300       v. : $b ill. ; $c 28 cm.
 15 310       Eight no. a year
 16 362 0     Vol. 1, no. 1 (1990)-
 17 500       Title from caption.
 18 510 1     Library literature $x 0024-2373
 19 610 20    Association for Library Collections & Technical Services $x
Periodicals.
 20 650  0    Processing (Libraries) $x Periodicals.
 21 650  0    Library science literature $x Periodicals.
 22 710 20    Association for Library Collections & Technical Services.
 23 780 00    RTSD newsletter $x 0360-5906
```

NOTES

[1] *Union List of Serials in Libraries of the United States and Canada*, 3rd ed. (New York, H. W. Wilson, 1965); coverage through 1949. *New Serial Titles: A Union List of Serials Commencing Publication after December 31, 1949* (Washington, D.C., Library of Congress, 1953-). *Standard Periodical Directory* (New York, Oxbridge Communications, 1964/65-). *Ulrich's International Periodicals Directory* (New York, Bowker, 1965-). *Ulrich's Update* (New York, Bowker, 1988-). *British Union Catalogue of Periodicals* (London, Butterworths, 1955-58; 4v.). *British Union Catalogue of Periodicals. New Periodical Titles* (London, Butterworths, 1964- ; quarterly).

[2] *Titles in Series: A Handbook for Librarians and Students* (Metuchen, N.J., Scarecrow Press, 1953-). *Books in Series in the United States 1966-1975: Original, Reprinted, In-Print, and Out-of-Print Books Published or Distributed in the U.S. in Popular, Scholarly, and Professional Series* (New York, Bowker, 1977; suppl.).

[3] Library of Congress, *Library of Congress Catalogs: Monographic Series* (Washington, D.C., 1974-1982).

SUGGESTED READING

Cannan, Judith Proctor. *Serial Cataloguing: A Comparison of AACR 1 and 2.* New York, New York Metropolitan Reference & Research Library Agency, 1980.

Leong, Carol L. H. *Serials Cataloging Handbook: An Illustrative Guide to the Use of AACR2 and LC Rule Interpretations.* Chicago, American Library Association, 1989.

Maxwell, Margaret F. *Handbook for AACR2, 1988 Revision.* Chicago, American Library Association, 1989. Chapter 11.

Saye, Jerry D., and Sherry L. Vellucci. *Notes in the Catalog Record Based on AACR2 and LC Rule Interpretations.* Chicago, American Library Association, 1989.

Soper, Mary Ellen. "Description and Entry of Serials in *AACR2.*" *Serials Librarian,* 4 (Winter 1979): 167-176.

Thomas, Nancy G., and Rosanna O'Neil. *Notes for Serials Cataloging.* Littleton, Colo., Libraries Unlimited, 1986.

Tseng, Sally C. "Serials Cataloging and *AACR2*: An Introduction." *Journal of Educational Media Science,* 19 (Winter 1982): 177-216.

Analysis 8

INTRODUCTION

Whether or not to describe parts of a work is an ever-present problem in cataloging. When does a part of a larger work deserve description of its own? When such description is warranted, how is it accomplished in relation to the larger work? These are questions addressed by *AACR2R* chapter 13, "Analysis."

In the Glossary of *AACR2R*, "analytical entry" is defined as "an entry for a part of an item for which a comprehensive entry is also made."[1] "Analytical note" is defined as "the statement in an analytical entry relating the part being analyzed to the item of which it is a part."[2] Analytical entries vary from complete bibliographic descriptions to simple added entries for parts mentioned in the description of the larger work. Obviously, preparing additional entries requires time. Usually, the decision in this matter depends on the administrative policy of an individual library and the local needs. In deciding whether analytical entries are needed, certain general principles may be taken into consideration:

1) The availability of printed indexes, bibliographies, and abstracting services that will locate the material to be analyzed.

2) The availability of analytics from LC or other sources.

3) The quantity and quality of material on the given subject already in the catalog.

4) The quantity of material by the same authors already in the catalog. The best example in this category is provided by the library's policy regarding books in sets that usually represent various types of collections or compilations of one or more authors—e.g., Harvard Classics or Harvard Shelf of Fiction. If the library has little material by an author, the need for analytics may be greater.

5) The parts to be analyzed have a special significance for a given library (e.g., parts written by local noted authors, etc.).

6) The parts occupy the major portion of a given work.

In addition, the rules in *AACR2R* give some guidance in deciding when and how analysis should be accomplished.

However, a basic descriptive question that must be answered before making the decision to analyze a multi-part item, and one for which there is no guidance in *AACR2R*, is: What is to be considered a multi-part item rather than two or more separate bibliographical entities for cataloging purposes?

A publication issued in two or more volumes may be defined as a set. Usually, monographs in collected sets represent various types of collections or compilations by one or more authors. Many reference books are examples of monographs in collected sets. The number of physical volumes making up such a set may cause problems in cataloging and classification. If the works of a single author are collected in several volumes, the cataloger may be tempted to class each volume separately. On the other hand, the cataloger may only have one volume of a multi-volume set to catalog and may consider classing it as if the library had the entire set. Although both of these approaches are arguable, the fact remains that neither is really right or wrong. There are no established codes for cataloging and classifying monographs in sets. The principles presented below are provided merely for the consideration of the cataloger; they are not meant to be followed slavishly.

One usually catalogs and classes a set of monographs together if,

1) they are issued in a uniform format,

2) the individual volumes are numbered in consecutive order, and

3) there is a general index to the entire set.

Two additional criteria are,

1) if patrons are likely to expect to find the monographs together as a set, and

2) if there is a possibility that supplements and/or additional volumes will appear at a later date.

However, one usually catalogs and classes a set of monographs separately if,

1) not all the volumes of the set are in the library, nor are likely to be added to the library's collection, and

2) each volume has a separate title, especially in the case of literary works.

Obviously, these two sets of principles are somewhat contradictory and demand individual application in actual practice. The following examples are designed to clarify these problems. First, it should be quite obvious that a set of books comprising an encyclopedia should be cataloged and classed together. An encyclopedia is uniform in format; the individual volumes are consecutively numbered; there is usually a general index to the entire encyclopedia; patrons do expect to find these books together as a set; and supplements and/or yearbooks often appear at a later date. Second, it similarly follows that a set of monographs that is a collection of great works (such as the *Harvard Classics* or the *Great Books of the Western World*) should be both cataloged and classed together. In both of these examples, however, individual volumes have one or more separate titles. Should individual volumes in either of these two sets (both of which, for example, include the plays of William Shakespeare) be classed with other collections of Shakespeare's plays or not? Should the non-literary material in either of these two sets be classed separately in its appropriate location? Either choice will create some problems. It is unwise in either case to try to avoid a record in the catalog for each separate bibliographical unit. The catalog may be the only key the patron uses for discovering the library's holdings. Analysis is one method of solving this particular problem. The use of analytical entries in Figs. 8.5 through 8.8 (under rules 13.5A, 13.5B, and 13.6) (see pages 185-186) allows these sets of monographs to be cataloged and classed together while also providing separate entries for individual bibliographical units.

The collected or complete works of one author present another problem of monographs in sets. For example, Winston Churchill's *A History of the English-speaking Peoples* may be cataloged together or separately. If this work is cataloged together as a set, the individual parts or volumes are listed in a contents note, and the set receives general subject added entries and a general subject classification number. *See* Fig. 8.1. On the other hand, if each of the parts of this work is cataloged separately, the relationship of each part to the main work is shown by a series note. This latter approach allows for a complete publication area, including the date, for each part, and for separate specific subject added entries. *See* Fig. 8.2. Cataloging each part separately allows the cataloger to choose whether to classify each part separately or in the more general number. The classification problems of collected sets versus cataloging as monographs are dealt with in chapter 16 of this textbook.

Fig. 8.1. Churchill's *A History of the English-speaking Peoples* cataloged as a set using a contents note for the individual bibliographical units.

Churchill, Winston, Sir, 1874-1965.

Title of   ⟶ A history of the English-speaking peoples / Winston S.
entire set   Churchill. — Toronto : McClelland and Stewart, 1988,
     c1956.
       4 v. : ill., maps, geneal. tables ; 22 cm.

       Includes bibliographical references and index.
       Contents: v. 1. The birth of Britain — v. 2. The new
     world — v. 3. The age of revolution — v. 4. The great
     democracies.
       ISBN 0-8103-4573-0

General   ⟶ 1. Great Britain—History. I. Title.
subject added
entry

Fig. 8.2. One part of Churchill's work cataloged as a separate biblio-graphical unit using a series note to relate to the collected set.

¹Title of individual volume

²Title of set

³Specific sub-ject added entries

1 Churchill, Winston, Sir, 1874-1965.
    The age of revolution / Winston S. Churchill. — Toronto : McClelland and Stewart, 1988, c1956.   2
        xi, 395 p. : ill., maps ; 22 cm. — (A history of the English-speaking peoples / Winston S. Churchill ; v. 3)

        Includes bibliographical references and index.

3   1. Great Britain—History—1689-1714. 2. Great Britain—History—18th century. I. Title. II. Series: Churchill, Winston, Sir, 1874-1965. A history of the English-speaking peoples.

SELECTED RULES AND EXAMPLES

RULE 13.1.   SCOPE

The scope of the analysis chapter in *AACR2R* is to give instructions for describing an item that constitutes a part or parts of a larger item. Various methods are suggested for doing this. Some of the suggestions here are also referred to in other chapters, but the point of this chapter is to gather together all the methods and to give suggestions for choosing one over another.

RULE 13.2.   ANALYTICAL ADDED ENTRIES

When the title of a part appears either in the title and statement of responsi-bility area or in the note area of the bibliographic record for a more comprehen-sive work, an added entry may be made to provide direct access to the part without having to make a separate bibliographic record for the part. Such an added entry is composed of the main entry heading and title, if title is not main entry. The title used is the uniform title if there is one, otherwise it is the title proper. *See* Fig. 8.3 (page 184).

RULE 13.3.   ANALYSIS OF MONOGRAPHIC SERIES AND MULTIPART MONOGRAPHS

The suggested criterion for deciding to describe a part of a monographic series or a multipart monograph independently concerns title. If the title of the part is not dependent on the title of the whole, a complete description of the part should be created, giving the title (and statement of responsibility, if applicable) of the whole set in the series area. The volume number of the part is also given in the series area. *See* Fig. 8.4 (page 184).

Fig. 8.3. Rule 13.2. Record for a comprehensive work with analytical added entry made for the second part.

Beethoven, Ludwig van, 1770-1827. Symphonies, no. 2, op. 36, D major. 1989.

Mozart, Wolfgang Amadeus, 1756-1791.
    [Symphonies, K. 543, E^b major]
    Symphony no. 39 in E flat, K. 543 / Wolfgang Amadeus Mozart. Symphony no. 2 in D, op. 36 / Ludwig van Beethoven [sound recording]. — [Netherlands] : Philips, p1989.
    1 sound disc (64 min.) : digital, stereo. ; 4¾ in. — (Digital classics)

    Philips: 422 389-2.
    Orchestra of the 18th century (on period instruments) ; Frans Bruggen, conductor.
    Recorded June 1988, Concertgebouw, Amsterdam.
    Compact disc.
    Durations: 32:00 ; 32:00.

    1. Symphonies. I. Bruggen, Frans, 1932-   . II. Beethoven, Ludwig van, 1770-1827. Symphonies, no. 2, op. 36, D major. 1989. III. Orchestra of the 18th century.

Fig. 8.4. Rule 13.3. Complete independent description of a monographic title with the title of the comprehensive series given in the series area.

Austrian fiction writers after 1914 / edited by James Hardin and Donald G. Daviau. — Detroit, Mich. : Gale Research, c1989.
    xi, 394 p. : ill. ; 29 cm. — (Dictionary of literary biography ; v. 85)

    Includes bibliographical references.
    ISBN 0-8103-4563-3

Rule 13.3 does not go on to say what one should do if the title of an individual part is dependent on the comprehensive title or if there is no individual title. The implication is that such works would not be described separately. However, when such items appear as parts of series that are analyzed in full or that are classified separately, a separate record is necessary. An LC rule interpretation gives rules and examples for handling such situations; it should be consulted when needed. (*CSB* 44: 34-36) Its basic idea is that the comprehensive title becomes part of the title proper, no series statement is given, and an explicitly traced series added entry is made.

RULE 13.4. NOTE AREA

If it is decided to describe the comprehensive work as a set, individual parts may be named in a contents note. This method was shown in Fig. 8.1 (page 182).

RULE 13.5. "IN" ANALYTICS

Another possible way to describe a part is to provide an "In" analytic record. This is useful when one wishes to provide more information than can be given in the note area of the record for the set.

LC makes "In" analytics only in very special cases. (*CSB* 44: 36)

13.5A. An "In" analytic shows first a description of the part. This is followed by a short description of the comprehensive work.

The description of the part contains all the elements of the eight areas of description that apply to the part, with the exception that in the publication, distribution, etc., area, only those elements that differ from the whole item are given.

The description of the whole item begins with the word *In*, emphasized in some manner (e.g., underlining), followed by: the name and/or uniform title heading (if appropriate); title proper; statement(s) of responsibility that are necessary for identification; edition statement; and numeric or other designation (if a serial) or publication details (if a monographic item). *See* Figs. 8.5 and 8.6.

> **Fig. 8.5. Rule 13.5A. "In" analytic where the part is contained in a monographic item.**
>
> The crisis in cataloging / Andrew D. Osborn. — p. 90-103 ; 25 cm.
> In Foundations of cataloging / edited by Michael Carpenter and Elaine Svenonius. — Littleton, Colo. : Libraries Unlimited, 1985.

> **Fig. 8.6. Rule 13.5A. "In" analytic where the part is contained in a serial item.**
>
> Uniform titles for music : an exercise in collocation / Richard P. Smiraglia. — p. 97-114 ; 22 cm.
> In Cataloging & classification quarterly. — Vol. 9, no. 3 (Spring 1989)

13.5B. Parts of "In" analytics

If an "In" analytic record is to be made for a part of a part already cataloged as an "In" analytic, the description following the word *In* should first give information about the part containing the part being analyzed. The information about the comprehensive work is then given as a series statement. *See* Fig. 8.7 (page 186).

Fig. 8.7. Rule 13.5B. "In" analytic where the part is contained in a work that is itself part of a larger work.

The last of the Mohicans : a narrative of 1757 / James Fenimore Cooper. — p. 467-878 ; 21 cm.
In Cooper, James Fenimore. [Selections. 1985]. The leatherstocking tales : volume 1 / [edited by] Blake Nevius. — New York, N.Y. : Literary Classics of the U.S. : Distributed to the trade in the U.S. and Canada by Viking Press, c1985. — (Library of America ; 26)

RULE 13.6. MULTILEVEL DESCRIPTION

An alternative to "In" analytic records is a technique called multilevel description. It is useful when one wishes to provide complete identification of both part and whole in a single record.

The first level of descriptive information shows the description of the whole item. The second level contains description (not repeating information given at the first level) of an individual part or groups of parts. If the second level describes a group of parts, then a third level may describe an individual part. *See* Fig. 8.8.

Fig. 8.8. Rule 13.6. Multilevel description showing three levels from most to least comprehensive.

The Library of America. — New York, N.Y. : Literary Classics of the U.S. : Distributed to the trade in the U.S. and Canada by Viking Press, 1982-   . — v. : 21 cm.

Vols. 26-27: [Selections. 1985]. The leatherstocking tales / James Fenimore Cooper ; [edited by] Blake Nevius. — c1985.

The last of the Mohicans : a narrative of 1757. — vol. 26, p. 467-878.

LC does not use the technique of multilevel description. (*CSB* 11: 17)

NOTES

[1]*AACR2R*, p. 615.

[2]*AACR2R*, p. 615.

SUGGESTED READING

Bloomberg, Marty, and G. Edward Evans. *Introduction to Technical Services for Library Technicians.* 5th ed. Littleton, Colo., Libraries Unlimited, 1985. pp. 189-190.

Hagler, Ronald. *The Bibliographic Record and Information Technology.* 2nd ed. Chicago, American Library Association, 1991. pp. 258-262.

Maxwell, Margaret F. *Handbook for AACR2, 1988 Revision.* Chicago, American Library Association, 1989. Chapter 12.

O'Neil, Rosanna M. "Analysis and 'In' Analytics," *Serials Review* 13, no. 2 (Summer 1987): 57-63.

Choice of Access Points

9

INTRODUCTION

The rules in *AACR2R*, chapter 21, deal with the choice of access points and not the form of entry. *Choice of access points* means choosing all names and titles under which the description of an item may be sought by a user. For any one item, one of the access points is chosen as a main entry, and the others become added entries. Originally this choice was necessary, in part, so that there could be one place in a printed catalog where all information about a work or item could be found, while other entries for the item in that catalog could be much shorter. Eventually, when *unit cards* (i.e., every card in a card set contains identical information) became standard, this need for a main entry became obsolete. However, the main entry is also used in printed catalogs as a secondary filing element (e.g., all items under the subject heading "Psychology" are subarranged by main entry). In the introduction to *AACR2R* there is a recognition that choice of one entry to be the main one may not be considered important in some libraries.[1] There is lack of agreement on this point in the cataloging community.

Proponents of main entry assert that one of the major outcomes of cataloging is to identify the work contained therein. This can only be done, they believe, by using one consistent means for citing the work. This, in turn, can only be done by adhering to a set of rules for choosing the main access point and then using this main entry in conjunction with other necessary elements to form a unit that identifies the work (e.g., if the main entry is the first of two authors, that name is combined with the item's title to form a unit that identifies the work). The unit thus formed is often referred to as the *uniform title*, although this can be misleading since the concept of uniform title is also used to refer to a standardized title for a work that may have variant titles or that may have only a generic title. In any case the unit formed to identify the work is used to collocate all editions, translations, criticisms, etc., of that work that may appear.

The introduction to *AACR2R* points out that it is necessary to distinguish the main entry from the others when one is creating a listing in which each record will be given only once or in any other situation when one must make a single citation for a work.[2] The latter situation occurs, for example, when a related work needs to be cited on the bibliographic record for the work to which it is related or when one work is the subject of another. *AACR2R* also points out that the concept of main entry is useful in creating uniform titles to draw those related works together. At one time it was thought that related works were probably a small proportion of all works, and therefore a great deal of time was spent choosing main entries for many works that would never have editions, translations, etc. However, ongoing research indicates that as much as one-third of all works have related works.[3]

Proponents of the idea that all access points for an item are basically equal question whether there is a need for main entry as a collocating device. They say that in most catalogs all access points are equally accessible; in online systems, the main entry is not necessarily used to subarrange records retrieved under other access points (e.g., subarrangement may be by date). Much has been written about this controversy,[4] and its resolution may not come about until there is a change in the basic underlying structure of the catalog.

This chapter covers basic choice of main entry under personal author, corporate body, and title (rule 21.2). More specific guidance is then given for choice of entry for 1) works where there have been changes in title proper (rule 21.2) or in persons or bodies responsible for the work (rule 21.3), 2) works of single responsibility (rules 21.4-21.5), 3) works of shared responsibility (rule 21.6), 4) collections and works produced under editorial responsibility (rule 21.7), 5) works of mixed responsibility (rules 21.8-21.27), and 6) works that are related to other works (rule 21.28). General rules for added entries are given (rules 21.29-21.30), followed by special rules for certain legal and religious publications (rules 21.31-21.39).

The rules covered in this text deal only with basic or general instances; for more complex problems and special cases, the student should consult *AACR2R*, chapter 21. Examples in this text allow the student to see not only the choice of main entry, but also the form of entry and the added entries. The following chapters deal with the rules for these specific forms.

SELECTED RULES AND EXAMPLES

RULE 21.0. INTRODUCTORY RULES

21.0B. Sources for determining access points

Access points for the item being cataloged are determined from the chief source of information or its substitute (*see* rule 1.0A). Other statements appearing formally in one of the prescribed sources of information should be taken into account, but the emphasis is to be on the chief source of information, making it unnecessary for the cataloger to search in the contents or outside the item for potential access points. A rule interpretation from LC indicates that when information in the prescribed sources is ambiguous, information may be taken from the contents or from outside the item. (*CSB* 45: 19-20)

21.0D. *Optional addition.* Designations of function

This option allows for abbreviated designations of function, such as *ed.* for *editor* and *tr.* for *translator*, to be added to a heading for a person. The Library of Congress has decided not to apply this option, with one exception: the abbreviation *ill.* is added to the headings for illustrators that appear as added entries on bibliographic records in the annotated cards (AC) series (i.e., for children's books). (*CSB* 18: 29-30)

RULE 21.1. GENERAL RULE

21.1A. Works of personal authorship

Personal author is defined as "the person chiefly responsible for the creation of the intellectual or artistic content of a work."[5] This can include composers, cartographers, photographers, performers, and others, as well as writers. The general rule is to enter works by one or more persons under the heading for the personal author according to the specific instructions given in rules 21.4A, 21.5B, 21.6, and 21.8-21.17 and to make added entries as instructed in rules 21.29-21.30. For example, the sound recording entitled "Where the Blue of the Night Meets the Gold of the Day," which includes songs from the original sound tracks of Bing Crosby's early films, would be entered under the heading:

Crosby, Bing, 1904-1977.

There would be an added entry for the title.

21.1B. Entry under corporate body

A corporate body is defined as "an organization or a group of persons that is identified by a particular name and that acts, or may act, as an entity."[6] Guidelines dictate that a corporate body should be considered to have a name: if the words referring to it are a specific appellation, not just a description; if the initial letters of important words are capitalized; and/or if the words are associated with a definite article. Corporate bodies include, for example, associations, institutions, business firms, governments, conferences, ad hoc events (e.g., exhibitions, festivals), and vessels (e.g., spacecraft).

LC has issued a rule interpretation that gives assistance in determining whether a conference is named. This interpretation should be consulted when needed. (*CSB* 46: 25-26)

21.1B2. The general rule states that a corporate body may be chosen as main entry if it falls into one or more of six categories:

a) A work that deals with the body itself, such as a report on finances or operations, or a listing of staff, or a catalog of the body's resources.

b) Certain legal, governmental, or religious types of works listed in this rule with rule numbers to consult for more guidance.

c) Works that deal with official pronouncements that represent the body's position on matters other than those covered in a) above.

d) Works of a *collective* nature that report on activities of conferences, expeditions, or events that can be defined as corporate bodies and whose names appear prominently in the publication.

e) Sound recordings, films, videorecordings, or written records of performances in which the responsibility of the group for the existence of the performance is more than a performance or execution of a previously existing script, score, etc. (e.g., improvized jazz or drama).

f) Cartographic materials for which a body does more than merely publish or distribute the materials.

A lengthy LC rule interpretation on this rule gives guidance in applying this rule and should be consulted for more information. (*CSB* 47: 42-46) *See* Figs. 9.5-9.7 under rule 21.4B (see page 194).

21.1B3. If a work falls outside the above categories, the main entry is chosen as if no corporate body were involved, but added entries may be made. Thus, the report of an exhibition entitled "130 Years of Ohio Photography" sponsored by and held in the Columbus Museum of Art would be entered under the heading "Columbus Museum of Art," and an added entry would be made under the title. However, a monograph entitled "Benue through Pictures" that has been put together in the Information Division of Benue, Nigeria, does not fall under one of the five categories of rule 21.1B2; therefore, the main entry would be under the title, with an added entry under the heading: Benue (Nigeria). Information Division.

21.1B4. If a subordinate unit of a corporate body is involved for a work that falls in a category in rule 21.1B2, the heading for the subordinate unit is used if the responsibility of that unit is stated prominently. Otherwise, the heading for the parent body is used. For example, the staff directory of the Women's Bureau of the Ministry of Labour in Ontario would be entered under the heading for the Women's Bureau, not that for the Ministry of Labour.

21.1C. Entry under title
    Entry under title is prescribed when there is no known personal author, or personal authorship is diffuse (*see* rule 21.6C2), *and* the work is not eligible for entry under corporate body; when the work is a collection of multiple authorship or is produced under editorial direction; or when the work is a text that a religious group accepts as sacred scripture.
    An LC rule interpretation adds a case for title entry that is not listed in *AACR2R*. It is the situation where a work seems to give technical credit of more than one kind to several persons, and the position and typography of the statement indicates lesser importance in relation to the title. (*CSB* 18: 34-35)

RULE 21.2. CHANGES IN TITLES PROPER
    This rule and the next one fill a need for guidance about when separate main entries should be chosen for different parts of a multipart monograph or of a serial. The cataloger is instructed to choose separate main entries (and thus make separate records) for each edition when the title proper of a monograph changes between editions. However, if the title proper of a multipart monograph changes between *parts*, one title proper (the one that predominates) is to be used for the whole monograph. If the title proper of a serial changes, a separate main entry is chosen for each title, and separate records are made.
    The cases in which a title proper is considered to have changed occur when:

1) any important words are added, deleted, or changed (e.g., *Cataloging Service* changed to *Cataloging Service Bulletin*)

2) the order of the first five words (not counting an initial article) changes (e.g., *Sell's Directory of Products & Services* changed to *Sell's Products and Services Directory*).

A title proper is not to be considered changed, however, if:

1) the change is one of word representation (e.g., *Teaching, Learning and Technology* versus *Teaching, Learning + Technology*).

2) the change is after the first five words (not counting an initial article) *and* does not change meaning or indicate different subject coverage.

3) the only change involves addition or deletion of issuing body at the end of the title.

4) the only change involves punctuation (e.g., *Out of Line!* versus *Out of Line*).

An LC rule interpretation adds cases to these categories and should be consulted as needed. (*CSB* 48: 12-13) A note should report changes not considered to constitute a change in title proper. Title added entries may also be made.

A rule interpretation from LC gives guidance for treatment of fluctuating serial titles. (*CSB* 42: 34-35)

RULE 21.3. CHANGES OF PERSONS OR BODIES RESPONSIBLE FOR A WORK

21.3A. Monographs

Monographs that have been modified by a person or body different from the one responsible for the original edition are to be treated according to rules 21.9-21.23. This means that in some cases, when the nature and/or content has been changed, the main entry will be different from that of the original. (*See* Fig. 9.1.) In other cases, when the modification abridges or rearranges, for example, the main entry of the original will be used. (*See* Fig. 9.2.)

Fig. 9.1. Rule 21.3A. Entry of a work whose nature has been changed from that of the original.

Bambi's fragrant forest : based on the original story by Felix Salten / Walt Disney Productions

Make added entries for persons or bodies responsible for the original and the modification:

I. Salten, Felix, 1869-1945. Bambi. II. Walt Disney Productions.

Fig. 9.2. Rule 21.3A. Entry of an abridged work.

Salten, Felix, 1869-1945.
Bambi [sound recording] / abridged by Marianne Mantell. Read by Glynis Johns

Make added entries for persons or bodies responsible for the modification:

I. Mantell, Marianne. II. Johns, Glynis. III. Title.

If responsibility in a multipart monograph changes between parts, the heading appropriate to the first part is used unless a later one predominates, just as with a change of title proper. However, if more than three persons or bodies are finally responsible for a multipart monograph, with none predominant, main entry is changed to title.

21.3B. Serials

AACR2R gives two conditions under which changes in persons or bodies could require a new entry for a serial:

1) when the serial has a corporate body main entry and the name of that body changes (e.g., *Financial Report* of the Board of Trustees of the Firemen's Pension Fund, formerly the Firemen's Pension and Relief Fund).

2) when the serial has a corporate body or personal author as main entry, and the person or body is no longer responsible for the serial.

An LC rule interpretation adds a third condition:

3) when the serial's main entry is under a uniform title heading that must be changed either because a corporate body used as a qualifier changes or because the title used in the heading for a translation changes. (*CSB* 42: 35-36)

RULE 21.4. WORKS FOR WHICH A SINGLE PERSON OR CORPORATE BODY IS RESPONSIBLE

21.4A. Works of single personal authorship (MARC field 100)

An item that contains a work or works by one personal author should have the heading for that person as its main entry. For example, the following title page is from a work of single personal authorship. The choice of main entry should be the single author, Pamela Bennetts (*see* Figs. 9.3 and 9.4 [page 194]).

Fig. 9.3. Title page.

Title   ➤ **MY DEAR LOVER ENGLAND**

Single author   ➤ Pamela Bennetts

New York
St. Martin's Press

Fig. 9.4. Rule 21.4A. A work of single personal authorship.

Personal ———→ Bennetts, Pamela.
author main   My dear lover England / Pamela Bennetts
entry

Make added entry for title:

    I. Title.

21.4B. Works emanating from a single corporate body (MARC field 110 or 111)

    An item that contains a work or works that emanate from one corporate body should have the heading for that body as its main entry if one or more of the categories given under rule 21.1B2 applies. *See* Figs. 9.5, 9.6, and 9.7.

Fig. 9.5. Rule 21.4B. A work of single corporate responsibility.

Corporate ———→ Al-Anon Family Group Headquarters.
body main   World directory of Al-Anon Family Groups and
entry (21.1B2,   Ala-teens
type a)

Make added entry for title:

    I. Title.

Fig. 9.6. Rule 21.4B. A work of single corporate responsibility.

Corporate ———→ United States. Congress. House. Select Committee to
body main   Investigate Covert Arms Transactions with Iran.
entry (21.1B2,   Report of the congressional committees investigating the
type c)   Iran-Contra Affair : with the minority views

Make added entry for title:

    I. Title.

Fig. 9.7. Rule 21.4B. A work of single corporate responsibility.

Corporate ———→ AIAA International Communication Satellite Systems
body main   Conference and Exhibit (13th : 1990 : Los Angeles, Calif.)
entry (21.1B2,   A collection of technical papers : 13th AIAA International
type d)   Communication Satellite Systems Conference and Exhibit, Los
                  Angeles, CA, March 11-15, 1990

Make added entry for title:

    I. Title.

21.4C. Works erroneously or fictitiously attributed to a person or corporate body

When a publication erroneously or fictitiously attributes responsibility to a person or body, enter it under the heading for the actual person or body responsible, if possible and appropriate, or else under the title. Make an added entry under the heading for the person or body attributed responsibility if such person or body is real. *See* Fig. 9.8.

Fig. 9.8. Rule 21.4C. Entry under the real author rather than the attributed author.

Actual ——►Farmer, Philip Jose.
author as   The adventure of the peerless peer / by John H. Watson ;
main entry   edited by Philip Jose Farmer

Note explaining statement of responsibility:

Written by P.J. Farmer in imitation of A.C. Doyle.

Make added entry for title:

I. Title.

Note: No added entry is made for the attributed author, John H. Watson, since he is a fictional character created by A. C. Doyle in his series of detective stories about Sherlock Holmes and Dr. Watson.

21.4D. Works by heads of state, other high government officials, popes, and other high ecclesiastical officials

21.4D1. Official communications

Two categories of official works are entered under the corporate heading (*see* rules 24.20 and 24.27B) for the official:

"a) an official communication from a head of state, head of government, or head of an international body (e.g., a message to a legislature, a proclamation, an executive order other than one covered by 21.31)

b) an official communication from a pope, patriarch, bishop, etc. (e.g., an order, decree, pastoral letter, bull, encyclical, constitution, or an official message to a council, synod, etc.)."[7]

An added entry is made under the personal heading for the person. *See* Fig. 9.9 (page 196).

Fig. 9.9. Rule 21.4D1. Official communication entered under corporate heading.

Main entry ──►Maine. Governor (1975-1979 : Longley)
under corpo-   Budget message address of James B. Longley, Governor of
rate heading   Maine, to the One hundred and seventh Legislature, State of
                Maine, February 6, 1975

Make added entries:

Added entry   I. Maine. Legislature. II. Longley, James B. III. Title:
under personal Budget message address of James B. Longley, Governor of
heading   Maine ...

21.4D2. Other works

Other works by a government or religious official are given the personal heading for the person as main entry. One explanatory reference is made under the corporate heading rather than making an added entry under the corporate heading for each such work. *See* Fig. 9.10. For examples of explanatory references see rule 26.2D in chapter 14 of this text.

Fig. 9.10. Rule 21.4D2. Other works entered under personal heading.

Main entry ──►Jefferson, Thomas, 1743-1826.
under personal   The portable Thomas Jefferson / edited and with an
heading   introduction by Merrill D. Peterson

Make added entry for person responsible for this edition of the work:

I. Peterson, Merrill D.

21.4D3. Collections of official communications and other works

A collection of official communications *and other works* by *one* person is entered under the personal heading, with an added entry under the corporate heading. A collection of official communications and other works by *more than one* person is entered as a collection (*see* rule 21.7), with an added entry for the heading for the office held, if all the persons held the same office.

A collection of official communications *only* of *more than one* holder of *one* of the offices listed in rule 21.4D1 is entered under the heading for the office, with an added entry for an openly named compiler. (This rule actually is stated in *AACR2R* under rule 21.4D1.)

There is no rule specifically stated for a collection of official communications *only* of more than one holder of *more than one* of the offices listed. Such a work should be treated as a collection and entered according to provisions given in rule 21.7.

RULE 21.5. WORKS OF UNKNOWN OR UNCERTAIN AUTHORSHIP OR BY UNNAMED GROUPS

21.5A. Enter under the title a work of unknown or uncertain responsibility or one that emanates from a body that lacks a name. *See* Fig. 9.11.

Fig. 9.11. Rule 21.5A. Work of unknown authorship entered under title.

Main entry under title

The Old non-conformist, touching the book of common-prayer and ceremonies.... — London : [s.n.], 1660.

21.5C. Enter a work under a characterizing word or phrase or under a phrase naming another work by the person, if that is the only clue to authorship and it appears in the chief source of information. For example, the title page shown in Fig. 9.12 is from a work with an unknown author, but provides a "characterizing phrase." It would be entered in the form given in Fig. 9.13.

Fig. 9.12. Title page.

¹Title

²Subtitle

³Unknown author

⁴Place

⁵Publisher

1——► **THE MANUAL OF FRENCH COOKERY**

2——► Dedicated to the Housekeepers and Cooks of England who Wish to Study the ART simplified for the benefit of the most unlearned by

3——► One who has tested the receipts

4——► London

5——► Chapman and Hall

Fig. 9.13. Rule 21.5C. A work of unknown authorship entered under characterizing phrase.

Entry under characteriz-ing phrase

One who has tested the receipts.
The manual of French cookery : dedicated to the housekeepers and cooks of England who wish to study the art : simplified for the benefit of the most unlearned / by one who has tested the receipts

Make added entry for title:

I. Title.

RULE 21.6. WORKS OF SHARED RESPONSIBILITY

21.6A. Scope

This rule is used for situations in which two or more persons or corporate bodies have made the same kind of contribution to a work. It also applies when the same kinds of contributions come from one or more persons *and* one or more corporate bodies.

Special types of collaborations are covered by rules on mixed responsibility (rules 21.8-21.27), but when those rules prescribe main entry under the heading for an adapter, for example, and when there is shared responsibility among two or more adapters, then this rule of shared responsibility is applied. This rule does not apply to works produced under editorial direction or to works that are collections of previously existing works; these are covered by rule 21.7.

21.6B. Principal responsibility indicated

21.6B1. Enter a work of shared responsibility under the heading for the principal person or body if one is indicated by wording or typography. Make added entries under the headings for other persons or bodies involved, if there are not more than two. Always make an added entry under the heading for the person or body, other than the principal one, whose name appears first on the title page. *See* Figs. 9.14 and 9.15. Since the principal author, Connie Haynes, is indicated on the title page of this work by the wording of the subsidiary authorship statement, the choice of main entry is the principal author.

Fig. 9.14. Title page.

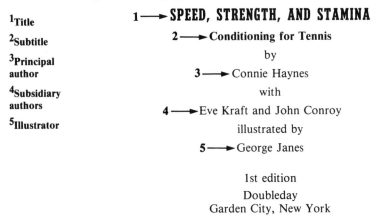

¹Title

²Subtitle

³Principal author

⁴Subsidiary authors

⁵Illustrator

1 ——► **SPEED, STRENGTH, AND STAMINA**

2 ——► Conditioning for Tennis

by

3 ——► Connie Haynes

with

4 ——►Eve Kraft and John Conroy

illustrated by

5 ——► George Janes

1st edition
Doubleday
Garden City, New York

Fig. 9.15. Rule 21.6B1. Principal author indicated.

Main entry——►Haynes, Connie
under princi-   Speed, strength, and stamina : conditioning for tennis /
pal author   by Connie Haynes, with Eve Kraft and John Conroy ; illustrated
by George Janes

Make added entries for subsidiary authors:

I. Kraft, Eve F. II. Conroy, John, 1908-   . III. Title.

21.6B2. When the chief source of information indicates that two or three persons or bodies have principal responsibility, main entry is made for the first named of these. Added entries are made under headings for the other principal author(s) and for a collaborator if there are two principal authors and one collaborator (i.e., there may be no more than two added entries).

21.6C. Principal responsibility not indicated

21.6C1. If principal responsibility is not indicated and if there are not more than three names, enter under the one that is named first and make added entries under the others. *See* Figs. 9.16 and 9.17.

Fig. 9.16. Title page.

¹Title

²Shared
author

³Shared
author

1 ⟶ **MODERN DANCE**

2 ⟶ Gay Cheney
3 ⟶ Janet Strader

second edition
Boston
Allyn and Bacon

In the case shown in Fig. 9.16, the principal author is not indicated; further, there are not more than three authors listed (i.e., two in this example), so the choice of main entry is the first named author (*see* Fig. 9.17). If there had been more than three authors on the title page, the choice of entry would have been the title (*see* Fig. 9.18).

Fig. 9.17. Rule 21.6C1. Principal author not indicated, and not more than three authors.

Main entry ⟶ Cheney, Gay.
under first   Modern dance / Gay Cheney, Janet Strader
named author

Make added entry for second named author:

I. Strader, Janet.

If different editions of a work have the responsible persons or bodies appearing in a different order in the chief sources of information, each edition is entered under the heading for the person or body named first in that edition.

21.6C2. If principal responsibility is not indicated and there are more than three persons or bodies, enter the work under the title and make an added entry under the heading for the person or body named first in the chief source of information. *See* Fig. 9.18.

Note: If the work is produced under the direction of an editor named in the chief source of information, apply rule 21.7.

Fig. 9.18. Rule 21.6C2. Principal author not indicated.

Title main ⟶ Europe reborn : the story of Renaissance civilization /
entry   contributors, Julian Mates ... [et al.]

Make added entry for first named author:

I. Mates, Julian, 1927-

21.6D. Shared pseudonyms

When two or more persons have used a single pseudonym for the result of their collaboration, the pseudonym is given as the heading in the appropriate place (either main entry or added entry). References are made from the real names to the pseudonym and, if the persons are also established singly, from the pseudonym to the real name(s) (*see* rules 26.2C and 26.2D1). *See* Figs. 9.19 and 9.20.

Fig. 9.19. Rule 21.6D. Shared pseudonyms.

Main entry⟶Ashe, Penelope.
under shared   Naked came the stranger / Penelope Ashe
pseudonym

It should be noted that Penelope Ashe is the shared pseudonym of 25 writers who wrote the book in collaboration. Because a number of unnamed persons were involved, explanatory references cannot be made. Such a reference might be made for Lillie Young, one of the contributors, who posed as Penelope Ashe, and who has since published a work under her own name.

Fig. 9.20. Rule 21.6D. Shared pseudonyms.

Coles, Manning.
    A toast to tomorrow / Manning Coles

In this case, the name is the shared pseudonym of Adelaide Frances Oke Manning and Cyril Henry Coles. References would be made from these names to the pseudonym.

RULE 21.7. COLLECTIONS AND WORKS PRODUCED UNDER EDITORIAL DIRECTION

21.7A. Scope

This rule is used for situations in which contributions by different persons or corporate bodies are brought together either as collections of previously existing independent works (or extracts from those works) or as contributions produced under editorial direction or as combinations of the two preceding situations.

One should not apply this rule to works that emanate from a corporate body and fall in the scope of rule 21.1B2 or to papers or proceedings of conferences. For the latter, one should use rule 21.1B2d if the conference, etc., is named prominently; rule 21.1B3 if it is not named prominently; or rule 21.5A if it is unnamed.

21.7B. With collective title

Main entry for a work covered by this rule is title if there is a collective title. Added entries are made under the headings for prominently named editors or compilers if there are not more than three or for the principal one or the one named first if there are more than three. *See* Figs. 9.21 and 9.22.

Fig. 9.21. Rule 21.7B. Collections and works produced under editorial direction with collective titles. Added entries are made for the first-named editors.

Title main———►Modern music librarianship : essays in honor of Ruth
entry   Watanabe / edited by Alfred Mann.

Make added entries for persons or bodies responsible for the item:

    I. Mann, Alfred, 1917-

Fig. 9.22.

Title main———►The New Cassell's French dictionary : French-English,
entry   English-French / completely revised by Denis Girard ;
       with the assistance of Gaston Dulong, Oliver Van Oss and
       Charles Guinness.

Make added entry for editor:

    I. Girard, Denis. II. Title: Cassell's French
dictionary.

Name-title added entries are made if there are only two or three contributions or independent works included in a work covered by this rule. A name-title added entry is composed of the name of a person or corporate body followed by the title of an item for which the person or body is responsible. *See* Fig. 9.23 (page 202) for an example of name-title added entries.

An added entry is made for each contributor when only two or three have contributed four or more works. In this case if one or two contributors have contributed only one work each, a name-title added entry is made for each.

An added entry is made for the first contributor named when more than three are named in the chief source of information.

A rule interpretation from LC indicates that the above provisions for added entries for contributors are to be followed when the work is a collection, but not when it is produced under editorial direction. In the latter case LC makes the name added entries prescribed but does not make name-title added entries. (*CSB* 45: 25-26)

21.7C. Without collective title

The main entry for a work that falls under this rule but does *not* have a collective title is the heading appropriate for the first work or contribution named in the chief source of information. If a chief source is lacking, the first work in the item is noted. Added entries are made as instructed in rule 21.7B. The LC rule interpretation is also like that under rule 21.7B. (*CSB* 45: 26-27) *See* Fig. 9.23.

Note: The rule does not mention separate title added entries for the separate titles in a collection without a collective title, nor does rule 21.30J suggest such title added entries. However, an LC rule interpretation for rule 21.30J gives instructions to trace separate title added entries for each of the titles listed in the title and statement of responsibility area if there are not more than three. (*CSB* 48: 13-14)

Fig. 9.23. Rule 21.7C. Collections without a collective title.

Main entry ──►Ellsworth, Ralph E., 1907-
under first ____ Buildings / by Ralph E. Ellsworth. Shelving / by Louis
named author ___ Kaplan. Storage warehouses / by Jerrold Orne

Make name-title added entries:

I. Kaplan, Louis, 1909- . Shelving. II. Orne, Jerrold,
1921- . Storage warehouses. III. Title. IV. Title: Shelving.
V. Title: Storage warehouses.

WORKS OF MIXED RESPONSIBILITY: SELECTED RULES AND EXAMPLES

RULE 21.8. WORKS OF MIXED RESPONSIBILITY

21.8A. Scope

In many works the responsibility is divided. This occurs when different persons or bodies have contributed to the intellectual or artistic content performing different kinds of functions, e.g., writing, adapting, illustrating, translating, etc. Determination of main entry depends to a large extent on the relative importance of such contributions.

The rules in this section are divided into two basic categories of mixed responsibility:

1) modifications of previously existing works, such as revised editions, adaptations, or translations (rules 21.9-21.23), and

2) new works that consist of different kinds of contributions, such as illustrated texts or musical works with words by persons other than the composers (rules 21.24-21.27).

Works That Are Modifications of Other Works

RULE 21.9. GENERAL RULE

Works that are modifications of other works may be entered under the heading appropriate to the new work or that appropriate to the original, depending upon the nature of the modification. If the modification has changed the nature or content of the original in a substantial way, or if the medium of expression is different, the new heading is chosen. However, if the modification is a rearrangement, abridgment, etc., where the original person or body is still seen as being responsible, the original heading is chosen. Rules 21.10-21.23 give specific guidance in applying this general rule.

Modifications of Texts (Rules 21.10-21.15)

RULE 21.10.   ADAPTATIONS OF TEXTS
Adaptations of texts are entered under the heading for the adapter or under title if the adapter is unknown. A name-title added entry is made for the original work. Examples of adaptations are paraphrases, changes of literary form (e.g., dramatization), and adaptations for children. *See* Fig. 9.24.

Fig. 9.24. Rule 21.10. Entry under adapter.

Adapter as ⟶ Taylor, Helen L. (Helen Louisa)
main entry   Little Pilgrim's progress / by Helen L. Taylor

Note expanding upon statement of responsibility:

Adaptation for children of: The Pilgrim's progress / John Bunyan.

Make name-title added entry for original author:

I. Bunyan, John, 1628-1688. Pilgrim's progress. II. Title.

RULE 21.11.   ILLUSTRATED TEXTS

21.11A.   General rule
When an illustrator has added illustrations to a text, the main entry is under the heading appropriate to the text. *See* Fig. 9.25. An added entry for the illustrator may be made if appropriate (*see* rule 21.30K2). Works of collaboration between an artist and a writer are treated in rule 21.24.

Fig. 9.25. Rule 21.11A. Illustrated text entered under author.

Main entry ⟶ Day, Jenifer W.
under author   What is a bird? / by Jenifer W. Day ; illustrated by Tony Chen

Make added entry for artist:

I. Chen, Tony. II. Title.

RULE 21.12.   REVISIONS OF TEXTS

21.12A.   Original author considered responsible
The main entry for the original work is used for a revision if *either* the name of the original author appears in a statement of responsibility in the revision *or* the name of the original author appears in the revision's title proper and no other person is named in a statement of responsibility or other title information. The reviser, condenser, etc., is given an added entry. *See* Fig. 9.26 (page 204). Such revisions include condensations, enlargements, revisions, and updates. Abridgments, however, are always entered under the original author, with an added entry made for the abridger. *See* Fig. 9.2 on page 192. Condensations that involve rewriting are considered to be adaptations and are entered according to rule 21.10.

Fig. 9.26. Rule 21.12A. Revised work entered under original author.

Main entry ⟶ Wynar, Bohdan S.
under original   Introduction to cataloging and classification / Bohdan S.
author   Wynar. — 7th ed. / by Arlene G. Taylor

Make added entry for reviser:

    I. Taylor, Arlene G., 1941-   . II. Title.

21.12B. Original author no longer considered responsible

If the wording of the chief source indicates that the original person or body is no longer responsible (i.e., it does not meet the conditions given in rule 21.12A), then entry is under the reviser, etc., or under title as appropriate. A name-title added entry is made under the original author and, if possible, the title of the latest edition to be entered under that name. *See* Fig. 9.27.

Fig. 9.27. Rule 21.12B. Revised work entered under reviser.

Main entry ⟶ Bedingfeld, A. L.
under reviser   Oxburgh Hall, Norfolk : a property of the National
    Trust / by A.L. Bedingfeld. — 2nd ed.

Note expanding upon statement of responsibility:

    "First edition, 1953, by Professor F. de Zulueta."

Make name-title added entry for original author:

    I. Zulueta, Francis de. Oxburgh Hall, Norfolk.
    II. Title.

RULE 21.13. TEXTS PUBLISHED WITH COMMENTARY

This rule applies to items comprising a text or texts by one person or body and a commentary or interpretation by another person or body. In essence, the rule calls for entry under the heading appropriate to the commentary if the chief source of information presents the work as a commentary, and entry under the heading for the original work if the chief source of information presents the work as an edition of the original. If the chief source is ambiguous, entry is determined by (in order of preference) emphasis in the preface, the typographic presentation of the text and commentary, or the relative extent of text and commentary. If there is still doubt, the work is treated as an edition with an added entry appropriate to the commentary. *See* Fig. 9.28.

Fig. 9.28. Rule 21.13. Text with commentary entered under commentator.

Main entry ➤ Fischer, John L.
under named   Annotations to the Book of Luelen / translated and edited
commentator   by John L. Fischer, Saul H. Riesenberg, and Marjorie G.
     Whiting

Note explaining the statement of responsibility:

     Annotations by J.L. Fischer, S.H. Riesenberg, and M.G.
     Whiting.

Make added entries appropriate to the text:

     I. Riesenberg, Saul H. II. Whiting, Marjorie G.
     III. Bernart, Luelen. Book of Luelen.

RULE 21.14. TRANSLATIONS

A single translation is entered under the heading appropriate to the original. An added entry for the translator may be made in accordance with rule 21.30K1. *See* Fig. 9.29.

Fig. 9.29. Rule 21.14. Translation entered under original author.

Main entry ➤ Flohr, Salo, 1908-
under original   Twelfth chess tournament of nations / Salo Flohr ;
author   [translated from the Russian by W. Perelman]

A collection of translations of works by different authors is treated as a collection (*see* rule 21.7).

RULE 21.15. TEXTS PUBLISHED WITH BIOGRAPHICAL/CRITICAL MATERIAL

Works that consist of a writer's work or works accompanied by biographical or critical material written by someone else are treated according to the way they are represented in the chief source of information. If the chief source presents the work as biography and/or criticism, the main entry is the biographer/critic. If the chief source presents the work as an edition with an editor, compiler, etc., then the original writer is used as main entry. In either case an added entry is made for the one not chosen as main entry. *See* Figs. 9.30 and 9.31 (page 206).

Fig. 9.30. Rule 21.15. Biographical work entered under biographer.

Main entry ➤ Morse, John T. (John Torrey), 1840-1937.
under   Life and letters of Oliver Wendell Holmes / by John T.
biographer   Morse

Make added entries for Holmes both as subject of the biography and as personal author:

     1. Holmes, Oliver Wendell, 1809-1894. I. Holmes, Oliver
     Wendell, 1809-1894. II. Title.

Fig. 9.31. Rule 21.15. Edited biographical work.

Main entry——►Dover, Thomas, 1660-1742.
under author Thomas Dover's life and Legacy / edited and introduced
by Kenneth Dewhurst

Make added entry for editor:

   I. Dewhurst, Kenneth. II. Title.

Art Works (Rules 21.16-21.17)

RULE 21.16. ADAPTATIONS OF ART WORKS

AACR2R defines art works as including "paintings, engravings, photographs, drawings, sculptures, etc., and any other creative work that can be represented pictorially (e.g., ceramic designs, tapestries, fabrics)."[8]

21.16A. When an art work is adapted from one medium to another, the main entry is the adapter, or the title if the adapter is unknown. A name-title added entry is made for the original. *See* Fig. 9.32.

21.16B. When an art work is reproduced, however, the main entry is the heading for the original, with an added entry for the person or body responsible for the reproduction, unless that person or body is only the manufacturer or publisher. *See* Fig. 9.33.

RULE 21.17. REPRODUCTIONS OF TWO OR MORE ART WORKS

21.17A. Without text

If a work consists of reproductions of an artist's works and there is no text, the main entry is the artist.

21.17B. With text

When text accompanies reproductions of an artist's works, entry is under the personal heading for the author of the text if that person is represented as author in the chief source of information; an added entry is made under the heading for the artist. Otherwise, or in case of doubt, entry is made under the heading for the artist with an added entry for the person mentioned in the chief source of information as having written the text. Catalogs of the holdings of a corporate body are governed by rule 21.1B2a. Art catalogs often present difficult choices. An LC rule interpretation gives guidance in this area. (*CSB* 45: 27-28) *See* Figs. 9.34 and 9.35.

Fig. 9.32. Rule 21.16A. Adaptation entered under heading for title because adapter is unknown.

¹Main entry under title (adapter unknown)
[Mona Lisa] [picture] / [computer representation of the original by Leonardo da Vinci, produced via program written at IBM]

Copies distributed at demonstration of IBM equipment.

²Name-title added entry for original work
I. Leonardo, da Vinci, 1452-1519. Mona Lisa.

³Added entry for responsible corporate body
II. International Business Machines Corporation.

Fig. 9.33. Rule 21.16B. Reproduction of art work entered under heading for the artist.

Main entry under artist
Hobbema, Meindert, 1638-1709.
View on a high road [picture] / Hobbema ; National Gallery of Art

Make added entry for body responsible for reproduction:
I. National Gallery of Art (U.S.). II. Title.

Fig. 9.34. Rule 21.17B. Art reproductions with text entered under author of text.

Main entry under author of text
Cassou, Jean, 1897-
Rembrandt / par Jean Cassou

Make added entry for artist:
I. Rembrandt Harmenszoon van Rijn, 1606-1669.

Fig. 9.35. Rule 21.17B. Art reproductions with text entered under artist.

Main entry under artist
Rembrandt Harmenszoon van Rijn, 1606-1669.
More drawings of Rembrandt / introduction by Stephen Longstreet

Make added entry for author of text:
I. Longstreet, Stephen, 1907-   II. Title.

Musical Works (Rules 21.18-21.22)

RULE 21.18. GENERAL RULE

21.18A. Scope
This rule applies to all kinds of arrangements of musical works where medium of performance has been changed; the original has been simplified; the new work is described as "based on," etc.; new material has been incorporated; or the harmony or style of the original has been changed.

21.18B. Arrangements, transcriptions, etc.
A musical arrangement is a musical work or part of a musical work that has been rewritten either for a different medium of performance or to provide a simplified version. The general rule for a musical arrangement is to enter it under the heading for the original composer whenever possible. An added entry is made for the name of the arranger. *See* Fig. 9.36.

Fig. 9.36. Rule 21.18B. Arrangement of musical work entered under original composer.

Main entry⟶Mozart, Wolfgang Amadeus, 1756-1791.
under   Eighth quintet, k. 614, fourth movement / W.A. Mozart ;
composer   arranged for 2 B^b trumpets, horn, trombone & tuba by Ralph
             Lockwood

Make added entry for arranger:

I. Lockwood, Ralph.

21.18C. Adaptations
A musical work that is an adaptation represents a more serious departure from the original work than does an arrangement. Thus, generally, the main entry is made under the heading for the adapter, with an added entry given to the author of the original work. Three types of adaptations of music are specified for entry under adapter:

"a) a distinct alteration of another work (e.g., a free transcription)
b) a paraphrase of various works or of the general style of another composer
c) a work merely based on other music (e.g., variations on a theme.)"[9]

In case of doubt about whether a work is an adaptation, it is to be treated as an arrangement, transcription, etc. *See* Fig. 9.37.

Fig. 9.37. Rule 21.18C. Adaptation of musical work entered under adapter.

Main entry   ⟶ Brahms, Johannes, 1833-1897.
under adapter   Variations and fugue on a theme by Handel, op. 24 / Johannes Brahms

Note explaining the scope of the item:

       The theme is that of the Aria con variazioni from Handel's Suite for harpsichord, 2nd collection, no. 1.

Make name-title added entry for original work:

       I. Handel, George Frideric, 1685-1759. Suites, harpsichord, HWV 434, B^b major. Aria con variazioni.

RULE 21.19. MUSICAL WORKS THAT INCLUDE WORDS

21.19A. General rule

If a musical work includes words, the main entry is for the composer with an added entry for the writer of the words, if the writer's work is represented, as in a full score or a vocal score, for example. A name-title added entry is made for an original text upon which the words have been based. Librettos are treated under another rule: 21.28. *See* Fig. 9.38.

Fig. 9.38. Rule 21.19A. Musical comedy entered under composer.

Main entry   ⟶ Adler, Richard.
under   The pajama game : a musical comedy / music and lyrics
composer   by Richard Adler and Jerry Ross ; book by George Abbott

Note expanding statement of responsibility:

"Based on the novel '7½ cents' by Richard Bissell."

Make added entries for shared composer and for writer and an added name-title entry for original text:

       I. Ross, Jerry, 1926-1955. II. Abbott, George, 1889-
III. Bissell, Richard. 7½ cents. IV. Title.

21.19C. Writer's works set by several composers

If the work or works of one writer are set in a collection of songs, etc., by two or more composers, entry is made according to the rule for collections, rule 21.7. *See* Fig. 9.39.

Fig. 9.39. Rule 21.19C. Collection of songs with words by one writer and music by several composers; entered as a collection under title.

Title main   ⟶ A Shakespeare song book / edited by H.A. Chambers.
entry

Make added entry for writer of words and for editor:

       I. Shakespeare, Willilam, 1564-1616. II. Chambers, H. A. (Herbert Arthur), 1880-

RULE 21.20. MUSICAL SETTINGS FOR BALLETS, ETC.

Main entry for the musical setting for ballets, etc., is the composer. Added entries are made for writers of librettos, choreographers, etc., if their names appear in the chief source of information. *See* Fig. 9.40.

Fig. 9.40. Rule 21.20. Music for a ballet entered under composer.

Main entry⟶Nabokov, Nicholas, 1903-
for composer   Don Quichotte : ballet en 3 actes / Nicolas Nabokov ; libretto par Nicolas Nabokov et Georges Balanchine

Make added entry for shared author of libretto:

I. Balanchine, Georges. II. Title.

RULE 21.21. ADDED ACCOMPANIMENTS, ETC.

If accompaniment or parts have been added to a musical work, main entry is made for the original work, with an added entry for the composer of the accompaniment or parts.

RULE 21.22. LITURGICAL MUSIC

Music that is officially part of a liturgy is treated under the rules for religious publications. *See* rule 21.39.

Sound Recordings (Rule 21.23)

RULE 21.23. ENTRY OF SOUND RECORDINGS

It should be noted that this rule applies only to sound recordings that are modifications of other works. This includes readings of texts and performances of musical works. There is no rule specifically for sound recordings considered to constitute new works, such as recordings of improvisations and lectures. These items would be entered according to the principles of responsibility found in the basic rules. Such works as interviews made as oral history could be entered according to the principles in rule 21.25.

It should be noted also that this rule must be used in conjunction with rule 6.1G. If under rule 6.1G it is decided that a sound recording lacking a collective title should be described as a unit, then one of rules 21.23B-21.23D will be applied. If, however, it is decided to make a separate description for each separately titled work, rule 21.23A will be applied.

21.23A. One work

Main entry for a sound recording of one work is the heading appropriate to that work. The rule specifically calls for added entries for the principal performers unless there are more than three, in which case an added entry is made for the first named principal performer. A rule interpretation from LC points out that added entries should also be made for those prescribed by the rules under which the choice of main entry for the work is made. (*CSB* 44: 37) *See* Fig. 9.41.

Fig. 9.41. Rule 21.23A. Sound recording entered under author of original work.

Main entry → Rey, Margret.
under author   Curious George learns the alphabet [sound recording] / Margret & H.A. Rey

Note expanding statement of responsibility:

     Read by Julie Harris.

Make added entry for shared author and for reader:

     I. Rey, H. A. (Hans Agusto), 1898-   . II. Harris, Julie. III. Title.

21.23B. Two or more works by the same person(s) or body(ies)

Main entry for a sound recording of works that are all the responsibility of the same person(s) or body(ies) is the heading appropriate to those works. Added entries are made for performers and for additional responsible persons or bodies as explained above under rule 21.23A. *See* Fig. 9.42.

Fig. 9.42. Rule 21.23B. Sound recording entered under composer of the several works performed.

Main entry → Chopin, Frédéric, 1810-1849.
under   The 24 preludes [sound recording] / Chopin
composer

Note expanding statement of responsibility:

     Alexander Brailowsky, pianist.

Make added entry for performer:

     I. Brailowsky, Alexander, 1896-1976. II. Title.

21.23C. Works by different persons or bodies. Collective title

Main entry for a sound recording of works by different persons or bodies that has a collective title is the person or body represented as principal performer. If there are two or three principal performers, main entry is the first named, with added entries for the others. A rule interpretation from LC gives guidance in deciding whom to consider "principal performers." This rule interpretation should be consulted for further detail. (*CSB* 45: 28-31) *See* Fig. 9.43.

Fig. 9.43. Rule 21.23C. Sound recording entered under principal performer.

Main entry → Boston Pops Orchestra.
under first   Greatest hits of the '50s [sound recording]
named performer

Note expanding statement of responsibility:

     Boston Pops Orchestra ; Arthur Fiedler, conductor.

Make added entry under second named principal performer:

     I. Fiedler, Arthur, 1894-1979. II. Title.

A sound recording with four or more principal performers or no principal performers is given main entry under title. *See* Fig. 9.44.

Fig. 9.44. Rule 21.23C. Sound recording entered under title.

Main entry ——► Firestone presents your favorite Christmas music
under title   [sound recording]

Note expanding statement of responsibility:

> Julie Andrews, Vic Damone, Dorothy Kirsten, James McCracken, vocals ; the Young Americans ; the Firestone Orchestra ; Irwin Kostal, conductor.

21.23D. Works by different persons or bodies. No collective title

This rule applies to a sound recording that contains works by different persons or bodies, that has no collective title, and that is to be cataloged as a unit. Treatment depends upon the decision about whether participation of the performer(s) goes beyond mere performance, execution, or interpretation.

Popular, rock, and jazz music are usually considered to have participation of performers beyond execution or interpretation. In these cases main entry is under principal performer, if there is one; under the first of two or three principal performers; or under the heading appropriate to the first work if there are four or more principal performers. Added entries are made for the performers not named as main entry if there are not more than three. *See* Figs. 9.45 and 9.46.

Fig. 9.45. Rule 21.23D. Sound recording entered under principal performer.

Main entry ——► Alan, Buddy.
under princi-   When I turn twenty-one / Merle Haggard. Adios, farewell,
pal performer   goodbye, good luck, so long / Buck Owens [sound recording]

Note expanding statement of responsibility:

> Buddy Alan, vocals ; James Burton's orchestra.

Fig. 9.46. Rule 21.23D. Sound recording entered under main entry for first work.

Main entry ——► Little white duck. Mary had a little lamb [sound
under title   recording]
of 1st work

Note expanding statement of responsibility:

> Recording sung by Betty Wells, Bill Marine and The Playmates with orchestra directed by Maury Laws (side A), The 4 Cricketones with orch. and chorus (side B).

Classical and other "serious" music is usually considered to have participation of performers that does not go beyond execution or interpretation. For these works, main entry is under the heading appropriate to the first work with added entries for the other works if appropriate as explained under rule 21.7C.

Mixed Responsibility in New Works

RULE 21.24. COLLABORATION BETWEEN ARTIST AND WRITER
If a work appears to be a collaborative effort between an artist and a writer, rather than an artist's illustrations of a writer's text (covered by rule 21.11A), main entry is under the one named first in the chief source of information, unless the other one is given greater prominence by typography, etc. *See* Fig. 9.47.

Fig. 9.47. Rule 21.24. Collaborative work entered under artist.

Main entry → Mair, A. J. (Alice Joy).
under artist   More homes of the pioneers and other buildings : pen and
named first   wash drawings / by A.J. Mair ; with text by J.A. Hendry
on title page

Make added entry for author:

     I. Hendry, J. A. (John A.). II. Title.

RULE 21.25. REPORTS OF INTERVIEWS OR EXCHANGES
Whether to give main entry to the reporter or to one of the other participants in an interview or exchange depends upon how much the words are those of the reporter and how much those of the other participant(s). If the report gives essentially the words of the interviewee or other participant, main entry is the principal participant, first named participant, or title if there are more than three equal participants. An added entry is made for an openly named reporter. If the report, for the most part, consists of the words of the reporter, main entry is for the reporter, with added entry(ies) for the persons interviewed if they are named in the chief source of information (or for only the first if there are more than three). *See* Figs. 9.48 and 9.49 (page 214).

Fig. 9.48. Rule 21.25. Interview entered under the first named participant.

Main entry → Scott, David Randolph.
under first   Interview from deep space [sound recording] / by David
named parti- Randolph Scott, Alfred Merrill Worden, and James
cipant   Benson Irwin

Make added entries for other participants:

     I. Worden, Alfred Merrill. II. Irwin, James B. (James Benson). III. Title.

Fig. 9.49. Rule 21.25. Interview entered under reporter.

Main entry ——►Schneider, Duane.
under reporter   An interview with Anaïs Nin / Duane Schneider

Make added entry for person interviewed:

      I. Nin, Anaïs, 1903-1977.

RELATED WORKS:
SELECTED RULES AND EXAMPLES

RULE 21.28. RELATED WORKS

21.28A. Scope

    According to rule 1.9, supplementary items may be described separately or dependently (i.e., described as accompanying material; or in a note; or in a multilevel description, further described in rule 13.6). This rule (21.28) applies only to separately cataloged works that are related to another work. It includes continuations, sequels, supplements, indexes, concordances, incidental music to dramatic works, cadenzas, scenarios, screenplays, choreographies, subseries, special numbers of serials, and collections of extracts from serials. It does not apply to works that have only subject relationship to other works or to the particular types of relationship covered in rules 21.8-21.27.

    In *AACR2R* proper, this rule includes librettos, but an alternative rule for librettos is given in a footnote. The Library of Congress has decided to apply the alternative rule for librettos because "librettos are normally sought as an adjunct to the music."[10] Therefore, librettos are entered by LC under the heading for the musical work, with an added entry under the personal heading for the librettist. A name-title added entry is also made under the heading for the original text on which the libretto is based, if this applies. *See* Fig. 9.50.

Fig. 9.50. Rule 21.28A, footnote 7. Libretto entered under heading appropriate to the musical work.

Main entry ——►Laderman, Ezra.
for composer   [Galileo Galilei. Libretto. English]
        Galileo Galilei : an opera-oratorio in three acts / libretto
    by Joe Darion ; music by Ezra Laderman

Note providing other title information:

      Original title: The trials of Galileo.

Make added entry for librettist:

      I. Darion, Joe, 1917-   . II. Title. III. Title: The trials
    of Galileo.

21.28B. General rule

    Main entry for a related work is the heading appropriate to it as if it were an independent work. An added entry is made for the name-title or title (whichever is main entry) of the related work. An added entry is not made, however, for the related work in the case of a sequel by the same author. LC has made some other exceptions to making added entries for the related works that apply to excerpts from serials, indexes, census data, and Bible texts. (*CSB* 47: 46-47) *See* Figs. 9.51-9.54 (page 216).

Fig. 9.51. Rule 21.28B. Supplement cataloged separately and entered under author.

Main entry ──▶Gore, Marvin.
for author   Elements of systems analysis for business data process-
of supple-   ing. Instructional supplement / Marvin Gore, John Stubbe
ment

Make added entry for co-author of supplement:

I. Stubbe, John. II. Title.

Note that a name-title added entry is not made because it would, in essence, be a duplication of the main entry and title given before the words *Instructional supplement.*

Fig. 9.52. Rule 21.28B. Concordance entered under its own author.

Entry under ──▶Williams, Mary.
compiler of the   The Dickens concordance, being a compendium of names
concordance   and characters and principal places mentioned in all the works
                of Charles Dickens ... / by Mary Williams

Make added entry for author of works to which this work is related:

I. Dickens, Charles, 1812-1870. II. Title.

Fig. 9.53. Rule 21.28B. Collection of extracts from a serial entered as a collection. [Joyce is the subject of these essays.]

Main entry ──▶James Joyce essays / by Brian Nolan ... [et al.]
appropriate to
related work in
hand

Note providing bibliographic history:

"These essays were first published in Envoy, 1951."

Make added entry for first named author and for serial from which essays were extracted:

I. O'Brien, Flann, 1911-1966. II. Envoy (Dublin).

Note: Flann O'Brien has written under many names, including Brian Nolan. All works are brought together by LC under: O'Brien, Flann, 1911-1966.

Fig. 9.54. Rule 21.28B. Index entered under its own author.

Main entry → Schneider, Ben Ross, 1920-
for compiler   Index to The London stage, 1660-1800 / compiled, with
of index   an introduction by Ben Ross Schneider, Jr. ; foreword by
    George Winchester Stone, Jr.

Make added entry for serial indexed:

    I. London stage, 1660-1800. II. Title.

ADDED ENTRIES:
SELECTED RULES AND EXAMPLES

RULE 21.29. GENERAL RULE

The preceding rules have indicated the added entries required in typical cir-cumstances to supplement the main entry by providing additional bibliographical access to materials represented in the catalog. In general, added entries are sug-gested to provide access to other names of persons or titles under which a work may be known and under which catalog users might reasonably search. Persons, corporate bodies, and works related to the work at hand are considered, provid-ing these are openly stated in the work. It is a matter of local library policy to establish whether or not to make all required added entries, a decision that must be related to the extent of the collection, the needs it serves, and some economic considerations.

It is prescribed here that if the cataloger believes an added entry is needed, and if the reason for an added entry is not clear from the body of the description, a note should be provided to justify the added entry.

An option provides for explanatory references in place of certain added en-tries (as in rule 26.5); the Library of Congress is not applying this option. (*CSB* 8: 12)

LC prescribes the following order for added entries:

"1) Personal name;

2) Personal name/title;

3) Corporate name;

4) Corporate name/title;

5) Uniform title (all instances of works entered under title);

6) Title traced as Title-period;

7) Title traced as Title-colon, followed by a title;

8) Series." (*CSB* 12: 24)

LC has given guidelines in addition to those in *AACR2R* for making added entries for audiovisual materials and for sound recordings. These should be con-sulted when appropriate. (*CSB* 45: 32-34)

RULE 21.30. SPECIFIC RULES

21.30A-21.30H, 21.30K, 21.30M. These specific rules for added entries for collaborators, writers, editors and compilers, corporate bodies, other related persons or bodies, related works, other relationships, translators, illustrators, and analytical entries have been touched on in the rules for choice of main entry. When particular guidance is needed for one of these cases, these rules in *AACR2R* should be consulted. One should also consult LC rule interpretations for rule 21.30E, Corporate bodies (*CSB* 13: 26-27); rule 21.30F, Other related persons or bodies (*CSB* 47: 47); rule 21.30G, Related works (*CSB* 28: 16-17); rule 21.30H, Other relationships (*CSB* 45: 34); and rule 21.30M, Analytical entries (*CSB* 45: 46-47). *See* Figs. 9.55 and 9.57 (page 218).

Two added entry rules are used with such frequency that they warrant special mention:

21.30J. Titles

There are only four instances in which an added entry for a title proper (that is not a main entry) should not be made:

> "a) the title proper is essentially the same as the main entry heading or a reference to that heading

or b) the title proper has been composed by the cataloguer

or c) in a catalogue in which name-title and subject entries are interfiled, the title proper is identical with a subject heading assigned to the work, or a direct reference to that subject heading

or d) a conventionalized uniform title has been used as the uniform title for a musical work (*see* 25.25-25.35)."[11]

See Figs. 9.55-9.57.

Added entries should also be made for any other version of the title (e.g., cover title) that differs significantly (according to rule 21.2A) from the title proper.

LC does not apply restrictions a) and c) in the above list. An extensive rule interpretation gives guidelines for making title added entries and for tracing them. Guidance is also given for tracing spelled-out forms of abbreviations, numerals, etc., as well as the non-spelled-out forms. (*CSB* 48: 13-21)

21.30L. Series

An added entry is made for a series on each record for each work in the series if it is judged to be a useful access point. Adding the numeric or other designation to each added entry is optional. This option is applied at the Library of Congress. (*CSB* 47: 47-48) *See* Fig. 9.56 (page 218).

Fig. 9.55. Rule 21.30D. Added entry for editor.

⟶ Hollindale, Peter.
Shakespeare, William, 1564-1616.
    As you like it / [by William Shakespeare] ; edited by Peter Hollindale

Added entry noted in tracing:

    I. Hollindale, Peter. II. Title.

Fig. 9.56. Rule 21.30L. Added entry for series.

⟶ Studies in folklore ; 2.
Dundes, Alan.
    Analytic essays in folklore / by Alan Dundes

Use of series area:

    — (Studies in folklore ; 2)

Added entry noted in tracing:

    I. Title. II. Series.

Fig. 9.57. Rule 21.30K1. Added entry for translator.

⟶ Wiemann, Rudolph.
Busch, Wilhelm, 1832-1908.
    The bees : a fairy tale / by Wilhelm Busch ; translated by Rudolph Wiemann

Notes providing information on translation and summary:

    Translation of: Schnurrdiburr.
    Verse.
    Summary: Relates in verse the adventures and misadventures of a hive of bees and the bee keeper, his daughter, and their neighbors.

Added entry noted in tracing:

    I. Wiemann, Rudolph. II. Title.

According to *AACR2R* series added entries are not made if the series shares only common physical characteristics or if the series numbering appears to be only publisher's stock control numbers.

For a number of years LC placed certain additional restrictions on tracing series, but at the end of 1989 a decision was made to begin tracing every series.[12] The cataloger should still consult LC's rule interpretation for assistance with the form of series added entry tracings. (*CSB* 47: 48-49)

SPECIAL RULES:
SELECTED RULES AND EXAMPLES

Certain Legal Publications

RULE 21.31. LAWS, ETC.

21.31A. Scope

This rule is applied to legislative enactments and decrees that have the force of law except for the following cases, which are treated in later rules: administrative regulations (rule 21.32), constitutions and charters (rule 21.33), court rules (rule 21.34), and treaties (rule 21.35).

21.31B. Laws of modern jurisdictions

21.31B1. Laws governing one jurisdiction

Laws governing one jurisdiction are entered under the heading for the jurisdiction they govern, with added entries for persons and corporate bodies (other than legislative bodies) that compiled or issued the laws. A uniform title is added as instructed in rule 25.15A (*see* chapter 13 of this text). *See* Fig. 9.58.

Fig. 9.58. Rule 21.31B1. Laws governing a single jurisdiction.

[1] Name of jurisdiction

[2] Uniform title, *see* rule 25.15A

United States. [2]
    [Tax reduction act of 1975]
    Tax reduction act of 1975, P.L. 94-12, as signed by the President on March 29, 1975 : law and explanation. — Chicago : Commerce Clearing House, [1975]

Make added entry for corporate body issuing or compiling the law:

    I. Commerce Clearing House. II. Title.

21.31B2. Laws governing more than one jurisdiction

A compilation of laws governing more than one jurisdiction is treated as a collection (*see* rule 21.7).

RULE 21.32. ADMINISTRATIVE REGULATIONS, ETC.

The purpose of this rule is to distinguish between administrative regulations that are promulgated by government agencies under authority granted by one or more laws (as in the United States) and those that are from jurisdictions in which such regulations are laws (as in the United Kingdom and Canada). The former are entered under the promulgating agency, while the latter are entered as instructed in rule 21.31. *See* Figs. 9.59 and 9.60.

Fig. 9.59. Rule 21.32. U.S. administrative regulation entered under promulgating agency.

Main entry under promulgating agency

United States. Internal Revenue Service.
    Estate tax regulations under the Internal Revenue Code of 1954 / [United States Treasury Department, Internal Revenue Service]

Make added entry under heading for uniform title for authorizing law:

    I. United States. [Internal Revenue Code of 1954]. II. Title.

Fig. 9.60. Rule 21.32. U.K. administrative regulation entered under the jurisdiction.

Main entry under jurisdiction

Great Britain.
    [Army Code No. 13206]
    The Queen's regulations for the Army, 1975 / United Kingdom, Ministry of Defence

Make added entry for promulgating agency:

    I. Great Britain. Ministry of Defence. II. Title.

It should be noted that although *AACR2R* uses *United Kingdom* instead of *Great Britain* in all its examples, LC and other national libraries have decided to continue using *Great Britain* on their records. See the discussion in chapter 11 of this text on page 249.

RULE 21.33. CONSTITUTIONS, CHARTERS, AND OTHER FUNDA-MENTAL LAWS

21.33A. Main entry for a constitution, charter, or other fundamental law of a jurisdiction is the jurisdiction. *See* Fig. 9.61.

Fig. 9.61. Rule 21.33A. Entry for constitution.

Political ———▶Wyoming.
jurisidction   Constitution of the State of Wyoming, adopted in convention at Cheyenne, Wyoming, September 30, 1889, including all amendments adopted to Nov. 2, 1976 / compiled by Linda Mosley

Make added entry for compiler:

        I. Mosley, Linda.

RULE 21.35. TREATIES, INTERGOVERNMENTAL AGREEMENTS, ETC.

21.35A. International treaties, etc.
A treaty between one national government and two others is given main entry for the government that is the only one on its side. Other types of treaties between two or three national governments are given main entry for the government whose heading is first in English alphabetic order. (*See* rule 24.3E for establishment of each heading.) Added entries are made for the other governments. A uniform title is also made according to rule 25.16B1.
A treaty among more than three national governments is given main entry under title—either title proper or uniform title according to rule 25.16B2. *See* Fig. 9.62.

Fig. 9.62. Rule 21.35A1. Treaty involving two countries.

1
¹Entry under ◤France.   ◢2
country alpha-   [Treaties, etc. United States, 1984 Jan. 3]
betically first   Atomic energy, radioactive waste management : arrange-
²Uniform title ment between the United States of America and France, signed
for main and at Washington and Paris January 3 and 10, 1984.
added entries

Make added entry for the second named country: ◢2

        1. United States. Treaties, etc. France, 1984 Jan. 3. II.
        Title. ◀——

Certain Religious Publications

RULE 21.37. SACRED SCRIPTURES

Main entry for a work that is accepted as sacred scripture by a religious group is title. The uniform title is constructed according to rules 25.17-25.18. Added entries are made for up to three persons associated with the work. *See* Fig. 9.63.

Fig. 9.63. Rule 21.37. Sacred scripture entered under uniform title.

Uniform title ↖Tipiṭaka. Suttapiṭaka. English. Selections.
main entry   Some sayings of the Buddha, according to the Pali canon /
             translated [from the Pali] by F.L. Woodward ; with an
             introduction by Christmas Humphreys

Make added entries for persons associated with the work:

I. Woodward, F. L. (Frank Lee), 1870 or 71-1952.
II. Humphreys, Christmas, 1901-   . III. Tipitaka. Vinayapiṭaka.
English. Selections.   IV. Title.

RULE 21.39. LITURGICAL WORKS

21.39A. General rule

Liturgical works include "officially sanctioned or traditionally accepted texts of religious observance, books of obligatory prayers to be offered at stated times, calendars and manuals of performance of religious observances, and prayer books known as 'books of hours.' "[13] These are to be entered under the heading for the church or denomination that uses them. An appropriate uniform title, using rules 25.19-25.23, is added to the main entry. *See* Fig. 9.64.

Fig. 9.64. Rule 21.39A. Liturgical work entered under heading for the church.

[1]Corporate ↖Catholic Church. ↙[2]
heading for   [Rite of ordination. English]
specific church   The ordination of deacons, priests, and bishops : pro-
[2]Uniform   visional text prepared by the International Committee on
title   English in the Liturgy, approved for interim use by the
             Bishops' Committee on the Liturgy, National Conference of
             Catholic Bishops, and confirmed by the Apostolic See

Make added entry for title:

I. Title.

21.39C. Jewish liturgical works

Main entry for a Jewish liturgical work is title, with the uniform title being constructed according to rules 25.21-25.22. An added entry is made for a body that makes special use of the work. *See* Fig. 9.65 (page 222).

Fig. 9.65. Rule 21.39C. Jewish liturgical work entered under uniform title.

Main entry ──► Maḥzor (1972). English & Hebrew.
under uniform   Maḥzor for Rosh Hashanah and Yom Kippur : a prayer
title   book for the Days of Awe / edited by Jules Harlow. — New
                  York : Rabbinical Assembly, [1972]

Make added entry for editor and for body that uses the work:

I. Harlow, Jules. II. Rabbinical Assembly of America.

NOTES

[1]*AACR2R*, p. 2 (paragraph 0.5).

[2]*AACR2R*, p. 2 (paragraph 0.5).

[3]Richard P. Smiraglia, "Authority Control and the Extent of Derivative Bibliographic Relationships," Ph.D. dissertation in progress, University of Chicago, draft, 1989.

[4]For example, see Seymour Lubetzky, "The Fundamentals of Bibliographic Cataloging and *AACR 2*," *in* International Conference on AACR 2, Florida State University, 1979, *The Making of a Code* (Chicago, American Library Association, 1980), pp. 18-23; Michael Gorman, "*AACR 2*: Main Themes," *in* ibid., pp. 45-46; Elizabeth L. Tate, "Examining the 'Main' in Main Entry Headings," *in* ibid., pp. 109-140.

[5]*AACR2R*, p. 312.

[6]*AACR2R*, p. 312.

[7]*AACR2R*, p. 321.

[8]*AACR2R*, p. 338.

[9]*AACR2R*, p. 340.

[10]"AACR 2 Options to Be Followed by the Library of Congress, Chapters 1-2, 12, 21-26," *Library of Congress Information Bulletin*, 37 (July 21, 1978): 425.

[11]*AACR2R*, p. 356.

[12]Typescript circulated at the ALA midwinter conference, January 1990.

[13]*AACR2R*, p. 376.

SUGGESTED READING

Chan, Lois Mai. *Cataloging and Classification*. New York, McGraw-Hill, 1981. Chapter 4.

Hagler, Ronald. *The Bibliographic Record and Information Technology*. 2nd ed. Chicago, American Library Association, 1991. pp. 64-74.

Maxwell, Margaret F. *Handbook for AACR2, 1988 Revision*. Chicago, American Library Association, 1989. Chapter 13.

Tate, Elizabeth L. "Examining the 'Main' in Main Entry Headings," *in* International Conference on AACR 2, Florida State University, 1979, *The Making of a Code*. Chicago, American Library Association, 1980. pp. 109-140.

Form of Headings for Persons

10

INTRODUCTION

The previous chapter dealt with choice of access points; this chapter and the next three chapters will present rules for the form of entry regardless of whether the access point is to be a main entry or an added entry. Once it has been decided what is to be the main entry or heading and what are to be added entries, it must be determined how those entries are to be displayed or written on the record. Choice of entry rules deal with who or what is to be the entry; form of entry rules deal with how an entry is to be written or recorded.

Most headings in American library catalogs consist of a personal name entered under the surname followed by forenames (like the white pages of a telephone directory). However, as the following rules for headings for persons show, there are certain complexities that must be considered in a library catalog. Rules — i.e., principles and practices — must be followed consistently for those persons known by more than one name. There are many possible instances when a person may be known and/or even write under more than one name. Some authors deliberately disguise their real names and write under a pseudonym or pen name — such as Charles Lutwidge Dodgson, who wrote his children's fantasies under the pseudonym of Lewis Carroll. Others consistently write under initialized forenames (e.g., H. G. Wells), while still others, such as Bernard Shaw, consistently omit one of their forenames. If someone's original name is written in a nonroman alphabet, different romanization systems may create different spellings of the name (such as Chekhov, Chekov, or Tchekhov). A married woman has two possible surnames — her birth surname and her husband's surname. Further, compound surnames — i.e., surnames consisting of two or more parts — create problems. Granville-Barker is an example of a compound, hyphenated English surname. Prefixes to surnames create another type of compound surname. De Gaulle and von Goethe are examples of surnames with prefixes; O'Brien and MacPherson are other examples. Individuals who are members of nobility may have two names — a titled name and a common surname (such as Lord Byron, George Gordon Byron). Certain individuals are known under their bynames or forenames rather than their surnames; these include royalty (Elizabeth II), saints (Joan of Arc), popes (Paul VI), and individuals in ancient and medieval periods prior to the development of surnames (Horace). Bynames or forenames often exist in different forms in different languages (such as Horace in English, but Horatius in Latin). The purpose of this chapter in this text is to demonstrate the general rules used to resolve all of these problems. For more complicated problems of personal names, the student should carefully examine *AACR2R*, chapter 22.

The *AACR2R* chapter is divided into four sections, the first three of which suggest the order of the steps taken by the cataloger to establish the form in which the name will appear as a heading in the catalog. The first section, rules 22.1-22.3, s entitled "Choice of name." This "choice" is a separate action from "choice of access points," discussed in the preceding chapter. Once it has been decided through choice of access points that a person will be given an access point, rules 22.1-22.3 prescribe the choice of name when that person has used more than one name or different manifestations of the same name. After making a choice of name, the cataloger uses the next section, rules 22.4-22.11, "Entry element," to decide which element of the chosen name will be the first and in what order the other elements will follow. The third step is to make any additions to the name that may be necessitated because of the kind of name involved (rules 22.12-22.16) or because two or more names are identical (rules 22.17-22.20). The fourth section of *AACR2R*, chapter 22, is "Special Rules for Names in Certain Languages." These are for selected languages in which heading form does not follow the typical "western" style.

It should be noted that the rules in this chapter apply to the choice and form of personal names whether they are access points because of some kind of responsibility for the creation of a work or because they are the subject of a work. That is, a personal name subject heading is constructed in the same manner and according to the same rules as is a personal name main or added entry heading for an author, painter, performer, etc.

The Library of Congress adopted *AACR2* for new names beginning January 2, 1981. It also abandoned the policy of superimposition at that time so that a number of already established name forms were changed to agree with the prescribed *AACR2* form. Superimposition was a policy established with the adoption of *AACR1* in 1967. Under that policy any name that had been established prior to *AACR1* continued to be used on new cataloging as already established, even if its form according to *AACR1* would have been different. Even though this policy was officially abandoned with the adoption of *AACR2*, in certain defined categories, established names were considered to be "*AACR2* compatible," and the established form continued to be used even on new records. However, after the initial impact of adopting *AACR2* was over, it became counterproductive to continue the "compatible" policy, because it took more time to decide on such headings than to change the old forms. Therefore, the "compatible" policy was abandoned on September 1, 1982.[1] All pre-*AACR2* headings coded as compatible between January 2, 1981, and September 1, 1982, remain in that form at LC. Thus, it is useful to be aware of some of the major cases. These are summarized with examples in an issue of *Cataloging Service Bulletin*, which should be consulted by anyone who works with cataloging copy from LC.[2]

A heading created using this chapter is coded 100, 600, 700, or 800 in the MARC format, depending upon whether it functions as a main entry, a subject heading, or an added entry or begins a series tracing.

CHOICE OF NAME:
SELECTED RULES AND EXAMPLES

RULE 22.1. GENERAL RULE

22.1A. The name by which a person is commonly known is the one that should be chosen, whether that name be the person's real name, nickname, pseudonym, shortened form of name, or other form of name customarily used by a person. Thus the following choices might be made:

Pseudonym
> Mathew James
> *not* birth name: James D. Lucey

Nickname
> Billy Graham
> *not* William Franklin Graham

Name in religion
> Maria Teresa dell'Eucaristia
> *not* birth name: Maria Teresa Tosi

Short form of name
> Virginia Knight Nelson
> *not* Alyce Virginia Knight Nelson

Real name
> Sally Benson
> *not* pseudonym: Esther Evarts

22.1B. The name by which a person is commonly known is to be determined from chief sources of information of works in that person's language. This, of course, may not be possible if the person is only a subject of works or creates only nonverbal works (e.g., unsigned paintings). In these cases the name is to be determined from reference sources in the person's language or from the person's country of residence or activity. A footnote to this rule in *AACR2R* indicates that "reference sources" include books and articles written about a person.

A rule interpretation from LC indicates that chief sources used for this rule may be from works published both during and after a person's lifetime. There are special instructions, also, about treatment of music composers, names without forenames, names containing abbreviations rather than initials, and other more unusual situations. (*CSB* 44: 38-41)

Throughout this chapter of *AACR2R* there are references to "commonly known" and "predominant" when referring to choosing one name or one form of name. *AACR2R* defines predominant name as, "The name or form of name of a person or corporate body that appears most frequently (1) in the person's works or works issued by the corporate body, or (2) in reference sources, in that order of preference."[3] At the time of implementation of *AACR2* in 1981 there was indication from those involved in its creation that "most frequently" should not be taken to mean 51 percent of the instances; yet there were no guidelines otherwise. For a number of years, the Library of Congress had used 75 percent in interpreting the "fullness of name" rule. That is, until a name appeared in a different form in an author's works 75 percent of the time (counting works by the person issued after the person's death as well as during the person's lifetime), the form of heading was not changed. They continued to apply this concept with *AACR2*, except the percentage was changed to 66⅔ percent during the early years of *AACR2* and later was changed to 80 percent. They are continuing this policy with *AACR2R*. A note with the interpretation that gives the figure of 80 percent to be used with the rule for fullness (22.3A) cautions that this figure is to be applied only to rule 22.3A—that no formula has been assigned to the other rules. (*CSB* 44: 45) However, other libraries might still use this as a guideline for changes. When a name is first established, "predominant" could be 51 percent or more; but a change would not be called for until the name had appeared differently 80 percent of the time.

22.1C-22.1D.   Terms and punctuation associated with a name

These rules refer to inclusion of titles of nobility or honor, diacritical marks, and hyphens. At first glance it may not be clear how these relate to choice of name. However, the intention here is to give rules for choosing those elements that should be included in the heading. The order in which these elements appear is the subject of rules 22.4-22.17.

The principle again is to follow the form customarily used by the person. Titles, words, or phrases that commonly appear with the name are included as are accents, other diacritical marks, and hyphens used by the person, except that a hyphen that is used between a forename and a surname is not included.

RULE 22.2.   CHOICE AMONG DIFFERENT NAMES

Rules 22.2 and 22.3 give more specific guidelines for adhering to the principle stated in rule 22.1. Rules in 22.2 help choose among different names for the same person, and those in rule 22.3 help in the choice among different forms of the same name. Both may have to be used in a particular instance, because a name chosen from among different names may itself appear in varying degrees of fullness or with variant spellings. For example, once it has been decided that the name used should be George Novack, not William Warde, one then has to decide whether to use George Novack, George E. Novack, or George Edward Novack.

22.2A.   Predominant name

This rule applies only when a pseudonym is not involved. If a person is *known* by more than one name, and if there is a name that is clearly most common, it is used. If not, the following order of preference is used in making a choice:

"a)   the name that appears most frequently in the person's works

b)   the name that appears most frequently in reference sources

c)   the latest name."[4]

LC has issued a rule interpretation to be used for an author who simultaneously uses different forms of a *real* name. (*CSB* 44: 41) Another rule interpretation notes that if a person's name is shown with a nickname in quotation marks or parentheses, the nickname should be omitted in the heading. (*CSB* 43: 32)

22.2B. Pseudonyms

22.2B1. One pseudonym

When a person has used one pseudonym on all works, it is used for the heading, with a reference from the real name, if known. *See* Fig. 10.1.

Fig. 10.1. Rule 22.2B1. Entry under the one pseudonym used by the author.

Ford, Ford Madox, 1873-1939.
It was the nightingale / Ford Madox Ford

Note: Refer from[5] real name: Hueffer, Ford Madox.

22.2B2. Separate bibliographic identities

The concept in this rule was new with *AACR2R*. When works of one type always appear under one pseudonym and works of another type always appear under the person's real name or under another pseudonym, the person is considered to have established different bibliographic identities, and each separate group of works is given as heading the name used for that identity. The cataloger is instructed to consult also rule 22.2B3 if the person involved is contemporary. *See* Fig. 10.2.

Fig. 10.2. Rule 22.2B2. Entry under each name used by a person with separate bibliographic identities.

Entry under real name Clemens, Samuel Langhorne, 1835-1910.
Republican letters / by Samuel L. Clemens

Note on bibliographic record:

Articles published in the Chicago Republican in 1868.

Entry under pseudonym Twain, Mark, 1835-1910.
A Connecticut Yankee in King Arthur's court / Mark Twain

Note: References are made from each name to the other and to Snodgrass, Quintus Curtius, 1835-1910—another pseudonym used by this author.

The impetus for a rule establishing bibliographic identities came from those who were dissatisfied with the previous provision for entering all works of a person using two or more names under the name that had been used predominantly in the person's works or had become predominant in reference sources. The result was that the scholarly works written under a person's real name (e.g., Charles L. Dodgson) sometimes were entered under the name that person used on works of fiction (e.g., Lewis Carroll). In addition manuscript writings from a person's personal life (e.g., letters to family members) could be entered under a pseudonym used in published works. Establishing bibliographic identities solves these problems, and with advances in authority control in online systems, the need for pulling a person's works together in the same catalog drawer is no longer as urgent.

22.2B3. Contemporary authors

When a contemporary author uses more than one pseudonym or a real name and one or more pseudonyms, each work is given a heading based upon the name used in it. References are made to connect the names. *See* Fig. 10.3.

Fig. 10.3. Rule 22.2B3. Entry under each name used by a contemporary author.

Entry under pseudonym

Cross, Amanda, 1926-
Death in a tenured position / Amanda Cross

Entry under real name

Heilbrun, Carolyn G., 1926-
Hamlet's mother and other women / Carolyn G. Heilbrun

Note: References are made from each name to the other. It should be noted that if this author were not a contemporary, both names would still be used because of separate bibliographic identities. She writes mysteries under the pseudonym of Cross and literary criticism under her real name of Heilbrun.

When different editions of a work of a contemporary author have appeared with different names of the author, the name most often used should be the heading for all editions. If no one name is predominant, one should use the name that appears in the latest available edition. In all cases name-title references are made from the other name(s) used for editions of that work.

22.2B4. When a person who falls under rule 22.2B is not a contemporary and does not have separate bibliographic identities under different names, one name is chosen based on the following order of preference:

1) the name used in later editions of his or her works

2) the name most used in critical works

3) the name by which the person has come to be identified in reference sources.

References are made from other names not chosen.

In a rule interpretation for all of rule 22.2B, LC points out that the intent of this rule is that for contemporaries who use at least one pseudonym, there will be as many headings as there are names. For non-contemporaries, the same may be true, but only if the cataloger can establish that there are separate bibliographic identities. If such identities cannot be identified, then there will be only one heading for non-contemporaries, regardless of number of names. The rule interpretation then gives guidelines for identifying "contemporary" and "separate bibliographic identities." (*CSB* 47: 49-52)

22.2C. Change of name

When a person who has not used a pseudonym has changed his or her name or has acquired and become known by a title of nobility, the latest name should be used for the heading. *See* Fig. 10.4.

Fig. 10.4. Rule 22.2C. Entry under latest name used.

Latest name used

Cochrane, Pauline A. (Pauline Atherton), 1929-
 Improving LCSH for use in online catalogs : exercises for self-help with a selection of background readings / Pauline A. Cochrane

Note: Refer from Atherton, Pauline, 1929- , name used in writings before author's marriage.

RULE 22.3. CHOICE AMONG DIFFERENT FORMS OF THE SAME NAME

22.3A. Fullness

When a name is found in forms that vary in fullness, the form most commonly found should be used as the heading, with references from the other forms when they would be useful. *See* Fig. 10.5.

Fig. 10.5. Rule 22.3A. Name entered under form most commonly found.

Hamilton, John P.
 Predominant form: John P. Hamilton
 Occasional form: J.P. Hamilton
 Rare form: "Bud" Hamilton

Note: Because Hamilton is a common surname, the second forename, Peter, may be required in parentheses to distinguish between two identical names (*see* rule 22.18). Also, references may be needed from the two forms of name not chosen.

When a form cannot be decided upon as most common, *AACR2R* prescribes using the latest form; but if the latest form is in doubt, then use the fullest form. LC skips the possibility of "latest form" and goes directly to fullest form if one form cannot be determined to be most common. (*CSB* 46: 39)

LC's rule interpretation also suggests that if the name appears in two or more forms in the same work, one should choose the form in the chief source. If the name does not appear in the chief source, then a form in another prominent source should be used, if the name appears only once in a prominent source. Otherwise, the fullest form should be chosen. (*CSB* 46: 39-40)

LC applies the "80% rule" when a heading is already coded as "AACR" but subsequent items are received showing the name in a different form. If an established heading is coded "AACR2 compatible" LC generally will not reconsider the heading with exceptions made in a few instances (e.g., when an author has notified LC that another form of name is preferred). (*CSB* 46: 39-40) *See* Figs. 10.6 and 10.7.

Fig. 10.6. Rule 22.3A. Fullness—LC practice.

Established heading: Rouse, John Edward, 1942-
Has written later as: John E. Rouse
Heading coded "AACR2 compatible."
Established heading retained.

Fig. 10.7. Rule 22.3A. Fullness—LC practice.

Established heading: Sánchez E., Rodrigo.
Has now written over 80% as: Rodrigo Sánchez Enríquez
New heading: Sánchez Enríquez, Rodrigo.

22.3B. Language

22.3B1. Persons using more than one language

The heading for a person who writes in more than one language should be the form that corresponds to the language of most of the works. *See* Fig. 10.8.

Fig. 10.8. Rule 22.3B1. Entry for person using more than one language.

Names found on works: William More
Guillermo Mora
Lived and worked in both U.S. and Venezuela.
Most works in Spanish.
Entry: Mora, Guillermo.

If there is doubt about which language is used in most of the works, the form found most in reference sources of the person's country of residence or activity should be used. LC practice when reference sources cannot be found, or the person is not listed, is to use the form of the name in the person's native language but to change to another language if 80% of the works eventually use the name in that language. (*CSB* 47: 52)

Note: The choice made according to this rule may be altered by application of rules 22.3B2, 22.3B3, or 22.3C.

22.3B2. Names in vernacular and Greek or Latin forms

The heading for a name that appears in both Latin or Greek and the vernacular in reference sources and/or in the person's works should be given in the form found most often in reference sources. For cases of doubt, the Latin or Greek is chosen for persons active before 1400 A.D. and the vernacular for persons active after 1400. *See* Fig. 10.9 (page 232).

Fig. 10.9. Rule 22.3B2. Entry of name found in both the vernacular and Latin.

Name in vernacular: Dante Alighieri (with various spellings)
Name in Latin: Dantes Aligerius
Form most commonly found in reference sources: Dante Alighieri
Entry: Dante Alighieri, 1265-1321.

22.3B3.   Names written in the roman alphabet and established in an English form

The heading for a person entered under given name according to rule 22.8 or for a Roman of classical times should be the English form if an English form is well established in English-language reference sources. The vernacular or Latin is used in cases of doubt. *See* Fig. 10.10.

Fig. 10.10. Rule 22.3B3. Entry of name with established English form.

Name of saint in Latin: Justinus
Name in English-language reference sources: Justin
Entry: Justin, Martyr, Saint.

22.3B4.   Other names

The heading for all other names found in two or more languages is the form found most often in reference sources of the person's country of residence or activity. *See* Fig. 10.11.

Fig. 10.11. Rule 22.3B4. Entry of name that is found in different language forms.

Name on original work: John Boyer Noss
Name on translation of original work: Jān B. Nūs
Place of author's residence: U.S.
Entry: Noss, John Boyer.

22.3C.   Names written in a nonroman script

Names that must be romanized or transliterated present many problems. Some languages have a number of systems for romanization, and use of the different systems results in different spellings. In addition, there may be one or more English-language forms of some better known names. The rules in 22.3C give some guidance.

22.3C1.   Persons entered under given name, etc.

This rule, like 22.3B3, calls for entry under an English-language form, if one has become well established in English-language reference sources. (If more than one exists, choose the one that appears most frequently.) *See* Fig. 10.12. If there is no English form, or if one romanization cannot be determined to be predominant, the name should be romanized according to the cataloging agency's adopted romanization table.

Fig. 10.12. Rule 22.3C1. Entry of name originally in nonroman script—given name.

Romanizations of name: Movses Khorenat̂si
Moses Xorenc'i
English-language form of name: Moses of Khoren
Entry: Moses, of Khoren, 5th cent.

A single LC rule interpretation addresses both rule 22.3C1 and rule 22.3C2. LC's policy for nonroman alphabet names entered under a given name or a surname is to search the name in *Academic American Encyclopedia, The Encyclopedia Americana,* and *Encyclopaedia Britannica* (15th ed.). If the name is in all three sources in a single form, that form is used. If it varies, the form in *Encyclopaedia Britannica* is used. If it is not found in all three sources, the systematic romanization is used. An exception is made for persons entered under *given* name who are not found in all three sources because of specialized fame. In such cases major specialized encyclopedias, such as *New Catholic Encyclopedia,* are used. Another exception is for persons of very recent fame. For these, yearbooks to the encyclopedias and indexes to major newspapers are consulted. (*CSB* 40: 29-31)

22.3C2. Persons entered under surname

Unlike the preceding rule, this one directs the cataloger to romanize a name entered under surname according to the table adopted by the cataloging agency. References are made from other romanized forms. If a name is found only in romanized form in the works involved, that form is used.

An alternative rule is given for 22.3C2: An English form, well established in English-language reference sources, may be used for the heading. This corresponds to the treatment of persons entered under given name, but is counter to the principle of entry under the name elements most commonly found in writers' works or in reference works in the language or country of residence or activity for persons other than writers. The Library of Congress is following the alternative rule. (*CSB* 40: 29-31) Their policy for application of the alternative rule is discussed above under discussion of rule 22.3C1. *See* Fig. 10.13.

Fig. 10.13. Rule 22.3C2—Alternative rule. Entry of name originally in nonroman script—surname.

Dostoyevsky, Fyodor, 1821-1881.

Entry in romanized form found in English-language reference sources

[Brat'i̐a Karamazovy. English]

The brothers Karamazov ; The brothers Karamazov : a novel in four parts with epilogue / Fyodor Dostoevsky ; translated and annotated by Richard Pevear and Larissa Volokhonsky

Note: Romanized form appearing in the item: Fyodor Dostoevsky

Systematic romanization according to LC's adopted tables:
Dostoevskiĭ, Fedor

Form most often found in English-language reference sources:
Dostoyevsky, Fyodor

Refer from:
Dostoevsky, Fyodor.
Dostoevskiĭ, Fedor.

It should be noted that the alternative rule makes no provision for names for which there are no entries in English-language reference sources, unless the person uses Hebrew or Yiddish, in which case the romanized form found in the person's works is called for. Otherwise, when there are no entries in English-language sources, presumably, one should use the provision given in rule 22.3C1 for persons entered under given name: "If no English romanization is found ... romanize the name according to the table for the language adopted by the cataloguing agency."[6] *See* Fig. 10.14.

Fig. 10.14.

Romanizations found in chief sources of information, but not in reference sources:
Maĭsiŭte, Regina
Maciŭte, Regina [romanization according to adopted table]
Entry: Maciŭte, Regina
Refer from: Maĭsiŭte, Regina.

22.3D. Spelling
If variant spellings occur that are not the result of different romanizations, the form that represents an official orthographic change should be used, if this is applicable. Otherwise, one should choose the predominant spelling, or, in case of doubt, the spelling found in the first item cataloged. *See* Fig. 10.15.

Fig. 10.15. Rule 22.3D. Entry of name with variant spellings.

Variant spellings found: Thomas Decker
Thomas Dekker
Thomas Deckar
Predominant spelling: Thomas Dekker
Entry: Dekker, Thomas, ca. 1572-1632.

ENTRY ELEMENT:
SELECTED RULES AND EXAMPLES

RULE 22.4. GENERAL RULE

22.4A. When a person's name consists of more than one part, a choice must be made about which part will be the entry element. In general the entry element is the one that would usually be used in authoritative alphabetic lists in the person's own country or language. "Authoritative" is defined as meaning "who's who" type publications, not telephone directory type. However, if it is known that the person prefers some other entry element than would be the usual usage for that language or country, the person's preference is followed.

22.4B. Order of elements
The entry element is chosen according to rules 22.5-22.9, but the order of other elements is given here.

22.4B1-22.4B2. If the entry element is the first element, the name is entered in direct order. If that first element is a surname, it is followed by a comma. *See* Fig. 10.16.

Fig. 10.16. Rule 22.4B1-22.4B2. Name entered under first element, which is surname.

Name on chief source of information: Wu Hsin-chung
Surname: Wu
Entry: Wu, Hsin-chung.

22.4B3. If the entry element is not the first one, the names preceding it are transposed to follow the entry element and a comma. *See* Fig. 10.17.

Fig. 10.17. Rule 22.4B3. Name entered under third element, which is surname.

Name on chief source of information: Jill S. Slattery
Surname entry element: Slattery
Entry: Slattery, Jill S., 1943-

22.4B4. If the entry element is the proper name in a title of nobility, according to rule 22.6, the personal name follows in direct order, and the term of rank follows that. *See* Fig. 10.18.

Fig. 10.18. Rule 22.4B4. Name entered under proper name of a title of nobility.

Name on chief source of information: Thomas Pitt, Baron
   Camelford
Entry element: Camelford
Entry: Camelford, Thomas Pitt, Baron, 1737-1793.
Refer from: Pitt, Thomas, Baron Camelford.

RULE 22.5.   ENTRY UNDER SURNAME

22.5A.   General rule

If a name contains a surname, the entry element should be the surname unless one of the following rules provides for a different entry element. (*See also* rules 22.6, 22.10, and 22.28.) When a surname is represented by an initial, and another element of the name is in full, the initial is treated as a surname. This is in contrast with the provisions of rule 22.10 for entry of names that consist only of initials. *See* Figs. 10.16 and 10.17.

22.5B. Element other than the first treated as a surname

A name that functions as a surname, even though it is not really a surname, is treated as if it were. *See* Fig. 10.19.

Fig. 10.19. Rule 22.5B. Entry under element treated as a surname.

Name on chief source of information: Muhammad Sa'īd
Bāyirlī
Entry: Bāyirlī, Muhammad Sa'īd.
Refer from: Muhammad Sa'īd Bāyirlī.

22.5C. Compound surnames

22.5C1. Preliminary rule

Compound surnames consist of two or more proper names. The rules under rule 22.5C treat these and also some names that appear to be compound surnames. The rules are applied in the order given. References should be made from elements of a compound surname not chosen for entry.

22.5C2. Preferred or established form known

The entry element for a compound surname of a person with a known preference should be the person's preferred entry element. Otherwise, the entry element should be the element under which it is given in reference sources from the person's country or in the person's language. *See* Fig. 10.20 and Fig. 10.25 under rule 22.5C5 (page 237).

Fig. 10.20. Rule 22.5C2. Entry under preferred or established form of compound name.

Lloyd George, David, 1863-1945.
War memoirs of David Lloyd George

Note: Refer from: George, David Lloyd. George is his correct paternal surname.

22.5C3. Hyphenated surnames

Compound surnames that are hyphenated (even if only sometimes) should be entered under the first element. *See* Fig. 10.21.

Fig. 10.21. Rule 22.5C3. Entry under hyphenated surname.

Entry under
first part of
hyphenated
surname

Ward Lock's encyclopedia / edited by Harold
Boswell-Taylor

I. Boswell-Taylor, Harold.

Note: Refer from: Taylor, Harold Boswell- .

22.5C4. Other compound surnames, except those of married women whose surname consists of surname before marriage and husband's surname

Compound surnames remaining, if the foregoing rules have not sufficed, should be entered under the first element, with the exception of Portuguese names, which should be entered under the last element. *See* Fig. 10.22.

Fig. 10.22. Rule 22.5C4. Entry of "other compound surnames."

Torres Ramírez, Blanca.
    Las relaciones cubanosovieticas / por Blanca Torres
Ramírez

Note: Refer from: Ramírez, Blanca Torres.

22.5C5. Other compound surnames. Married women whose surname consists of surname before marriage and husband's surname
    If the woman's language is Czech, French, Hungarian, Italian, or Spanish, the entry element is the first element of the compound surname. In all other cases, the husband's surname (usually the last element) is the entry element. Hyphenated names, however, are treated above under rule 22.5C3. *See* Figs. 10.23 and 10.24.

Fig. 10.23. Rule 22.5C5. Entry of married French-speaking woman.

Entry under
surname
before
marriage

Mendès France, Joan.
    L'anglais juridique et le droit anglais : textes bilinques et exercises / Joan Mendès France et Hélène Bourrouilhou

Note: Refer from: France, Joan Mendès.

Fig. 10.24. Rule 22.5C5. Entry of married English-speaking woman.

Graves, Kathleen George.
    Our Union County heritage : a historical and biographical album of Union County, people, places, and events / by Kathleen George Graves and Winnie Palmer McDonald

Entry under ⟶ I. McDonald, Winnie Palmer.
husband's
name

However, as in earlier rules, if a married woman is known to prefer some other entry element than prescribed here, rule 22.5C2 takes precedence. *See* Fig. 10.25.

Fig. 10.25. Rule 22.5C2. Entry of married English-speaking woman under preferred entry element.

Entry under
surname
before
marriage

Rutherford Carr, Deborah.
    Individuals / by Deborah Rutherford Carr and Thomas J.
Carr

Note: Author is known to prefer combination of surname before marriage and husband's surname as compound surname.
    Refer from: Carr, Deborah Rutherford.

22.5D. Surnames with separately written prefixes

LC's rule interpretation should be consulted for guidance on placement of constituent parts of a name in headings and references once the appropriate entry element has been determined according to the following rules. (*CSB* 23: 31-33)

22.5D1. Articles and prepositions

Names that contain an article or a preposition or a combination of the two as part of the surname should be entered under the element that would normally be used in alphabetical lists from the person's country or in the person's language.

In *AACR2R* this rule contains many specific examples of names in different languages. Only the most basic of those rules are cited here.

DUTCH. Dutch names are entered under the part following the prefix with one exception: a name with the prefix *ver* is entered under the prefix. *See* Fig. 10.26.

Fig. 10.26. Rule 22.5D1. Entry of Dutch name.

Schuit, Steven R.
    Dutch business law : legal, accounting, and tax aspects of business in the Netherlands / by Steven R. Schuit and Jan M.

Entry under part follow-ing prefix   van der Beek

    I. Beek, Jan M. van der.

Note: Refer from: Van der Beek, Jan M.

ENGLISH. English names are entered under the prefix. *See* Fig. 10.27.

Fig. 10.27. Rule 22.5D1. Entry of English name beginning with prefix.

Nuclear or not? : choices for our energy future : a Royal Institution forum / edited by Gerald Foley and Ariane van Buren

Entry under prefix   I. Van Buren, Ariane.

Note: Refer from: Buren, Ariane van.

FRENCH. French names in which the prefix is an article or a contraction of an article and a preposition are entered under the prefix. *See* Fig. 10.28.

Fig. 10.28. Rule 22.5D1. Entry of French name beginning with article.

Entry under the article   Le Bihan, Alain.
    Francs-maçons et ateliers parisiens de la Grande Loge de France au XVIIIe siècle : 1760-1795 / Alain Le Bihan. — Paris : Bibliothèque nationale, 1973.

Note: Refer from: Bihan, Alain Le.

All other French names with prefixes are entered under the element following the prefix. *See* Figs. 10.29 and 10.30.

Fig. 10.29. Rule 22.5D1. Entry of French names that include prepositions.

Entry under part of name following the preposition

Richemont, Jean de.
L'intégration du droit communautaire dans l'ordre juridique interne : article 177 du Traité de Rome / Jean de Richemont ; préface par Marcel Ancel

Fig. 10.30.

Entry under the article following the preposition

La Fontaine, Jean de, 1621-1695.
Fables / La Fontaine ; préface et commentaires de Pierre Clarac

Note: Refer from: Fontaine, Jean de la.

GERMAN. German names are entered like French names. Articles or contractions of articles and prepositions are entry elements. *See* Fig. 10.31.

Fig. 10.31. Rule 22.5D1. Entry of German name under prefix.

Vom Scheidt, Jürgen, 1940-
Alles über Rauschdrogen / Jürgen vom Scheidt, Wolfgang Schmidbauer

Note: Refer from: Scheidt, Jürgen vom.

All other German names with prefixes are entered under the element following the prefix. *See* Fig. 10.32.

Fig. 10.32. Rule 22.5D1. Entry of German name with preposition.

Entry under part of name following the preposition

Weizsäcker, Carl Christian von.
Modern capital theory and the concept of exploitation / Carl Christian von Weizsäcker

ITALIAN. Modern Italian names are entered under the prefix. *See* Fig. 10.33.

Fig. 10.33. Rule 22.5D1. Entry of modern Italian name.

Entry under the prefix

De Filippo, Peppino.
La lettera di mammà : farsa in due parti / Peppino De Filippo

Note: Refer from: Filippo, Peppino de.

In order to determine the correct entry element for medieval and early modern Italian names, reference sources should be consulted. Example:

Medici, Lorenzo de'

SPANISH. Spanish names that have a prefix that consists only of an article are entered under the prefix. Otherwise, a name is entered under the element following the prefix. *See* Fig. 10.34.

Fig. 10.34. Rule 22.5D1. Entry of Spanish name.

Entry under
part of name
following
prefix

Lorenzo, Pedro de.
 Libros de la vocación / Pedro de Lorenzo

22.5D2-22.5E. Other prefixes
 In all languages, when the prefix is not an article or a preposition or a combination of the two, or when the prefix is hyphenated or combined with the name, the entry element should be the prefix. *See* Fig. 10.35.

Fig. 10.35. Rule 22.5D2-22.5E. Entry under the prefix. "Mac" is an attributive prefix.

MacIntyre, Elisabeth.
 The purple mouse / by Elisabeth MacIntyre

RULE 22.6. ENTRY UNDER TITLE OF NOBILITY
 If a person is commonly known by a title of nobility, the proper name in that title should be the entry element. This rule applies to persons who use titles rather than surnames in their works or, if there are no textual works to consult, to those persons who are listed by title in reference sources that do not list all members of the nobility under title. The proper name in the title is followed by the personal name in direct order, and the personal name is followed by the term of rank. Unused forenames are not included. A reference is made from the personal surname unless it is the same as the proper name in the title. *See* Fig. 10.18. If the person does not use a term of rank, and the proper name in the title is used as a surname, then the personal surname is omitted (e.g., John Julius Norwich was born John Julius Duff Cooper and became Viscount Norwich, but the name appears as John Julius Norwich). If the title includes a territorial designation that is an integral part of the title, it should be included. *See* Fig. 10.36.
 This rule is closely related to rules 22.4B4 and 22.12. The three result in the same form of name, but they approach this type of name from the three viewpoints of order of elements, entry element, and additions to names.

Fig. 10.36. Rule 22.6. Entry under title of nobility.

Joint Advisory Committee on Pets in Society.
 Dogs in the United Kingdom : report of the Joint Advisory Committee on Pets in Society

Note clarifying statement of responsibility:
 Chairman: Lord Houghton of Sowerby.

Make added entry under title of nobility with territorial designation:
 I. Houghton of Sowerby, Douglas Houghton, Baron,
1898-

RULE 22.8. ENTRY UNDER GIVEN NAME, ETC.

If a person is not identified by a title of nobility and the name does not include a surname, the entry element should be the part of the name that is the entry element in reference sources. Any words or phrases that are commonly associated with the name in that person's works or in reference sources should be included, preceded by a comma. *See* Fig. 10.37.

Fig. 10.37. Rule 22.8. Entry of a name under given name.

Paul, of Aleppo, Archdeacon, fl. 1654-1666.
The travels of Macarius, patriarch of Antioch / written by his attendant archdeacon, Paul of Aleppo

Specific parts of this rule address names that include a patronymic and names of royal persons. Library of Congress rule interpretations give guidelines for more complicated given name entries and should be consulted for more guidance. (*CSB* 13: 29; *CSB* 44: 46)

22.10-22.11.

These rules give instructions for entry elements when all one has for a name are initials, letters, numerals, or phrases. These are to be entered in direct order if they do not contain a real name. Example: One who has tested the receipts (*see* Fig. 9.12 in the preceding chapter). More specialized rules cover entry of phrases that contain names, and these should be consulted when needed.

ADDITIONS TO NAMES: SELECTED RULES AND EXAMPLES

General

RULE 22.12. TITLES OF NOBILITY AND TERMS OF HONOUR

22.12A. If a nobleman or noblewoman is not entered under title according to rule 22.6, but the title or a part of the title usually appears with the name, the title of nobility should be added in the vernacular to the personal name. *See* Fig. 10.38.

Fig. 10.38. Rule 22.12A. Addition of title of nobility to given name entry.

Title of   John, of Gaunt, Duke of Lancaster, 1340-1399.
nobility   John of Gaunt's register, 1379-1383 / edited from the original record by the late Eleanor C. Lodge and Robert Somerville

22.12B. British terms of honour

There are four British terms of honour that are to be added to a name if they usually appear with the name in the person's works or in reference sources. They are: Sir, Dame, Lord, Lady. Note that the terms "Hon." and "bart." formerly used in headings are not now authorized. LC no longer uses them and revises existing headings that contain them. (*CSB* 11: 25)

In *AACR2R* this rule goes on to distinguish the times when such terms should be added after the forenames and when they should be inserted before forenames. However, the Library of Congress, because of the incapability of their computer system to handle these as nonfiling characters, places all terms of honour and address after the forenames. (*CSB* 18: 55) *See* Figs. 10.39 and 10.40.

Fig. 10.39. Rule 22.12B. Addition of term of honour.

Term of honour

Stephen, James Fitzjames, Sir, 1829-1894.
A digest of the law of evidence / by Sir James Fitzjames Stephen. — 5th ed. / by Sir Herbert Stephen and Harry Lushington Stephen

Note: Position of term is LC practice. According to *AACR2R*, heading should be:

Stephen, Sir James Fitzjames, 1829-1894.

Fig. 10.40. Rule 22.12B. Addition of term of honour.

Term of honour

Hepworth, Barbara, Dame, 1903-1975.
Barbara Hepworth / J.P. Hodin. — London : Lund Humphries

Note: Position of term is LC practice. *AACR2R* form:

Hepworth, Dame Barbara, 1903-1975.

RULE 22.13. SAINTS

The word *Saint* is added after a saint's given name unless the person was a pope, emperor, empress, king, or queen. In those cases the latter epithet takes precedence over *Saint*, and one follows rules 22.16A-22.16B. *See* Fig. 10.41.

Fig. 10.41. Rule 22.13. Addition of *Saint*.

Addition of designation *Saint*

Jeanne d'Arc eine Heilige? : Sceptische Studien gelegentlich des Canonisation-processes.

I. Joan, of Arc, Saint, 1412-1431.

RULE 22.15. ADDITIONS TO NAMES ENTERED UNDER SURNAME

22.15A. When a name consists only of a surname with an accompanying word or phrase in the person's works or in reference sources, the associated word or phrase should be added after the surname. A reference is made from the name in direct order if it would be useful. LC generally makes the direct order reference only when such a heading is a pseudonym or assumed name. (*CSB* 39: 13) *See* Fig. 10.42.

Fig. 10.42. Rule 22.15A. Addition of phrase associated with surname alone.

Jefferson, Mr., of Gray's Inn.
    Tales of old Mr. Jefferson, of Gray's Inn / collected by young Mr. Jefferson, of Lyon's Inn

Note: Refer from: Mr. Jefferson of Gray's Inn.

22.15B. Terms of address of married women

When a woman is identified only by "Mrs." with her husband's name, the term "Mrs." is added. *See* Fig. 10.43.

Fig. 10.43. Rule 22.15B. Entry for married woman identified only by husband's name.

¹Husband's name   Bruce, William, Mrs.

²Term of address

    Some intermarriages of some old Springfield, Ohio, families / compiled by Mrs. Wm. Ultes, Jr., as dictated by her mother, Mrs. Wm. Bruce

Note: Form above is LC practice. *AACR2R* form:

Bruce, Mrs. William.

22.15C. Titles or terms other than those in the preceding rules are not added to names entered under surname except when necessary to distinguish between otherwise identical names for which dates are not available. *See* Fig. 10.44.

Fig. 10.44. Rule 22.15C. Omission of unneeded term of address.

Name on chief source of information: Dr. Mary Lyon
Entry: Lyon, Mary.

RULE 22.16. ADDITIONS TO NAMES ENTERED UNDER GIVEN NAME, ETC.

22.16A. Royalty

This rule in *AACR2R* has four specific subsections with accompanying examples. The essence of the rule is that royal persons are entered under the names by which they are known. A royal name may include a house, dynasty, or surname (*see* rule 22.8C in *AACR2R*) or a roman numeral. A phrase (in English, if possible) consisting of title and state governed follows the name of a person with the highest royal status in a state. Other epithets are not added, but are referred from. Consorts, children, and grandchildren of rulers have a title added to their names (again in English, if possible) plus the name of the ruler to whom related. *See* Figs. 10.45 and 10.46 (page 244).

Fig. 10.45. Rule 22.16A. Entry of royalty.

1Entry under
royal forename
Nikolaĭ Mikhaĭlovich, Grand Duke of Russia, 1859-
1919.
2Title and
name of state
[Pis'ma vysochaishikh osob k grafinie A.S.
Protasovoi]

Письма высочайшихъ особъ къ графинѣ А.С. Прота-
совой / Великій князь Никогай Михайловичъ

Fig. 10.46. Rule 22.16A. Addition to names of royalty.

Moncreiffe of that Ilk, Iain, Sir, 1919-
    Royal Highness : ancestry of the royal child / Sir Iain
Moncreiffe of that Ilk

Addition of name of ruler to whom related:

... 3. William, Prince, grandson of Elizabeth II, Queen of
Great Britain, 1982-

22.16B.   Popes

22.16C.   Bishops, etc.

22.16D.   Other persons of religious vocation

These rules call for addition of the words *Pope, Bishop, Archbishop,
Cardinal*, and other titles in English (if there is an English equivalent) to the
names of persons who are high ecclesiastical officials. The name of the latest see
is also added to some titles. For other persons of religious vocation who are
entered under given name, titles or terms of address are added in the vernacular.
Initials of a Christian religious order regularly used by the person are also added.
See Figs. 10.47 and 10.48.

Fig. 10.47. Rule 22.16B. Additions to names of popes.

Title added
in English
John Paul II, Pope, 1920-
    Easter vigil and other poems / translated from the Polish
by Jerzy Peterkiewicz

Fig. 10.48. Rule 22.16D. Additions to names of persons of religious
vocation.

Mead, Jude.
    Dove in the cleft : the life of Mother Mary Crucified
of Jesus, C.P., the first Passionist nun, 1713-1787 / Jude
Mead

Title added in vernacular:

1. Maria Crocifissa di Gesu, madre, 1713-1787.

Additions to Distinguish Identical Names

RULE 22.17.   DATES

Birth and death dates are added as the last element of a heading in order to distinguish between two otherwise identical headings. An option to this rule allows adding the date(s) even when there is no conflict. LC is applying this option when the date is known at the time the heading is first established or later if the heading must be revised anyway. For persons living in the twentieth century, LC only adds precise dates. Less precise dates may be added to the headings for pre-twentieth century persons. (*CSB* 46: 40-41) *See* Figs. 10.49-10.54.

Fig. 10.49. Rule 22.17. Addition of dates for a living person.

Vieweg-Marks, Karin, 1957-

Fig. 10.50. Rule 22.17. Addition of dates when references differ as to year of birth; 1496 is probable.

Fox, Edward, Bishop of Hereford, 1496?-1538.

Fig. 10.51. Rule 22.17. Addition of dates when year of birth is unknown.

Timberlake, Henry, d. 1626.

Fig. 10.52. Rule 22.17. Addition of dates when years of birth and death are unknown, but date of activity is known. (Not used for twentieth century.)

Gardiner, Richard, fl. 1599-1603.

Note: "fl." is the *AACR2R* abbreviation for "flourished."

Fig. 10.53. Rule 22.17. Day, month, and year of birth added to distinguish from others of same name and same year of birth.

Fischer, John, 1910 Apr. 27-

Fig. 10.54. Rule 22.17. Addition of probable dates.

Ford, John, 1586-ca. 1640.

RULE 22.18.   FULLER FORMS

When two names as prescribed by the preceding rules are identical and a fuller form of one or both names is known, the fuller form is added in parentheses in order to distinguish between the two names. The rule calls for a reference from the full form when appropriate. In many catalogs such references are superfluous, especially when the initial in the name is for a second or later forename. *See* Fig. 10.55 (page 246).

Fig. 10.55. Rule 22.18. Addition to name containing initials.

Full form
of name
added in
parentheses

Roberts, J. O. (Jack O.)
    Coal and nuclear : a comparison of the cost of generating
baseload electricity by region / J.O. Roberts

Note: Refer from: Roberts, Jack O.

This rule allows the option of making the above additions even when not necessary to distinguish identical names except that, when following the option, one is not to add:

    "[1]   unused forenames to headings that contain forenames

    [2]   initials of names that are not part of the heading

    [3]   unused parts of surnames to headings that contain surnames."[7]

LC is following the option when the information is known with certainty. A rule interpretation gives guidelines for how much of the name to include in the parenthetical statement and where to place it. Once a heading has been established without the names in parentheses, they are not added if they become known later unless the heading must be changed for some other reason (e.g., it comes in conflict with another heading). (*CSB* 44: 50-52)

RULE 22.19.   DISTINGUISHING TERMS

RULE 22.20.   UNDIFFERENTIATED NAMES
    When dates or fuller forms are not available to distinguish between identical names, certain other additions may be made following rule 22.19. For given names, a brief term may be devised (e.g., "poet") and added in parentheses. For surname entries, a term of address, title of position, initials of academic degree, etc., that appears with the name in works or reference sources may be added. *See* Fig. 10.56. Otherwise, according to rule 22.20 the same heading is used for all persons with the same name.

Fig. 10.56. Rule 22.19. Distinguishing term added.

Chapman, William H., M.A.

22.21-22.28.
    These are special rules for names in certain languages and should be consulted as needed.

NOTES

[1]*Cataloging Service Bulletin*, no. 17 (Summer 1982): 31.

[2]*Cataloging Service Bulletin*, no. 18 (Fall 1982): 49-51.

[3]*AACR2R*, p. 621.

[4]*AACR2R*, p. 384.

[5]For examples of references, see the chapter on references in this text.

[6]*AACR2R*, p. 390.

[7]*AACR2R*, p. 416.

SUGGESTED READING

Chan, Lois Mai. *Cataloging and Classification*. New York, McGraw-Hill, 1981. pp. 99-107.

Hagler, Ronald. *The Bibliographic Record and Information Technology*. 2nd ed. Chicago, American Library Association, 1991. pp. 145-151.

Maxwell, Margaret F. *Handbook for AACR2, 1988 Revision*. Chicago, American Library Association, 1989. Chapter 14.

Form of Headings for Geographic Names

11

INTRODUCTION

This chapter covers chapter 23 in *AACR2R*, which treats the form of heading for any geographic name that may be used as a main or added entry heading. This includes names for places that now are or once were jurisdictional entities. It does not include names that cannot be jurisdictions, such as continents, mountains, and rivers. Yet there is an attempt in *AACR2R* to separate rules for place names that are "only" geographic names from those that are names of jurisdictions. Therefore, one rule in chapter 24, "Headings for Corporate Bodies" (rule 24.6), deals with what seem to be geographic names; but the rule actually deals with jurisdictions. Another rule, 24.3E, covers "conventional" names of governments and gives instructions to use the geographic name as constructed in chapter 23. Other rules throughout chapter 24 cover additions of geographic names to corporate names for the purpose of identification or distinction. It can be seen, then, that the cataloger cannot rely solely on chapter 23 for the construction of names that appear to be geographic.

In chapter 23 of *AACR2R* there are rules for choice of name (rules 23.2-23.3), additions to place names (rule 23.4), and modification of place names (rule 23.5). Problems involved in choice of name often involve choice between an English form and a form in some other language. Choice may also involve which name to use when the name of a place has changed. For additions to place names, problems may involve decisions about which larger place names are most useful for identification. (For example, should the name of the county, state, and/or country be added to the name of a town?) A problem that may require modification of a name involves the use of a term indicating type of jurisdiction. The problem is whether that term comes first, while the name is commonly known or listed under another element of the name (e.g., Kreis Lippe, a county in Germany, is commonly listed under Lippe). The purpose of this chapter is to demonstrate the rules used to resolve these problems.

A heading created according to the rules in this chapter is coded 110, 651, 710, or 810 in the MARC format, depending upon whether it functions as a main entry, subject heading, or added entry or begins a series. Codes 110, 710, and 810 are for corporate names, and in these cases the name of a jurisdiction alone is coded as a corporate name. However, in the subject fields there are separate numbers for corporate names (610) and geographic names (651). Jurisdictions that stand alone are coded as geographic names.

SELECTED RULES AND EXAMPLES

RULE 23.2. GENERAL RULES

These general rules involve choice of a name from among variant forms of a name that may be found.

23.2A. English form

AACR2R calls for use of the English form of a place name and specifies that this form should be determined from gazetteers and other reference sources from English-speaking countries. When there is doubt as to whether the English form is generally used, the vernacular form is to be used. *See* Fig. 11.1.

Fig. 11.1. Rule 23.2A. Geographic name entered under English form of name.

[1]English form
in general use

Forms of name found: Brasil
Brazil ◄—1
AACR2R heading: Brazil.

Forms of name found: Bucharest ◄—1
Bucuresti
Bucuresci
Bukharest
Bucarest
AACR2R heading: Bucharest (Romania)

Forms of name found: Rome ◄—1
Roma
AACR2R heading: Rome (Italy)

The Library of Congress bases headings for United States names on the *Rand McNally Commercial Atlas and Marketing Guide*. Names from Great Britain, Australia, and New Zealand are based on the form found in a recently published gazetteer. For names in Canada, LC uses headings provided by the National Library of Canada. For other names, the heading is based on the form found in the work being cataloged, considered with the form found in a recent gazetteer, or it may be based on the form approved by the U.S. Board on Geographic Names (BGN). An English form in general use is always used even when the BGN approves only a vernacular form. (*CSB* 48: 21-25)

Certain of the examples given in *AACR2R* for geographic names are not being followed by LC. BGN approves both *Union of Soviet Socialist Republics* (the form used in *AACR2R*) and *Soviet Union* (the form used by LC in the past). LC is continuing to use *Soviet Union*. *AACR2R* uses *United Kingdom* in examples where *Great Britain* was used in the past. However, *Great Britain* can be thought of as the conventional name for *United Kingdom of Great Britain and Northern Ireland*. In addition, libraries in Britain wish to continue using *Great Britain*. Therefore, LC continues to use the heading *Great Britain*. Other decisions include use of *Germany (West)* for Federal Republic of Germany, *Germany (East)* for German Democratic Republic, *Germany* for the government prior to division and for the post-reunification government, *Korea (North)* for Democratic People's Republic of Korea, *Korea (South)* for Republic of Korea. For

Washington, D.C., LC uses *District of Columbia* as the heading for the government of this name, with *Washington (D.C.)* used only as a location qualifier or as the entry element for cross references from place. In dealing with London, LC uses *Corporation of London* or *Greater London Council* for jurisdictional headings and *London (England)* as the qualifier added to corporate names or as the entry element for a cross reference from place. (*CSB* 48: 21-25)

23.2B. Vernacular form

23.2B1. If there is no English form in general use, the form in the official language of the country is used. *See* Fig. 11.2.

Fig. 11.2. Rule 23.2B1. Geographic name entered under vernacular form of name.

AACR2R headings: Pistoia (Italy)
[no English form   Tétaigne (France)
in use]   Tromsø (Norway)

AACR2R heading: Braunschweig (Germany)
[English form not   [English form: Brunswick]
in general use]

In cases where there is more than one official language in a country, the most common form found in English-language reference sources is used. *See* Fig. 11.3.

Fig. 11.3. Rule 23.2B1. Geographic name entered under most common form found.

Forms of name found: Bruxelles
                    Brüssel
                    Brussels

Form most often found in English-language sources:
                    Brussels

AACR2R heading: Brussels (Belgium)

Note: There is no rule for variations of spelling of the name in the same language. Because of the close association in the rules of geographic names and corporate names, it is assumed that needed rules, such as the one for spelling, may be taken from *AACR2R* chapter 24 and applied to geographic names. Rule 24.2C states that for a name with variant spellings, the one that represents an official change in orthography should be used if this applies or else the predominant spelling should be used. *See* Fig. 11.4.

Fig. 11.4. Entry of name with variant spellings.

Original spelling: Tandjungpinang, Indonesia
New official spelling: Tanjungpinang, Indonesia
Variants also found: Tandjoengpinang
                   Tandjung Pinang
                   Tanjung Pinang
AACR2R heading: Tanjungpinang (Indonesia)

RULE 23.3.   CHANGES OF NAME
The essence of this rule is that if the name of a place changes, one should use on catalog records as many of the names as are required by rules in *AACR2R*, chapter 24. The rule mentions specifically rules 24.3E, 24.4C6, and 24.7B4 but allows for other relevant rules as well. *See* Figs. 11.5 and 11.6.

Fig. 11.5. Rule 23.3. Use of more than one name for the same place.

In 1971, the Town of Whitchurch-Stouffville was created, incorporating the Village of Stouffville in Ontario.

An item requiring Stouffville as a heading prior to 1971 would use the heading:
> Stouffville (Ont.)

An item requiring Stouffville as a heading in 1971 or later would use the heading:
> Stouffville (Whitchurch-Stouffville, Ont.)

Fig. 11.6. Rule 23.3. Use of latest geographic name as an addition to a corporate body.

In 1971 East Pakistan became Bangladesh. A corporate body whose lifetime spanned the change would have the latest name of the country added, even for items relevant only to the body during the time the country was known as East Pakistan, e.g.,
> Institution of Engineers (Bangladesh)
> *not* Institution of Engineers (East Pakistan)

RULE 23.4.   ADDITIONS

23.4A.   Punctuation
Additions to place names that are used as entry elements are made in parentheses. Example:

Staunton (Va.)

When the whole place name is used as an addition, it is enclosed in parentheses with a comma preceding the larger place. Example:

Second Presbyterian Church (Staunton, Va.)

23.4B.   General rule
Any place name (other than that of a country or that of a state, etc., listed in rule 23.4C1 or rule 23.4D1) should have added to it the name of a larger place, following rules 23.4C-23.4F. Additional instructions for place names used as headings for governments are given in rule 24.6. Instructions for abbreviations for additions are given in Appendix B of *AACR2R*.

In a rule interpretation for this rule, LC addresses three situations not covered by rules 23.4C-23.4F: (*CSB* 41: 44-45)

1) If an island or island group is a jurisdiction, the name of the larger jurisdiction should be added only when the island or island group is located near the larger jurisdiction. Example:

   Guardia Island (Spain)
   Madeira Islands

2) When a larger place that is being added has changed its name and if the smaller place existed through the name change, the current larger place name should be added, with a reference from the place with the earlier larger place name. Example:

   Georgetown (Guyana)

   make a reference from:

   Georgetown (British Guiana)

3) The additions prescribed in rule 24.6 should not be added as part of the qualifier being added under rule 23.4B. Example:

   St. Romuald (Québec)
   not St. Romuald (Québec, Province)

23.4C. Places in Australia, Canada, Malaysia, the United States, U.S.S.R., or Yugoslavia

23.4C1. States, etc.

No addition should be made to the name of a state, province, etc., of one of the countries covered by this rule. Examples:

California
not California (U.S.)

Hrvatska Croatia
not Hrvatska Croatia (Yogoslavia)

LC makes references from the names of states of Malaysia qualified with "(Malaysia)." (*CSB* 41: 46) Example:

Kedah

make reference from:

Kedah (Malaysia)

For the constituent republics of the Soviet Union, LC uses the following headings: (*CSB* 51: 41-42)

Armenian S.S.R.	Lithuania
Azerbaijan S.S.R.	Moldavian S.S.R.
Byelorussian S.S.R.	Russian S.F.S.R.
Estonia	Tajik S.S.R.
Georgian S.S.R.	Turkmen S.S.R.
Kazakh S.S.R.	Ukraine
Kirghiz S.S.R.	Uzbek S.S.R.
Latvia	

23.4C2. Other places

Add the name of the state, province, or territory to a place located in one of the countries covered by this rule. Places located in cities are treated according to rule 23.4F2. Examples:

Delmont (Pa.)
Montreal (Québec)
Melbourne (Vic.)

23.4D. Places in the British Isles

23.4D1. No addition should be made to the names of the parts of the British Isles: England, the Republic of Ireland, Northern Ireland, Scotland, Wales, the Isle of Man, and the Channel Islands.

23.4D2. For a place located in one of the above-named parts of the British Isles, one of the following names is added to the heading, as appropriate: England, Ireland (for the Republic of Ireland), Northern Ireland, Scotland, Wales, Isle of Man, or Channel Islands. Examples:

Antrim (Northern Ireland)
Warwickshire (England)
Ayrshire (Scotland)
Cambridge (England)
Mold (Wales)
Tralee (Ireland)

23.4E. Other places

If a place is not covered by 23.4C-23.4D, the name of the country in which it lies is added. Examples:

Lund (Sweden)
Siena (Italy)
Rio de Janeiro (Brazil)

23.4F. Further additions

If two places with the same name are not sufficiently distinguished with additions as instructed in rules 23.4C-23.4E, a word or phrase commonly used with them may be used or an appropriate smaller place may be added before the larger place. Examples:

Mount Vernon (Westchester County, N.Y.)
Mount Vernon (Erie County, N.Y.)

A place otherwise difficult to identify, such as a community within a city, may also have an appropriate smaller place added before the larger place. Examples:

Bregninge (Svendborg, Denmark)
Chinatown (San Francisco, Calif.)

RULE 23.5. PLACE NAMES INCLUDING OR REQUIRING A TERM INDICATING A TYPE OF JURISDICTION

23.5A. When the first element of a place name indicates a type of jurisdiction but the place is usually listed under another name element in reference sources of the country, the term indicating type of jurisdiction should be omitted. Example:

Kreis Lippe in Germany is commonly listed under Lippe in German lists.

Heading: Lippe (Germany : Kreis)

Note: In this example, *Kreis* is omitted from the first element according to this rule, but it is added in the qualifier to distinguish it from the principality that had the name *Lippe*, as called for in the *AACR2R* chapter on corporate names.

The type of jurisdiction is included in all cases that do not fit the above criteria. Example:

Dutchess County (N.Y.)

Note: The term *county* should be included for U.S. counties, even though many U.S. atlases list counties by name only under the caption *counties* and therefore omit the word *county* with the name. Note that *county* is now spelled out. Most U.S. counties have been established by LC and other libraries in the past using *Co.* and are being changed by LC as new occasions for use of each county name arise.

23.5B. Occasionally a place name does not include a term indicating type of jurisdiction, but such a term is required for differentiating between two identical names. If this is the case, rule 24.6 should be applied. Example:

Chimaltenango (Guatemala : Department)
[there is also a municipality named Chimaltenango]

Note: LC continues to abbreviate *Department* as *Dept.*, even though it is not allowed to be abbreviated in headings according to *AACR2R*, Appendix B, "Abbreviations." (*CSB* 32: 58)

SUGGESTED READING

Hagler, Ronald. *The Bibliographic Record and Information Technology.* 2nd ed. Chicago, American Library Association, 1991. pp. 161-163.

Maxwell, Margaret F. *Handbook for AACR2, 1988 Revision.* Chicago, American Library Association, 1989. Chapter 15.

Form of Headings for Corporate Names

12

INTRODUCTION

This chapter covers the rules for construction of names of corporate bodies. *Corporate body* is defined in rule 21.1B1 of *AACR2R* as "an organization or a group of persons that is identified by a particular name and that acts, or may act, as an entity."[1] In general, entry of a corporate body is under the name the body itself uses except when the rules specify entry under a higher or related body or under the name of a government. Like the principle in use for personal names, the principle for corporate names is to choose the name the corporate body generally uses (including conventional names), even if that name is not the official one. Unlike personal names, however, when the name of a corporate body changes, a new heading is made under that name with cross references to and from various other former and related names.

Following the general rule (rule 24.1) in this chapter, there are rules for choice of names (rules 24.2-24.3) and for additions, omissions, and modifications (rules 24.4-24.11). These are followed by rules for subordinate and related bodies in general (rules 24.12-24.16), for government bodies and officials (rules 24.17-24.26), and for religious bodies and officials (rule 24.27). Problems involved in choice of name include choice among variant forms found in items issued by a body, such as official name or acronym or short form, choice among variant spellings (including differences in romanization), and choice among different languages. Problems requiring additions, omissions, or other modifications include the need to distinguish between two or more bodies with the same name, the need to provide adequate identification for a name that does not convey the idea of a corporate body, and the desire to omit unnecessary or excess terms such as *incorporated* or *biennial*. In dealing with a subordinate body, the cataloger must decide whether the body can be entered directly under its own name or must be entered under a higher body, and because government and religious bodies present special problems in this area, the cataloger must know whether a subordinate body belongs in one of these two groups before applying the rules. The purpose of this chapter is to demonstrate only the most important problems of corporate entry. For more detail, the cataloger should consult *AACR2R*, chapter 24.

As with personal names, there are certain previously established headings for corporate bodies that LC considered "*AACR2* compatible" from January 2, 1981, to September 1, 1982 (see discussion on page 225 in the chapter on form of headings for persons). These are summarized with examples in *Cataloging Service Bulletin*. (*CSB* 45: 52-54)

A heading created according to the rules in this chapter is coded 110, 111, 610, 611, 710, 711, 810, or 811 in the MARC format, depending upon whether it functions as a main entry, subject heading, or added entry or begins a series. The codes ending in "11" are for conference names. The codes ending in "10" are for all other corporate names.

GENERAL RULES:
SELECTED RULES AND EXAMPLES

RULE 24.1. GENERAL RULE

24.1A. A corporate body is to be entered directly under its own name unless later rules instruct that it be entered subordinately to a higher body or to a government. Although the rule does not say so, there are also religious bodies that must be entered subordinately. Therefore, the cataloger must first determine whether a body is a government or religious body and start with those rules if it is: rules 24.17-24.26 for government bodies; rule 24.27 for religious bodies. If a body is neither government nor religious but is subordinate to another body, rules 24.12-24.16 must be consulted. In many cases one will be referred back to this rule (rule 24.1), because the body can be entered under its own name even though it is a subordinate body.

The form of the name of a corporate body is determined from items issued by the body in its language, if possible, or from reference sources. The punctuation usage of the body should be followed (e.g., whether or not periods are included after initials depends upon the predominant usage by the body).

References from different forms of a corporate body name are prescribed in the *AACR2R* reference chapter, rule 26.3. Examples:

Lawyer's Committee for Civil Rights Under Law.

W. K. Kellogg Arabian Horse Center.
 Refer from: Kellogg Arabian Horse Center.

Nelliston Community Group.

Pro Musica Antiqua, Prague.
 Refer from: Symposium "Pro Musica Antiqua" Prag.

A rule interpretation from LC gives guidance for punctuating and spacing corporate names. (*CSB* 45: 51-52)

It should also be noted here that for a corporate name that includes the name of a place at the end, the punctuation used by the body is retained. This means that some names may be established ending with a place preceded by a comma and a space, and others may be established with a place enclosed in parentheses. These have nothing to do with the additions prescribed in rule 24.4 and should not be interpreted as "errors." Example:

California State University, San Diego
 not California State University (San Diego)

24.1B. Romanization

The name of a body that is written in a nonroman script is romanized using the table adopted by the cataloging agency. This means that even if a romanized form of the name appears in items issued by a body, that form may be used only if it corresponds to the table adopted by the cataloging agency. References are made from other romanizations.

A footnote in *AACR2R* allows an alternative to this rule: a romanized form appearing in items issued by the body is used with references from other romanizations. The Library of Congress is not applying the alternative rule. (*CSB* 44: 53) *See* Fig. 12.1.

Fig. 12.1. Rule 24.1B. Romanization of names originally in nonroman script. Also illustrates rule 24.3A: Use of the form in the official language of the body. Refer from the English form of the names.

Corporate names entered under romanized form

Akademiiâ nauk SSSR.◀
    Noctilucent clouds : optical properties / Academy of Sciences of the U.S.S.R., Soviet Geophysical Committee, and Institute of Physics and Astronomy of the Academy of Sciences of the Estonian S.S.R.

Make added entries using romanized forms of names:

    I. Akademiiâ nauk SSSR. Mezhduvedomstvennyĭ geofizicheskiĭ komitet. II. Füüsika ja Astronoomia Instituut (Eesti NSV Teaduste Akadeemia).

24.1C. Changes of name

When a corporate body changes its name, a new heading is established for the new name. A bibliographic record for an item relating to the old name has the old name as a heading, while a bibliographic record for an item relating to the new name has the new name as a heading. References are made referring to each name from the other. *See* Fig. 12.2.

Fig. 12.2. Rule 24.1C. Entry under each name a corporate body has used.

The Long Range Planning Service of the Stanford Research Institute became the Business Intelligence Program in April 1976. On May 16, 1977, the Institute changed its name to S.R.I. International.
    Works by these bodies are found under the following headings according to the name used at the time of publication:

Entry under two names ⟶ Stanford Research Institute. Long Range Planning Service. Business Intelligence Program (SRI International)

RULE 24.2. VARIANT NAMES. GENERAL RULES

Variant names here do not include those resulting from official changes of names. Such changes are covered by 24.1C. LC has a rule interpretation that explains what are to be treated as variant names. (*CSB* 47: 54-55)

24.2B. When different name forms are found in various places in items issued by a corporate body, the form found in chief sources of information should be used. *See* Fig. 12.3 (page 258).

Fig. 12.3. Rule 24.2B. Entry of name having variant forms.

Name on title page: Michael Bradner Associates
Forms of name found elsewhere in work:
  Mike Bradner & Associates
  Mike Bradner and Associates
AACR2R heading: Michael Bradner Associates.
Refer from: Mike Bradner and Associates.
      Bradner Associates.

24.2C. When there are variant spellings of a name in items issued by the body, the one that represents an official change in orthography should be used, if this applies, or if not, the predominant spelling should be chosen. *See* Fig. 12.4.

Fig. 12.4. Rule 24.2C. Entry of name having variant spellings.

Name on some title pages:
  Allgemeines deutsches Commersbuch
Name on most title pages:
  Allgemeines deutsches Kommersbuch
AACR2R heading: Allgemeines deutsches Kommersbuch.
Refer from: Allgemeines deutsches Commersbuch.

24.2D. When different name forms appear in the chief source of information, the one presented formally should be used if that is applicable, or the predominant form should be used if no form is presented formally or all are equally presented. *AACR2R* prescribes that if no form is predominant, a short form that distinguishes this body from others with a similar name should be used in preference to a longer form. However, a rule interpretation from LC indicates that if a body's initials or acronym appear formally with the full form, the full form should be chosen for the heading. (*CSB* 44: 53-54) *See* Fig. 12.5.

Fig. 12.5. Rule 24.2D. Entry under brief form of name.

Names on title page: GAAG, the Guerrilla Art Action Group
Neither form formally presented. No predominant form.
AACR2R heading: GAAG.
Refer from: Guerrilla Art Action Group.
LC choice of heading: Guerrilla Art Action Group.

If a brief form does not differentiate a body from another with the same name, a form found in reference sources or the official form, in that order of preference, should be used. For example, the short form *NEA* for the National Education Association of the United States does not distinguish it from other bodies known as NEA: Nouvelles Editions africaines, National Endowment for the Arts, or the OECD Nuclear Energy Agency.

RULE 24.3. VARIANT NAMES. SPECIAL RULES

24.3A. Language

This rule sets up an order of precedence to follow when the name of a body appears in different languages:

1) the form in the official language of the body

2) an English-language form if there is more than one official language and one is English

3) the predominant language

4) English, French, German, Spanish, or Russian, in that order

5) the language that comes first in English alphabetic order

An LC rule interpretation inserts another criterion between 3) and 4); if one does not know the official language of the body, the official language of the country in which the body is located is used (if the country has a single official language). (*CSB* 45: 54) *See* Fig. 12.6.

Fig. 12.6. Rule 24.3A. Entry of name found in different languages.

Names on publications:
Schweizerische Hochschulrektoren-Konferenz,
Kommission für Hochschulplanung
Commission de planification de la Conférence
des recteurs des universités suisses
Official language: German
AACR2R heading: Schweizerische Hochschulrektoren-
Konferenz. Kommission für Hochschulplanung.
Refer from French form.

An alternative to this rule allows use of a form of language appropriate to the catalog's users if the application of the rule results in a language not familiar to the users. LC is not following this alternative. (*CSB* 45: 54)

24.3B. Language. International bodies

The English form of an international body is used if the name appears in English in its publications. Otherwise, the preceding rule, rule 24.3A, is used. *See* Fig. 12.7.

Fig. 12.7. Rule 24.3B. Entry of international body when the name appears in English.

Names on title page:
al-Maṣrif al-'Arabī lil-Tanmiyah al-Iqtiṣādiyah fī Afrrīqyā
Arab Bank for Economic Development in Africa
Banque Arabe de développement économique en Afrique
AACR2R heading: Arab Bank for Economic Development
in Africa.
Refer from the names in Arabic and French.

24.3C. Conventional name

24.3C1. General rule

A conventional name that is often used to identify a corporate body in reference sources in its own language should be used in place of an official name. *See* Fig. 12.8.

Fig. 12.8. Rule 24.3C1. Entry under conventional name.

¹Conventional name   Abbey of Bury St. Edmunds.◄——¹

²Official name   The customary of the Benedictine Abbey of Bury St. Edmunds in Suffolk : (from Harleian MS. 1005 in the British Museum) / edited by Antonia Gransden

24.3C2. Ancient and international bodies

When an English form of name of an ancient body or of a body of international character has become very well known in English-language usage, this form should be used. A footnote comments that this rule applies to such bodies as religious bodies, fraternal and knightly orders, church councils, and diplomatic conferences. *See* Fig. 12.9.

Fig. 12.9. Rule 24.3C2. Entry under English form of conventional names of international bodies.

Orthodox Eastern Church.
[Hēmerologion tēs Ekklēsias tēs Hellados]
Ἡμερολόγιον τῆς Ἐκκλησίας τῆς Ἑλλάδος

English form of names   Catholic Church. Canadian Catholic Conference.
Messages des évêques canadiens à l'occasion de la Fête du travail (1956-1974) / présentation de Richard Arès

24.3D. Religious orders and societies

The best known form of name for a religious order or society should be used. An English form is preferred, if one exists. Otherwise, the language of the country of origin is used. *See* Fig. 12.10.

Fig. 12.10. Rule 24.3D. Entry of religious orders and societies.

Name of religious order or society   White Fathers.◄——
Annexes des Archives de la Maison généralice des Pères blancs = Documents in the Annexe of the Archives of the Generalate of the White Fathers

24.3E. Governments

The conventional name of a government is preferred unless there is an official name in common use. The name of the geographic area over which the government has jurisdiction serves as the conventional name. Examples:

Jersey City (N.J.)
not City of Jersey City

Korea (North)
not Democratic People's Republic of Korea

San Marino
not Most Serene Republic of San Marino

24.3F. Conferences, congresses, meetings, etc.
When variant forms of a conference name appear in the chief source of information, one that includes the name (or initials) of a body associated with the conference should be chosen, if possible. If, however, the meeting is *subordinate* to the body, rule 24.13A, Type 6 should be applied. *See* Fig. 12.11.

Fig. 12.11. Rule 24.3F. Entry of a conference under form of name that includes initials of the bodies associated with the meeting.

Name of meeting: ALI-ABA Course of Study: Partnerships: UPA, ULPA, Securities, Taxation, and Bankruptcy
Name appears both with and without the initials of the American Law Institute and the American Bar Association.
AACR2R heading: ALI-ABA Course of Study: Partnerships: UPA, ULPA, Securities, Taxation, and Bankruptcy (1990 : Seattle)
Refer from: Course of Study: Partnerships: UPA, ULPA, Securities, Taxation, and Bankruptcy.

ADDITIONS, OMISSIONS, AND MODIFICATIONS: SELECTED RULES AND EXAMPLES

RULE 24.4. ADDITIONS

24.4A. General rule
The subrules under rule 24.4 give general directions for making additions to corporate names. Special types of corporate names may need more specialized types of additions, which are covered in rules 24.6-24.11. All additions to corporate names are enclosed in parentheses.

24.4B. Names not conveying the idea of a corporate body
When a corporate name does not sound like that of a corporate body, a designation is added in English. A rule interpretation from LC that gives guidance in determining when such designations are needed (e.g., for ships, performing groups, etc.) should be consulted when needed. (*CSB* 34: 39-41)
Examples:

ABBA (Musical group)

International Road Safety (Association)

But (Yacht)

24.4C. Two or more bodies with the same or similar names

24.4C1. General rule

When two or more corporate name headings are identical or so similar that they could be easily confused, a word or phrase must be added to each according to the subrules under rule 24.4C. Such additions may also be made when they would merely assist understanding. A rule interpretation explains how LC is applying this rule. In general additions are made to every government body name that is entered under its own name unless the government's name (or an understandable substitute for it) is already part of the name. An exception is made for government institutions (e.g., schools, libraries, hospitals). If one of these or if a nongovernment body is entered under its own name, a qualifier is added if it is needed for understanding the nature or purpose of the body. The rule interpretation goes on to elaborate upon choice of qualifiers and the forms qualifiers should take. (*CSB* 47: 55-57)

24.4C2-24.4C9. Rules 24.4C2-24.4C6 authorize addition of place names— country, state, province, etc.—for a body that is national, provincial, etc., in character or of local place names for a body whose character is essentially local. If a place is not appropriate, rules 24.4C7-24.4C9 provide for addition of the name of an institution, the inclusive years of existence, or some other appropriate general designation in English. See Fig. 12.12.

Fig. 12.12. Rule 24.4C2. Addition of country to corporate name.

National Committee on the Status of Women (India)
    Status of women : report to the government / National
Committee on the Status of Women

Note: This name could be held by similar groups in several countries. Therefore, the name of the country is added.

It should be noted that when a place is used as a qualifier, if it is a place that is itself qualified by a larger place according to *AACR2R* chapter 23, the smaller and the larger place are both used in the qualifier of the corporate body. Thus, for a corporate body in Oklahoma City, the name of the city alone cannot be used as qualifier. It must be: (Oklahoma City, Okla.). *See also* Fig. 12.13.

RULE 24.5. OMISSIONS

24.5A-24.5C. These rules require omission of certain elements from corporate names: initial articles are omitted unless the heading is to be filed under the article; terms indicating incorporation, etc., are omitted unless they are an integral part of the name or are needed to clarify the fact that the name is that of a corporate body. Other required omissions occur in rare instances, and the cataloger should consult *AACR2R* for them. *See* Figs. 12.13-12.15.

Fig. 12.13. Rule 24.5A. Entry of name omitting initial article.

The "Peterborough" book II / selected and compiled by
   Michael Green

. . .

Note giving title as shown on item in hand:

At head of title: The Daily Telegraph.

Added entry made with initial article omitted:

I. Green, Michael. II. Daily Telegraph (London, England).

Fig. 12.14. Rule 24.5C1. Entry of name omitting term indicating incorporation.

Name appearing on publications:
   Firestone Tire and Rubber Company, Inc.
Cataloger's judgment: *Inc.* not necessary for clarification
   as a corporate body
AACR2R heading: Firestone Tire and Rubber Company.

Fig. 12.15. Rule 24.5C1. Entry of name retaining term indicating incorporation.

A Week full of Saturdays [motion picture]

Information about corporate body:

[Produced and distributed by Alternate Choice, Inc.]

Added entry made for body with term of incorporation retained:

I. Alternate Choice, Inc.

RULE 24.6.   GOVERNMENTS. ADDITIONS

As mentioned in the chapter on geographic names, this rule is an attempt to give directions for entry of names of jurisdictions—distinct from the rules given for strictly geographic names. However, they are not totally separate, because this rule says that if names have not been differentiated by use of rule 23.4, then further addition according to rule 24.6 should be made.

LC has elaborated upon how it will interpret this rule (*CSB* 46: 41-43), because it is not clear from the rule whether additions should be made to *both* conflicting names in all cases.

A succession of jurisdictions that have had the same name are all entered under one heading. Examples:

North Carolina
not North Carolina (Colony)
North Carolina (State)

Hawaii
not Hawaii (Kingdom)
Hawaii (Republic)
Hawaii (State)

The name of a sovereign nation that is the same as the name of another place is not qualified. Example:

Italy
Italy (Tex.)

A third elaboration on this rule distinguishes between situations where the name of a place within a jurisdiction conflicts with the name of the jurisdiction and situations where the name of a jurisdiction conflicts with the name of a place in another jurisdiction. In the first situation, the name of the larger jurisdiction is qualified with the name of the type of government. Example:

Québec (Québec)   [name of city]
Québec (Province)   [name of larger jurisdiction]

In the second situation, only the name of the place in another jurisdiction is qualified. Example:

Alberta (Va.)
Alberta
not Alberta (Province)

An exception is made for the state of Washington. It is entered:

Washington (State)

24.6B. If a jurisdiction is not a city or town and must have an addition because of conflict with another name, the type of jurisdiction is given in English, if there is an English equivalent; otherwise, it is given in the vernacular. Examples:

São Paulo (Brazil)
São Paulo (Brazil : State)
Alessandria (Italy : Province)
Esberg (Denmark : Kommune)

RULE 24.7. CONFERENCES, CONGRESSES, MEETINGS, ETC.

24.7A. Omissions
Words that express number, frequency, or year of meeting are omitted from the name of a conference. *See* Fig. 12.16.

Fig. 12.16. Rule 24.7A. Omission of number from name of conference.

Name on title page: II Jornadas de Derecho Natural
AACR2R heading: Jornadas de Derecho Natural

24.7B. Additions
The number of a conference, etc., the year, and the place in which it was held are added in parentheses to the name. If any of these elements are not known, they are omitted. *See* Figs. 12.17 and 12.18.

Fig. 12.17. Rule 24.7B. Additions to names of conferences.

¹Name of
conference

²Number

³Date

⁴Place

¹⟶International Ocular Trauma Conference (1st : 1988 :
Zhengzhou, Henan, China)◄—4 ⬊2 ⬊3
First International Ocular Trauma Conference : April
15-19, 1988 : directory of conference

Fig. 12.18. Rule 24.7B. Additions to names of conferences.

¹Name of
conference

²Date

³Place

¹⟶International Symposium on Viral Hepatitis and Liver Disease
2—►(1987 : Barbican Centre for Arts and Conferences) ◄—3
Viral hepatitis and liver disease : proceedings of the International Symposium on Viral Hepatitis and Liver Disease, held
at the Barbican Centre, London, May 26-28, 1987 / editor,
A.J. Zuckerman

For further guidance in selecting qualifiers for conferences, etc., the LC rule interpretation on this rule should be consulted. (*CSB* 45: 57-58)

SUBORDINATE AND RELATED BODIES

The problem of entry of corporate bodies that are subordinate to or closely related to other bodies is a difficult one. No completely unambiguous set of rules (including *AACR2R*) has yet been devised to handle it. The last sixteen rules in chapter 24 of *AACR2R* (rules 24.12-24.27) deal with this issue; yet even with this exhaustive treatment the end result may still depend upon the judgment of the individual cataloger.

There are three parts to this section: general rules, government body rules, and religious organization rules. The cataloger must first know if a body is a government or religious body. This is important because, in some cases, the results of applying the nongovernment rules to a government body may yield a heading not intended by the makers of the code. However, once into the sequence for government or religious bodies, the cataloger may be referred back to the general sequence for further instructions.

If it is determined that a body is a government body, rules 24.17-24.26 must be consulted before any others in chapter 24, because a government body is always a subordinate body—that is, it is always subordinate to a jurisdiction. Once into the rules, the cataloger may find that the result is the same as if subordination were not involved—that is, the body may be entered under its own name. (For example, the University of California, Los Angeles, a state institution, and the University of Southern California, a private institution, both end up entered under "University of....") But if the body is one of the types listed in rule 24.18, it will be entered subordinately, and then rule 24.19 for direct or indirect subheading must be consulted; and if it is one of Types 6 through 11, one of rules 24.20-24.26 must also be consulted. The cataloger must also be concerned with the level of subordinate body involved. If it is subordinate to another government body that is entered under its *own name* because it is not one of the types listed in rule 24.18, then general rules 24.12-24.14 must be consulted for formulation of the heading for the subordinate body. If it is subordinate to another body that is entered under *jurisdiction*, then the cataloger continues to use government body rules 24.17-24.19 for formulation of the heading for the subordinate body.

If it is determined that a body is a religious body, rule 24.27 and its subparts are consulted first. Certain kinds of religious subordinate bodies are specified for subordinate entry in these rules. All others are to be treated according to general rules 24.12-24.14.

For all subordinate bodies other than government or religious, the cataloger uses general rules 24.12-24.16, which refer back to rules 24.1-24.3 for construction of headings for subordinate bodies that should be entered under their own names.

SUBORDINATE AND RELATED BODIES: SELECTED RULES AND EXAMPLES

RULE 24.12. GENERAL RULE

If a subordinate body is not a government body entered under jurisdiction, it is to be entered under its own name according to rules 24.1-24.3 unless it is one of the types listed under rule 24.13. A reference is made from the name formulated as a subheading of its higher body to the name as an independent heading. *See* Figs. 12.19 and 12.20. (Note the similarity of this rule to rule 24.17 for government bodies.)

Fig. 12.19. Rule 24.12. Entry of subordinate body under its own name.

Information on title page of exhibition catalog:
    Baxter Art Gallery, California Institute of Technology,
        Pasadena
AACR2R heading: Baxter Art Gallery.
Refer from: California Institute of Technology. Baxter
    Art Gallery.

Fig. 12.20.

Information on title page: National Affiliation for Literacy
    Advance, Laubach Literacy International's programming
        arm in the U.S. and Canada
AACR2R heading: National Affiliation for Literacy
    Advance.
Refer from: Laubach Literacy International. National
    Affiliation for Literacy Advance.

RULE 24.13. SUBORDINATE AND RELATED BODIES ENTERED SUBORDINATELY

When a subordinate or related body's name belongs to one of Types 1-6 below, the heading for that body is constructed so that the higher body is named first, followed by the name of the subordinate or related body. If the name or abbreviation of the higher body is included in the name of the subordinate body in noun form, it is omitted from the subheading, unless it does not make sense to omit it. There may or may not be names of intervening bodies that are part of the hierarchy, depending on the application of rule 24.14. (Note the similarity of this rule to rule 24.18 for government bodies. Note also that Types 1-4 in the two rules are nearly identical, but that the other types are quite different.)

Type 1.   If a name contains a term that implies the body is part of another body, it is entered subordinately. Examples of such terms: *department, division, section, branch,* and their equivalents in other languages. *See* Fig. 12.21.

Fig. 12.21. Rule 24.13, Type 1. Subordinate entry of body that is part of another.

Current legal aspects of doing business in the Pacific Basin / Section of International Law and Practice, American Bar Association

I. American Bar Association.   Section of International Law and Practice.

A major LC departure from *AACR2R* affects headings constructed by many rules, but it can be illustrated here. LC continues to abbreviate *Department* as *Dept.* even though this is not authorized for use in headings by *AACR2R,* Appendix B, "Abbreviations." (*CSB* 32: 58) *See* Fig. 12.22.

Fig. 12.22. Rule 24.13. Illustration of LC's decision on use of the abbreviation *Dept.*

Previously established heading: Notre Dame, Ind. University. Dept. of Economics.
LC's new heading under *AACR2R*: University of Notre Dame. Dept. of Economics.
Note: Even though the heading must be reconstructed for other reasons, the abbreviation *Dept.* is retained.

Type 2.   If a name contains a term that implies that the body is subordinate to another in an administrative sense, it is entered subordinately *if* the name of the higher body is required to identify the subordinate body. *See* Fig. 12.23. *AACR2R* gives two words as examples: *committee* and *commission.* LC has created lists of words in English, French, and Spanish that imply administrative subordination. (*CSB* 41: 52-53) For the second part of the rule, judgment is to be used by LC's catalogers to determine whether the name of the higher body is required for identification.

Fig. 12.23. Rule 24.13, Type 2. Subordinate entry of body that is administratively subordinate to another.

Information on title page: NAIS Teacher Services Committee
AACR2R heading: National Association of Independent Schools. Teacher Services Committee.
Refer from: NAIS Teacher Services Committee.

Type 3. If a name is "general in nature" or indicates only that it is a geographic, chronological, numbered, or lettered subdivision of a higher body, it is entered subordinately. For LC "general in nature" means that the name has no distinctive elements, such as proper names, nor does it have subject words. (*CSB* 25: 67-68) *See* Fig. 12.24.

Fig. 12.24. Rule 24.13, Type 3. Subordinate entry of body that has a name that is general in nature.

Name in credits of motion picture: Brigham Young University, Media Productions
Cataloger's judgment: *Media Productions* is general in nature
AACR2R heading: Brigham Young University. Media Productions.

Type 4. If a name does not give the impression of being that of a corporate body, it is entered subordinately. *See* Fig. 12.25.

Fig. 12.25. Rule 24.13, Type 4. Subordinate entry of body that has a name that does not give an impression of being that of a corporate body.

Name on title page: National Student Ministries
Cataloger's judgment: Name does not clearly give the impression of being that of a corporate body
AACR2R heading: Southern Baptist Convention. National Student Ministries.

Type 5. If a name of a unit of a university simply indicates that it encompasses a particular field of study, it is entered subordinately. A rule interpretation adds *college* as well as *university* and also adds *interest* and *activity* to *field of study* as criteria for the type of field encompassed by the unit. (*CSB* 44: 58) *See* Fig. 12.26.

Fig. 12.26. Rule 24.13, Type 5. Subordinate entry of body that has a name that simply indicates a field of study.

Name on title page: School of Graduate and Professional Studies, Emporia State University
AACR2R heading: Emporia State University. School of Graduate and Professional Studies.

Type 6. If the name of a subordinate or related body includes the entire name of the higher or related body, it is entered subordinately. LC has issued a lengthy rule interpretation for rule 24.13, Type 6, including exceptions and exclusions and discussing its application to named meetings. (*CSB* 44: 58-62) *See* Fig. 12.27.

Fig. 12.27. Rule 24.13, Type 6. Subordinate entry of body that has a name that includes the name of the higher body.

Name on title page: Chaucer Group of the Modern Language Association of America
AACR2R heading: Modern Language Association of America. Chaucer Group.

RULE 24.14.   DIRECT OR INDIRECT SUBHEADING

A body that belongs to one of the types listed in rule 24.13 and that, therefore, is to be entered subordinately is entered as a subdivision of the element closest above it in its hierarchy that is entered under its own name. If there are elements in the hierarchy that fall between the subdivision and the name that is to be the entry element, they are omitted unless they are needed to distinguish this body from another that does or might have the same entry form (e.g., several sections of the same institution might have an office called the "Personnel Office"). A reference is made from the form that includes the name of an intervening body that has been omitted from the heading. (Note the similarity of this rule to rule 24.19 for government bodies.) *See* Figs. 12.28 and 12.29.

Fig. 12.28. Rule 24.14. Indirect subordinate entry of a section.

Name on title page: University of Washington Libraries, Manuscripts Section
AACR2R heading: University of Washington. Libraries. Manuscripts Section.

Note: Even though the University of Washington is a government body, its subordinate bodies are entered according to rules 24.12-24.14 because the university is entered under its own name, not under jurisdiction.

Fig. 12.29. Rule 24.14. Direct subordinate entry of a laboratory.

Name on title page: Radiological Research Laboratory, Department of Radiology, Columbia University, New York, N.Y.
AACR2R heading: Columbia University. Radiological Research Laboratory.
Refer from: Columbia University. Dept. of Radiology. Radiological Research Laboratory.

Omission of elements of a hierarchy is another area where the results of various catalogers' judgments may vary. The words *or is likely to be* often mean differences in judgment. The Library of Congress has identified for its catalogers two categories where judgment should not vary. In the first category, names of bodies performing functions common to many higher bodies (e.g., Personnel Office; Planning Dept.), the hierarchy should be included. In the second category, names of bodies performing major functions unique to the higher body (e.g., Division of Fisheries; Division of Transport [under the Ministry of Transport, Industry, and Engineering]), intervening elements of the hierarchy should be omitted. Common sense must dictate the inclusion of hierarchy for the great middle ground. The cataloger should consider whether the name would be appropriate for another subordinate body within the same higher body structure and whether some word or phrase in a name in the hierarchy expresses an idea necessary to the identification of the subordinate body. (*CSB* 18: 76-78)

GOVERNMENT BODIES AND OFFICIALS: SELECTED RULES AND EXAMPLES

RULE 24.17. GENERAL RULE

A government body that is not one of Types 1-11 below is entered under its own name according to rules 24.1-24.3 or is entered subordinately to a higher body that is entered under its own name according to rules 24.12-24.14. A reference is made from the form the name would have if it were a subheading under the name of the government. *See* Fig. 12.30.

Fig. 12.30. Rule 24.17. Entry of a government body under its own name.

AACR2R heading: National Institutes of Health (U.S.)
Refer from: United States. National Institutes of Health.
        N.I.H.
        United States. Public Health Service. National
           Institutes of Health.
        United States. Federal Security Agency. National
           Institutes of Health.

The Library of Congress treats the United Nations as a government body when applying these rules. (*CSB* 45: 58)

RULE 24.18. GOVERNMENT AGENCIES ENTERED SUBORDINATELY

When a government body's name belongs to one of Types 1-11 below, it is entered subordinately. If the name or abbreviation of the government is included in the name of the subordinate body in noun form, it is omitted from the subheading, unless it does not make sense to omit it. There may or may not be names of intervening bodies between the name of the government and the name of the subordinate body being established, depending on the application of rule 24.19.

A rule interpretation from LC should be consulted for guidance when a government agency name contains the entire name of its parent body (there is no equivalent to rule 24.13, Type 6, under rule 24.18). (*CSB* 44: 62-64)

Type 1. If a name contains a word that implies the body is part of another body, it is entered subordinately. The same terms given as examples under rule 24.13, Type 1, apply here. *See* Fig. 12.31.

Fig. 12.31. Rule 24.18, Type 1. Entry of subordinate government body that has a name implying it is part of another body.

Name on title page: Division of Planning, City of Jersey City
AACR2R heading: Jersey City (N.J.). Division of Planning.

Type 2.   If a name contains a word that implies that the body is subordinate to the government in an administrative sense, it is entered subordinately *if* the name of the government is required to identify the agency. *See* Fig. 12.32.

Fig. 12.32. Rule 24.18, Type 2. Entry of subordinate government body that has a name implying administrative subordination.

Information on title page: Legislative Commission on
Correctional Programs [seal]: The Great Seal of the
State of North Carolina
AACR2R heading: North Carolina. Legislative Commission
on Correctional Programs.

In LC's rule interpretation for catalogers at LC, there are two tests to be applied here. One is a judgment as to whether the name contains a word that implies "administrative subordination." The cataloger should ask whether the word is commonly used in a particular jurisdiction for names of government subdivisions. If in doubt, the word is considered *not* to have such an implication. The same list of terms in English, French, and Spanish given for rule 24.13, Type 2, is given under the rule interpretation for this rule and should be consulted when needed. (*CSB* 41: 53-54)

If the name passes the first test, it is then evaluated as to whether the name of the government is required for identification. "If the name of the government is stated explicitly or implied in the wording of the name, enter it independently; in all other cases, enter the name subordinately."[2] Thus, the United States Travel Service, which includes the government in its name, is entered independently: United States Travel Service. The Soil Conservation Service, however, is entered subordinately: United States. Soil Conservation Service.

If the body is entered independently according to this interpretation, the name of the government is added as a qualifier unless the name or an understandable surrogate for the name of the government (e.g., *American* for U.S.) appears in the name. (*CSB* 41: 54) *See* Fig. 12.30.

Type 3.   If a name is "general in nature" or indicates only that it is a geographic, chronological, numbered, or lettered subdivision of a government or a government agency, it is entered subordinately. *See* Fig. 12.33.

Fig. 12.33. Rule 24.18, Type 3. Entry of subordinate government body that has a name that is general in nature.

Name on title page: U.S. Public Health Service. Region V
Cataloger's judgment: Region V is a name that is general in
nature
AACR2R heading: United States. Public Health Service.
Region V.

LC policy for interpreting this rule states that if the body is at the national level, it is to be considered general and entered subordinately if the name contains neither distinctive words nor subject words and does not contain either the term *national* or *state* or one of their foreign language equivalents. (*CSB* 44: 63) For example, enter subordinately:

    Research Center
    Library
    Technical Laboratory

but enter independently:

    Population Research Center (U.S.)
    Nuclear Energy Library (U.S.)
    Technical Laboratory of Oceanographic Research (U.S.)
    National Gallery (U.S.)

If the body is below the national level and it is not any of the other types under rule 24.18, LC enters it under the name of the government unless that name is explicitly or implicitly included in the subordinate body's name or the name contains some other word that tends to make it absolutely unique (e.g., a proper noun). (*CSB* 44: 63)

As under rule 24.18, Type 2, a body entered independently under Type 3 will have the name of the government added as a qualifier unless it is already part of the body's name. (*CSB* 44: 63)

Type 4. If the name does not give the impression of being that of a corporate body *and* it does not contain the name of the governing jurisdiction, it is entered subordinately. *See* Fig. 12.34.

Fig. 12.34. Rule 24.18, Type 4. Entry of name that does not give the impression of being a corporate body and does not contain the name of the government.

Name on title page: Naval Oceanography and Meteorology
AACR2R heading: United States. Naval Oceanography and Meteorology.

Type 5. If the name represents a major executive agency (as defined by official publications of the government) it is entered subordinately. *See* Fig. 12.35.

Fig. 12.35. Rule 24.18, Type 5. Entry of a major executive agency.

Name on title page: Oyo State Executive Council
AACR2R heading: Oyo State (Nigeria). Executive Council.

LC restricts application of this rule to major executive agencies of *national* governments. (*CSB* 44: 63)

Type 6. Government legislative bodies are entered subordinately according to the provisions in rule 24.21. *See* Fig. 12.39 (page 274).

Type 7. Government courts are entered subordinately according to the provisions in rule 24.23. *See* Fig. 12.40 (page 275).

Type 8. Principal armed services are entered subordinately according to the provisions in rule 24.24. *See* Fig. 12.41 (page 275).

Type 9. Chiefs of state and other heads of government are entered subordinately according to the provisions in rule 24.20. *See* Fig. 12.38 (page 274).

Type 10. Embassies, consulates, etc., and Type 11, Delegations to international and intergovernmental bodies, are also entered subordinately.

RULE 24.19. DIRECT OR INDIRECT SUBHEADING

This rule is the same as rule 24.14 except that the body is entered under the heading for the government instead of under the lowest element in the hierarchy that is entered under its own name. Other elements in the hierarchy are interposed or omitted in the same way and with the same difficulties in judgment. (*See* discussion under rule 24.14.) *See* Figs. 12.36 and 12.37.

Fig. 12.36. Rule 24.19. Indirect subordinate entry of an office.

Name on title page: Office of the Executive Director,
    Colorado Department of Natural Resources
AACR2R heading: Colorado. Dept. of Natural Resources.
    Office of the Executive Director.

Fig. 12.37. Rule 24.19. Direct subordinate entry of an office.

Name on title page: U.S. Department of Commerce
    Maritime Administration, Office of Commercial
    Development, Office of Port and Intermodal Development
AACR2R heading: United States. Office of Port and
    Intermodal Development.
Refer from: United States. Maritime Administration.
        Office of Port and Intermodal Development.
        United States. Maritime Administration. Office
        of Commercial Development. Office of Port
        and Intermodal Development.

Special Rules

RULE 24.20. GOVERNMENT OFFICIALS

24.20B. Heads of state, etc.

The heading for a head of state who is acting in an official capacity is made up of the name of the government followed by the title of the office in English, if possible, the inclusive years the person held that office, and a brief form name of the person in the language used for the person's personal heading. Non-sexist terminology is used, e.g., *Sovereign*, not *Queen* or *King*. See Fig. 12.38.

Fig. 12.38. Rule 24.20B. Entry of governor as an official.

[1]Govern-
ment

[2]Title

[3]Dates

[4]Surname

New York (State). Governor (1983-   : Cuomo)
Public papers of Governor Mario M. Cuomo

An explanatory reference should be made to the incumbent as a person (*see* rule 26.3C1 in *AACR2R*).

24.20C.   Heads of governments and of international governmental bodies

For heads of governments who are not also heads of state and for heads of international intergovernmental organizations, the subheading is the title of the office in the vernacular or in the official language of the organization, without dates or names.

RULE 24.21.   LEGISLATIVE BODIES

A legislature is entered under the name of the jurisdiction for which it makes laws. Chambers of legislative bodies are entered subordinately to the legislative body, and committees are entered subordinately to the legislature or to a chamber, whichever is appropriate. A subcommittee of the U.S. Congress is entered as a subheading of the committee to which it is subordinate. If legislatures are numbered, the number and year(s) are added [e.g., United States. Congress (95th : 1977-1978)]. Session numbers may also need to be added. *See* Fig. 12.39.

Fig. 12.39. Rule 24.21. Entry of a state legislative committee.

Name on title page: Committee on Motor Vehicles, Illinois
House of Representatives
AACR2R heading: Illinois. General Assembly. House of
Representatives. Committee on Motor Vehicles.

It should be noted that, although *AACR2R* shows in its examples "United States. Congress. House of Representatives," which is the official name of that body, the Library of Congress continues to use the conventional name "House" in its headings for the body. (*CSB* 44: 64)

RULE 24.23.   COURTS

Civil and criminal courts are entered as subheadings of the jurisdiction. A place name for the place a court sits or the area it serves is omitted but added as a conventional addition if needed to distinguish it from others of the same name. *See* Fig. 12.40.

Fig. 12.40. Rule 24.23. Entry of a court under jurisdiction with addition of area it serves.

Name on title page: Court of Common Pleas of Crawford County, Pa.
AACR2R heading: Pennsylvania. Court of Common Pleas (Crawford County)

RULE 24.24. ARMED FORCES

A principal service of the armed forces of a government is entered as a subheading of the government. A branch, district, or unit is entered as a subheading for the principal service, and if it is numbered, the numbering in the style used in the name follows the name. *See* Fig. 12.41.

Fig. 12.41. Rule 24.24. Entry of an armed service branch under the principal service.

Name on chief source of information: Air Defense Command, U.S. Air Force
AACR2R heading: United States. Air Force. Air Defense Command.

RELIGIOUS BODIES AND OFFICIALS: SELECTED RULES AND EXAMPLES

RULE 24.27. RELIGIOUS BODIES AND OFFICIALS

24.27A. Councils, etc., of a single religious body

Councils, etc., of a single religious body are entered as subheadings of that body. Appropriate additions may be made as for conferences, etc. (rule 24.7B). General councils are entered according to the general rules for subordinate bodies (rules 24.12-24.13). *See* Fig. 12.42.

Fig. 12.42. Rule 24.27A. Entry of a religious council.

Name on title page: Il Concilio romano del 1725
AACR2R heading: Catholic Church. Concilio romano (1725)

24.27B. Religious officials

The heading for a religious official acting in an official capacity looks very much like the heading for a head of state (rule 24.20B). It consists of the heading for the diocese, order, patriarchate, etc., followed by the title in English (unless there is no English equivalent), the inclusive years of incumbency, and the name of the person. *See* Fig. 12.43 (page 276).

Fig. 12.43. Rule 24.27B. Entry of a religious official.

Name on title page: His Holiness John Paul II
AACR2R heading: Catholic Church. Pope (1978-   : John Paul II)
Refer in an explanatory reference to the personal heading for John
  Paul II.

24.27C. Subordinate bodies

Provinces, dioceses, synods, and other subordinate units having jurisdiction over geographic areas are entered as subheadings of the religious body. For the Catholic Church, the English form of name should be used. *See* Fig. 12.44.

Fig. 12.44. Rule 24.27C. Entry of religious subordinate body.

Name on title page: Arzobispado del Cuzco
AACR2R heading: Catholic Church. Archdiocese of Cuzco
  (Peru)
Refer from: Catholic Church. Arzobispado del Cuzco.

NOTES

[1]*AACR2R*, p. 312.

[2]*Cataloging Service Bulletin*, no. 41 (Summer 1988): 54.

SUGGESTED READING

Hagler, Ronald. *The Bibliographic Record and Information Technology.* 2nd ed. Chicago, American Library Association, 1991. pp. 151-166.

Maxwell, Margaret F. *Handbook for AACR2, 1988 Revision.* Chicago, American Library Association, 1989. Chapter 16.

Uniform Titles   **13**

INTRODUCTION

When a work has appeared under more than one title, a uniform or conventional title may be used for cataloging purposes in order to bring all editions of the work together. Uniform titles have traditionally been used for sacred scriptures, creeds, liturgical works, and anonymous classics. *Bible* is a very common example of a uniform title in library catalogs; similarly, editions of the Mother Goose verses are assembled under the uniform title *Mother Goose.* In these cases the uniform titles represent main entry headings. In other instances the uniform title follows the main entry, as in the case of music, laws, liturgical works, and translations. *AACR2R*, chapter 25, contains many further suggestions for extending these rules to other instances.

One of the problems faced in constructing uniform titles is the choice of a title when titles of a work appear in more than one form. Titles may be in different languages, in one or more long forms and one or more short forms, or in two simultaneous versions (as when a work is published simultaneously in England and the United States under different titles). Some works may be published in parts and need identification of the part *without* identification of the whole (as in the case of one title from a trilogy) or *with* identification of the whole (as in the case of a book from Homer's *Iliad*, called only "Book 1"). Further additions may be needed to distinguish uniform titles from each other or from other headings, to identify the language in which the work appears, to identify the version, or to date the particular edition. The purpose of this chapter is to demonstrate the general rules used to resolve these problems. Much more detail can be found in *AACR2R*, chapter 25.

In addition to the first rule, which sets down the conditions for use of uniform titles, the *AACR2R* chapter comprises three groups of rules: basic rules for choice and form of the title itself (rules 25.2-25.4 and 25.12), rules for additions to uniform titles (rules 25.5-25.11), and special rules for certain materials (rules 25.13-25.35). The materials given special treatment are manuscripts (rule 25.13), incunabula (rule 25.14), legal materials (rules 25.15-25.16), sacred scriptures (rules 25.17-25.18), liturgical and other religious works (rules 25.19-25.24), and music (rules 25.25-25.35).

A heading created using this chapter is coded 130, 240, 630, 730, or 830 in the MARC format, depending upon whether it functions as a main entry, a supplementary title between main entry and the title proper, a subject heading, an added entry, or a series tracing.

RULE 25.1. USE OF UNIFORM TITLES

Whether or not uniform titles are needed depends on the type and size of catalog one has. *AACR2R* gives five criteria to use in deciding whether to use uniform titles:

"1) how well the work is known

2) how many manifestations of the work are involved

3) whether the main entry is under title (see 21.1C)

4) whether the work was originally in another language

5) the extent to which the catalogue is used for research purposes."[1]

In essence this rule states that the entire set of rules on uniform titles is optional, and a policy decision should be made in each cataloging agency as to whether some or all of the rules should be applied.

GENERAL RULES:
SELECTED RULES AND EXAMPLES

RULE 25.2. GENERAL RULE

25.2A. The basic rule gives an instruction to choose one title from among various ones that may appear on different manifestations of a work. (Revised editions are not included when considering variant titles of a work. *See* rule 25.2B.)

On the bibliographic record for a particular item the uniform title should be used if:

1) the title proper differs from the uniform title;

2) an addition of another element must be made because the title proper is not sufficient to organize the file (e.g., a uniform title is identical in form to the heading for a person or corporate body or another uniform title);

3) a title main entry or a title added entry must be differentiated from that of another work (e.g., two different serials are entered under their titles, which are identical); or

4) the title proper contains elements that obscure the title of the work (e.g., there are introductory words about the presentation of the work that precede the title proper but must be transcribed in grammatical order).

The uniform title is given before the title proper and enclosed in square brackets. If the main entry is title, *AACR2R* calls for it also to be enclosed in brackets, but an option allows omitting the brackets if the uniform title is used as main entry.

The Library of Congress is following the option, which is a continuation of LC's past practice. In addition it is LC practice not to enclose uniform titles in brackets when used in added entries. (*CSB* 27: 31) Brackets are used as prescribed when a uniform title falls between a main entry and a title proper. This is evident only in LC's printed products, however. Display of brackets in machine-readable products is dependent upon the programming of the system that displays the records. The examples in this text follow LC practice.

It is also LC practice in the case of anonymous classics that have been published in many editions, translations, and differing titles to use the uniform title for all editions, even when it does not differ from the title proper. (*CSB* 27: 31) *See* Fig. 13.1.

Fig. 13.1. Rule 25.2A. Uniform title as main entry without square brackets – LC practice.

Uniform ⟶ Beowulf.
title as   Beowulf : an edition with manuscript spacing notation
main entry   and graphotactic analyses / Robert D. Stevick

25.2B. Uniform titles are not used for revisions or updated versions of a work in the same language as the original. Instead, these are related by giving a note about the earlier edition in the bibliographic record for the later edition. *See* Fig. 13.2.

Fig. 13.2. Rule 25.2B. New title, not uniform title, is used for new edition in the same language.

Hawker, Pat.
    Amateur radio techniques / Pat Hawker. — 6th ed. —
London : Radio Society of Great Britain, 1978.
    336 p. : ill. ; 25 cm.
Note giving
title of   ⟶ First ed. published with title: Technical topics for the
earlier   radio amateur.
edition

25.2C. Initial articles

Initial articles are omitted unless the uniform title is to be filed under that article. *See* Fig. 13.3.

Fig. 13.3. Rule 25.2C. Initial article is not included in uniform title.

Initial   Dickens, Charles, 1812-1870.
article   ⟶ [Pickwick papers]
omitted   The Pickwick papers / Charles Dickens ; edited with an
    introduction and notes by James Kinsley

Individual Titles

RULE 25.3. WORKS CREATED AFTER 1500

25.3A. For a work created after 1500 the title in the original language by which the work has become known is used as its uniform title. The "known" title is judged from its use in manifestations of the work or in reference sources. *See* Fig. 13.4.

Fig. 13.4. Rule 25.3A. Uniform title in original language.

Suder, Joseph, 1892-
  [Dona nobis pacem]
  Festmesse in D [sound recording] / Joseph Suder

Other titles given to this work:

  Messe Dona nobis pacem
  Grosse Messe Dona nobis pacem

25.3B. If none of the titles in the original language can be established as being the "best known," the title proper of the original edition is used. In using such original titles, one should omit introductory phrases and statements of responsibility that can be grammatically separated. LC also omits alternative titles. (*CSB* 44: 65) *See* Fig. 13.5.

Fig. 13.5. Rule 25.3B. Use of title proper of the original edition when there are variant titles in the original language.

Original title   Cross, Amanda, 1926-
  ⟶ [Death in a tenured position]
  A death in the faculty / Amanda Cross. — London : Virago, 1988, c1981.

Note explaining uniform title:

  Originally published as: Death in a tenured position. New York : Dutton, 1981.

25.3C. Simultaneous publication under different titles

25.3C1. When a work is published in two or more editions simultaneously in the same language with different titles, the cataloger should use as uniform title the one for the edition published in the cataloging agency's country, if this applies. If it does not apply, the title of the edition received first should be used. *See* Fig. 13.6.

Fig. 13.6. Rule 25.3C1. American title used as uniform title for work whose British title is different.

Mansfield, Peter, 1928-
   [Arab world]
   The Arabs / Peter Mansfield. — Harmondsworth : Penguin, 1928.

Note explaining uniform title:
   American ed. published under title: The Arab world.

RULE 25.4. WORKS CREATED BEFORE 1501

25.4A. If a work was created before 1501, the title in the original language by which the work is identified in modern reference sources is used. If none of the titles can be established in reference sources, the title found most frequently in modern editions, early editions, or manuscript copies (in that order of preference) is used. This rule, however, is superseded by rules 25.4B-25.4C and 25.14, if they apply. *See* Fig. 13.7.

Fig. 13.7. Rule 25.4A. Uniform title for pre-1501 work as identified in reference sources.

Uniform ——▶Gawain and the Grene Knight.
title   Sir Gawain and the Green Knight / translated with an introduction by Brian Stone

25.4B-25.4C. In general, a well-established English title, if there is one, is used for a pre-1501 Greek work or anonymous work in nonroman script. *See* Fig. 13.8.

Fig. 13.8. Rules 25.4 and 25.5C1. Anonymous pre-1501 work originally in nonroman script entered under established English title with the language of the translation in hand added.

     1↘
[1]Uniform   ▶Arabian nights. English.◀—2
title   More fairy tales from the Arabian nights / edited and
[2]Language   arranged by E. Dixon ; illustrated by J.D. Batten

RULE 25.5. ADDITIONS TO UNIFORM TITLES

25.5B. Conflict resolution

25.5B1. If uniform titles used as main entries are identical to each other or to the form used as the heading for a person, corporate body, or reference, additions are made in parentheses to the uniform title. *See* Fig. 13.9 (page 282).

Fig. 13.9. Rule 25.5B1. Additions in parentheses to distinguish between two otherwise identical uniform titles.

Jungle book (1942)
    Jungle book [motion picture]

Jungle book (1967)
    The jungle book [motion picture]

Identical uniform titles that are entered under the same personal or corporate heading also need additions in parentheses to distinguish them. Example:

United States.
    [Census (1960]

United States.
    [Census (1970)]

For this rule LC has made a lengthy rule interpretation that prescribes the kinds of additions that are to be made to distinguish between otherwise identical titles of different serials, including monographic series. (*CSB* 50: 41-48) In general such conflicts are handled by adding a uniform title to the bibliographic record for the serial in hand, not to the one cataloged earlier.

Place of publication is LC's preferred qualifying term for conflicting serial titles. Example:

Times (Charleston, S.C.)

Times (Kansas City, Mo.)

However, if the title consists only of an indication of type and/or periodicity of publication, or if the place is inadequate to resolve the conflict, or if the conflicting titles include initials of their issuing bodies' names, then the heading for the body that originated or issued the serial is used as the qualifying term. Examples:

Occasional paper (Canberra College of Advanced Education. Library)

Occasional paper (London Public Library and Art Museum (Ont.))

European physics series (McGraw-Hill)

European physics series (Wiley)
    [both works published in New York, N.Y.]

Other qualifiers may be added when the above provisions do not suffice. Other qualifiers may be place and date, corporate body and date, date, edition statement, other title information, etc. The LC rule interpretation should be consulted for elaboration on these qualifiers and on other special situations such as may occur with radio and television programs, comics, motion pictures, and computer programs.

25.5C. Language

25.5C1. When the item in hand is in a different language from the original, the name of the language of the item is added to the uniform title. LC catalogers use the language name as established in the latest edition of *USMARC Code List for Languages*. (*CSB* 44: 66) *See* Figs. 13.8 and 13.10.

Fig. 13.10. Rule 25.5C1. Modern translation with original title as uniform title, followed by language of translation.

^{1}Uniform
title

^{2}Language

Leys, Simon, 1935- ^{2}

1——▶[Habits neufs du président Mao. English]

The Chairman's new clothes : Mao and the cultural revolution / Simon Leys ; translated by Carol Appleyard and Patrick Goode

AACR2R rule 25.5C and LC's rule interpretation on multilingual works should be consulted when more than one language is involved. (*CSB* 44: 66-67)

25.5D. An option allows addition of General Material Designations (GMDs) at the end of uniform titles. LC is not applying this option. (*CSB* 44: 67)

RULE 25.6. PARTS OF A WORK

This rule is not applied to parts of the Bible and certain other sacred scriptures (*see* rules 25.17-25.18) or to parts of musical works (*see* rule 25.32).

25.6A. One part

25.6A1. When a separately cataloged part of a work has a title that is not dependent for its meaning upon the title of the collected work, the title of the part alone is used as the uniform title. A reference is made from the form the heading would have if the title of the part were a subheading of the title of the whole work. *See* Fig. 13.11.

Fig. 13.11. Rule 25.6A1. Separately cataloged part with its own title as uniform title.

Hesse, Hermann, 1877-1962.
[Tractat vom Steppenwolf. English]
Treatise on the Steppenwolf / Hermann Hesse ; [translated from the German] ; paintings by Jaroslav Bradac

Note: The title of the whole work is *Der Steppenwolf.*
Refer from: Hesse, Hermann, 1877-1962.
Steppenwolf. Tractat vom Steppenwolf. English

25.6A2. When a separately cataloged part of a work has a title that *is* dependent for its meaning upon the title of the whole work, the uniform title is the title of the whole work followed by the title of the part as a subheading. Arabic numerals are used to record part numbers. *See* Fig. 13.12 (page 284).

Fig. 13.12. Rule 25.6A2. Separately cataloged part given as subheading of the title of the whole work.

¹Whole
work   Milton, John, 1608-1674.   ^²

1 ——▶[Paradise lost. Book 4]

²Part   Paradise lost, book IV / John Milton ; edited by S.E. Goggin

25.6B. More than one part

When an item consists of consecutively numbered parts, the designation of the parts in the singular is used as a subheading of the title of the whole work and is followed by the inclusive numbering of parts. *See* Fig. 13.13.

Fig. 13.13. Rule 25.6B. Separately cataloged consecutive parts of a work given as subheading of the title of the whole work.

¹Whole
work   Milton, John, 1608-1674.   ^²

1——▶[Paradise lost. Book 9-10]

²Singular
form of name   Paradise lost, books IX and X / John Milton ; edited
of part   by Cyril Aldred

When an item has two parts not consecutively numbered, the uniform title is made for the first part, and a name-title added entry is made for the second. When an item has three or more parts not consecutively numbered, the uniform title of the whole work is used, followed by "Selections."

RULE 25.7. TWO WORKS ISSUED TOGETHER

25.7A. When an item contains two works entered under a personal or corporate main entry, uniform titles are assigned to the two works. The uniform title of the first work is given following the main entry, and a name-title added entry using the second uniform title is made for the second work. *See* Fig. 13.14.

Fig. 13.14. Rule 25.7A. Separate uniform titles made for two works appearing in the same item.

Poe, Edgar Allan, 1809-1849.
    [Tell-tale heart]
    The telltale heart ; and, The cask of Amontillado [sound recording]

Added entry for second work:
    I. Poe, Edgar Allan, 1809-1849. Cask of Amontillado.

Collective Titles

Collective titles can be general (e.g., "Works," "Selections") or more specific (e.g., "Novels," "Poems," "Laws, etc."). When these are used alone, the effect is to separate originals from translations, different editions from each other, etc., if the titles proper are different. They also are inadequate when being used in added entries. Therefore, LC emphasizes using the principle found in rule 25.5B in conjunction with collective titles when needed to bring together items with different titles proper or to refer to a work in an added entry. The designation to be enclosed in parentheses may be title proper, editor, translator, publisher, etc. — whichever best fits each case. Example:

Maugham, W. Somerset (William Somerset), 1874-1965.
[Short stories (Heinemann)]
Complete short stories

This technique is applied only after the need arises; thus, earlier entries must be revised. (*CSB* 45: 72-73)

RULE 25.8.   COMPLETE WORKS
If an item contains, or claims to contain, the complete works of a person, the collective title "Works" is used as uniform title. *See* Fig. 13.15.

Fig. 13.15. Rule 25.8. Collective title "Works" used as uniform title.

Posada, José Guadalupe, 1852-1913.
[Works. English & German. 1976]
Das Werk von Jose Guadalupe Posada = The works of José Guadalupe Posada / edited and with an introduction by Hannes Jähn

A rule interpretation from LC indicates that "Works" occurs so frequently that there should always be additions made to such uniform titles to make them distinctive. The interpretation outlines the additions to be made. (*CSB* 45: 70-72)

RULE 25.9.   SELECTIONS
When an item contains three or more works in various forms, all by the same person, the collective title "Selections" is used as uniform title. *See* Fig. 13.16.

Fig. 13.16. Rule 25.9. Collective title "Selections" used as uniform title.

Twain, Mark, 1835-1910.
[Selections. 1987]
The outrageous Mark Twain : some lesser-known but extraordinary works : with "Reflections on religion" now in book form for the first time / selected and edited, with an introduction, by Charles Neider

LC calls for the same additions here that are made to the collective title "Works." (*CSB* 45: 73)

RULE 25.10. WORKS IN A SINGLE FORM
The following collective titles are used for a collection of the works of a person all in one form:

Correspondence   Poems
Essays   Prose works
Novels   Short stories
Plays   Speeches

LC applies this rule only when the title proper of the collection is not distinctive or when there is no collective title proper. (*CSB* 45: 73-74)

SPECIAL RULES FOR CERTAIN TYPES OF WORK:
SELECTED RULES AND EXAMPLES

Laws, Treaties, Etc.

RULE 25.15. LAWS, ETC.

25.15A. Modern laws, etc.

25.15A1. Collections
A collection of legislative enactments is given the uniform title "Laws, etc.," unless the compilation is on a particular subject. LC, when using "Laws, etc.," makes further additions, in parentheses, and revises existing records that lack the additions. The additions may consist of a brief title and, if needed, edition or date. The LC rule interpretation should be consulted. (*CSB* 36: 33-38) *See* Fig. 13.17.

> **Fig. 13.17. Rule 25.15A1. Collective title "Laws, etc.," used as uniform title.**
>
> India.
>   [Laws, etc. (Statutes of India)]
>   The statutes of India : a manual of central arts & rules : exhaustive commentary on all central acts with important central rules

When a compilation of laws is on a particular subject, a citation title, if there is one, should be used as uniform title. If there is no citation title, a uniform title should be constructed according to rule 25.3. LC adds that if a subject compilation lacks both a citation title and a collective title, the uniform title of the first law in the collection should be used. (*CSB* 36: 38)

25.15A2. Single laws, etc.
Single laws are assigned as uniform title one of the following (in order of preference): an official citation title (or official short title), an unofficial short or citation title used in legal literature, the official title, or any other official designation. *See* Fig. 13.18.

Fig. 13.18. Rule 25.15A2. Official short title used as uniform title.

[1]Govern-
ment   1➤Québec (Province)   3

[2]Uniform
title   2➤[Labour code. English & French]
Code du travail : Titre 1, des relations du travail =
Labour code : Title 1, labour relations

[3]Language

RULE 25.16. TREATIES, ETC.

The uniform title for treaties is "Treaties, etc." Various additions are made depending upon the circumstances: the second party for a collection of treaties between two parties or for single treaties between two parties; the date or earliest date of signing (in the form: year, abbreviated name of the month, number of the day) for a single treaty. A single treaty between four or more parties is entered under the name by which the treaty is known (in English, if possible) followed by the year of signing in parentheses. Added entries for individual signers, if made, are formulated with the uniform title "Treaties, etc.," followed by date of signing. *See* Fig. 13.19.

Fig. 13.19. Rule 25.16. Uniform title for a treaty between two parties.

[1]Conventional
uniform title   Soviet Union—1   2   3
[Treaties, etc. United States, 1990 June 1]

[2]Second
country   Agreement between the government of the United States of America and the government of the Union of Soviet Socialist Republics on the supply of grain

[3]Date

Sacred Scriptures

RULE 25.17. GENERAL RULE

The uniform title for a sacred scripture should be the title that is usually used in English-language reference sources that discuss the particular religious group that uses the scripture.

RULE 25.18. PARTS OF SACRED SCRIPTURES AND ADDITIONS

25.18A. Bible

When appropriate, the testaments (designated O.T. and N.T.) are added after the word *Bible*. Then books are designated. If the books are numbered, the number is given as an ordinal arabic numeral after the name. The name of a group of books may also be a subdivision of the testament (e.g., Minor Prophets, Apocrypha, Gospels). Next are added, as appropriate: 1) language; 2) version, translator, name of manuscripts or repository, or reviser; and 3) year. A single selection with a distinctive title is entered directly under that title with a reference from the appropriate "Bible" uniform title. If a work consists of more than two selections, they are entered under the most specific Bible heading appropriate to all, with the term *Selections* added after language and version but before the year. Examples:

> Bible. [parts] [language] [versions] [selections] [date]
> Bible. N.T. Gospels ...
> Bible. O.T. Historical books ...
> Bible. O.T. Genesis XII, 1 – XXV, 11 ...
> Bible. N.T. Corinthians, 1st ...
> Bible. English. New Jerusalem Bible. 1990.
> Bible. N.T. English. Stern. 1989.
> Bible. O.T. Leviticus. Hebrew. Samaritan. 1959.
> Bible. English. New Century. Selections. 1990.

See Figs. 13.20 and 13.21.

Fig. 13.20. Rule 25.18A. Uniform title for the Bible.

¹Uniform title

²Language

³Version

⁴Date

Bible. English. New Life. 1990.
Precious moments children's Bible : easy-to-read New Life Version

Fig. 13.21. Rule 25.18A. Uniform title for part of the Bible.

¹Uniform title

²Parts

³Language

⁴Date

Weinbach, Mendel.
Turnabout : the Malbim on Megilas Esther / by Mendel Weinbach

Note on part of Bible included:

"Scroll of Esther" in Hebrew: p. 1-50 (2nd group)

Added entry made for part from Bible:

I. Bible. O.T. Esther. Hebrew. 1990.

25.18B-25.18M. These are special rules for the Talmud, Mishnah and Tosefta, Midrashim, Buddhist scriptures, Vedas, Aranyakas, Brahmanas, Upanishads, Jaina Āgama, Avesta, and Koran. Rules are given for parts and additions as for the Bible.

Liturgical Works

RULE 25.19. GENERAL RULE

When a liturgical work is entered under an English-language corporate body name, the uniform title should also be in English if there is an established English title; if not, the uniform title is given in the language of the liturgy. *See* Fig. 13.22.

Fig. 13.22. Rule 25.19. Uniform title for a liturgical work.

[1]Corporate
name

[2]Uniform
title

[3]Language

Catholic Church. ◀—1
2—▶[Mass, Epiphany. German]
Messe an Epiphanias ◀—3

RULES 25.20-25.23.

These are special rules for Catholic and Jewish liturgical works, for variant and special texts, and for parts of liturgical works.

Musical Works

RULE 25.25.   GENERAL RULE

The general rule outlines the rules in the remainder of the chapter.

Uniform titles for:	Rule(s):
one musical work	25.26-25.31
one or more parts of a musical work	25.32
two works of a composer issued together	25.33
collections of music	25.34

The last rule, rule 25.35, is for additions to a uniform title to designate a particular manifestation. The cataloger is instructed to use rules 25.1-25.7 whenever they are applicable and are not contradicted by rules 25.26-25.35.

Individual Titles

RULE 25.26.   GENERAL RULE

The initial title element of the uniform title for a musical work is created as instructed in rules 25.27-25.29. Rules 25.30-25.32 and 25.35 give instructions for additions to the initial title element, although additions are not always required.

RULES 25.27-25.31.

Uniform titles are frequently used in cataloging music because the same musical composition is often issued in numerous editions with variations in the language and the wording of the title pages. Composer-title references are made from forms of the title not used as uniform title, as needed. The examples shown on page 290 are typical.

Beethoven, Ludwig van, 1770-1827.
Battle of Vitoria
see
Beethoven, Ludwig van, 1770-1827.
Wellingtons Sieg

Beethoven, Ludwig van, 1770-1827.
Cantata on the death of Emperor Joseph II
see
Beethoven, Ludwig van, 1770-1827.
Kantate auf den Tod Kaiser Josephs II

In the selection and construction of uniform titles the most reliable biblio-graphical sources are consulted, such as thematic indexes, bibliographies, music encyclopedias, etc. Information given in the work cataloged is not used without an attempt at verification. The Library of Congress catalogs are useful in con-structing a uniform title, but only after the cataloger has identified the work in thematic or other musical sources.

Rules 25.27-25.31 give the principles for construction of a uniform title for a single work. The basic rule for choice of uniform title instructs the cataloger to use the composer's original title unless a later title in the same language has become better known. If the title is distinctive, it is left unmodified unless there is a conflict. Example:

Bach, Johann Sebastian, 1685-1750.
[Kunst der Fuge]

If the title is distinctive and there *is* a conflict, the title is followed by some modification as instructed under rule 25.31B1. Example:

Bach, Johann Sebastian, 1685-1750.
[Wachet auf, ruft uns die Stimme (Cantata)]

Bach, Johann Sebastian, 1685-1750.
[Wachet auf, ruft uns die Stimme (Chorale prelude)]

However, if the title consists solely of the name of one type of composition, the title is constructed as instructed under rule 25.29A. Additions are then made according to rule 25.30: the medium of performance (the instruments for which it was written), followed by further identifying elements to distinguish the work from other compositions by the same composer, generally the serial number, opus (or thematic index) number, and the key. Examples:

Mozart, Wolfgang Amadeus, 1756-1791.
[Quartets, strings, K. 387, G major]
Quartett für 2 Violinen, Viola und Violoncello

Dvořák, Antonín, 1841-1904.
[Symphonies, no. 8, op. 88, G major]
From the new world : symphony no. 8 by Dvořák

Titles of works in the larger vocal forms (operas, oratorios, etc.) generally require additional modification because of the various versions in which they are likely to be issued. Example:

Puccini, Giacomo, 1858-1924.
    [Manon Lescaut]
    [Manon Lescaut. Vocal score]
    [Manon Lescaut. Libretto. English]

RULE 25.32. PARTS OF A WORK

A separately published part of a musical work uses the title of the whole work, followed by the title of the part. This is counter to rule 25.6A1 for other types of works. Examples:

Arne, Thomas Augustine, 1710-1778.
    [Artaxerxes. Soldier tir'd]

Schumann, Robert, 1810-1856.
    [Fantasiestücke, piano, op. 12. Nr. 7. Traumes Wirren]

Collective Titles

RULES 25.33-25.34

These rules give principles for construction of a uniform title for items containing more than one work. Two works published together (rule 25.33) are treated as in rule 25.7. Complete works (rule 25.34A) are treated as in rule 25.8. A collection of selections of various types of compositions originally composed for various instrumental and/or vocal media is assigned the uniform title "Selections" (rule 25.34B). However, if a collection contains works of various types all in a broad or specific medium, the designation of that medium is used (rule 25.34C1). For example:

[Instrumental music]
[Vocal music]
[Brass music]
[Piano music]
[Violin, piano music]

If the collection contains works of one type, the name of that type is used, with the addition of medium in appropriate cases (rule 25.34C2). For example:

[Operas]
[Quartets, strings]
[Sonatas, piano]

Additions

RULE 25.35.   ADDITIONS FOR MUSICAL WORKS

Further additions are made to distinguish sketches for a musical composition, arrangements of a musical work, translations of texts of vocal works, etc. Example:

Cowell, Henry, 1897-1965.
　　[Concerto brevis; arr.]
　　Concerto brevis : for accordion and orchestra

NOTES

[1]*AACR2R*, p. 484.

SUGGESTED READING

Hagler, Ronald. *The Bibliographic Record and Information Technology.* 2nd ed. Chicago, American Library Association, 1991. pp. 166-171.

Maxwell, Margaret. *Handbook for AACR2, 1988 Revision.* Chicago, American Library Association, 1989. Chapter 17.

Smiraglia, Richard P. *Cataloging Music: A Manual for Use with AACR2.* 2nd ed. Lake Crystal, Minn., Soldier Creek Press, 1986. Chapter 3.

_____. *Music Cataloging: The Bibliographic Control of Printed and Recorded Music in Libraries.* Englewood, Colo., Libraries Unlimited, 1989. pp. 54-61.

References

INTRODUCTION

All the rules in the preceding four chapters have referred to "references" needed when one name or form of heading is chosen from among more than one possible name or form of heading. This chapter is a summary of all those situations where references are called for explicitly or implicitly in the earlier rules. This chapter also gives examples of the different types of references. Chapter 26 of *AACR2R*, "References," begins with introductory notes that define different kinds of references, explain the form to use, and set up the conditions under which references should be made. Following this introduction are specific rules for and examples of references for persons, corporate bodies and geographic names, and uniform titles. Finally, there is a rule allowing references instead of certain added entries that are common to many editions.

References are not included in the bibliographic records for the items being cataloged when the references are made. Instead they are recorded in a record called an authority record. An authority record is a separate record for each name or title established as a heading to be used in the library's public catalog. It contains the established form for the heading, the forms from which references should be made to the established form, and, often, notes about the sources of information used in establishing the heading. In manual authority files the forms from which references are to be made are preceded by x's—one x precedes a *see from* reference, and two x's precede a *see also from* reference. In a machine-readable authority file headings and references are preceded by codes similar to those used in bibliographic records. There is a separate MARC format for authority records. In this format 1xx codes precede headings, 4xx codes precede *see from* references, and 5xx codes precede *see also from* references. Sample authority records and further information about authority files are given in chapter 25 of this text.

SELECTED RULES AND EXAMPLES

RULE 26.1. GENERAL RULE

26.1A. References are to be made as instructed in the previous four chapters and also according to the more general instructions in *AACR2R*, chapter 26. References should be made only to a heading for which there is an entry in the catalog. (References made to headings that are not there are called *blind references* because they direct a user to something that cannot be seen.) A record of every reference made should be kept under the heading to which the reference refers. (This record is usually kept on an authority record for the heading that is being referred to. The record, among other things, enables one to correct or delete a reference when the heading is changed or deleted.)

26.1B. *See* references

See references are used to direct users from a form of name or title of a work that they have looked under to the form that has been chosen as the heading for that name or title. A *see* reference says to the user, "No, you won't find what you're looking for here; but if you'll look under _____, you will find something."

26.1C. *See also* references

See also references are used to direct users from a name or uniform title heading to a related name or uniform title heading. A *see also* reference says to the user, "Yes, there is some information here, and you may also be interested in related information that you can find under _____."

26.1D. Name-title references

Name-title references are used when a title has been entered under a personal or corporate name and either *see* or *see also* references are needed from another form of the title. When such references are needed, the name is given before the title in both the form referred from and the form referred to.

26.1E. Explanatory references

Explanatory references are used when more guidance or explanation than can be given in simple references is necessary.

Terminology used in references is undergoing change with the expansion of online catalogs. In an online environment the codes 4xx and 5xx can be translated into other words or phrases than *see* and *see also*, if the creator of the system believes that other terminology would be more understandable to users. Popular substitutes are "search under" or "the heading used in this catalog is" for *see*, and "search also under" or "related information may be found under" for *see also*. Because *AACR2R* uses *see* and *see also*, these terms are used in the remainder of this chapter for ease of explanation.

There is a lengthy LC rule interpretation that explains the forms that references should take on LC authority records, explaining, for example, how references for "compatible headings" might differ from those for "pure" *AACR2* headings. (*CSB* 47: 57-60)

26.1F. Form of references

AACR2R suggests that the form of name from which a reference is made should have the same structure it would have if it were the heading rather than a reference to the heading. *AACR2R* also calls for making only one reference rather than two or more when one form is used to refer to more than one catalog heading. Examples:

Taylor, J. R.
    see also
Taylor, James Robert.
Taylor, John Roberts.

ACU
    see
Arbeitskreis Computer im Unterricht (Germany)
Association of Commonwealth Universities.
Association of Computer Users (U.S.)

The Library of Congress makes individual references rather than combined references in these instances. (*CSB* 44: 79) Presumably this is because of the difficulty of maintaining records of such combined references in an automated system. However, in most online systems that have access to authority records a search for initials brings up a response screen that lists all the headings with authority records that have a reference from those initials. The wording of the examples of references in *AACR2R* and in this text is not intended to be prescriptive, but only to provide examples.

RULE 26.2.   NAMES OF PERSONS

26.2A.   *See* **references**

26.2A1.   Different names
When a person has used a name different from that chosen for the heading for that person, or when a different name is found in reference sources, a reference is made from the different name to the heading. (*See also* rule 26.2C1 and rule 26.2D1.) Examples:

Tosi, Maria Teresa, 1918-
    see
Maria Teresa dell'Eucaristia, suor, 1918-

Beyle, Marie Henri, 1783-1842
    see
Stendhal, 1783-1842.

Sklodowska-Curie, Maria, 1867-1934
    see
Curie, Marie, 1867-1934.

26.2A2.   Different forms of the name
If a form of name used by a person is significantly different from the form used for the heading for the person, a reference is made. For LC catalogers the policy for normal inverted headings is to make references from forms that have any variations to the left of the comma or in the first element to the right of the comma. (*CSB* 45: 75) Examples:

Burt, Stanley G.
    see
Burt, S. G. (Stanley G.).

Abe, Suehisa, 1622-1709
    see
Abe, Suenao, 1622-1709.

(Examples continue on page 296.)

Ruth, George Herman, 1895-1948
    see
Ruth, Babe, 1895-1948.

Homerus
    see
Homer.

26.2A3. Different entry elements

A reference should be made from any element of a name heading under which a user might reasonably look for a name. Examples:

Van Zuidam, R. A.
    see
Zuidam, R. A. van.

Buren, Ariane van
    see
Van Buren, Ariane.

Damas, Bernardo Valverde
    see
Valverde Damas, Bernardo.

Ram Acharya
    see
Acharya, Ram.

Wellesley, Arthur, Duke of Wellington, 1769-1852
    see
Wellington, Arthur Wellesley, Duke of, 1769-1852.

26.2C. *See also* references

When a person is entered under two headings (e.g., two pseudonyms), *see also* references are made at each heading to direct the user also to search under the other heading. Example:

Baker, Ray Stannard, 1870-1946
    see also
Grayson, David, 1870-1946.

Grayson, David, 1870-1946
    see also
Baker, Ray Stannard, 1870-1946.

LC also makes a *see also* reference from a form of name from which a *see* reference should be made but which is exactly the same as another heading already established in the catalog and there are no data to resolve the conflict. Example:

Goldstein, Charles
   see also
Goldstein, Chaim Itsl.

Note: Goldstein, Charles is already established. (*CSB* 45: 77-78)

26.2D. Explanatory references

26.2D1. Explanatory references are provided when more information is needed for guidance than can be given with a *see* or *see also* reference. Examples:

Stone, Rosetta
   The joint pseudonym of Michael K. Frith and Dr. Seuss.
   For separate works entered under each name search also under:
   Frith, Michael K.
   Seuss, Dr.

Hunter, Evan, 1926-
   For works of this author written under pseudonyms, see
   Collins, Hunt, 1926-
   McBain, Ed, 1926-
   Marsten, Richard, 1926-

26.2D2. An option allows making an explanatory reference under each separately written prefix that can be used in a number of surnames. The purpose of such a reference is to explain how names with this prefix are entered in the catalog. Example:

Van
   Some names beginning with this prefix are also entered under the
   name following the prefix (e.g., Zuidam, R. A. van)

The Library of Congress is not applying this option. Instead, individual references are traced for each heading. (*CSB* 30: 22)

RULE 26.3. GEOGRAPHIC NAMES AND NAMES OF CORPORATE BODIES

26.3A. *See* references

26.3A1. Different names
   When a corporate body or place has appeared in works or reference sources with a different name or names than that used for the catalog heading, a reference is made from the different name. If, however, the name represents a name *change*, use rule 26.3C1. Example:

Detroit (Mich.). Police Dept. God Squad
   see
Detroit (Mich.). Police Dept. Chaplain Corps.

26.3A3. Different forms of the name

If a different form of name for a body or place is found in works or reference sources or if different romanizations result in different forms, references are made from the differing form(s). Examples:

A.B.E.D.I.A.
    see
Arab Bank for Economic Development in Africa.

Wien (Austria)
    see
Vienna (Austria)

Pharmaceutical Society of Korea
    see
Taehan Yakhakhoe.

Carlsruhe (Germany)
    see
Karlsruhe (Germany)

Kellogg Arabian Horse Center
    see
W.K. Kellogg Arabian Horse Center.

General Aniline and Film Corp. Ansco
    see
Ansco.

Society of Jesus
    see
Jesuits.

Bradner Associates
    see
Michael Bradner Associates.

Torup (Denmark)
    see
Hammer, Torup (Denmark)

26.3A5. Numbers

If the catalog is filed so that numbers expressed as words are in a different place than numbers expressed as numerals, make references from the opposite form to the one used in the heading, if the number is in a position to affect the filing. Example:

3 Bridges Reformed Church (Three Bridges, N.J.)
    see
Three Bridges Reformed Church (Three Bridges, N.J.)

26.3A6. Abbreviations

If the catalog is filed so that abbreviations are in a different place than the equivalent words, refer from the full form to an abbreviation, if the abbreviation is in a position to affect the filing. Example:

Mount Auburn Associates (Somerville, Mass.)
>   see
>   Mt. Auburn Associates (Somerville, Mass.)

LC includes ampersands or other symbols that represent *and* here. If such a symbol occurs in the first five words, a reference from the name using *and* or its equivalent in the language of the heading is made. For other abbreviations to get a reference, LC requires that they be in the first five words, not be listed in Appendix B.9 of *AACR2R, and* not represent a proper name. (*CSB* 21: 45)

26.3A7. Different forms of heading

References are made from different forms of a corporate name that seem to be reasonable forms under which a user might search. Examples:

Cambridge University
>   see
>   University of Cambridge.

California Institute of Technology. Baxter Art Gallery
>   see
>   Baxter Art Gallery.

Project Introspection
>   see
>   Virgin Islands of the United States. Project Introspection.

United States. Maritime Administration. Office of Commercial Development. Office of Port and Intermodal Development
>   see
>   United States. Office of Port and Intermodal Development.

Treviso (Italy). Cathedral
>   see
>   Treviso Cathedral.

26.3B. *See also* references

26.3B1. *See also* references are made between corporate headings that are related. This includes names that represent corporate name changes. LC calls these "earlier/later heading references," and instead of reading *see also*, the message of the reference reads "search also under the earlier heading" or "search also under the later heading." (*CSB* 27: 41-42) Examples:

Gemeentelijke Archiefdienst Amsterdam
>   see also
>   Amsterdam (Netherlands). Gemeentearchief.

(Examples continue on page 300.)

Automotive Transport Association of Ontario
search also under the later heading
Ontario Trucking Association.

Ontario Trucking Association
search also under the earlier heading
Automotive Transport Association of Ontario

26.3C. Explanatory references

26.3C1. General rule

Explanatory references are made when more guidance is required. Examples:

United Nations. Missions.
Delegations, missions, etc. from member nations to the United Nations
and to its subordinate units are entered under the name of the nation
followed by the name of the delegation, mission, etc., e.g.

United States. Mission to the United Nations.
Uruguay. Delegación en las Naciones Unidas.

A. Harris & Co.
Sanger Brothers was established in 1857. A. Harris & Co. was established in 1886. In 1961 they merged to form Sanger-Harris.
Works by these bodies are found under the following headings
according to the name used at the time of publication:

Sanger Brothers.
A. Harris & Co.
Sanger-Harris.

The Library of Congress no longer makes references of this type. Instead
each related body is connected with the earlier or later name by a *see also* reference. References like the "United Nations. Missions" example above are handled
by tracing specific *see* references on each applicable authority record. (*CSB* 27:
41-51)

26.3C2. Acronyms

When a filing system files initials separated by periods in a different place
from initials not separated by periods, *AACR2R* allows for making an explanatory reference. Examples:

N.A.C.
see
National Automobile Club
Naval Avionics Center (U.S.)
When these initials occur in a title or other heading without spaces
or periods, they are filed as a single word.

NAC
see
National Automobile Club
Naval Avionics Center (U.S.)
When these initials occur in a title or other heading with spaces or periods, they are filed as if each initial is a single word.

The Library of Congress no longer makes explanatory references for acronyms. They are converted to simple *see* references on the authority record for each name involved. (*CSB* 27: 51-52)

RULE 26.4. UNIFORM TITLES

26.4A. A rule calling for a reference to or from a uniform title, in some cases, means that the reference may require a name heading preceding the uniform title.

26.4B. *See* references

26.4B1. Different titles or variants of the title
When different titles have been used in other editions of a work than the one(s) held by the library, or when variant titles have been used to cite a work in reference sources, references may be made from these variants. Examples:

Laderman, Ezra.
Trials of Galileo
see
Laderman, Ezra.
Galileo Galilei

Córdoba (Argentina : Province)
Ley no. 4051
see
Córdoba (Argentina : Province)
Ley orgánica del poder judicial (1942)

Suder, Joseph, 1892-
Festmesse, in D
see
Suder, Joseph, 1892-
Dona nobis pacem

Revueltas, Silvestre, 1899-1940.
Chit-chat music
see
Revueltas, Silvestre, 1899-1940.
Música para charlar
[Title page title: Música para charlar = Chit-chat music. Title added entries would be made for both titles. In the other cases, a title added entry would be made for the title proper of the edition being cataloged.]

When translated titles are involved, the reference is made from the translated version of the title to the uniform title followed by the appropriate language subheading. Examples:

Song of Roland
see
Chanson de Roland. English

Naft, Stephen, 1878-1956.
Kyōsanshugi ni taisura nijū no shitsumon
see
Naft, Stephen, 1878-1956.
Answer please! Questions for communists. Japanese

26.4B2. Titles of parts of a work cataloged independently

When a part of a work is cataloged so that the part is entered independently, a reference is made from the uniform title of the whole work with the part as a subheading to the title of the part as an independent entry. Example:

Hesse, Hermann, 1877-1962.
Steppenwolf. Tractat vom Steppenwolf
see
Hesse, Hermann, 1877-1962.
Tractat vom Steppenwolf

26.4B3. Titles of parts cataloged under the title of the whole work

When a part of a work is cataloged so that the part is a subheading of the whole work, and if the title of the part is distinctive, a reference is made from the title of the part to the uniform title of the whole work with the part as a subheading. Examples:

Strauss, Richard, 1864-1949.
Breit über mein Haupt dein schwarzes Haar
see
Strauss, Richard, 1864-1949.
Lieder, op. 19. Breit über mein Haupt dein schwarzes Haar

Muʿawwidhatān
see
Koran. Muʿawwidhatān.

26.4B4. Collective titles

If a collection or selection of works of one person has been given a collective uniform title, and if the title proper is distinctive, a name-title reference is made from the title proper to the uniform title. Example:

Shepp, Archie.
Further fire music
see
Shepp, Archie.
Instrumental music. Selections

SUGGESTED READING

Chan, Lois Mai. *Cataloging and Classification: An Introduction.* New York, McGraw-Hill, 1981. pp. 117-121.

Smiraglia, Richard P. *Cataloging Music: A Manual for Use with AACR2.* 2nd ed. Lake Crystal, Minn., Soldier Creek Press, 1986. pp. 75-83.

Part III

SUBJECT ANALYSIS

Subject Arrangement of Library Materials **15**

INTRODUCTION

Subject analysis is the part of cataloging that deals with determining what the intellectual content of an item is "about," translating that "aboutness" into the conceptual framework of the classification or subject heading system being used, and then translating the conceptual framework into the specific classificatory symbols or specific terminology used in the classification or subject heading system.

First, one must have a clear idea about the level of exhaustivity that is to be applied. Exhaustivity has to do with the number of concepts that will be considered in the conceptual framework of the system. A. G. Brown identifies two basic degrees of exhaustivity: depth indexing and summarization.[1] Depth indexing aims to extract all the main concepts dealt with in an item, recognizing many subtopics and subthemes. Summarization recognizes only a dominant, overall subject of the item, recognizing only concepts embodied in the main theme. In library cataloging subject analysis has traditionally been carried out at the summarization level, reserving depth indexing for other enterprises such as periodical indexes.

Determining what an item is about at the summarization level can be a difficult matter. In chapter 1 of this text, Cutter's statement of the basic functions of a catalog was quoted, including "To show what the library has ... on a given subject." (See p. 7). The implication of this is that it is obvious what being "on a given subject" means. Patrick Wilson has discussed this matter at some length and has suggested that part of the problem is that catalogers and others are taught to look for *the* subject of an item.[2] He observes that if a person is writing a book or paper, and you ask what the person is writing about, he or she can tell you. If you go further and ask what is the subject about which the person is writing, this seems to be an equivalent question; but using the definite article *the* in front of *subject* implies that there will be just one thing to mention in answer to the question. Wilson's further explication demonstrates the fallacy of this assumption.[3]

Although some items *seem* to have an easily determined subject, it may not be so. A work entitled *History of Mathematics* is about the discipline of mathematics; but it is more specifically about mathematics from a historical perspective while not being about the discipline of history. This distinction has a certain subtlety that is learned through education in our present-day Western tradition. It is possible that in another place and time history would be considered to be the major subject of anything historical, regardless of the specific topic. Let us take another example: *Nature in Italian Art: A Study of Landscape Backgrounds from Giotto to Tintoretto*. This work is about landscape painting—specifically in Italian art during a set period of time. Is it *about* Italian art? Who is to say that it would not be useful to someone searching for information on Italian art? Is it about Giotto and Tintoretto and all the landscape artists in between? Of course it is, and if one were doing depth indexing, all would be indexed; but if one is looking for *the* subject, a listing of names of numerous artists will not do.

Determining what something is about depends to some extent upon one's knowledge or opinions about the world and upon understanding a work in different ways depending upon one's experiences. Many people could read a list of names that included Giotto and Tintoretto and not know that the list was a list of Italian artists, not to mention that they were landscape painters. A person could understand each individual sentence in a writing and still not know what the writing as a whole was about.

In addition determination of "aboutness" may depend on judgment. This problem has been elaborated upon by Sayers:

> If [a] book on Scotland is not mainly geographic and historical, but consists of descriptive and narrative chapters together with a melange of literary and scientific observations and reflections on the national traits and institutions, also considerable social philosophy in the last chapters, the judgment is indeed complex and the decisions may be uncertain.[4]

Because it is difficult to define what "on a given subject" means, and because determining "aboutness" depends upon the indexer's or cataloger's knowledge, opinions, experiences, and judgment, Marcia Bates has observed that "it is practically impossible to instruct indexers or catalogers [on] how to find subjects when they examine documents. Indeed, we cataloging instructors usually deal with this essential feature of the skill being taught by saying such vague and inadequate things as 'Look for the main topic of the document.'"[5]

Wilson describes some of the methods that people use to come to their own understanding of what a work is about:[6]

1. Purposive method — This is an attempt to understand what the author "is trying to describe, report, narrate, prove, show, question, explain."[7] One tries to determine what the author is up to and what the objective, aim, or purpose is. There may be a statement of purpose, or the author may describe an attempt, and if we assume that a person knows what he or she is doing, we can then "know" what the work is about. But some authors aim at several things at the same time and may accomplish them unequally. Some have secondary purposes that, upon reading, may appear to be primary. And many authors say nothing about their aims.

2. Figure-ground method — The cataloger attempts to determine the "central figure" (which can be an individual item or a group of items) that stands out from the background of detail. By the impression of dominance, or by reference to what stands out, the cataloger determines the subject of the work. But what stands out depends on the reader as well as the author. What catches one's interest and absorbs one's attention will not be the same for everyone or, indeed, for the same person at different times.

3. Objective method—This method involves counting references to items (e.g., name or topic), including references where the item is not named explicitly. If references to one item vastly outnumber references to anything else, then that item is the subject. Unfortunately, an item constantly referred to might be a background item (e.g., Washington, D.C., in a work about presidents). It is also possible for the words of a subject never to appear (Wilson gives the example of a writing said to be on the subject of the political career of a person but that contains no occurrence of the words *political career*).[8] Counting references also may require grouping references according to a principle supplied by the cataloger, which may differ from person to person.

4. Method of appealing to unity or to rules of selection and rejection—When using this method the reader tries to determine what unity and completeness there is. What makes the work cohesive? What has been said (selection) and *not* said (rejection)? The result again depends upon the reader; discovery of how a work seems to be cohesive may be one of several possible ways in which it can appear to be unified. Obviously, in order to use this method one must know quite a lot about the subject area into which the work falls. Otherwise, how could one know what had been rejected? In addition, authors do not always attain the ideal of a work that is cohesive with all parts connected and with no loose ends.

As the foregoing discussion indicates, there is no one correct way to determine "aboutness." Catalogers can use any or all of these methods, but the different methods will not necessarily lead to the same result. Yet, Wilson points out, "each seems to have a reasonable claim to being *a* way of picking out the subject of a writing."[9] If they *do* give the same result, one might be reasonably assured of having found *the* subject. However, a single cataloger might arrive at three or four different subjects using the different methods, and several catalogers might arrive at different results using the same method.

Two other works besides Wilson's that are useful for someone faced with the need to determine "aboutness" are *Documentation: Methods for Examining Documents, Determining Their Subjects and Selecting Indexing Terms*, published by the International Organization for Standardization, and *Subject Analysis: Principles and Procedures*, by D. W. Langridge.[10] These give suggested guidelines on what to look for when doing subject analysis.

Evidence of the difficulty in determining subjects consistently is found in studies in which people have been asked to give subject headings they would use to find specific books. In one such study by Oliver Lilley, 340 students looked at six books and suggested an average of 62 different headings for each book.[11] Given the difficulty of predicting the subject analysis even a trained cataloger will pull from an item, one might wonder if subject cataloging is worth the effort. Prior to the 1980s there was considerable antipathy toward subject access in the United States based in part on studies that showed that academic library card catalog users used a subject approach only about 30 percent of the time. However, Karen Markey has constructed a grid of card catalog use studies in several types of libraries completed between 1967 and 1981 that shows that subject approaches in card catalogs varied from 10 percent to 62 percent and the median was about 40 percent.[12] More recently studies of online catalog users have showed that subject access in online catalogs is quite popular—one study of many types of libraries with different online systems showed that subject approaches were about 59 percent of all catalog uses.[13] It must be assumed, therefore, that subject analysis has been done well enough that people find it useful, if not perfect.

Once the cataloger has decided what he or she thinks an item is about, that "aboutness" must be translated into the conceptual framework of the system. If one is classifying, this usually means one must determine disciplines, sub-disciplines, subtopics, space (i.e., place in which the subject is set), time, and form (e.g., fictional treatment, dictionary). A. G. Brown gives an excellent introduction to the process of learning to place one's subject into a conceptual framework necessary for classification.[14] If one is using a verbal subject system, the conceptual framework of the system usually also requires that the subject be thought of from general to specific, although the discipline and sub-discipline levels are not often required.

Finally, the cataloger assigns classification symbols from the particular classification scheme being used and subject headings according to a set of rules, as is the case with PRECIS headings (see discussion of PRECIS in chapter 24), or from a list of headings, which may also have rules for using the list, as is the case with Library of Congress Subject Headings (LCSH) or with the *Sears List of Subject Headings* (*Sears*). (See discussion of LCSH and *Sears* in chapters 22 and 23.) The classification notation is usually used as the basis for a call number, which will determine the position of the item on the library's shelves. The subject term(s) most often appear as access points for the item in the library's catalog.

CLASSIFIED VERSUS ALPHABETIC APPROACH
TO INFORMATION

During cataloging, the cataloger must take into account the dual manifestations of the items to be added to the collection. Items are both intellectual and physical entities. In descriptive cataloging the physical description addresses the physical entity while access points are constructed to allow for approach to the intellectual work. In subject analysis, classifiers traditionally choose only one classification, which will place in one location on the shelves all copies of a given item. On the other hand, catalogers may choose more than one subject term or classification under which to represent an item in a catalog or index. Classifiers strive for the optimum location in view of the content of the item, the accepted classification schedule, and the needs of the clientele. Such decisions are not always easy to make. For instance, the same historical treatise might go equally well into political or economic history, or perhaps under social history or biography. In the choice of subjects to be represented in the catalog or index for this hypothetical treatise, all the aspects can be brought out through choice of multiple access points.

Inquirers who want information on a certain subject will approach the catalog with questions formulated in their own words. These terms must be translated into the predetermined access categories of the catalog. Such communication between inquirer and catalog, with the possible intervention of a librarian, must take place regardless of the type of catalog consulted or the arrangement of its entries. Two systems of arranging entries in a library catalog were discussed in chapter 1. Classified catalogs were said to be the older of the two, although in present-day libraries they are less numerous than alphabetical catalogs of either the dictionary or the divided type. In the case of the classified catalog, the user's search terms must be converted to retrieval by means of classification. More than one category of the schedules may represent a significant aspect of the same item, thus allowing more than one entry or access point for that item. Skilled users may know the schedules well enough to go directly to those categories that correspond to their needs. However, any classified catalog must be accompanied by an alphabetical index, to help users translate their search terms into classification notations that represent them in the catalog.

The alphabetical catalog might facilitate the information retrieval process for most users, but it is similar in principle to the classified catalog index. In either case, the search for relevant information usually starts with an alphabetical list of subject terms. If the user's terminology coincides with that of the list, the search process will be quite direct. If not, the user must follow references or try to adjust his or her vocabulary to that of the system.

Still, each type of catalog requires a different pattern of communication. The classified catalog offers a "vertical" (hierarchical) approach to the collection through its closely related classes and categories, under which materials can be identified by means of logical, orderly sequences from general to specific. The alphabetical catalog gives a "horizontal" approach through its random scattering of access points throughout the entire linguistic finding apparatus.

Classified Arrangement

Certain advantages of a classified catalog were cited in chapter 1. They include:

1. *A controlled order of academic disciplines, as well as of popular topical sequences.* This order fosters direct, efficient searching at either catalog or shelf for those users familiar with the classification scheme. A reader interested in psychology, for instance, can initially consult and study a single section of the catalog with assurance of its relevance.

2. *Extensive opportunities for in-depth searching.* Based on logical relationships rather than linguistic associations, this arrangement not only offers a better comprehension of subject matter, but also directly stimulates the learning experience. It expands the frequently discussed values of browsing in an open-shelf library. Directly related is the opportunity to search in both directions, from general to specific as well as from specific to general.

3. *Denotative symbols (notation) objectively signifying topics and categories.* They reduce to a minimum the connotative implications and prejudices often associated with linguistic terms. The notation further allows one class number to be used for shelving, while others may designate supplementary entries in the catalog.

There are, on the other hand, disadvantages which account for the relatively few classed catalogs in modern libraries in the United States:

1. *Much of our cultural heritage, as recorded in documentary collections, cannot be satisfactorily systematized.* Any classification scheme has inherent deficiencies. The most effective classed catalogs are in special libraries, chiefly those for one or more scientific or technological disciplines. These areas are the most susceptible to rigid logical systematization. Even traditional academic disciplines tend to crumble nowadays before the onslaught of inter- and multi-disciplinary studies. Systems of arrangement within any subject field can be made obsolete by the advancing frontiers of knowledge.

2. *Systematic arrangements are almost never such ready vehicles of common knowledge as is the alphabet.* While factual information, study, and research slowly became less and less the province of aristocrats alone, due to the spread of democracy and popular education, the older, more esoteric patterns of organization, however worthy, were often sacrificed to the rote mechanisms of arithmetic and alphabetic progression.

With online catalogs it is possible to have both approaches in the same catalog, and some experimentation with this is being done. For the most part, so far, access by classification notation in online catalogs is a shelflist approach— that is, there is only one classification notation for any one item. Karen Markey and Anh Demeyer have experimented with making the verbal terms associated with Dewey Decimal classification numbers in the scheme itself searchable alongside the subject headings assigned. They found that searchers locate approximately equal numbers of relevant items using either the traditional subject headings or the terminology associated with the classification, but the groups of relevant items retrieved by the two methods are different from each other.[15]

The alphabetic index accompanying a classified catalog usually gives access only to spans and categories of classification, unlike an alphabetical catalog, which identifies specific titles. It points the user to both the classified catalog, where *all* the library's holdings are recorded, and the shelves, where actual documents can be examined, but where items may be missing, being at the moment in use elsewhere. It may be a published index to a particular classification scheme, e.g., the "relative index" of the Dewey Decimal Classification. It may be a list of separately published subject headings that are locally associated with class numbers from a given system, e.g., *Library of Congress Subject Headings*, which carries many LC classification numbers, although it is not specifically designed to be a classification index. Or it may be a specially generated index, such as a chain index, based on the extracted vocabulary of the classification used. The major advantage of a chain index in this context is that specific rules for controlling the index vocabulary may be based on the classification scheme being used. For example, the concept "alcoholic beverages" is listed in the index of the *Dewey Decimal Classification*, 20th edition (*DDC20*), with 10 different class numbers in 10 contexts. Four of these contexts are outlined below:

100	Philosophy
170	Ethics
172-179	Applied ethics
178	Ethics of consumption
178.1	In use of alcoholic beverages

300	Social sciences
390	Customs, etiquette, folklore
394	General customs
394.1	Drinking
394.13	Alcoholic beverages

600	Technology
660	Chemical engineering and related technologies
663	Beverage technology
663.1	Alcoholic beverages

640	Home economics
641	Food and drink
641.2	Beverages
641.21	Alcoholic beverages

From these sequences and categories, the following chain index entries could result:

Alcoholic beverages: applied ethics 178.1
Alcoholic beverages: beverage technology: chemical engineering and related technologies 663.1
Alcoholic beverages: customs 394.13
Alcoholic beverages: home economics 641.21
Applied ethics 172-179
Beverage technology: chemical engineering and related technologies 663
Beverages: home economics 641.2
Chemical engineering and related technologies 660
Customs 394
Customs, etiquette, folklore 390
Drinking: customs 394.1
Ethics of consumption: philosophy 178
Ethics: philosophy 170
Food and drink: home economics 641
Home economics 640
Philosophy 100
Social sciences 300
Technology 600

Alphabetical Arrangement

Some of the more obvious advantages of an alphabetical catalog or index are:

1. *Simplicity and popularity.* The apparent simplicity of alphabetical filing can be deceptive, however. Filing problems inevitably arise, especially in dictionary catalogs, where interfiling personal and corporate authors, titles, subjects, references, etc., becomes something like the old dilemma of adding apples and oranges to pears. (The filing of LC subject headings is discussed in chapter 22, and chapter 28 addresses general filing systems and problems.)

2. *Direct access to bibliographic data and holdings.* In spite of its filing pitfalls, a consolidated, single-strike catalog is in many ways more efficient. The "double look-up," and even more extended serial searching, is reduced to a minimum. The user may in most cases move directly from the catalog to the shelves.

3. *Greater freedom in introducing new groupings.* Descriptive subject headings need not bear the same logical relationship to one another as do classes in a systematic arrangement.

On the other hand, the alphabetic approach has serious drawbacks:

1. *Fragmentation of subject matter.* Most published subject heading lists for libraries indulge in a kind of surreptitious "classing" through the use of inversions, subdivisions, and the like. The urge to group like topics in one place, to make subject searching more efficient, is almost irresistible.

2. *Exacerbation of semantic problems.* In the absence of short, specific words for many subject concepts, awkward compound and prepositional phrase headings soon appear, complicating the filing and confounding the user.

3. *Inherent weakness in the conceptual structure of subject headings.* With no systematic framework to regulate its growth, an alphabetic subject list inevitably stumbles over the problems of the plurality and specificity of its terms. The concept of specific entry is difficult to control, as we shall see in a later chapter.

CONCLUSION

This chapter has discussed the topic of subject analysis and arrangement of library materials both by classification and by verbal/alphabetical approaches. In the chapters that follow these two approaches are considered separately along with systems and schemes for implementing each approach. The student should remember, however, that these are two sides of the same coin and that both are attempts to provide users access to the intellectual contents of the items being analyzed.

NOTES

[1]A. G. Brown, in collaboration with D. W. Langridge and J. Mills, *An Introduction to Subject Indexing*, 2nd ed. (London, Bingley, 1982), frames 48 and 51.

[2]Patrick Wilson, "Subjects and the Sense of Position," in *Theory of Subject Analysis: A Sourcebook*, edited by Lois Mai Chan, Phyllis A. Richmond, and Elaine Svenonius (Littleton, Colo., Libraries Unlimited, 1985), p. 309.

[3]Wilson, "Subjects and the Sense of Position," pp. 309-320.

[4]W. C. Berwick Sayers, *Sayers' Manual of Classification for Librarians*, 3rd ed. rev. by Arthur Maltby (London, Andre Deutsch, 1955), pp. 235-236.

[5]Marcia Bates, "Subject Access in Online Catalogs: A Design Model," *Journal of the American Society for Information Science* 37, no. 6 (November 1986): 360.

[6]Wilson, "Subjects and the Sense of Position," pp. 312-318.

[7]Wilson, "Subjects and the Sense of Position," p. 312.

[8]Wilson, "Subjects and the Sense of Position," p. 317.

[9]Wilson, "Subjects and the Sense of Position," p. 318.

[10]*Documentation: Methods for Examining Documents, Determining Their Subjects and Selecting Indexing Terms* (Geneva, Switzerland, International Organization for Standardization, 1985); D. W. Langridge, *Subject Analysis: Principles and Procedures* (London, Bowker-Saur, 1989).

[11]Oliver L. Lilley, "Evaluation of the Subject Catalog," *American Documentation* 5, no. 2 (April 1954): 41-60, as cited in Bates, "Subject Access in Online Catalogs," p. 361.

[12]Karen Markey, *Subject Searching in Library Catalogs: Before and After the Introduction of Online Catalogs* (Dublin, Ohio, OCLC, 1984), pp. 75-77.

[13]*Using Online Catalogs: A Nationwide Survey*, edited by Joseph R. Matthews, Gary S. Lawrence, and Douglas K. Ferguson; sponsored by the Council on Library Resources (New York, Neal-Schuman, 1983), p. 144.

[14]Brown, *Introduction to Subject Indexing*, frames 91-130.

[15]Karen Markey and Anh Demeyer, *Dewey Decimal Classification Online Project: Evaluation of a Library Schedule and Index Integrated into the Subject Searching Capabilities of an Online Catalog: Final Report to the Council on Library Resources* (Dublin, Ohio, OCLC, 1986).

SUGGESTED READING

Brown, A. G., in collaboration with D. W. Langridge and J. Mills. *An Introduction to Subject Indexing.* 2nd ed. London, Bingley, 1982.

Chan, Lois Mai. *Cataloging and Classification: An Introduction.* New York, McGraw-Hill, 1981. Chapter 3.

Documentation: Methods for Examining Documents, Determining Their Subjects and Selecting Indexing Terms. Geneva, Switzerland, International Organization for Standardization, 1985.

Foskett, A. C. *The Subject Approach to Information.* 4th ed. London, Bingley; Hamden, Conn., Linnet Books, 1982.

Hagler, Ronald. *The Bibliographic Record and Information Technology.* 2nd ed. Chicago, American Library Association, 1991. Chapter 7.

Langridge, D. W. *Subject Analysis: Principles and Procedures.* London, Bowker-Saur, 1989.

Wellisch, Hans, ed. *Subject Retrieval in the Seventies: New Directions: Proceedings of an International Symposium*, edited by Hans Wellisch and Thomas D. Wildon. Westport, Conn., Greenwood, 1972.

Wilson, Patrick. "Subjects and the Sense of Position," in *Theory of Subject Analysis: A Sourcebook*, edited by Lois Mai Chan, Phyllis A. Richmond, and Elaine Svenonius. Littleton, Colo., Libraries Unlimited, 1985.

Classification of Library Materials

16

INTRODUCTION

Collections in libraries of any appreciable size are arranged according to some system, and the arrangement is generally referred to as classification. Classification provides formal, orderly access to the shelves.

No matter what scheme is chosen, or how large the library, the purpose of classification is to bring related items together in a helpful sequence from the general to the specific. Ease of access is especially important if the collection is heterogeneous. It is convenient and desirable—particularly in the open-shelf collections to which many libraries in the United States are committed—to have, for example, all histories of the United States together, or all books on symbolic logic, or all symphony scores, so that the patron, who may or may not have one title in mind, can find related works in one location.

The ultimate aim of any classification system is to lead the patron to the items required. Traditionally in the United States this has been accomplished either through direct search of the shelves (open stacks) or through the help of a library attendant whose duty is to retrieve the materials on demand (closed stacks). Each system has its virtues. Open stacks encourage browsing, and thus stimulate intellectual awareness and foster serendipity. They work best with a logical, fairly comprehensible system of classification that encourages the patron's self-reliance in seeking items on a particular subject or its specific aspects. Closed stacks lessen the chances that materials will be mishandled, misplaced, or stolen, but they force the patron to limit his or her own searching to the catalog (and perhaps the shelflist) and to wait for a library employee to bring items specifically requested. Closed stacks are valuable in a storage library situation where items may not be shelved in subject groups at all, but ranged in more or less fixed location by size, with consecutive numbers assigned as addresses. "Fixed location" means that each item has one specific, fixed position on the shelf in the library as was the case in many libraries prior to the mid-nineteenth century. "Relative location" is a fluid, constantly changing arrangement of items according to their relationship to one another and resulting from the addition of new materials or the removal of old, weeded, or lost materials. In this system items may be moved from shelf to shelf without altering or disturbing their classified sequence.

No matter what the classification scheme or the type of shelving, the library catalog, as primary source of reference, must be complete and current. It provides information about particular items or types of items through various access points—usually by author(s) or other names associated with an item, by any title given to a work, by subject headings, and, occasionally, by classification numbers themselves. Along with information found via these access points is usually a call number (i.e., the shelf address where an item may be found). One element of the call number is usually the classification.

LIBRARY CLASSIFICATION

Organized documentary collections have existed since early civilizations learned to convert their spoken languages to written form. Even before the codex book appeared, early record depositories received some form of utilitarian arrangement. Groupings were made by title, by broad subject, by chronology, by author, by order of acquisition, by size, etc. One of the earliest catalogs was the one known as *Pinakes* (Greek for "tablets with wax in the middle") compiled for the great Alexandrian library by the poet Callimachus in the third century B.C. Although this catalog did not survive, it is known that it arranged the entries in at least 10 (and possibly more) main classes, subdivided alphabetically by author. In the Middle East and in the Byzantine Empire it served as a model for other catalogs and bibliographies until the early Middle Ages. The monastery libraries of that time in Western Europe were mostly small and had almost no need for classification, but the university libraries of the late Middle Ages arranged books corresponding to the Trivium and Quadrivium, the traditional seven subject fields taught. Within the classes, books had fixed locations on the shelves. Beginning in the sixteenth century, librarians devised many different classification schemes for the arrangement of books, but fixed locations predominated in most European and early American libraries until the mid-nineteenth century. The most substantive developments in the arrangement of library collections were concurrent with the rapid growth of libraries and their use during the nineteenth century. At that time librarians felt a definite need for better methods of arrangement, so that the content of their holdings would be available, and more apparent, to the user.

The history of modern library classification corresponds to the various attempts to adapt and modify existing philosophical systems of knowledge to the arrangement of materials and to users' needs. One of the best known early American classifiers was Thomas Jefferson, third president of the United States. He adapted certain elements of Francis Bacon's outline of knowledge, not only to his own library, but also to his plans for the organization of the University of Virginia and the reorganization of the College of William and Mary.

Bacon's system classified materials as functions of the three basic faculties: history (natural, civil, literary, ecclesiastical) as the function of memory; philosophy (including theology) as that of reason; and poetry, fables, and the like as that of imagination.[1] Its influence was widespread. Jean Le Rond d'Alembert used the Baconian system for the arrangement of the famous *Encyclopédie ou dictionnaire raisonné des sciences des arts et des métiers* of the French Enlightenment (1751-1765). Jefferson's classification was based on that modification as was the *Catalogue* of Benjamin Franklin's Library Company of Philadelphia (1789). Three years before Jefferson's *Catalogue of the Library of the United States* was installed at the Library of Congress, a variant of the Philadelphia scheme was used to produce the 1812 *Catalogue of the Library of Congress*.[2]

Among other early followers of the Baconian system were Thaddeus Mason Harris, librarian at Harvard (1791-1793); Edward William Johnson, librarian of the College of South Carolina and later of the St. Louis Mercantile Library; and, finally, Johnson's successor, William Torrey Harris, a Hegelian who inverted the Baconian system, creating an independent American classification. At the same time, various adaptations of the Brunet utilitarian classification scheme existed in several American libraries as a direct result of its use to arrange parts of the British Museum and the Bibliothèque Nationale.

In 1876 Melvil Dewey devised his famous Dewey Decimal Classification (DDC), based in large part on W. T. Harris's system, with a decimal notation. Soon DDC was spreading its influence throughout the world. At about the same time, Charles A. Cutter began his work at the Boston Athenaeum. Cutter sought to achieve, not a classification of knowledge, but a practical, useful method for arranging library materials. Nevertheless, his Expansive Classification shows the definite influence of Spencer and Comte, especially in the development of its subordinate classes.

At the beginning of the present century, when the Library of Congress had grown from several thousand books to nearly one million, it was apparent that the library would need a new classification system. After much deliberation, J. C. M. Hanson and Charles Martel decided to design an independent system governed by the actual content of the collection (literary warrant). This form of classification differs from a purely philosophical approach in that it is based on the books as entities. For this reason it is enumerative. An *enumerative* classification attempts to assign designations for (to enumerate) all the single and composite subject concepts required in the system. *Hierarchical* classification is based on the assumption that the process of subdivision and collocation must exhibit as much as possible the "natural" organization of the subject, proceeding from classes to divisions to subdivisions and following, at least in part, the rules of division as set down by "logic." *Synthetic* classifications confine their explicit lists of designations to single, unsubdivided concepts, giving the local classifier generalized rules with which to construct headings for composite subjects (see below, "Faceted Classification").

In summary, established philosophical systems of knowledge, with various modifications, underlie most traditional library classifications. The frequent distinction between classification of knowledge and classification of materials seems to have confused the thinking of many librarians. The two processes have important interactions. Even cursory examination of any library classification, including those purporting to organize "the items themselves," reveals an intellectual concept of the item as an expression of certain ideas in one of many available media. Philosophical classification organizes knowledge itself—registering, evaluating, and classifying thoughts, ideas, and concepts for the universal purpose of adequately representing the field of human learning. Library classification arranges the records that express and preserve knowledge, making adjustments as needed because of the physical format of such records.

TRADITIONAL CLASSIFICATION SCHEMES

Most traditional classification systems are basically enumerative. By contrast, the more recent schemes tend to be synthetic. In this introductory text the discussion will apply quite generally to both kinds of order. All printed schedules of library classifications reflect adjustments for the media in which the information may appear and provide detailed analysis of the scope and sequence of topics covered. But it is well to remember that materials on shelves or in files are arranged in a single order. Most items can be requested by author, title, subject, or form, but they can be organized by only one of these at a time. Linear arrangement imposes certain limitations on the classifier. Over the years efforts to meet such limitations have resulted in techniques or features that are characteristic of nearly every worthwhile library classification.

One such feature is a generalia or general works class, which accommodates items that are too broad in scope for inclusion in any single class. Such works usually overlap several traditional disciplines or "classes," e.g., encyclopedias, dictionaries, general periodicals, etc.

In addition, form classes organize materials according to their form of presentation rather than to their subject content. Literary works, e.g., poetry, drama, fiction, etc., are the most obvious, but books of etchings, photographs, musical scores, etc., also fall into this group.

Form divisions group items in a class according to their form or mode of treatment. For example, notations for outlines, dictionaries, or periodicals are used to pull together items in those physical forms; and notations for philosophical treatments, research in a subject, histories, and biographies show the "inner form" of items.

A notation is a shorthand code for the class, division, and subdivisions chosen for an item. It may be composed of letters, numerals, arbitrary signs, or a mixture of these. Notation can be of two types, pure or mixed. Pure notation uses only one kind of symbol. DDC, for example, uses numbers only (e.g., 974.1, meaning history of Maine). Mixed notation uses two or more kinds of symbols. Library of Congress Classification (LCC), for example, uses letters and numbers (e.g., BF575.G7, meaning psychology of the emotion of grief).

A final feature of traditional classification schemes is the index. The index provides an alphabetical approach to the classified part of the scheme.

FACETED CLASSIFICATION

A faceted classification differs from a traditional one in that it does not assign fixed slots to subjects in sequence, but uses clearly defined, mutually exclusive, and collectively exhaustive aspects, properties, or characteristics of a class or specific subject. Such aspects, properties, or characteristics are called facets of a class or subject, a term introduced into classification theory and given this new meaning by the Indian librarian and classificationist S. R. Ranganathan and first used in his Colon Classification in the early 1930s. Although the term was then new to classification, the idea was not (as Ranganathan freely admitted). It had its roots in Dewey's device of place (location) using a standard number (e.g., the United States always being 73) appended to any subject number by means of digits 09, a device now known as a facet indicator. Dewey recognized three things: 1) that certain characteristics such as "belonging to a place," "being in the form of a periodical," and some others are general and should be applicable to all subjects; 2) that such a number must be clearly distinguished from the class notation for the main subject to avoid confusion; and 3) that two or more facets could be combined to express a complex subject—his "number building" device (e.g., the subject "frost damage to oranges" can be expressed by adding to the class notation 634.31 for oranges the facet indicator 9 and the last two digits taken from the subject "plant injuries: low temperatures" 632.11, to result in 634.31911).

Most other classification schemes designed after Dewey also provided generally applicable facets for places and time periods, and often also for forms. Even LCC, which is an entirely enumerative scheme, included such facets, although they were specially developed for each class as a part of the enumerative structure and are not uniformly applicable in all classes. The Universal Decimal Classification (UDC) expanded Dewey's "standard subdivisions" to about a dozen generally applicable "auxiliaries" (see section on UDC in chapter 17 of this text). Finally, the Colon Classification introduced the fully faceted approach by means of synthetic class notations (i.e., those constructed entirely from individual facets in a prescribed sequence from the most specific to the most general).

Originally, Ranganathan postulated five basic facets: personality (i.e., the focal or most specific subject), material, energy (i.e., any activity, operation, or process), space, and time, known as the "PMEST formula." These basic facets were used to analyze a class or subject and to construct a composite class notation for it. For example, the subject "the design of metal ploughshares in the 19th century U.S." shows all five facets: from the most general to the most specific, 19th century is the time facet; U.S. is the space (or place) facet; design (an activity) is the energy facet; metal is the material facet; and ploughshares, the focal subject, is personality. It was soon found that these five basic facets were too broad and that most classes or disciplines needed tailor-made facets; e.g., the field of education can be broken down into facets for students, educators, teaching methods, subjects taught, level of instruction, etc.; agriculture has the facets crops, operations (sowing, harvesting, etc.), implements and tools, etc.

Each facet must have a distinctive notation and a facet indicator to show the sequence of facets unambiguously. Thus, in an imaginary faceted scheme the notation of the example given above might be

$$AfsM3d5U13Z18$$

where Afs is the class notation for ploughshares (in the tool facet of agriculture), M3 stands for iron in the material facet, d5 is the class notation for design, U13 means U.S., and Z18 stands for the 19th century.

Thus, a faceted structure relieves a classification scheme from the procrustean bed of rigid hierarchical and excessively enumerative subdivision that resulted in the assignment of fixed "pigeonholes" for subjects that happened to be known or were foreseen when a system was designed but often left no room for future developments and made no provision for the expression of complex relationships and their subsequent retrieval. Enumeration is, however, not entirely absent from faceted schemes: the Colon Classification has some 50 main classes, largely corresponding to traditional disciplines, and an astronomy classification would certainly list the planets of the sun in their order of distance.

While all traditional schemes are essentially based on the strictly hierarchical genus-species relationship for most of their subdivisions, faceted schemes, while recognizing this relationship where warranted, also display others, such as whole-part, operations and processes, agents and tools, substances, physical forms, organizational aspects, and many more, as needed for each specific field or subject. The design of faceted classification schemes is treated in detail by Vickery[3] and Foskett.[4]

A faceted class notation such as the one in the example above is not necessarily meant to serve as a shelving device or "call number" (although all or part of it may be so used) but rather for the arrangement of items in bibliographies and access service databases, where the synthetic notation provides a helpful sequence, and the individual facets can be accessed and retrieved either alone or in any desired combination. This feature is especially important for computerized retrieval, which has been successfully applied to faceted classification,[5] and in online retrieval as a complement to verbal retrieval methods by subject headings or keywords.[6] The faceted approach is indeed not limited to the construction and assignment of class notations. It is clearly discernible also in verbal subject indication, e.g., a subject heading such as **"Newspapers — United States — Bibliography"** shows "United States" as the place facet and "bibliography" as the form facet. The "List of subdivisions" in the *Sears List of Subject Headings* is actually a list of generally applicable facets (although it is not arranged systematically as it would be in a faceted classification).

Since the 1960s all major classification schemes (with the exception of LCC) either have been partially restructured on a faceted basis or display a fully faceted structure. The influence of faceted classification theory has been most conspicuous in DDC, which now offers facets not only for its traditional "standard subdivisions" and areas, but also for individual literatures and languages, for racial, ethnic, and national groups, for persons, and in a completely revised schedule for music that relies heavily on faceting in its internal structure. Special faceted classifications have been designed for broad fields such as education or business management, as well as for more specialized ones such as occupational safety, the diamond industry, library and information science, and many others (see section titled "Special Classification Schemes" in chapter 20 of this text).

CRITERIA FOR A SUCCESSFUL CLASSIFICATION SCHEME

Classification schemes, as indicated earlier, vary widely. Besides providing for the subject organization of the collection, a successful classification scheme may also contain devices for indicating method of treatment or form of materials treated, time periods, places, peoples, various types of persons, and other special categories.

Any or all of these devices may be justifiably and successfully used for a special situation such as a rare book collection or a collection concerned with a particular subject area or period. Following is a list of a few criteria that may be generally applied to judge a successful classification system:

1. It must be inclusive as well as comprehensive. That is, it must encompass the whole field of knowledge as represented in collectible media of communication and information. It must therefore include all subjects that are, have been, or may be recognized, allowing for possible future additions to the body of knowledge. It must make provision, not only for the records themselves, but also for every actual and potential use of the records.

2. It must be systematic. Not only must the division of subjects be exhaustive, but it must also bring together related topics in logical, comprehensible fashion, allowing its users to locate easily whatever they want

that is available. It must be so arranged that each aspect of a subject can be considered a separate, yet related, part of the scheme, and it must be so arranged that new topics and aspects can be added in a systematic manner.

3. It must be flexible and expansible. It must be constructed so that any new subject may be inserted without dislocating the general sequence of classification. It must allow for recognized knowledge in all its ramifications, and it must be capable of admitting new subjects or new aspects of well-established subjects. The flexibility of the notation is of first importance if the classification scheme is to be expansive and hospitable in the highest degree. It should also be current. Both the Dewey Decimal Office and the Library of Congress send subscribing libraries periodic lists of all changes in their schedules, noting additions and deletions. These notices and revisions are especially important in subject areas in which a great deal of new work is being done.

4. It must employ terminology that is clear and descriptive, with consistent meaning for both the user and the classifier. The arrangement of terms in the schedule and the index should help reveal the significance of the arrangement. The terms themselves should be unambiguous and reasonably current, correctly identifying the concepts and characteristics present in the materials being classified.

BROAD AND CLOSE CLASSIFICATION

Close classification means classing each work as specifically as possible, using all available subdivisions in the classification scheme. Broad classification groups works under the main divisions and main subdivisions of the scheme, without using its minute breakdowns into narrower concepts. When a library has relatively few items in a given subject area, broad classification might actually be more useful than isolating each item under its own specific class. A library using the DDC with a large collection of Bibles, for example, may need to classify the King James Version in 220.5203, whereas a smaller collection might cut back to the broad number 220. Generally speaking, DDC provides small libraries with more opportunities than does LCC to cut back to broader notations, because its enumeration stresses hierarchies of subject matter, while the Library of Congress has relatively few notations that signify broad categories.

GENERAL PRINCIPLES OF CLASSIFYING

Most of this chapter has been directed to the broad principles, methods, and problems of constructing classification systems. Some attention should now be given to choosing the optimum location for each item.

When classifying an item with respect to a particular library's holdings, it is often tempting to arrange items with local needs in mind, but classification schemes vary in their hospitality to local manipulation. It is assumed that such possibilities and difficulties were considered when the choice was made of one scheme over all others for use in a local library.

Once the particular system of arrangement is chosen, certain general precepts enable the classifier to apply it meaningfully to the items acquired by the library. The following summary is designed to aid that process. These principles apply primarily to both the DDC and the LCC schemes.[7]

1. **Class the item first according to subject, then by the form in which the subject is represented, except in the generalia class and in literature, where form might be paramount.** The classifier must determine the subject matter or form of the item and then use the classification schedules as a matrix for choosing the best position in the scheme. (See chapter 15 of this text for a discussion of the steps involved in this process.) For example:

   598.2/03

   Subject (birds)   Form (encyclopedia)

   but

   811

   Form (American poetry)   No subject represented in the number.

2. **Class an item where it will be most useful.** The classifier has to consider the nature of the collection and the needs of the user. For example, should a sports biography be shelved with sports or with biography? The answer to this question might be quite different in a school library than in a library that specializes in sports materials.

3. **Place the item in the most specific subject division that will contain it, rather than with the general topic.** This principle, of course, may be affected by a decision to use broad rather than close classification. Most libraries, for example, classify general French histories together and then subdivide the rest of the items dealing with the history of France by the specific time periods or local places they cover. To assign the same number to all would result in a discouragingly large assortment of volumes under one number. On the other hand, small libraries might prefer to classify all of their few volumes dealing with this subject in the general number.

4. **When the book deals with two or three subjects, place it with the predominant subject or with the one treated first. When the book deals with more than three subjects, place it in the general class that combines all of them.** This principle requires little explanation. The subject that is treated most fully should take predominance over secondary subjects. If two subjects are coordinate (e.g., electricity and magnetism treated equally in the same volume) the item should be placed with whichever topic comes first.

There are some refinements to this general principle. For example, if the work covers two subjects, one of which is represented as acting upon or influencing the other, such a work should be classed under the subject influenced or acted upon. Thus, a work discussing French influence on English literature should be classed with English literature. On similar grounds a work such as *Religious Aspects of Philosophy* should be classed under philosophy, not religion, since a treatment of some particular aspect of a subject should be classed with the subject, not with the aspect.

Another, perhaps more involved difficulty arises with the monographic series or collected set. (See chapter 8 of this text.) Winston Churchill's *A History of the English-Speaking Peoples* can be classed as an author's collection of four related volumes under a broad "history" number. Or the classifier can place volume 1 with other works on very early Britain, volume 2 with those on discovery and growth of the New World, and so on. The Library of Congress, as mentioned earlier, often classifies series and collected sets together, but has in recent years provided, for optional use by other libraries, an alternative, volume-specific class number on most of its separate records for monographs belonging to serial sets.

CONCLUSION

Critics have noted limitations in existing classification systems used by most libraries today.[8] A few are summarized here only as a basis for further study. There is a long-standing argument over the logical arrangement of various systems. Although a scheme may be logical within itself, it can also have inconsistencies. For example, in DDC, language is separated from literature, and history from social sciences. In LCC language is classified with literature, and history is shelved close to the social sciences. Arguments can be advanced for both approaches. Language is closely related to literature, but it is also an essential to all disciplines. History throws much light on the social sciences, but every discipline and every literature has its own history that influences, and is influenced by, general social history. There is some evidence that the current trend away from hierarchical enumeration toward synthesis has lessened concern over achieving the one incontestably correct logical arrangement.

As mentioned above, DDC and LCC, the two most popular library classifications, are both linear and therefore uni-dimensional. However, concepts found in works are multi-dimensional, but because classification is used to arrange items on shelves, only one number is assigned to each title whether it covers one subject or many. Classified catalogs address this problem to a certain extent because they allow the classifier to assign as many numbers to the catalog record as are appropriate. But classified catalogs have not gained acceptance in the United States. Instead, the many subject relationships among items and works are shown through a verbal, alphabetical approach—i.e., subject headings with references (see chapters 21-24 of this text).

Other limitations include problems of reorganization and relocation arising from the need to keep any classification scheme up-to-date. DDC and LCC both are regularly revised with new numbers being added for new concepts and with some concepts being moved to more logical locations in the scheme (e.g., computer science in DDC was moved from 001.6 to 004-006 to give this rapidly growing area room to expand). Occasionally, a section of a scheme is completely reorganized so that the old numbers are reused with new meanings (e.g., 780 for music was completely reorganized for the twentieth edition of DDC). While such reorganizations and relocations are very logical from a theoretical point of view, they may wreak havoc for orderly browsing in libraries. Most libraries cannot afford to reclassify older items, so they either push all items belonging to a reorganized section together on the shelves and start a new section for the new items, or they simply give up and say that the number is only a location address in any case. A more in-depth discussion of this problem may be found in *Subject Analysis in Online Catalogs*, by Aluri, Kemp, and Boll.[9]

Another problem arising from the process of keeping a classification scheme up-to-date is that the notation tends to become more complex and awkward as the schedules are expanded to include new subjects and to define old topics more specifically. In LCC, for example, digits are added after decimal points to place a new concept with older equivalent concepts. For example, in QB, Astronomy, "Meteors" are covered by the numbers QB740-QB753. QB748 is for "Orbits," and QB749 is for "Relation between meteors and comets." When "Streams," a concept equivalent to "Orbits," was added it was placed at QB748.2.

Related to the problem of keeping up with revisions in classification schemes is the fact that in most libraries, most of the classification numbers are taken from cataloging provided by an outside agency (e.g., a centralized processing facility or LC). These numbers are only as current as the time period in which they were assigned. A more in-depth discussion of this problem may be found in Taylor's *Cataloging with Copy*.[10]

In an international context classification is taken much more seriously than it has been in the United States. In a setting where many languages are involved it is believed that numerical and other symbols can transcend the language barriers imposed upon verbal subject approaches. As computer technology becomes more sophisticated many of the limitations mentioned above have the potential to be overcome, and classification may become an international means for subject communication. This possibility is discussed in more detail by Sweeney.[11]

In chapters 17-20 some of the better-known modern classifications devised by librarians and used in various contexts are discussed. Their resemblances and differences are briefly examined, to show their actual and possible uses, strengths, and limitations.

NOTES

[1] Cf. Bacon's *Advancement of Learning* (1605) and *De augmentis scientarium*.

[2] Leo E. LaMontagne, "Historical Background of Classification," in *The Subject Analysis of Library Materials* (New York, Columbia University School of Library Service, 1953), p. 20.

[3] B. C. Vickery, *Faceted Classification: A Guide to the Construction and Use of Special Schemes* (London, Aslib, 1960).

[4] A. C. Foskett, *The Subject Approach to Information*, 4th ed. (London, Bingley, 1982), pp. 150-175.

[5]R. R. Freeman, "The Management of a Classification Scheme: Modern Approaches Exemplified by the UDC Project of the American Institute of Physics," *Journal of Documentation* 23 (1967): 304-320.

[6]Karen Markey, "Subject Searching Experiences and Needs of Online Catalog Users: Implications for Library Classification," *Library Resources & Technical Services* 29 (January/March 1985): 34-51.

[7]This discussion summarizes the principles stated by several authors, including William Stetson Merrill, *Code for Classifiers, Principles Governing the Consistent Placing of Books in a System of Classification*, 2nd ed. (Chicago, American Library Association, 1939); and W. C. Berwick Sayers, *A Manual of Classification for Libraries and Bibliographers*, 3rd ed. (London, Andre Deutsch, 1955). The reader will observe that for the purpose of this discussion we selected Sayers' third edition rather than more recent ones.

[8]A helpful list of articles and books on classification theory can be found in the brief bibliography: Phyllis A. Richmond, "Reading List in Classification Theory," *Library Resources & Technical Services* 16 (Summer 1972): 364-382.

[9]Rao Aluri, D. Alasdair Kemp, and John J. Boll, *Subject Analysis in Online Catalogs* (Englewood, Colo., Libraries Unlimited, 1991), pp. 184-187.

[10]Arlene G. Taylor, *Cataloging with Copy*, 2nd ed. (Englewood, Colo., Libraries Unlimited, 1988), pp. 170-246.

[11]Russell Sweeney, "The Atlantic Divide: Classification Outside the United States," in *Classification of Library Materials*, edited by Betty G. Bengtson and Janet Swan Hill (New York, Neal-Schuman, 1990), pp. 40-51.

SUGGESTED READING

Buchanan, B. *Theory of Library Classification*. London, Bingley, 1979.

Dunkin, Paul S. *Cataloging U.S.A.* Chicago, American Library Association, 1969. Chapter 6.

Foskett, A. C. *The Subject Approach to Information*. 4th ed. London, Bingley, 1982. Chapter 8.

Herdman, M. M. *Classification: An Introductory Manual*. 3rd ed., revised by Jeanne Osborn. Chicago, American Library Association, 1978.

Decimal
Classification

17

INTRODUCTION

Of modern library classification schemes, the Dewey Decimal Classification (DDC) is both the oldest and the most widely used in the United States. It also has a substantial following abroad. Such widespread use is a tribute to Melvil[le Louis Kossuth] Dewey, whose original plan was adaptable enough to incorporate new subjects as they emerged and flexible enough to withstand the changes imposed by the passage of time. Born on December 10, 1851, and graduated from Amherst in 1874, Dewey became assistant college librarian. He developed the first draft of his system for arranging books at that time. He soon became a leader in American librarianship, helping to found both the American Library Association and the first American library school at Columbia University. Being a man of many interests, he was also an advocate of spelling reform. He shortened his forename to "Melvil," dropped his two middle names, and even attempted to change the spelling of his surname to "Dui." Throughout his career he promoted librarianship by his teaching, writing, and speaking. In recognizing and acting upon the need to systematize library collections for effective use, he knew of various previous attempts, but found them inadequate.

Dewey never claimed to have originated decimals for classification notation, but earlier systems used them merely as shelf location devices with no significant relation to the subject matter. What Dewey did claim as original, and with some justification, was his "relative index," compiled as a key to the "diverse material" included in his tables. His most significant contribution was perhaps the use of decimals for hierarchical divisions. Combined with the digits 0 to 9, decimals provide a pure notation that can be subdivided indefinitely.

The first edition of Dewey's scheme, prepared for the Amherst College Library, was issued anonymously in 1876 under the title *A Classification and Subject Index for Cataloguing and Arranging the Books and Pamphlets of a Library*. It included schedules to 1,000 divisions numbered 000-999, together with a relative index and prefatory matter—a total of 44 pages. The second, "revised and greatly enlarged" edition was published under Dewey's name in 1885. Since that time 18 more full editions and 12 abridgments have appeared. The fourteenth edition, published in 1942, remained the standard edition for many years because an experimental index to the fifteenth edition, published in 1951, was unsuccessful. In 1958 the sixteenth edition appeared with many changes and additions, including a complete revision of sections 546-47, "Inorganic and Organic Chemistry." Since that time each successive edition has carried, besides other, less sweeping changes, totally new developments of one or more targeted portions of the system. The present twentieth edition (*DDC20*) was published in 1989.[1] The associated twelfth abridged edition was published in 1990.[2]

DDC notations are assigned the tag 082 in the MARC format when they have been created for a particular item by the Library of Congress. A DDC notation created by a local library participating in a network is placed in MARC field 092. DDC complete call numbers are also placed in field 092, regardless of who assigned the DDC notation to the item involved.

Closely related to DDC is the Universal Decimal Classification (UDC), which was based on DDC. It is discussed briefly at the end of this chapter.

BASIC CONCEPTS

The system is called "decimal" because it arranges all knowledge as represented by library materials into ten broad subject classes numbered from 000 to 900. Using Arabic numerals for symbols, it is flexible only to the degree that numbers can be expanded in linear fashion to cover special aspects of general subjects. Theoretically, expansions may continue indefinitely. The more specific the work being classified, the longer the number combination will tend to grow. Library of Congress records have been known to carry suggested Dewey numbers containing 21 digits, i.e., 18 decimal places. But such long numbers, however accurate, are unwieldy; it is hard to crowd them onto book spines and catalog cards, and dangers of miscopying and mis-shelving are multiplied. For these and related reasons many larger libraries have turned from DDC to some other system, such as LC, which has a more economical notation.

Nevertheless, the Dewey Decimal Classification system has many advantages. Its content is compact, consisting in *DDC20* of a volume for introductory matter, auxiliary tables, and a list of relocations and schedule reductions; two volumes for schedule summaries and schedule development; and a fourth volume for the index and the manual. It incorporates many mnemonic devices that can be transferred from one class to another (e.g., "-03" at the end of a class number of any length often indicates a dictionary of the subject at hand). The classifier, once familiar with the system, can apply it to incoming materials quite rapidly. It provides a limited number of optional alternative locations and allows for great detail of specification. The patron is likely to be familiar with it, because it is the system most frequently used in school and small public libraries. Furthermore, it arranges subjects from the general to the specific in a logical order, which often can be traced by analogy through more than one class. It is philosophical in conception, being based on a systematic outline of knowledge that allows for subjects not yet known. Even so, the overall arrangement is not preemptively theoretical or logical. Dewey's intent was to provide a practical system for classifying books. This primary application to the books generally found in American libraries remains one of its notable limitations, although efforts have been made in later editions to rectify that bias.

A basic premise of the Dewey approach is that there is no one class for any given subject. The primary arrangement is by discipline. Any specific topic may appear in any number of disciplines. Various aspects of such a topic are usually brought together in the relative index. For example, a work on "families" may be classed in one of several places depending on its emphasis, as can be seen in the table below. Besides the aspects shown there, other material on families may be found in still different DDC numbers. Use of the relative index would lead the classifier to some of them.

Some DDC Class Numbers Pertaining to the Family

173	Ethics of family relationships
241.63	Christian family ethics
296.4	Religious family rites, celebrations, services
304.666	Family planning
306.8	Marriage and family
362.82	Families with specific problems
392.3	Dwelling places [including those for families]
616.89156	Family psychotherapy
796.0191	Sports for families
929.2	Family histories

The basic concepts of the system are covered in two "official" sources: the introduction in volume 1 and the manual in volume 4 of *DDC20*. In addition to the manual in *DDC20*, the editor John P. Comaromi has revised a long-standing detailed guide to the Dewey Decimal system originally authored by Jeanne Osborn.[3] The DDC introduction gives detailed explanations of the schedules and tables and detailed instructions in classifying and building numbers with DDC. The manual is devoted to a discussion of the tables and schedules by number, pointing out areas of difficulty and explaining what should or should not be included in certain numbers.

SCHEDULE FORMAT

Summaries

At the beginning of volume 2, DDC provides three summaries, showing successively the 10 main classes, the 100 divisions, and the 1,000 sections of the basic scheme. Each class from 100 to 900 consists of a group of related disciplines. The 000 class is reserved for materials too general to fit anywhere else.

Summary of the 10 Main DDC Classes

000	Generalities
100	Philosophy & psychology
200	Religion
300	Social sciences
400	Language
500	Natural sciences & mathematics
600	Technology (Applied sciences)
700	The arts
800	Literature & rhetoric
900	Geography & history

Each main class is separated into 10 divisions, although a few of these, as well as some further subdivisions, may seem to be rather artificially located within the class. The hundred divisions are shown in the "Second Summary," e.g.:

Summary of the Divisions of a Typical DDC Class

600 Technology (Applied sciences)
610 Medical sciences Medicine
620 Engineering & allied operations
630 Agriculture
640 Home economics & family living
650 Management & auxiliary services
660 Chemical engineering
670 Manufacturing
680 Manufacture for specific uses
690 Buildings

Each division is subdivided into 10 sections. Again some of these may seem artificially located. The one thousand sections are shown in the "Third Summary," e.g.:

Summary of the Sections of a Typical DDC Division

610 Medical sciences Medicine
611 Human anatomy, cytology, histology
612 Human physiology
613 Promotion of health
614 Incidence & prevention of disease
615 Pharmacology & therapeutics
616 Diseases
617 Surgery & related medical specialties
618 Gynecology & other medical specialties
619 Experimental medicine

Volume 2 presents in detail the subjects placed in 000 through 599. Fully detailed schedules for subjects placed in 600 through 999 are in volume 3. In the full schedules each of the 1,000 numbers that has subdivisions extending over more than two pages gives a summary of the "tens" place past the decimal point, e.g.:

612   Human physiology

SUMMARY

612.01-.04   [Biophysics, biochemistry, control processes, tissue and organ culture, physiology of specific activities]
.1   Blood and circulation
.2   Respiration
.3   Digestion
.4   Secretion, excretion, related functions
.6   Reproduction, development, maturation
.7   Motor functions and integument
.8   Nervous functions Sensory functions
.9   Regional physiology

At eight places within the schedules, multilevel summaries are provided. An example of this can be found at "610 Medical sciences Medicine."

Entries in Schedules

In the full schedules the 1,000 sections are listed separately, followed in detail by any subdivisions they may have. There are often asymmetrics attesting to the fact that the phenomena of the world cannot always be subdivided and re-subdivided into groups of 10:

Extended Decimal Subdivision of a DDC Topic

612	Human physiology
612.1	Blood and circulation
612.11	Blood
612.12	Blood chemistry
612.13	Blood vessels and vascular circulation
612.14	Blood pressure
612.17	Heart
612.18	Vasomoters

Successive lengthening of the base number by one (occasionally two or three) digit(s) achieves step-wise division. This pyramidal structure means that, in subject relationships, what is true of the whole is true of the parts. For instance, the medical sciences are a branch of technology; physiology is a medical science, etc.

A Typical DDC Hierarchical Sequence

600	Technology (Applied sciences)
610	Medical sciences Medicine
612	Human physiology
612.1	Blood and circulation
612.11	Blood
612.112	White corpuscles

As the notation expands beyond the decimal point, DDC editors introduce a space after every third number. The spaces are inserted merely to facilitate reading the closely listed digits. On library materials and bibliographic records they should be omitted, so that the number will occupy no more space than is absolutely necessary. Thus the schedules show "331.873 2 Membership and membership policies [in labor unions]" or "351.878 31 [Administration of ground transportation] Traffic control." The schedules rarely display numbers with more than four decimal places, although the relative index sometimes expands numbers to eight or even nine decimals. Thus in the index we find "Radio — production economics 338.476 213 84." Yet the schedules proper expand "338 — Production" only as far as "338.47 Goods and services." Instructions at 338.47 in the schedules allow the building of the longer number found in the index. The concept of building numbers is explained later in this chapter.

Certain places in the schedules where fully symmetrical expansion cannot be maintained are given *centered entries*, which represent concepts for which there is no specific number in the notational hierarchy and which, therefore, cover an abbreviated span of numbers. These appear with centered inch-long lines immediately above them and with the symbol ">" at their left margins. Centered entries are always followed by a note that tells where to class comprehensive works that cover the subject represented by the centered entry, e.g.:

A Typical DDC Centered Entry

> 439.7-439.8   East Scandinavian languages

Class comprehensive works in 439.5

Other useful formatting devices are the section numbers and running titles at the top of each page of volumes 2 and 3 (the schedules), the use of boldface and light-face type in various sizes, lefthand marginal indentions to indicate hierarchical structure, and the use of square brackets for numbers from which a topic has recently been shifted (or "relocated").

Notes

Perhaps the most helpful sources of information for the DDC classifier are the notes. There are seven major kinds of notes in the twentieth edition: 1) notes that tell what is found at a classification, 2) notes that tell what is found at other classifications, 3) notes that identify topics in "standing room," 4) notes that explain changes in schedules and tables, 5) notes that instruct the classifier in number building, 6) notes that prescribe precedence order, and 7) notes that explain options.

1. Notes that tell what is found at a classification include scope notes (also called definition notes), former heading notes, variant name notes, general aspect notes, and class-here notes. An example of a scope or definition note is found at "025.6 Circulation services." The first note there reads, "Lending and renting materials, keeping records of loans and rentals." The second note at this classification is an example of a class-here note: "Class here document delivery." Such notes are used to list major topics that are included at a class and also to indicate where interdisciplinary and comprehensive works are to be classified. Former heading and variant name notes begin with those words and seem self-explanatory. An example of a general aspect note found at the centered entry "069.55-069.57 Special collections" is: "General aspects: classification, arrangement, housing." Such notes list general aspects that are applicable to all the subdivisions of a number.

2. Notes that tell what is found at other classifications begin with the words *class, for,* or *see also.* For example, at "070.9 Historical and persons treatment of journalism and newspapers" is found the note, "Class geographical treatment in 071-079." At "338.5 General production economics" is the note, "For organization of production, see 338.6."

   Notes found in categories 1 and 2 have what is called "hierarchical force." This means that they are applicable to all the subdivisions under the number that has the note, as well as to the number with the note. For example, the two previously quoted notes found at "025.6 Circulation services" would apply also to the subdivision "025.62 Interlibrary loans." That is, a work about keeping records of loans carried out via interlibrary loans would be appropriate at 025.62, even though there is no specific note to this effect at 025.62.

3. Notes that identify topics in "standing room" provide a location for topics that do not yet have enough works about them to justify a separate number. It is assumed that there may be more works in the future, in which case the topics could be assigned their own number. Therefore, the rules for applying DDC do not allow number building of any kind (including additions of standard subdivisions) for topics in "standing room." The assumption is that the number in which the topic stands will be subdivided to create a number for the topic, and so, if no number building has been done, all items on that topic can be classed in the new number for the topic simply by adding new digits to the general number. Standing-room notes begin with the words *common names, contains, example(s),* or *including.* For example, in the library and information sciences section at "025.313 Form [of the catalog]" is the note, "Examples: book, card, microform catalogs." The topic "Online catalogs" has its own number: "025.3132."

4. Notes explaining changes in schedules and tables tell a user of the schedules that there have been changes at a particular number since the last edition of DDC. There may have been revisions of contents covered, a discontinuation of coverage either for a whole number or for a part of its contents, or a relocation of all or part of the contents.

5. Notes that instruct the classifier in number building provide ways to gain greater depth of analysis at a particular classification. Number building is discussed in detail below.

6. Notes that prescribe precedence order help a classifier decide which of more than one aspect or characteristic to use for classification when the situation is such that only one can be chosen. For example:

   006   Special computer methods

   . . .

   Unless other instructions are given, class complex subjects with aspects in two or more subdivisions of 006 in the one coming last, e.g., natural language processing in expert systems 006.35 (*not* 006.33)

7. Notes that explain options are given in parentheses and may be of benefit in providing alternative methods for handling certain situations. International users find that options for religions, languages, and literatures allow them to give preferred treatment for local needs. One option often followed even in the United States is:

> 016   Bibliographies and catalogs of works on specific subjects or in specific disciplines
>
>   . . .
>
> (Option: Class with the specific discipline or subject, using notation 016 from Table 1, e.g., bibliographies of medicine 610.16)

COMPLETELY REVISED SCHEDULES

In *DDC20* there are two relatively confined but significant areas that have undergone complete remodeling. In earlier editions such changes were referred to as "phoenix" schedules, but this term has been dropped in *DDC20*, and they are simply referred to as being completely revised. One of the changed areas is music at 780. The other is in the table for geographic areas at −711, British Columbia. These changes are summarized at the end of volume 1, where the *DDC19* and *DDC20* numbers are listed in parallel columns. The new music schedule allows building of numbers through use of facets and the facet indicators 0 and 1. It is now possible, for example, to express all relevant facets for a recording of military marches for brass instruments. The change in the area notation for British Columbia has resulted in a more accurate representation of that geographic area.

Another major change in *DDC20* is a major relocation of computer science from 001.6 to 004-006. In the process it was expanded dramatically. There are hundreds more minor relocations and reductions. These are listed in a section at the end of volume 1.

NUMBER BUILDING

A premise in working with Dewey Classification is that all possible numbers are not specifically printed in the schedules, but more precise numbers than those printed can be built or synthesized using tables or other parts of the schedules.

Adding from Auxiliary Tables

Auxiliary tables 1 through 7, found in volume 1 of *DDC20*, give the classifier one way to expand existing numbers in the schedules. Each number in these tables is preceded by a dash to show that it cannot stand alone as a class number. The dash should be omitted when the number is attached to a class notation.

Table 1. Standard Subdivisions

As was noted under the "General Principles of Classifying" section of chapter 16, all shelf classifications provide a dual approach. Some items are grouped on the basis of their subject content, while others are placed according to their format. The standard subdivisions supplied in auxiliary Table 1 derive from what was called in earlier editions a table of "form divisions." The present-day "standard subdivisions" include examples other than form. Some actually do treat format (e.g., dictionaries, encyclopedias, periodicals, etc.). Others represent "modes of treatment," covering theoretical or historical aspects of the subject, such as philosophy and theory, history, etc. The following illustrates some of the categories to be found in Table 1.

—01 **Philosophy and theory.** An exposition of any subject treated from the theoretical point of view.
Example: 701 Philosophy of the Arts

—03 **Dictionaries, encyclopedias, concordances.**
Example: 720.3 Dictionary of Architecture

—05 **Serial publications.** Used for publications in which the subject is treated in articles, papers, etc.
Example: 720.5 Architectural Record

—08 **History and description with respect to kinds of persons.**
Example: 720.8 Architectural Adaptations for People with Specific Needs

—09 **Historical and geographical treatment.**
Example: 720.9 Fletcher's History of Architecture

Most of the standard subdivisions are further subdivided in Table 1. For example, under "-01 Philosophy and theory" the following subtopics are listed:

—011 Systems
—012 Classification
—013 Value
—014 Languages (Terminology) and communication
—015 Scientific principles
—019 Psychological principles

The —09 standard subdivision can be geographically divided, through the addition of area digits from Table 2, e.g., "720.973 History of Architecture in the United States." This is explained in detail below in the section titled "Table 2. Geographic Areas, Historical Periods, Persons."

Unless specific instructions indicate otherwise, standard subdivisions may be used with any number if such application is meaningful. One specific instruction not to add standard subdivisions is found only in the introduction in volume 1 and is often overlooked. When a work does not "approximate the whole of the subject of the number," the standard subdivision usually should not be added. This was mentioned above in the discussion of notes that identify topics in "standing room." If, for example, a book is about research on card catalogs, it should be given the number "025.313" for "Form" of catalogs. Because the book is not about research on all forms of catalogs, and because there is no specific number for card catalogs, the standard subdivision "−072" for research should not be attached to the number.

Although in the table each number is preceded by a single zero, e.g., "−03 Dictionaries, etc.," it is sometimes necessary in the schedules to apply a double or triple zero to introduce the subdivision. This happens when single zero subdivisions are already appropriated in the schedules for special purposes. The instructions that cover such situations are explicit and should be followed carefully. A few examples will illustrate certain basic principles:

a) **Standard subdivisions printed in the schedules**

In some parts of the schedules a concept that is ordinarily expressed as a standard subdivision is printed with its own number. For example, "803 Dictionaries, encyclopedias, concordances" is printed in the schedule following "800 Literature..." Therefore, this is the number used for a dictionary of literature, not 800.3 or 800.03. Likewise, "501 Philosophy and theory" is printed after "500 Natural sciences and mathematics." None of the standard subdivision breakdown for −01 found in Table 1 is printed after "501," but one can use this breakdown at this number if appropriate. Thus, a work on the concept of theoretical value in the natural sciences would be classed "501.3."

b) **Standard subdivisions not printed and no instructions given**

The most common situation is that in which standard subdivisions are not printed and no instructions are given. In such cases a single-0 introduces the standard subdivision. For example, the schedules give the number "371.4" for educational guidance and counseling. A work on the philosophy and theory of educational guidance and counseling would be given the class number "371.401."

c) **0-divisions utilized for a specific purpose; standard subdivision to be introduced by a double-0**

An example of the double-0 appears at "271 Religious congregations and orders in church history." Single-0 subdivisions are used for specific kinds of religious congregations, e.g., "271.01 Contemplative," "271.03 Teaching," "271.04 Preaching," etc. Here the instruction is to use 271.001-271.009 for standard subdivisions. Therefore, a dictionary of religious congregations and orders in general is classed in 271.003.

d) **00-divisions utilized for special purposes; standard subdivisions to be introduced by a triple-0**

An example of the triple-0 appears at "351 Administration of central governments." 351.001-351.009 are reserved for bureaucracy and specific aspects of the chief executive, while 351.01-351.09 are used for specific executive departments and ministries of cabinet rank. 351.1-351.9 encompass specific aspects of public administration such as personnel management, lists of officials and employees, civil service examinations, etc. Here the instruction is to use 351.0001-351.0009 for standard subdivisions of this general subject. Therefore, a dictionary of public administration in general is classed 351.0003.

Table 2. Geographic Areas, Historical Periods, Persons

When a given heading can be subdivided geographically and the library has many books dealing with that subject, it is recommended that the classifier use Table 2 (the area table), which allows one to expand the number systematically by region or site. It is by far the bulkiest of the seven auxiliary tables accompanying the DDC schedules. Its general arrangement is as follows:

−01-05	Historical periods
−1	Areas, regions, places in general
−2	Persons regardless of area, region, place
−3	The ancient world
−4	Europe Western Europe
−5	Asia Orient Far East
−6	Africa
−7	North America
−8	South America
−9	Other parts of world and extraterrestrial worlds Pacific Ocean islands

Area −1 is used for the treatment of any subject geographically but not limited by continent, country, or locality. It allows diverse elements that have natural ties to regions or groups (e.g., frigid zones, temperate zones, land forms, or types of vegetation) to be brought together under certain subjects. Area −2 permits subdivision by biography, diaries, reminiscences, correspondence, and the like of persons associated with any subject for which the schedule instructions say to add the "areas" notation directly instead of adding "standard subdivision" notation -092 from Table 1. Area −3 offers specific subdivisions for ancient countries and areas up to the fall of the Roman Empire. Area notations −4 through −9 are for specific continents and modern countries. For example, area number "−4 Europe" has the following summary subtopics:

−41	British Isles
−42	England and Wales
−43	Central Europe Germany
−44	France and Monaco
−45	Italian Peninsula and adjacent islands Italy
−46	Iberian Peninsula and adjacent islands Spain
−47	Union of Soviet Socialist Republics (Soviet Union) Russia (Russian Soviet Federated Socialist Republic)
−48	Scandinavia
−49	Other parts of Europe

The area notations −41 and −42 were extensively revised in the nineteenth edition to reflect a thorough reorganization of British local administration. The area concepts of "British Isles," "United Kingdom," and "Great Britain" were at the same time relocated from area −42 to area −41.

Area notations may be added directly to schedule numbers where so instructed. For example, a general treatise on higher education in Dundee, Scotland, will be classed in 378 in the Dewey Decimal Classification. The schedule at 378.4-.9 instructs "Add to base number 378 notation 4-9 from Table 2." The index refers to "T2−412 7" as the number for "Dundee (Scotland)." This number is therefore applied to 378, giving 378.4127, as the following analysis shows:

378	Higher education
378.4	Europe
378.41	British Isles
378.412	Northeastern Scotland
378.4127	Dundee, Scotland

Where specific instructions (as in 378.4-.9) are not given for geographical treatment in the schedules, the classifier can apply the standard subdivision "−09 Historical and geographical treatment" to any number that lends itself to that approach, unless localized instructions mandate a double- or triple-0 in place of the single-0. For example, the specific DDC number for savings banks is 332.21. To class a work on savings banks in London, the schedule gives no specific direction to use Table 2, nor does it give any direction for specific subdivisions. So the standard subdivision −09 may be used directly. In Table 1 a note under "−093-099 Treatment by specific continents, countries, localities; extra-terrestrial worlds" says to "Add to base number −09 notation 3-9 from Table 2." So books on savings banks in London will be classed in 332.2109421. The number may be analyzed to show:

332.21	Savings banks
332.2109	Standard subdivision for historical and geographical treatment
332.21094	In Europe
332.210942	In England and Wales
332.2109421	In Greater London

Although these examples result in long numbers, they are quite simple to construct.

Table 3. Individual Literatures

Table 3, "Subdivisions for Individual Literatures, for Specific Literary Forms," is actually three tables: Table 3-A, "Subdivisions for Works by or about Individual Authors," Table 3-B, "Subdivisions for Works by or about More than One Author," and Table 3-C, "Notation to be Added Where Instructed in Table 3-B and in 808-809." The titles of these tables are descriptive of their uses. They are never used alone, but are used following the instructions given under 808-809 and 810-890. Numbers "−1-8 Specific forms" in Tables 3-A and 3-B develop and expand the summary form numbers that appear in the full schedules under "810 American literature in English." These mnemonic form divisions for kinds of literature are:

−1	Poetry	(e.g., 831 German poetry)
−2	Drama	(e.g., 842 French drama)
−3	Fiction	(e.g., 839.313 Dutch fiction)
−4	Essays	(e.g., 869.4 Portuguese essays)
−5	Speeches	(e.g., 845 French speeches)
−6	Letters	(e.g., 836 German letters)
−7	Satire and humor	(e.g., 869.7 Portuguese satire & humor)

[−7 does not appear in Table 3-A and is not used for individual authors.]

−8	Miscellaneous writings	(e.g., 839.318 Dutch miscellaneous writings)

Flow charts for building literature numbers can be found at the Table 3 instructions in the Manual in volume 4 of *DDC20*. These are of great assistance in following the massive amount of instructions found in the literature schedules and with Table 3.

Table 4. Individual Languages

Table 4, "Subdivisions of Individual Languages," is used with base numbers for individual languages, as explained under 420-490. In a fashion similar to that of Table 3 it provides mnemonic form divisions for languages, e.g.,

−1   Writing systems and phonology of the standard form of the language.
    (e.g., 431 Writing systems and phonology of standard German)
−2   Etymology of the standard form of the language.
    (e.g., 442 Etymology of the standard form of French)
−3   Dictionaries of the standard form of the language.
    (e.g., 439.313 Dictionaries of the standard form of Dutch)
etc.

Table 5. Racial, Ethnic, National Groups

Table 5, "Racial, Ethnic, National Groups," is used according to specific instructions at certain places in the schedules or in other tables, or through the interposition of "−089 [Treatment among specific] racial, ethnic, national groups" from Table 1. These applications are exactly parallel to the use of Table 2, which is used either on direct instructions in the schedule or on interposition of "−09 Historical and geographical treatment" from Table 1. The Table 5 summary includes:

−03-04	[Basic races, mixtures of basic races]
−1	North Americans
−2	British English Anglo−Saxons
−3	Nordic (Germanic) people
−4	Modern Latin peoples
etc.	

An example to illustrate the use of Table 5 could be a work dealing with special education for American blacks. The number for special education, as found in the index and the schedules, is 371.9. An instruction under subdivision "371.97 Students exceptional because of racial, ethnic, national origin" says, "Add to base number 371.97 notation 03-99 from Table 5." The number in Table 5 for "United States blacks (Afro-Americans)" is −96073. Thus, the full class number 371.9796073 may be analyzed as follows:

371.9	Special education
371.97	Students exceptional because of racial, ethnic, national origin
371.979	Racial, ethnic, national groups other than North American or major European nationalities
371.9796	Africans and people of African descent
371.97960	Digit used to expand the notation, here geographically
371.979607	In North America
371.9796073	In the United States

Table 6. Languages

Table 6, "Languages," is a basic mnemonic table used to indicate the particular language of a work or the language that is the subject matter of a work. It is used as instructed in the schedules or other tables. The summary includes:

−1	Indo-European (Indo-Germanic) languages
−2	English and Old English (Anglo-Saxon)
−3	Germanic (Teutonic) languages
−4	Romance languages
etc.	

To illustrate the application of this table let us class a Bible in French, starting from the entry given in both index and schedules, "220.5 Modern versions and translations [of the Bible]." For "220.53-59 Other languages [than English]" the schedule direction says, "Add to base number 220.5 notation 3-9 from Table 6." The notation for French in Table 6 is −41. The resulting whole number for a modern French Bible may be analyzed as follows:

220	The Bible
220.5	Modern versions
220.54	In the Romance languages
220.541	In modern French

Table 7. Groups of Persons

Table 7, "Groups of Persons," is used as instructed in the schedules or other tables. It deals with various characteristics of persons, as the following partial summary shows:

—01	Individual persons
—02	Groups of persons
—03-08	Persons by various nonoccupational characteristics
	—03 Persons by racial, ethnic, national background
	—04 Persons by sex and kinship characteristics
	—05 Persons by age
etc.	

—1-9	Specialists
	—1 Persons occupied with philosophy, parapsychology and occultism, psychology
	—2 Persons occupied with or adherent to religion
	—3 Persons occupied with the social sciences and socioeconomic activities
etc.	

From −09 to −9 this table is based on the 10 main classes of DDC. A book on Shakers as a social group furnishes the following example. The number for adherents of religious groups in social contexts is 305.6. The direc-tions in the schedule at the number say, "Add to base number 305.6 the numbers following −2 in notation 21-29 from Table 7." The Table 7 number for Shakers is −288. Thus our book would be classed 305.688. The analysis of the number proceeds as follows:

305	Social stratification (Social structure)
305.6	Adherents of religious groups
305.688	Shakers

Adding from Other Parts of the Schedules

There are a number of places in the schedules where the classifier is in-structed to find a number elsewhere in the schedules and to add it whole to the number at hand, as demonstrated by the following example:

750	Painting and paintings
. . .	
758	Other subjects
. . .	
758.9	Other
	Add to base number 758.9 notation 001-999, e.g., paintings of historical events 758.99 . . .

If one wanted to classify paintings of library buildings, the number for the architecture of library buildings, 727.8, would be attached to 758.9, resulting in 758.97278.

In many other places the classifier is instructed to take a part of another number and add to a base number given in the instruction. The following example will illustrate:

574.921-.928 Marine biology
Add to base number 574.92 the numbers following 551.46 in 551.461-551.468, e.g., Mediterranean Sea life 574.922; however, class Antarctic waters of Atlantic Ocean in 574.924, of Pacific Ocean in 574.9258, of Indian Ocean in 574.927; comprehensive works on Antarctic waters in 574.924

Under "551.46 Oceanography" we find that the full sequence referred to may be summarized as follows:

551.461   Atlantic Ocean
551.4611   North Atlantic
551.4613-.4614   Northeast and northwest Atlantic
551.462   Mediterranean Sea
551.463   Caribbean Sea and Gulf of Mexico
551.464   South Atlantic Ocean
551.465   Pacific Ocean
551.466   East Pacific Ocean
551.467   Indian Ocean
551.468   Arctic Ocean (North Polar Sea)

In this sequence the Mediterranean Sea is represented by 551.462. The number following 551.46 is "2." Thus, "2" is attached to the base number 574.92 to arrive at 574.922 for Mediterranean Sea life.

More complicated instructions may give more than one directive for building a number. For example:

616.99411-.99415 Cancers [Malignant tumors] of cardiovascular organs
Add to base number 616.9941 the numbers following 611.1 in 611.11-611.15, e.g., cancer of heart 616.99412; then add further as instructed under 618.1-618.8

At 618.1-618.8 is a table of digits to be added where instructed. This table may be summarized as follows:

001-009   Standard subdivisions
01-04   Microbiology, special topics, rehabilitation, special classes of diseases
05   Preventive measures and surgery
06   Therapy
07   Pathology

So a work on therapy for cancer of the heart could be given the classification number 616.9941206. "Add tables" of this type are found in many places in the schedules and must be used only as instructed.

When a single work treats multiple aspects of a subject, such as age, gender, and physical characteristics, the classifier must be careful to observe citation and precedence order. Citation order allows a number to be built that takes into account two or more of the aspects. Instructions are given in such cases as to the order in which the aspects may be represented in the number. If a citation order is not given, then one must choose among the aspects according to instructions for precedence. Sometimes one is instructed to prefer the aspect that comes first (or last) in the schedule, while at other times there may be a table of precedence given. The important point to remember is to follow instructions. More detail about number building can be found in the Introduction to *DDC20*.

THE RELATIVE INDEX

The "relative" index is so called because it is claimed to show relationships of each specific topic to one or more disciplines and to other topics. It contains terms found in the schedules and tables, and synonyms for those terms; names of countries, states, provinces, major cities, and important geographic features; some names of persons. It does not contain phrases that begin with the adjectival form of languages and countries (e.g., "French plays") or phrases that contain concepts represented by standard subdivisions (e.g., "Medical education"). Many *see also* references are given (e.g., "Organizations ... *see also* Religious organizations"). Geographic name entries usually refer the user to the appropriate area table [e.g., "Macerata (Italy : Province) T2—456 73"]. A few referrals occur to the standard subdivisions and to other auxiliary tables (e.g., "Repairs ... T1—028 8").

The DDC relative index enumerates alphabetically all the main headings in the classification schedules, plus certain other specific entries not actually listed in the schedules. One such instance was discussed on page 332.

In other places index terminology varies from that found in the schedules for the same class number, although the general meanings coincide. Thus, the schedule entry "612.7921 Glands and glandular secretions, Example: perspiration" is a generalized representation of the index entry "Sebaceous glands—human physiology 612.792 1."

The classifier should, of course, consult the index, especially in cases in which the location of the desired topic, or the precise nature of its relation to other topics, is in doubt. Yet the relative index should never become a substitute for the schedules. It is coordinated with them, but is limited for reasons of space and cannot show hierarchical progressions or topical groupings. It will guide the classifier to some, but not necessarily all, aspects of a given subject. The next important step in the classification process is to consult the schedules for verification, perspective, and possible further instructions. Only by using the two types of display together can the full potential of the scheme be realized.

BROAD AND CLOSE CLASSIFICATION

Because it offers a wide variety of techniques and nearly limitless expansions in number building, Dewey Decimal Classification is hospitable to all the titles that a large library might add in any subject. It also offers various ways to meet the limited needs of smaller libraries. The classifier must remember that, in general, when there are relatively few books in a given subject area, DDC encourages broad classification. Digits in class notations after decimal points may be cut off at any appropriate place. The present policy of the Library of Congress is to provide bibliographic records with Dewey Decimal numbers of from one to three segments. The segments are indicated by prime marks or slash marks, e.g., "940.53/1743/092," which stands for "World War II — Concentration camps in Germany — Biographies." A small library with a limited collection of materials on World War II might prefer to keep them all together under 940.53. If the library has several dozen items on the war, it might keep the ones on concentration camps in Germany together by using 940.531743. If it maintains a separate resource collection for use by researchers, it could add the standard subdivision "−092" to distinguish the biographies. When a library decides to retain one or more of the DDC segments to achieve close classification at a particular point in the collection, it omits the prime marks, which were used in the LC record merely to suggest break-points.

In catalog records created by other members of a network, the DDC classification numbers do not have prime marks. If a shorter number is desired, one must consult the schedules to find an appropriate break-point. For example, in the World War II concentration camp number above, breaking the number at 940.531 would place the item with other works on social, political, and economic history of the war — not a very logical option. Breaking it at 940.5317 would place it with items on concentration camps, not subdivided by place — quite logical. The number 940.53174 would be for concentration camps in all of Europe, not subdivided by country. The classifier needs to check the schedules and not just cut the number at an arbitrary number of digits past the decimal point, which could result in an illogical placement.

UPDATING

New editions of Dewey Decimal Classification have been published every eight years or so. Between editions, updating is accomplished via the publication of *Dewey Decimal Classification Additions, Notes and Decisions* (affectionately known as *DC&*, "&" being the symbol for "AND," the acronym for "Additions, Notes and Decisions").[4] *DC&* is published annually. It contains corrections of errors, clarifications, updating, and expansions. A policy for "continuous revision" has been adopted by Forest Press, which means that major revisions are released as separates between editions, and new editions appear as cumulations.

ABRIDGED EDITIONS

The first *Abridged Decimal Classification and Relativ Index for Libraries, Clippings, Notes, etc.*, appeared in 1894, the year in which the fifth edition of the full schedules was published. Abridged edition 12 is based on *DDC20* and was published in 1990. Like its predecessors, it is designed primarily for general collections of 20,000 titles or less, such as are found in small public and school libraries. It contains many fewer entries than the full edition, and tables, schedules, index, and manual all appear in one volume. The numbers used are compatible with *DDC20* so that growing libraries can expand from the abridged to the full edition as their collections increase.

CONCLUSION

Among the difficulties built into the Dewey Decimal Classification system are its long numbers, which increase rather than diminish as the system grows, nullifying much of the mnemonic character of the basic system. Thus the number 338.47621384, which was cited on page 332 as coming from the relative index entry for production economics relating to the radio, is so long that any mnemonic associations between it and the number 621.384 (from which it was built) are obscured. Librarians who wish to retain these long numbers because of extensive holdings in one or more fields should write them on cards and items to be shelved in several lines. The above number could be written in short meaningful segments as follows:

338
.47
621
384

Related to the long number difficulties are the rapid, often sweeping, topical relocations from one edition to another. Such drastic surgery is forced upon the system by its limited notational base and the swift growth and change in the world of knowledge and of publication. An article by Pat Thomas in the first *DC&* to appear after *DDC20* gives pointers on adjusting to DDC's expansions, reductions, relocations, and revised schedules.[5] While the big rush, particularly in academic libraries, to change from Dewey to the Library of Congress classification seems to have run its course, no library can afford to ignore all efforts to keep shelf arrangement contemporary with the shifts in knowledge as reflected in the literature.

UNIVERSAL DECIMAL CLASSIFICATION (UDC)

The UDC was developed in 1885 by two Belgian lawyers, Paul Otlet and Henri LaFontaine, for the classification of a huge card catalog of the world's literature in all fields of knowledge. It was based on the DDC (then in its fifth edition) but was, with Dewey's permission, expanded by the addition of many more detailed subdivisions and the use of typographical signs to indicate complex subjects and what we know today as facets. DDC's decimal notation was retained (except for final zeros), and the 10 main classes as well as some subdivisions are still the same in UDC as they are in DDC, but class 4 (i.e., DDC 400) has been amalgamated with class 8 and is currently vacant. Many major and almost all minor subdivisions are now quite different from those in DDC. The main difference lies, however, in the synthetic structure of UDC. Thus, a work dealing with two or more subjects can be classed by two or more UDC class notations, linked by a colon sign (the most commonly used of the typographical symbols), as in the following example:

362.1 : 658.3 : 681.31 Hospital : Personnel management : Computers

for a work on the use of computers in the management of hospital personnel. Such a class notation is, however, not a "call number" but is intended for a classified catalog in which each of the three class notations may serve as an access point, while the other two are shown in rotation, e.g.,

658.3 : 681.31 : 362.1 and *681.31* : 362.1 : 658.3

If UDC is to be used for shelf classification, one of the three class notations may be chosen as a call number for a book on this complex subject.

UDC's faceted structure has its roots in DDC's device for indication of place, namely, the intercalation of −09 followed by the class notation for a country or region, e.g., −0973 for the United States. UDC uses largely the same place notations as DDC but encloses them in parentheses. Thus, "plant cultivation in the U.S." is 631.50973 in DDC but 631.5(73) in UDC (note that the main class notation is the same in both). In addition to the place facet UDC has also specific symbols and notations for the language of a work, its physical form, races and peoples, time periods, materials, persons, specific points of view, and recurring subdivisions in certain classes, all of which can be appended to basic notations either alone or in combination, as in the following example:

631.5 = 82	Plant cultivation — written in Russian
631.5(038)	— Glossary
631.5"17"	— 18th century
631.5(= 97)(85)	— By American Indians in Peru

Due to this highly faceted structure and largely expressive notation the UDC has been used successfully in computerized information retrieval.[6]

UDC schedules were first published in 1905 in French, followed later by full editions (each one containing about 150,000 class notations) in English (published as British Standards in several dozens of separate booklets for main classes and their major subdivisions), German, Japanese, Russian, Spanish, and eight other languages. Medium-size editions containing about 30 percent of the full schedules exist in 11 languages, the most recent one being in English.[7] Abridged editions are published in 17 languages and 5 scripts, including Hebrew, Japanese, and Korean.[8] In addition, there are special editions for certain subject fields, e.g., geology, building construction, and agriculture.

UDC is managed by the International Federation of Documentation (FID) in The Hague (Netherlands), which coordinates a continuous revision and expansion process by means of a network of committees and experts, the results of which are published annually.[9] UDC is widely used in many European countries, Latin America, Japan, and the Soviet Union. In the United States it is used mainly in some scientific and technical libraries and by one abstracting database.[10] A U.S. Information Center for the UDC exists at the College of Library and Information Services of the University of Maryland in College Park, Maryland, where a complete collection of current English UDC editions and their updating as well as pending proposals for revision are available. More detailed descriptions of the UDC, its development, and its application may be found in a number of publications.[11]

NOTES

[1]*Dewey Decimal Classification and Relative Index*, 20th ed., edited by John P. Comaromi et al. (Albany, N.Y., Forest Press, 1989), 4v.

[2]*Abridged Dewey Decimal Classification and Relative Index*, 12th ed. (Albany, N.Y., Forest Press, 1990).

[3]Jeanne Osborn, *Dewey Decimal Classification, 20th Edition: A Study Manual*, revised and edited by John Phillip Comaromi (Englewood, Colo., Libraries Unlimited, 1991).

[4]*Dewey Decimal Classification Additions, Notes and Decisions*, vol. 5, no. 1- (Albany, N.Y., Forest Press, 1990-).

[5]Pat Thomas, "Implementing *DDC20*," *DC&*, vol. 5, no. 1 (March 1990): 7-8.

[6]Malcolm Rigby, *Automation and the UDC, 1948-1980*, 2nd ed. (The Hague, FID, 1981), (FID 565).

[7]British Standards Institution, *UDC: International Medium Edition* (London, BSI, 1985), (BS 1000M:1985). Available in printed or machine-readable form.

[8]*Bibliographic Survey of UDC Editions* (The Hague, FID, 1982), (FID 573).

[9]*Extensions and Corrections to the UDC* (The Hague, FID, 1951-). Annual.

[10]*Meteorological and Geoastrophysical Abstracts* (Boston, American Meteorological Society, 1950-).

[11]W. Boyd Rayward, "The UDC and FID: A Historical Perspective," *Library Quarterly* 37 (July 1967): 259-278; A. C. Foskett, "The Universal Decimal Classification," in *The Subject Approach to Information*, 4th ed. (London, Bingley, 1982), pp. 349-371; *Principles of the UDC and Rules for Its Revision and Publication* (The Hague, FID, 1981), (FID 598); Geoffrey Robinson, *UDC: A Brief Introduction* (The Hague, FID, 1979), (FID 574).

SUGGESTED READING

Foskett, A. C. *The Subject Approach to Information.* 4th ed. London, Bingley, 1982. Chapters 17-18.

Osborn, Jeanne. *Dewey Decimal Classification, 20th Edition: A Study Manual.* Revised and edited by John Phillip Comaromi. Englewood, Colo., Libraries Unlimited, 1991.

Robinson, Geoffrey. *UDC: A Brief Introduction.* The Hague, FID, 1984. (FID 574). Also available in French (FID 612), Italian (FID 583), and Spanish (FID 608).

Library of Congress Classification

18

INTRODUCTION

The Library of Congress was founded in 1800. Its earliest classification system was by size (folios, quartos, octavos, etc.), subdivided by accession numbers. But by 1812 the collection had grown to about 3,000 volumes, and a better method of classification was needed. The solution was to arrange the works under 18 broad subject categories similar to the Bacon-d'Alembert system used in the 1789 *Catalogue* of Benjamin Franklin's Library Company of Philadelphia. Soon after, in 1814, British soldiers burned the Capitol, where the collection was housed. To re-establish it, Thomas Jefferson offered to sell Congress his library of around 7,000 volumes. Jefferson had cataloged and classified the works himself, using 44 main classes and divisions based on a different interpretation of the Bacon-d'Alembert system. After some debate, Congress agreed to purchase the Jefferson books. Although many were destroyed in a later fire, the classification that came with them was used until the end of the nineteenth century. By that time it had undergone so much ad hoc modification, largely based on shelving and other physical limitations, that it was barely recognizable and completely inadequate.

Many significant changes occurred at the Library of Congress near the turn of the century. In 1899 Dr. Herbert Putnam, the new Librarian, with many new staff appointments and a brand new building, decided to reorganize and reclassify his rapidly growing collection. Since it was to be moved into more adequate shelving areas, the time was right to develop a better, more detailed classification system. There were already in existence the first five editions of the *Dewey Decimal Classification* and the first six expansions of Cutter's *Expansive Classification*. LC classifiers studied both, as well as the German *Halle Schema* devised by Otto Hartwig. They did not adopt any in full, but the experience they gained was invaluable, and their debt, especially to Cutter, is implicit in the basic structure of their system. While the outline and notation of their main classes are very similar to those of the *Expansive Classification*, there are no main classes I, O, W, X, or Y, as there are in the Cutter system.[1] All five letters do appear, however, as second or third symbols in the notation for various Library of Congress subclasses. The other major similarity to the *Expansive Classification* is in the structure of class "Z — Bibliography and Library Science," which was the first class devised and was adopted from Cutter with only minor variations.

After Putnam and his Chief Cataloger, Charles Martel, determined the broad outlines of the new classification, different subject specialists were asked to develop each individual schedule, or portion of the system. Within a broad general framework set up to ensure coordination, each topic or form of presentation identified as a class or subclass was further organized to display the library's holdings and to serve anticipated research needs. Schedules comprising single classes or parts of classes were separately published as they were completed. Most of them first appeared between 1899 and 1940. Many have since gone through several editions. In one sense, the scheme represents a series of special classifications. Yet special libraries, with narrowly defined collecting and service goals, often find the LC Classification (LCC), which serves broader, more interdisciplinary uses, unsatisfactory for their purposes.

To keep the system functionally up-to-date, individual schedule volumes are frequently reviewed in committee. Revisions, re-allocations, and additions keep it flexible and hospitable to new subjects or points of view. For example, in the 1960s interest in Eastern religions and the increase in materials from Asia occasioned a re-allocation in 1972 of the topic "Buddhism" from the span BL1400-1495 into a whole new subclass, BQ. Revisions were likewise made in subclass PL, particularly in the sections for Chinese, Japanese, and Korean literatures. There have also been block revisions in the "D—General and Old World History" class. In subclass DZ, Hungary was released at last from Austrian capativity. Number spans now reflect political changes in Albania, Bangladesh, Korea, Namibia, Somalia, and the like. A triple-letter subclass "DJK—Eastern Europe" was developed in 1976. Intensified foreign acquisitions programs under PL480, the National Program for Acquisitions and Cataloging (NPAC), the revised copyright law, and other developments, stimulated increased expansion and revision of the system.

Hundreds of different number-letter combinations compatible with the notation have not yet been employed or have been retired in favor of new locations. The scheme will continue to accommodate for a long time the many new subjects and aspects of subjects not yet anticipated. It is particularly useful for large university and research collections because of its hospitality and inherent flexibility. It has been used effectively in smaller academic and public libraries, although its adaptability for broad classification is limited. Even special libraries frequently base their own more technical constructs on it, extending its schedules or parts of schedules to cover their unique materials. Some foreign libraries also use the system, although, in spite of LC's large foreign holdings, it is primarily designed from an American perspective.

In the MARC format call numbers based on LCC that are assigned by LC or the British Library are placed in field 050. Those assigned by the National Library of Canada, the National Library of Medicine, or the National Agricultural Library are entered in field 055, 060, or 070, respectively. In the OCLC system, members are asked to enter locally assigned call numbers based on LCC in field 090.

CLASSIFICATION TOOLS AND AIDS

The working schedules are contained in over 45 separate volumes. Besides the basic schedules, there are a separately published partial index for P-PM subcategories in the Language and Literature class, and a short general *Outline*, now in its sixth edition, which gives the secondary and tertiary subclass spans for most classes. Several volumes are devoted to subclass coverage of broad areas, such as related language and literature groups. They comprise:

A	General Works; Polygraphy (4th ed., 1973)
B-BJ	Philosophy; Psychology (4th ed., 1989)
BL, BM, BP, BQ	Religion: Religions, Hinduism, Judaism, Islam, Buddhism (3rd ed., 1984)
BR-BV	Religion: Christianity, Bible (1987)
BX	Religion: Christian Denominations (1985)
C	Auxiliary Sciences of History (3rd ed., 1975)
D-DJ	History (General): History of Europe, Part 1 (3rd ed., 1990)
DJK-DK	History of Eastern Europe: General, Soviet Union, Poland (1987)
DL-DR	History of Europe, Part 2 (3rd ed., 1991)
DS	History of Asia (1987)
DT-DX	History of Africa, Australia, New Zealand, etc. (1988)
E-F	American History (3rd ed., 1958; Reissue with supplementary pages, 1965)
G	Geography; Maps; Anthropology; Recreation (4th ed., 1976)
H-HJ	Social sciences: Economics (4th ed., 1981)
HM-HX	Social Sciences: Sociology (4th ed., 1980)
J	Political Science (2nd ed., 1991 revision)
K	Law (General) (1977)
KD	Law of the United Kingdom and Ireland (1973)
KDZ, KG-KH	Law of the Americas, Latin America, and the West Indies (1984)
KE	Law of Canada (1976)
KF	Law of the United States (Prelim. ed., 1969)
KJ-KKZ	Law of Europe (1989)
KJV-KJW	Law of France (1985)
KK-KKC	Law of Germany (1982)
L	Education (4th ed., 1984)

M	Music; Books on Music (3rd ed., 1978)
N	Fine Arts (4th ed., 1970)
P-PZ	Language and Literature Tables (supersedes the tables in the P Schedules, 1982)
P-PA	General Philology and Linguistics; Classical Languages and Literatures (1928; Reissue with supplementary pages, 1968)
PA supplement	Byzantine and Modern Greek Literature; Medieval and Modern Latin Literature (1942; Reissue with supplementary pages, 1968)
PB-PH	Modern European Languages (1933; Reissue with supplementary pages, 1966)
PG	Russian Literature (in part) (1948; Reissue with supplementary pages, 1965)
PJ-PK	Oriental Philology and Literature, Indo-Iranian Philology and Literature (2nd ed., 1988)
PL-PM	Languages of Eastern Asia, Africa, Oceania; Hyperborean, Indian, and Artificial Languages (2nd ed., 1988)
P-PM supplement	Index to Languages and Dialects (4th ed., 1991)
PN, PR, PS, PZ	General Literature; English and American Literatures; Fiction in English; Juvenile Belles Lettres (3rd ed., 1988)
PQ, pt. 1	French Literature (1936; Reissue with supplementary pages, 1966)
PQ, pt. 2	Italian, Spanish, and Portuguese Literatures (1937; Reissue with supplementary pages, 1965)
PT, pt. 1	German Literature (2nd ed., 1989)
PT, pt. 2	Dutch and Scandinavian Literatures (1942; Reissue with supplementary pages, 1965)
Q	Science (7th ed., 1989)
R	Medicine (5th ed., 1986)
S	Agriculture (4th ed., 1982)
T	Technology (5th ed., 1971)
U	Military Science (4th ed., 1974)
V	Naval Science (3rd ed., 1974)
Z	Bibliography; Library Science (5th ed., 1980)
A-Z	Outline (6th ed., 1991)

Updating is accomplished by a variety of publications, most of which are available directly from the Library of Congress.

1. **Revised editions of individual schedules.** As the above list shows, the various schedules differ widely in the number and kinds of revisions made. Pre-1970 volumes were letter-press printed on both sides of each leaf and issued in beige paper covers. As changes came, some schedules were thoroughly revised and issued in new editions. In other cases, "reissues" showed the new material cumulated at the back in a separate sequence, with a separate index. Users had to remember to look in both sections each time they consulted one of these "reissues." Since 1970 all revisions show a new format. They are photo-offset from keyboarded copy, printed on only one side of each leaf, and bound in blue-and-white paper covers. Automated production techniques now make fully integrated revisions feasible, so the confusing double-sequence reissues no longer appear. However, the new editions do not always render prior editions obsolete. For example, the second and third editions of the PN, PR, PS, PZ schedule omit not only the first edition index entries for personal names but also long-established, heavily used author cutters from the *Additions and Changes* because they were never incorporated into the "official schedules."[2] Instructive prefaces are frequently dropped from new editions. When buying recent editions of the schedules, classifiers should check their older issues, to ensure that no valuable information would be inadvertently lost if they were discarded. All schedules and the *Outline* are sold individually by the Library's Cataloging Distribution Service at nominal prices.

2. **Library of Congress Classification – Additions and Changes.** This stapled paper publication reports quarterly on the latest adjustments in all schedules and schedule indexes of LCC. Subscriptions may be placed with the Cataloging Distribution Service.

3. **Library of Congress Classification Schedules: A Cumulation of Additions and Changes.** These periodic cumulations of the quarterly *Additions and Changes* have been published since 1974 by Gale Research Company on contract with the Library of Congress.[3] The class and subclass coverage of each separate booklet corresponds to that of the basic schedule volumes. Each volume updates a basic schedule volume from its cutoff date to the close of a given year. Gale Research Company also has published since 1988 a set of complete cumulations of basic schedules combined with all additions and changes through the close of the previous year. Both publications are annual.[3]

4. *Cataloging Service Bulletin.* This channel for recent decisions and experiments in technical processing at the Library of Congress has been offered since 1945.[4] It now has a regular quarterly publication schedule, carrying valuable data on LCC and shelflisting practice, as well as other aspects of subject and descriptive cataloging.

5. **Library of Congress Subject Headings.** There is no official comprehensive index to the LCC scheme. Most of the schedules carry their own indexes, which are largely self-contained, although they occasionally refer to other schedules where related materials can be found on an indexed topic. For example, the index to class "T — Technology" provides the following sequence of entries under "Baths, Public":

> Baths, Public
>   Architecture: NA7010
>   Building: TH4761-4763
>   Plumbing: TH6518.B3
>   Public health: RA605-606

At best, this type of cross-schedule indexing is spotty. The class "N — Fine Arts" index entry reads:

> Baths, Public (Architecture): NA7010

and the class "R — Medicine" entry reads:

> Public baths: RA605 +

The most obvious substitute for an official comprehensive index is the printed edition of *Library of Congress Subject Headings.*[5] While it was never designed to function as a true index, many entries and subdivisions refer in brackets to one or more class numbers, often including terminology used in the schedules. In it, under the heading "Baths, Public" one finds the following:

> **Baths, Public** *(May Subd Geog)*
>   *[RA605 (Public hygiene)]*
>   *[TH4761 (Building)]*

LC makes no effort to maintain class notations in LCSH, and it can be seen that under the heading "Baths, Public" one would miss the entry from the N schedule. However, sometimes LCC notations relating to a given concept can be grouped more quickly through LCSH than through the many schedule indexes, as shown in the following example:

> *Schedule B-BJ — Philosophy; Psychology:*
>   Hypnotism (Parapsychology): BF1111 +

> *Schedule BL, BM, BP, BQ — Religion: Religions, Hindiusm, Judaism, Islam, Buddhism:*
>   Hypnotism: BL65.H9

> *Schedule HM-HX — Social Sciences: Sociology:*
>   Hypnotism and crime: HV6110

(Examples continue on page 356.)

Schedule Q—Science:

Hypnotic conditions (Neurophysiology): QP425

Schedule R—Medicine:

Hypnotics: RM325
Hypnotism and hypnosis
 Anesthesiology: RD85.A9
 Dentistry: RK512.H95
 Forensic medicine: RA1171
 Psychiatry: RC490 +

LCSH14:

Hypnotics *(May Subd Geog)*
 [RM325]
 . . .
Hypnotism
 [BF1111-BF1156 (Parapsychology)]
 [HV6110 (Hypnotism and crime)]
 [RC490-RC499 (Psychiatry)]
 . . .
Hypnotism in dentistry *(May Subd Geog)*
 [RK512.H95]
 . . .
Hypnotism in surgery
 [RD85.H9]

It can be seen that one would miss the entries at BL, QP, and RA when using LCSH, but more entries are grouped there than are not.

6. **Library of Congress Shelflist in Microform.** In 1978 the six and one-half million cards of the LC shelflist, arranged by call number, were offered for purchase in various microformats (35mm roll film, 16mm cartridge, and microfiche) as well as in Copyflo hard copy. The United States Historical Documents Institute, Inc., and University Microfilms International jointly sponsored the filming and respectively sell different formats of the full shelflist, or selected portions of it. This tool can be used most effectively for fine-tuning class number and shelflist assignments through comparison of proposed numbers for new materials with those already grouped in a given area.

7. **Commercially prepared indexes.** Just as the Gale *Additions and Changes* cumulations and the LC shelflist reproductions are commercial aids based on official, publicly accessible LC data, so a number of indexing ventures have reflected similar trade manipulation of publications or automated processing available from the Library of Congress. They have not had commercial backing for updating purposes, however. The most comprehensive of these was:

Olson, Nancy B. *Combined Indexes to the Library of Congress Classification Schedules.* Washington, D.C.: United States Historical Documents Institute, 1974. These 15 volumes comprise 5 major subsets based on schedule indexes to the close of 1973, proper names with associated LCC numbers from the *LC Catalog, Books: Subjects* for 1965-1969, and portions of the official LC shelflist as microfilmed on a variety of dates from early 1970 through mid-1974:

> Set I: Author/number index. Alphabetical by literary authors' names. 2v.
>
> Set II: Biographical subject index. Alphabetical by subjects' names. 3v.
>
> Set III: Classified index to persons. All entries from Set II arranged in LCC number order. 3v.
>
> Set IV: Geographical name index. Nouns only, in permuted alphabetical order. 1v.
>
> Set V: Subject keyword index. Includes all entries from Set IV as well as topical subjects. 6v.

8. **Texts and general discussions.** Through the years many perceptive discussions of LCC have appeared. The list of suggested readings at the end of this chapter gives those titles that are most likely to help introduce the scheme to the beginning student.

BASIC FEATURES

Since LCC was developed as a utilitarian scheme for books at the Library of Congress, it is an enumerative, rather than a deductive, system. Among the basic features borrowed from C. A. Cutter are its order of main classes, its use of capital letters for main and subclass notation, its use of Arabic numerals for further subdivision, and its modification of the Cutter author-mark idea to achieve alphabetic subarrangements of various kinds. While most LC call numbers follow a simple, recurring letter-number-letter-number pattern, various other combinations sometimes reflect special situations or more detailed subdivisions.

All the LC schedules have similar, but not identical, sequencing arrangements and physical appearance. Within each sequence of class numbers the order proceeds as a rule from general aspects of the topic or discipline to its particular divisions and subtopics. Chronological sequences may trace historical events, publication dates, or other useful time frames. Geographical arrangements are frequently alphabetical, but just as frequently are given in a "preferred order," starting with the Western Hemisphere and the United States. Class "G—Geography, etc." is distinct from the history classes, although located next to them. This distribution differs from the DDC location of "910—Geography and Travel" within class "900—History." Neither scheme quite succeeds in solving the problem of ambiguous relationships between popular works of description and travel and other, perhaps more scholarly, books on national or regional social life and customs. The user must search both the history and the geography shelves to find all available materials on these topics.

There are other significant differences from the Dewey Decimal theory of organizing some materials. In class "J – Political Science," which is largely devoted to constitutional history of various modern governments, the primary groupings are national or jurisdictional. Each topical aspect (e.g., political parties or electoral systems) is treated as a subdivision of the governmental unit under which it functions. In DDC materials are grouped first by topic (e.g., "324 – The political process") and then subdivided by geography or jurisdiction.

Similarly, the Library of Congress provides broad subclasses in class P for the various national literatures, subdividing next by chronology and then by individual author. Seldom, except for anthologies, does it group literary works by form. DDC also starts in its 800 class with a basic separation into national literatures, but it subdivides next by form, e.g., poetry, drama, fiction, etc. Only subordinately does it provide for time divisions or individual authors.

The LC preference for grouping national literatures by time period and author extends to class "B – Philosophy" but not to music or the graphic arts. In subclass "M – Music and Scores" works are classed first by form (e.g., opera, oratorio, symphony, chamber music), then by composer. There is no attempt to keep time periods, national schools, or genres of expression (e.g., classical, romantic, modern) distinct. Subclass "ML – Literature, History and Criticism of Music" does use national, chronological, and similar groupings. In class "N – Fine Arts" materials are grouped first by form (e.g., sculpture, drawing, painting), then by nationality or chronology, and finally by artist.

The major LC use of literary grouping by form formerly was its infamous subclass "PZ – Fiction in English; Juvenile Belles Lettres." Here a concession was made to a "reader interest" orientation that proved to be most controversial and a stumbling block to the full use of LCC by other research libraries with large holdings in literature. Therefore, beginning July 1, 1980, LC discontinued use of PZ1, PZ3, and PZ4. American fiction is now classed in PS, English fiction in PR, and translations of fiction into English with the original national literature. Otherwise, LC's handling of literature has met with general approval. A recurring pattern of organization within each literature affords the shelf or shelflist browser a useful guide:

1. History and criticism, subdivided
   a. Chronologically
   b. Then by form
2. Collections or anthologies, subdivided by form
3. Individual authors, subdivided
   a. Chronologically
   b. Then alphabetically by author
      1) Collective works
      2) Individual works
      3) Biography and criticism

LCC breaks the "Generalia" class familiar to DDC users into two classes at opposite ends of the alphabet. The "A – General Works" schedule employs for its subclasses rare instances of mnemonic notation. General encyclopedias are located in subclass AE, general indexes in AI, general museum publications in AM, and so forth. By contrast, the Z class, containing bibliographies and works on the book industries and on libraries, has no two-letter subclasses at all. While its subject bibliographies are arranged alphabetically by topic in the Z5001-Z8000 span, there is nothing mnemonic about their notation. The only other notable instances of mnemonic class letter associations are for class "G—Geography, etc.," class "M—Music," subclass "ML—Music Literature," and class "T—Technology."

SCHEDULE FORMAT

Most of the LCC schedules exhibit certain common features of external and internal format. Many of these format features are missing from certain schedules, a reminder that the scheme was intentionally decentralized in its development. Subject specialists were encouraged to adopt standard modes of organization, but were never forced to maintain a rigid formal pattern.

External Format

The gross physical format, or external appearance, of the schedules has already been described. Both old and new editions, regardless of typography or binding, tend to follow a familiar pattern of organization:

1. **A preface or prefatory note** nearly always follows the title page. As was said, these introductory remarks in recent editions have become briefer and less helpful for classification purposes than they formerly were.

2. **Brief synopses** next appear in over one-third of the schedules, to show the primary subdivisions contained in those volumes. In most cases these broad subclasses are readily identifiable by their brief double-letter notation, but class "K—Law" is issued in double-letter subclass volumes with synopses that frequently show mnemonic triple-letter divisions. We can learn at a glance that the law of Ontario is found in subclass KEO, while that of Quebec is in KEQ. A similar mnemonic arrangement applies to the American states in subclass KF, but their notation is more complicated since several states share certain initial letters. Moreover the KF schedule is one of those that carries no synopsis. A typical synopsis is:

    SYNOPSIS

H	SOCIAL SCIENCES (GENERAL)
HA	STATISTICS
HB	ECONOMIC THEORY
HC	ECONOMIC HISTORY AND CONDITIONS
HD	ECONOMIC HISTORY AND CONDITIONS
HE	TRANSPORTATION AND COMMUNICATIONS
HF	COMMERCE
HG	FINANCE
HJ	PUBLIC FINANCE

3. **An outline,** consisting not only of alphabetic subclasses, but also of significant alphanumeric subspans, is present in nearly every schedule. In schedules without synopses the outlines tend to be briefer and to show broader subdivisions; in schedules with synopses, they are longer and more detailed. Occasionally, as in the schedule for class "J – Political Science," the "synopsis" is really an outline. These two kinds of preliminary overview lend a counterweight to the detail of the schedule indexes. They offer the user supplementary techniques for arriving quickly at any given portion of the schedules. The outline for the first two subclasses of class H appears in the schedule as follows:

OUTLINE

H		SOCIAL SCIENCES (GENERAL)
HA		STATISTICS
	29-31.9	Theory and method of social science statistics
	36-37	Organizations. Bureaus. Service
	38-39	Registration of vital events. Registration (General)
	154-4737	Statistical data
	154-155	Universal statistics
	175-4737	By region or country
HB		ECONOMIC THEORY
	71-74	Economics as a science. Relation to other subjects
	75-130	History of economics. History of economic theory
		Including special economic schools
	131-145	Methodology
	135-145	Mathematical economics. Quantitative methods
		Including econometrics, input-output analysis, game theory
	201-205	Value. Utility
	221-236	Price. Regulation of prices
	238-251	Competition. Production. Wealth
	501	Capital. Capitalism
	522-715	Income. Factor shares
	531-551	Interest. Usury
	601	Profit
	615-715	Entrepreneurship. Risk and uncertainty. Property
	801-843	Consumption. Demand
	846-846.8	Welfare theory
	848-3697	Demography. Vital events
	3711-3840	Business cycles. Economic fluctuations

One cannot assume that the numbers and spans given in a schedule outline will coincide precisely with those in the corresponding portion of the general *Outline*. Decentralized classification and intermittent revisions of the different publications result in slightly varying "summaries" of schedule contents in print at the same time. The section of the H and HA subclasses in the sixth edition of the *Outline* reads like a synopsis:

SOCIAL SCIENCES

H	1-99	Social sciences (General)
HA	1-4737	Statistics
		Including collections of general and census statistics of special countries. For mathematical statistics, *see* QA

4. **The schedule proper** enumerates specific class number assignments and sequences in their most explicit form. Page formatting devices, standard in most published schemes, demonstrate hierarchical subordinations and progressions. LCC schedules show left-margin indentions, with nested running titles on nearly every page to demonstrate hierarchy. These devices are not so carefully worked out, nor so consistently displayed, as they are in the Dewey Decimal Classification. Size and quality of typeface also indicate levels of subordination in the pre-1970 letter-press LCC schedules, as well as in DDC. But current production from typed copy permits the use of only two typographical devices (underlining and full capitals) to identify topics of greater generality or inclusiveness. Many broad headings not listed in the schedule outline, but which offer a useful survey of subtopics, are interpolated just ahead of the specific numbers that they embrace. They often carry no single class number of their own. For this and related reasons LCC does not work well for classifying small general collections or parts of collections. Nor are these spans very often accompanied by internal summary tables such as DDC uses.

Most schedules do carry internal tables at key junctures, to provide schematic patterns for further localized development of class numbers or sequences. While LCC is basically enumerative (that is, its topical number assignments are usually not made until there is at least one book to go into the category), these generalized tables open up patterned arrangements that are usually not fully realized on the shelves.

A related space saver is the "Divide like" or "Subarranged like" note, which appears infrequently, but very specifically, in simple one-to-one equivalencies, without the complications encountered in the more abstractly contrived DDC notation. Scope notes and footnotes occasionally refer to auxiliary tables, etc., or they sometimes give useful instructions for number building. The following page from the "T — Technology" schedule shows most of these features:

TD   **ENVIRONMENTAL TECHNOLOGY. SANITARY ENGINEERING**

→   The promotion and conservation of the public health, comfort and convenience by the control of the environment

Cf. GF, Human ecology

HC68, HC95-710, Environmental policy (General)

HD3840-4730, Economic aspects (Government ownership, municipal industries, finance, etc.)

QH75-77, Landscape protection

RA565-604, Public health

S622-627, Soil conservation

S900-972, Conservation of natural resources

TC801-978, Reclamation of land

TH6014-7975, Building environmental engineering

Periodicals and societies, by language of publication

1	English
2	French
3	German
4	Other languages (not A-Z)
5	Congresses
6	Exhibitions. Museums

→   Subarranged like TA6

7	Collected works (nonserial)
9	Dictionaries and encyclopedias
12	Directories

History

15	General works
16	Ancient
17	Medieval
18	Modern to 1800
19	Nineteenth century
20	Twentieth century
21-126	Country and city subdivisions. Table I[1]

→   Including municipal reports of public sanitary works

Under each country (except as otherwise specified):

(1) .A1A-Z General works

.A6-Z   States, provinces, etc.

(2)   Local (Cities, etc.), A-Z

Biography

139	Collective
140	Individual, A-Z

General works

144	Early to 1850
145	1850-
146	Elementary textbooks
148	Popular works
151	Pocketbooks, tables, etc.
153	General special
155	Addresses, essays, lectures
156	Environmental and sanitary engineering as a profession
157	Study and teaching
.5	Research
158	Municipal engineering organization and management

→ [1]For Table I, *see* pp. 263-265. Add country number in table to 0

5. **Auxiliary tables** designed for use with more than one specific class notation or span are located externally to the schedules proper in many volumes. If, as in the "B—Philosophy" and "J—Political Science" schedules, they apply to only one subclass, they follow that subclass. Otherwise, they appear after the full schedule, immediately preceding the index. Sometimes a table number is given in parentheses beside an entry in the schedule, to warn the user that the entry should be further subdivided. More often a footnote cites the table with its page number and occasionally indicates how the interpolation should be made. Such a footnote can be seen on the subclass TD page reproduced above. A part of the table to which it refers appears on page 364.

This auxiliary Table I from the T schedule is "simple" because it carries only one sequence of numbers that can be interpolated directly into the corresponding number spans in the schedule. Other tables are "compound." That is, they supply more than one number sequence for the same list of subtopics. Number spans from the schedule and the table are matched according to the quantity of materials that the LC classifiers anticipate at any given location. The following excerpt from the "N—Fine Arts" external Tables I to III-A shows how spans of from 100 to 300 numbers can be distributed by reference to the same list of terms.

N   **TABLES OF SUBDIVISIONS**

Tables I to III-A

I (100)		II (200)	III (300)	III-A (300)
01	America	01	01	01
	Latin America	02	02	02
02	North America	03	03	03
03	United States	05	05	05
.5	Colonial period; 18th (and early 19th) century	06	06	06
.7	19th century	07	07	07
04	20th century	08	08	08
05	New England	10	10	10
.5	Middle Atlantic States	.5	.5	.5
06	South	11	11	11
07	Central	14	18	18
08	West	17	23	23
09	Pacific States	19	25	25
10	States, A-W	25	35	35
11	Cities, A-Z	27	38	38
12	Special artists, A-Z	28	39	39
13	Canada	29	41	41
14	Mexico	31	44	44

For instance, the span "N5801-5896—Classical Art in Other [i.e., Non-Greek or Italian] Countries" is to be distributed according to Table I, starting from class number N5800. On the other hand, "NB1501-1684—Sculptured Monuments in Special Countries" uses Table II as a guide for

T TABLES OF SUBDIVISIONS

TABLE I

HISTORY AND COUNTRY DIVISIONS

	History
15	General works
16	Ancient
17	Medieval
18	Modern
19	19th century
20	20th century
	Special countries

Under each country with two numbers:

(1) General works

(2) Local or special, A-Z

The numbers for "Cities or other special," "Local or special," "Provinces or special" may be used in some cases for the local subdivision, in other cases for special canals, rivers, harbors, railroads, or bridges, as specified in the particular scheme to which this table is applied

Under both general and local subdivisions arrange as follows:

.A1-5 Official documents

.A6-Z Nonofficial. By author, A-Z

e.g. TD257.A5, 1966, Gt. Brit. Water Resources Board. Water supplies in South East England

TD264.T5P6, 1967, Port of London Authority. The cleaner Thames.

TD224.C3A53, 1963, California. Dept. of Water Resources. Alameda County investigation

21	America
22	North America
23	United States
.1	Eastern states. Atlantic coast
.15	New England
.2	Appalachian region
.3	Great Lakes region
.4	Midwest. Mississippi Valley
.5	South. Gulf states
.6	West
.7	Northwest
.8	Pacific coast
.9	Southwest
24	States, A-W ⟵
	e.g. .A4 Alaska
	.H3 Hawaii
25	Cities (or other special), A-Z
26	Canada
27	Provinces (or other special), A-Z
.5	Latin America
28-29	Mexico ⟵
30	Central America
31	Special countries, A-Z

adding country numbers to NB1500. Similarly, "ND2601-2876 — Mural Painting in Special Countries" uses Table III to add country numbers to ND2600.

Geographical and chronological subdivisions are often relegated to auxiliary tables. Frequently the two concepts are combined, as in the above excerpt from the N schedule. But other principles of division may also be found in tabular form. A compound table external to subclass "JS — Local Government" contains such categories as "Periodicals," "Executive administration," "Legislative organization," and the like. The heavily used PN, PR, PS, PZ schedule has a separately published extensive set of simple and compound tables designed for use with literary author numbers, running the gamut from long spans for prolific, often translated and discussed authors to brief expansions of cutter designations for recent or little-published authors.

A few auxiliary tables, especially certain geographic lists from the H schedule, are said to "float." That is, they appear, usually in slightly variant forms, in other schedules. Thus, the Table of Countries in One Alphabet from the H schedule shows up in mutation as an auxiliary table for schedules C, D, E-F, T, U, and V.

6. **A detailed index** accompanies each schedule except PA Supplement, Parts 1 and 2 each of the PQ and PT subclasses, and the 1991 revision of Class J. These indexes vary in coverage and depth, but most of them list specific topics from their schedule. References from synonyms or related terms, alphabetized and indented subordinate topical lists, and suggestions for placing related materials in other schedules are occasionally included. An excerpt from the class "T — Technology" index is given on page 355.

7. **Supplementary pages of additions and changes** appear at the back of many schedules published before 1970. These were discussed under "Revised editions of individual schedules" on page 354.

Internal Format

While Herbert Putnam and Charles Martel left the local arrangement of topical and form divisions very much to the discretion of their subject specialists, they nevertheless identified certain basic orientation features for use throughout the system. These organizational concepts were generally known as "Martel's Seven Points" of internal format. They could be incorporated into the schedules at any level of hierarchical subdivision appropriate within the given context. They encompassed:

1. **General form divisions.** The approach here was similar to Dewey's Form Division Table, which has evolved in recent DDC editions into the Table of Standard Subdivisions. It assumes that library materials can often be effectively grouped according to their mode of presentation. Examples are periodicals; society publications; collections; dictionaries or

encyclopedias; conference, exhibition, or museum publications; annuals or yearbooks; directories; and documents. Because of their general application they belong near the beginning of any disciplinary or topical section, but LCC imposes no rigid order upon their location. Their importance in subclass "L – Education (General)" is best observed in the following schedule outline:

L	EDUCATION (GENERAL)
7-97	Periodicals. Societies
101	Yearbooks
106-107	Congresses
111-791	Official documents, reports, etc.
797-899	Educational exhibitions and museums
999-991	Directories of educational institutions

By contrast, subclasses "LD-LG – Individual Educational Institutions" show no obvious use of the form division concept. Only in their auxiliary tables do a few of the forms emerge as useful ordering concepts.

2. **Theory. Philosophy.**

3. **History. Biography.**

4. **Treatises. General works.** Works falling under these three of Martel's Seven Points are often intermixed with those arranged according to physical form and with other locally useful groupings, as the excerpt on page 367 shows (QE – Geology).

5. **Law. Regulation. State relations.** Until the publication in 1969 of the first "K – Law" subclass, this ordering principle was handy for grouping legal materials with their related topics, especially in the social sciences. The belated, still unfinished development of class K inverts the relationship. Whenever possible we now classify such works first as legal materials and only subordinately as being discipline-oriented. For example, books dealing with government regulations for control of drugs as economic commodities were originally classed in HD9665.7-9. Those dealing with regulations for the manufacture, sale, and use of drugs were classed in RA402. Subclass "KF – Law of the United States" now places drug laws in KF3885-3894. In years to come, most works dealing with U.S. drug legislation and regulation will be placed there.

QE	GEOLOGY
1	Periodicals, societies, congresses, serial collections, yearbooks
3	Collected works (nonserial)
4	Voyages and expeditions
5	Dictionaries and encyclopedias
→ 6	Philosophy
7	Nomenclature, terminology, notation, abbreviations
→	History
11	General works
13	By region or country, A-Z
→	Biography
21	Collective
22	Individual, A-Z
	e.g. .D25 Dana, J.D.
	.L8 Lyell
23	Directories
25	Early works through 1800
→	General works, treatises, and advanced textbooks
26	1801-1969
.2	1970-
	Elementary textbooks
28	General
.2	Physical geology
.3	Historical geology

6. **Study and teaching. Research. Textbooks.** Unlike DDC, LCC some-times allows a unique place for textbooks, as well as for more theoretical works on how to study, teach, or research a topic. Thus, under "QL — Zoology" (see page 368) there appears the following sequence.

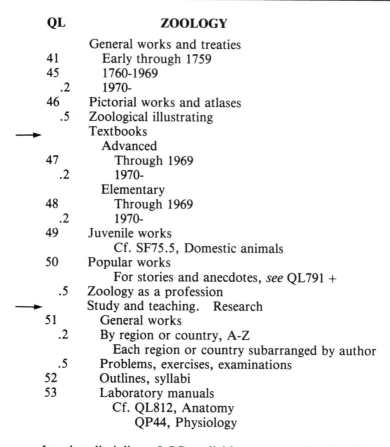

QL	ZOOLOGY
	General works and treaties
41	Early through 1759
45	1760-1969
.2	1970-
46	Pictorial works and atlases
.5	Zoological illustrating
⟶	Textbooks
	Advanced
47	Through 1969
.2	1970-
	Elementary
48	Through 1969
.2	1970-
49	Juvenile works
	Cf. SF75.5, Domestic animals
50	Popular works
	For stories and anecdotes, *see* QL791 +
.5	Zoology as a profession
⟶	Study and teaching. Research
51	General works
.2	By region or country, A-Z
	Each region or country subarranged by author
.5	Problems, exercises, examinations
52	Outlines, syllabi
53	Laboratory manuals
	Cf. QL812, Anatomy
	QP44, Physiology

In other disciplines, LCC explicitly groups textbooks with general works and treatises. Under one subtopic we find:

QH	CYTOLOGY
573	Periodicals, societies, congresses, serial collections, yearbooks
574	Collected works (nonserial)
575	Dictionaries and encyclopedias
	History
577	General works
578	By region or country, A-Z
⟶	General works, treatises, and textbooks
581	Through 1969
.2	1970-
.5	Addresses, essays, lectures
582.5	Juvenile works
⟶ 583	Study and teaching. Research
.2	Laboratory manuals

7. **Subjects and subdivisions of subjects.** Most modern classification systems are disciplinary rather than topical. That is, they normally proceed from broad general divisions of knowledge to narrower subdivisions, with more or less comprehensive coverage provided for each special topic in relation to the hierarchy. Any linear arrangement of books or other materials on shelves must resort to a series of cyclic progressions if it displays subject-related groupings based on logical considerations or practical associations. Just as Martel's fourth point reminds classifiers that "general works" should be shelved together, usually near the beginning of each new topical group, so this seventh point provides for further subject breakdown based on "literary warrant" or the amount of material requiring classification in such a group. One intermediate type that LCC frequently places just after "general works" is a potpourri called "general special" or "special aspects." These works treat the topic from particular points of view. Sometimes, as in TD153 (see page 362), such books have a single class number. At other places they must be spread out over several pages of the schedules.

NOTATION

The typical LCC notation contains a mixed notation of one to three letters, followed by one to four integers, and possibly a short decimal. Decimal numbers were not used much until it became necessary to expand certain sections where no further integers were available. Decimals do not usually indicate subordination, but allow a new topic or aspect to be inserted into an established context. In the above excerpt from the "QH573-583.2 — Cytology" schedule the decimals belie the left-margin indentions of their associated topics. Clearly, "QH581.5 — Addresses, essays, lectures" is hierarchically equivalent to "QH575 — Dictionaries and encyclopedias."

Another method of expanding LCC notations is by means of mnemonic letter-number combinations, which look like Cutter's "Author numbers" but are derived from a different matrix (see chapter 19, "Creation of Complete Call Numbers"). These "cutter numbers" may represent geographic, personal, corporate, or topical names. They are subordinated to schedule notations where an instruction to subdivide "A-Z" appears. Since they are part of the class notation, many of the actual LC assignments, or at least a significant number of examples, are included within the schedule (see "QE22 — Individual Biography of Geologists, A-Z" above). Geographic cutter numbers are generally omitted, however, unless they happen to be available in an auxiliary table to one or another of the schedules (see "QH578 — History of Cytology, by region or country, A-Z" above). In the excerpt from class T, Table I (page 364), the table number 24 is associated with American states "A-W," together with a rare inclusion of two examples. The class T user will find that auxiliary Table III is a complete list of state cutter numbers that corroborates the examples in Table I.

Alphabetic geographic sequences normally appear at subordinate places in the schedules, where they subdivide a single integer or decimal number. For broader disciplines or subjects, where the geographic arrangement covers an extensive number span, the organization follows a "preferred pattern" as was noted in the section on external format (see page 363). The excerpt from class N,

Tables I to III-A, shows how such sequences begin with "home base" (i.e., the Western Hemisphere and the United States), following a pattern that covers the earth pretty much according to our American perceptions of the nearness and importance of our neighbors.

Library of Congress interpretation of "cutter numbers" is always decimal. In a typical letter(s)-number(s)/letter-number(s) combination, the primary letter(s)-number(s) group should be arranged first alphabetically, then by integer(s) until a fifth digit is introduced following a decimal point. All schedules make the basic ordering by integer quite evident, as when PR509 follows PR51, but precedes PR5018. The secondary letter-number(s) combination, by contrast, should be filed decimally. The Library of Congress carefully inserts a decimal point in front of it, even if, as at "QH541.15.M3—Mathematical Models in Ecology," a decimal is already part of the primary notation. Some libraries using LCC drop the cutter decimal from their notation, on the premise that users will remember to follow the convention. The practice may possibly cause confusion in long cutter number runs where it is not clearly understood that a class notation like PR4972.M33 should follow PR4972.M3 but precede PR4972.M5.

Occasionally a class notation, or series of notations, appears in the schedules in parentheses. These were formerly termed "shelflist numbers," but today more often are called "alternative class numbers." Some of them represent locations once actively used, but now retired by the Library of Congress. Class notation G1020, for instance, was assigned to school atlases in schedule G, third edition (1954). By 1966 the *Additions and Changes* showed it as G(1020) with an instruction to see G1019 for school atlases. In the 1976 fourth edition of class G, there is no G1020 at all.

Other class notations appear to have been reserved in parentheses for possible future use and have since been activated. The span "PA2023-2027—Congresses and Collections of Papers Dealing with Latin Philology and Language" was so reserved in the original 1928 edition of the P-PA schedule, but all parentheses were removed by 1962. Alternative class notations are nearly always accompanied by "prefer notes." Thus subclass SF (Animal culture) has an entry "SF(112) Weight tables, see HF5716.C2, etc." Libraries using LCC are welcome to adopt these alternative class notations if their own classification needs are better realized by so doing.

Following are a few examples of number building using LCC.

Example 1

DC203.4   Ashton, John, b. 1834.
             English caricature and satire on Napoleon I . . .

D	History and Topography (except America)
DC	France
139-249	Revolutionary and Napoleonic period, 1789-1815
203-212	Biography of Napoleon
203	General works
.4	Caricature and satire

Example 2

QL696	Turner, Angela K.
.P247	Swallows & martins . . .

Q	Science
QL	Zoology
605-739.3	Chordates. Vertebrates
671-699	Birds
696	Systematic divisions. By order and family, A-Z
.P2	Passeriformes
.P247	Hirundinidae (Swallows)

Example 3

RA407.3	American Hospital Association
	Comparative statistics on health facilities and population : metropolitan and nonmetropolitan areas . . .

R	Medicine (General)
RA	Public aspects of medicine
1-418.5	Medicine and the state
407-409.5	Medical statistics and surveys
407.3-407.5	By region or country
407.3	United States. General works

CONCLUSION

Most libraries using LCC will continue to appropriate officially assigned call numbers for any of their own materials that the Library of Congress has already classified. However, it is a rare library that holds only titles, editions, and issues available in the Library of Congress collection. Librarians and library users should be able to break down an LC call number into its components. Classifiers should be able to create reasonably consistent supplementary notations with which to fit their unique holdings into the system. Users may stumble over special practices at local points, but the general principles of arrangement are nearly always decipherable, especially if a shelflist of LC call numbers is available to compare with the schedules. Highly specific shelflisting (i.e., the rationale underlying many cutter numbers, as explained in chapter 19) is, on the other hand, not always so easy to explain. The perfectionist classifier, geared to the invariabilities of DDC, must remember that LCC is loosely coordinated and essentially pragmatic. It aims first to class closely, then to identify uniquely, particular works, or issues of works, using the most economical notation available within its broad parameters of theory and practice.

NOTES

[1]A table comparing the main classes of the Cutter and the LC schemes is given on page 384.

[2]*Cataloging Service Bulletin*, no. 2 (Fall 1978): 45.

[3]*Library of Congress Classification Schedules: A Cumulation of Additions and Changes through ...* (Detroit, Gale Research Company, 1974-); *Library of Congress Classification Schedules Combined with Additions and Changes through ...: Classes A-Z*, edited by Rita Runchock, Kathleen Droste, and Victoria A. Coughlin (Detroit, Gale Research Company, 1988-).

[4]Library of Congress, *Cataloging Service*, bulletin 1 (June 1945)-125 (Spring 1978); *Cataloging Service Bulletin*, no. 1 (Summer 1978)-date.

[5]*Library of Congress Subject Headings*, 14th ed. (Washington, D.C., Library of Congress, 1991), 3v. For a detailed discussion of this work, see chapter 22.

SUGGESTED READING

Chan, Lois M. *Immroth's Guide to the Library of Congress Classification*, 4th ed. Englewood, Colo., Libraries Unlimited, 1990.

Foskett, A. C. *The Subject Approach to Information*. London, Bingley, 1982. Chapter 21.

Matthis, Raimund E., and Desmond Taylor. *Adopting the Library of Congress Classification System: A Manual of Methods and Techniques for Application or Conversion*. New York, R. R. Bowker, 1971.

Creation of Complete Call Numbers

19

INTRODUCTION

Library call numbers serve a double function. The class notation portion groups related materials together. The second portion of the complete call number uniquely identifies different works in the same class. Traditionally, this second part of the call number is based on the main entry, which has been chosen for the work through descriptive cataloging. Various terms such as *author number, book number,* and *cutter number* have been applied, but *author number* does not allow for those works with title main entries, while *book number* implies that it cannot be applied to nonbook materials. *Cutter number* is also misleading because the LC method of deriving it differs from the original tables devised by C. A. Cutter. However, the name *cutter number* has come into general use in practice regardless of the classification scheme used. Its general usage is a tribute to C. A. Cutter, who conceived the idea of using alphanumeric symbols to keep items in alphabetical order within a particular classification notation. In this text *cutter number* is used for any notation serving this function.

CUTTER NUMBERS DEVISED BY
C. A. CUTTER

Providing a classification notation with a supplementary cutter number enables the cataloger to design a fully unique call number for each title in a collection. The cutter numbers most often used with DDC class notations are taken from a set of tables devised by Charles Ammi Cutter. These tables equate surnames and other words with alphanumeric sequences. Cutter initially produced a table in a single alphabet of all consonants except *S*, followed by an alphabet of vowels and the letter *S*.[1] This "two-figure" table (most of its combinations consist of a capital letter plus two digits) was later expanded by Kate E. Sanborn to provide more differentiation among names for use with larger collections.[2] However, since she did not adhere to Cutter's schema, Cutter then developed his own expansion to permit growing libraries to assign more specific book numbers without disrupting the sequences they had already established from his two-figure table.[3] There are thus three different "Cutter" tables. The Cutter-Sanborn version is perhaps the most widely used today, being preferred by many larger libraries because of its simpler design and notation.

While cutter numbers are most commonly used to arrange material by main entries (usually authors' surnames, but occasionally forenames, corporate names, or titles), they are also used in some instances to alphabetize material by subject, as in the case of biography. To illustrate the use of each table, let us suppose that we wish to assign a cutter number for the English poet John Donne. The three tables carry the following sequences:

Cutter Two-figure Table

Doll	69	Foh
Dom	71	Folg
Doo	72	Foll

Cutter Three-figure Table

Donk	718	Folk
Donnet	719	Folke
Doo	72	Foll

Cutter-Sanborn Table

Donk	684	Fonti
Donn	685	Fontr
Donner	686	Foo

According to the Cutter two-figure table, the number for Donne is D71. By the Cutter three-figure table it is D718 (an expansion of the D71 assignment). But by the Cutter-Sanborn table it is D685. The above examples also demonstrate the typical three-column display used in the original form of the tables. In 1969 Paul K. Swanson of the Forbes Library, Northampton, Massachusetts, and Esther M. Swift, editor of the H. R. Huntting Company, revised this arrangement into single continuous alphabets of two columns, with letters on the left corresponding to numbers on the right. The new arrangement appears to be easier to use.

The work letter (or workmark) is the first letter of the title of the work, exclusive of articles. It follows the cutter number on the second line of the call number. Thus, the complete Dewey Decimal call number of Henry James's novel *Wings of the Dove* is 813.4 J27w. Work letters do not inevitably ensure that a book will be placed in alphabetical sequence within the author grouping; this depends upon the sequence of acquisition of the books. One additional letter from the title may be added if necessary. Thus, a copy of James's *Washington Square* might be classified 813.4 J27wa. If the third acquisition is a volume entitled *The Works of Henry James*, it would most probably be given the call number 813.4 J27, with no workmark, as most libraries prefer to place collected works of an author ahead of the individual works.

With an author such as Erle Stanley Gardner, who began the title of all of his Perry Mason mysteries with *The Case of the ...*, such a scheme is not feasible. Depending on the library's policy, the cataloger can choose one of several alternatives. For example, the cataloger can ignore completely the common phrase *the case of the* and proceed directly to the distinctive part of the title, or use two work letters: *c* for *case*, plus an additional letter for the distinctive title (e.g., *The Case of the Mischievous Doll* might be assigned the work letters *cm*).

Biographies and criticism of a specific author pose a particular problem of library policy. Two procedures are common. In the Dewey schedule, 928 is the biography number for literary figures (920 for Biography; 8 for Literature). Thus, biographies of authors might be classified in 928, with subdivision for nationality. Another way of classifying biography is to use the standard biography subdivision, 092. A third possibility is to classify biographies of authors with their work, in order to keep everything by and about a literary figure in one place. In such cases, a common method of distinguishing works "by" from works "about" an author is to insert an arbitrary letter — usually one toward the end of the alphabet — after the cutter number and to follow it with the initial of the author of the biography. This device puts all books about an author directly behind all books by that author. Thus, if the letter z is chosen as the biographical letter, a biography or criticism of Henry James by Leon Edel would be cuttered J27zE, and it would follow, in shelflist order, J27w. If James had written a novel beginning with the letter z only the work letter z would be used for the novel; thus, the novel would still come before all criticism and biography.

The problem of a variety of editions occurs most frequently in literature, but classic works in all other fields are also reprinted by the same or another publisher, especially now that paperbacks have revived many worthwhile books that have been long out of print.

One cataloging practice is to assign the date of publication as part of the call number to all editions of a single work issued by the same publisher and to assign a number following the work letter to all editions of the same work published by different publishers. Thus, the first acquired copy of *Wings of the Dove* would be classified 813.4 J27w. If the library acquired a second copy of the novel, issued by a different publisher, the number would be 813.4 J27w2. Assume that the second publisher was Modern Library and that the library received another edition of the novel, also published by Modern Library, in 1985. The call number might then be 813.4 J27w2 1985. A completely different edition published by a third publisher would be classified 813.4 J27w3.

CUTTER NUMBERS DEVISED
BY LC

Library of Congress call numbers also consist, in general, of two principal elements: class notation and cutter number, to which are added, as required, symbols designating a particular work. While it is possible to use Cutter-Sanborn numbers with LC classification, most libraries prefer to use Library of Congress cutter numbers constructed from a table composed by LC for this purpose.

Policies and procedures used at the Library of Congress in completing call numbers have been published in the form of a shelflisting manual.[4] This manual should be consulted for more detailed information than is discussed below.

Library of Congress cutter numbers are composed of the initial letter of the main entry heading, followed by Arabic numerals representing the succeeding letters on the following basis:

Cutter Table

(1) After initial *vowels*

for the second letter:	b	d	l-m	n	p	r	s-t	u-y
use number:	2	3	4	5	6	7	8	9

(2) After initial letter *S*

for the second letter:	a	ch	e	h-i	m-p	t	u	w-z
use number:	2	3	4	5	6	7	8	9

(3) After initial letters *Qu*

for the second letter:	a	e	i	o	r	t	y
use number:	3	4	5	6	7	8	9

For initial letters *Qa-Qt*,
use: **2-29**

(4) After other initial *consonants*

for the second letter:	a	e	i	o	r	u	y
use number:	3	4	5	6	7	8	9

(5) For *expansion*

for the letter:	a-d	e-h	i-l	m-o	p-s	t-v	w-z
use number:	3	4	5	6	7	8	9

The following examples show cutters that could be used only when the entries already shelflisted conform to the table above. In most cases, the cutters must be adjusted to file an entry correctly and to allow room for later entries.

Vowels		S		Q		Consonants	
IBM	.I26	Sadron	.S23	*Qadduri	.Q23	Campbell	.C36
Idaho	.I33	*Scanlon	.S29	*Qiao	.Q27	Ceccaldi	.C43
*Ilardo	.I4	Schreiber	.S37	Quade	.Q33	*Chertok	.C48
*Import	.I48	*Shillingburg	.S53	Queiroz	.Q45	*Clark	.C58
Inman	.I56	*Singer	.S57	Quinn	.Q56	Cobblestone	.C63
Ipswich	.I67	Stinson	.S75	Quorum	.Q67	Cryer	.C79
*Ito	.I87	Suranyi	.S87	Qutub	.Q88	Cuellar	.C84
*Ivy	.I94	*Symposium	.S96	*Qvortrup	.Q97	Cymbal	.C96

*These cutters reflect the adjustments made to allow for a range of letters on the table, e.g., **l-m**, or for letters not explicitly stated, e.g., **h** after an initial consonant.[5]

Some points need further comment. Note first of all that the numeral *1* appears nowhere in the table. The Library of Congress avoids its use, and the use of zeros, as decimals to preserve alphabetic order. If, for instance, the name *Abbott* were given the cutter *.A1*, a subsequent cutter at the same location for *Aamodt* would have to be, say, *.A09*, while *Aagard* would go to *.A085* or something like it. While most type-fonts and computer print-chains distinguish between the digit zero and the capital letter *O*, typewriters often do not. In actual practice, LC shelflisters would more likely give *Abbott* a cutter such as *.A15* so later assignments for names such as *Aagard* and *Aamodt* could have *.A12* and

.A128, or similar decimals to ensure space for unlimited further alphabetical expansion if needed.

All this brings out another trait of LC shelflisting. There is nothing sacrosanct about the above table. It has been officially changed as shelflisting problems were encountered and new needs were perceived. The present LC shelflist contains a jumble of old and new assignments. Recently devised numbers may reflect accommodation to outmoded practices, to avoid extensive re-shelflisting, rather than following current practice as outlined in the table. Cutter numbers assigned for the same person may also vary significantly from one class notation to another. The examples below illustrate such a variation:

TL561	Splaver, Sarah, 1921-
.S65	Some day I'll be an aerospace engineer . . .
. . . .
Z682	Splaver, Sarah, 1921-
.S735	Some day I'll be a librarian . . .

Since cutter numbers are used by the Library of Congress to extend some class notations, as well as for shelflisting alphabetically by main entry, many works have at least two cutter segments in their call numbers. One example is Niles M. Hansen's *French Regional Planning*, for which the LC call number HT395.F7H35 can be analyzed as follows:

H	Social sciences
HT	Communities. Classes. Races
395	Regional planning: countries or regions other than the United States, A-Z
.F7	France
H35	The cutter number for Hansen

While double cutters are commonplace, triple cutters are exceedingly rare. They have been used in class G for certain kinds of subject maps, but with a special disclaimer added. An example is the *New York City Community Health Atlas 1988* prepared by Melvin I. Krasner, et al. Its call number, G1254.N4 E55 K7 1988, is analyzed as follows:

G	Geography. Anthropology. Recreation
1-9980	Geography (General). Atlases. Maps
1000.3-3122	Atlases
1254	New York State sub-area atlas
.N4	New York City
E55	Public Health [from Table IV—Subject subdivisions: "These numbers are not Cutter numbers and have no alphabetical significance."]
K7	Cutter number for Krasner
1988	Date of atlas publication

In the few instances where double cutters are prescribed in the schedules to stand for two separate subdivisions of the subject, the second cutter is made to accommodate both the subject for which it stands and the alphabetical arrangement for which it stands. For example:

HD3561   Hydén, Göran, 1938-
.A6E227   Efficiency versus distribution in East African
                     cooperatives

In the classification schedules under HD3441-3570.9, the notation run assigned to industrial cooperation by country, the notation for the country is first cuttered by *.A6* for general cooperative societies and then is subdivided further "by state, province, etc." Thus, *E227* stands both for East Africa and for the alphabetical arrangement of *Hydén* among other works on the subject.

Reserved cutter numbers. The LC schedules and tables frequently set aside the first few *.A* or the last several *.Z* possibilities in a cutter sequence for special purposes. Observe the example at "TD21-126 — Country and City Subdivisions of Environmental Technology and Sanitary Engineering" on page 362 of this text. Assume that class T, Table I, and the internal table in the schedule have been applied to derive the class number TD28.A1 for a general work on sanitary engineering in Mexico. Let us suppose that the first book classified here was written by a Ricardo Gomez. Using the LC cutter number table, we could complete the call number as TD28.A1G6 or TD28.A1G65. A second work on the same topic by a Rachael Goode might then receive the call number TD28.A1G66, while still a third treatise by a Ralph Goddard could be given something like TD28.A1G58.

Assume now that we have a book on sanitary engineering in the Mexican state of Aguascalientes. It cannot receive the usual cutter *.A3* or *.A33* because the internal table at TD21-126 has "reserved" .A1 through .A5 for general works and other possible future needs. Therefore we must accommodate the reservation by assigning the class number TD28.A68 or TD28.A7, followed by an appropriate cutter number for main entry. Now suppose that still another book covers sanitary engineering in the city of Aguascalientes. Our class number will probably be TD29.A33, plus a second cutter for the main entry.

.A cutters are likely to be reserved for serials, society publications, documents, etc., where these general forms of material have not been given integer or decimal class numbers. Such special reservations are often called "official" cutters. The following schedule excerpt, with two LC call number assignments, illustrates this practice:

HA   **STATISTICS**
175-4010   By country
195-730   United States
730   Cities, A-Z
                        Under each:
                        .A1-5 Official
                        .A6-Z Nonofficial

. . . .

(Example continues on page 379.)

| HA730 | Houston, Tex. Division of Vital Statistics. |
| .H67A3 | Facts about Houston : population, births, deaths, maternal and infant deaths . . . |

HA730	Houston, Tex. Chamber of Commerce. Census Tract
.H67H6	Division.
	1970 Census data for the Houston area . . .

In both of the above call numbers *.H67*, identifying the city of Houston, is a geographical extension of the class number. Publications of the city government's Division of Vital Statistics are considered to be "official publications." Therefore, *A3* is added in accordance with schedule instructions and the LC shelflist entries, to serve as the cutter number for the main entry. Houston Chamber of Commerce publications, not being considered "official," have their cutters based on the traditional first word of the main entry.

.Z cutter reservations are most common in class P, where researchers like to have biography and criticism of an author shelved immediately following that author's works. In this class, separate integers frequently designate all authors of a given period whose surnames start with the same initial. The first cutter number is then based on the second letter of the surname (i.e., the letter beginning the cutter is the second letter of the author's name, followed by a number representing the third, or third and fourth, letter[s]). A second cutter, based usually on an auxiliary table of reserved numbers, identifies collected works, selections, titles of separate works, adaptations, translations, or biography and criticism. *The Selected Letters of Robinson Jeffers, 1897-1962* carries the LC call number PS3519.E27Z53, exemplifying application of auxiliary Table XL in the *Language and Literature Tables* volume of the LC classification schedules.

Workmarks, in the traditional sense of lowercase letters added to cutter numbers to alphabetize titles or writers of biographies, are not used by the Library of Congress. Lowercase letters do serve a few special purposes in LC call numbers. They are sometimes used following dates, as discussed below. In addition, in subclass "PZ Fiction in English. Juvenile Belles Lettres" a unique combination of upper- and lowercase letters (instead of second cutter numbers) alphabetizes the titles of a given author, while dates designate reissues or new editions. For example, the original 1938 Vanguard Press edition of Dr. Seuss' *The 500 Hats of Bartholomew Cubbins* was given the call number PZ8.G326 Fi, while the 1990 Random House edition has the call number PZ8.G326 Fi 1990. (*Fi* was used in the time when this title was to be filed as if spelled out: "Five Hundred Hats ....") Formerly, numerals were used with juvenile literature call numbers to designate new editions, so the 1966 Collins edition of this work was given the call number PZ8.G326 Fi2.

Additions to LC call numbers. The adding of dates to LC call numbers has increased with multiple publication in more than one country, in different imprints, in paperback as well as hardcover, in later editions, and in reprints. The Library of Congress began in 1982 to add dates to all monographic call numbers.[6] One use of lowercase letters is to identify bibliographically distinct issues of the same title published in the same year. For example, Andrew M. Greeley's *Love Song* was published by G. K. Hall in a large print version the same year it was published by Warner Books. The second one to be cataloged was assigned the call number PS3557.R358 L68 1989b, the use of the letter *b* being the only difference between the two call numbers. Another use of lowercase letters following dates is to distinguish among works on the same subject and published in the same year that have the same corporate body as main entry.[7]

A few other exceptional notations show up in some schedules. For example, dates are used not only as final elements, to distinguish issues of the same title. They occasionally become secondary elements of class numbers, taking precedence over cutter numbers. Class numbers "BX830-831—Medieval and Modern Councils Within Roman Catholicism" use this device to arrange church councils by date of opening. An example is John W. O'Malley's *Tradition and Transition: Historical Perspectives on Vatican II*, which carries the LC call number BX830 1962 .O45 1989. Also, in schedule "BL-BX—Religion" some Bible texts are so specifically classed that LC shelflisters merely add dates (no cutter numbers) to keep them in order. For example, the *NRSV-NIV Parallel New Testament in Greek and English*, with interlinear translation by Alfred Marshall, has been assigned the LC call number BS1965.5 1990.

CONCLUSION

Call numbers are of particular concern in libraries with open stacks where browsing allows patrons to find materials on similar subjects in proximity, to find works of one author on a subject together, and to find editions of a work together. Where there are closed stacks, an accession number can serve as well as a call number.

While use of cutter numbers is the most common method of creating complete call numbers, other means may sometimes be found more useful. In a science and technology collection, for example, where recency of material may be of utmost importance, subarrangement under each class notation may be by year of imprint. In very small general collections, on the other hand, one or more letters of the first word of the main entry may be added after the class notation, with no additional numbers given. This method, however, will usually not result in unique call numbers, which may be needed for circulation control.

NOTES

[1]Charles Ammi Cutter, *Two-Figure Author Table*, Swanson-Swift revision, 1969. Distributed by Libraries Unlimited, Inc., Littleton, Colo. (formerly distributed by H. R. Huntting Co.).

[2]*Cutter-Sanborn Three-Figure Author Table*, Swanson-Swift revision, 1969. Distributed by Libraries Unlimited, Inc., Littleton, Colo. (formerly distributed by H. R. Huntting Co.).

[3]Charles Ammi Cutter, *Three-Figure Author Table*, Swanson-Swift revision, 1969. Distributed by Libraries Unlimited, Inc., Littleton, Colo. (formerly distributed by H. R. Huntting Co.).

[4]*Subject Cataloging Manual: Shelflisting* (Washington, D.C., Subject Cataloging Division, Library of Congress, 1986).

[5]*Subject Cataloging Manual: Shelflisting*, G060, p. 26.

[6]*Cataloging Service Bulletin*, no. 19 (Winter 1982): 25-26.

[7]*Subject Cataloging Manual: Shelflisting*, G220.

SUGGESTED READING

Comaromi, John P. *Book Numbers: A Historical Study and Practical Guide to Their Use.* Littleton, Colo., Libraries Unlimited, 1981.

Lehnus, Donald J. *Book Numbers: History, Principles, and Application.* Chicago, American Library Association, 1980.

Other Classification Systems

20

INTRODUCTION

This chapter provides a brief overview of some of the more significant modern classifications besides DDC and LCC. Those discussed are Cutter's Expansive Classification, Brown's Subject Classification, Bliss' Bibliographic Classification, and some special classifications. UDC was discussed at the end of chapter 17, "Decimal Classification," and Ranganathan's Colon Classification was used as an example in the discussion of faceted classification in chapter 16. While the classifications discussed here by no means exhaust modern classification research and practice, they do illustrate many of the problems and solutions, or failures, of both the seminal and the well-entrenched systems discussed in the contemporary literature.[1]

CUTTER'S EXPANSIVE CLASSIFICATION

The Expansive Classification, like the Dewey Decimal Classification, is the brainchild of an eminent library pioneer. Charles Ammi Cutter (1837-1903) was 15 years older than Melvil Dewey (1851-1931) but took 15 years longer to publish his scheme. Both men devised their systems as practical efforts to organize collections that they knew and served. Just as DDC came out of Dewey's student employment in the Amherst College Library, so Cutter's cataloging efforts in the Harvard College Library, and for much longer at the Boston Athenaeum, flowered into his Expansive Classification.

While the lives and achievements of the two men show many parallels, there are also significant differences. In classification, Dewey chose his pure decimal notation early on, making it such a key feature of his approach that it more or less governed all subsequent growth patterns. He saw that a simple basic design, easy-to-master mnemonic devices, and a certain sturdy inflexibility could provide a general system that would be applicable to the many libraries that were being established. With characteristic energy, he started a schedule of periodic revision to keep his system responsive to the rapidly changing cultural and publishing milieu. And he marketed his invention with zest and conviction. Cutter was of a more delicate physique and temperament, less exuberant, more institution-oriented. But he, too, imbued with the gregarious optimism of his era, worked diligently to establish librarianship as a helping profession, with "scientific" organization as one of its basic assumptions.

Cutter's scheme stressed a sequence of "classifications," or expansions, from a very simple set of categories for a small library to an intricate network of inter-related, highly specific subdivisions for the library of over a million volumes.[2] He did not live to finish his ultimate seventh expansion or to embark on a successive-edition program, but he did have the satisfaction of seeing the Library of Congress prefer many features of his scheme to that of his friendly rival. His willingness to take suggestions, and to compromise, worked to his credit and to the continuing influence of his system in spite of its limited adoption.

Cutter found the 10 broad classes of DDC too narrow a base for large collections. He therefore turned to the alphabet, with its easily ordered sequence of up to 26 primary groupings. For collections that "could be put into a single room" his first "classification" used only seven letters, with an eighth double-letter subclass, as follows:

A   Works of reference and general works that include several of the following sections, and so could not go to any one

B   Philosophy and Religion

E   Biography

F   History and Geography and Travels

H   Social sciences

L   Natural sciences and Arts

Y   Language and Literature

YF   Fiction

If a small library should grow to require closer, more specific classes, Cutter's second classification, or expansion, introduced a mixed alphanumeric notation. It also subdivided the "F – History" and the new "G – Geography" classes by adding two Arabic numerals to the letter to signify identical geographic areas for each class. For example, F30 means History of Europe, while G30 means Geography of Europe. The second expansion holds 14 main classes, some redefinition of the original seven, and further differentiation of two classes along geographic lines.

The third expansion completes all but "P – Vertebrates" of the base 26 divisions and separates Religion from Philosophy, moving it to a second double-letter subclass. Part of the debt that LCC owes to Cutter can easily be traced through the outline comparison shown on page 384.

The fourth expansion subdivides 12 main classes for the first time, increasing the double-letter subclasses to 50. It also carries an extensive supplementary table expanding the double-digit geographic numbers from the F and G classes into a "place" or "local" list.

The fifth expansion introduces the twenty-sixth single-letter class "P – Vertebrates" and subdivides all remaining undivided classes, using many triple- and a few quadruple-letter sections. The sixth "classification" introduces no new techniques – only new expansions of existing classes and subclasses.

The seventh classification was published in 18 parts, edited and to some extent developed by William Parker Cutter after the originator's death.[3] All expansions were prepared on the theory that as a library outgrew its simpler modes of organization, partial dislocation and reclassification of the existing collection was preferable to complete reorganization. Although some books would have to be reclassed and relocated, not all would be, and certainly not all at once.

	Cutter's Expansive		Library of Congress
A	General works	A	General works
B	Philosophy	B	Philosophy. Religion
BR	Non-Judaeo-Christian religions		
C	Judaism and Christianity	C	History. Auxiliary sciences
D	Ecclesiastical history	D	History (except America)
E	Biography	E-F	History of the Americas
F	History		
G	Geography	G	Geography. Anthropology
H	Social sciences	H	Social sciences
I	Sociology		
J	Political science	J	Political science
K	Law	K	Law
L	Natural sciences	L	Education
M	Natural history	M	Music
N	Botany	N	Fine arts
O	Zoology		
		P	Language and literature
Q	Medicine	Q	Science
R	Technology	R	Medicine
S	Engineering	S	Agriculture
T	Manufactures and Handicrafts	T	Technology
U	Defensive and preservative arts	U	Military science
V	Athletic and recreative arts	V	Naval science
W	Fine arts		
X	Languages		
Y	Literature		
YF	Fiction		
Z	Book arts	Z	Bibliography and Library science

While it was never widely adopted, some 67 American, Canadian, and British libraries have been identified as past or present Cutter System users.[4] Perhaps even more important is the influence it exerted on later, more popular classifications, such as that developed soon after at the Library of Congress.

BROWN'S SUBJECT CLASSIFICATION

Next in chronological development is a British scheme. James Duff Brown (1864-1914) was a Scottish counterpart of Dewey and Cutter, if somewhat younger. Coming to the profession from an early apprenticeship to publishers and booksellers, he became deeply involved in the public library movement in Great Britain. It is debatable whether his advocacy of open stacks was directly influenced by his travels in the United States, in 1893. Without benefit of a university education, his breadth of knowledge was legendary, and his interest in music resulted in several music reference tools that he either compiled or sponsored.

Brown recognized the lack of good organization of materials in most British libraries. To make open stack access feasible he and John Henry Quinn published in 1894 a "Classification of Books for Libraries in Which Readers Are Allowed Access to Shelves." Brown's own "Adjustable Classification" followed in 1898. As the name implies, it allowed for insertion of new divisions or topics as needed, but it was not worked out or indexed in much detail. Growing out of it, in 1906, was the first edition of the *Subject Classification*. In 1914, shortly after Brown's death, came a second edition, and in 1939 James Douglas Stewart issued a revised and enlarged third edition.[5]

The basic scaffold of Brown's *Subject Classification* consists of 11 main classes, expressing 4 broad divisional concepts in orderly sequence. Primary notation is alphabetical, with some classes assigned more than one capital letter, to cover all subtopics without making the notation unduly long:

A	Generalia	} Matter and Force
B C D	Physical Science	
E F	Biological Science	
G H	Ethnological and Medical Science	} Life
I	Economic Biology and Domestic Arts	
J K	Philosophy and Religion	} Mind
L	Social and Political Science	
M	Language and Literature	
N	Literary forms	} Record
O - W	History, Geography	
X	Biography	

Each initial letter is followed by three Arabic numerals. Sequence, rather than length of number, reveals hierarchy, e.g.,

D600	METALLURGY
601	Smelting
602	Blast Furnaces
603	Open Hearth Furnaces
604	Ores

These schedule numbers may be expanded like decimals (without the decimal point) when new topics require insertion. The scheme allows several methods of building numbers: geographic numbers from the O-W classes may be attached to topical numbers when needed. There is a "Categorical Table" of "forms, etc. for the subdivision of subjects." Numbers from this table are attached after a period, which is not to be regarded as a decimal point. A plus sign is used to connect two facets from the same class. The underscore is used to "stack" parts of a number. Its purpose is to keep an extended notation compact.

While Brown's *Subject Classification*, like Cutter's *Expansive Classification*, never received the widespread adoption received by its American rivals, timing and the lack of a consistent, continuing update program may be the explanation, rather than the comparative merits of the four schemes. Brown's system stimulated research and development in British classification theory, much as Cutter's did in the United States. Both are now milestones of classification history, rather than popular modern schemes for arranging library materials.

BLISS'S BIBLIOGRAPHIC CLASSIFICATION

Henry Evelyn Bliss (1870-1955) was Librarian of the College of the City of New York, where he spent some 30 years developing and testing his ideas on library classification. After several periodical articles and books, he finished publication of his magnum opus only two years before his death.[6]

A "bibliographic" classification is, in Bliss's terminology, one designed to organize documentary materials (i.e., library collections, chiefly in print format). The sequence of main classes nonetheless preserves the discipline (rather than topical) orientation that Bliss interpreted as the basic structure of knowledge. Paul Dunkin called it "a sort of reader interest classification for scholars."[7]

According to Bliss, it is important in classifying a book to decide in what main classes it falls. The literature on concrete topics like "bees" is not kept in one place (as Brown would try to do) but is distributed, as in DDC, according to the "aspect" from which it is viewed. For example, a book on bees from a scientific aspect goes to class "G – Zoology," whereas a book on beekeeping is classed in "U – Useful Arts."

The Bliss system soon grew more popular in Great Britain than in the United States.[8] A British Committee for the Bliss Classification, which changed its name in 1967 to the Bliss Classification Association, draws its membership largely from libraries using the scheme. It publishes an annual *Bliss Classification Bulletin* and has commissioned its chair, Jack Mills, to edit a thoroughly revised and enlarged second edition in 20 separate parts. After various delays, the first volumes of this edition appeared in 1977, and new volumes have been published at various times since then.[9]

The second edition makes full use of principles that Bliss developed over the years but had little opportunity to apply consistently to his original edition. It also derives techniques of facet analysis, as well as of explicit citation and filing orders, from Ranganathan's monumental contributions to classification theory.

Second edition notation consists of capital letters and numerals, omitting zero because of its similarity to the letter O. Bliss wished to keep his numbers as brief as possible, consistent with full expression of the various aspects of a topic.

He was not interested much in expressiveness, that is, showing position in the logical hierarchy of the system by the length or configuration of the individual class number. Rather, he tried to make his notation show flexibly, but specifically, all the auxiliary features (facets and arrays) that might be used to modify the basic subject of a work. He further strove to provide alternative locations and treatments so that the individual classifier could select the one most appropriate to the library's holdings.

The future of the *Bibliographic Classification* is dependent in large part on the timing and public acceptance of the new edition. That Bliss's theory and practice had many advantages is a fact recognized by anyone who knows it well enough to compare it with more widely accepted schemes. That it badly needed updating and further development is also clear. The gargantuan job of complete overhaul by a few aficionados on a shoestring budget, if finished, should permit future sequential revision of different class schedules as needed (somewhat resembling the present revision program at the Library of Congress). Meanwhile, some libraries using the original schedules are falling away.[10] Establishment of the Bliss scheme as a major contender for library adoption will require not only efficient, dedicated work, but also a great deal of luck.

SPECIAL CLASSIFICATION SCHEMES

Classification schemes comprising the entire universe of knowledge must of necessity be general and cannot deal with specialties or fine detail. They are also largely inflexible, presenting the particular viewpoint of their designers (which in the case of DDC and LCC represents the late nineteenth century), and they often disperse subjects that, for the purposes of specialists, ought to be dealt with in close proximity (e.g., DDC has chemistry in 540 but chemical technology in 660, which is very unhelpful for a chemistry library). Even UDC, although providing for very fine detail, suffers from many of the faults inherited from DDC (e.g., the chemistry dispersal) and often has long notations.

Librarians of collections devoted mainly or exclusively to one specific field of knowledge, a discipline, or one of its subfields have therefore often found it necessary to design special classification schemes. The British Classification Research Group (CRG) was particularly active in designing special faceted classifications during the 1960s and 1970s, whereas in the United States special classifications were more often the work of individuals and organizations.

Special classification schemes are mainly of two types: "general-special" schemes, which classify a special field or subject exhaustively while providing only very general class marks to peripheral or extraneous subjects, and "special" schemes, dealing only with a particular specialty in sometimes very fine detail but leaving the classing of other subjects to one of the general schemes. Hybrids of the two types are those schemes that expand an existing class of a general scheme or make use of an unused notation under which a special subject field is developed in detail.

Two examples of the latter type are widely used in U.S. libraries. *The National Library of Medicine Classification*[11] uses class W (which is vacant in LCC) and the medical parts of LCC's class Q for the entire biomedical field. Subdivision of W is by all letters of the alphabet, including even I and O (which are avoided by LCC because of possible confusion with the digits 1 and 0), followed by up to three digits used enumeratively and an occasional fourth digit used decimally, followed by more detailed subdivision using cuttering, e.g.,

WD 200   Metabolic diseases
WD 205.5.A5   Amino acid metabolism

Since NLM's W class notations now appear on MARC records for medical books, most medical libraries use the W special classification.

A Classification Scheme for Law Books,[12] which expands class K of LCC, found wide acceptance in law libraries after its publication in 1968, but completion of many parts of class K by LC in recent years has reduced the need for the separate scheme. Another expansion of LCC is for a highly specialized subject. *An Alternative Classification for Catholic Books*[13] takes a section of the LC classification that was not in use by LC when the schedule was developed in 1937 and develops it as Christian literature with three major subclasses: BQT, theology; BQV, canon law; and BQX, church history, all further subdivided by enumerative digits and cuttering. The introduction gives detailed instructions on how to integrate these schedules into either LCC or DDC when these are used to class other subjects in a library.

The following examples are representatives of the special type that combine a faceted structure and high flexibility with brief notations. The *London Education Classification*[14] fulfills a double role as a classification and thesaurus and uses a letter notation, with uppercase letters serving as facet indicators, e.g.,

Mab   Curriculum
Mabb   Curriculum development
Mabf   Curriculum classification

The *Physics and Astronomy Classification Scheme*[15] of the American Institute of Physics (AIP) uses a mixed notation of two decimal groups followed by a letter, e.g.,

84   Electromagnetic technology
84.30   Electronic circuits
84.30 L   Amplifiers

Except for two sections, the AIP scheme is identical with the *International Classification for Physics*,[16] and parts of it have been adopted by the Institution of Electrical Engineers in London for its *INSPEC Classification for Physics, Electrotechnology, Computers and Control*.[17] Thus, a physics library could choose among three major special schemes, all of which have the backing of professional societies.

The *London Classification of Business Studies*[18] has five major classes: management responsibility in the enterprise (A-G), environmental studies (J-R), analytical techniques (S-X), library and information science (Y), and auxiliary schedules (1-7). The notation consists of up to four uppercase letters, e.g.,

K   Industries
KCL   Alcoholic drinks industry
KCLB   Wine industry

and notations can be combined by an oblique stroke, e.g.,.

EE/KCLB   Financial management in the wine industry

The scheme is used in a number of British libraries and in libraries elsewhere. The London Business School is responsible for updating and development of the scheme.

An example of a special scheme relying on another classification for extraneous subjects is the *Classification of Library and Information Science*,[19] designed by the CRG and used by *Library and Information Science Abstracts* (*LISA*) for the arrangement of entries. This scheme, too, makes use of a letter notation with capitals as facet indicators, resulting in notations such as TogsNjrFv, which expresses the topic "Online systems:centralized:Public libraries," or ZmRnM(57), "Databases:Information Services:By subject:Biology," with 57 taken from UDC for a subject not germane to the central topic of library and information science.

Special classifications are sometimes developed for extremely narrow subjects, such as the *Classification for London Literature*,[20] concerned with works only on that city, with decimal subdivisions for every place and event in its long history, e.g.,

10   Religion
12   St. Paul's Cathedral
12.4   Dome and roof

A bibliography of classification schemes and subject heading lists for hundreds of different subjects lists 2,250 items in several languages.[21]

A special classification scheme may initially have the advantage of being more detailed and more up-to-date than any of the general schemes, but it is unfortunately often the case that such schemes, once designed, are not further developed and therefore become obsolete and lacking in detail much quicker than general schemes. When adopting a special scheme, one must take care to choose a scheme that has a reasonably good chance of being further developed and updated — that is, one that is backed by an organization rather than being the one-time effort of a librarian in a special collection. Such homemade classification schemes are generally motivated by the fact that sooner or later almost any librarian will find that the scheme he or she uses, whether general or specific, is insufficiently detailed or does not contain a class notation for a new subject. It is then easy to succumb to the temptation to create a new subdivision or an entirely new scheme for the missing topics or for sections of a scheme that seem to be misplaced. The proper design of a special classification is, however, a task best left to someone thoroughly familiar with the theory and principles of classification design, and the novice should refrain from attempting this enterprise until some considerable experience has been gained. Many a hastily conceived and improperly designed special classification scheme has had to be abandoned sooner or later, to be replaced with an existing and proven scheme at great cost and inconvenience to the library and its users.

CONCLUSION

The classification systems briefly reviewed here differ from each other, and from the better known DDC and LCC systems, in many ways. In basic theory of the organization of knowledge, some emphasize the specific subject approach, clustering these unitary topics in related sequences, whereas most start from a broad disciplinary orientation, subdividing hierarchically, so that the various aspects or unitary topics become scattered to different parts of the system. In providing a schedule framework to arrange books on shelves, some systems (the more traditional) are primarily enumerative, whereas most newer ones are synthetic or faceted. Some maintain a comparatively pure notation, whereas others use combinations of letters and Arabic numerals, while upper- and lowercase letters, roman numerals, Greek letters, and a variety of arbitrary relational signs and symbols appear in still others. Timeliness is a constant problem. Some systems maintain a serials program to announce additions and changes or issue new editions at intervals of 5 to 25 years. Many have outlived their originators, but some suffer more than others from age and lack of funds or organized promotion. Each has unique attractive features; each has practical and theoretical problems. Some are more useful for shelf arrangement of books and related formats. Others are better suited to in-depth indexing of periodical articles, technical reports, books, and the like. Centripetal forces such as networking seem at the moment to favor general acceptance of one or two well-known, widely used schemes, overlooking functional disadvantages to achieve standardization and administrative coherence. Yet classification research, like that in all other areas of bibliographic organization, is very brisk and busy in the modern world of information science. Time may show that all the schemes we study and use today, regardless of their present achievements or popularity, are chiefly important for the historic part they play as heralds of still better solutions to the problems of subject access.

NOTES

[1]Four examples of specific applications using the systems discussed in this chapter, as well as DDC and LC, are given in Bohdan S. Wynar, *Introduction to Cataloging and Classification*, 5th ed., prepared with the assistance of John Phillip Immroth (Littleton, Colo., Libraries Unlimited, 1976), pp. 314-328.

[2]Charles Ammi Cutter, *Expansive Classification, Part I: The First Six Classifications* (Boston, Cutter, 1891-1893).

[3]Charles Ammi Cutter, *Expansive Classification, Part II: Seventh Classification*, largely edited by William Parker Cutter (Boston and Northampton, Mass., Cutter, 1896-1911), 2v. with supplementary pages.

[4]Robert L. Mowery, "The Cutter Classification: Still at Work," *Library Resources & Technical Services* 20 (Spring 1976): 154.

[5]James Duff Brown, *Subject Classification: With Tables, Indexes, etc. for the Subdivision of Subjects*, 3rd ed., rev. and enl. by James Douglas Stewart (London, Grafton, 1939).

[6]Bliss's major works are the following: *The Organization of Knowledge and the System of the Sciences* (New York, Holt, 1929); *The Organization of Knowledge in Libraries*, 2nd ed., rev. and partly rewritten (New York, H. W. Wilson, 1939); *A Bibliographic Classification: Extended by Systematic Auxiliary Schedules for Composite Specification and Notation* (New York, H. W. Wilson, 1940-1953), 4v.

[7]Paul S. Dunkin, *Cataloging U.S.A.* (Chicago, American Library Association, 1969), p. 126.

[8]See, for instance: School Library Association (England), *The Abridged Bliss Classification: The Bibliographical Classification of Henry Evelyn Bliss Revised for School Libraries*, with corrections and minor amendments (London, The Association, 1970).

[9]H. E. Bliss, *Bibliographic Classification*, 2nd ed., edited by Jack Mills and V. Broughton (London, Butterworths, 1977-).
  Introduction and Auxiliary Schedules, 1977.
  Class A: Philosophy, Logic, Mathematics, Statistics, Natural Science in General, 1990.
  Class H: Health Sciences, Medicine, 1981.
  Class I: Psychology, Psychiatry, 1978.
  Class J: Education, 1990 revision, 1990.
  Class K: Social Science, Sociology, and Social Anthropology, 1984.
  Class P: Religion, the Occult, Morals and Ethics, 1977.
  Class Q: Social Welfare, 1977.
  Class T: Economics, Management of Economic Enterprises, 1986.

[10]See, for instance: "Ibadan Abandons Bliss," *Library Association Record* 79 (May 1977): 241, which tells how the University of Ibadan (Nigeria), after using Bliss for 25 years, converted to LCC because of the inadequacy of outdated, unrevised Bliss schedules.

[11]*National Library of Medicine Classification: A Scheme for the Shelf Arrangement of Books in the Field of Medicine and Its Related Sciences*, 4th ed., rev. (Bethesda, Md., NLM, 1981).

[12]E. M. Moys, *A Classification Scheme for Law Books* (Hamden, Conn., Archon Books, 1968).

[13]Jeannette Murphy Lynn, *An Alternative Classification for Catholic Books*, 2nd ed., rev. by G. C. Peterson; supplement (1965) by Thomas G. Pater (Washington, D.C., Catholic University of America Press, 1965).

[14]D. J. Foskett and J. Foskett, *The London Education Classification: A Thesaurus/Classification of British Education Terms*, 2nd ed. (London, University of London Institute of Education Library, 1974).

[15]American Institute of Physics, *Physics and Astronomy Classification Scheme* (Woodbury, N.Y., AIP, 1990).

[16]International Council of Scientific Unions, Abstracting Board, *International Classification for Physics* (Paris, ICSU/AB, 1975).

[17]Institution of Electrical Engineers, *INSPEC Classification: A Classification Scheme for Physics, Electrotechnology, Computers and Control* (London, IEE, 1988).

[18]K. D. C. Vernon and V. Lang, *The London Classification of Business Studies*, 2nd ed., rev. by K. G. B. Bakewell and D. A. Cotton (London, Aslib, 1979).

[19]Classification Research Group, *A Classification of Library and Information Science* (London, CRG, 1965). (A second edition was published in 1975 but is not used by LISA. Used instead is the unpublished 1971 draft revision.)

[20]Guildhall Library, *Classification for London Literature*, 3rd ed. (London, The Library, 1966).

[21]*Classification Systems and Thesauri, 1950-1982* (Frankfurt, West Germany, Indeks Verlag, 1982). (International Classification and Indexing Bibliography 1.)

SUGGESTED READING

Chan, Lois Mai. *Cataloging and Classification: An Introduction.* New York, McGraw-Hill, 1981. Chapter 14.

Foskett, A. C. *The Subject Approach to Information.* London, Bingley, 1982. Chapters 9, 13, 18-20.

Verbal Subject Analysis

21

INTRODUCTION

We have seen in the preceding chapters that classification provides a library with a systematic arrangement of materials according to their subject content, mode of treatment, or even their physical format. In addition to classification, there is another commonly used means of access to the intellectual contents of a library— namely indexing through the use of a subject heading list of controlled vocabulary terms and references. Whereas classification provides a logical, or at least a methodical, approach to the arrangement of documentary materials, subject headings give a more random alphabetic approach to the concepts inherent in those materials, thus adding another dimension to the linear arrangement characteristic of classification. The two techniques offer alternative, and to some extent complementary, modes of access to the collection, comprising that aspect of bibliographic control and access known as subject cataloging.

There are many theoretically sound objectives for subject cataloging. Shera and Egan summarized them as follows:

1. To provide access by subject to *all* relevant material.

2. To provide subject access to materials through all suitable *principles of subject organization*, e.g., matter, process, applications, etc.

3. To bring together references to materials which treat of substantially the *same subject* regardless of disparities in terminology, disparities which may have resulted from national differences, differences among groups of subject specialists, and/or from the changing nature of the concepts with the discipline itself.

4. To show *affiliations among subject fields*, affiliations which may depend upon similarities of matter studied, or method, or of point of view, or upon use or application of knowledge.

5. To provide entry to any subject field at any *level of analysis*, from the most general to the most specific.

6. To provide entry through any *vocabulary* common to any considerable group of users, specialized or lay.

7. To provide a *formal description of the subject content* of any bibliographic unit in the most precise, or specific, terms possible, whether the description be in the form of a word or brief phrase or in the form of a class number or symbol.

8. To provide means for the user to make *selection* from among all items in any particular category, according to any chosen set of criteria such as: most thorough, most recent, most elementary, etc.[1]

BASIC CONCEPTS AND STRUCTURE
OF SUBJECT HEADINGS

Subject heading has been defined as "an access point to a bibliographic record, consisting of a word or phrase which designates the subject of the work(s) contained in the bibliographic item."[2] Today, information analysts distinguish pre-coordinate indexing, by which appropriate terms are chosen and coordinated at the time of indexing, from post-coordinate indexing, with which coordination takes place after the encoded documents have been stored.[3] Libraries traditionally prefer the former method of compiling alphabetical subject catalogs. All standard published lists of "subject headings" were developed with pre-coordinate indexing techniques.

Subject headings have dual objectives: 1) to identify pertinent material on a given subject or topic; 2) to enable the inquirer to find material on related subjects. Both objectives pose problems of communication; both demand a set of terms that match, as far as possible, the terms likely to be in the minds of inquirers wishing to locate material on a given topic or in a given discipline. E. J. Coates warns:

> This would be fairly simple to achieve if there were an uncomplicated, one-to-one relationship between concepts and words: that is to say, if there were a single word corresponding to each separate concept and a single concept corresponding to each separate word. In fact, we have on the one hand concepts that can be rendered by any one of a number of words, and on the other hand, concepts for which no single word equivalent exists in the natural language.[4]

Modern subject heading practice has its roots in Charles A. Cutter's *Rules for a Dictionary Catalog.*[5] Immroth reminds us that Cutter's "rules for subject entries are the basis for two major American lists of subject headings—the *Library of Congress Subject Headings* and the *Sears List of Subject Headings.*"[6] Later theorists refined and expanded Cutter's work in various ways. David Judson Haykin, former Chief of the Library of Congress Subject Cataloging Division, enumerates the principles on which the choice of terms for a subject list must rest.[7] They may be summarized as follows:

1. *The reader as focus.* "[T]he heading, in wording and structure, should be that which the reader will seek in the catalog, if we know or can presume what the reader will look under.... [In] the face of a lack of sufficient objective, experimental data, we must rely for guidance in the choice of terms upon the experience of librarians and such objective findings as are available."

2. *Unity.* "A subject catalog must bring together under one heading all the books which deal principally or exclusively with the subject, whatever

the terms applied to it by the authors of the books and whatever the varying terms applied to it at different times. [It] must [use] a term which is unambiguous and does not overlap in meaning other headings in the catalog, even where that involves defining the sense in which it is used."

3. *Usage.* "The heading chosen must represent common usage or, at any rate, the usage of the class of reader for whom the material on the subject within which the heading falls is intended.... Whether a popular term or a scientific one is to be chosen depends on several considerations. If the library serves a miscellaneous public, it must prefer the popular to the scientific term."

4. *Specificity.* "The heading should be as specific as the topic it is intended to cover. As a corollary, the heading should not be broader than the topic; rather than use a broader heading, the cataloger should use two specific headings which will approximately cover it."

The following discussion touches on some of the most important problems encountered in construction and use of subject headings.

The Choice of Subject Headings

Linguistic usage determines correctness of form in natural language, as all grammarians and dictionary compilers well know. Language changes constantly, not only in response to new discoveries and formulations of knowledge, but also in response to dynamic forces of its own, some but not all of which have been codified by linguists. In choosing subject terms, librarians try to consider both the author's usage and the patron's needs and preferences. But authors and patrons are likely to use different terms for the same subject. Without a record of choices, the cataloger may enter the same subject under two or more different headings. Two types of decision are especially likely to miscarry: those for which more than one adequate term is available and those for which no adequate term is available.

Selecting a term from among verbal equivalents. The cataloger or compiler of a subject heading list must sometimes choose one subject term from among several synonyms or very similar terms. Cutter suggests the following sequence of preferences when selecting from synonymous headings:[8]

1. *The term most familiar to the general public.* Cutter no doubt was thinking of the local library's public. We shall see that one of the major differences between LCSH and *Sears* is that LCSH, being designed for use in a comprehensive research library, favors scientific terminology (e.g., "**Arachnida** NT Spiders"), whereas *Sears* tends to use more popular terms (e.g., "Arachnida. *See* **Spiders**").

2. *The term most used in other catalogs.* Since patrons frequently change libraries or consult more than one library catalog, it is comforting to find that terminology remains stable, even standardized, so long as it

does not violate the usage of the local library's public. Broad automated networks, using consolidated computer files, make reliably standardized terminology even more desirable. A different, but related, argument is that new concepts and terms are often introduced into the periodical literature before they form the topics of full-scale books. If a library's subject heading list does not yet include such a term, the cataloger might well consult the *New York Times Index*, or commonly used periodical indexes and abstracting tools, to discover what usage, if any, has been established.

3. *The term that has fewest meanings.* The clear intent here is to avoid ambiguity wherever possible.

4. *The term that comes first in the alphabet.* This is the type of arbitrary, procedural decision that can and should be invoked when semantic considerations have been exhausted.

5. *The term that brings the subject into the neighborhood of other, related subjects.* It was previously noted that a serious drawback of alphabetic arrangement is its fragmentation of subject matter and that most alphabetic subject lists indulge in some "classing." Here is Cutter's recognition that the technique is valid, but only after all other modes for choosing among synonymous terms have been exhausted.

Supplying a term that is not contained in a single word. Some concepts must be expressed by phrases (combinations of words). Phrase headings present certain disadvantages. As Coates indicates, most catalog users try to formulate search topics in single words, even when a phrase would be used in natural language.[9] Various uncertainties shadow the introduction of phrases into a controlled vocabulary. In determining the order of words, should a heading always retain the order of natural language, or should modifications and transpositions be allowed in the interests of brevity and clarity? Should a variety of syntactic forms be used, or should the syntax of phrase headings be confined to a few simple forms that occasionally make them seem awkward and artificial? Some theorists feel that, lacking cleanly enunciated rules, phrase-makers have produced a number of troublesome headings. Modern usage condones several varieties, which different subject lists usually adapt to their own uses. The specific rules printed in *Sears List of Subject Headings* and in *Library of Congress Subject Headings* simplify but do not solve this problem, since they are purely arbitrary.[10] The problem of communication still exists. Many books are listed under subject headings that patrons would not immediately think of as the appropriate ones under which to search. For the most part they can be roughly categorized as follows. All examples are taken from the Library of Congress list:

1. *Modified nouns.* Modifiers can take different syntactic forms:
   a) Nouns preceded by adjectives or other modifiers, e.g., **"Regional planning," "Fur-bearing animals,"** or **"Country life"**

   b) Nouns followed by adjectives or other modifiers, e.g., **"Insurance, Malpractice,"** or **"Molds (Botany)"**

2. *Conjunctive phrases.* The conjunction is nearly always *and*, e.g., **"Mills and mill-work," "Instrumentation and orchestration,"** or **"Mind and body"**

3. *Prepositional phrases. In* and *of* are most common, but other prepositions may be used to form phrases, e.g., **"Segregation in education,"** or **"Freedom of speech"**

4. *Serial phrases*, e.g., **"Hotels, taverns, etc.," "Rewards (Prizes, etc.),"** or **"Plots (Drama, novel, etc.)"**

5. *Complex phrase forms*, e.g., **"Artificial satellites in telecommunication," "Glass painting and staining," "Libraries, University and college," "Cities and towns, Ruined, extinct, etc.," "Justice, Administration of," "Right and left (Political science),"** or **"Fortune-telling by tea leaves"**

6. *Subdivided topical phrases*, e.g., **"Book industries and trade – Exhibitions," "Mines and mineral resources – United States,"** or **"Military service, Voluntary – Law and legislation"**

The Number of Subject Headings

The number of subject headings entered into a catalog for a single item depends on many factors. As long as library catalogs are in card form, rapidly increasing bulk is both an economic and a use hazard. Maintenance costs (housing, filing, revising) are high, while users grow confused, or waste considerable time, moving from one point to another in a roomful of several thousand trays. The larger the number of subject entries provided, the greater is the cost of cataloging a title. On the other hand, the assignment of more headings per item makes the total resources of the library more available and may bring out special aspects and bits of unusual or significant information.

The current trend toward online catalogs makes increasing the number of subject entries proportionately less expensive in time, effort, or cost of retrieval. Catalogs in either book form or microform also occupy little space and can be consulted in one spot. Moreover, the simultaneous display of either complete or truncated entries in an ordered column often makes filing practices self-evident. In the early 1980s the Library of Congress was adding about two subject entries per cataloged item. This was up from fewer than two entries per record prior to the implementation of *AACR2*. The tendency over the decades prior to 1980 was to reduce the average number of subject entries. However, this trend has reversed, and more entries per record are being made. Indexes and abstracting tools in science and technology, by contrast, tend to use specific subject entries to a point of minute analysis. Twenty to forty subject terms for one brief article are not rare. It is probable that subject analysis of library titles will expand with the increased use of automated bibliographic control. The computer is facilitating more, and better, studies of library use, to discern optimum types and quantities of subject headings for full subject retrieval. A Council on Library Resources (CLR) study of online catalog use of 15 online catalogs showed that in catalogs with subject access, about 59 percent of all searches were for subject information rather than for "known items."[11] This is quite different from studies of card catalog use, which showed that over two-thirds of searches were known-item searches. The CLR study recommended that system designers implement keyword searching for subjects and browsing of the subject index or thesaurus. It also recognized that such systems can only find subject terms that exist in bibliographic records and recommended increased subject information in bibliographic records along with strict authority control to restrict the number of synonymous and related terms.[12]

Location of Material on Related Subjects

Consistency is one of the most important criteria for assigning subject headings. The cataloger should choose one subject term, and one alone, to index all materials on the same topic. References should then be made to the chosen heading from all other likely headings. They help the inquirer to locate available material on the topic, plus collateral topics, at the level of specificity and from the point of view most useful for the particular need. References consist primarily of three types: references from unused terms, hierarchical references, and coordinate references.

An unused term is one under which no items are entered. Instead, a reference is made from that term to the one that is used, e.g., "Lunar expeditions *See* **Space flight to the moon**." The instruction given may be something other than the word *See*, e.g., "For material on this subject search under" or "Use." It is also possible for an online catalog to give no reference at all in a situation where a *see* reference would be given in a manual catalog. A user searching under "lunar expeditions" might be given automatically a list of the library's material that had been given the heading "space flight to the moon." This practice is called "invisible referencing."

Hierarchical references and coordinate references are most often related term references that suggest to the user that if the material already located is more or less relevant, there are other related headings that might also yield some relevant material. The instruction given is usually "*See also*" or "Related material on this topic may be found under"; e.g., "**Deafness** *See also* **Hearing**," or "**Hearing disorders**. Related material on this topic may be found under **Deafness**."

Hierarchical references move vertically, rather than horizontally, leading the user to topics at a different level of specificity. In current library practice references of this type nearly always move "down" from a general term to one or more specific topics subsumed under it, e.g., "**Cruelty** NT **Atrocities**" (LCSH) or "**Cruelty** *See also* **Atrocities**" (*Sears*), although in indexing practice, many systems provide for moving either up or down the hierarchy. (See discussion of this issue in chapter 22 of this text.)

The connections and relationships shown by coordinate references (often called "related terms") are horizontal rather than vertical. They usually overlap in such ways that reciprocal or multilateral entries are deemed to be necessary, e.g., "**Reforestation** *See also* **Tree planting**," "**Tree planting** *See also* **Reforestation**." Others suggest associative rather than overlapping relationships, e.g., "**Corruption (in politics)** *See also* **Misconduct in office**," "**Misconduct in office** *See also* **Corruption (in politics)**."

While unused term references are most often synonymous terms, they are occasionally hierarchical or coordinate in their relationship to the used term. A few of them move "up" from a specific term that is not used to the broader term that contains it, e.g., "Heirs *See* **Inheritance and succession.**" A few others show an "illustrative" relationship, e.g., "Economic entomology USE **Beneficial insects.**"

Besides simple references, subject heading lists sometimes include scope notes to define and delimit a subject term. These may or may not suggest further terms for the user to consult. Some libraries copy these notes for guides to precede all subject entries under those given terms in their catalogs. Other libraries, wishing to avoid unnecessary catalog entries, keep one or more copies of the printed list near the catalog for public consultation. The following two examples come from LCSH:

Community and school
> Here are entered works on ways in which the community at large, as distinct from government, may aid the school program.

Migrant labor
> Here are entered works on laborers who migrate from one section to another section of the same country. Works on nationals of one country working in another country are entered under "**Alien labor.**" Works on employment opportunities in foreign countries are entered under "**Employment in foreign countries.**"

Some lists include key headings or pattern headings, with instructions to the cataloger on how to construct other headings of similar form that have been omitted from the list for reasons of brevity. The following example is from *Sears*:

Hijacking of airplanes
> Use same form for the hijacking of other modes of transportation.

To assure maximum consistency, a careful, up-to-date record of all subject term selections and references should be kept, either by checking the terms used and the additions made in a standard printed list or by maintaining a separate subject authority file. Such a record can save the cataloger time in the long run and provide the following summary information:

1. Unused terms from which *See* references have been made.

2. Scope notes describing a heading or distinguishing its use in instances where one of its two or more meanings has been chosen.

3. Less comprehensive, subordinate headings, to which *See also* references have been made from more comprehensive terms.

4. More comprehensive, broad headings, from which *See also* references have been made to more specific headings.

5. Coordinate headings from which and to which references have been made from related or associated headings.

The Concept of Specific Entry

One of Haykin's principles on which the choice of terms for a subject list must rest was "specificity." The idea had been enunciated a half century earlier by Cutter:

> Enter a work under its subject heading, not under the heading of the class which includes that subject.... Put Lady Cust's book on "the cat" under "Cat," not under Zoology or Mammals, or Domestic animals.... Some subjects have no name. They are spoken of by a phrase or phrases not definite enough to be used as headings. It is not always easy to decide what is a *distinct* subject.... Possible matters of investigation ... must attain a certain individuality as objects of inquiry and be given some sort of *name*, otherwise we must assign them class-entry.[13]

It should be noted that the concept of specific entry is not the same as the concept of coextensive entry. At least one system for subject analysis, PRECIS (discussed in greater detail in chapter 24), attempts to make subject headings coextensive with the concept/topics covered in the item analyzed. That is, the subject heading will cover all, but no more than, the concepts or topics covered in the item. A very simple example can be drawn by elaborating upon the idea from Cutter above. If one had a book about cats and dogs, the concept of *specific* entry would require two headings: "Cats" and "Dogs." There is no one specific term to cover these two kinds of animal. In order to have a heading that is *coextensive* with the subject of the item the heading would have to be "Cats and dogs."

A great weakness of the concept of specific entry is that subjects must be described in terms that are constantly changing. Material very often has to be cataloged before a suitable term has been added to any standard list. Many subjects now represent a cross-fertilization among once traditional disciplines. As Coates indicates,

> New subjects are being generated around us all the time, and while subjects may still be more or less distinct, there can be no hard and fast separation of the "distinct" subjects from the others.[14]

Not only do particular terms fluctuate in meaning, but a constant, obtrusive tendency of any alphabetic subject list based on the ideal of specific entry is to develop sequences of topical subdivisions or modifications that, as was previously noted, convert true random access into an inadvertent classing device. All such lists show marks of a split personality in this respect. The two most popular American lists, LCSH and *Sears*, are reviewed in the next two chapters; chapter 24 presents some indexing systems that have been proposed as supplements to, or replacements for, these two lists as a primary mode of subject access to organized library collections.

NOTES

[1] Jesse H. Shera and Margaret E. Egan, *The Classified Catalog* (Chicago, American Library Association, 1956), p. 10.

[2] *ALA Glossary of Library and Information Science* (Chicago, American Library Association, 1983), p. 220.

[3] A. C. Foskett, *The Subject Approach to Information*, 4th ed. (London, Clive Bingley; Hamden, Conn., Linnet Books, 1982), p. 86.

[4] E. J. Coates, *Subject Catalogues: Headings and Structure* (London, Library Association, 1960), p. 19.

[5] Charles Ammi Cutter, *Rules for a Dictionary Catalog*, 4th ed. (Washington, D.C., GPO, 1904), republished, London, Library Association, 1972). The original version of this work was Charles A. Cutter, "Rules for a Printed Dictionary Catalogue," in *Public Libraries in the United States of America: Their History, Condition, and Management*, U.S. Bureau of Education (Washington, D.C., GPO, 1876), Part II.

[6] John Phillip Immroth, "Cutter, Charles Ammi," in *Encyclopedia of Library and Information Science*, vol. 6 (New York, Marcel Dekker, 1971), p. 382.

[7] David Judson Haykin, *Subject Headings: A Practical Guide* (Washington, D.C., GPO, 1951), pp. 7-9.

[8] Cutter, *Dictionary Catalog*, p. 19.

[9] Coates, *Subject Catalogues*, p. 19.

[10] For the development of phrase heading forms in *Sears List of Subject Headings* and in *Library of Congress Subject Headings*, see chapters 22 and 23.

[11] *Using Online Catalogs: A Nationwide Survey*, edited by Joseph R. Matthews, Gary S. Lawrence, and Douglas K. Ferguson (New York, Neal-Schuman Publishers, 1983), pp. 144-146.

[12] *Using Online Catalogs*, pp. 177-179.

[13] Cutter, *Dictionary Catalog*, pp. 66-67.

[14] Coates, *Subject Catalogues*, p. 32.

SUGGESTED READING

Chan, Lois Mai, Phyllis A. Richmond, and Elaine Svenonius. *Theory of Subject Analysis: A Sourcebook.* Littleton, Colo., Libraries Unlimited, 1985.

Coates, E. J. *Subject Catalogues: Headings and Structure.* London, Library Association, 1960.

Foskett, A. C. *The Subject Approach to Information.* 4th ed. London, Clive Bingley, 1982; Hamden, Conn., Linnet Books, 1982. Chapter 7.

Harris, Jessica Lee. *Subject Analysis: Computer Implications of Rigorous Definition.* Metuchen, N.J., Scarecrow Press, 1970.

Pettee, Julia. *Subject Headings: The History and Theory of the Alphabetical Approach to Books.* New York, H. W. Wilson, 1946.

Library of Congress Subject Headings

22

INTRODUCTION

The official list of Library of Congress subject headings consists of terms, with references, that have been established over the years since 1897 for use in that library's subject catalogs. Although developed to give subject access to the vast collections of one particular library, this list can be, and has been, adopted by libraries of all sizes, including many with non-LC classification schemes. The National Library of Canada, for example, has for many years used it as basic, supplementing it with a special set of terms for Canadian material.[1] It is used by most large public libraries, college and university libraries, and special libraries that do not have more technical subject lists of their own. Since bibliographic records created by LC usually carry Dewey Decimal classification numbers as well as LC call numbers but have only LC subject headings, some smaller libraries also use the LC subject list. Others retain the shorter, less frequently revised *Sears* list as their primary source, but consult the LC list for suggestions when *Sears* cannot provide the specificity or the diversity they want.[2]

BACKGROUND

Library of Congress subject headings come from a long tradition of theory and practice that is generally held to begin with Charles Ammi Cutter's *Rules for a Dictionary Catalog*.[3] A brief review of Cutter's approach and of the major developments stemming from his work can be found in chapter 21, "Verbal Subject Analysis." The purpose in the present chapter is to highlight trends leading directly to the current manifestations of LC subject headings.[4]

On July 1, 1909, J. C. M. Hanson, Chief of the Catalog Division of the Library of Congress, addressed the Catalog Section of the American Library Association at its Bretton Woods Conference "The Subject Catalogs of the Library of Congress."[5] He alluded to a two-volume subject catalog published by the Library in 1869, but called the subject heading developments of the intervening 40 years too radical to permit a meaningful comparison. The many changes attendant upon the new classification scheme and the move into the new building required a new approach to subject indexing. LC catalogers agreed to start from the *ALA List of Subject Headings for Use in Dictionary Catalogs* (1895), which embodied much of Cutter's theory and which originally formed an appendix to his *Rules*. It was designed for smaller libraries of "generally popular character," but with LC's printed card distribution plans, such an orientation was not altogether disadvantageous.

When the first cards carrying the new headings were published, subject terms were given only if an LC call number was available to print. Since many class schedules were still undeveloped, the list of subject headings grew slowly in the first decade. Proposed new headings were compared to those in the *ALA List* before final selection. Separate publication of the new list did not start until 1909, when the annotated and interleaved copies of the *ALA List* grew unwieldy. It was assumed from the first that cumulations of additions and changes would be issued periodically to supplement the main list, which itself appeared in parts until March 1914.

The practice of subordinating place to subject in scientific and technical headings, as well as under many economic and educational topics, was established at this time. But other subjects—historical, political, administrative, social, and descriptive—were to be subordinated to place, although Hanson admitted to "a number of subjects so nearly on the border line, that it has been difficult in all cases to preserve absolute consistency in decisions."[6] Besides the place/subject versus subject/place precedents, other syntactic forms evolved:

> There is undeniably a strong tendency in the Library of Congress catalog to bring related subjects together by means of inversion of headings, by combinations of two or more subject-words, and even by subordination of one subject to another.[7]

Hanson recognized that subordination within the dictionary arrangement of his new subject list was a concession to the alphabetic-classed or systematic organization of the 1869 catalog. He argued:

> the student and the investigator ... are best served by having related topics brought together so far as that can be accomplished without a too serious violation of the dictionary principle.[8]

The practice of inversion of certain types of modified headings was firmly established by 1951 when David Judson Haykin wrote:

> It is unlikely that the reader will look under an adjective denoting language, ethnic group, or place for material on a subject limited by language, ethnic group, or place, although, in the case of ethnic groups particularly, the interest in the group may outweigh that in the subject. On this basis it has been assumed, although it has not been demonstrated, that a reader interested in French art ... would be much more likely to look under *Art, French* (or *Art—France*) ... than under the respective uninverted forms.[9]

These and other practices have been questioned and modified in recent years but remain as basic premises in the establishment of subject headings at the Library of Congress.

FORMATS AND SUPPLEMENTARY TOOLS

The Library of Congress subject headings are made available in several forms. The longest running format is the printed and bound version. For many years these lists were published in new editions every five years or so, but starting in 1988 with the 11th edition, they have been published annually.[10] Beginning with the 9th edition, it was necessary to publish the list in two volumes, which quickly expanded to three volumes by the 11th edition. The volumes have for many years been published in red bindings and are affectionately known as "The Big Red Books." The print format can be supplemented with *L.C. Subject Headings Weekly Lists*, which are issued in packets of four or five lists monthly.[11] These give information about new and changed subject headings, class numbers, references, and scope notes. A fully updated list can be purchased each quarter on microfiche.[12] It saves the bother of consulting several alphabets to find the most current status of any given term.

MARC format authority records for LC subject headings became available online through OCLC in 1987 and through RLIN in 1988. LC sends update tapes to subscribers weekly, and so the online version provides the most current data. The complete subject authority file is also available on CD-ROM under the title *CDMARC Subjects.*[13] This version is distributed quarterly, fully updated each time.

The concept of the official headings authorized by LC is referred to in this chapter as LCSH (standing for LC subject headings). When an edition of the printed list version is being referred to, it is so stated (e.g., the 13th edition is referred to as *LCSH13*).

When catalogers make use of LCSH there are several supplementary tools that must be used. The rules and guidelines used by LC catalogers when applying LCSH have been published as *Subject Cataloging Manual: Subject Headings* (*SCM: SH*), issued in looseleaf form with periodic updates.[14] It is an essential tool for anyone who wishes to apply the LC subject headings correctly.

Catalogers also keep up-to-date on LCSH through the *Cataloging Service Bulletin* (*CSB*).[15] *CSB* gives information about changes to *SCM: SH*, lists some new subject headings that have been established, lists headings that have been changed, and gives information about new publications that may be useful to the subject cataloger.

TYPES OF TOPICAL
SUBJECT HEADINGS
(MARC bibliographic field 650;
MARC authority field 150)

Library of Congress subject headings are constructed in a variety of ways, ranging from a single noun to complex descriptive phrases. As was discussed in chapter 21, Cutter enumerated six varieties according to their grammar or syntax.[16] They covered only primary headings, i.e., headings without further subdivision. The categories below are his, but the examples come from the current LC list:

1. A single word (e.g., **"Skating"**)

2. A noun preceded by an adjective (e.g., **"Administrative law"**)

3. A noun preceded by another noun used like an adjective (e.g., **"Energy industries"**)

4. A noun connected with another by a preposition (e.g., **"Radioisotopes in cardiology"**)

5. A noun connected with another by *and* (e.g., **"Libraries and society"**)

6. A phrase or sentence (e.g., **"Show driving of horse-drawn vehicles"**)

While Cutter did tolerate modifier inversions (e.g., **"Etching, Anonymous"**) "only when some other word is decidedly more significant or is often used alone with the same meaning as the whole name," he made no explicit provision for parenthetical qualifiers (e.g., **"Kairós (The Greek word)"**) or other such complicated forms as **"Internal combustion engines, Spark ignition,"** which, like subdivisions, are usually reminiscent of the alphabetico-classed approach. There are various alternative groupings. This discussion follows those used by Lois Mai Chan in her treatise on LC subject headings.[17]

Single Noun or Substantive

Cutter's Rule No. 172 reads: "Enter books under the word which best expresses their subject, whether it occurs in the title or not." He worked primarily in terms of the simple concept-name relationship on which the noun forms of all languages are based. The Library of Congress over the years has experimented with slight variations of this single-word heading, for example, inclusion of an initial article (e.g., **"The West"**), sometimes inverted (e.g., **"State, The"**) in the interests of clarity. Subject headings are no longer established with an English article in initial position. **"The West"** has been changed to **"West (U.S.)."**[18]

Another variation was the distinction drawn, particularly in literature and art, between singular nouns (denoting the activity or the form, e.g., **"Essay"** and **"Painting"**) and plural nouns (denoting the objects, e.g., **"Essays"** and **"Paintings"**). In general no new plural noun headings are being established, and some old plurals (e.g., **"Paintings"**) have been cancelled in favor of the singular form.

Adjectival Headings

These headings start with a modifier followed by a noun or noun phrase (e.g., **"Municipal officials and employees"**). The modifier may be an adjective or it may be a noun used as an adjective. Examples of some of these are:

Common adjective (e.g., **"Dental records"**)

Ethnic, national, or geographic adjective (e.g., **"Afro-American librarians"**)

Participial modifiers (e.g., **"Applied anthropology"** or **"Hearing aids"**)

Common noun used as a modifier (e.g., **"Household pests"**)

Proper noun used as a modifier (e.g., **"Bernstein polynomials"**)

Conjunctive Phrase Headings

Headings composed of two or more nouns, with or without modifiers, connected by *and* or ending with *etc.* belong in this group. Those that are additive may comprise similar elements (e.g., **"Wit and humor"** or **"Hotels, taverns, etc."**) or the elements may be contradictory (e.g., **"Right and wrong"**). Headings of this type are now established only when a work being cataloged discusses a relationship between two topics from both perspectives and in such broad terms that the relationship could not be described by use of a main heading with a subdivision.[19] Many older additive headings, such as the former **"Buddha and Buddhism,"** have been separated.[20]

Prepositional Phrase Headings

Prepositions sometimes enable the subject cataloger to express single but complex ideas for which there is no one word. Some express relationships for which an "and" phrase would be artificial (e.g., **"Photography in psychiatry"** or **"Police services for juveniles"**). Some are inverted (e.g., **"Plants, Effect of heat on"**). Examples of other prepositions used are:

against (e.g., **"Offenses against the person"**)

as (e.g., **"Alfalfa as feed"**)

from (e.g., **"Theft from motor vehicles"**)

to (e.g., **"Ceramic to metal bonding"**)

with (e.g., **Double bass with band"**)

Many of these circumlocutions are replaced when a simpler expression gains currency (e.g., **"Psychoanalysis in historiography"** was replaced by **"Psychohistory"**). "As" headings for classes of persons have been restricted to certain situations where the resulting connotation will not be seen as disparaging. **"Children as collectors"** or **"Physicians as authors"**). Old headings in which men or women are identified as professionals (e.g., **"Men as nurses"** or **"Women as teachers"**) have been replaced by adjectival phrases (e.g., **"Men nurses"** and **"Women teachers"**).[21]

Parenthetical Qualifiers

Nouns or phrases in parentheses following primary terms have in the past occasioned a variety of linguistic ineptitudes. The Library of Congress no longer adds them to designate special applications of a general concept, although it has no plans to change established headings such as:

Vibration (Marine engineering)
Cookery (Frozen foods)
Excavations (Archaeology)

For newly established situations, three different techniques are available:

1. "In" and "of" headings:

   Information theory in biology (*not* **Information theory (Biology)**)

   Abandonment of automobiles (*not* **Abandonment (Automobiles)**)

2. Phrase headings:

   Combinatorial enumeration problems (*not* **Enumeration problems (Combinatorial analysis)**)

3. Subdivisions under a primary heading (preferred when practicable):

   Public health—Citizen participation (*not* **Citizen participation (Public health)**)

Two situations are recognized in which it may be necessary to use parenthetical qualifiers:

1. To specify a definition if several can be found in the dictionary (e.g., **"Analysis (Philosophy)"**)

2. To remove ambiguity or to make an obscure word or phrase more explicit (e.g., **"Cluttering (Speech pathology)"**)[22]

Inverted Headings

Inversions, while awkward syntactically (e.g., **"Aged, Writings of the, American"**), serve the alphabetico-classed function of subordinating specific descriptors under their broad generic categories (e.g., **"Education, Bilingual"** or **"Asylum, Right of"**). Here too, much inconsistency is apparent.

In the course of its efforts to modernize and systematize LCSH, the Library of Congress has attempted to set policy for creation of new inverted headings. For example, topical headings modified by adjectival qualifiers referring to ethnic groups are to be established in the inverted form (e.g., **"Proverbs, Korean"**) with certain exceptions, one of which is for ethnic groups of the United States (e.g., **"Mexican American proverbs"**).[23] LC occasionally changes an existing inverted heading, especially in cases where every instance of the concept but one is in direct order.

SEMANTICS

Not only have syntactic forms of LC subject headings come under close scrutiny and revision in recent years, but also LCSH terminology has been reconsidered. Word meanings, particularly their connotative aspects, mutate rapidly; social and political upheavals cause many changes, and scientific and technological developments account for many more. The problem of shifting terminology is particularly troublesome for a subject access list based on specific entry, avoidance of synonyms, and controlled references, designed for use with card or printed book catalogs.

A ringing complaint that LCSH terminology was obsolete and prejudicial came from Sanford Berman in 1971.[24] As Head of the Hennepin County, Minnesota, Library Catalog Department, Berman edits the *HCL Cataloging Bulletin*, a bimonthly carrying lists of subject headings and references currently added to the HCL catalogs.[25] Many new concepts are added as headings at HCL before they are added by LC, and LC subject catalogers frequently consult the *HCL Cataloging Bulletin* when establishing new headings.

Other writers have criticized the stance at the Library of Congress on conceptual and linguistic shifts. Doris Clack's 1975 analysis of black literature resources started from a critique of LC subject analysis. She observed:

> Inadequate subject analysis is not just a problem with black literature — though admittedly there the level of adequacy is critically low — nor has it only in recent years been brought to the attention of the library world.[26]

Clack devoted the bulk of her treatise to various lists of LC class numbers and subject terms from the black perspective. Since her book was published the Library of Congress has made many changes. The one cited below involved changing approximately 12,000 cards:

> A basic function in the maintenance of a subject heading system is that of updating headings to conform to changing terminology or altered concepts. In general, the Library of Congress is and has been conservative in making changes since it involves altering reference structures surrounding a given heading as well as accommodating the change in both the card catalogs and the machine-readable data base. However, after a long period of great reluctance in effecting major changes, the Library has recently been involved in a number of changes represented in the following list ...

> **Negroes.** This heading discontinued February 1976.
> See **Afro-Americans** for later materials on the permanent residents of the United States. See **Blacks** for later materials on persons outside the United States....[27]

It can be seen in this statement that a major deterrent to LC's making changes was the card catalog. Since they closed the card catalog at the beginning of 1981 and have had only machine-readable records to update, terminology changes have been made much more readily.

Reflecting another socio-linguistic revolution was Joan K. Marshall's 1977 critique of sex bias in LCSH.[28] She used six principles developed by the American Library Association's Social Responsibilities Round Table Task Force Committee on Sexist Subject Headings to replace logically and consistently the guesswork that evolved over the years from Cutter's concern for the "convenience of the public." Basing her work on the six principles, she submitted an alphabetical, annotated "Thesaurus for Nonsexist Indexing and Cataloging." As in the case of blacks, the Library of Congress has overhauled most of its more obsolete or offensive sexist headings.

PROPER NAME HEADINGS

Any proper names can be used as subject headings in the LC system. They are not, however, all included in the subject list or given a subject authority record. The only ones appearing in the list are those that are used as pattern headings (see discussion below) or examples or that need special subject subdivisions or instructions printed under them.

Personal and Corporate Names and Uniform Titles
(MARC bibliographic fields 600, 610, 611, 630;
MARC authority fields 100, 110, 111, 130)

The correct forms of personal names, names of corporate bodies, names of jurisdictions, names of conferences and meetings, and uniform titles are found in LC's Name Authority File. (If one thinks of a uniform title as the "name" of a *work*, then this file is correctly named.) When any of these is the subject of a work, the correct form is taken from the Name Authority File and placed in a subject field in the bibliographic record. These names are established in accordance with LC's interpretation of *AACR2R*.

Geographic Names
(MARC bibliographic field 651;
MARC authority field 151)

Geographic, jurisdictional, and physiographic names form a large part of any library's subject network. Prior to the mid-1970s, only key examples to illustrate modes of entry and types of subdivision were listed in LCSH. Libraries had to locate bibliographic records using the names to verify them. With the acceptance of *AACR2* in 1981 it was decided to create subject geographic names in a form consistent with the jurisdictional forms controlled by *AACR2*. Subject authority records are now created for all non-jurisdictional geographic and physiographic names, except for those that are created as free-floating phrase headings (see discussion below), and are listed in the printed versions of LCSH. Although the form of jurisdictional names is taken from the Name Authority File, subject records are sometimes made and printed when needed in order to add a topical or chronological subdivision (e.g., "**Chicago (Ill.) — History — To 1875**").

Place names reflecting political or jurisdictional changes are treated somewhat differently as subject headings than as descriptive cataloging access points. In descriptive cataloging, the name used for the place at the time of the creation of the work is used as the access point. In subject cataloging, however, when the name of a country, state, city, etc., has been changed without substantially affecting the jurisdictional area covered, it is LC's policy to make all subject entries under the new name regardless of the time period covered. Subject entries under an old name are changed to the new name. These changes are referred to as "linear jurisdictional name changes."[29] This policy is followed regardless of whether the government changed the jurisdiction name or the change was made to accommodate cataloging rules. Examples:

Old Form	Latest Form
Argentine Republic	**Argentina**
British Honduras	**Belize**
Congo (Democratic Republic)	**Zaire**
Formosa	**Taiwan**

HEADINGS OMITTED FROM LCSH

A troublesome corollary of the principle of specific entry is the inevitable, and seemingly endless, proliferation of subject terms for individual members of certain subject categories. Until the early 1980s the Library of Congress omitted from its printed list a wide variety of such terms. These terms were included in the library's official records but were not spelled out in the printed editions of LCSH. They included such categories as names of sacred books, fictitious and legendary characters, works of art, chemicals, geographic regions, archaeological sites, and buildings. Authority records are now being made for the individual names in such groups, but only those established after 1976 (1981 if affected by *AACR2*) are in the file. There are still many general *See also* references to cover such situations (e.g., "**Lumber**, SA *kinds of lumber*, e.g. Cypress; Walnut"). These are gradually being replaced as the narrower headings are established.

Categories of headings currently intentionally omitted from the list are: headings residing in the Name Authority File; free-floating phrase headings; and certain music headings. Headings in the Name Authority File are discussed above. Free-floating phrase headings are composed as needed without creation of authority records. In free-floating phrase headings the initial word changes. This type is still limited to a very few pattern phrases. The following are listed in the *Subject Cataloging Manual*:

[personal name] in fiction, drama, poetry, etc.
    e.g., **Jesus Christ in fiction, drama, poetry, etc.**

[topic or name heading (except personal names)] in literature
    e.g., **Horses in literature**

[topic or name heading (except personal names)] in art
    e.g., **Manhattan (New York, N.Y.) in art**

[name of city] Metropolitan Area ([geographical qualifier])
    e.g., **Atlanta Metropolitan Area (Ga.)**

[name of city] Region ([geographical qualifier])
    e.g., **Dallas Region (Tex.)**

(List continues on page 412.)

[name of city] Suburban Area ([geographic qualifier])
    e.g., **Atlanta Suburban Area (Ga.)**

[name of geographic feature] Region ([geographic qualifier, if part of the name as established])
    e.g., **Himalaya Mountains Region**

[name of river] Estuary [Region, Watershed, or Valley] ([geographic qualifier, if part of name as established])
    e.g., **Kobuk River Valley (Alaska)**[30]

The local cataloger should not take any other "... in ..." phrase found in LCSH as a pattern phrase. For example, the heading "**Color in clothing**" does not of itself give license to coin other phrases ending with "**... in clothing.**" The Library of Congress formerly used pattern phrases of the form "**... as a profession**" (e.g., "**Medicine as a profession**"). It now uses the subdivision "**— Vocational guidance**" instead (e.g., "**Medicine — Vocational guidance**").

For an explanation of the music headings that are omitted from the list, the reader should consult the introduction to a printed edition of LCSH.[31]

It should be pointed out that this list of categories of headings omitted from LCSH refers only to main headings. In the discussion under "Subdivisions" below it can be seen that there are *many* headings with subdivisions that are not individually listed in the subject authority file.

GENERAL CHARACTERISTICS OF LCSH

The physical characteristics differ depending upon whether one is dealing with a printed version or with an online version. In the printed book version all primary subject terms appear in boldface type, while subdivisions and reference tracings, as well as references interfiled with the main headings, are in lightface type. In the microfiche version, of course, bold- and lightface type cannot be used, and the primary terms must be distinguished from references by what follows them. References interfiled with primary terms are followed in both book and microfiche versions by the instruction USE, which is in turn followed by the preferred term. The instruction SA (*See also*) is given in some authority records and precedes terms, phrases, etc., that show related headings or subdivisions. The directions UF (used for), BT (broader term), RT (related term), and NT (narrower term) precede reference tracings in authority records.

In the MARC authorities format functions of terms are identified by coding. Primary terms are given a three-digit code beginning with *1* (e.g., 150, 151). "Used for" terms are preceded by codes beginning with *4* (e.g., 450, 451); "see also" references are preceded by code 360; and broader and related terms are preceded by codes beginning with *5* (e.g., 550, 551). Narrower terms are not shown in MARC authority records except in the relatively few cases where general "reference records" are made showing the unused term coded 150 and the preferred term in a field coded 260. In such a record there is a fixed field code to show that the record is a reference record and that the term in the 150 field should not be used as a heading.

Syndetic (Reference) Structure

The following examples illustrate the usages of the abbreviations in the print formats and of the codes in the MARC format.

Example from *LCSH14*

Maintenance
    UF   Preventive maintenance
           Upkeep
    BT   Maintainability (Engineering)
    RT   Repairing
           Service life (Engineering)
    SA   *subdivision* Maintenance and repair
            under kinds of objects, including machinery, vehicles, structures, etc., e.g. Automobiles—Maintenance and repair; Dwellings—Maintenance and repair; Nuclear reactors—Maintenance and repair
    NT   Automatic checkout equipment
           Buildings—Repair and reconstruction
           Grounds maintenance
           Military bases—Maintenance
           Plant maintenance

The two terms following UF serve as tracings to indicate that there are references in the "P" and "U" sections of the list that read:

Preventive maintenance
    USE   Maintenance

Upkeep
    USE   Maintenance

This also serves as an instruction that when the heading "Maintenance" is first entered into the catalog, these two references should be added to the catalog also.

The BT line not only indicates that the term following BT is a broader term in the hierarchy of the concept, but also serves as a tracing to indicate that there should be a reference in the catalog that reads:

Maintainability (Engineering)
    See also   Maintenance

In traditional library practice it has been considered improper to provide a reference from a narrower term to its broader term, on the assumption that there would be no place to stop until one arrived at "General Knowledge," and the catalog would be overflowing with reference cards.

The terms following RT are related terms. Neither is hierarchically above the other. The instruction here is to make references both from and to these terms:

Maintenance
> *See also*   Repairing
>   Service life (Engineering)

Repairing
> *See also*   Maintenance

Service life (Engineering)
> *See also*   Maintenance

SA means "see also" and is currently used for special instructions concerning how the concept embodied in this heading may be used as a subdivision or to refer to groups of headings that are all related to the heading concept. In the example shown above the concept as a subdivision may be expressed as "Maintenance and repairs" under kinds of objects.

The terms following NT are narrower in the concept hierarchy, and there is an implicit instruction to make a reference that reads:

Maintenance
> *See also*   Automatic checkout equipment
>   Buildings—Repair and reconstruction
>   Grounds maintenance
>   Military bases—Maintenance
>   Plant maintenance

This last reference would most likely be combined with the "related terms" reference from "Maintenance" shown above.

The MARC format version of the same record (see page 415) shows the heading coded 150. The "used for" terms are coded 450. In some records a term coded 450 may be followed by "$w nne" ("e" meaning "earlier"), which indicates that the now unused term was once used as the heading for the concept, but the correct heading now is the one in the 150 field. The broader term and the related terms are all coded 550. The broader term is distinguished from the two related terms by the "$w g" following the term. The special instructions about the concept used as a subdivision are coded 360. Narrower terms are not included in MARC authority records on the assumption that if all references are made from broader terms listed in all authority records in an online system, references to the narrower terms will automatically be taken care of. This does, in fact, work, as can be seen in the sample screen display from OCLC (see page 415) in which headings and references beginning with "MAINT" are displayed.

Example from MARC Authority File as formatted in OCLC*

```
ARN:      2080919        Rec stat:    c
Entered:  19871218       Replaced:    19891024
Type:     z     Enc lvl:    n     Source:        Lang:
Roman:    |     Upd status:  a    Mod rec:       Name use: b
Govt agn: |     Ref status:  b    Subj:      a   Subj use: a
Series:   n     Auth status: a    Geo subd:  |   Ser use:  b
Ser num:  n     Auth/ref:    a    Name:      n   Rules:    n
1 010        sh 85079931
2 040        DLC $c DLC $d DLC
3 150   0    Maintenance
4 360        $i subdivision $a Maintenance and repair $i under kinds of
objects, including machinery, vehicles, structures, etc., e.g. $a
Automobiles--Maintenance and repair; Dwellings--Maintenance and repair;
Nuclear reactors--Maintenance and repair
5 450   0    Preventive maintenance
6 450   0    Upkeep
7 550   0    Maintainability (Engineering) $w g
8 550   0    Repairing
9 550   0    Service life (Engineering)
```

*This is not the default display in the OCLC PRISM service, which was implemented in 1991. In the default display the fixed field and $w codes are replaced by English equivalents for the most used codes. (See Fig. 25.10 in the chapter on authority control and the authority record for "Lumbering" on page 425 in this chapter.)

Example from OCLC**

```
1   Maintainability (Engineering)
2   Maintainability (Engineering) >> Nuclear power plants Maintainability
3   Maintainability (Engineering) >> Reliability (Engineering)
4   Maintaining, Preparing, and Producing Executive Reports (Computer
        system) >> MAPPER (Computer system)
5   Maintenance
6   Maintenance >> Automatic checkout equipment
7   Maintenance >> Buildings Repair and reconstruction
8   Maintenance >> Grounds maintenance                  Narrower terms
9   Maintenance >> Military bases Maintenance            under "Maintenance"
10  Maintenance >> Plant maintenance
11  Maintenance >> Repairing
12  Maintenance >> Service life (Engineering)
13  Maintenance and champerty
14  Maintenance (Domestic relations) >> Support (Domestic relations)
```

**This display is not the default display in the OCLC PRISM service, but can be viewed if one asks for the "brief" display.

The instructions for references imbedded in the abbreviations and codes are not to be followed blindly, but should be applied where useful and needed. If, for example, a catalog lacks entries under the narrower terms "Grounds maintenance," "Military bases—Maintenance," and the related term "Service life (Engineering)," then the *See also* reference from "Maintenance" would omit these and read only:

Maintenance
> *See also*   Automatic checkout equipment
>   Buildings—Repair and reconstruction
>   Plant maintenance
>   Repairing

If all seven headings are lacking, then the reference should not be made at all.

The related and broader term references *to* "Maintenance" present a complicated problem. If there were no entries in the catalog under "Repairing," strictly speaking it would be inaccurate to make a reference reading:

Repairing
> *See also*   Maintenance

Some theorists argue that it is nonetheless justifiable to make such *See also* references on the assumption that the term referred from will eventually be activated. Even if it is not, they say, the reference serves to move users from a term not included in the catalog to one where there may be pertinent materials. Some libraries convert such ambiguous *See also* references into *See* references:

Repairing
> *See* Maintenance

If the term referred from is later activated, they add the word *also* to *See* on the reference. This system is difficult to handle, and as more catalogs are automated it is necessary to write unambiguous programs that create references only as authorized in the authority file. The problem might be solved by using *Broader terms, Narrower terms*, etc., in catalogs instead of *See also*, or *Search also under* (a phrase currently gaining acceptance). There should be no semantic problem with telling a user that a related term for "Repairing" is "Maintenance," even if there are no entries under "Repairing." In fact, the traditional ban on referring users from narrower terms to broader terms could also be lifted.

A number of writers have criticized LCSH's syndetic structure and its lack of ability to show hierarchical relationships. Coates wrote in 1960 that LCSH merely linked an "indeterminate selection" of related terms—that at times there was more than one level of hierarchy in a list under one primary term, while at other times intermediate hierarchical terms were omitted from the chain of references.[32] Sinkankis demonstrated in his 1972 study, in which he followed the *See also*s under the heading "Hunting," that a user was quickly led away from the subject. By following the references he was led to "Migrant labor," "Pimps," "Liturgy and drama," and "Panic," among other terms.[33] Petersen wrote in 1983 that during a project to create the Art and Architecture Thesaurus, the designers chose to keep LCSH terms as a base and to modify and expand them. But the *See also*s and *See* *also from*s in LCSH had to be ignored because they could not be converted to broader, narrower, and related terms. There were too many types of reference present.[34] Dykstra was critical in 1989 of the format LC began using in *LCSH11*, the first edition to use the abbreviations BT, RT, NT, etc., instead of the previous system that used *x* and *xx* to trace *See* and *See also* references. Dykstra believed that LC was trying to make *LCSH* look like a true thesaurus, which it is not because of its use of "headings" instead of "terms."[35]

LC has recognized the problems but has not been able to eliminate most inappropriate references created in the past; staff time has not been available for "clean-up" projects. However, beginning in the mid-1980s, subject catalogers at LC put into effect a fairly strict policy for creating new references for all *new* headings created. The general rule is to make a broader term reference from the class of which the heading is a class member (e.g., "**Cinematography**, BT Photography"), to make a reference for a whole/part relationship (e.g., "**Toes**, BT Foot"), and to make a reference for cases in which a specific heading is an instance or example of a broader category (e.g., "**Erie, Lake**, BT Lakes—United States"). Broader term references are made only from the next broader level in a hierarchy. Related terms are used to link two headings not in the same hierarchy (e.g., a concept and an object). One of the headings should be strongly implied whenever the other is considered (e.g., "**Boats and boating**, RT Ships").[36] While this reference policy moves LCSH toward answering its critics, the problem will not be solved completely unless "clean-up" projects can be undertaken.

Scope Notes

Scope notes are sometimes inserted into the full list between subject terms and their suggested references. Such notes specify the range of application for a term or draw distinctions between related terms. Some libraries with card catalogs copy these notes on cards and file them in the catalog just ahead of the subject entries under the same heading. Other libraries provide one or more copies of LCSH near the catalog for reference use by patrons doing subject searches. A typical example of an entry with a scope note is the following from *LCSH14*:

> **Sexism** *(May Subd Geog)*
>   Here are entered works on sexism as an attitude
> as well as works on attitude and overt discrimina-
> tory behavior. Works dealing solely with discrim-
> inatory behavior directed toward both of the sexes
> are entered under Sex discrimination.
>   UF Sex bias
>   BT Attitude (Psychology)
>   Prejudices
>   Sex (Psychology)
>   Social perception
>   RT Sex role
>   NT Sex discrimination

In the MARC authorities format the scope note is in a field coded 680 as can be seen in the following copy of the record for "Sexism" as it is formatted in the OCLC database:

```
ARN:     2102436        Rec stat:    n
Entered:   19871218     Replaced:      19871218
Type:     z    Enc lvl:    n      Source:          Lang:
Roman:    |    Upd status:  a     Mod rec:         Name use: b
Govt agn: |    Ref status:  b     Subj:      a     Subj use: a
Series:   n    Auth status: a     Geo subd: i      Ser use:  b
Ser num:  n    Auth/ref:    a     Name:      n     Rules:    n
 1 010        sh 85120678
 2 040        DLC $c DLC $d DLC
 3 150   0    Sexism
 4 450   0    Sex bias
 5 550   0    Attitude (Psychology) $w g
 6 550   0    Prejudices $w g
 7 550   0    Sex (Psychology) $w g
 8 550   0    Social perception $w g
 9 550   0    Sex role
10 680        $i Here are entered works on sexism as an attitude as well
as works on attitude and overt discriminatory behavior. Works dealing
solely with discriminatory behavior directed toward both of the sexes
are entered under $a Sex discrimination.
11 681        $i Note under $a Sex discrimination
```

In online catalogs with linked authority records it is possible to give users the option of viewing scope notes.

Subdivisions
(MARC subfields $x, $y, $z)

It was mentioned earlier that the practice of establishing subdivisions for headings was firmly set in Hanson's time as a concession to alphabetic-classed organization of catalogs. The introduction to *LCSH14* states:

> The application of Library of Congress subject headings requires extensive use of subject subdivisions as a means of combining a number of different concepts into a single subject heading. Complex topics may be represented by subject headings followed by subdivisions. Some subdivisions are printed in *LCSH 14* but a greater number of subdivisions may be assigned according to rules specified in the *Manual*. Only a fraction of all possible heading-and-subdivision combinations are listed in *LCSH*.[37]

Subdivisions fall into four broadly defined categories: topical and chronological subdivisions specific to particular headings; geographic subdivisions; free-floating subdivisions; and subdivisions under pattern headings.

Topical and Chronological Subdivisions
Specific to Particular Headings
(MARC subfields $x, $y)

Some headings need topical and/or chronological subdivisions that are specific to the concepts in the headings and that, therefore, must be authorized specifically for the headings. Such subdivisions in printed versions of LCSH are introduced by a long dash; if two subdivisions are used, there are two long dashes; etc. The following example from *LCSH14* shows printed subdivisions for the heading "**Lumber**":

> **Lumber**
> > *[TS800-TS837]*
> > BT   Forests and forestry
> > > Wood products
> > RT   Timber
> > SA   *kinds of lumber, e.g.* Cypress; Walnut
> > NT   Hardwoods
> > > Pit-wood
> > > Planing-mills
> > > Sawmills
> > **−Drying**
> > > *[TS837]*
> > > UF   Lumber−Seasoning
> > > > Lumber drying
> > > > Wood−Drying
> > > BT   Wood−Preservation
> > **−Law and legislation**   *(May Subd Geog)*
> > **−Mensuration**
> > **−Rate-books**
> > > *[HE2116.L8]*
> > −Seasoning
> > > USE   Lumber−Drying
> > **−Storage**
> > **−Transportation**
> > > *[HE199.5.L]*
> > **−−Law and legislation**
> > > *(May Subd Geog)*

The interpretation of these subdivisions should be:

Lumber−Drying
Lumber−Law and legislation
Lumber−Mensuration
Lumber−Rate-books
Lumber−Storage
Lumber−Transportation
Lumber−Transportation−Law and legislation

In the MARC version of LCSH, each of these headings is given a separate authority record:

```
ARN:       2070743          Rec stat:     c
Entered:   19871218         Replaced:     19871218
Type:      z      Enc lvl:     n      Source:            Lang:
Roman:     |      Upd status:  a      Mod rec:           Name use: b
Govt agn:  |      Ref status:  b      Subj:      a       Subj use: a
Series:    n      Auth status: a      Geo subd:  |       Ser use:  b
Ser num:   n      Auth/ref:    a      Name:      n       Rules:    n
 1 010        sh 85078804
 2 040        DLC $c DLC $d DLC
 3 053        TS800 $b TS837
 4 150  0     Lumber
 5 360           $i kinds of lumber, e.g. $a Cypress; Walnut
 6 550  0     Forests and forestry $w g
 7 550  0     Wood products $w g
 8 550  0     Timber
```

```
ARN:       2070757          Rec stat:     n
Entered:   19871218         Replaced:     19871218
Type:      z      Enc lvl:     n      Source:            Lang:
Roman:     |      Upd status:  a      Mod rec:           Name use: b
Govt agn:  |      Ref status:  b      Subj:      a       Subj use: a
Series:    n      Auth status: a      Geo subd:  |       Ser use:  b
Ser num:   n      Auth/ref:    a      Name:      n       Rules:    n
 1 010        sh 85078805
 2 040        DLC $c DLC
 3 053        TS837
 4 150  0     Lumber $x Drying
 5 450  0     Lumber $x Seasoning
 6 450  0     Lumber drying
 7 450  0     Wood $x Drying
 8 550  0     Wood $x Preservation $w g
```

```
ARN:       2070772          Rec stat:     n
Entered:   19871218         Replaced:     19871218
Type:      z      Enc lvl:     n      Source:            Lang:
Roman:     |      Upd status:  a      Mod rec:           Name use: b
Govt agn:  |      Ref status:  n      Subj:      a       Subj use: a
Series:    n      Auth status: a      Geo subd:  i       Ser use:  b
Ser num:   n      Auth/ref:    a      Name:      n       Rules:    n
 1 010        sh 85078806
 2 040        DLC $c DLC
 3 150  0     Lumber $x Law and legislation
```

* * *

```
ARN:      2070790        Rec stat:     n
Entered:    19871218     Replaced:     19871218
Type:     z     Enc lvl:      n     Source:           Lang:
Roman:    |     Upd status:   a     Mod rec:          Name use: b
Govt agn: |     Ref status:   n     Subj:       a     Subj use: a
Series:   n     Auth status:  a     Geo subd:   |     Ser use:  b
Ser num:  n     Auth/ref:     a     Name:       n     Rules:    n
 1 010        sh 85078810
 2 040        DLC $c DLC
 3 053        HE199.5.L
 4 150    0   Lumber $x Transportation
```


```
ARN:      2070794        Rec stat:     n
Entered:    19871218     Replaced:     19871218
Type:     z     Enc lvl:      n     Source:           Lang:
Roman:    |     Upd status:   a     Mod rec:          Name use: b
Govt agn: |     Ref status:   n     Subj:       a     Subj use: a
Series:   n     Auth status:  a     Geo subd:   i     Ser use:  b
Ser num:  n     Auth/ref:     a     Name:       n     Rules:    n
 1 010        sh 85078811
 2 040        DLC $c DLC
 3 150    0   Lumber $x Transportation $x Law and legislation
```

In these records the dashes that appeared in the printed list are represented by the code $x.

Chronological subdivisions appear in the printed list as in this example:

> **Irian Jaya (Indonesia)** *(Not Subd Geog)*
> UF   Irian Barat (Indonesia)
>   Netherlands New Guinea
> **— Description and travel**
> **— — To 1963**
> **— — 1963-**
> **— Politics and government**
> **— — To 1963**
> **— — 1963-**

In MARC authority records chronological subdivisions are preceded by the code $y. Again, every heading/subdivision combination has its own separate authority record:

```
ARN:        2121120         Rec stat:      n
Entered:    19871218        Replaced:      19871218
Type:      z      Enc lvl:     n     Source:          Lang:
Roman:     |      Upd status:  a     Mod rec:         Name use: b
Govt agn:  |      Ref status:  n     Subj:       a    Subj use: a
Series:    n      Auth status: a     Geo subd:   |    Ser use:  b
Ser num:   n      Auth/ref:    a     Name:       n    Rules:    n
 1 010      sh 85068058
 2 040      DLC $c DLC
 3 151   0  Irian Jaya (Indonesia) $x Description and travel
```

```
ARN:        2121123         Rec stat:      n
Entered:    19871218        Replaced:      19871218
Type:      z      Enc lvl:     n     Source:          Lang:
Roman:     |      Upd status:  a     Mod rec:         Name use: b
Govt agn:  |      Ref status:  n     Subj:       a    Subj use: a
Series:    n      Auth status: a     Geo subd:   |    Ser use:  b
Ser num:   n      Auth/ref:    a     Name:       n    Rules:    n
 1 010      sh 85068059
 2 040      DLC $c DLC
 3 151   0  Irian Jaya (Indonesia) $x Description and travel $y To 1963
```

```
ARN:        2121127         Rec stat:      n
Entered:    19871218        Replaced:      19871218
Type:      z      Enc lvl:     n     Source:          Lang:
Roman:     |      Upd status:  a     Mod rec:         Name use: b
Govt agn:  |      Ref status:  n     Subj:       a    Subj use: a
Series:    n      Auth status: a     Geo subd:   |    Ser use:  b
Ser num:   n      Auth/ref:    a     Name:       n    Rules:    n
 1 010      sh 85068060
 2 040      DLC $c DLC
 3 151   0  Irian Jaya (Indonesia) $x Description and travel $y 1963-
```

```
ARN:        2121129         Rec stat:      n
Entered:    19871218        Replaced:      19871218
Type:      z      Enc lvl:     n     Source:          Lang:
Roman:     |      Upd status:  a     Mod rec:         Name use: b
Govt agn:  |      Ref status:  n     Subj:       a    Subj use: a
Series:    n      Auth status: a     Geo subd:   |    Ser use:  b
Ser num:   n      Auth/ref:    a     Name:       n    Rules:    n
 1 010      sh 85068061
 2 040      DLC $c DLC
 3 151   0  Irian Jaya (Indonesia) $x Politics and government
```

(Text continues on page 424.)

```
ARN:      2121131          Rec stat:    n
Entered:    19871218       Replaced:    19871218
Type:     z     Enc lvl:      n      Source:          Lang:
Roman:    |     Upd status:   a      Mod rec:         Name use: b
Govt agn: |     Ref status:   n      Subj:       a    Subj use: a
Series:   n     Auth status:  a      Geo subd:   |    Ser use:  b
Ser num:  n     Auth/ref:     a      Name:       n    Rules:    n
 1 010       sh 85068062
 2 040       DLC $c DLC
 3 151   0   Irian Jaya (Indonesia) $x Politics and government $y To
1963
```

```
ARN:      2121132          Rec stat:    n
Entered:    19871218       Replaced:    19871218
Type:     z     Enc lvl:      n      Source:          Lang:
Roman:    |     Upd status:   a      Mod rec:         Name use: b
Govt agn: |     Ref status:   n      Subj:       a    Subj use: a
Series:   n     Auth status:  a      Geo subd:   |    Ser use:  b
Ser num:  n     Auth/ref:     a      Name:       n    Rules:    n
 1 010       sh 85068063
 2 040       DLC $c DLC
 3 151   0   Irian Jaya (Indonesia) $x Politics and government $y 1963-
```

Geographic Subdivisions
(MARC subfield $z)

The code words *"(May Subd Geog)"* in parentheses after any entry in the printed list tell us that place names may be added without having been spelled out in the list. In a MARC authority record the code for geographic subdivision is given in a byte of the fixed field. The letter *i* indicates that geographic subdivision is allowed. In the OCLC system the fixed field byte is labeled "Geo subd:". The printed and MARC codes are illustrated in the following copies of the printed and MARC records for the same heading:

Lumbering *(May Subd Geog)*
[SD538-SD557 (Forestry)]
[TS800-TS837 (Manufactures)]
    Here are entered works on the manufacturing of logs into lumber. Works on the felling of trees through the transporting of logs to sawmills or to a place of sale are entered under Logging.
  BT   Forestry engineering
        Forests and forestry
        Trees
  RT   Lumber trade
  NT   Communication in lumbering
        Explosives in lumbering
        Logging
        Lumbermen

```
ARN:       2070847        Rec stat:    n
Entered:   19871218       Replaced:    19871218
Type:      z       Enc lvl:    n    Source:         Lang:
Roman:     |       Upd status: a    Mod rec:        Name use: b
Govt agn:  |       Ref status: b    Subj:      a    Subj use: a
Series:    n       Auth status: a   Geo subd:  i    Ser use:  b
Ser num:   n       Auth/ref:   a    Name:      n    Rules:    n
 1 010     sh 85078820
 2 040     DLC $c DLC $d DLC
 3 053     SD538 $b SD557 $c Forestry
 4 053     TS800 $b TS837 $c Manufactures
 5 150   0 Lumbering
 6 550   0 Forestry engineering $w g
 7 550   0 Forests and forestry $w g
 8 550   0 Trees $w g
 9 550   0 Lumber trade
10 680     $i Here are entered works on the manufacturing of logs
into lumber. Works on the felling of trees through the transporting of
logs to sawmills or to a place of sale are entered under $a Logging.
11 681     $i Note under $a Logging
```

It will be noted that in the earlier example shown for the heading "Lumber" (see page 420), geographic subdivision is not called for. The code shown following "Geo subd:" in that record is a "fill character" (shown in the example as "|"). The default display for subject authority records in the OCLC PRISM service uses the word INDIRECT to indicate that geographic subdivision is allowed:

```
AUTHORITY RECORD                                           NOT EVALUATED
  ARN: 2070847            REC STAT: NEW                    VERIFIED
  ENTERED: 19871218       REPLACED: 19871218

  SUBJECT                 ESTABLISHED HEADING
  LC                      INDIRECT

   1  010       sh 85078820
   2  040       DLC $c DLC $d DLC
   3  053       SD538 $b SD557 $c Forestry
   4  053       TS800 $b TS837 $c Manufactures
   5  150    0  Lumbering
   6  550    0  Forestry engineering [BROADER TERM]
   7  550    0  Forests and forestry [BROADER TERM]
   8  550    0  Trees [BROADER TERM]
   9  550    0  Lumber trade
  10  680       $i Here are entered works on the manufacturing of logs into
lumber. Works on the felling of trees through the transporting of logs to
sawmills or to a place of sale are entered under $a Logging.
  11  681       $i Note under $a Logging
```

The code "i" stands for the word "indirect" which was a former code used to indicate that geographic subdivision was allowed. It still describes the manner in which LCSH goes about providing geographic subdivision. Indirect subdivision means that the elements of the geographic name are to be arranged hierarchically, with a broader place name preceding the local name, e.g., "Chestnut — Oregon — Portland." Each sequential part of the subdivision is filed in its proper alphabetical order, regardless of its political, administrative, or regional scope.

Formerly, "direct" subdivision was allowed (and is still used in the *Sears List of Subject Headings*, as explained in chapter 23). This meant that the place name was written as it would be written to address a letter (e.g., "Opera — Santa Fe, N.M."). Late in 1976, "direct" subdivision was abandoned, although there are a few exceptions, which are well defined. The advantage of indirect subdivision is the collocation of material on one topic in one country or state, while direct subdivision separated such material by the first letters of the names of cities. On the other hand, indirect subdivision can sometimes be difficult to apply (e.g., when a geographic entity falls within two countries), whereas direct subdivision allowed use of the established name without alteration.

The following are subdivided "direct" in exception to the "indirect" policy:[38]

Names of countries

Names of geographical entities not wholly within one country

Names of first order subdivisions (e.g., states) of the United States, Soviet Union, Canada, and Great Britain. (While there are seven countries that are qualified by first-order subdivision rather than country under *AACR2R*, only four of these are subdivided indirectly this way.)

Inverted terms with name of the country, etc., first (e.g., **"Italy, Northern"**)

Three cities: New York, Washington, and Jerusalem. (Hong Kong and Vatican City are treated as countries and are thus also assigned directly.)

Islands "at a distance" from "owning" land masses.

The following list shows some results of the above policy:

Catholic Church – France – Paris
Expeditions – Pyrenees (France and Spain)
Children – Ontario – Toronto
Children – Australia – New South Wales [only two levels are allowed; so a city in New South Wales would follow **"Australia –"**:
Children – Australia – Newcastle (N.S.W.)]
Education – New York (N.Y.)
Geology – Islands of the Aegean
Geology – Indonesia – Ambon Island

For geographic subdivisions, as for geographic headings, local name changes are observed. For instance, works that formerly would have received the heading **"Banks and banking – Leopoldville, Belgian Congo"** are now found under **"Banks and banking – Zaire – Kinshasa."** In card catalogs it was very difficult to keep up with such subdivision changes because of the difficulty of finding all occurrences of, for example, "Belgian Congo" used as a subdivision. In online catalogs, keyword searching is making such changes easier, although some critics still object to making such changes "regardless of the form of the name used in the work cataloged."[39]

If both geographical and topical subdivisions are established in the same heading, the last provision for geographical subdivision prevails. For example, the subject heading "Children" may be subdivided geographically. The subdivision "costume" is not divided. Therefore, a correct heading would be:

Children – Illinois – Costume

The subdivision **"Dental care"** under "children" *is* divided. Therefore, a correct heading would be:

Children – Dental care – Illinois

Other explanations and illustrations of geographic headings and subdivision practice are issued from time to time. Their best sources are the *Cataloging Service Bulletin*, and the *Subject Cataloging Manual: Subject Headings*.

Free-Floating Subdivisions
(MARC subfield $x)

For many kinds of primary headings there are a number of identical, or nearly identical, subdivisions that can be applied in specifically defined situations, according to LC's rules, policies, and practices, and that, therefore, do not have separate authority records made for each heading with subdivision combination in which they appear. These are collectively designated "free-floating," but they may not be assigned indiscriminately, for they fall into different groups, each with its own rules and examples. There are five broad groups: general free-floating subdivisions; subdivisions used under classes of persons and ethnic groups; subdivisions used under names of corporate bodies, persons, and families; subdivisions used under place names; and subdivisions controlled by pattern headings. All free-floating subdivisions are listed in *Free-Floating Subdivisions: An Alphabetical Index.*[40] In this list they are in alphabetical order, each with a reference to the category in which it appears in *SCM: SH* and with citations to special instructions in the manual when applicable.

General Free-Floating Subdivisions

General free-floating subdivisions are listed in *SCM: SH*, H1095. Along with each subdivision is a scope note, followed by *See also* references to other subdivisions, when applicable. With some there are also references to other memo numbers in the manual because the concept represented by the subdivision has an entire instruction sheet about it. A few also include the instruction *"(May Subd Geog)."* Example:

> —**Political aspects** *(May Subd Geog)*   *H1942*   *sh85-104440*
> Use under individual religions and topical headings for works on the political dimensions or implications of nonpolitical topics.
> See also —**Politics and government** [under] names of countries, cities, etc., and under ethnic groups.

An example of a heading using this subdivision is:

Environmental education—Political aspects

Subdivisions Used under Classes of Persons and Ethnic Groups

These subdivisions are listed in *SCM: SH*, H1100 and H1103. The primary headings under which the list in H1100 may be used include all kinds of classes of persons except ethnic groups and nationalities, which is covered by H1103. Examples of classes of persons are: **Mothers; Youth; Political prisoners; Lung—Cancer—Patients; Baseball—Coaches;** and even **Afro-American dentists,** because this is a class of persons even though qualified by an ethnic adjective. Examples of ethnic groups are: **French Canadians; Dinka (African people); Jews.**

Headings for nationalities (e.g., **Ukrainians**) are included when they designate those nationalities *outside* their native countries. Many of the subdivisions in these two lists carry the instruction *"(May Subd Geog)."* Only a few have scope notes. Examples: **Women – Information services; Cuban Americans – Job stress.**

Subdivisions Used under Names of Corporate Bodies, Persons, and Families

Subdivisions to be used under names of corporate bodies are given in H1105. H1110 lists subdivisions used under names of persons, and H1631 lists those for family names. The subdivisions in H1105 may be used under all types of corporate bodies except conferences, congresses, meetings, or names of jurisdictions. The list has no scope notes as such, but does have footnotes that limit the use of some subdivisions. Example: **Princeton University. Art Museum – Catalogs.**

Subdivisions listed in H1110 may be used under persons of all categories except literary authors. The latter are covered by a pattern heading and are discussed below. This list is like the one for general subdivisions in that there are scope notes and references to other subdivisions. Example: **Lincoln, Abraham, 1809-1865 – Correspondence.**

The list of subdivisions to be used under family names is relatively short with no notes. Example: **Lull family – Coin collections.**

Subdivisions Used under Place Names

Subdivisions to be used under place names are given in two lists: H1140 lists subdivisions used under names of regions, countries, cities, etc., and H1145.5 lists those to be used with names of bodies of water. As for subdivisions under corporate bodies, the list of subdivisions in H1140 is simply a list with no scope notes but with footnotes that limit the use of some subdivisions. Example: **Chicago (Ill.) – Ethnic relations.** The list of subdivisions used with names of bodies of water is very short. Example: **Okmulgee Lake (Okla.) – Recreational use.**

Until 1985 LC had a separate list for use under cities. This list contained a number of terms that were (and still are) acceptable as subject headings alone and could be subdivided geographically. When this situation occurred the heading could not be divided down to the city level, but was used instead as a subdivision under the name of the city, e.g., **"Chicago (Ill.) – Buildings."** The heading used since 1985 has been **"Buildings – Illinois – Chicago,"** but card catalogs continue to hold many cards with the headings constructed according to "the city flip" (as the policy was called).[41]

Subdivisions Controlled by Pattern Headings

Pattern headings are examples of a particular primary heading type that have been entered into the LCSH authority file to show all the possible subdivisions that might be used with other specific headings of the same type. A very few may not even apply to the heading under which they are found. For instance, under "**Shakespeare, William, 1564-1616**" a scope note warns us:

> The subdivisions provided under this heading represent for the greater part standard subdivisions usable under any literary author heading, and do not necessarily pertain to Shakespeare.

Besides literary authors, several other categories of specific subjects have distinctive sets of subdivisions applicable to all examples of their genre. These include such categories as educational institutions, monastic and religious orders, languages, musical instruments, industries, military services, animals, diseases, and sports. Pattern headings are represented by examples in the printed LCSH and in the online authority file, but one must have a table to find them. A table in alphabetical order by category is found in the introduction to the printed list. A table grouped by subject field is found in *SCM: SH*, H1146. There is also a separate memo in *SCM: SH* for each pattern heading that explains what is included in the category and lists all allowable subdivisions for that category.

The following table shows some of the pattern headings available:

Subject Field	Category	Pattern Heading(s)
Religion	Theological topics	**Salvation**
History and geography	Legislative bodies	**United States. Congress**
Recreation	Sports	**Soccer**
Social sciences	Individual educational institutions	**Harvard University**
The arts	Music compositions	**Operas**
Science and technology	Organs and regions of the body	**Heart; Foot**

Thus, if one were cataloging a work about "football" it would be appropriate to find "**Soccer**" in LCSH and choose appropriate subdivisions found there to be used with the heading "**Football**." General free-floating subdivisions are not usually printed under pattern headings, but they may also be used as appropriate.

Classification Aids
(MARC field 053)

Many primary subject terms, and some subject subdivisions under those terms, are accompanied by LC classification notations. Sometimes more than one LC class notation is given, with a term from the schedule to show the various aspects of classification represented by the subject heading or a range of notations may be supplied:

> **Chestnut** *(May Subd Geog)*
> *[QK495.F14 (Botany)]*
> *[SB401.C4 (Nut trees)]*
> *[SD397.C5 (Forestry)]*
> UF   Castanea sativa
>   Castenea vesca
>   Castanea vulgaris
>   Chestnut tree
>   Common European chestnut
>   English chestnut
>   European chestnut
>   Italian chestnut
>   Spanish chestnut
>   Sweet chestnut
> BT   Castanea

In the MARC authorities format the class numbers are given in a field with the tag 053. When a term is used to identify the particular aspect the classification represents, that term is coded $c in the 053 field:

```
ARN:      2140296        Rec stat:    n
Entered:    19871219     Replaced:      19871219
Type:     z     Enc lvl:    n     Source:          Lang:
Roman:    |     Upd status: a     Mod rec:         Name use: b
Govt agn: |     Ref status: b     Subj:      a     Subj use: a
Series:   n     Auth status: a    Geo subd: i      Ser use:  b
Ser num:  n     Auth/ref:   a     Name:     n      Rules:    n
 1 010       sh 85023154
 2 040       DLC $c DLC $d DLC
 3 053       QK495.F14 $c Botany
 4 053       SB401.C4 $c Nut trees
 5 053       SD397.C5 $c Forestry
 6 150   0   Chestnut
 7 450   0   Castanea sativa
 8 450   0   Castanea vesca
 9 450   0   Castanea vulgaris
10 450   0   Chestnut tree
11 450   0   Common European chestnut
12 450   0   English chestnut
13 450   0   European chestnut
14 450   0   Italian chestnut
15 450   0   Spanish chestnut
16 450   0   Sweet chestnut
17 550   0   Castanea $w g
18 681       $i Example under $a Nuts
```

These notations are usually supplied when a term is first established. Occasionally they are added at a later time. But there is no systematic checking or revision of these notations unless changes are being made in an existing record for some other reason. Thus, a classification notation could be changed or its meaning revised in the LC Classification Schedules, but it might not be changed in LCSH. Therefore, these notations are only a guide and should not be assigned without verification.

Filing Arrangement

The list proper in printed versions is given in alphabetical order. Filing rules were revised in 1980 to facilitate computer manipulation, and the revised rules continue to be used. Basic arrangement is word by word. Numbers given in digits precede alphabetic characters in the order of increasing value. Initials separated by punctuation file as separate words. Abbreviations without interior punctuation file as single whole words:

4-H clubs
A3D bomber   USE Skywarrior bomber
A4D (Jet attack plane)   USE Skyhawk (Jet attack plane)
A-36 (Fighter-bomber planes)   USE Mustang (Fighter planes)
A.D.C.   USE Child welfare
A priori
Aage family   USE Agee family
ACI test   USE Adult-child interaction test
ACTH
AK 8 motion picture camera
Alaska
ALGOL (Computer program language)

Punctuation of subject terms affects filing order more immediately than it does in lists such as *Sears*, which sacrifice categorical to straight alphabetical arrangement. LC subject headings that contain subordinate elements preceded by one or more dashes fall into three groups:

a) period subdivisions (MARC subfield $y), arranged chronologically according to explicit dates, regardless of whether a descriptive term is used,

b) form and topical subdivisions (MARC subfield $x), arranged alphabetically, and

c) geographical subdivisions (MARC subfield $z), arranged alphabetically.

The secondary subdivisions under **"United States — Foreign relations"** faithfully illustrate all three groups in order:

a) **United States — Foreign relations — Revolution, 1775-1783**
    United States — Foreign relations — 1783-1865
    United States — Foreign relations — Constitutional period, 1789-1809
    United States — Foreign relations — War of 1898

b) **United States — Foreign relations — Executive agreements**
    United States — Foreign relations — Historiography
    United States — Foreign relations — Juvenile literature
    United States — Foreign relations — Law and legislation
    United States — Foreign relations — Speeches in Congress
    United States — Foreign relations — Treaties

c) **United States — Foreign relations — Canada**
    United States — Foreign relations — France
    United States — Foreign relations — Japan
    United States — Foreign relations — Soviet Union

In actual practice these three groups generally collapse into two, for nearly all period subdivisions follow such topical subdivisions as **"—Civilization,"** **"—Economic conditions," "—Politics and government,"** or **"—History."** All period subdivisions have explicit dates to allow for computer filing:

> **United States — History — 1849-1877**
> **United States — History — Civil War, 1861-1865**
> **United States — History — 1865-**
> **United States — History — 1865-1898**
> **United States — History — 1865-1921**

Prior to 1974 period subdivisions were sometimes indicated only by descriptive terminology (e.g., **"United States — History — Civil War"**), and one may still find these forms in old card catalogs.

All subject subdivisions (identified by dashes) file ahead of inverted modifiers, which are punctuated by commas. Inverted modifiers, in turn, file ahead of parenthetical qualifiers. Last of all come phrases that start with the primary term:

> **Children**
> **Children — Attitudes**
> **Children — Growth**
> **Children — Quotations**
> **Children, Adopted**
> **Children, Deaf**
> **Children, Vagrant**
> **Children (Christian theology)**
> **Children (International law)**
> **Children (Roman law)**
> **Children and animals**
> **Children and strangers**

Children as witnesses
Children in literature
Children of working parents

SUBJECT HEADINGS FOR
CHILDREN'S LITERATURE
(2nd MARC indicator 1 in 650 field)

Since 1965 the Library of Congress has issued a special service for children's catalogers. Known as the Annotated Card Program, it provides "more appropriate and in-depth subject treatment of juvenile titles."[42] A list of specially tailored subject headings given in each printed edition of LCSH is accompanied by a review of commonly used subdivisions, another of subdivisions and qualifiers not used, and general instructions for applying and modifying standard LC subject terms. LC's printed cards carry the children's heading forms in brackets. In the MARC format they are tagged specifically as subject terms for children with a second indicator of *1* in fields beginning with *6*. Some comparative examples are:

LCSH	Annotated Card List
Alpine fauna	Alpine animals
Life-saving	Lifesaving
Phytogeography	Plant distribution
Picture-books for children	Picture books
Zoogeography	Animal distribution

CONCLUSION

In spite of perennial criticisms on grounds of its outdated terminology, illogical syntax, and general inefficiency for precise subject retrieval, LCSH is the most widely accepted controlled vocabulary list in use in English-language libraries today. The Library of Congress, with considerable prompting from interested bystanders, now and again assesses its virtues and disadvantages, in comparison with other, more scientifically constructed systems. PRECIS (Preserved Context Index System), inaugurated for the *British National Bibliography* in 1971, received perhaps the strongest consideration as an alternative to, if not a replacement for, LCSH. After cost studies, however, the decision went against any such replacement or supplement. Instead, more intensive efforts are under way to modernize and systematize the existing tool. Many of the features discussed in this chapter represent steps in that direction. For the foreseeable future, this venerable subject list gives every sign of retaining its vitality and preeminence for subject access to library collections.

In the spring of 1991 a special conference was sponsored by LC to bring together experts to discuss possible ways of restructuring LCSH. Among the possibilities discussed was that of specifying a prescribed order of subdivisions following a main heading (i.e., geographical, chronological, and form subdivisions, in that order). The reader should be aware that changes to LCSH may soon be implemented.

NOTES

[1] *Canadian Subject Headings*, 2nd ed. (Ottawa, National Library of Canada, 1985).

[2] *Sears List of Subject Headings*, 14th ed., edited by Martha T. Mooney (New York, H. W. Wilson, 1991).

[3] Charles Ammi Cutter, *Rules for a Dictionary Catalog*, 4th ed., rewritten (Washington, D.C., GPO, 1904; republished, London, The Library Association, 1972). The original version of this work was: Charles A. Cutter, "Rules for a Printed Dictionary Catalogue," in *Public Libraries in the United States of America: Their History, Condition, and Management*, United States Bureau of Education (Washington, D.C., GPO, 1876), Part II.

[4] For fuller information on the origin and development of the *LC Subject List*, see: Lois Mai Chan, *Library of Congress Subject Headings: Principles and Application*, 2nd ed. (Littleton, Colo., Libraries Unlimited, 1985); and Richard S. Angell, "Library of Congress Subject Headings — Review and Forecast," in *Subject Retrieval in the Seventies: New Directions*, edited by Hans (Hanan) Wellisch and Thomas D. Wilson (Westport, Conn., Greenwood Publishing Co., 1972), pp. 143-163.

[5] J. C. M. Hanson, "The Subject Catalogs of the Library of Congress," *Bulletin of the American Library Association* 3 (September 1909): 385-397.

[6] Hanson, "Subject Catalogs," p. 387.

[7] Hanson, "Subject Catalogs," p. 389.

[8] Hanson, "Subject Catalogs," p. 390.

[9] David Judson Haykin, *Subject Headings: A Practical Guide* (Washington, D.C., GPO, 1951), p. 11.

[10] *Subject Headings Used in the Dictionary Catalogues of the Library of Congress*, [1st]-3rd eds. (Washington, D.C., Library of Congress, Catalog Division, 1910-1928); *Subject Headings Used in the Dictionary Catalogs of the Library of Congress*, 4th-7th eds. (Washington, D.C., Library of Congress, Subject Cataloging Division, 1943-1966); *Library of Congress Subject Headings*, 8th-12th eds. (Washington, D.C., Library of Congress, Subject Cataloging Division, 1975-1989); *Library of Congress Subject Headings*, 13th- eds. (Washington, D.C., Library of Congress, Office for Subject Cataloging Policy, 1990-).

[11] *Library of Congress Subject Headings Weekly Lists* (Washington, D.C., Library of Congress, Subject Cataloging Division, January 1984-).

[12] *Library of Congress Subject Headings in Microform* (Washington, D.C., Library of Congress, Subject Cataloging Division, current issue supersedes all previous issues).

[13] *CDMARC Subjects* (Washington, D.C., Library of Congress, Subject Cataloging Division, current issue supersedes all previous issues).

[14] *Subject Cataloging Manual: Subject Headings*, 4th ed. (Washington, D.C., Office of Subject Cataloging Policy, Library of Congress, 1991).

[15]*Cataloging Service Bulletin*, no. 1- (Washington, D.C., Library of Congress, Processing Services, 1978-).

[16]Cutter, *Rules*, 4th ed., pp. 71-72.

[17]Chan, *Library of Congress*, pp. 48-59.

[18]*Subject Cataloging Manual: Subject Headings*, H290; H690, p. 7.

[19]*Subject Cataloging Manual*, H310.

[20]The two new headings replacing the older compound heading are **"Buddhism"** and **"Gautama Buddha."**

[21]*Subject Cataloging Manual*, H360.

[22]*Subject Cataloging Manual*, H357.

[23]*Subject Cataloging Manual*, H320, H350, H351.

[24]Sanford Berman, *Prejudices and Antipathies: A Tract on the LC Subject Heads Concerning People* (Metuchen, N.J., Scarecrow, 1971).

[25]Hennepin County Library, Cataloging Section, *Cataloging Bulletin*, May 1973- .

[26]Doris H. Clack, *Black Literature Resources: Analysis and Organization* (New York, Marcel Dekker, 1975), p. 10.

[27]*Cataloging Service*, bulletin 119 (Fall 1976): 22, 24.

[28]Joan K. Marshall, comp., *On Equal Terms: A Thesaurus for Nonsexist Indexing and Cataloging* (Santa Barbara, Calif., American Bibliographical Center – Clio Press, 1977).

[29]*Subject Cataloging Manual*, H708.

[30]*Subject Cataloging Manual*, H362.

[31]*LCSH14,* pp. xvi-xvii.

[32]E. J. Coates, *Subject Catalogues: Headings and Structure* (London, Library Association, 1960).

[33]George M. Sinkankis, "A Study in the Syndetic Structure of the Library of Congress List of Subject Headings" (Pittsburgh, Pa., University of Pittsburgh, 1972).

[34]Toni Petersen, "The AAT: A Model for the Restructuring of LCSH," *Journal of Academic Librarianship* 9 (September 1983): 207-210.

[35]Mary Dykstra, "LC Subject Headings Disguised as a Thesaurus," *Library Journal* 113 (March 1, 1988): 42-46.

[36]*Subject Cataloging Manual*, H370.

[37]*LCSH14*, p. xi-xii.

[38]*Subject Cataloging Manual*, H830, H807.

[39]*Cataloging Service*, bulletin 120 (Winter 1977): 10.

[40]*Free-Floating Subdivisions: An Alphabetical Index* (Washington, D.C., Library of Congress, 1989).

[41]*Subject Cataloging Manual*, H832.

[42]*LCSH14*, p. xli.

SUGGESTED READING

Chan, Lois Mai. *Library of Congress Subject Headings: Principles and Application.* 2nd ed. Littleton, Colo., Libraries Unlimited, 1985.

Foskett, A. C. *The Subject Approach to Information.* 4th ed. London, Bingley, 1982. Chapter 22.

"Introduction," in *Library of Congress Subject Headings.* 13th- eds. Washington, D.C., Library of Congress, Office for Subject Cataloging Policy, 1990- .

Sears List of Subject Headings

23

INTRODUCTION

The *Sears List of Subject Headings*, now in its fourteenth edition, is widely used by small public libraries and by school libraries. It is very much smaller in scope and more general in treatment than *Library of Congress Subject Headings* (*LCSH*), which is commonly used in academic and research libraries. Its history of continuous publication is not so long-standing as that of the LC list. The current preface states:

> Minnie Earl Sears prepared the first edition of this work in response to demands for a list of subject headings that was more suitable to the needs of the small library than the A.L.A. and the Library of Congress lists. Published in 1923, the *List of Subject Headings for Small Libraries* was based on the headings used by nine small libraries that were known to be well cataloged. However, Minnie Sears early recognized the need for uniformity, and she followed the form of the Library of Congress subject headings with few exceptions. This decision was important and foresighted because it allowed a library to add Library of Congress headings as needed when not provided by the Sears List and to graduate to the full use of Library of Congress headings when collections grew too large for a limited subject headings list.[1]

The reliance of *Sears* editors and users on LCSH as a kind of sturdy big brother has never ceased. The following hypothetical situation should help make this clear. Suppose that a library using *Sears* acquires a book on the chemical effects of high energy radiation on matter. *Sears* offers the following headings:

Radiation, which seems too broad
Radiation — Physiological effect, which seems too narrow
Chemistry, Physical and theoretical, which seems much too broad
Radiochemistry, which seems to fit the book's contents most closely.

However, the cataloger checks the library holdings for which the term "**Radiochemistry**" has been used and finds that the new work has a distinctly different focus. By consulting LCSH he or she learns that the difference is important enough to merit another heading," "**Radiation chemistry**." A scope note carefully distinguishes it from "**Radiochemistry**," making its application to the book at hand clear. The local library can incorporate the borrowed term into its subject authority file, using the references suggested by LCSH to relate it to existing *Sears* terminology.

TERMINOLOGY

New headings for the fourteenth edition of *Sears* were suggested by librarians representing various sizes and types of libraries and by H. W. Wilson catalogers responsible for the Standard Catalog series and the *Book Review Digest*. Wilson also publishes a special interest companion volume for Canadian libraries and a Spanish language translation.[2] *Sears* headings are based on LCSH, but modifications for LC subject headings are made to meet the needs of smaller collections. Included among these are many terms from LC's "Subject Headings for Children's Literature." Terms considered by the editor to be sexist, racist, or pejorative have been changed or eliminated. Aside from its comparative brevity and simplicity, the following *Sears* differences from LCSH are worthy of note:

1. More current terminology and spelling. *Sears* uses **"Crisis centers"** and **"Litigation"**; LCSH uses **"Crisis intervention (Psychiatry)"** and **"Actions and defenses"** as primary headings.

2. Less emphasis on specificity. *Sears* uses **"Hallucinogens"** and **"Silk screen printing"**; LCSH uses only narrower terms: **"Hallucinogenic drugs," "Hallucinogenic plants," "Screen process printing,"** and **"Serigraphy."**

Elimination of Racist, Sexist, and Pejorative Headings

Sears has undergone the same attempts to eliminate racist, sexist, and pejorative headings that have been made with LCSH. For example, the heading **"Negro actors,"** was replaced by **"Black actors,"** while **"Air lines – Hostesses"** became **"Airlines – Flight attendants."**

Other headings with prejudicial connotations disappeared or underwent purification rites. The tenth edition's **"Jewish question"** disappeared along with **"Women in aeronautics"** and most other **"Women in ..."** and **"Women as ..."** headings. **"Underdeveloped areas"** was downgraded into a *see* reference to **"Developing areas"** in the eleventh edition, changed to a *see* reference to **"Third World"** in the twelfth edition, and then became a *see* reference to **"Developing countries"** in the thirteenth edition. **"Insanity"** was likewise converted into a *see* reference to **"Mental illness – Jurisprudence."** **"Man, Primitive"** became **"Nonliterate man."** (It is noted that **"Man"** is to be used only in its generic sense.)

Problems of Updating Terminology

Some linguistic change would have occurred, no doubt, regardless of the social climate. However, formal subject lists are notoriously conservative in their response to new terminology. In attempting to retain the goodwill of their constituents, they are understandably sensitive to the disruptions caused to a library's cataloging routines when an unduly large number of new subject forms are mandated at one time. Still, the argument that an obsolete form reflects usage in the bulk of the literature indexed is specious. Furthermore, it becomes misleading as new materials with new terminology are added. On the other hand, librarians with card catalogs fear not only the time and effort required to change large numbers of entries, but also the stresses placed on the filing apparatus when revised cards must be moved from one section of the catalog to another. As online catalogs become more numerous, this problem is easing.

Various proposals have been advanced for coping with large-scale subject heading revision. Taylor suggests three major options:[3]

1. For card catalogs, interfiling of "over-printed" cards (on which the subject term is printed above the main entry) or "highlighted" cards (on which one subject tracing is underlined for use as the filing element). Interfiling is seldom fully successful unless there is considerable erasing and retyping, although its purpose is to avoid just those problems. An analogous technique bypasses any marking of the subject entries themselves, preceding them instead with a "guide term" that, through typography or other marks of format and design, shows the full group of subject entries ranged behind or under it. The guide term principle works better in book, microform, and online catalogs than in the more traditional card catalog.

2. References connecting the old and revised heading forms. The *See also* references might well carry brief explanations, particularly showing the dates of publication, or of cataloging, covered by each form of the altered headings.

3. Changing old headings to the new forms. We have already suggested that the "interfiling" option for card catalogs usually requires some erasing and retyping of subject cards. The "full change" method extends such revisions to every entry affected by the new heading. Some libraries attempt to remove old markings and reword the entry. Others prepare complete new subject entries. Either mode involves labor that is both intensive and wasteful. As card catalogs have given way to online catalogs, quick, easy, and accurate subject heading change through computer commands has made this a much less serious problem.

SEARS'S USE OF
SUBJECT HEADING THEORY

The general philosophy of *Sears List of Subject Headings* is contained in two phrases, both of which the cataloger should remember as he or she makes specific application of the list to the individual materials in the library's collection.[4]

"The theory of specific entry" means that a specific heading is preferred to a general one. For a book about cats alone, **"Cats"** is preferred to **"Domestic animals."** On the other hand, the headings **"Siamese cats"** or **"Seal-point Siamese cats"** would likely be too specific for most libraries, except possibly a veterinary library. The cataloger must know the collection, know its emphases, and know something of the way people use it to be prepared to assign subject headings to it.

"The theory of unique heading" means that one subject heading, and one alone, is chosen for all items on that subject. The choice of subject headings must be logical and consistent. References should be inserted in the catalog wherever it is anticipated that patrons are likely to approach the topic through different terminology. A few general principles or guidelines are useful for constructing subject headings:

1. Prefer the English word or phrase unless a foreign one best expresses the idea. *Sears*, for example, carries the reference "Laissez faire. *See* **Industry—Government policy.**"

2. Try to use terms that are used in other libraries as well, unless the library in question is highly specialized or otherwise unique.

3. Try to use terms that will cover the field, i.e., terms that will apply to more than one item.

4. Try to use no more than three subject headings per cataloged item. This rule is not tyrannical; some items may require more than three.

References

Sears breaks down references into three main categories, and the introduction discusses each in some detail: specific *See* references; specific *See also* references; and general references.[5]

See references are considered essential to the success of the catalog. Yet the cataloger in a local library may not find necessary every *See* reference suggested in the list. For example, *Sears* proposes "Copybooks *See* **Handwriting.**" But if the library's holdings on handwriting contain nothing about copybooks, then it is potentially misleading to put such a reference into the catalog. The most frequent and helpful varieties of *See* references direct the user from:

1. Synonyms or terms so nearly synonymous that they would cover the same kind of material, e.g., "Chemical geology *See* **Geochemistry**" and "Pay equity *See* **Equal pay for equal work.**"

2. The second part of a compound heading, e.g., "Illusions *See* **Hallucinations and illusions**" and "Motels *See* **Hotels, motels, etc.**"

3. The second part of an inverted heading, e.g., "American music *See* **Music, American.**"

4. Some inverted forms to the heading in normal order, e.g., "Libraries, Music *See* **Music libraries.**"

5. Variant spellings or initialisms to the accepted spelling or full form, e.g., "Gipsies *See* **Gypsies**" and "H.B.O. *See* **Home box office.**"

6. Opposites when they are included without being specifically mentioned, e.g., "Disobedience *See* **Obedience**" and "Truth in advertising *See* **Deceptive advertising.**"

7. The singular to the plural when the two forms would not file together, e.g., "Goose *See* **Geese.**"

See also references pose theoretical and practical problems that jeopardize their efficacy. Yet both *Sears* and LCSH make heavy use of them. The above warning against making references simply because they are suggested in a standard list holds as true for *See also* references as it does for *See* references.

It was stated in chapters 21 and 22 that *See also* references normally move downward from a general term to a more specific term or terms, e.g., "**Conservation of natural resources** *See also* **Energy conservation; Nature conservation.**" In this example the general term refers to two more specific terms. The user who pursues the reference by looking under "**Nature conservation**" will find a still more specific downward reference to more headings: "**Nature conservation** *See also* **Endangered species; Landscape protection; Natural monuments; Plant conservation; Wildlife conservation.**"

Sears also indulges in a high number of bilateral or reciprocal references, where the movement is horizontal, between related subjects of more or less equal specificity. The following examples have been pruned of extraneous terms, to make their reciprocity more visible:

Gods and goddesses *See also* **Mythology; Religions**
Mythgology *See also* **Gods and goddesses**
Religions *See also* **Gods and goddesses**

Mollusks *See also* **Shells**
Shells *See also* **Mollusks**

In the case of general *See* and *See also* references, the more specific terms being referred to are so diverse or numerous that the standard list cites only one or two noteworthy illustrations, adding an "etc." to launch the cataloger on his or her own list of additional headings of similar format as needed to describe the local library collection. The problem raised by these general or "blanket" references is one of control. When *Sears* uses "**Forage plants** *See also* **Grasses** ... also names of specific forage plants, e.g. **Corn; Hay; Soybean;** etc." but the only book in the library on a specific forage crop is on clover, it seems fairly obvious that the cataloger should change the illustration to read "**Forage plants** *See also* **Grasses** ... also names of specific forage plants, e.g. **Clover.**" Or perhaps the format could be simply "**Forage plants** *See also* **Grasses; Clover.**"

If, on the other hand, there are books on several specific topics, not all of which serve as examples in the reference, should the cataloger add each new term at the time it first becomes a subject heading? That is, when the list gives "**Illustrations** *See* subjects with the subdivision *Pictorial Works*; e.g. **Animals—Pictorial works; United States—History—1861-1865, Civil War—Pictorial works;** etc." and the library that has subject entries for both referrals adds a book consisting largely of pictures of children, should the cataloger revise the reference entry by inserting **"Children — Pictorial works"** as a third illustration? Or can he or she depend on the "etc." to cover all subsequent examples? Most libraries follow the second option, thus throwing the burden of search on the user, who probably either will not understand the instructions or, after a bit of desultory searching, will give up. However well the user copes, valuable materials may be overlooked.[6]

Sears enumerates seven major types of general references:

1. Common names of different species of a class, e.g., **"Dogs** *See also* classes of dogs, e.g. **Guide dogs; Hearing ear dogs;** etc.; also names of specific breeds, e.g. **Collies;** etc."

2. Names of individual persons, e.g., **"Presidents — United States** *See also* names of presidents, e.g. **Lincoln, Abraham, 1809-1865;** etc."

3. Names of particular institutions, buildings, societies, etc., e.g., **"Bridges** *See also* names of bridges, e.g. **Golden Gate Bridge (San Francisco, Calif.);** etc."

4. Names of particular geographic features, e.g., **"Natural Monuments** *See also* **Wilderness areas;** also names of natural monuments, e.g. **Natural Bridge (Va.);** etc."

5. Names of places subdivided by subject, e.g., **"Defenses, National** *See* **Industrial mobilization;** and names of countries with the subdivision *Defenses*, e.g. **United States — Defenses;** etc."

6. Form divisions, e.g., **"Case studies** *See* subjects with the subdivision *Case studies*, e.g. **Juvenile delinquency — Case studies;** etc."

7. National literatures, e.g., **"Essays** ... Collections of literary essays by American authors are entered under **American essays;** by English authors, under **English essays;** etc."

STRUCTURE OF SUBJECT HEADINGS

Like LC subject headings, *Sears* terms consist of a variety of forms, ranging from a single noun to different kinds of complex descriptive phrases:[7]

1. The single noun is the most desirable form of subject heading if it is specific enough to fit the item at hand and the needs of the library. In general, if there is a significant difference between the singular and plural forms, the plural is preferred (e.g., **"Mouse** *See* **Mice"**). However, there are situations where the singular form is used to cover abstract ideas or general usage (e.g., **"Sonata"** as a musical form), while the plural designates individual examples of the form, frequently collected into anthologies or the like.

2. The modified noun takes at least three forms: a) normal word order (e.g., **"Health maintenance organizations"**), b) inverted word order (e.g., **"Artificial satellites, Soviet"**), and c) explanatory modifier added in parentheses (e.g., **"Hotlines (Telephone counseling)"**). There is usually no reliable way of predicting which form of modification will be used.

3. The compound heading is usually two nouns joined by *and*, but the nouns are sometimes also modified (e.g., **"Coal mines and mining"**). The terms are conjoined for various reasons:

   a) To link related topics. Usually both ideas are covered in a single treatise, e.g., **"Anarchism and anarchists," "Bicycles and bicycling," "Clocks and watches,"** and **"Puppets and puppet plays."**

   b) To link opposites. Again, the pairs are often discussed together, e.g., **"Corrosion and anticorrosives," "Good and evil,"** and **"Joy and sorrow."**

   c) To dispel ambiguity when the primary term is susceptible to more than one interpretation, e.g., **"Files and filing."** The second term is added to distinguish storage files from the tools used by carpenters and mechanics. LCSH, as might be expected, is even more precise with these homonyms. It uses two subject headings: **"Filing systems"** and **"Files and rasps."**

In most cases, usage dictates the order of terms, but when that fails, alphabetical order is preferred. If a library should acquire enough materials under one of two such terms (e.g., **"Fraternities and sororities"**) to make searching difficult or tiresome, the cataloger might consider splitting the subject heading into its two components, with linking references. For example, LCSH has broken its former heading **"Antigens and antibodies"** into **"Antigens"** and **"Immunoglobulins."**

Recently there has been concern about the fact that the use of *and* in compound headings can cause searching difficulties in systems that use *and* as a combining term in the searching process. In the fourteenth edition of *Sears* a number of compound headings were reworded, where possible, to eliminate the word *and*, e.g., **"Steel industry and trade"** was changed to **"Steel industry"**; **"Information storage and retrieval systems"** was changed to **"Information systems."**

4. The phrase heading may be prepositional (e.g., **"Cost of living"**), serial (e.g., **"Plots (Drama, fiction, etc.)"**), or an intriguing combination of forms (e.g., **"Oil pollution of rivers, harbors, etc."** or **"Life support systems (Medical environment)"**).

TYPES OF SUBDIVISIONS

Subject subdivisions indicate a specialized aspect of a broad subject or point of view, e.g., "**Artificial satellites—Orbits.**" They are set off from the primary heading by a dash and are presumably distinguishable from inverted modifiers, which restrict or narrow the topic, e.g., "**Artificial satellites, American.**" Yet *Sears* no longer separates the two categories, but interfiles all entries in straight alphabetical order, letter by letter to the end of each word, disregarding punctuation.[8]

A primary purpose of the subject subdivision is to subdivide topics that are broad in scope or that have much written about them (e.g., "**Education**"). Without subdivision, there would be many entries under such headings sub-arranged only by main entry or by date. Such headings with large numbers of entries can be tedious for a catalog user to search. Subdivision allows grouping of the entries in meaningful ways, e.g.,

Education—Aims and objectives
Education—Curricula
Education—Experimental methods

Subdivisions may be compounded under a given topic. As many as three are used for such a subtopic as "**United States—History—1861-1865, Civil War—Medical care.**" In it are displayed several of the different types of subdivisions:

1. Form divisions are used, like the Dewey Decimal Classification form divisions, to indicate the physical (e.g., "... **—Bibliography**") or philosophical (e.g., "... **—Research**") form of the work and may be used by the cataloger to divide practically any subject heading in the list. In addition there are many general and topical subdivisions that may be used under subjects as appropriate. As in LCSH, these form, general, and topical subdivisions are known as "free-floating subdivisions" and are found in a "List of Commonly Used Subdivisions" that precedes the alphabetical list of subject headings.

2. *Sears*, like LCSH, has a group of headings that serve as patterns for the subdivisions that may be used under all headings of the same type. In *Sears* they are called "Key Headings":

Persons:

Presidents—United States	(to illustrate subdivisions that may be used under presidents, prime ministers, and other rulers)
Shakespeare, William, 1564-1616	(to illustrate subdivisions that may be used under any voluminous author)

Peoples:

Indians of North America	(to illustrate subdivisions that may be used under names of peoples and linguistic families)

Places:

United States	(to illustrate subdivisions—except for his-
Ohio	torical periods—under geographic names)
Chicago (Ill.)	

Languages and Literatures:

English language	(to illustrate subdivisions that may be used
English literature	with any language or literature)

Wars:

World War, 1939-1945	(to illustrate subdivisions that may be used
	under any war or battle)

In order to use the subdivisions under the key headings, one finds the appropriate example (e.g., **"English language—Idioms"**) and then applies the subdivision to the heading for the item in hand (e.g., **"French language—Idioms"**).

3. Some special topic divisions cannot readily be transferred from one heading to another because they are specially tailored to bring out important aspects of individual topics, e.g., **"Deaf—Means of communication"** or **"Airplanes—Piloting."** One could not reasonably use **"Deaf—Piloting"** or **"Airplanes—Means of communication."** Such divisions are listed in full in the body of the list, being for the most part nontransferable.

4. Time divisions, which apply most frequently to history, define a specific chronology for the primary topic. Some consist merely of dates (e.g., **"Europe—History—1789-1900"**). Often the date or dates are followed by a descriptive phrase (e.g., **"Church history—30(ca.)-600, Early church"**). Prior to the twelfth edition the descriptive phrase preceded the dates in such headings. The change in position was made to facilitate filing in chronological order both manually and by machine. Occasionally the chronological designation is an inverted qualifier rather than a subdivision. It may be used without dates (e.g., **"Civilization, Ancient"**), but more often dates are added (e.g., **"Gettysburg (Pa.), Battle of, 1863"**).

5. Geographic divisions are of two forms: a) area—subject, e.g., **"Chicago (Ill.)—Foreign population,"** and b) subject—area, e.g., **"Geology—Bolivia."** *Sears* adds parenthetical instructions to those headings in its list that may be divided by place, e.g., **"Geology (May subdiv. geog.)."** Under some headings the instructions are more detailed, e.g., **"Hostages, American (May subdiv. geog. except U.S.)."** Or the place term might be an inverted modifier, e.g., **"Ethics (May subdiv. geog. adjective form, e.g. Ethics, American; etc.)."**

Unlike LCSH, *Sears* does not dictate the form of geographic subdivisions. The introduction to the fourteenth edition specifies that *Sears* prefers direct place subdivision (in which the name of the place discussed in the work is used directly as the subdivision) over indirect place subdivision (in which the name of a larger geographic area is interposed between the subject and a smaller area discussed in the work). *Sears* uses the *AACR2* form of a place name in using direct subdivision (i.e., "—Chicago (Ill.)," not just "—Chicago"), but it does not mandate this usage for the libraries using its list. Some libraries may wish to follow LCSH practice and use indirect place subdivision. If direct place subdivision is chosen, it is wise to use *AACR2* form for the sake of consistency.

Area—subject situations are less conspicuous in the list, but play an important role in most library catalogs. Instructions may take the form: **"Italy** ... May be subdivided like U.S. except for *History*."** A similar example is: "**Neutrality** *See also* names of countries with the subdivision *Neutrality*, e.g., **United States—Neutrality;** etc."

Subject headings in various fields, especially in the fields of science, technology, and economics, usually are subdivided by place. Those in history, geography, and politics usually are made subdivisions under place.[9] It is assumed that the real subject of a book about Colorado history, and the one the patron will most likely consult, is **"Colorado,"** not **"History."** In *Sears*, the subject entry **"History"** is used only for general works on history as an intellectual discipline.

HEADINGS FOR BELLES-LETTRES

Individual works of belles-lettres (e.g., novels, plays, and poetry) are not always assigned subject headings. It is assumed that patrons are more likely to seek access to these materials through author or title. However, there are many themes of literature that may be used as subject headings. In the list of form subdivisions supplied by *Sears* "... —Fiction" appears as a suggested option for libraries that prefer to make subject headings for fictionalized history or biography. Thus, a novel about the Six Day War in the Middle East might be given the subject heading, **"Israel-Arab War, 1967—Fiction."** Other common headings include **"Mystery and detective stories"** (which can be assigned to any book of this genre) or **"Science fiction"** (a heading popular with patrons who want to read every such book in a collection but which the *Sears* scope note actually limits to materials about the genre or to collections of such stories).

Literary anthologies are also likely to receive subject headings. It is common to list a genre with the subdivision "—Collections" (e.g., "Poetry—Collections"; "American drama—Collections") but *Sears* sometimes uses the plural noun (e.g., **"Essays"**) rather than using the subdivision.[10] Topical headings reflecting themes of the work as a whole are also common (e.g., **"Love poetry"; "Dogs—Fiction"**).

PHYSICAL CHARACTERISTICS AND
FORMAT OF *SEARS*

The fourteenth edition of *Sears* opens with a preface that gives its historical setting and identifies the authoritative sources and the new features incorporated in it. It is followed by an explanatory essay that has become a *Sears* tradition, undergoing considerable expansion in scope and detail over the years. This essay is called "Principles of the Sears List of Subject Headings."[11] It treats both the theoretical and practical aspects of subject heading work. It merits careful reading, not only by those planning to use the *Sears* list, but also by anyone wishing to gain knowledge of traditional subject list usage.

In the list proper, the right half of each page is blank. All entries, references, and instructions are confined to the left columns, to leave space for the local cataloger to add any new headings, references, or comments needed to convert the volume into an authority file. Subject entries are printed in boldface type. *See* references appear in lightface type in the same alphabet. Filing in *Sears* has already been discussed under "Types of Subdivisions." The following excerpt shows the various elements that may be included under a subject entry, although not every entry requires all of these elements:

> **Children's poetry 808.81; 809.1; 811, etc.;**
> **811.008, etc.; 811.009, etc.**
> Use for collections of poetry for children by one
> or more authors and for materials about
> children's poetry. For poetry written by chil-
> dren use **Children's writings**. Materials
> about poetry written by children are entered
> under **Child authors**.
> *See also* **Children's songs; Lullabies; Nonsense**
> **verses; Nursery rhymes; Tongue twisters**
> *x* Poetry for children
> *xx* **Children's literature; Poetry;**
> **Poetry — Collections**

Dewey Decimal Classification numbers from the twelfth abridged edition of DDC are given with the permission of the publisher, Forest Press, a division of OCLC Online Computer Library Center. The above example shows the associated DDC numbers in their customary place, on the same line with the subject entry. Note that three numbers are specifically included, together with an "etc.," to remind the user that he or she might profitably seek further in the Dewey Decimal Classification to find the best number for the particular need.

Scope notes have been used more extensively in each new edition of *Sears*. The one in the example above is typical. The reader receives first a positive instruction on appropriate use of the entry. Then comes a negative instruction (albeit stated positively) on the kinds of material that should be placed under a different entry.

The words *See also* in italics normally follow the scope note or, if there is no scope note, the entry proper. They precede a list in boldface type of closely related and/or more specific headings that the user might like to explore. Each boldface entry in this list is a legitimate subject heading. Reference to these *See also* headings might very well lead to further *See also* headings that could help expand or modify the search to reveal the full range of materials available in the particular collection. But a *See also* reference is not usually made unless the catalog actually has material under the heading referred to (see discussion of this issue in chapter 22).

The letter x before one or more terms means that a *See* reference is recommended from each such term to the heading under which the x appears. Terms preceded by an x are never used as subject headings. The letters xx before one or more terms mean that a *See also* reference should be made from each such term used in the catalog to the heading under which the xx appears. Thus, *Sears* suggests the following references for the subject entry **"Children's poetry,"** but the local cataloger is expected to consider each on its merits, in view of the terminology used by the library's clientele and the presence of other subject entries in the catalog:

Children's poetry *See also* **Children's songs**
                                 Lullabies
                                 Nonsense verses
                                 Nursery rhymes
                                 Tongue twisters

Poetry for children *See* **Children's poetry**

Children's literature *See also* **Children's poetry**

Poetry *See also* **Children's poetry**

Poetry—Collections *See also* **Children's poetry collections**

The x and xx are tracings of a sort, to help the cataloger fit the most appropriate specific subject entries to each individual item in the collection and keep track of their interrelationships. The *"x* Poetry for children" under **"Children's poetry"** is there as a reminder that a user might very well go first to the P's, looking under "Poetry for children." If so, a simple reference could save both time and frustration. **"Poetry—Collections"** is one of three headings in boldface following the *xx*. It might be a subject entry in the catalog, but according to the theory of specific entry it is too broad for a work confined to children's poetry. However, the *"xx* **Poetry—Collections"** serves the dual purpose 1) of reminding the cataloger to make a **"Poetry—Collections** *See also* **Children's poetry"** reference and 2) of helping anyone who has access to the printed list to work back to the broader heading, where some entries may lead to poetry anthologies that actually contain some poetry for children. In most libraries the *see also* reference will be filed after all the subject entries bearing the heading **"Poetry—Collections."**

Sears supplies two pages of instructions for checking and adding headings.[12] Here the technique of checking all terms in the list that have been transferred to the local catalog, and the uses of the blank right-hand columns to record the headings and references added by the local cataloger, are fully explained. Many smaller libraries find this type of subject authority file the simplest and quickest to prepare. There is one serious drawback, however. When a new edition of *Sears* appears, all checks and entries must be laboriously recopied, or the library's subject control will suffer. If the older edition is retained for its authority records, all new headings and changes must be entered, making it increasingly messy and difficult to read. If the new edition is adopted without reviewing and checking former practices, inconsistencies will soon weaken the power of the subject access structure. That is why many *Sears* users prefer to use the public catalog as the authority list.[13]

Sears includes a list of "Headings to Be Added by the Cataloger."[13] Eight varieties of proper names and five each of corporate names and common names, are identified, for which there is no attempt to include all possibilities in the printed list. One or two obvious names of each variety can be found in the list proper, to serve as examples or because important or typical subdivisions have been given. The cataloger is also reminded that general *See also* references imply other specific names that the cataloger is to add as needed, using available reference sources to establish correct entry forms.

UPDATING

Sears updates its usage by successive editions. The current intention is to produce new print editions every three years. Machine-readable versions are also available on tape and CD-ROM, and these are intended to be updated annually. The relatively limited scope of *Sears*, for use in small and medium-size libraries, makes comprehensive revision manageable for both editors and users. The results are more coherently integrated than the ad hoc revisions issued for LCSH. However, some may believe that one to three years is too long to wait for updated terminology in today's rapidly changing environment. The Library of Congress's publication of the "Weekly Lists" and weekly updating of the online LCSH permit (if they do not always ensure) easy professional response on the part of one enormous library to inevitable, but generally unpredictable, shifts in publishing interests and emphases. Actually neither approach monopolizes all the advantages. What matters is that every viable subject access mode remain under constant surveillance and revision, offering a dynamic compromise between rigid custom and assimilative change.

CONCLUSION

The assigning of subject headings is a discipline that inevitably seems complicated and bewildering to the neophyte cataloger. Unlike other cataloging disciplines, it has no logical progression other than the linguistic development of knowledge itself. Even the assigning of a classification number to a book is less forbidding, for the novice usually has some sort of previous orientation to the Dewey system and can see, if dimly, the divisions of knowledge and why they should exist. Subject headings are, however, not difficult once the cataloger learns to handle them. Both *Sears* and LCSH are quite explicit in their directions; both contain lists of general subdivisions with specific instructions for their use. If followed consistently, they will provide useful reference guides for the user, including the reference librarian.

A beginning cataloger should study the subject list used in the local library. It would be helpful to choose a subject in which he or she is personally interested, tracing it throughout the list and observing the interrelation of *see also, x,* and *xx* references. There are other aids, such as the reference tools in the library. They amplify subjects and clarify aspects not immediately understood, especially in an age when no one can expect to know everything. The library's shelflist and public catalog are also helpful. The former can suggest subject headings if the cataloger has a classification number in mind, since most shelflists consist of full unit records, with tracings for the subject entries of each cataloged item. The public catalog can suggest classification numbers if the would-be cataloger has a subject heading in mind. Neither is a completely reliable crutch. Books are very often written about new subjects and about more than one subject. The vagaries of past and present individual catalogers, however experienced, may mislead. Yet both resources are generally helpful; both serve to characterize the practices of the local library. To become a successful cataloger, one must know what is current local practice and work within that frame of reference. Major changes should not be put into effect until the reasons for what is done are fully understood and the reactions of other users and fellow librarians can be anticipated.

NOTES

[1] *Sears List of Subject Headings*, 14th ed., edited by Martha T. Mooney (New York, H. W. Wilson, 1991), p. vii.

[2] Ken Haycock and Lynne Lighthall, comps., *Sears List of Subject Headings: Canadian Companion*, 3rd ed., revised by Lynne Lighthall (New York, H. W. Wilson, 1987); *Sears—Lista de Encabezamientos de Materia: Traducción y Adaptación de la 12a. Edición en Inglés*, ed. por Barbara M. Westby; trans. por Carmen Rovira (New York, H. W. Wilson, 1984).

[3] Arlene G. Taylor, *Cataloging with Copy: A Decision-Maker's Handbook* (Englewood, Colo., Libraries Unlimited, 1988), pp. 139-151.

[4] For more detailed discussion of the theory of subject headings, refer to chapter 21, "Verbal Subject Analysis." See also *Sears*, pp. 2-4.

[5] The list of reference types is adapted from *Sears*, p. 15, but the examples are changed, to give alternative insights.

[6] *Sears*, pp. 16-17, also discusses this problem.

[7] For a review of the structure of LC headings and further comment on some of the points mentioned here, see "Types of Topical Subject Headings" in chapter 22 and "The Choice of Subject Headings" in chapter 21.

[8] See pp. 431-433 of this text to compare the filing used in the printed versions of LCSH with that found in *Sears*. Chapter 28 presents still other filing options.

[9] *Sears*, p. 9.

[10] *Sears*, p. 13.

[11] Much of the foregoing discussion is based on this essay.

[12] *Sears*, pp. 24-25.

[13] *Sears*, p. 26.

SUGGESTED READING

Foskett, A. C. *The Subject Approach to Information*. 4th ed. London, Bingley, 1982. Chapter 23.

"Principles of the Sears List of Subject Headings," in *Sears List of Subject Headings*. 14th ed. Edited by Martha T. Mooney. New York, H. W. Wilson, 1991. pp. 1-23.

Other Types of Verbal Analysis

24

INTRODUCTION

For well over a century libraries have provided subject retrieval from their holdings through the use of pre-coordinate lists of integrated and cross-referenced topical headings. The preceding chapters have discussed *Sears* and LCSH, which remain the most universally recognized linguistic tools for analyzing library collections. But recent developments in information science offer new modes of indexing that throw both practical and theoretical light on traditional subject lists. Some of the techniques are offered as supplements, or even substitutes, for traditional subject catalogs. This chapter reviews those enterprises most pertinent to library subject retrieval and explains briefly the applications of the more successful ones.

DEVELOPMENTS IN DOCUMENT INDEXING

The word *index* still connotes book and periodical indexes more often than it does subject catalogs for library collections. However, library indexes and catalogs are nearly as old as alphabets, being present in some form with almost every organized collection of written records as far back as the early Mesopotamian and Egyptian archives. In the final years of the nineteenth and the early years of the twentieth centuries, catalogers frequently made numerous "analytics" to significant informational works in their libraries. Books were expensive. The high cost of acquisitions and the relative scarcity of printed materials were countered with efforts to exploit collections intensively. Librarians were a captive labor force, often with "disposable time" on the job. And what more profitable "pickup work" could there be than making analytic indexes to anthologies and treatises? If the cards followed standard cataloging practices they were filed into the official catalog. If they were less carefully constructed, they might be kept in a desk drawer or a shoe box in the reference department. John Rothman points to a continuing reciprocity between library classification and indexing:

> Although indexing is often clearly differentiated from cataloging and classification, there is considerable overlapping in practice, and the development of new cataloging techniques or new classification systems is bound to affect indexing practices. Thus the development of the Dewey and other decimal classification systems for library catalogs was paralleled by the development of decimal, coded, and faceted topical indexing systems.[1]

452

Coordinate Indexing

The post-World War II information explosion dramatized the values of good indexing. Older methods that had gone into eclipse were revived and improved. New theories sprang up to support other techniques. A major departure from the relatively simple hierarchical use of subordinate divisions and inverted modifiers in traditional subject heading lists was the idea of post-coordinate searching, in which the searcher could play a more active role. A coordinate index consists of a list of subject terms in a standard format. Each term is independent of all others, except for references, and is designed to retrieve all documents for which it is specifically relevant. A user can stop at the single-term level of search if he or she is satisfied with the results. However, true coordinate searching moves on to a second level. Taking two or more terms that together delimit a still more specific search topic, and comparing the records indexed under each, the searcher retrieves only those items that have been indexed under all the chosen terms.

Suppose the searcher is looking for material on the use of solar energy for drying grain. The index might offer the terms "Solar energy," "Heat engines," and "Grain." Perhaps five document citations emerge because they are all entered under all three terms. The searcher makes the matches and consults those documents. In a traditional printed subject catalog this type of post-coordinate searching is awkward and difficult. The underlying assumption is that the list itself is pre-coordinate. That is, the assimilation and matching of concepts has already been done by the cataloger and is implicit in the terminology of the list. Thus, LCSH offers the subject headings **"Solar energy in agriculture"** and **"Grain—Drying"** as subject identifiers for the above items. In a printed catalog there would be no way of matching the two concepts to specify the available items except by comparing subject entries under each heading or examining full bibliographic records to find those on which both headings were traced.

In post-coordinate indexing, the coordination of terms is the responsibility of the searcher, rather than of the subject cataloger. The terms are usually single nouns, and the specific document citations frequently take the form of accession numbers (rarely hierarchical class or call numbers). In 1953 Mortimer Taube introduced what he called the Uniterm index, to emphasize its post-coordinate use of single terms as opposed to composite headings.[2] It was primarily a manual system, using cards with headings displayed at the top and ten columns in which document accession numbers could be entered according to the number's final digit. For example, documents 56A, 306, 96, 1176, and 1006 might all be listed in column 6 of each of the three cards bearing the Uniterms "Solar energy," "Heat engines," and "Grain." The technique, known as terminal digit posting, has been most successful in its computerized applications, where some of the tediousness and error-proneness of manual listing is forestalled.

To overcome the disadvantages of a visual search, other modes of post-coordinate indexing soon developed. Mechanical scanning devices were based on the fact that cards could be precisely gridded for punched holes to replace the columns of written or printed numbers. Two or more of these punched cards (e.g., the three carrying the headings "Solar energy," "Heat engines," and "Grain") could be laid together and held up to the light, or otherwise probed, to extract the reference numbers that they indexed in common. Various brands of these cards have been marketed. Foskett prefers to call them all optical coincidence cards, but he recognizes other popular names such as "peek-a-boo," "peephole," and "feature" cards.[3]

The newest form of coordinate indexing is that created by keyword access in online catalogs. This has been described by Bates (italics original):

> [I]n fact, *online search capabilities themselves constitute a form of indexing.* Subject access to online catalogs is thus a combination of original indexing and what we might call "search capabilities indexing." ...
>
> Typical online search capabilities are keyword searching, Boolean searching, truncation, and multi-index searching (that is, combining query terms from more than one index, e.g., "FIND TITLE Grapes AND FIND AUTHOR Steinbeck").
>
> ... When an online catalog simply possesses the capability of being searched by title keyword, in effect a whole new index is added to the catalog, with every title word an index term, even though the whole index is not seen printed out.[4]

Typically, online catalogs with keyword access allow the user to input several search terms to be searched at once with an implicit Boolean "and" in operation. That is, a search may be made to "FIND KEYWORDS solar energy grain," which the system interprets to mean "Find bibliographic records that have the words 'solar' AND 'energy' AND 'grain'." While this method can yield false drops (e.g., "Electrical energy characterization of grain boundaries in gallium arsenide and their relationship to solar cell performance"), it can also yield a number of useful retrievals in much less time than that needed for manual indexing. It cannot be a complete substitute for manual indexing, however, because keyword vocabulary is not controlled (i.e., no connections are made between synonyms, variant word forms, related terms, etc.), and not all titles contain subject-content words.

Hierarchic or Subordination Indexing

The subsuming of narrower terms or subdivisions under broader terms is familiar to librarians in many contexts. We spoke in previous chapters of its use for library subject catalogs. Book indexes frequently indent secondary words under primary ones and make use of *see* and *see also* references. *The New York Times Index* and most of the H. W. Wilson indexes, such as *Readers' Guide to Periodical Literature*, do the same. The rapid growth of online databases that analyze periodical articles, books, report literature, patents, and the like for rapid retrieval in nearly all disciplines has led to the publication of search-oriented thesauri to aid users with their search strategies.

The terms *thesaurus* and *subject heading list* are often used interchangeably in the literature, but they are not really the same. Since 1974 there have been international standard guidelines for thesauri.[5] There are no such standards for subject heading lists. Another difference is that thesauri are composed of "terms," while subject heading lists are composed of "subject headings." This difference has been described by Dykstra.[6] She says that in general a term denotes a single concept, while a subject heading may consist of composites of terms, although a subject heading may also consist of a single concept. Yet another difference lies in the way terms and subjects are related to each other (i.e., the syndetic structure). The guidelines for thesauri give rules for establishing hierarchical relationships and for assigning related (or associative) terms. While LCSH now also has rules that are used when establishing new headings, composite headings are more difficult to relate than terms, and there remain many headings and relationships that were established before the rules were made. Dykstra argues that by adopting the abbreviations used by thesauri to show these relationships, LCSH has exacerbated the confusion that already exists.[7] A final difference is that a thesaurus is likely to cover a limited discipline or cross-disciplinary area, whereas subject heading lists tend to be designed for unrestricted subject application.

Thesauri usually have introductory material that explains how to use them. One very simple example of a search strategy manual is the *Thesaurus of Psychological Index Terms*.[8] Its users' guide explains:

> Each *Thesaurus* term is listed alphabetically and, as appropriate, is cross-referenced and displayed with its broader, narrower, and related terms (i.e., subterms). In many cases, a scope note (**SN**) provides a definition and/or information on proper use of the term. The date of the term's inclusion in the *Thesaurus* appears as a superscript....

Term Relationships

The terms in the Relationship Section are displayed to reflect the following relationships:

> **Use.** Directs the user from a term that cannot be used (nonpostable) to a postable term that can be used in indexing or searching. The **use** reference indicates preferred forms of synonyms, abbreviations, spelling, and word sequence:
>
> Language Handicaps
>   **Use**   Language Disorders
>
> **UF (used for).** Reciprocal of the **Use** reference. Terms listed as **UF** (used for) references represent some but not all of the most frequently encountered synonyms, abbreviations, alternate spellings, or word sequences:
>
> **Language Disorders**[82]
>   **UF**   Language Handicaps
>
> **B (broader term)** and **N (narrower term).** Reciprocal designators used to indicate hierarchical relationships:
>
> **Achievement**[67]
>   **N**   Academic Achievement[67]
>
> **R (related term).** Reciprocal designators used to indicate relationships that are semantic or conceptual but not hierarchical.

Related-term references indicate to searchers or indexers terms that they may not have considered but that may have a bearing on their interest:

Achievement Motivation[67]
   R   Fear of Success[78]

Array Terms

Index terms that represent conceptually broad areas are designated array terms and are identified by a slash (/) following the term. These terms are used in indexing and searching when a more specific term is not available. Array terms are displayed in the *Thesaurus* with only selected related terms:

Communication/[67]
   R   Animal Communication[67]
           Censorship[78]
           Communication Skills[73]

It can be seen that such designations of terms and term relationships influenced the usages now found in LCSH.

The *Thesaurus of ERIC Descriptors* uses the abbreviations for the relationships that were adopted by LCSH: UF—*Used for*; NT—*Narrower term*; BT—*Broader term*; RT—*Related term*.[9] "Use" is the mandatory reciprocal of UF, putting what the *ERIC Thesaurus* calls a "non-postable" term into place. Unlike LCSH, however, SN precedes a scope note. Under postable terms other kinds of information are also given. The date is the "add" (first entry) date. Search strategies for materials entered into the database prior to that time should in most instances use different terminology. Posting counts (the number of citations available when the *ERIC Thesaurus* was published) are given for both the *Current Index to Journals in Education* (*CIJE*) and *Resources in Education* (*RIE*). A Group Code (GC) number is given to assist the user in identifying other Descriptors that are conceptually related to the term. Examples of *ERIC Thesaurus* entries are:

Dress Design
   Use   CLOTHING DESIGN

Drill Presses
   Use   MACHINE TOOLS

DRINKING   May 1974
    CIJE: 548   RIE: 480   GC: 210
- SN   Consumption of alcoholic beverages
- UF   Alcohol Consumption
       Alcohol Use
       Social Drinking
- NT   Alcohol Abuse
- BT   Behavior
- RT   Alcohol Education
       Alcoholic Beverages
       Drug Use
       Health Education
       Recreational Activities

A final, more complex example comes from the *INSPEC Thesaurus* of the Institution of Electrical Engineers (INSPEC stands for Information Services for the Physics and Engineering Communities).[10] It uses the following abbreviations:

UF: *Used for*	indicates a 'lead-in' term from which reference is made
NT: *Narrower Term(s)*	indicates one or more specific terms, one level lower in the hierarchy
BT: *Broader Term(s)*	indicates one or more general terms, one level higher in the hierarchy
TT: *Top Term(s)*	indicates the most general term(s) in the hierarchy
RT: *Related Term(s)*	indicates conceptual relationships between terms, not related hierarchically
CC: *Classification Code(s)*	one or more INSPEC classification codes used to indicate subjects related to that represented by the Thesaurus term
DI: *Date of Input*	indicates the date the term was first used in the Thesaurus
PT: *Prior Term(s)*	indicates terms used for the concept before establishment of the current preferred term.

Examples of *INSPEC Thesaurus* listings are:

dynamic braking
   USE   braking

dynamic nuclear polarisation
   UF   dynamic nuclear polarization
   NT   CIDNP
           Overhauser effect
           solid effect
   BT   magnetic double resonance
   TT   resonance
   RT   nuclear polarisation
           nuclear polarisation in liquids and solids
   CC   A0758   A3335D   A7670E
   DI   January 1977
   PT   magnetic double resonance

The programs written to retrieve information from computer-stored data-bases nearly all make use of the Boolean logic operators *and*, *or*, and *not*. With these machine-manipulated instructions, search commands that are highly sophisticated and very powerful examples of post-coordinate searching can be executed. For example, someone using the ERIC database might want to examine material on the consumption of alcohol in clubs, at social gatherings, and the like, but not have to wade through all those discussing related problems of health. Using the *ERIC Thesaurus*, he or she could construct the search command "(Drinking *or* Alcoholic Beverages) *and* ((Behavior *or* Recreational Activities) *not* (Health *or* Health Education))." Since the commands within parentheses are executed first, all documents indexed under the following rubrics would be retrieved:

Drinking *and* Behavior *but not* Health
Drinking *and* Behavior *but not* Health Education
Drinking *and* Recreational Activities *but not* Health
Drinking *and* Recreational Activities *but not* Health Education
Alcoholic Beverages *and* Behavior *but not* Health
Alcoholic Beverages *and* Behavior *but not* Health Education
Alcoholic Beverages *and* Recreational Activities *but not* Health
Alcoholic Beverages *and* Recreational Activities *but not* Health Education

THE PRESERVED CONTEXT
INDEXING SYSTEM (PRECIS)

In chapter 15 chain indexing was discussed in connection with classified cata-log access. Chain indexes, while bearing a format resemblance to keyword in-dexes (see discussion of KWIC and KWOC indexes on pages 464-466) usually are built upon a more selective, indexer-controlled vocabulary. They delete unneces-sary context, and all subheadings are superordinate terms. Key entries are as spe-cific as possible. Where they are hierarchically subordinate to broader terms in the search vocabulary, the next broader term is added for context. This type of alphabetical chain index was used for subject access to *The British National Bibliography* (*BNB*) from 1950 to 1970. From 1970 through 1990, a different system, based on a set of working procedures, rather than an established list of terms, was used. It was called PRECIS, an acronym for Preserved Context Indexing System. Derek Austin states:

> The system is firmly based upon the concept of an open-ended vocabulary, which means that terms can be admitted into the index at any time, as soon as they have been encountered in literature. Once a term has been admitted, its relationships with other terms are handled in two different ways, distinguished as the syntactical and the semantic sides of the system.[11]

The Library of Congress developed its Machine Readable Cataloging (MARC) tapes in the mid-1960s. *BNB*, which is now part of the National Bibliographic Service of the British Library, launched its cooperative UK/MARC Project in 1968. But *BNB* was not satisfied with the subject access provided by existing MARC fields, such as the title, DDC, and LC classification and subject heading fields. Drawing on its twenty-year chain indexing experience, it constructed under the direction of Derek Austin, the PRECIS system.[12]

Austin often starts his descriptions of PRECIS with a series of negative points, to dispel misconceptions. It is not a fully computer-generated program, but requires human processing for preparation of input. It is not a subject heading list, but is characterized by a set of established procedures rather than a set of accepted terms. Also, it is not a library classification, although its computerized thesaurus, like those of the hierarchical indexing systems examined above, embodies certain principles of classification. PRECIS operates with an open-ended vocabulary, so that terms can be adopted as soon as they appear in the literature. Entries are pre-coordinated, context-dependent strings of terms in which each term is semantically defined and syntactically related by *see* and *see also* references to synonyms and other associated words of different specificity. A Reference Indicator Number (RIN) is the computer address where the particular term, plus all references to it, may be accessed.

From established index strings, with their separate terms and RINs, all of the verbal parts of a PRECIS printed index can be generated. For reasons of bulk and cost, actual bibliographic citations are not included in such indexes. Instead, citations are usually sequenced and systematically grouped elsewhere by serial number according to a classification scheme. For bibliographic records in the MARC Project prior to January 1991, *BNB* provided each index string with a packet of subject data consisting of the string itself, a DDC number, an LC class number, LC subject headings as required, and the pertinent RINs to ensure appropriate references. A Subject Indicator Number (SIN) was then assigned as a computer address for each packet. The indexer did not write the chosen subject terms or strings on the worksheet of the item being cataloged. Rather, he or she tagged the worksheet with the appropriate SINs and the document retrieval number. If a new topic, with new references, was needed in the thesaurus, the indexer made the various necessary subject decisions, assigning corresponding RINs and SINs. Figure 24.1 (see page 460) shows a pre-1991 MARC record created at the British Library, as displayed in OCLC. It shows the PRECIS-related information in fields that OCLC has coded 886, while the terms chosen for the PRECIS string are also displayed as free text in field 653.

Fig. 24.1. OCLC MARC record created at the British Library before 1991. The subject package includes LC classification number, Dewey classification number, LC subject headings, PRECIS coded string, and RINs for the syndetic structure.

```
OCLC:      19774652      Rec stat:     p
Entered:    19900314     Replaced:      19900421      Used:      19910205
Type: a          Bib lvl: m        Source:    d        Lang:   eng
Repr:            Enc lvl:           Conf pub: 0        Ctry:   enk
Indx: 1          Mod rec:           Govt pub:          Cont:
Desc: a          Int lvl:           Festschr: 0        Illus:
                 F/B:      0        Dat tp:    s        Dates: 1990,
  1  010      gb89-39996
  2  040      UKM $c UKM
  3  015      GB89-39996
  4  020      0333463986 (cased) : $c £25.00
  5  020      0333463994 (pbk) : $c £6.95
  6  043      e-uk---
  7  050 14   HV9345.A5  ◄—1
  8  082 04   364.630941 $2 20  ◄—2
  9  092      $b
 10  049      YCLM
 11  100 1    Pitts, John, $d 1943-
 12  245 10   Working with young offenders / $c John Pitts.
 13  260      Basingstoke : $b Macmillan, $c 1990.
 14  300      xii, 164 p. ; $c 23 cm.
 15  440  0   Practical social work
 16  504      Bibliography: p. 148-158.
 17  500      Includes index.
 18  650  0   Probation $z Great Britain.
 19  650  0   Social work with delinquents and criminals $z Great}◄—3
Britain.
 20  653      Great Britain $a Welfare work with probationers◄—4
 21  886 2    $2 UK MARC $a 690 $b 00 $z 00030 $d Great Britain $z 21030}◄—5
$a welfare work with probationers
 22  886 2    $2 UK MARC $a 691 $b 00 $a 2534487}◄—6
 23  886 2    $2 UK MARC $a 692 $b 00 $a 0787418}
```

Key to Fig. 24.1:

[1]LC classification number

[2]Dewey classification number

[3]LC subject headings

[4]Terms from PRECIS string

[5]PRECIS coded string

[6]PRECIS RINs

In the PRECIS system, indexers use a complex coding scheme to show the syntactical relationship of each word in the string to the words that precede it and follow it. The purpose is so that in printed indexes, every important word in the string can be placed into the lead position and can then be followed by the remaining words in such a way that the string always makes contextual sense no matter which word is used as the entry point.

Suppose, for instance, that an item to be cataloged is about the training of personnel in the cotton industries in India. The indexer would start by establishing a context-dependent, hierarchical concept string such as: "India—Cotton industries—Personnel—Training." The terms form a sequence in which, much as in a traditional subject heading, each is directly related to the next one in the string. Standard permutation (e.g., a KWIC index) would generate entries under each term as follows:

INDIA. Cotton industries. Personnel. Training
COTTON INDUSTRIES. Personnel. Training. India
PERSONNEL. Training. India. Cotton industries
TRAINING. India. Cotton industries. Personnel

Simple permutation indexes are most successful in retrieving natural language forms, such as book and article titles, or loosely controlled terminology such as that used in the indexes to the Library of Congress Classification schedules. However, in subject heading strings simple transposition of each term to the entry position may raise serious ambiguities, as in the entry above under "TRAINING," where directly dependent terms in the original string are no longer adjacent, which raises the question of whether the personnel are doing or receiving the training.

To meet this inherent danger as economically and elegantly as possible, PRECIS developed a two-line printout that can be diagramed:

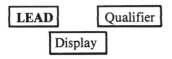

The Lead, as the filing element, is printed in boldface type. The Qualifier position carries any broader term that gives the Lead context. Each successive Qualifier term broadens that context. The Display represents hierarchic movement in the opposite direction. Each successive Display term narrows the context. Not all entries must have Qualifier or Display terms attached. If the topic has no broader, or narrower, context, those positions are blank. Setting our example into the printout matrix gives entries as shown on page 462.

The thesaural aspect is the second important part of the PRECIS system. After a PRECIS string is constructed, each important term is examined. If it is new to the system, it is assigned a RIN, and its relationships to other terms are established, including relationships that are synonymous, hierarchical, and related. Each RIN is coded to show all relationships with other RINs in the system. These codes are used by the system to generate references. If the term is not new, the already established RIN is attached to the record being assigned the PRECIS string. As mentioned earlier, a subject package is created for each

INDIA
    Cotton industries.   Personnel.   Training

COTTON INDUSTRIES.   India
    Personnel.   Training

PERSONNEL.   Cotton industries.   India
    Training

TRAINING.   Personnel.   Cotton industries.   India

PRECIS string. It includes the closest DDC number, LCC number, and LC subject headings. The package is assigned a SIN so that the next time the concept is needed, the bibliographic record can be assigned the SIN without all the work having to be repeated.

PRECIS indexing has been applied successfully to all sorts of subject disciplines and formats: films, instructional aids, books, periodical articles, abstracts, technical reports, etc. While it is a complex tool, developed to perform a complex job, its designers claim that beginners can learn to construct simple strings in a matter of hours. They freely admit that, like any human-based indexing system, it can never ensure that different indexers will arrive systematically at the same entries for the same document. However, it provides a climate of semantic control that fosters adaptability and creativity without degenerating into anarchy. At the same time, its syndetic structure, as represented in its three-part entry format, allows full statement of a compound subject under any of its significant terms without loss of either meaning or concepts. More than in any other known system of subject indexing, terminological access is both controlled and presented in a logical context.

The widespread availability of online keyword searching and the time-consuming nature of syntactic analysis and coding of PRECIS concept strings led the *BNB* to discontinue use of PRECIS at the end of 1990.[13] When a subject string is retrieved via keyword in an online system, it need not be displayed with the keyword in the lead position. It can always be displayed with the keyword in its context as it was placed in the original string.

The new British Library subject system abandons use of MARC fields 650, 651, 690, 691, and 692. Two new fields, 660 for subject topical descriptors and 661 for subject geographical descriptors, are used instead. The new subject system takes from PRECIS its basic components: an authority file of controlled terms and subject statements, and a network of relationships among terms.

The new subject authority file is made up of two types of records: those for terms and those for strings. Terms can be either single words or compound expressions of simple concepts (e.g., "Music" or "Foreign relations"). These may be either topical or geographical (e.g., "France" or "Great Britain"). String authority records are for expression of complex concepts. They consist of combinations of two or more topical terms (e.g., "Bridges. Design. History."). Neither geographical terms nor names as subjects are incorporated into string authority records. When a bibliographic record needs a name or a geographical term as a subject in addition to a subject term or a subject string, they are entered into separate fields in the record.

In bibliographic records appropriate topical terms are placed in MARC field 660 with a first indicator of 0. Topical strings are placed in field 660 with a first indicator of 1. Appropriate subject geographical descriptors are placed in field 661. Names as subjects are placed in field 600. Figure 24.2 shows a British Library record created after implementation of the new subject system.

Fig. 24.2. OCLC MARC record created at the British Library after 1990.

```
OCLC:      22806745        Rec stat:     n
Entered:   19910117        Replaced:    19910117      Used:      19910419
Type: a          Bib lvl: m       Source:    d         Lang:   eng
Repr:            Enc lvl: I       Conf pub: 0           Ctry:   enk
Indx: 1          Mod rec:         Govt pub:             Cont:   b
Desc: a          Int lvl:         Festschr: 0           Illus:  ac
                 F/B:       0b    Dat tp:    s          Dates:  1990,
 1  010     gb91-10306
 2  040     UKM $c UKM
 3  020  1  0094685509 : $c £20.00
 4  082     759.5 $2 20
 5  049     YCLM
 6  100  1  Rose, June, $d 1926-
 7  245 10  Modigliani : $b the pure bohemian / $c June Rose.
 8  260     London : $b Constable, $c 1990.
 9  300     249 p. : $b ill. (some col.), ports. ; $c 24 cm.
10  504     Bibliography: p. 238-239.
11  500     Includes index.
12  600 10  Modigliani, Amedeo, $d 1884-1920.  ◄—2
13  886 2     $2 UK MARC $a 660 $b 00 $a Paintings ◄—3
14  886 2     $2 UK MARC $a 661 $b 00 $a Italy ◄—4
```

Key to Fig. 24.2:

1 Dewey classification number

2 Name as subject

3 Topical term

4 Geographic descriptor

G. Donald Cook, addressing "The Practical Possibilities of PRECIS in North America," found that PRECIS assigned an average of 5.52, as compared to LCSH's 4.09, distinctive words per bibliographic record. The average PRECIS string, without its manipulation codes, is some 25 percent longer than the average LCSH entry for the same record. He warned that in neither system would all such words serve as useful access points, but he affirmed that, with permutation, access through PRECIS is triple that through LCSH.[14] It remains to be seen whether the new British Library subject system will outperform LCSH in the same way.

An indexing technique similar to PRECIS is POPSI (Postulate-based Permuted Subject Indexing). This approach was developed at the Documentation Research and Training Centre in Bangalore, India, where Ranganathan was the director until his death. It is often thought to be a particular string index language associated with the Colon Classification. However, it can be applied to different languages, according to the postulates recognized. The postulates comprise the definitions and the rules of grammar or syntax, which control associative as well as hierarchical relationships. Both POPSI and PRECIS are rotated pre-coordinate indexing systems, but whereas PRECIS developed out of a set of linguistic terms and a thesaurus, POPSI indexing developed directly from classification schedules and chain indexing.[15]

AUTOMATIC INDEXING METHODS

Indexers, like other human beings, are fallible, often are inconsistent, are subject to extraneous influences on their work, operate at a slow pace, and are therefore the most expensive component of an indexing operation. The idea of replacing human indexers by feeding part or all of a text into a machine that would assign index terms automatically, impartially, and with unfailing consistency and accuracy arose, therefore, quite early in the computer age. Success has, however, largely eluded the best efforts of many investigators and inventors.

KWIC and KWOC Indexing

The earliest automatic indexing method relying on the power of computers to perform repetitive tasks at high speed was invented by Hans Peter Luhn, an IBM engineer, who in 1958 produced what became known as KWIC (Key Word In Context) indexing. Luhn reported his system in 1960.[16] On the assumption that titles of scientific and technical articles generally include words indicating the most significant concepts dealt with, he wrote a program that printed strings of title words, each word appearing once in alphabetical order in the center of a page, with all other words to the left or right of the center word printed in the order in which they appeared in the title; when the right-hand margin was reached, the rest of the title (if any) was "wrapped around" to the left-hand margin and continued inward. A user had only to scan the left-justified middle column for a desired keyword and could, when the word was found, read the rest of the title "in context." The method worked indeed fully automatically (i.e., without any human intervention other than the keyboarding) and resulted in a quickly and inexpensively produced display of potentially sought terms. Most KWIC programs also employ so-called stop lists to eliminate common words such as articles, prepositions, and conjunctions from the middle column where they presumably would not be sought. A specimen of a typical KWIC index is shown in Fig. 24.3. This earlier and rather crude form of automatic indexing has, ironically, remained the only one that has proven itself to be practical and is still being used.

An adaptation of the KWIC method, known as KWOC (Key Word Out Of Context), simply prints the sought words in the left-hand margin instead of in the middle of the page, the rest of the title (or the entire title, including the keyword itself) being printed to the right or beneath the keyword (see Fig. 24.4).

KWIC and KWOC indexing have, however, some severe limitations: only words that appear in titles can be sought, while the article itself may deal with many other concepts not mentioned in the title; since there is absolutely no vocabulary control (other than the elimination of stop-list words), synonymous terms

Fig. 24.3. Sample from a KWIC index.

```
ORMATION AT THE NUCLEAR  SAFETY INFORMATION CENTER.    & INF   AINPBX-0005-0346A
UNCEMENT MEDIA ON CFSTI  SALES.=              & OF VARIOUS ANNO  AINPBX-0005-0327
          IMPACT OF A LARGE  SCALE COMPUTERIZED SDI SYSTEM ON A  AINPBX-0005-0223
WITH NASA/SCAN, A LARGE  SCALE SELECTIVE ANNOUNCEMENT SERVI  AINPBX-0005-0217
     OF INFORMATION-SMALL  SCALE. DISSEMINATION - CHOOSE IT     AINPBX-0005-0239
     OF INFORMATION-SMALL  SCALE. EXPERIMENTAL TRIAL OF SELEC   AINPBX-0005-0243
     OF INFORMATION-LARGE  SCALE. IMPACT OF A LARGE SCALE       AINPBX-0005-0223
OF INFORMATION.  LARGE  SCALE. KWOC INDEX AS AN AUTOMATIC    AINPBX-0005-0211
     OF INFORMATION-SMALL  SCALE. MANAGEMENT OF SMALL, SPECIA   AINPBX-0005-0233
     OF INFORMATION-LARGE  SCALE. OPERATING EXPERIENCE WITH     AINPBX-0005-0217
ON OF INFORMATION-LARGE  SCALE. POOR MAN/S SDI.&DISSEMINATI   AINPBX-0005-0227
EXPERIENCE WITH NASA/  SCAN, A LARGE SCALE SELECTIVE         AINPBX-0005-0217
TO THE DISSEMINATION OF  SCIENTIFIC AND EDUCATIONAL INFORMA  AINPBX-0005-0350A
          FOR FEDERAL  SCIENTIFIC AND TECHNICAL INFORMATI   AINPBX-0005-0311
FORUM FOR SPECIALIZED  SCIENTIFIC COMMUNICATION.=           AINPBX-0005-0031
ATION.  LARGE SCALE. &  SCIENTIFIC DISSEMINATION OF INFORM  AINPBX-0005-0211
ATION-LARGE SCALE. &  SCIENTIFIC DISSEMINATION OF INFORM    AINPBX-0005-0217
ATION-LARGE SCALE. &  SCIENTIFIC DISSEMINATION OF INFORM    AINPBX-0005-0223
ATION-LARGE SCALE. &  SCIENTIFIC DISSEMINATION OF INFORM    AINPBX-0005-0227
```

Fig. 24.4. Sample from a KWOC index.

CHEMICUS	Index Chemicus 4377.400 Q	
CHEMISTRY	Abstracts of Bulgarian Scientific Literature: Chemistry 0554.515 X	
	Berichte: Physiologie Physiologische Chemie und Pharmakologie (Chemistry)	1936.870
	Bibliographic Series: Institute of Paper Chemistry 1967.700	
	Bibliography on the High Temperature Chemistry and Physics of Materials	2002.870
	Current Abstracts of Chemistry and Index Chemicus 3494.030 Q	
	Current Titles in Electro Chemistry 3504.860 X	
	Key to Turkish Science Chemistry 5091.830	
	Papers and Patents from Olin Research (Chemistry) 6394.700	
	Selected Bibliography of Pure Chemistry 8233.005	
	Selected Bibliography of Applied Chemistry 8233.006	
	USSR and East Europe Scientific Abstracts: Chemistry 9135.1014 X	
CHEMISTS	Bibliographies of Chemists 1993.120	
CHEMOTHERAPY	Cancer Chemotherapy Abstracts 3046.465	
CHEST	Journal of Specialist Medicine: Heart and Chest including Tuberculosis	5066.130
CHEST DISEASES	Excerpta Medica: Chest Diseases Thoracic Surgery and Tuberculosis	3835.824 X
CHILD DEVELOPMENT	Child Development Abstracts and Bibliography 3172.942	
CHILD EDUCATION	Exceptional Child Education Abstracts 3835.200	
CHILDREN'S	'Courrier' of the International Children's Centre 3482.600	
CHINA	Index to People's Republic of China Press etc. 4385.100	

are not available to users as potential access points for searching (i.e., there are no *see* references, say, from AGRICULTURE to FARMING or from SODIUM CHLORIDE to SALT); and many titles are not representative of the subject dealt with or are on purpose written to catch the attention of prospective readers without indicating the subject at all, e.g., "On the care and construction of white elephants" (on cataloging) or "The money-eating machines" (on computer management). In addition, lengthy KWIC indexes are tiresome to scan, especially when they are printed in small type and in all capitals, as is often the case. Thus, contrary to the pun intended by the acronym KWIC, such indexes are neither quick for the user nor really indexes to concepts dealt with in texts but rather are listings of words that authors happened to put into titles. On the other hand, since the introduction of KWIC indexes, titles of scientific and technical articles have become more indicative of their contents because authors and editors became aware of the fact that inexpressive titles would be overlooked in KWIC and similar indexing techniques.[17] In the social sciences and humanities, however, the custom of authors to give catchy and uninformative titles to their papers is continuing unabated.

Extraction of Words

KWIC indexing was only the first of the so-called derivative indexing methods, all of which are based on the principle of extracting words from machine-readable text – a title, an abstract, or even the full text of a document. Automatic extraction of words is generally coupled with *truncation* in searching, that is, the possibility of searching for a word stem without regard to its prefixes or suffixes, in order to retrieve a maximum of potentially useful occurrences of that word. Thus, a physicist looking for the presence of the concept "pressure" may search for *PRESS* (the asterisks indicating that prefixes and suffixes are also to be searched), which may give:

COMPRESS
COMPRESSION
IMPRESSION
SUPPRESSION
PRESS
PRESSER
PRESSES
PRESSURE
PRESSURIZE
PRESSURIZATION
PRESSWORK

While truncation (or "stemming") does increase recall, it lowers precision because it may result in unwanted and irrelevant items being retrieved (the latter known as "false drops"). This may occur because of at least two phenomena: 1) homonyms cannot be detected by mere extraction methods – that is, in the example just cited, IMPRESSION, SUPPRESSION, and PRESSWORK do not pertain to "pressure" in the physical sense, while PRESS may pertain both to mechanical equipment and to newspapers, the latter being of no interest to a physicist; 2) the elimination of "common" words by a stop list may also result in false drops whenever relationships are of importance, e.g., a Boolean search for TEACHERS *and* STUDENTS *and* EVALUATION will retrieve both teachers' evaluation of students and students' evaluation of teachers, because the elimination of the crucial words "of" and "by" makes it impossible to know who does what to whom.

For a time it was tried to correct the lack of indicators of relationships in derivative indexing by so-called *links* and *roles*, the former making explicit which words were linked to each other in a relationship, while the latter indicated functions (e.g., acting "as" or "for" something). These devices led indeed to higher precision, but they had to be assigned at the input stage by human beings. As that greatly diminished any gains made by automatic extraction of terms, the method was soon abandoned.

Term Frequency Methods

On the assumption that terms (other than common words) to be indexed are those occurring either very frequently in a text (and therefore indicating concepts dealt with) or very seldom (indicating a topic mentioned expressly only once or twice in the title or first paragraph but then being referred to by "it" or "this" and the like), methods were designed to perform automatic indexing on the basis of frequency of occurrence and co-occurrence of terms, using probabilistic models. Some investigators tried to couple such methods of determining how often a term is used (term frequency methods) with term weighting, i.e., assigning different degrees of importance to terms on the basis of what terms are used in a search request or on the basis of where and how terms appear (e.g., in the title, in an abstract, or in the first or last paragraph of a text, and whether they are italicized or capitalized), all of which can to some extent be determined automatically. While these methods are of interest to statisticians and mathematicians, and some have produced acceptable results under tightly controlled laboratory conditions when applied to very limited subject fields, they have as yet not found any practical large-scale application.

Linguistic Methods

A quite different approach to automatic indexing is by syntactic and semantic analysis. The former is concerned with the automatic recognition of significant word order in a phrase or sentence and with inflections, prefixes, and suffixes that indicate grammatical relationships, while the latter approach seeks to analyze noun phrases automatically with the aid of stored dictionaries and other linguistic aids (thus having affinities to automatic translation). The two methods are also often used in conjunction. Most research in this direction has been performed in the Soviet Union, Germany, France, and Japan, while relatively little interest in purely linguistic methods have been shown by English-speaking researchers.[18]

Computer-Aided Indexing

As indicated above, except for KWIC and KWOC indexing, none of the other automatic indexing methods have been applied on a large scale. For the time being, the large access services and databases still use human indexers and abstractors, even though their work is far from perfect or consistent, because none of the methods of automatic indexing invented so far has shown itself to be able to compete in terms of indexing quality or economic viability. According to Lancaster,[19] automatic indexing methods are now no longer the focus of interest of researchers, but computers will increasingly aid information retrieval in various other ways. Microcomputers are now widely used by indexers in *computer-aided* indexing, relying on stored dictionaries of synonyms and homonyms, lists of authors' names for automatic verification, lists of trade names and names of chemical compounds, plants and animals, etc. They are also used to take the drudgery out of indexing by automatically arranging entries in alphabetical order or subordinating subheadings and cross references in exact sequence under a heading, and by performing many other functions that previously had to be done manually and therefore were quite expensive and often subject to errors.

SWITCHING LANGUAGES

We have made a cursory examination of a number of subject access systems available for use in modern library cataloging. Most are self-contained, providing their own categories and terminology, with syntactical rules designed to express complex or multi-faceted concepts. Each exhibits both strengths and weaknesses. Not one has yet proved sufficient to meet all needs nor is demonstrably better than all others in every situation.

The information explosion, together with rapid developments in automation, has made intercommunication among subject disciplines, libraries, and nations both a possibility and a growing necessity. Several possible solutions to this problem have been proposed. One has been a movement toward "switching languages." With a multilateral translation program, materials already indexed would be more readily available, while libraries and information centers could avoid future duplication by joining systems of shared cataloging without discarding or revamping their own catalogs and indexes.

Many enthusiasts favored an umbrella classification, a coarse approach recognizing only two to four hierarchical levels, for use by several agencies to construct a cumulative thesaurus or to share indexing on a general level. One example is the Committee on Scientific and Technical Information's *COSATI Subject Category List*, a scheme of 22 broad research-oriented topical areas, each with one or two levels of subdivision. It is used by a number of government agencies and research organizations to order their abstracting and indexing tools and for similar purposes. But the problems of depending on such an ad hoc system are obvious. Lacking breadth as well as specificity, it does not provide a satisfactory universal switching language.

Another effort, backed by the Fédération Internationale de Documentation (FID) and Unesco, produced a subject code schedule called the Broad System of Ordering (BSO).[20] It is basically a classification system designed to serve as a switching mechanism between various indexing languages. Its proponents claim:

A classification, more than any other form of indexing language, is amenable to easy, predictable, yet at the same time fully controlled updating. This is the essential ground upon which it is the preferred form of indexing language for the universal switching application. That existing universal classifications have failed, or are visibly failing, precisely in this respect does not vitiate the argument.[21]

Criteria established for BSO include flexibility, structural simplicity, and easy manipulation in either manual or automated information systems. In its present form it is an umbrella mechanism for shallow indexing and collocation of large blocks of related information, rather than for retrieving specific documents from different in-depth indexing systems. Several other illuminating experiments have taken place. The interested student will have no trouble finding descriptions of most of them in the literature.[22]

Because creation of a master switching vocabulary proved so difficult, researchers turned to other approaches to the problem. Linda C. Smith reports an effort to "map" a portion of the *Medical Subject Headings (MeSH)*, which the National Library of Medicine uses in its preparation of *Index Medicus*, to three other controlled vocabularies, namely, *Subject Headings for Engineering (SHE)*, used in *Engineering Index*; the *NASA Thesaurus*, used for *Scientific and Technical Aerospace Reports (STAR)*; and *Subject Headings Used by the USAEC*.[23] The effort was only partially successful. Test searches showed that *Index Medicus* alone could retrieve 81 percent of the materials retrieved through mapping all four sources. Where the mapping increased the number of documents retrieved, some loss of precision occurred. The experiment did suggest possible alternative approaches to the clerical conversion of terms from one index language to another.

A somewhat different approach is that of the BRS/TERM database, which was created to enhance online searching.[24] The vocabularies of six thesauri have been organized into concept records that include hierarchical information and free-text searching suggestions. This kind of approach has an inherent linguistic interest that has led researchers to reexamine the structure and properties of indexing languages.

Also being explored are software interfaces and various applications of artificial intelligence. The hope is that such systems eventually can take a user's natural language query and translate it into indexing terms used in any indexing system.

NOTES

[1] John Rothman, "Index, Indexer, Indexing," in *Encyclopedia of Library and Information Science*, Vol. 11 (New York, Marcel Dekker, 1974), p. 289.

[2] Mortimer Taube and Associates, *Studies in Coordinate Indexing* (Washington, D.C., Documentation, Incorporated, 1953).

[3] A. C. Foskett, *The Subject Approach to Information*, 4th ed. (London, Clive Bingley; Hamden, Conn., Linnet Books, 1982), p. 436.

[4] Marcia J. Bates, "Rethinking Subject Cataloging in the Online Environment," *Library Resources & Technical Services* 33, no. 4 (October 1989): 401.

[5] International Organization for Standardization, *Documentation: Guidelines for the Establishment and Development of Monolingual Thesauri*, 2nd ed. ISO 2788 (Geneva, ISO, 1986; first edition published in 1974); British Standards Institution, *British Standard Guide to Establishment and Development of Monolingual Thesauri*, BS 5723 (London, BSI, 1987; first edition published in 1979); American National Standards Institute, *American National Standard Guidelines for Thesaurus Structure, Construction, and Use*, ANSI Z39.19-1980 (New York, ANSI, 1980).

[6] Mary Dykstra, "LC Subject Headings Disguised as a Thesaurus," *Library Journal* 113 (March 1, 1988): 42-46.

[7] Dykstra, "LC Subject Headings Disguised," p. 43.

[8]*Thesaurus of Psychological Index Terms*, 5th ed. (Washington, D.C., American Psychological Association, 1988).

[9]*Thesaurus of ERIC Descriptors*, 12th ed. (Phoenix, Ariz., Oryx Press, 1990).

[10]*INSPEC Thesaurus*, 1989 [ed.] (London, Institution of Electrical Engineers, 1989).

[11]Derek Austin, "Progress in Documentation: The Development of PRECIS: A Theoretical and Technical History." *Journal of Documentation* 30 (March 1974): 47. In addition to this excellent article, the serious student is referred to: Derek Austin, *PRECIS: A Manual of Concept Analysis and Subject Indexing*, 2nd ed. (London, British Library, 1984); *The PRECIS Index System: Principles, Applications, and Prospects*, Proceedings of the International PRECIS Workshop, ed. by Hans H. Wellisch (New York, H. W. Wilson, 1977); and M. Mahapatra and S. C. Biswas, "PRECIS: Its Theory and Application—An Extended State-of-the-Art Review from the Beginning up to 1982," *Libri* 33 (December 1983): 316-330.

[12]Derek Austin and Jeremy A. Digger, "PRECIS: The Preserved Context Index System," *Library Resources & Technical Services* 21 (Winter 1977): 13-30; Derek Austin, "PRECIS: Theory and Practice," *International Cataloguing* 13 (January/March 1984): 9-12; and Phyllis A. Richmond, "PRECIS Compared with Other Indexing Systems," in *The PRECIS Index System*, p. 113.

[13]National Bibliographic Service, *Newsletter* no. 1 (June/July 1990): 3-4.

[14]C. Donald Cook, "The Practical Possibilities of PRECIS in North America," in *The PRECIS Index System*, p. 189.

[15]G. Bhattacharyya and A. Neelameghan, "Postulate-Based Subject Heading for Dictionary Catalogue System," in Documentation Research and Training Centre, *Annual Seminar* 7 (1969): 221-254; and G. Bhattacharyya, "Chain Procedure and Structuring of a Subject," *Library Science with a Slant to Documentation* 9 (1972): 585-635.

[16]Hans Peter Luhn, "Keyword in Context Index for Technical Literature (KWIC Index)," *American Documentation* 11 (1960): 288-295.

[17]J. J. Tocatlian, "Are Titles of Chemical Papers Becoming More Informative?" *Journal of the American Society for Information Science* 21 (1970): 345-350.

[18]Hans H. Wellisch, "Vital Statistics on Abstracting and Indexing Revisited," *International Classification* 12 (1985): 11-16.

[19]F. W. Lancaster, "Trends in Subject Indexing from 1957 to 2000," in *New Trends in Documentation and Information: Proceedings of the 39th FID Congress, 1978* (London, Aslib, 1980), pp. 223-233.

[20]Eric J. Coates, et al., *BSO, Broad System of Ordering: Schedule and Index* (The Hague, IFLA; Paris, Unesco, 1978).

[21]Eric J. Coates, et al., *The BSO Manual: The Development, Rationale and Use of the Broad System of Ordering* (The Hague, FID, 1979), p. 35.

[22]For example: Robert Niehoff and Greg Mack, "The Vocabulary Switching System: Description of Evaluation Studies," *International Classification* 12, no. 1 (1985): 2-6.

[23]Linda C. Smith, "Systematic Searching of Abstracts and Indexes in Interdisciplinary Areas," *Journal of the American Society for Information Science* 25 (November-December 1974): 344.

[24]Sara D. Knapp, "Creating BRS/TERM, a Vocabulary Database for Searchers," *Database* 7, no. 4 (December 1984): 70-75.

SUGGESTED READING

Austin, Derek. "PRECIS: Theory and Practice." *International Cataloguing* 13 (January/ March 1984): 9-12.

Bates, Marcia J. "Rethinking Subject Cataloging in the Online Environment." *Library Resources & Technical Services* 33, no. 4 (October 1989): 400-419.

Dykstra, Mary. *PRECIS: A Primer.* London, British Library, 1985.

Foskett, A. C. *The Subject Approach to Information.* 4th ed. London, Clive Bingley; Hamden, Conn., Linnet Books, 1982. Chapters 14-15, 24-27.

Soergel, Dagobert. *Organizing Information: Principles of Data Base and Retrieval Systems.* Orlando, Fla., Academic Press, 1985. Chapters 12-15.

Part IV

AUTHORITY CONTROL

Authority
Control

25

INTRODUCTION

Authority control, as currently practiced, is the process of maintaining consistency in the verbal form used to represent an access point in a catalog and the further process of showing the relationships among names, works, and subjects. The goal is to make possible the identifying and collocating functions of the catalog.

IDENTIFYING FUNCTION

Authority control enhances the identifying, or finding, function of the catalog through the use of consistent forms of access points with references from forms not used. In a system under authority control, a user can assume that all works relating to a name will be found together or will at least be connected with references. Once one determines, for example, that records are found under Cochrane, Pauline A., and not under Atherton, Pauline, one can assume that everything by this person will be found at this heading. It is not necessary to look under Cochrane, P. A., or the alternate spelling, Cochran, P., or to try to think of other possible spellings or forms.

It is possible to identify titles through use of a consistent heading for works that have different titles. A particular edition of the Bible, for example, can be found under "Bible." One does not have to remember an exact title such as *Holy Bible*, or *Good News for Modern Man*, although they can also be found under these titles if one remembers them. Identification of works on a particular subject is made easier by using only one of two synonyms, for example, or by always using the words of a phrase in the same order—e.g., "Serials control systems," not "Control systems (Serials)."

COLLOCATING FUNCTION

Authority control enhances the collocating, or gathering, function of the catalog through the linking of consistent headings in a syndetic structure. *Syndetic* is an adjective meaning "connective, connecting." It is used to characterize the nature of a catalog under authority control because of the connecting that is brought about by using consistent headings and by providing references to and among those headings.

Names are collocated by bringing everything by and about a person or corporate body together under the same form of name; or in some cases where a person or body actually has used two or more different *names* (not just different forms), collocation may be accomplished by connecting the names with references. Examples of the latter are:

472

University of North Carolina at Chapel Hill.   School of Information and Library Science

For works issued by this body under its earlier name see:

University of North Carolina at Chapel Hill.   School of Library Science.

Dodgson, Charles Lutwidge, 1832-1898

For works written under this author's pseudonym see:

Carroll, Lewis, 1832-1898.

Works are collocated by creating a uniform title for every work that has appeared under more than one title and by providing references from titles not chosen for the heading. In this way all manifestations of the Bible can be found together; and Dickens's *Life and Adventures of Nicholas Nickleby* can be found with his *Nicholas Nickleby*. Uniform titles also aid in showing relationships among works. Bibliographic records for the musical stage play and the film version of *Nicholas Nickleby* contain added entries for the uniform title for Dickens's original work, and thus can be found collocated with it. References also can help to show relationships among works. An example of this is:

Tolkien, J. R. R. (John Ronald Reuel), 1892-1973.   Lord of the rings. 2, Two towers

see

Tolkien, J. R. R. (John Ronald Reuel), 1892-1973.   Two towers.

The heading chosen for the work in this example collocates the bibliographic records for the work under the title of the part, but the reference collocates with the title of the whole larger work, letting the user know that parts of the whole work are available in addition to the whole work.

Authority control assures that subjects are collocated by providing consistent headings for discrete concepts, by assuring that there are references to those headings from terms not used, and by providing a network of references to and among broader terms, narrower terms, and related terms. For example, let us suppose that someone is using a catalog in which the subjects are from the Library of Congress Subject Headings (LCSH) and in which appropriate references have been provided. If this person looks up "Heart attack," a reference will show that this term is not used, but that "Heart — Infarction" is used instead (*see* Fig. 25.1a, page 474). At "Heart — Infarction," in addition to finding bibliographic records representing works on the subject, the user will find a reference to the narrower term "Cardiogenic shock" (*see* Fig. 25.1b, page 474). In an ideal world there would also be a reference to the broader term "Coronary heart disease," although, traditionally, library catalogs have referred only to narrower and related terms because it was felt that to refer to broader terms made an impossibly complicated network. (This was true in manual systems. Most libraries even gave up providing related and narrower term references in manual catalogs.) If the broader term reference *were* made, however, the user could follow up with a search under "Coronary heart disease" and would be referred to the related term "Type A behavior" and two other narrower terms besides the one that led to this term: "Angina pectoris" and "Coronary vasospasm." There could also be a reference to the broader term "Heart—Diseases."

Fig. 25.1a. Reference from unused term to term used.

```
LUIS SEARCH REQUEST:  S=HEART ATTACK
 Subject Index (LCSH) -- 1 entries found, 1 - 1 displayed

    HEART ATTACK
              *Search under
    1             HEART--INFARCTION




TYPE LINE NO. FOR LUIS RECORD, & TO REFINE SEARCH.
TYPE ia FOR AMPLIFIED INDEX, e TO START OVER, h FOR HELP.
TYPE COMMAND AND PRESS ENTER
```

Fig. 25.1b. Result of typing "1" at the screen shown in Fig. 25.1a.

```
LUIS SEARCH REQUEST:  S=HEART--INFARCTION
 Subject Index (LCSH) -- 95 entries found, 1 - 14 displayed

    HEART
     --INFARCTION
                *Search also under
    1             CARDIOGENIC SHOCK
    2         .ACUTE MYOCARDIAL INFARCTION <1978> (HS)
    3         .ACUTE MYOCARDIAL INFARCTION <1987> (HS)
    4         .CARDIAC EMERGENCIES <1977> (HS)
    5         .CLINICAL STRATEGIES IN ISCHEMIC HEART DISEAS <1979> (HS)
    6         .CORONARY CARE <1981> (HS)
    7         .ELECTROCARDIOLOGY OF CORONARY ARTERY DISEASE <1975> (HS)
    8         .HEART ATTACK HANDBOOK <1978> (HS)
    9         .HEART ATTACK SURVIVAL MANUAL <1981> (HS)
   10         .HEART PATIENT RECOVERS <1977> (HS)
   11         .HEMIBLOCKS IN MYOCARDIAL INFARCTION <1976> (HS)
   12         .MYOCARDIAL INFARCTION <1979> (HS)
   13         .MYOCARDIAL INFARCTION AND CARDIAC DEATH <1983> (HS)
   14         .MYOCARDIAL INFARCTION IN WOMEN <1986> (HS)

TYPE m FOR MORE ENTRIES, LINE NO. FOR LUIS RECORD,  & TO REFINE SEARCH.
TYPE ia FOR AMPLIFIED INDEX, e TO START OVER, h FOR HELP.
TYPE COMMAND AND PRESS ENTER
```

SYSTEM DESIGN

It should be emphasized that authority control of the terminology does not ensure that everything on a subject will be found together. The latter depends upon the subject analysis that has been done, as discussed in chapter 15. That is, only if an item were determined to be about "heart attacks" will it be found under "Heart — Infarction." And in library catalogs, even that will be true only if the whole item, and not just, let's say, one chapter is on the subject. It should also be pointed out that not all terms thought of by a user will match a reference if they do not match a heading. For example, a user of an authority-controlled online catalog with references who searches for "heart attacks" will be told there are no matches, because the reference is from "heart attack" in the singular (*see* Fig. 25.2). This can be a problem in searching for names and titles as well as for subjects. For example, a person may search for a name spelled as it sounds (e.g., "Kirshenbaum, Baruch" instead of "Kirschenbaum, Baruch"). Systems can be designed with enhanced search capabilities to supplement authority control in such situations.[1]

Fig. 25.2. Search result showing no matches for term searched.

```
LUIS SEARCH REQUEST:   S=HEART ATTACKS
                       NO SUBJECT HEADINGS FOUND
Possible reasons:

   1. Your subject term is not an authorized subject heading. Choose
      another term to represent the topic.
   2. Your term is not authorized in the subject heading list you
      searched. Type s for information on selecting a subject heading list.
   3. Your term may be valid, but there are no materials in LUIS.
      Check the card catalog for older materials.
   4. Your search term includes a typographical error.
   5. Your subject term includes an incorrectly formatted subject
      subdivision. Type two hyphens (and no spaces) between the subject
      term and each succeeding subdivision:
                    s=united states--history--civil war
   6. Improper use of pound sign (#) or ampersand (&).

IMPORTANT: When unsure of spelling or form, try shortening the search term.
      Also consider using the "#" technique or advanced searching methods.
      Type # or & to learn about these techniques.

TYPE t, a, or s FOR AN INTRODUCTION TO TITLE, AUTHOR, OR SUBJECT SEARCHES.
TYPE e FOR AN INTRODUCTION TO LUIS.
TYPE COMMAND AND PRESS ENTER
```

LACK OF AUTHORITY CONTROL

In systems without authority control, it is up to the user to try to think of all possible ways that a name, work, or subject could be verbally represented, while at the same time eliminating all possible representations that will not satisfy the need. For example, a user wanting material on MERCURY as a metal must eliminate that which concerns the planet or the Roman god; and a user wishing to consult works by John F. Murphy on cash management (*see* Fig. 25.3, page 476) must sort out these from works by other John F. Murphys who write about Christian education, law, parenting, and other subjects and who do not always use titles that are descriptive of their contents. [In fact, in many of today's supposedly

Fig. 25.3. Partial authority records for four authors who use the name "John F. Murphy".

```
1 010      n  83175165
2 040      DLC $c DLC
3 100 10   Murphy, John F. [AACR2]
4 670      Murphy, A.M. Successful parenting, c1983 (a.e.) $b CIP t.p.
(John F. Murphy, Ed. M.)


1 010      n  83016187
2 040      DGPO $c DLC
3 100 10   Murphy, John F. $q (John Francis), $d 1913- [AACR2]
4 670      His Sound cash management and borrowing, 1981: $b t.p.
(John F. Murphy, retired bank exec. and member Manasota SCORE Chapter,
Sarasota, Fla.)
5 670      Phone call 3/28/83 to John F. Murphy $b (John Francis
Murphy, b. 3/4/13)


1 010      no 90025472
2 040      DGPO $c DGPO
3 100 10   Murphy, John F. $q (John Francis), $d 1922- [AACR2]
4 670      Richmond, G.M. Preliminary quaternary geologic map of the
Dinwoody Lake area, Fremont County, Wyoming [MI], 1989?: $b t.p. (John F.
Murphy; U.S. Geological Survey)
5 670      Phone call to author, 11/26/90 $b (John Francis Murphy, b.

8/27/22)


1 010      n  80072584
2 040      DLC $c DLC
3 100 10   Murphy, John F., $d 1922- [AACR2]
4 400 10   Murphy, Jack, $d 1922-
5 670      His Mary's immaculate heart, 1951.


1 010      n  78011669
2 040      DLC $c DLC
3 100 10   Murphy, John Francis, $d 1937- [COMPATIBLE]
4 400 10   Murphy, John F. $q (John Francis), $d 1937-
5 670      American Society of International Law. Legal aspects ...
1978 (a.e.) $b t.p. (John F. Murphy)
6 670      Dir. Amer. scholars, 1974 $b (Murphy, John Francis;
b. 5/23/37)
```

authority-controlled online catalogs, users must do this same sorting because works by all John F. Murphys, regardless of variant qualifiers or birthdates, are interfiled and subarranged alphabetically by the titles of their various works, and there is no reference to the John F. Murphy who is entered as "Murphy, John Francis, 1937- ". (*See* Fig. 25.4.) This is a step backward from card catalogs where all works by the person whose heading is "Murphy, John F. (John Francis), 1913- " are filed together before works by the person whose heading is "Murphy, John F. (John Francis), 1922- ".]

Fig. 25.4. Partial alphabetical listing of titles in OCLC of at least six different authors named "John F. Murphy".

```
OLUC   dp murp,joh,f                                      Records: 95

Rec#   Name             Title                      Publisher      Date L
  1    Murphy, John F.  Across the western ocean : Fr              1982
  2    Murphy, John F., The catechetical experience Herder and Her 1968 D
  3    Murphy, John F., Catechetics from A to Z /   Ave Maria Pres 1982 D
  4    Murphy, John F.  A Comparison study of patient             1989
  5    Murphy, John F.  The condensation of aliphatic             1940
  6    Murphy, John F.  Countdown to communication : Distributors, 1973
  7    Murphy, John F.  Countdown to communication : Sullivan Broth 1973
  8    Murphy, John F.  Developing language with youn Educators Pub. 1973
  9    Murphy, John F.  Developing oral language with Educators Pub. 1974
 10    Murphy, John F.  Developing oral language with Educators Pub. 1975
 11    Murphy, John F., Doing, dance & drama /      Ave Maria Pres 1980 D
 12    Murphy, John F.  Eighty photographic views-- o John F. Murphy 1890
 13    Murphy, John F.  Fifty photographic views of P John F. Murphy 1900
 14    Murphy, John F., Geology of the Sheldon-Little The Survey,  1956
 15    Murphy, John F.  Implications of the Irish pas             1983
 16    Murphy, John F.  In the Supreme Court of the s             1909
 17    Murphy, John F.  Knowledge is power: foreign p             1975
 18    Murphy, John F.  Listening, language & learnin Educators Pub. 1970
 19    Murphy, John F., Mary's Immaculate Heart; the Bruce        1951 D
 20    Murphy, John F.  The mathematical fundamentals s.n.],      1972
```

It has been argued by some that users have for some time now been finding material in uncontrolled online databases that index papers and articles. This is true, but the process is not without some frustration. A series of articles in 1985 and 1986 in *DATABASE* and *ONLINE* addressed the problem of searching for names in such databases.[2] Upon reading these articles one is struck by the immense number of complications waiting to sabatoge the uninitiated, and one must wonder how any searcher could possibly remember all the tricks necessary for a complete name search. These articles are mini-lessons in performing authority work, except that it is up to the user, not the cataloger, to do the work over and over as searches are performed.

AUTHORITY WORK

Authority control, of course, cannot be achieved automatically. It requires authority work to be done by catalogers. First, it is necessary to discover all available evidence relative to the naming of a person, body, work, topic, etc., and then to choose the form to use as the heading and the forms to use as references according to some rule. Then there must be creation of authority records. A carefully prepared authority record contains the form chosen for use as the heading, a list of variant forms or terms that may be used as references, and a list of sources consulted in the process of deciding upon the heading.

The process followed for names, uniform titles, and series is somewhat different from that used for subjects. The first step in the process used for names, uniform titles, and series is verification, which means determining the existence of an author or other entity and the accepted form of heading to use. The name or title is first recorded as it appears in the work being cataloged. The next step usually is to check the library's catalog and authority files to determine if the heading already has been established for the library. If it has, the authorized form is noted and used in the cataloging in hand. If the heading is not already established, the cataloger checks the LC authority file (LCAF) either online through the utility in which the library holds membership or in the microfiche or CD-ROM version. If the name or title is in the LCAF and is coded as being in *AACR2* form, the record is copied for the local file. This may be accomplished by downloading the authority record from the bibliographic utility to the local system, if the library has an online catalog. Another method, if the library relies on cards, is to download the authority record from the bibliographic utility onto a personal computer. Then the record can be printed on card stock from the machine-readable record. There are several programs available for this operation.

If the name or title is not in the LCAF or is not coded as being in *AACR2* form, *AACR2R* is consulted for the appropriate rules for form. If verification problems emerge, such as the existence of different names or different forms of the same name, further sources of information must be consulted. Such sources that might be consulted include other works by the same author or issued by the same body, *National Union Catalog, Cumulative Book Index, American Book Publishing Record, New Serial Titles*, reliable directories or biographical dictionaries, or other reference sources. An authority record must then be made. The one or more sources used as authoritative may be cited on the authority record. Pertinent references are listed. References also should be made, as well as a revised authority record, for any conflicting heading that had to be changed in the process of creating the authority heading for the name or title in hand.

Figure 25.5 shows one format that a manual name authority card might take. In this format the rules used are indicated in the upper right corner, the heading is given on the top line at the left martin, sources are given next, and references follow. A single *x* means that there will be a *see* reference from that form to the heading. A double *xx* would be used to mean that a *see also* reference would be made from that form, in cases where headings have been created for two or more names for the same person or body, e.g.:

Carroll, Lewis, 1832-1898.

xx   Dodgson, Charles Lutwidge, 1832-1898

Fig. 25.5. Sample name authority card.

```
                                          AACR2
    Van Buren, Ariane.

    LCAF:   n   79022593

    Work cat.:  Nuclear or not? 1978 (a.e.): t.p. (Ariane
    van Buren) jkt. (E. Ariane van Buren, research assoc.,
    International Inst. of Environment & Development)

    x   Buren, Ariane van
    x   Van Buren, E. Ariane




                        O
```

Many authority records are created in the MARC format by the Library of Congress and by libraries in special cooperative relationships with LC, and most libraries try to use these as much as possible in order to reduce their local authority work. Figure 25.6 shows the name authority record from Fig. 25.5 coded according to the MARC authorities format and formatted as is done in the OCLC system. In the MARC format the authorized heading is given in a field beginning with 1 (100, 110, 111, 150, 151). *See from* references (those preceded by *x* in a manual file) are given in fields beginning with 4 (400, 410, etc.). *See also from* references (those preceded by *xx* in a manual file) are given in fields beginning with 5 (500, 510, etc.). Notes are given in fields beginning with 6 (667, 670, 675, 678, 680, 681). Special kinds of references are given in fields 663 through 666. MARC records, of course, can be displayed in any fashion that a system programmer chooses. In the OCLC PRISM service, implemented in 1991, a default display eliminates the fixed field area of an authority record and replaces it with English equivalents of the most used fixed field codes. In name authority records it also displays "[AACR2]" or "[COMPATIBLE]" in place of "c" or "d" that appears following the word "Rules" in the display format illustrated in Fig. 25.6 (*see* Fig. 25.7).

Fig. 25.6. MARC authority record for name in Fig. 25.5.

```
ARN:       256371        Rec stat:    n
Entered:   19840818      Replaced:    19840818
Type:      z       Enc lvl:    n     Source:          Lang:
Roman:     |       Upd status: a     Mod rec:         Name use: a
Govt agn:  |       Ref status: a     Subj:        a   Subj use: a
Series:    n       Auth status: a    Geo subd: n      Ser use:  b
Ser num:   n       Auth/ref:    a    Name:     a      Rules:    c
  1 010       n  79022593
  2 040       DLC $c DLC
  3 100 10    Van Buren, Ariane.
  4 400 10    Buren, Ariane van
  5 400 10    Van Buren, E. Ariane
  6 670       Nuclear or not? 1978 (a.e.) $b t.p. (Ariane van Buren) jkt.
(E. Ariane van Buren, research assoc., International Inst. of Environment
& Development)
```

Fig. 25.7. Default display of name authority record in OCLC PRISM service.

```
AUTHORITY RECORD                                     EVALUATED
  ARN: 256371            REC STAT: NEW               VERIFIED
  ENTERED: 19840818      REPLACED: 19840818

  NAME/SUBJECT           ESTABLISHED HEADING
  LC

  1  010       n  79022593
  2  040       DLC $c DLC
  3  100 10    Van Buren, Ariane. [AACR2]
  4  400 10    Buren, Ariane van
  5  400 10    Van Buren, E. Ariane
  6  670       Nuclear or not? 1978 (a.e.) $b t.p. (Ariane van Buren) jkt.
(E. Ariane van Buren, research assoc., International Inst. of Environment &
Development)
```

Subject authority work is almost always done by verifying a heading as being the latest terminology used in the official list used by the library. In the case of LCSH, the online version of the Library of Congress Subject Authority File (LCSAF) can be searched through a bibliographic utility, or the latest microfiche, CD-ROM, or book version may be checked. In a manual system it is then necessary to determine which of the headings following the codes for *see also from* references are already represented in the catalog. The cataloger must also choose from the list of recommended terms those from which *see* references should be made. Figure 25.8 is an example of a subject authority card, indicating the source of the information. In manual subject authority records, the initials NT (narrower term), UF (used for), RT (related term), and BT (broader term) are often used instead of *x* and *xx*. Fig. 25.9 shows the corresponding MARC authority record. Terms coded 550 can be either related terms or broader terms. The difference is made known through use of "$w g" following the broader terms. MARC authority records do not show narrower terms on the assumption that when the system is programmed to display all the references from broader terms on a record, the narrower terms are automatically taken care of. As with names, the OCLC PRISM default display of subject authority records replaces the fixed field with English equivalents of the most used codes. It also displays "[BROADER TERM]" in place of "$w g" (*see* Fig. 25.10).

Fig. 25.8. Sample subject authority card.

```
      LITERATURE AND SCIENCE    (PN55; English literature,
        PR149.S4)

      NT   SCIENCE FICTION

      UF   Poetry and science
           Science and literature
           Science and poetry

      BT   SCIENCE AND THE HUMANITIES


                                   LCSH 13th ed.

                         O
```

instead of *x* and *xx*. Fig. 25.9 shows the corresponding MARC authority record. Terms coded 550 can be either related terms or broader terms. The difference is made known through use of "$w g" following the broader terms. MARC authority records do not show narrower terms on the assumption that when the system is programmed to display all the references from broader terms on a record, the narrower terms are automatically taken care of. As with names, the OCLC PRISM default display of subject authority records replaces the fixed field with English equivalents of the most used codes. It also displays "[BROADER TERM]" in place of "$w g" (*see* Fig. 25.10).

Fig. 25.9. Sample MARC authority record.

```
ARN:        2060424        Rec stat:     n
Entered:    19871218       Replaced:     19871218
Type:       z     Enc lvl:     n    Source:        Lang:
Roman:      |     Upd status:  a    Mod rec:       Name use: b
Govt agn:   |     Ref status:  b    Subj:       a  Subj use: a
Series:     n     Auth status: a    Geo subd: i    Ser use:  b
Ser num:    n     Auth/ref:    a    Name:       n  Rules:    n
 1 010        sh 85077571
 2 040        DLC $c DLC
 3 053        PN55 $c General
 4 053        PR149.S4 $c English literature
 5 150    0   Literature and science
 6 450    0   Poetry and science
 7 450    0   Science and literature
 8 450    0   Science and poetry
 9 550    0   Science and the humanities $w g
```

Fig. 25.10. Default display of subject authority record in OCLC PRISM service.

```
AUTHORITY RECORD                             NOT EVALUATED
  ARN: 2060424         REC STAT: NEW         VERIFIED
  ENTERED: 19871218    REPLACED: 19871218

  SUBJECT              ESTABLISHED HEADING
  LC                   INDIRECT

  1   010     sh 85077571
  2   040     DLC $c DLC
  3   053     PN55 $c General
  4   053     PR149.S4 $c English literature
  5   150   0 Literature and science
  6   450   0 Poetry and science
  7   450   0 Science and literature
  8   450   0 Science and poetry
  9   550   0 Science and the humanities [BROADER TERM]
```

CREATION OF AUTHORITY FILES

Following creation of authority records, the next step in authority work is the addition of the records into an authority file, either manual or machine-readable. In order for the authority file to serve its purpose it must be linked in some way to the bibliographic file. In card or paper systems the link is implicit. That is, the link is in the mind of a human who perceives the presence of an identical form on both the authority record and the catalog record and also perceives the presence in both files of the appropriate reference(s).

In many machine systems, also, the authority system linkage is implicit. In those systems, such as OCLC and RLIN, the authority file, although automated, is a completely separate file from the bibliographic file, and authority control of new records is dependent upon the cataloger finding the correct form of a heading in the authority file and then entering it correctly into the bibliographic record. There are no references in these files, although the authority files may be searched under the forms from which references are authorized. In such systems changes in headings mean that unless there are strict procedures for checking headings already in a file against every new heading entered, two or more forms of a heading may appear simultaneously with different bibliographic records displayed at each heading. Fig. 25.11 (11a through 11d) shows four screens of an online catalog in which bibliographic records related to the same person are entered under two forms of the name of a person who changed her name in 1983.

Fig. 25.11. Non-authority-controlled catalog with entries under two names for the same person, although only one is authorized.

Fig. 25.11a. Search for first name.

```
MSU=>AU DOWELL, ARLENE

    3 RECORDS MATCHED THE SEARCH

----Type DI 1-3  to Display the records
```

Fig. 25.11b. Display of hits found in Fig. 25.11a.

```
Screen 001 of 001                                                Catalog MSU
NMBR DATE  --------------------TITLE-------------------  -------AUTHOR------
0001 1976  Cataloging with copy : a decision-maker's ha  Dowell, Arlene Taylo
0002 1983  Cataloging nonbook materials :  problems in t  Frost, Carolyn O.,
0003 1980  Introduction to cataloging and classification  Wynar, Bohdan S.

-----Type DI NMBR(s) to Display specific records
```

Fig. 25.11c. Search for second name.

```
MSU=>AU TAYLOR, ARLENE

    2 RECORDS MATCHED THE SEARCH

-----Type DI 1-2  to Display the records
```

Fig. 25.11d. Display of hits found in Fig. 25.11c.

```
Screen 001 of 001                                            Catalog MSU
NMBR DATE  -------------------TITLE------------------ -------AUTHOR------
0001 1988  Cataloging with copy : a decision-maker's ha Taylor, Arlene G.,
0002 1985  Introduction to cataloging and classification Wynar, Bohdan S.

-----Type DI NMBR(s) to Display specific records

MSU=>
```

Figures 25.12a and 25.12b (see page 484) show two screens of an online catalog in which a subject heading that LC changed in 1989 appears on new materials in the new form, but still appears with many entries in its older form. In such situations it is possible occasionally to run the bibliographic file against the authority file to check for headings that match references and to change any matches found to the new form; but it usually is not feasible to do this often, and in the meantime multiple forms exist unless someone notices and changes them individually.

Fig. 25.12a. New form of LC subject heading has some current entries under a number of subdivisions.

```
CLIO SEARCH REQUEST:   S=SAVINGS AND LOAN
  SUBJECT HEADING GUIDE -- 12 HEADINGS FOUND   1 - 12 DISPLAYED
     SAVINGS AND LOAN ASSOCIATIONS
   1    --GOVERNMENT GUARANTY OF DEPOSITS
   2    --GOVERNMENT POLICY - UNITED STATES
   3    --TEXAS - HISTORY - 20TH CENTURY
   4    --UNITED STATES
   5    --UNITED STATES -CONGRESSES
   6    --UNITED STATES -CORRUPT PRACTICES
   7    --UNITED STATES -DEREGULATION
   8    --UNITED STATES -DIRECTORIES
   9    --UNITED STATES -GOVERNMENT GUARANTY OF DEPOSITS
  10    --UNITED STATES -HISTORY -20TH CENTURY
  11    --UNITED STATES -PERIODICALS
  12    --UNITED STATES -STATISTICS -PERIODICALS



Type line no. for titles under a heading.
Type r to revise, h for help, e for CLIO introduction.
Type your search and press ENTER==>
```

In more sophisticated systems the linkage between authority file and bibliographic file is explicit. That is, a direct internal linkage exists between a heading stored in the authority file and the same heading stored in the bibliographic file. In such systems the headings for every new record are checked against the authority file, and new or changed headings are flagged for review. In these systems also, references are displayed from unused terms to used ones and from used terms to narrower terms and sometimes also to related terms. References to

Fig. 25.12b. Old form of LC subject heading has many entries under the heading and a number of its subdivisions.

```
CLIO SEARCH REQUEST:  S=BUILDING AND LOAN
 SUBJECT HEADING GUIDE -- 15 HEADINGS FOUND  1 - 15 DISPLAYED
  1 BUILDING AND LOAN ASSOCIATIONS
  2    --CANADA -PERIODICALS
  3    --GERMANY
  4    --GOVERNMENT GUARANTY OF DEPOSITS
  5    --GOVERNMENT POLICY -UNITED STATES -CONGRESSES
  6    --GREAT BRITAIN
  7    --GREAT BRITAIN -HISTORY
  8    --LAW AND LEGISLATION -UNITED STATES -CONGRESSES
  9    --UNITED STATES
 10    --UNITED STATES -CONGRESSES
 11    --UNITED STATES -COSTS -STATISTICS
 12    --UNITED STATES -DIRECTORIES
 13    --UNITED STATES -PERIODICALS ⁻
 14    --UNITED STATES -STATE SUPERVISION
 15    --UNITED STATES -STATISTICS -PERIODICALS



Type line no. for titles under a heading.
Type r to revise, h for help, e for CLIO introduction.
Type your search and press ENTER==>
```

broader terms are not usually displayed, however. Figures 25.13a and 25.13b show two screens of an online catalog in which bibliographic records for works written under two forms of a person's name are consolidated under the later form with a reference from the earlier form. Figures 25.14a and 25.14b show two screens of an online catalog in which entries for a subject heading that LC changed in 1989 are consolidated under the later form with a reference from the earlier form.

Fig. 25.13a. Reference found under name searched.

```
LUIS SEARCH REQUEST:  A=DOWELL ARLENE
 Author Index -- 1 entries found, 1 - 1 displayed

    DOWELL ARLENE TAYLOR 1941
             *Search under
 1           TAYLOR ARLENE G 1941




TYPE LINE NO. FOR LUIS RECORD, & TO REFINE SEARCH.
TYPE ia FOR AMPLIFIED INDEX, e TO START OVER, h FOR HELP.
TYPE COMMAND AND PRESS ENTER
```

Fig. 25.13b. Result of typing "1" at the screen shown in Fig. 25.13a.

```
LUIS SEARCH REQUEST:  A=TAYLOR ARLENE G
 Author Index -- 6 entries found, 1 - 6 displayed

    TAYLOR ARLENE G 1941
  1   .CATALOGING NONBOOK MATERIALS <1983> (NU)
  2   .CATALOGING WITH COPY <1976> (GE)
  3   .CATALOGING WITH COPY <1988> (GE)
  4   .INTRODUCTION TO CATALOGING AND CLASSIFICATION <1980> (GE)
  5   .INTRODUCTION TO CATALOGING AND CLASSIFICATION <1985> (GE)
  6   .NOTES FOR SERIALS CATALOGING <1986> (NU)




TYPE LINE NO. FOR LUIS RECORD, & TO REFINE SEARCH.
TYPE ia FOR AMPLIFIED INDEX, e TO START OVER, h FOR HELP.
TYPE COMMAND AND PRESS ENTER
```

Fig. 25.14a. Reference found under form of subject heading searched.

```
              SUBJECT: building and loan



Building And Loan Associations    is not used in this library's catalog;

Savings And Loan Associations    is used instead.


Do you wish to search for Savings And Loan Associations?  (y/n)


                 INNOPAC(4) ----- Columbia Law Library
```

Fig. 25.14b. Result of typing "y" at the screen shown in Fig. 25.14a.

```
You searched for the SUBJECT: Savings And Loan Associations
20 SUBJECTS found, with 59 entries; SUBJECTS 1-8 are:

    1    Savings And Loan Associations Government Guaranty Of      1 entry
    2    Savings And Loan Associations Law And Legislation Gre     3 entries
    3    Savings And Loan Associations Law And Legislation Ire     1 entry
    4    Savings And Loan Associations Law And Legislation Uni    12 entries
    5    Savings And Loan Associations Pennsylvania ..........     1 entry
    6    Savings And Loan Associations Pennsylvania Law ......     1 entry
    7    Savings And Loan Associations Taxation United States .    1 entry
    8    Savings And Loan Associations United States ........    14 entries


Please type the NUMBER of the item you want to see, or
  F> Go FORWARD                    P> PRINT
  N> NEW Search                    D> DISPLAY Title and Call #
  A> ANOTHER Search by SUBJECT     O> OTHER options
Choose one (1-8,F,N,A,P,D,T,L,J,O)
                   INNOPAC(4) ----- Columbia Law Library
```

Typographical errors are possible in any system, of course, but if the authority link is only implicit, the system does not aid in identifying them. The result can be complete loss of information for users. Suppose, for example, someone is looking for all novels a library has by Hamilton Cochran. Fig. 25.15 shows the results of a search for this author in an online catalog. Most users would assume from this response that there is only one novel. However, if one searches just the surname "Cochran" and then becomes curious about the strange name "Cochranm" at the end of the list (*see* Fig. 25.16a), one will find a second novel by Hamilton Cochran (*see* Fig. 25.16b). In a system with explicit authority linkage, "Cochranm, Hamilton, 1898- " would have been brought to a cataloger's attention as a new heading, at which time the typographical error likely would have been noticed.

Fig. 25.15. Results of a search for novels of Hamilton Cochran.

```
CLIO SEARCH REQUEST:  A=COCHRAN HAM
BIBLIOGRAPHIC RECORD -- NO. 1 OF 1 ENTRIES FOUND

Cochran, Hamilton, 1898-
   The dram tree.  Indianapolis, Bobbs-Merrill [1961]
   286 p. 22 cm.
   SUBJECT HEADINGS (Library of Congress; use s= ):
      United States--History--Civil War, 1861-1865--Fiction.

LOCATION: BUTLER STACKS
CALL NUMBER:  812C6434 P5 (copy 1)




Type r to revise, h for help, e for CLIO introduction.
Type your search and press ENTER==>
```

Fig. 25.16a. Results of a search for all surnames "Cochran."

```
CLIO SEARCH REQUEST:  A=COCHRAN
  AUTHOR/TITLE GUIDE -- 116 DISPLAYED
    1      COCHRAN A
    2      COCHRAN B
    4      COCHRAN C
    7      COCHRAN E
    8      COCHRAN G
   10      COCHRAN H
   12      COCHRAN J
   19      COCHRAN L
   26      COCHRAN M
   27      COCHRAN P
   28      COCHRAN R
   29      COCHRAN S
   32      COCHRAN T
   46      COCHRAN W
   59      COCHRANE
  116      COCHRANM


Type no. of guide term that matches or precedes desired entry to see index.
Type r to revise, h for help, e for CLIO introduction.
Type your search and press ENTER==>
```

Fig. 25.16b. Result of typing "116" at the screen shown in Fig. 25.16a.

```
CLIO SEARCH REQUEST:  A=COCHRAN
BIBLIOGRAPHIC RECORD -- NO. 116 OF 116 ENTRIES FOUND

Cochranm, Hamilton, 1898-
    Rogue's holiday, a novel by Hamilton Cochran.  Indianapolis, New York, The
Bobbs-Merrill company [1947]
    297 p. 22 cm.
    "First edition."

LOCATION: BUTLER STACKS
CALL NUMBER  812C6434 V5 (copy 1)




Type i for index, g for guide.
Type r to revise, h for help, e for CLIO introduction.
Type your search and press ENTER==>
```

In the most sophisticated systems there is a linkage that uses relational file techniques to link a bibliographic record without any headings to a complex of authority records that store all the headings. The advantage here is that each heading is stored only once, and thus matching of bibliographic and authority headings is unnecessary. In addition when a heading has to be changed, the change is made only in the authority record. What the user sees in such a system is no different from what is seen in the previously described linked systems.

CATALOG AS AUTHORITY FILE

While it is possible to do authority work without making separate authority records, this is done less and less often. In manual card catalogs, libraries formerly would let the catalog itself serve as the authority file. That is, the heading used in the catalog was assumed to have been verified, and necessary references were kept track of on the back of one of the main entry cards for the heading in question. This method became difficult, however, when notes were needed to resolve conflicting headings or when the set of cards on which the references were recorded were withdrawn from the catalog.

In online catalogs, too, the bibliographic record may be considered to contain the authoritative heading in situations where no notes or references are required. In some systems authority work is done for every heading, but authority records are made only when references or notes are required, and then the heading index is created from authority file headings and references combined with headings from bibliographic records that have no associated authority records. The advantage of this system is the saving of disk space necessary to store MARC authority records that contain no information not available in bibliographic records. This advantage is offset in systems using relational file techniques, because in the latter, much space is saved by storing each heading only once instead of in every associated bibliographic record.

MAINTENANCE OF AUTHORITY SYSTEMS

In order to maintain an authority system, it is necessary to have routine error checking between authority and bibliographic files. There must also be routine error checking among authority records for consistency. For example, if a changed heading authority record does not replace the older heading record properly, it would be possible to have a response to a search for one term refer to another term only to have a reference at that term referring back to the first (*see* Fig. 25.17).

Fig. 25.17. Possible result of a changed heading in a system without error checking.

```
SEARCH REQUEST:  S=PHONOTAPES
   Subject Index -- 5 entries found, 1 - 5 displayed

            PHONOTAPES
               *Search under
      1        AUDIOTAPES
      2        --CATALOGS
      3        --REVIEWS -INDEXES
      4     PHONOTAPES IN EDUCATION
      5     PHONOTAPES IN RADIO JOURNALISM


[Result of pressing "1" at this screen:]


SEARCH REQUEST:  S=AUDIOTAPES
   Subject Index -- 1 entries found, 1 - 1 displayed

         AUDIOTAPES
               *Search under
      1        PHONOTAPES
```

Updating is necessary when a library is using LC authority data as the basis of its authority system. Names are changed to reflect new usages by some authors; subjects are constantly changed to update terminology, add references, etc.; and new headings are added. There must be procedures for replacing the changed records and adding the new ones. Changed LC records are particularly difficult because there is not yet a mechanism for notifying a library that has used an LC bibliographic record in the past that its terminology or name form has now been changed. For example, the authority record for "Cochrane, Pauline Atherton, 1929- " was changed in 1990 to "Cochrane, Pauline A. (Pauline Atherton), 1929- " because 80 percent of her works as represented in OCLC's database were found to use the form with the initial "A." (*See* Fig. 25.18.) Records that appeared in LC's MARC file at the time were changed and reissued, but many records in the utilities and in local online catalogs remain in the old form. (*See* Fig. 25.19.) One problem in such a case is that the titles of such authors appear in two or more separate alphabetical subsets—the same problem that can result when no authority work was done in the first place.

Fig. 25.18. Authority record for Pauline A. Cochrane.

```
ARN:        66085          Rec stat:    c
Entered:    19840817       Replaced:    19900703
Type:     z      Enc lvl:  n       Source:          Lang:
Roman:    |      Upd status: a     Mod rec:         Name use: a
Govt agn: |      Ref status: a     Subj:       a    Subj use: a
Series:   n      Auth status: a    Geo subd: n      Ser use:  b
Ser num:  n      Auth/ref:   a     Name:       a    Rules:    c
  1 010       n 50030719
  2 040       DLC $c DLC $d DLC
  3 100 10    Cochrane, Pauline A. $q (Pauline Atherton), $d 1929-
  4 400 10    Atherton, Pauline, $d 1929-
  5 400 10    Atherton, P. $q (Pauline), $d 1929-
  6 400 10    Cochrane, Pauline Atherton, $d 1929-
  7 670       Her Development of a computer-based laboratory for library
science students ... 1970: $b t.p. (Pauline Atherton)
  8 670       Meadow, C. Basics of online searching, c1981: $b t.p.
(Pauline (Atherton) Cochrane)
  9 670       Her Redesign of catalogs and indexes ... 1985: $b CIP t.p.
(Pauline A. Cochrane) book t.p. (Pauline Atherton Cochrane)
 10 670       Her Improving LCSH for use in online catalogs, 1986: $b
t.p. (Pauline A. Cochrane)
 11 670       OCLC data base, 10-12-89: $b (Pauline A. Cochrane [80%
form], Pauline Atherton Cochrane, Pauline Atherton, Pauline A. Atherton,
P. Atherton)
```

Fig. 25.19. OCLC truncated display for Pauline Cochrane, showing two alphabetical subsets.

```
OLUC   dp coch,pau,a                            Records: 65

Rec#  Name               Title                  Publisher      Date L
   1  Cocheis, Pauline Au P'edagogie des travaux a l'au Librarie Ch. D 1885
   2  Cocheris, Pauline A Les parures primitives avec u Furne,         1914
   3  Cocheris, Pauline A P'edagogie des travaux 'a l'a C. Delagrave,  1882
   4  Cochrane, Pauline A Aid-to-indexing forms : a pro American Insti 1963
   5  Cochrane, Pauline A American Institute of Physics American Insti 1965
   6  Cochrane, Pauline A Basics of online searching /  Wiley,         1981 D
   7  Cochrane, Pauline A Critical views of LCSH - the  ERIC Clearingh 1981
   8  Cochrane, Pauline A Development of a computer-bas  School of Libr 1970 D
   9  Cochrane, Pauline A Executive summary, project bi Syracuse Unive 1981
  10  Cochrane, Pauline A Final report of the research  American Insti 1968
  11  Cochrane, Pauline A Guidelines for the organizati Unesco,        1975 D
  12  Cochrane, Pauline A Handbook for information syst Unesco,        1977 D
  13  Cochrane, Pauline A Humanization of knowledge in  School of Libr 1972
  14  Cochrane, Pauline A Improving LCSH for use in onl Libraries Unli 1986 D
  15  Cochrane, Pauline A Librarians and online service Knowledge Indu 1977 D
  16  Cochrane, Pauline A Libraries and automation; a s School of Libr 1970 D
  17  Cochrane, Pauline A A method for producing journa American Insti 1964
  18  Cochrane, Pauline A Putting knowledge to work; an Vikas Pub. Hou 1973 D
  19  Cochrane, Pauline A Redesign of catalogs and inde Oryx Press,    1985 D
  20  Cochrane, Pauline A The role of "letters" journal American Insti 1964
  21  Cochrane, Pauline A A suggested method for produc American Insti 1963
  22  Cochrane, Pauline A Aid-to-indexing forms : repor American Insti 1964
  23  Cochrane, Pauline A Books are for use : final rep School of Info 1978
  24  Cochrane, Pauline A Critical views of LCSH--the L ERIC Clearingh 1981
  25  Cochrane, Pauline A An ERIC information analysis   ERIC Clearingh 1981 G
  26  Cochrane, Pauline A An ERIC information analysis   ERIC Clearingh 1983
  27  Cochrane, Pauline A An ERIC information analysis   ERIC Clearingh 1984
  28  Cochrane, Pauline A Evaluation of the retrieval o Clearinghouse  1968
  29  Cochrane, Pauline A File organization and search  American Insti 1967
  30  Cochrane, Pauline A Free text retrieval evaluatio Syracuse Unive 1972
  31  Cochrane, Pauline A Guidelines for the organizati United States  1975
  32  Cochrane, Pauline A Humanization of knowledge in  School of Libr 1973
  33  Cochrane, Pauline A Identification of research pa American Insti 1963
  34  Cochrane, Pauline A Indexing physics research pap                1963
  35  Cochrane, Pauline A Indexing requirements of phys                1962
  36  Cochrane, Pauline A The journal literature of phy American Insti 1964
  37  Cochrane, Pauline A On tap : on-line training and ERIC Clearingh 1978
  38  Cochrane, Pauline A Online public access catalogs ERIC Clearingh 1982
```

[1]Start of first alphabetical sequence

[2]Start of second alphabetical sequence

CONCLUSION

There is great potential for use of authority control that has not yet been realized. One is the idea mentioned earlier of providing access to broader subject terms. Another is the potential for controlling elements of records not now even given as access points (e.g., names of publishers). A third potential lies in further control of works. Editions of works, for example, are now related only by either the fact of their having identical author and title access points or the provision of notes on bibliographic records giving earlier titles or authors. If authority control of works, which is only in its infancy, were extended to such relationships as editions and other derivative works, identifying works in fields such as music and literature would be greatly enhanced.

NOTES

[1]For discussion of how system design can supplement authority control, see: Marcia Bates, "Subject Access in Online Catalogs: A Design Model," *Journal of the American Society for Information Science* 37, no. 6 (November 1986): 357-376; Arlene G. Taylor, "Authority Control and System Design," in *Policy and Practice in the Bibliographic Control of Nonbook Media*, edited by Sheila S. Intner and Richard P. Smiraglia (Chicago, American Library Association, 1987), pp. 64-81.

[2]Catherine E. Pasterczyk, "Russian Transliteration Variations for Searchers," *DATABASE* 8 (February 1985): 68-75; Anne B. Piternick, "What's in a Name? Use of Names and Titles in Subject Searching," *DATABASE* 8 (December 1985): 22-28; David M. Pilachowski and David Everett, "What's in a Name? Looking for People Online – Social Sciences," *DATABASE* 8 (August 1985): 47-65; David M. Pilachowski and David Everett, "What's in a Name? Looking for People Online – Current Events," *DATABASE* 9 (April 1986): 43-50; David Everett and David M. Pilachowski, "What's in a Name? Looking for People Online – Humanities," *DATABASE* 9 (October 1986): 26-34; Bonnie Snow, "Caduceus: People in Medicine: Searching Names Online," *ONLINE* 10 (September 1986): 122-127.

SUGGESTED READING

Authority Control in Music Libraries: Proceedings of the Music Library Association Preconference, March 5, 1985. Edited by Ruth Tucker. MLA Technical Report No. 16. Canton, Mass., Music Library Association, 1989.

Burger, Robert H. *Authority Work: The Creation, Use, Maintenance, and Evaluation of Authority Records and Files.* Littleton, Colo., Libraries Unlimited, 1985.

Clack, Doris Hargrett. *Authority Control: Principles, Applications, and Instructions.* Chicago, American Library Association, 1990.

Tillett, Barbara B., ed. *Authority Control in the Online Environment: Considerations and Practices.* New York, Haworth Press, 1989. (Also issued as *Cataloging & Classification Quarterly*, v. 9, no. 3 [1989].)

Part V

ORGANIZATION

Processing Centers, Networking, and Online Systems

26

INTRODUCTION

With the continued growth in volume of published materials and increased use of computers and telecommunications to transmit bibliographic information and documents from producer to consumer, the resultant need is for more and better library service. The impact of computerization has significantly changed the traditional patterns of cataloging and processing of library materials. Most libraries and library systems of any size have either centralized their technical services or entered into cooperative arrangements with other libraries through various levels of networking. Smaller institutions often purchase their processing from commercial vendors or non-commercial suppliers, such as the Library of Congress. Thus we have centralized processing, cooperative processing, and commercial processing, most of which are automated.

For nearly all American libraries, the Library of Congress has been the primary source of bibliographic data for decades. With the advent of automation, LC's bibliographic products have been repackaged or reformatted by vendors, networks, and individual libraries. The result has been the development of large databases with LC records as the core. These databases are used directly by some libraries for their cataloging operations, are accessed by other libraries through a bibliographic utility, and are also used by commercial vendors who provide processing for still other libraries.

Major cataloging operations usually have two production lines: copy cataloging and original cataloging. The copy cataloging operation is usually the larger unit, staffed by well-trained technicians called "copy catalogers," who edit existing bibliographic records either found in machine-readable form, on printed cards or proofslips, in the *National Union Catalog*, or in other bibliographic tools. The original cataloging operation is usually/staffed by a handful of professionally trained "original catalogers" who prepare bibliographic records when no cataloging "copy" has been found for the work in hand.

Cataloging operations are now closely tied to automated processing. The development of networking using telecommunications and computers has enhanced cooperation for processing services and systems. Automation has virtually eliminated the isolated individual library doing its own ordering, cataloging, and physical preparation of materials.

CENTRALIZED PROCESSING

In integrated library systems serving an entire region, county, municipality, university, public school district, commercial enterprise, or government agency, a central processing office normally handles the acquisition and preparation of materials for all public service branches. Subunits may do a final checking of

493

records and file those records in their branch catalogs, but if any significant revision of the work is needed, it usually goes back to the central office. This type of organization received strong emphasis with the rapid growth of library systems after World War II.

The term *centralized processing* may be broadly defined as any consolidated effort to bring under one control the technical operations necessary to prepare library materials for access and use at different service points. In the ensuing discussion several comments will be made that apply equally well—perhaps with some slight modification—to cooperative efforts and even to commercial sources of cataloging. The reader can carry over such observations into those discussions where they have a bearing.

Processing centers take a variety of forms, but can generally be grouped into broad categories according to one or more notable characteristics. Grouping by type of services rendered gives: 1) centers responsible for acquisition and complete technical processing, down to the physical marking and/or jacketing, 2) centers that order, catalog, and classify, and 3) centers that only catalog and classify.

There are, of course, advantages to setting up a processing center for a group of libraries or branches. They include:

1. Increased efficiency in handling more material at less cost

2. Higher quality cataloging

3. Centralization and simplification of business routines

4. Better deployment of staff through specialization

5. Use of more sophisticated equipment

6. Opportunities to create union catalogs

But there are problems as well. Local variations in practice have to be identified and coordinated, or, if necessary, eliminated. Economic justification must be carefully determined, both before and after decision-making, to ensure that it is real, not imaginary. Many descriptive reports of individual centers lack critical self-appraisal and follow-up studies, especially in their cost analyses. Efficiency of operation is often the function of size. The "optimum" volume of processing in a given center should be determined. Combining several different types of libraries (e.g., school and public) within one system may lead to problems that even a highly structured organization cannot solve. We often learn as much from our failures as from our more successful attempts at consolidation.

COOPERATIVE SYSTEMS

The chief trait differentiating cooperative from centralized processing is that the cooperative approach involves several independent libraries or systems. Each member usually continues to perform some of its own technical service work, depending on exchange of data to achieve broader coverage or leaving a sizeable portion of its processing to be performed as a group project. Again, better use of resources, personnel, and equipment, as well as higher discounts on bulk purchases, are anticipated. The need for more standardization in ordering, cataloging, and processing may become either an advantage or a disruptive factor.

There are a number of cooperative arrangements in which several libraries share a single terminal connected to a bibliographic utility. Several libraries with small budgets and small staffs can pool resources to share one membership in a utility. Some such libraries may use the terminal only a few hours a month; others may use it one day a week. The librarians must commute to the location of the terminal and must schedule terminal time carefully.[1]

UNION CATALOGS

Union catalog projects are not, strictly speaking, a type of processing arrangement, but they are essential to a successful processing center and can be a *sine qua non* of a cooperative system. For example, the Bibliographical Center for Research (BCR) in Denver started in 1936 with a WPA grant to develop a union catalog based on a depository set of Library of Congress cards marked to show the holdings of member libraries in the Rocky Mountain area. The catalog was designed chiefly to serve BCR as a clearinghouse for regional interlibrary loans. In 1975, after a period of waning membership and reduced revenues, new objectives were announced, including the brokerage of OCLC services, with aid to members in other, related fields of communication, systems study, and network stimulation. The union catalog and interlibrary loan (ILL) services continued, but were de-emphasized in favor of newer forms of cooperation. As at BCR, most union catalog projects in printed card form are now valued primarily for having fostered early efforts at library cooperation that are presently coming to fruition in many kinds of consortia and networks.

Some of those consortia and networks have produced online union catalogs at various levels:

- international online union catalogs of the major bibliographic utilities

- multi-institutional regional or state networks, such as the union catalog for libraries in Illinois

- single institution union catalogs, ranging from the statewide nine-campus online union catalog of the University of California to the union catalog for the branches of an individual public library

There are also specialized union catalogs for types of materials such as the Union Catalog of Newspapers on OCLC and numerous union lists of serials, including those available through the bibliographic utilities.

COMMERCIAL PROCESSING

Over a century ago, Charles C. Jewett, librarian of the Smithsonian Institution, proposed "A Plan for Stereotyping Catalogues by Separate Titles...." The Smithsonian was at that time a copyright depository. As it produced bibliographic records, they could, he suggested, be preserved on stereotype plates for a variety of applications, including the printing of cards for sale to other libraries on demand. While Jewett's proposal did not itself endure, it presaged the marketing of printed cards undertaken by the Library of Congress in 1901. Neither venture was "commercial" in the strict sense. However, they were later imitated by a host of business concerns. Barbara Westby defines *commercial cataloging* as "centralized cataloging performed and sold by a non-library agency operating for profit."[2] In most cases it is a by-product of other commercial interests, e.g., the Standard Catalog compilations of H. W. Wilson, the vending emphasis of a book jobber such as Baker & Taylor, or the promotional activities of a corporation like the Society for Visual Education.

The Wilson Printed Catalog Card Service supplied many school and public libraries with simple but adequate card copy at nominal cost for widely read books from 1938 to 1975. During that period over 100 other distributors and publishers followed the Wilson example of supplying a packet of cards with each book sold. In 1976 the first edition of *Cataloging with Copy* listed 15 commercial processing services and 5 additional commercial sources of card sets.[3] Technological advances have caused considerable changes in the scene since then. Some of the services are no longer in business. Most of the others have radically changed their character. They have supplemented their print services with microform, CD-ROM, and/or online data retrieval systems. Changes are occurring so rapidly that no reliable recommendations of particular systems or services can be made, but the Commercial Processing Services Committee of the Resources and Technical Services Division (RTSD) does offer a set of guidelines that any cataloger interested in making an intelligent choice should apply.[4]

BIBLIOGRAPHIC SERVICES OF THE LIBRARY OF CONGRESS

LC's bibliographic records offer complete coverage for materials, both foreign and domestic, cataloged by the Library. LC is, of course, the copyright depository for domestic works. Two federal legislative acts significantly increased LC's coverage of foreign materials starting in the early 1960s. One authorized certain foreign countries to pay some of their debts to the United States by sending printed materials. The other authorized LC to acquire, catalog, and distribute bibliographic records for all materials of research value published in foreign countries. The thrust of the legislation benefited not only the Library of Congress, but also all American research libraries.

In 1975 the Card Division of the Library of Congress changed its name to the Cataloging Distribution Service (CDS).[5] The change reflected a trend from print to machine-readable format (i.e., MARC tapes) in its distribution of bibliographic records. The print formats are still widely used. This distribution of print formats includes the sale of Alert Service cards as well as printed cards, the Cataloging-in-Publication (CIP) program, and the publication of book catalogs and cataloging tools, including the *National Union Catalog* (*NUC*), various bibliographies, the *Library of Congress Classification* schedules, *Library of Congress Subject Headings, New Serial Titles*, etc. Many of LC's bibliographic tools are now available only in non-print formats. For example, since 1983, the *National Union Catalog* has been produced only in microfiche. Other tools are available in CD-ROM format, such as LC's authority records for names and subjects and also their bibliographic records, all of which are, of course, also available on MARC tapes.

Library of Congress Cards

Most of today's card output is produced on demand from MARC tapes and packaged by machine through use of automated optical scanning equipment, although orders for non-MARC cards must still be filled manually from inventory stocks. *The Complete Catalog* from CDS, available on request, gives information on how to open an account and interpret the various order codes and pricing structures. Standard order slips of the kind reproduced below are furnished free to subscribers; multiple order forms compatible with LC optical character recognition devices are available from all major library supply houses.

Card Order Form

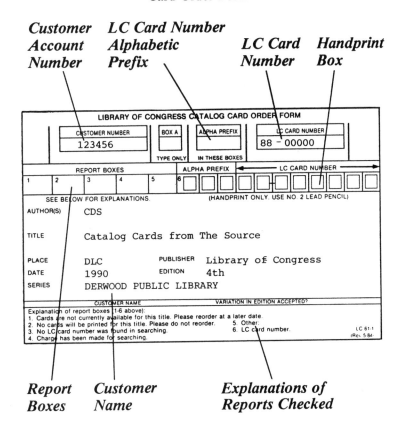

Ordering by LC card number rather than by author or title is more economical, and usually more satisfactory. This number can be found in standard bibliographies and book selection tools, such as the *Cumulative Book Index* (*CBI*), the *Weekly Record* (*WR*), the *American Book Publishing Record* (*BPR*), *Library Journal* (*LJ*), etc. It is also included, along with CIP data, on the title-page verso of most current books.

CDS Alert Service

The CDS Alert Service is a notification service that issues subject selections of bibliographic records produced at LC. The notices are printed on 3x5-inch white lightweight card stock. They are sent weekly to subscribers, and the content depends upon a subscriber's profile. The subscriber chooses from any of 2,155 subject categories identified in *LC Classification Outline for Alert Service* and/or any of 21 broad subject categories (which are basically the class letters of the LC classification). With this service the subscriber receives full LC cataloging for the subject areas of interest. Subscribers may choose to receive English-language records only, non-English records only, or both, and may also choose to receive only MARC records, only non-MARC records (i.e., records in the nonroman alphabets that are not yet being input to MARC), or both. CIP records are included, thus providing three to six months' advance notice of a book's publication. *The Complete Catalog* describing the procedures for ordering, is available on request.

Depository card sets were formerly maintained by many research libraries, but the *NUC* now serves the same purpose at very real economy of both filing time and storage space. Even more economical is access to LC's bibliographic and authority records on CD-ROM or online through the bibliographic utilities.

Cataloging in Publication

Most current American books carry a partial bibliographic description, namely author, title, series statement, notes, subject and added entries, LC call number, DDC number, and LC card number, on the verso of the title page. The program responsible for providing this bibliographic information is known as Cataloging in Publication, or CIP. This program was initiated in 1971. Publishers cooperate by sending data sheets and front matter for books nearing publication to the Library of Congress for preliminary cataloging prior to publication of their books. CIP records are available on MARC tapes, being later supplanted when the full record becomes machine-readable. CIP records are useful as a ready source of LC card numbers. They can also be used to assist in the establishment of name headings. Some libraries use the CIP records for preliminary cataloging and later enhance the record when full LC records appear. Other libraries may use the brief CIP record instead of full cataloging, satisfied with the minimal-level record it provides. The illustration below shows the format and appearance of CIP data.

Library of Congress Cataloging-in-Publication Data

Sears, Minnie Earl, 1873-1933.
    Sears list of subject headings. -- 14th ed. / edited by Martha T. Mooney.
      p.   cm.
    Includes bibliographical references.
    ISBN 0-8242-0803-X : $42.00
    1. Subject headings. I. Mooney, Martha T. II. Title.
Z695.S43 1991

        91-10290
        CIP

LC Publications Displaying Cataloging

A wealth of bibliographic information can be obtained from the printed catalogs of the Library of Congress. The *Catalog of Books Represented by Library of Congress Printed Cards Issued to July 31, 1942* has been continued by cumulative serial publication of the *NUC*. A separate retrospective set published by Mansel is entitled *National Union Catalog, pre-1956 Imprints*. Library of Congress book catalogs include *Audiovisual Materials*; *Music, Books on Music, and Sound Recordings*; *Monographic Series*; and the *Subject Catalog*. 1989 was the last year for the printed version of *Music, Books on Music, and Sound Recordings*. Starting in 1990, it is published in microfiche. Since January 1983 the *NUC* has been published in 48X microfiche and has replaced the publication of the other LC book catalogs. *NUC* is issued as a register with complete bibliographic entries accompanied by indexes for name, title, subject, and series access to the registers. *NUC Books* adds new registers monthly and *NUC Audiovisual Materials* and *NUC Cartographic Materials* add new registers quarterly. The corresponding indexes cumulate monthly and quarterly, respectively. Also published in microfiche format is the *National Union Catalog: Register of Additional Locations* (*RAL*). The *RAL* contains additional location symbols of libraries contributing bibliographic records to the *NUC* since 1968. It is updated quarterly and includes over 40 million locations with about 3 million new location symbols added each year. A final *NUC* product, the *National Union Catalog of Manuscript Collections*, has been available in print since 1959.

Another LC publication displaying cataloging is *New Serial Titles*. Cataloging entries are supplied by the Library of Congress and more than 500 cooperating libraries in the United States and Canada. All of the records contributed to the CONSER file (see description below) are included. Annual and 5-year cumulations are available. The 1986-1990 cumulation is published only in microfiche.

Machine-Readable Cataloging (MARC)

The importance of the Library of Congress for setting catalog practice became even more evident with the introduction of the MARC Distribution Service. The initial study began in 1964; since that time, extensive experimentation proceeded in the MARC I and MARC II, the Retrospective Conversion (RECON), the Cooperative Machine-Readable Cataloging (COMARC), and the British UK/MARC pilot projects.[6]

At first, records were available only for English-language monographs, but now there are formats available for archival materials, audiovisual materials, computer files, films, manuscripts, maps, music, and serials as well as for books. In addition, over 130 roman-alphabet languages and several non-roman-alphabet languages are now being input.

The proliferation of different formats for different types and patterns of publications has been a problem because, while the formats are the same in basic ways, they differ in some of their details. A field may be legal in one format but not in others, and occasionally indicators or subfield codes differ in meaning across formats. To remedy this, an integrated format has been constructed. It is to be implemented in 1993. A publication that explains and lists the integrated format, *Format Integration and Its Effect on the USMARC Bibliographic Format*, is available from CDS.

The Conversion of Serials (CONSER) automated database was sponsored by the Council on Library Resources, using the online facilities of OCLC, and distributed through the MARC Distribution Service—Serials. Starting in mid-1976 with nearly 30,000 LC/MARC serial records, and accepting input from 14 North American libraries, it amassed over 200,000 records in its initial two years. Only one-third of them were authenticated by the Library of Congress and the National Library of Canada (the Designated Centers of Responsibility), but the number of verifications increased each year. Original plans were for LC to take over full support at the close of the two-year pilot program, but when it ran into difficulties in expanding its automation capacity, OCLC agreed to retain the database, assuming managerial responsibility as well.

Another project to add machine-readable bibliographic records for materials previously cataloged on cards was the REMARC project, a retrospective conversion project. The REMARC database was created by Carrollton Press starting in 1980. The goal was to convert to MARC format over five million titles cataloged by LC between 1897 and 1968 (the year that most English-language LC cataloging of monographs became available in MARC format). Carrollton also converted some items cataloged by LC since 1968 that were not input into the MARC database by LC (e.g., foreign-language items that were phased into the MARC program throughout the 1970s).

Other projects to add to the LC MARC database began as experiments in cooperative cataloging. In the early 1980s the University of Chicago and Harvard University joined with the Library of Congress to create cataloging records in MARC format. Library staff at both Harvard and Chicago directly input bibliographic records into the LC database, which were then distributed along with LC records to MARC subscribers. This project has now expanded to become the National Cooperative Cataloging Project (NCCP).

Expanding on the idea of online data entry using computer to computer connections rather than direct terminal to computer connection to LC's computers, the Library of Congress initiated the Linked Systems Project (LSP) to connect the major bibliographic utilities in the United States with the Library of Congress. LSP currently links the OCLC and RLIN systems (with plans to also include the Western Library Network [WLN]) with the Library of Congress for the creation and maintenance of authority records. LSP is in the process of expanding to include creation and maintenance of bibliographic records with the NCCP libraries.

The growth and nearly universal acceptance of the MARC formats, and even more, the publication of *AACR2* and *AACR2R*, highlighted the need for machine-readable authority records. A MARC format for name authority records was developed in the late 1970s, and LC began inputting name authority records in 1978. Later the MARC format for authorities was expanded to accommodate subjects, series, and uniform titles. All new names, series, uniform titles, and subjects are currently entered into the LC database in the MARC authorities format, and many records have been retrospectively converted. The NACO project (Name Authority Cooperative Project) complements LC's internal creation of machine-readable authority records by the addition of records from other cooperating libraries. As noted above, this is now done online by the participating libraries through RLIN and OCLC connections to the Library of Congress using LSP.

It is possible to obtain a subscription to one or more of the MARC tape services. One can receive only books, films, maps, or serials, or any combination of these. Also available are CONSER records, Name Authorities, and Subject Authorities. *The Complete Catalog*, available on request, describes this service. All of the major bibliographic utilities subscribe to the MARC tape services.

In addition to the USMARC records created by the Library of Congress, other countries have accepted the MARC format with slight variations for creating machine-readable cataloging records. Canada uses CANMARC, the United Kingdom uses UKMARC, and many other countries utilize the UNIMARC format established through the International Federation of Library Associations and Institutions (IFLA).

ONLINE BIBLIOGRAPHIC NETWORKING

Various definitions of networking spell out theoretical criteria or conditions. In practice, however, the term covers any systematic interchange of materials, bibliographic data, services, information, or occasionally, the transfer of such resources from a central office to a number of libraries. *Network* has been used to describe multi-library organizations designed to facilitate interlibrary loan, reference, duplicate exchange, processing, and the like. Our concern in this section is with the last named activity.

There are at present three major online bibliographic networks in the United States: OCLC Online Computer Library Center, the Research Libraries Information Network (RLIN), and the Western Library Network (WLN). A fourth network, Utlas International, also serves some libraries in the United States, although the majority of its members are in Canada. The Network Development Office of the Library of Congress uses the term *bibliographic utility* for these online processing systems.[7] This term refers to providers of computerized cataloging records as distinguished from bibliographic service centers or regional networks, e.g., the Southeastern Library Network (SOLINET), which serve as regional brokers, providing intermediate communication, training, and service for participating libraries.

Bibliographic utilities seek to make catalog data widely and conveniently available, to foster processing speed and efficiency, to reduce the staff and cost of technical operations, and to facilitate resource sharing. Emphasis varies with the types of library a utility is designed to serve. RLIN, for example, caters to the needs of major research libraries, while OCLC appeals to a wider spectrum. As most bibliographic utilities evolved, their goals broadened to include support for different library functions.

Although the objectives of the three major bibliographic utilities are similar, their services, costs, and operating procedures differ considerably. Each offers unique features that involve advantages and disadvantages for different members. The library that has potential access to more than one utility must consider carefully such factors as cost, size of database, adaptation to its needs, types of service contracts, training and support arrangements, and the membership among neighboring libraries. One of the goals of the Linked Systems Project is to provide an interface to the databases of all utilities regardless of an individual library's primary affiliation.

OCLC Online Computer Library Center

This oldest and largest of the bibliographic networks was incorporated in 1967 as the Ohio College Library Center, establishing an online, shared cataloging system with an online union catalog to the academic libraries of Ohio. Online operations began in 1971 and expanded rapidly. By 1990 there were over 10,400 member libraries throughout the world, cataloging 94 percent of their incoming materials through use of the existing online records, and inputting their original catalog records for cooperative use by other members. In 1978 it changed its name to the acronym OCLC, Inc., downplaying the former regional connotation. At the same time, the governing structure was altered to allow libraries outside Ohio equal participation in its governance. In 1981 it changed the official name to OCLC Online Computer Library Center in response to the fact that many people thought "OCLC" should stand for something. A Users' Council, elected from participants grouped in the regional service networks, chooses from among its members 6 of the 15 who serve on the Board of Trustees. The Users' Council also advises the Board, which is the corporation's governing body. Additionally, there is a Research Libraries Advisory Committee (RLAC) made up of 12 directors of research libraries. RLAC meets three times a year to articulate the special needs and concerns of research libraries that are members of OCLC.

OCLC serves individual libraries for the most part through broker networks such as AMIGOS, NELINET, OHIONET, SOLINET, SUNY, and BCR. The western states and Europe each have a regional service center maintained by OCLC itself, and there are a few scattered independent members. The brokers negotiate group contracts on behalf of their affiliates, perform profiling and staff training according to each one's specific needs, handle billing and other business procedures, and offer general assistance in effective utilization of OCLC services. Most regional networks are financed through membership fees plus surcharges on OCLC's first-time use charges.

The primary OCLC service has always been the online cataloging subsystem creating a database called the Online Union Catalog (OLUC). Because of its widespread use, it is described briefly here, but this overview is not intended to be a full introduction to its operation.[8] A library using the subsystem has access to a database that numbers over 24 million bibliographic records, for which there are over 350 million locations listed. LC MARC tapes and additional cataloging by affiliates are constantly expanding the database at the rate of about 35,000 records per week. An authorized library staff member at any one of the terminals connected to the system via dedicated line or dial access may access any record, then edit the data to agree with the item being processed, and add holdings statements, locations, or other in-house data. For those libraries with card catalogs, cards are produced offline at OCLC headquarters in Dublin, Ohio, and shipped daily. They come arranged in packs according to member specifications, ready for immediate filing in local catalogs. Other libraries receive their records on magnetic tapes, while still others download bibliographic and authority records directly into their local automated systems.

In 1990 OCLC began operation of a new online service called PRISM. It uses the same database that was created in the first online system, but there is a new computer system architecture that results in enhanced capabilities. The OLUC may be searched by personal, corporate, or conference name; a combination of name and title; title; LC control number (also called LC card number); ISBN; ISSN; CODEN; or OCLC control number through use of special search keys. Any of these searches except the OCLC control number may be modified by type of material or by date of publication. A major new feature of PRISM allows any two of these search keys (except OCLC control number) to be combined using the Boolean operator *AND*. PRISM also has a title browsing capability in which users enter as much or as little of a title as they know. In response the appropriate place in the title index appears and users can scroll up or down the list to find the desired title.

In addition to the OLUC, authority files from LC are available. These are also searched with search keys. When found, an authority record may be placed in "Copy Display," and the user may then toggle between it and a bibliographic record in "Main Display." This feature may also be used to toggle between two authority records or between two bibliographic records. And, using this feature in the editing process, one may "cut and paste" blocks of text into bibliographic records from either authority records or other bibliographic records.

Another service available through OCLC is their CJK system for cataloging materials in Chinese, Japanese, and Korean. Special terminals and a printer are used to create catalog cards and machine-readable records with fields in the vernacular characters. Also, a copy of the OLUC is used for the EPIC service and the First Search service. EPIC started in 1990 to offer subject access, keyword, and Boolean searches of the OLUC and to serve as a gateway to other databases. First Search, begun in 1991, offers end user searching of the OLUC, whereas EPIC is targeted for use by reference librarians.

Records are held in the OLUC and in the authority databases in the MARC formats, although responses to searches may first be displayed in truncated or brief formats. New cataloging is entered in a MARC format. There are, of course, standard protocols for cataloging at the OCLC terminals. For one, member libraries are obliged to follow the *Anglo-American Cataloguing Rules*, 2nd ed. (*AACR2R*). They are also requested, when inputting original cataloging, to check all name, uniform title, and series headings in the LC MARC authority file. Headings found in the authority file that are coded as being *AACR2* are to be input in that form into original cataloging. However, the system is highly flexible, allowing members to adapt local records to meet local practices and conventions.

Quality control exists in published standards to which participating libraries are expected to adhere. Participants are encouraged to report any errors they find in the database. OCLC staff members check and correct the master records from these reports. Certain authorized libraries have been able to correct errors directly since 1984. Unnecessary duplication of records has been a problem. James Schoenung reported in 1981 that 17 percent of the records in his study could be eliminated without the loss of a unique title.[9] LC records, when received, replace some duplicates, and OCLC staff eliminate others when they are reported.

Consultation of training manuals and, above all, hands-on use are needed to gain skill in tagging, searching, and operating the terminals. Most people who have been properly trained find the techniques simple to master. Suggested sources for further information include *OCLC Workbook: Using the PRISM Service* and other texts produced by participating networks. It must be remembered, however, that the online catalog subsystem is constantly developing and changing. Only recent tools should be used. In fact, it is often necessary to supplement published manuals with the serial *OCLC Technical Bulletin* to learn the latest instructions for using the system.

Although the subsystem was originally designed specifically for cataloging support, online access to a bibliographic database of over 24 million records is in fact a general service resource. Other subsystems have been introduced that interface with it or use it as a point of reference. Other subsystems that have been offered include serials control, acquisitions, and interlibrary loan. Experience with these subsystems has led to the conclusion that some operations (e.g., serial check-in) are best handled at the local level. The rapid development of microcomputers has made such designs quite feasible, and OCLC has created a number of software packages that allow certain tasks to be completed at the local level with an interface to the OLUC where needed. OCLC's adoption of personal computers as official workstations (adapted especially for use with OCLC and called M300, M310, M386, M386SX, etc., Workstations) has made development and use of local software packages easier.

Research Libraries Information Network (RLIN)

RLIN resulted from adoption of Stanford University's Bibliographic Automation of Large Library Operations (BALLOTS) by the Research Libraries Group (RLG). RLG, Inc., was originally formed in 1974 by Columbia, Harvard, and Yale universities and the New York Public Library. Harvard withdrew at the time RLIN was formed, to be replaced by Stanford University. Membership exceeded 100 in 1990. Several hundred other institutions purchase RLG's services (e.g., "search only" access to RLIN).

The corporate objective is to foster interinstitutional support of scholarly communication and instruction in a rapidly changing climate of increasing costs and shrinking resources. Voting officers are elected annually by the member institutions to a Board of Directors. Together with the President — RLG's executive officer whom the Board elects and who then serves on the Board ex officio — they establish policies, programs, budgets, and fee structures and appoint committees. Over them is a Board of Governors, to which each member library sends a representative. At its quarterly meetings it reviews the actions of the Board of Directors, as well as those of other officers and committees.

The primary programs of RLG are bibliographic control and access, shared resources, collection management and cooperative development, preservation of research materials, and RLG's subject programs. The bibliographic component, called RLIN, consists of a computerized set of data files and data manipulation programs. Like OCLC, the RLIN system can transmit data in either a "full-face" (covering an entire screen) or a "line-by-line" mode, depending on the user's hardware. It provides catalog worksheets, printed cards, and magnetic tapes in the USMARC communications format; a variety of other acquisitions and in-process forms; and interlibrary loan capabilities.

Unlike OCLC, RLIN preserves a separate bibliographic record for every title cataloged by each library. Thus each library has online access to its own records showing whatever local changes may have been made. Local holdings, etc., are available to each local library, and selected data are available from records of other institutions.

All entries are in one of the MARC formats, including added copy cataloging and record maintenance. One of RLIN's strengths is its powerful query potential. Search terms can be used singly or in any sequence. They include LC card numbers, all or part of call numbers, and LC subject headings. Truncation searching on main and added entry words includes personal surnames and names of corporate bodies and geographic entities. The Boolean logic operators *and*, *or*, and *not* help tailor search strategies. All searches are interactive and can be negotiated or changed as searching progresses. Searching is also available on authority records. If a library has reason to believe an item will be cataloged by a national agency, brief bibliographic information can be keyed in once. It then is automatically searched against all new records entering the system.

The RLIN database is considerably smaller than that of OCLC. However, RLIN does have an excellent system to support Chinese, Japanese, and Korean (CJK) scripts. In addition RLIN supports Hebrew and Cyrillic and is developing Arabic scripts. The cost for cataloging is comparable to that of OCLC, but fixed costs for telecommunications are substantially higher to some areas of the country. This high cost may have contributed to the current reevaluation of RLG's priorities. If events proceed as they are moving at the time of publication of this book, some of RLIN's activities will be phased out by the end of 1992.

Western Library Network (WLN)

WLN was initiated by the State Library of Washington to give public and private libraries of the state a comprehensive bibliographic control system. While online operations began in 1977 with only ten pilot libraries, it has developed rapidly to become the most complete, although still the smallest, of the three major U.S. bibliographic utilities. It can be accessed online either by leased telephone lines or by dial-up. Its first out-of-state clients, the Alaska State Library at Juneau and the University of Alaska Library at Fairbanks, joined in the spring of 1978. By mid-1979 WLN extended its coverage to much of the Pacific Northwest, with state, public, academic, community college, and special libraries participating. While WLN gives first priority to libraries in its region, it agreed in early 1979 to sell its software to the National Library of Australia (NLA) in Canberra. Since then it has sold its software to others, including the University of Illinois at Urbana-Champaign and the Southeastern Library Network (SOLINET). But WLN has determined to restrict membership to the Pacific Northwest (with the exception of some member libraries in Arizona). In 1985 it changed its name from Washington Library Network to Western Library Network to reflect its regional character.

Like its two counterparts, WLN reached a point where its growing constituency called for representation in its administrative decisions. The Washington State Library Commission established a Computer Services Council, elected by participants, in 1979. Its name was later changed to Network Services Council. In 1988 WLN was established as a private, not-for-profit corporation.

WLN's Bibliographic Subsystem provides catalog support services notable for their quality control. All MARC formats are used. WLN, like the other networks, conforms to Library of Congress policy in adopting *AACR2R* headings. Headings are linked to a network-wide authority database that is more sophisticated than those of either OCLC or RLIN. When a cataloger is ready to enter original cataloging into the database, a check command is given, whereupon each heading is checked automatically against the authority file. A code is returned to tell the cataloger whether each heading is identical to a heading already in the authority file, is identical to a *see* reference in the file, or does not match any term in the authority file. If a heading matches a *see* reference, the form referred to is given on the screen so that the cataloger can determine which form to delete or alter.[10]

Local catalog records can be accessed and edited online as in RLIN. Passwords, which may be changed as a precaution against unauthorized use, give access to specific files. Authorized participants are intensively trained in MARC tagging and input/edit techniques. All contributed bibliographic records are given either computer or human review in a system designed to maintain a high quality database.[11]

The Inquiry Module uses algorithms that are both powerful and flexible enough to support reference services as well as the Bibliographic Subsystem. They include subject and keyword, as well as author (personal, corporate, and conference names), title (including keyword and uniform titles), series, LC card number, ISBN, and ISSN search keys. Boolean operators expand the search capabilities.

Book catalogs, COM catalogs, printed cards, and processing kits are producible offline, to fit the individual client's profile. A COM union catalog in quarterly issues is supplemented with biweekly local library accessions lists. Holdings information facilitates interlibrary loan and other searches. In addition to the Bibliographic Subsystem, WLN supports acquisitions and interlibrary loan subsystems.

Part of the success of the WLN system can be attributed to its adoption of the system design with a quadraplanar data structure developed at the University of Chicago, although never fully utilized at Chicago or at WLN.[12] At a demonstration given at the Library of Congress, WLN representatives showed:

> The redundant storage of data is minimized in the system by interrelating the principal files: holdings, authorities, bibliographic, and local data. Thus, an individual institution may hold data unique to it, while more general data will be stored in the central system to be implemented at the level most appropriate for its operation.[13]

Utlas International

Canadian efforts toward computer-based network cataloging were sparked largely by the University of Toronto Library Automation Systems (UTLAS), which became a separate corporation in 1983 and changed its name in 1988 to Utlas International, although the uppercase form of the name is retained in some product literature.[14] In 1963 the Ontario New Universities Library Project started work on computer-produced book catalogs representing the initial library collections for five new campuses in the province.[15] The project was to facilitate selection, acquisition, and cataloging, while remaining flexible in its record format, access, and products. Implementation in 1965 led to the University's participation in the Library of Congress MARC project. By 1970 it was producing cards from MARC tapes for sale to clients, including in 1971 the College Bibliocentre, a processing center for 19 colleges of applied technology. It started supplying computer-based systems and services to libraries in 1973.

Membership in UTLAS has been primarily among Canadian libraries, although UTLAS signed an agreement in 1981 with a Japanese firm to broker its services in Japan, and an UTLAS branch office was opened in New York in 1984.[16]

The UTLAS Catalogue Support System (CATSS) provides original, derived, and shared cataloging in all formats. Like the other utilities, CATSS provides online interactive editing with generation of various offline products: cards, book and COM catalogs, lists, and forms. Like RLIN, UTLAS maintains online separate copies of every record produced by every user. However, these are kept in separate files, which can be searched, but not altered, by other users. Like WLN, UTLAS offers online verification of headings for authority control.

Searching of CATSS includes keyword capabilities along with the ability to "browse" personal, corporate, and conference names; titles; series; and subjects. One can also search LCCNs, ISBNs, and other control numbers. Boolean capabilities assist in narrowing keyword searches.

Cooperation

The obvious duplication of resources and effort among the utilities has been of concern for some time. It has been felt that there should be some means for exchanging data across utilities. However, there are political, technical, and economic factors that must be taken into account. In 1980 a study of this subject was completed by Battelle Institute under a grant from the Council on Library Resources. It recommended either batch processing of search requests to be exchanged among the utilities or allowing a user of one utility direct online access to the others. The recommendations were not implemented, but the report drew attention to the need for cooperation. As a result there have been policy changes, and cooperative projects have been initiated.[17] In 1982, for example, OCLC began allowing partial membership and tapeload membership status. At reduced cost over full membership, this allows members of other networks (particularly RLIN) to have access to the OCLC database. Partial members may use noncataloging subsystems or search the database without entering their cataloging. For tapeload members, the location identifier is added to the OCLC master record for records on the library's archive tapes, which are run against the OCLC database. Most of RLG's full members have become tapeload members of OCLC. Similarly, RLIN has loaded some OCLC tapes. A number of RLG members that were formerly OCLC members desired access to the records they had created on OCLC. By loading their archive tapes into RLIN, they were allowed that access. WLN has a somewhat different approach. Any library or system that purchases the WLN software agrees to allow its archive tapes to be run against the WLN database for the purpose of adding to WLN any records not already in the file.[18]

Another cooperative venture that has implications for improved cataloging is the Linked Systems Project (LSP), mentioned above. RLIN, WLN, and LC have been working on this since 1980. OCLC has joined in the effort since then. The goal is to be able to exchange all data in an online mode through a standard network interconnection (SNI). Authority data is currently being sent to LC in this manner. The standard network interconnection being tested and developed internationally is known as the Open System Interconnection (OSI). It allows end users to use the searching techniques of their home system to search any other system on the network following standard protocols, known as *Z39.50*. There are also developments in national networks themselves, such as the Internet and NREN, that will increasingly facilitate access to other libraries' catalogs or bibliographic utilities' databases.

General Considerations

In most libraries, the professional cataloger's role with respect to online cataloging procedures is supervisory and managerial, although it is not uncommon for professionals to edit machine records, to revise nonprofessionals' input, and to use the database in problem solving routines. Even direct supervision of terminal operators is considered paraprofessional in many libraries. The essential professional contribution is to organize policies and procedures to make the most efficient use of the system.

Research shows that use of an online cataloging system does not always result in major organizational or procedural change.[19] However, the introduction of such a tool into a traditional catalog department is potentially a powerful change agent. It should at least stimulate reevaluation of long-standing policies and procedures. The measures taken by librarians to adapt their operations to the new environment affect their success in reducing per-unit cataloging costs, speeding the flow of materials through the processing department, and achieving related objectives. Some of the factors to be considered when utilizing network services and designing efficient interface procedures are described below.

Cataloging Networks as a General Bibliographic Resource

Library managers should encourage use of the bibliographic utility's database for pre-order verification, for location spotting in ILL work, for public service uses such as citation verification, and for bibliographic problem solving. It is unfortunate that many libraries overlook these potential uses of the system. Not only can full use of the system improve such tasks as pre-order searching, but it also can foster goodwill and acceptance by introducing more staff to use of the terminals. Staff resistance to online cataloging comes most often from those who do not use the terminals in their jobs. It is generally good policy to introduce the full staff to the fundamentals of terminal operation, encouraging them to use the system as part of their daily routines if possible.

It is true, however, that administrative emphasis on full utilization of the system complicates matters such as terminal placement, scheduling, and decisions to purchase additional ones. These problems are cited most often where use has been restricted to the catalog department. On the other hand, noncataloging uses seldom require large amounts of terminal time, in comparison to cataloging use. It is usually possible to schedule these functions, either with an "interrupt priority" or with one or more terminals completely unscheduled for catalog production.

Unfortunately, sometimes a perceived encroachment on cataloging time is actually the result of inefficient, wasteful cataloging procedures. Time must be treated as a valuable resource if the system is to provide optimum support to all appropriate technical and public service functions. Cataloging routines should proceed in a manner that conserves terminal time. This point will be further discussed in the section on procedural design.

Also related to maximizing use of some online cataloging systems is the decision to acquire a library's archive tapes, the machine-readable records of all transactions the library makes on the system. While cards are the principal system product for a decreasing majority of libraries, the possibility of owning, very inexpensively, a machine-readable record of a library's holdings is an important byproduct. Even though there may be no immediate need for the archive tapes, it is a good idea to place a subscription when a library joins such an online system. In many libraries machine-readable bibliographic products such as COM, CD-ROM, and online catalogs are making use of these tapes.

Many local automated systems now facilitate downloading of machine-readable records into the local database in addition to tape loading of the archival tapes. Such records are then immediately available for the online catalog.

Cataloging Policy

It is more convenient to edit copy to local standards with online cataloging than when using printed cards from LC or other sources. Still, a high degree of local variation from standard LC practice tends to slow work-flow, due largely to the need to consult local authority files and shelflist records.

To profit most from online cataloging, it is a good idea to review all local variations from standard practice at the time a library joins a bibliographic utility or network. This is not to suggest that all variations are misguided. Many local prerogatives are necessary because of inconsistent precedents over the years on the part of LC itself. Others may be justified by special local conditions. However, librarians should review all such variations in the light of their costs and their effects on processing efficiency. Any decision will affect online cataloging in areas such as terminal staffing, policies on the use of other libraries' records, and the organization of authority (integration) procedures.

The majority of titles added to a member library's collections will be cataloged in accordance with records existing in the database. Policies related to accepting and modifying records created by another institution are now among the most critical ones a library makes — even more important than those related to original cataloging. Arlene G. Taylor's *Cataloging with Copy*, 2nd ed., is a detailed examination of copy cataloging, which includes guidelines for accepting and modifying records.[20]

Procedural Design

Local cataloging procedures related to online networking fall into seven general groups:

1) The pre-cataloging search for copy, either as an acquisitions or as a cataloging responsibility

2) Cataloging with exact-match copy from the database

3) Cataloging with copy that requires editing

4) Inputting original cataloging

5) Record maintenance, including the enhancement of master records

6) Dealing with the offline products from the central office

7) Dealing with exporting bibliographic and authority records between the local online system and the bibliographic utility or online union catalog.

For best results, these functions must be well coordinated to avoid duplicate effort. They must be assigned to appropriate staff, with proper supervision and revision. They must also be integrated into an organizational structure designed to fit the new conditions resulting from network membership. Many issues arise when catalogers set up interface procedures with an online system. Among them are the following:

1) To what extent should clerical operators be restricted to using exact copy or be allowed to edit "near copy" at the terminal?

2) To what extent should they be allowed to accept non-LC records?

3) What information should the pre-order search, or a special pre-catalog search, provide them?

4) How should the Acquisitions Department sort and route incoming items in accordance with the availability and type of database copy?

5) Where should authority work take place for name, series, uniform title, and subject entries?

6) To what extent must the shelflist be consulted in the course of cataloging?

7) What amount of revision is needed for each type of terminal operation?

8) Who should perform the revision?

Obviously, the above questions are interrelated. For example, appropriate revision of clerical operators' work will depend on the amount of editing and authority determination they may perform and on the type of copy they are permitted to use. Collectively, the answers to such questions will decide a library's program for interfacing with the network. The system's efficiency helps determine whether the library meets its goals for network participation. To reduce turn-around time, cut the cost spiral, and improve cataloging quality, the interface must be as efficient as possible.

No single combination of procedures and policies would fit the majority of situations, since each interface emerges from the meshing of network capabilities with unique library conditions. A few simple guidelines may be useful, however, when setting up or evaluating such procedures:

1) **Conserve terminal time.** The point has been made that cataloging should be designed to avoid needless waste of time. Techniques can be used such as batching offline activities (particularly authority processing), avoiding unnecessary transcription (such as nonproductive printing of information from the terminals), and avoiding unnecessary call-ups of records (e.g., using a second or third call-up to produce cards if all the processing information is available the first time).

2) **Coordinate authority procedures.** One task that an online cataloging system does not do for a library is to ensure that the cataloging it initiates is compatible with that already existing at the library. Authority control is still largely manual and, if poorly executed, can nullify the advantages of online operation. Establishing authority records for names, for series, and for subjects should be handled as separate processes. A decision on whether to do any one of them before, during, or after cataloging at the terminal should be carefully weighed.

3) **Take advantage of the special capabilities of the system.** Major differences between online cataloging and the manual techniques it replaces are the speed of copy work and that of card production. It is no longer necessary to backlog bibliographic records while waiting for cards to arrive or for typists to produce them. With appropriate priorities, a library can expedite books for which exact LC copy is available, thus considerably reducing the familiar cataloging gap. Some of these capabilities are:

   a) Priority staffing such that the copy-cataloging work remains fully staffed regardless of attrition in the department as a whole.

   b) Special staff assignments on a temporary basis to meet peak load conditions in copy-cataloging work.

   c) Expeditious sorting of recently acquired books according to the types of catalog copy available. Some libraries follow a "first in, first out" rule, which mixes all categories of materials regardless of their difficulty or the availability of catalog copy.

   d) Frequent recycling of arrearages for which catalog copy is likely to become available.

As has been previously said, it is a good idea to reevaluate continually a library's procedures in the light of systems capability within the network. Such changes inevitably include the constant growth of the database and the evolution of operating procedures and subsystems. In the volatile network environment no cataloging interface can become so immutable as the techniques it replaces long appeared to be.

ONLINE PUBLIC ACCESS CATALOGS

Although experimentation with online public-access catalogs (OPACs) began in the 1960s, they did not become really functional until the 1980s. OPACs are now at the stage of development at which card catalogs were at the beginning of the twentieth century, when there was little agreement on size of cards, amount and order of data to be included, etc. OPACs have been developed locally in libraries and commercially. Some have expanded out of circulation systems that became fully functional in the 1970s. Others have been designed solely to serve as OPACs. Still others have grown up as one component of multipurpose systems that incorporate acquisitions and serials control functions as well as circulation and catalog functions. OPACs all differ in the way in which data are displayed, the amount of data displayed, and the manner in which a user must interact with them. There are varying amounts of authority control from none at all to a complete authority record for every heading fully linked to the bibliographic records. OPACs also provide for very different kinds of access ranging from those that essentially duplicate the access points available in a card catalog to those that offer sophisticated levels of searching using keywords, Boolean operators, truncation, and qualifiers.

OPACs differ further in the way in which bibliographic records are entered. Some allow direct downloading of records from the bibliographic utility to which the library belongs. Most allow loading of records from archive tapes, but the tapes usually must first be processed to eliminate superseded records, consolidate duplicates, etc. Some allow direct input of cataloging data for a record into a MARC work form. Still others require direct input of records in a mode that has come to be known as "conversational cataloging," where the inputter is prompted for each line of the record.

Although there has been some research on existing OPACs,[21] more is needed along with more experimentation before standards can be set for future design.

FUTURE PROSPECTS

Trends in computer technology and progress in developing bibliographic standards are encouraging. Recent advances in computer technology indicate that minicomputers have the capacity to operate local online catalogs and other processing functions, such as acquisitions and serials control, at reasonable cost. Advances in telecommunication make possible distributed networks, consisting of a series of separate individual library catalogs interconnected by telecommunications links. Such a configuration is especially attractive in areas where many libraries engage in extensive resource sharing and coordinated collection development.

Even with local online catalogs, libraries still find the large network databases valuable as sources for extended record searching. It appears that cataloging will continue in much the same way as today, except for the transfer of the edited machine-readable record into the local online database rather than to card stock. Closing of card catalogs, at least in some libraries, has been a major step in the evolution of materials processing toward quality improvement and control in standardized entry, descriptive detail, filing, physical preparation, and economical production of records.

The professional cataloger's contribution to an exclusively online situation is sometimes questioned. It is possible that many libraries that acquire only standard trade books and accept existing cataloging without modification will no longer need professional processing staff. On the other hand, there will likely be greater coordination of the national cataloging effort. The Library of Congress cannot maintain timely coverage of the world's entire publication output. Other libraries at home and abroad will no doubt take responsibility for cataloging in specific languages or subject categories. Consistently high standards will be kept in relatively few cataloging centers throughout the world. The number of professional catalogers may well be reduced, but the highly skilled cataloger with special language or subject competency will be in greater demand than ever. Moreover, public service librarians are finding that in-depth knowledge of catalog codes and conventions, machine search strategies, and MARC or other machine-readable formats immeasurably increases their effectiveness in reference work, information exchange, bibliographic problem solving, and implementation of online public-access catalogs.

NOTES

[1]OCLC, *Annual Report 1983/84* (Dublin, Ohio, OCLC, 1984), pp. 15-16.

[2]Barbara M. Westby, "Commercial Services," *Library Trends* 16 (July 1967): 46.

[3]Arlene Taylor Dowell, *Cataloging with Copy: A Decision-Maker's Handbok* (Littleton, Colo., Libraries Unlimited, 1976), pp. 248-257.

[4]American Library Association, Resources and Technical Services Division, Commercial Processing Services Committee, "Guidelines for Selecting a Commercial Processing Service," *Library Resources & Technical Services* 21 (Spring 1977): 170-173.

[5]*Cataloging Service*, bulletin 113 (Spring 1975): 7-8.

[6]Henriette D. Avram, *MARC: Its History and Implications* (Washington, D.C., Library of Congress, 1975).

[7]Library of Congress, Network Development Office, "A Glossary for Library Networking," *Network Planning Paper*, no. 2 (Washington, D.C., Library of Congress, 1978): 7.

[8]For general descriptions and comparisons of the major utilities see Dennis Reynolds, *Library Automation: Issues and Application* (New York, R. R. Bowker, 1985), pp. 55-63, 327-360; and William Saffady, "Six Bibliographic Utilities: A Survey of Cataloging Support and Other Services," *Library Technology Reports* (November-December 1988): 723-839.

[9]James Gerald Schoenung, "The Quality of the Member-Input Monographic Records in the OCLC On-Line Union Catalog" (Ph.D. Thesis, Drexel University, 1981), p. 129.

[10]Arlene G. Taylor, Margaret F. Maxwell, and Carolyn O. Frost, "Network and Vendor Authority Systems," *Library Resources & Technical Services* 29 (April/June 1985): 199.

[11]Saffady, "Six Bibliographic Utilities," p. 796.

[12]Maurice J. Freedman, "Some Thoughts on Public Libraries and the National Bibliographic Network," *Journal of Library Automation* 10 (June 1977): 128.

[13]*Library of Congress Information Bulletin* 36 (December 30, 1977): 845.

[14]Saffady, "Six Bibliographic Utilities," p. 779.

[15]Gordon H. Wright, "The Canadian Mosaic—Planning for Shared Partnership in a National Network," *ASLIB Proceedings* 30 (February 1978): 96-102; and Harriet Velazquez, "University of Toronto Library Automation System," *Online Review* 3 (September 1979): 254.

[16]Reynolds, *Library Automation*, p. 63.

[17]Reynolds, *Library Automation*, pp. 349-350.

[18]Reynolds, *Library Automation*, pp. 350-352.

[19]Joe A. Hewitt, *OCLC, Impact and Use* (Columbus, Ohio State University Libraries, Office of Educational Services, 1977), pp. 122-124.

[20]Arlene G. Taylor, *Cataloging with Copy: A Decision-Maker's Handbook*, 2nd ed., with the assistance of Rosanna M. O'Neil. (Englewood, Colo., Libraries Unlimited, 1988).

[21]See, for example: Jean Dickson, "An Analysis of User Errors in Searching an Online Catalog," *Cataloging & Classification Quarterly* 4 (Spring 1984): 19-38; Karen Markey, "Subject-Searching Experiences and Needs of Online Catalog Users: Implications for Library Classification," *Library Resources & Technical Services* 29 (January/March 1985): 34-51; Joseph R. Matthews and Gary S. Lawrence, "Further Analysis of the CLR Online Catalog Project," *Information Technology and Libraries* 3 (December 1984): 354-376; and Arlene G. Taylor, "Authority Files in Online Catalogs: An Investigation of Their Value," *Cataloging & Classification Quarterly* 4 (Spring 1984): 1-17.

SUGGESTED READING

Avram, Henriette D. *MARC: Its History and Implications.* Washington, D.C., Library of Congress, 1975.

Crawford, Walt. *MARC for Library Use: Understanding Integrated USMARC.* 2nd ed. Boston, G. K. Hall, 1989.

Dickson, Jean. "An Analysis of User Errors in Searching an Online Catalog." *Cataloging & Classification Quarterly* 4 (Spring 1984): 19-38.

Matthews, Joseph R., and Gary S. Lawrence. "Further Analysis of the CLR Online Catalog Project." *Information Technology and Libraries* 3 (December 1984): 354-376.

Reynolds, Dennis. *Library Automation: Issues and Applications.* New York, R. R. Bowker, 1985. Chapters 2-4, 10-14.

Rohrbach, Peter T. *Find: Automation at the Library of Congress: The First Twenty-five Years and Beyond.* Washington, D.C., Library of Congress, 1985.

Taylor, Arlene G. *Cataloging with Copy: A Decision-Maker's Handbook*, 2nd ed., with the assistance of Rosanna M. O'Neil. Englewood, Colo., Libraries Unlimited, 1988.

Taylor, Arlene G., Margaret F. Maxwell, and Carolyn O. Frost. "Network and Vendor Authority Systems." *Library Resources & Technical Services* 29 (April/June 1985): 195-205.

Catalog
Management 27

INTRODUCTION

Efficiency of bibliographic retrieval, and the quality of bibliographic description, are affected not only by the care and standards used to catalog each item, but also by several other important factors. One is the recording of local decisions and practices and keeping the department files and records current; another is the organization and routines facilitating each phase of the process; a third is the continuing maintenance and editing of the catalog. Each of these factors should be carefully evaluated and efficiently administered. Here we will consider briefly the major responsibilities, summarizing those features for which patterns of implementation may vary from library to library. Organizational structure, including the specification of staff duties, is not within the scope of this text.[1]

CATALOGING RECORDS AND FILES

A catalog department maintains files essential for accuracy, efficiency, standardization, and record keeping. Until recently, such files were nearly always formatted on cards or slips. Technology now offers new formats, which have been successfully introduced into many libraries. From the cataloger's, as well as the user's, viewpoint each embodies certain advantages, as well as some less attractive features.

Alternative Catalog Formats

The historical development and present uses of various catalog formats were briefly reviewed in chapter 1, "Cataloging in Context." Although the dictionary catalog on 3x5-inch cards still predominates in most libraries, active vendor merchandising of proprietary machine-readable databases now brings alternative catalogs within the reach of smaller public and school libraries or systems. In many cases the existing card catalog remains in use, while another format is adopted to supplement and continue it.

Book catalogs may be produced in several ways, as was noted in chapter 1. In photoreproduction the book pages carry images of catalog cards, filed in order and reduced in size, but still in most cases quite legible. Varied type faces, type sizes, and local characteristics are all preserved. The original card catalog should, of course, be carefully groomed before it is photographed. Many manual operations, such as correcting errors, retyping poor quality cards, and checking the filing, are unavoidable prerequisites. Computer-based book catalogs have also been produced with varying degrees of success. Entries in such works are less likely to reflect a card-type appearance, being amenable to a denser column-and-line presentation.

Book catalogs are frequently limited to author (or main entry) lists, to title lists (especially for serials), or to subject lists. They are far more compact and easy to scan than are card files, but they cannot be continuously cumulated, as can card files. Periodically cumulated reprints are possible, but expensive. Most libraries prefer to supplement the latest book edition with a card file, an acquisitions list, or some other means of showing recent additions to the collection. The human tendency to overlook, or neglect to search, more than one file makes multiple access lists an ever-present hazard.

Computer output microform (COM) catalogs, like the other alternatives, are primarily a technological innovation. Still, their impact on cataloging procedures is significant.[2] While initially expensive, COM per-unit cost is significantly reduced by mass production. Particularly in large libraries, where many service points need ready and full information about the entire collection, extra issues of the catalog at minimum cost are a real benefit. To be sure, other expenses, such as the purchase or lease of reading machines and the keyboarding of all bibliographic records for the computer's database, must be met. COM catalogs, like book catalogs, cannot be constantly expanded and updated. They are static and instantly out of date. New cumulations must be reissued from time to time. Or supplements must provide the records for incoming materials in a separate alphabetical file, and possibly in a different format. Moreover, since microforms cannot be read with the naked eye, some simple form of indexing must accompany them. Microfiche indexing is more precise and easier to use than film indexing, which depends on sequential searching, but both are somewhat awkward. Another drawback is the reluctance of many people to work with microforms, which require different reading skills and attitudes than do print materials. Yet some large public systems still use them, and they are frequently used as a backup for online catalogs.

At the initial conversion stage, machine-readable records may be stored in a large network database, in commercial automated service facilities, on archival tapes, or in the in-house computers of individual libraries. Whatever the storage arrangements, COM catalogs, in either fiche or film, at various reduction ratios, can be issued in batch mode — that is, at times when online demands for computer power are minimal. Record and format quality depends on the needs and budget of the library. There are grades of difference, at varying prices. For example, the use of lower- as well as uppercase type faces or the inclusion of special characters will raise the cost of production, but will also result in a more pleasing, and usually a more readable, appearance.

Machine-readable records can also be used to generate a CD-ROM catalog. These PC-based catalogs have the same drawbacks as book and COM catalogs, in that they are static, a snapshot of the library's database. However, the searching capabilities are usually enhanced over the author, title, and subject lists of book and COM catalogs, often allowing searching by keyword using Boolean operators in addition to the more traditional access.

The number of online machine-readable catalogs in libraries is growing rapidly. Some administrators feel that it will be ultimately more satisfactory to wait until they can put their bibliographic records directly online, rather than adopting interim solutions in the forms of book or COM catalogs. The online catalog retains the continuous expansion features of the card catalog, along with the compactness, speed, and ease of access characteristic of book and COM catalogs. Cost is still prohibitive for many libraries but will probably go down, rather than up, as computer services are expanded and refined.

All of the files discussed in the remainder of this section can and do exist in card, COM, CD-ROM, or online formats. (The only one likely to appear in book format is the catalog department manual, which is beginning to be found also online.)

The Shelflist

The shelflist is a complete record of all titles in a collection, arranged by call number as the library materials are found on the shelves. Its primary purpose is to provide an official inventory record of the collection. Its classified arrangement shows what titles have been placed in a specific class notation. It serves, then, as an important classification aid, for catalogers consult it to verify their library's past use of each notation. The shelflist also displays, within certain limitations, related materials more general and more specific on either side of the notation referred to. In addition, it furnishes the matrix on which unique cutter numbers and workmarks are assigned, to differentiate titles collocated in the same class.

If the shelflist is in card format, the cataloger may insert a temporary hold slip, or other place marker, for each new item entered, to avoid duplication of call numbers and to provide some information (not necessarily full cataloging) until the permanent record is made. That permanent record very likely will be a unit card, showing the entire bibliographic description plus tracings. Multiple volumes and copies, including location symbols for duplicates in reference, children's rooms, branches, and the like, are noted. This information makes it not only easier, but also more accurate, to browse the shelflist than to go directly to the shelves, where a number of items may be out in circulation or otherwise displaced. The shelflist is thus useful not only to catalogers, but also to acquisitions staff, to circulation staff, to reference staff, and to knowledgeable patrons. For these reasons many libraries make their shelflists available to the public. Others keep the official shelflist in the catalog department, sometimes placing a less detailed one near the card catalog.

Some libraries keep on their shelflist cards brief records of costs, accession numbers, acquisition dates, sources, missing and withdrawn copies, or anything else considered pertinent to the current status of each title. A typical "full information" shelflist card is shown in Fig. 27.1. It indicates that two copies were purchased, but one is missing and has been replaced. In addition, the purchase source, date, and price of each copy are shown. On an official card, of which this card is a copy, the cataloger has checked the tracings that were actually used.[3]

If the library has an online system searchable by call number, this can serve as the shelflist. This is more likely to occur in situations where there is an integrated system that is used for acquisition functions as well as for cataloging. In such a system a record is initiated with the order of an item. Dates, costs, etc., are part of the record and can be maintained for as long as the item is part of the system or even after the item is withdrawn or reported missing. Some libraries, however, maintain a card form shelflist as a backup to the online system.

Fig. 27.1. Sample shelflist card.

```
Z
693
.W94    Wynar, Bohdan S.
1985        Introduction to cataloging and classification / Bohdan S. Wy-
            nar. — 7th ed. / by Arlene G. Taylor. — Littleton, Colo. :
            Libraries Unlimited, 1985.
                xvi, 641 p. ; 25 cm. — (Library science text series)
                Includes bibliographies and index.
                ISBN 0-87287-512-1 : $35.00. — ISBN 0-87287-485-0 (pbk.) : $21.50
        c.1   Baker & Taylor    3-20-86   $35.00    msg   9-30-87
        c.2    "     "    "         "      $35.00

            ⅈ. Cataloging.  2. Anglo-American cataloguing rules.  3. Classification—
            Books.  I. Taylor, Arlene G., 1941-   II. Title.
            Z693.W94   1985              025.3—dc19            85-23147
        c.1(repl.) Libraries                                AACR 2   MARC
                   Unlimited            12-9-87    $21.50
            Library of Congress          ⭕   ⟨r86⟩rev
```

Authority Files

The purpose of an authority file, or files, is to standardize and control a library's use of name, title, and subject headings and their respective references. (See also chapter 25.) In many smaller libraries its upkeep has often been more honored in the breach than in the observance. Such libraries obviously depend on their prime cataloging sources (e.g., the Library of Congress) to suggest references and to keep the use of heading forms in standard order. The inconsistencies that inadvertently creep in, through rule changes, error, and the like, are remedied if and when found. In a limited operation there may be some economic justification for this ad hoc approach. However, in larger libraries, where inconsistent and erroneous entries cause misfiling, result in loss of entries in online catalogs, and otherwise obscure valuable entries in extensive files, the interest in authority files has escalated in the last 15 years.[4] As discussed in chapter 26, the Linked Systems Project facilitates exchange of authority data on a national scale online.

Many libraries use the public catalog as their authority list, but some information that should be available to the acquisitions or catalog librarian does not lend itself to inclusion in a public file. Such information may include the series treatment or the locations of catalogs where the heading and its references were used. Moreover, the introduction of dramatic changes in cataloging rules, such as those that occurred with *AACR2* in 1978, lead to total review of the use of authority records and to decisions of how to integrate old and new forms of headings into the library's catalog.

As noted in chapter 25, there is a difference between the existence of an authority file and the processes of creating and using an authority file. *Authority work* is "the process of determining the form of a name, title, or subject concept that will be used as a heading on a bibliographic record; determining cross references needed to that form; and determining relationships of this heading to other authoritative headings."[5] The record of that work is given in a printed or machine-readable unit that is entered into the authority file. The file is then used for the process of *authority control*, i.e., for maintaining the consistency of headings in a bibliographic file and for showing relationships among names, works, and subjects. In increasing numbers of online systems, the process of *authority control* is becoming at least partially automated, but the process of *authority work* remains highly tied to human endeavor.

Western Library Network (WLN), Utlas International, a number of commercial suppliers of online systems, and some locally developed in-house systems have well-developed authority control programs. Some commercial suppliers of bibliographic services, such as Blackwell North America, provide magnetic tape processing in which a library's archive tapes from a bibliographic utility may be edited to change older forms of heading to new forms. OCLC (Online Computer Library Center) and Research Libraries Information Network (RLIN) provide their members with LC's authority file online but give no control over headings in their databases. In the systems that provide automated authority control, incoming headings on bibliographic records are automatically checked against the machine-readable authority file. For systems where the bibliographic and authority records are linked, a heading on a new bibliographic record that matches one in the authority file automatically links the bibliographic record to the authority record. When a heading does not match, it is either referred to the cataloger for checking or the system creates a mini-authority record for it.[6] For systems where the bibliographic and authority records are unlinked, a match with a reference will generate an invalid headings report and a non-match will generate a new heading report.

Most libraries that maintain authority files still do so in card form. However, many libraries with online catalogs are moving to online authority files. Name authority files bring together in an alphabetic list all name headings, personal, corporate, conference, or geographic, that are used in a given catalog as main, added, analytic, or subject entries. Authority records for series, uniform titles, and topical subjects may be added, creating a general authority file. Or they may be handled in separate files.

In-Process Files

Certain areas of acquisitions and cataloging overlap. Each library's requirements must be studied to avoid duplication of record keeping, verification, etc. This is a continuous administrative responsibility. Some file, whether maintained by the cataloger or by the order librarian, must show "items in process." Its records continuously trace the status of each item from the time it is received in the library until it goes to the shelf, with its permanent catalog record available to the public. Libraries that use multiple order forms can reserve one copy of the form for the in-process record. Some use the original requisition slip, once the book has been invoiced. Others with online systems may be able to use the order record as the in-process record and later enhance that record for the catalog record. Since the correct main entry may not be established until the item is cataloged, most libraries arrange their in-process files by title rather than by author.

If printed cards are ordered separately from the works they describe, a separate file may be necessary for those card sets that arrive ahead of the books.

Catalog Department Manuals

The purpose of a department manual is to codify all pertinent decisions and procedures. A copy should be readily available to every member of the library staff, and it should contribute to the in-service training of every new cataloging employee. Even public service staff should be able and willing to consult it on problems of local catalog interpretation and use. It is most effective in looseleaf format, so the various tagged and indexed sections can be withdrawn and replaced by updated material as needed. Foster recommends that it give complete coverage of responsibilities and practices and that it be easy to use, to read, and to revise. He gives the following points to remember during its preparation:

1. Arrange material in logical order so that related information is found together.

2. Use precise and concrete words, not abstract words. And illustrate whenever possible.

3. Be alert to details. Write the manual so that there is no question about procedures and so that the newcomer can easily understand and follow each routine.

4. But do not over-detail. Too much detail provides no room for individual variation and will not allow for minor changes without complete rewriting.

5. Anticipate future revisions and additions.

6. Before adding a new procedure into the manual, test it out to discover and correct unforeseen problems.

7. Take advantage of auxiliary sources, particularly publications from the Library of Congress and, if the library is part of a network, publications distributed by network headquarters.[7]

On the last point, the department manual may contain guidelines for input standards for automated systems or refer to those input standards of the bibliographic utility or network to which the library belongs.

Some catalog department manuals also contain expectations for cataloging staff job performance with specific guidelines for performance standards. Such guidelines are very useful for a clear understanding of expectations when it is time for performance evaluations.

CATALOGING ROUTINES

Copy Cataloging

We know that most cataloging performed in the United States today derives from LC copy in either print or machine-readable form.[8] Since the Library of Congress uses ISBD and *AACR2R*, most present-day descriptive cataloging embodies the precepts of these two compatible and internationally recognized paradigms. Local catalogers may use the description as it stands or may alter it to reflect differences in a copy of an item received locally, to correct occasional errors made on LC copy, to adjust headings to fit the local authority file, or to add name or title added entries.

As for subject analysis, the Library of Congress provides with many of its records a suggested DDC class number, as well as its own full call number, with possible alternative LC and DDC class numbers for such materials as bibliographies, biographies, and the separate parts of a monographic series. It also shows the subject headings it has chosen for the work. Local copy catalogers may use LC decisions as they stand, or may modify them to reflect variations in edition, impression, or format, to complete the DDC class numbers, to adjust official LC call numbers to their local shelflists, to substitute *Sears* or other subject list terms for the LC subject headings, and to omit, add, or change other tracings. Original cataloging is usually necessary for a work without an available record from the Library of Congress or some other reliable bibliographic agency.

Original Cataloging

Descriptive Cataloging

Most libraries follow the Library of Congress in conforming to ISBD and *AACR2R* requirements, or some modification thereof. Bibliographic description requires transcription from the chief sources of information according to prescribed guidelines in *AACR2R* and *Library of Congress Rule Interpretations* as modified in local practice. Much of descriptive cataloging is straightforward and is a task assigned to paraprofessional staff in many libraries. *AACR2R* outlines three levels of description, with increasing detail included at each of the two higher levels. It also offers options throughout, which frequently have to do with adding further details to the record. Main and added (non-subject) entries are determined in accordance with *AACR2R*, or perhaps with some adjustments for established practice. Any changes from LC practice, or *AACR2R* options exercised, should be described in the catalog department manual. All new headings should be recorded in the local authority list, along with references as indicated. Authority control was discussed earlier.

Subject Cataloging

The subject heading list and subject authority file used by the library must be consulted for consistent selection and recording of accepted headings and references. Obsolete terminology may be caught and changed at once, although it is usually better to postpone major overhauls to a designated time, in order to expedite new cataloging in progress.

For original cataloging, classifying an item requires judgment. The task requires the selection of an appropriate classification number that fits the existing collection in subject emphasis and then requires adjusting the resulting call number to uniquely fit into the existing collection. This activity is usually performed by professionally trained librarians when no classification is provided on cataloging copy, as well as for original cataloging. After examining the item to be cataloged in the light of the classification schedules used by the library, the cataloger usually consults the shelflist to see if the class number chosen, or its possible alternative, has been previously used for similar or different materials. When the appropriate class number is selected, the distinguishing cutter number, with any necessary additions, such as workmark, edition date, or location symbol, is added. The full call number may be recorded in the shelflist, on the item proper (with volume and copy number if needed), and on the work form. If catalog and shelflist are in card form, a temporary slip may be inserted in the shelflist, with possibly another in the catalog in main entry position, pending arrival of permanent cards. Libraries using COM or book catalogs frequently maintain card shelflists for recent additions, until a new cumulated catalog is available. In machine-readable files new entries are likely to be held or "saved" online until an authorized reviser has approved them, but this routine does not take so long that a temporary substitute is considered necessary.

Use of Work Forms

Work forms are useful to routinize procedures and ensure full coverage of essential points. In print format they may be sheets, cards, or slips pre-printed to exhibit the standard categories of information that catalogers must consider. Some catalogers still use typewriters. For them, some form of the 3x5-inch card or a larger work slip may be sufficient. Some libraries use one part of the multiple copy order forms available from library supply houses, but these leave little room for corrections and additions. If printed cards are purchased, especially from a commercial vendor, necessary changes to fit the local item may be made directly on the card set, or perhaps on one unit card, which can then be reproduced to give added copies for secondary entries, departmental or branch libraries, and shelflists.

Many catalogers prefer to use long work sheets that are forwarded to typists for card production or inputting into machine-readable files. In a library in which catalog cards are produced in house, the work form can carry instructions for the typist or keyboard operator to use when preparing added entries, tracings, new references, subject analytics, etc. If the cataloging is based primarily on a large union file of machine-readable records and done at a terminal, the operator usually can call up prepared work forms. These are completed in substantive detail directly at the keyboard. Where the MARC format is used, pre-selected fields and tags are changed or expanded as needed. On the other hand, the cataloger may prefer to start in longhand on a printed form (see Fig. 27.2, page 524), handing the completed sheet to a terminal operator for inputting. Figure 27.3 (see page 525) shows the MARC record for the item in Fig. 27.2.

(Text continues on page 525.)

Fig. 27.2. An OCLC participant's work form.

Type: a	Bib lvl: m	Source: d	Lang: *eng*
Repr:	Enc lvl: *I*	Conf pub: ∅	Ctry: *fr*
Indx: ∅	Mod rec:	Govt pub: *i*	Cont: *b*
Desc: a	Int lvl:	Festschr: ∅	Illus: *ab*
	F/B: ∅	Dat tp: *s*	Dates: *1984,*

010 LCCN	041 _ Lang.
040 Cat. Source IVE $c IVE	043 Geog. area code *a-io- - - -*
020 ISBN	090 Local call no. *TK5101 $b .B37 1984*

1∅∅ *1*   Main entry *Battu, Daniel Pierre.*

24_ _ _   Uniform title

245 *1∅* Title *Telecommunication services for the transfer of information and data : $b a case study in Indonesia / $c prepared by Daniel Pierre Battu and John B. Rose.*

250   Edition

260   Publication info. *Paris : $b General Information Programme and UNISIST, United Nations Educational, Scientific and Cultural Organization, $c 1984.*

300   Physical description *vii, 83 p. : $b ill., maps ; $c 30 cm.*

49∅ *1 _*   Series *PGI ; $v 84/WS/1∅*

5∅4   Note *Bibliography: p. 67-68.*

5___   Note

5___   Note

65∅ *∅* Subject *Telecommunication systems.*

65∅ *∅* Subject *Telecommunication policy $z Indonesia.*

6___ _ Subject

7∅∅ *1∅* Added entry *Rose, John B.*

7__ _ _   Added entry

83∅ _ *∅* Series traced differently *PGI (Series) ; $v 84/WS/1∅.*

9__ _ _   User option

Fig. 27.3. OCLC record produced from preceding work form.

```
OCLC:      11851699        Rec stat:    c
Entered:   19850326        Replaced:    19870607      Used:     19860623
Type: a          Bib lvl: m      Source:    d         Lang:   eng
Repr:            Enc lvl: I      Conf pub: 0           Ctry:   fr
Indx: 0          Mod rec:        Govt pub: i           Cont:   b
Desc: a          Int lvl:        Festschr: 0           Illus:  ab
                 F/B:     0      Dat tp:    s          Dates:  1984,
   1  040      IVE $c IVE $d m/c
   2  043      a-io---
   3  090      TK5101 $b .B37 1984
   4  092      $b
   5  049      YCLM
   6  100 1    Battu, Daniel Pierre. $w cn
   7  245 10   Telecommunication services for the transfer of information and
data : $b a case study in Indonesia / $c prepared by Daniel Pierre Battu and
John B. Rose.
   8  260      Paris : $b General Information Programme and UNISIST, United
Nations Educational, Scientific and Cultural Organization, $c 1984.
   9  300      vii, 83 p. : $b ill., maps ; $c 30 cm.
  10  490 1    PGI ; $v 84/WS/10
  11  504      Bibliography: p. 67-68.
  12  650  0   Telecommunication systems.
  13  650  0   Telecommunication policy $z Indonesia.
  14  700 10   Rose, John B. $w cn
  15  830  0   PGI (Series) ; $v 84/WS/10.
```

Following the preparation of work forms, the item is generally ready for final preparation. In many libraries the work form is manually translated by a typist into pockets and labels before the item can have its final processing. Other libraries have this step performed by commercial suppliers, by a network central office, or by in-house automated printers.

Card Catalog Maintenance

Like any ongoing function, a catalog is subject to wear and tear, obsolescence, inadvertent clerical and professional errors, inconsistency, and a variety of related ills. It therefore requires continual editing and maintaining, although libraries, being traditionally shorthanded, often neglect or postpone the responsibility, to the detriment of effective service. As collections grow, the efforts needed to keep a card catalog in satisfactory condition tend to increase exponentially. Outdated and disreputable cards, call number changes, location changes (e.g., transfers in or out of the Reference department), filing backlogs, and blind references (i.e., references to or from headings once used but incompletely or inaccurately withdrawn) are among the major maintenance problems encountered. Maintenance is also necessary to remedy the inconsistencies resulting from years of different rules for headings. Attention to physical elements such as repair of damaged drawers or replacement of worn and soiled cards is important. Tray labels, guide cards, and instructions for use inside and outside the file should be altered whenever improvements are possible. Expansion inevitably requires occasional shifting of cards.

Catalog editing is needed to eliminate unnecessary entries, to suggest improvements, and to plan for future growth and development. Old entries may not have been pulled during cancellation of a title. Inconsistent headings, misleading or blind references, filing errors, missing cards, wrong call numbers, etc., all cause perplexity and ill will. The normal, rapid obsolescence of terminology mandates constant surveillance to modify or expand existing terms and references. The intricacies of connecting references between old and new headings, as established according to changes in rules of entry, must be adjudicated. Changes in filing rules also present problems. Some entries may need to be refiled, to keep pace with shifting needs of the library and its users. Foster describes a number of grooming functions that should be assigned as full- or part-time responsibilities, depending on the size and age of the catalog.[9]

Maintenance of Other Types of Catalogs

Maintenance of book, COM, CD-ROM, and online catalogs involves editing, as discussed above, to guard against obsolescence of terminology and to take care of call number changes, location changes, and heading inconsistencies resulting from rule changes. These catalogs are particularly vulnerable to typographical errors because these errors cause major retrieval problems. References must be maintained, and old name and title entries must sometimes be changed when there are conflicts with new entries to the catalog. In addition, for COM, CD-ROM, and online catalogs there must be concern for maintenance of the equipment necessary for their use. However, the equipment maintenance usually is not performed by catalog department staff.

Reproducing Catalog Cards

Catalog cards can be produced by typing each one individually. More often, however, they are purchased in sets. One of the most common sources of such sets is the bibliographic utility of which the library may be a member. In addition to the card sets mailed from the bibliographic utility, card sets may be produced from the utility's online records by downloading to a printer (as is done for OCLC's CJK system) or by downloading to the library's own computer or personal computer. Cards are then printed using special card production software. It is also possible to photocopy a set from one master unit card by either using copy received through LC's CDS Alert Service, adapting information from CIP or NUC, or typing one copy of one's original cataloging.[10] There are also several computer programs on the market that will produce a catalog card set when main entry information is typed into the screen form.

Reclassification and Recataloging

There is inevitably a certain amount of recataloging to be performed in any library. Recataloging may be either a mass production affair or an individualized, single item performance. During the 1960s and early 1970s many medium-sized and larger libraries, especially academic ones, mounted full reclassification projects from DDC to LC classification. Large-scale reclassification was sometimes undertaken on special collections or a selected part of a collection. In the course of most such efforts, brief, inaccurate, or obsolete cataloging could be caught and redone. Many collections were at the same time weeded and surveyed for needed new materials.

More commonly, however, recataloging is performed on individual items for which the former records prove unsatisfactory. Class numbers within a given classification scheme (e.g., DDC or LCC) may need changing because the schedules have been revised or because of new interpretations and needs within the collection. Recataloging on a greater or lesser scale is also the consequence of adopting a new or revised descriptive cataloging code. For instance, *AACR2* called for many more corporate names to be entered directly under the body's own name rather than subordinately under a higher body as was done under earlier rules (e.g., "Library of Congress" *not* "United States. Library of Congress"). Catalogers whose libraries are not yet ready to close their card files and start new ones based strictly on the changed rules must decide what to do about superseded usages, particularly changed headings for already used entries that are likely to be used again. Not all practices have been officially standardized to meet this dilemma. Some attempt to solve it with full sets of *see also* references linking old and new forms of headings in unified or split files without actually recataloging the older works. Others refile old headings under guide-cards carrying the new heading forms, leaving *see* references at the old positions to assist users who still search under those outdated forms. Still other libraries recatalog under the new forms, particularly if there are only a limited number of entries under the obsolete forms. Old and new forms are often identified and corrected during preprocessing for an online catalog's database or in subsequent cleanup of the database. Ongoing maintenance of changed forms of headings in online catalogs may be simplified through a "global update" capability.

Closing Card Catalogs

In 1965 studies were made at the New York Public Library that confirmed that a staggering number of the cards (actually 29 percent) in the public catalog of the Research Libraries Division were illegible, damaged, dirty, badly worn, or otherwise unfit to remain. The problem was aggravated by the fact that some entries had been there for over 100 years. It was a dramatic instance of a malaise that was reaching epidemic proportions in many long-established research libraries. Besides the deterioration problem, upkeep and maintenance were expensive and unsatisfactory. Space, lighting, and furniture pose real logistics problems in files of over 10 million cards. Labor costs for filing and revising have increased considerably since the 1960s.

The NYPL studies led to a decision to photograph the existing catalog prior to discarding it in favor of conversion to book format.[11] All new cataloging would be made available in a combination of card and book formats from a store of machine-readable records.[12]

The NYPL venture, along with other, similar experiments, encouraged the Library of Congress to announce in late 1977 that it would soon implement a similar solution to its card catalog proliferation.[13] LC's original plans were to "freeze" its existing files on January 1, 1980. The particular point in time was intentionally orchestrated to the appearance of *AACR2*, but other research libraries, fearful of the consequences of so "precipitous" an action, persuaded the Library of Congress to postpone the change until January 1, 1981.

The Library proposed to abandon at the same time its practice of "super-imposition," by which it retained most of its established headings regardless of rule changes, following *AACR1* dictates only for those headings being established for the first time. Superimposition had been an attempt to avoid the Herculean task of updating all forms rendered obsolete by the new rules. But even with liberal use of references, it confounded catalogers and catalog users alike, with its legacy of inconsistent access forms in a single file. Starting in 1981 with all obsolete headings officially frozen in a searchable but defunct catalog, headings for new materials were established according to *AACR2* regardless of whether a given entry was identified differently in the old catalog. In situations where libraries have closed old catalogs, complete bibliographic access to all the records in *both* catalogs under many personal, corporate, and geographic headings requires that the search be conducted under heading forms that differ from one catalog to the other. The kind and number of references to be used in one or both catalogs have occasioned much discussion.

Not all librarians in 1981 were convinced that a step as radical as closing one catalog and starting afresh on another was the best solution to problems of catalog lag. For the most part, only large research collections tried it. Most libraries maintained one catalog, using combinations of interfiling, split files, references, and revising old headings.

The advent of online catalogs is precipitating more catalog closings than did *AACR2*. Once an online system can provide as many access points as does the card or other printed catalog, the old catalog can be closed. Most online catalogs do not have a distinct "opening" date. Several years' worth of entries appear in both the closed catalog and the online catalog. However, all new entries after a certain date appear only in the online catalog.

The cleanup of headings for an online or other machine-readable catalog may involve four steps: 1) retrospective conversion to transform every record in the card shelflist into machine-readable form; 2) preprocessing of archival tapes and retrospective conversion tapes by a commercial service on contract; 3) systematic database cleanup projects using global update capabilities of the online system; and 4) ongoing database maintenance. During retrospective conversion and preprocessing operations outdated headings may be changed to current forms. Retrospective conversion is a major concern as more and more libraries move to online catalogs and close not only their card catalogs, but also their card shelflists. This is often done through a utility by searching for the records in the database and, when a match is found, adding that record to the library's archive tape. Retrospective conversion can also be done by a commercial service on contract.[14]

NOTES

[1]Other reliable texts are available for this purpose. See, for example, Marty Bloomberg and G. Edward Evans, *Introduction to Technical Services for Library Technicians*, 5th ed. (Littleton, Colo., Libraries Unlimited, 1985); and Donald L. Foster, *Managing the Catalog Department*, 3rd ed. (Metuchen, N.J., Scarecrow, 1987).

[2]Ellen Altman, "Reactions to a COM Catalog," *Journal of Academic Librarianship* 3 (November 1977): 267-268; Richard W. Meyer and Bonnie Juergens, "Computer Output Microfiche Catalogs: Some Practical Considerations," *Journal of Micrographics* 11 (November 1977): 91-96; and William Saffady, *Computer-Output Microfilm: Its Library Applications* (Chicago, American Library Association, 1978).

[3]For additional examples of shelflist cards and explanations, see Bloomberg and Evans, *Technical Services*.

[4]See, for instance, S. Michael Malinconico, "Bibliographic Data Base Organization and Authority File Control," *Wilson Library Bulletin* 54 (September 1979): 36-45.

[5]Arlene G. Taylor, "Authority Files in Online Catalogs: An Investigation of Their Value," *Cataloging & Classification Quarterly* 4 (Spring 1984): 1.

[6]For more detailed information on automated authority control see Arlene G. Taylor, Margaret F. Maxwell, and Carolyn O. Frost, "Network and Vendor Authority Systems," *Library Resources & Technical Services* 29 (April/June 1985): 195-205.

[7]Foster, *Managing the Catalog Department*, pp. 225-226.

[8]For discussion of adapting copy in the cataloging process, see Arlene G. Taylor, *Cataloging with Copy: A Decision-Maker's Handbook*, 2nd ed., with the assistance of Rosanna M. O'Neil (Englewood, Colo., Libraries Unlimited, 1988).

[9]Foster, *Managing the Catalog Department*, pp. 15-22.

[10]Taylor, *Cataloging with Copy*, pp. 5-7.

[11]S. Michael Malinconico and James A. Rizzolo, "New York Public Library Automated Book Catalog Subsystem," *Journal of Library Automation* 6 (March 1973): 3-36.

[12]James W. Henderson and Joseph A. Rosenthal, *Library Catalogs: Their Preservation and Maintenance by Photographic and Automated Techniques* (Cambridge, Mass., M.I.T. Press, 1968), p. ix.

[13]"LC to Freeze Card Catalog," *Library of Congress Information Bulletin* 36 (November 4, 1977): 743-744; "Freezing the Library of Congress Catalog," *Library of Congress Information Bulletin* 37 (March 3, 1978): 152-156; and "Information on Freezing the Catalog Updated," *Library of Congress Information Bulletin* 37 (July 21, 1978): 415-419.

[14]For in-depth discussions of retrospective conversion, see Ruth C. Carter and Scott Bruntjen, *Data Conversion* (White Plains, N.Y., Knowledge Industry Publications, 1983); and Dennis Reynolds, *Library Automation: Issues and Applications* (New York, R. R. Bowker, 1985), pp. 280-324.

SUGGESTED READING

Bloomberg, Marty, and G. Edward Evans. *Introduction to Technical Services for Library Technicians.* 5th ed. Littleton, Colo., Libraries Unlimited, 1985. Chapters 24-25.

Burger, Robert H. *Authority Work: The Creation, Use, Maintenance, and Evaluation of Authority Records and Files.* Littleton, Colo., Libraries Unlimited, 1985.

Foster, Donald L. *Managing the Catalog Department.* 3rd ed. Metuchen, N.J., Scarecrow, 1987.

Reynolds, Dennis. *Library Automation: Issues and Applications.* New York, R. R. Bowker, 1985. Chapter 10.

Taylor, Arlene G. *Cataloging with Copy: A Decision-Maker's Handbook.* 2nd ed., with the assistance of Rosanna M. O'Neil. Englewood, Colo., Libraries Unlimited, 1988. Chapters 1, 9.

Taylor, Arlene G., Margaret F. Maxwell, and Carolyn O. Frost. "Network and Vendor Authority Systems." *Library Resources & Technical Services* 29 (April/June 1985): 195-205.

Tillett, Barbara B., ed. *Authority Control in the Online Environment: Considerations and Practices.* New York: Haworth Press, 1989. (Also issued as *Cataloging & Classification Quarterly,* v. 9, no. 3 [1989].)

Filing

28

INTRODUCTION

Neophyte catalogers are surprised to discover many alternative filing codes. They learn not only that choice of catalog arrangement (dictionary or divided) affects filing decisions, but also that choice of entry is to some extent interactive with filing questions. Arbitrary groupings, exceptions from strict alphabetical order, and other complexities are directly related to the forms of subject headings and other catalog entries. Filing problems resulting from entry conflicts between the old *ALA Cataloging Rules* and *AACR1* were a major impetus to the closing of such large catalogs as those of the New York Public Library and the Library of Congress. Some libraries attempt to interfile old and new forms of the same entry, while others file all forms exactly as they appear. In either case, ample use of references is necessary.

Before the advent of online catalogs, some people thought that filing would become a nonissue in online catalogs. However, we are now learning that when more than ten or so entries are retrieved in response to a search, they need to appear on the screen in some logical order. Catalog users are not happy with responses in which the entries appear in the order in which the items happened to be acquired by the library. Filing order is somewhat less of a problem, however, in online, book, and microform catalogs than it is in card catalogs. It is easier to scan one or more columns of entries and to discern their order than it is to determine the order of cards.

Research libraries have long adhered to one or another of various kinds of "categorical filing," particularly in those parts of their catalogs where relatively large numbers of highly formalized entries are concentrated. Categorical filing is based on the assumption that the user knows enough about a subject to prefer a partially classified arrangement over straight adherence to the alphabet. Less scholarly libraries generally prefer a simpler and therefore more readily grasped alpha-arrangement. Even the big academic and research collections are gradually succumbing to popular demand, and to the requirements of computer filing. For instance, the Library of Congress used to arrange its entries for individual books and groups of books of the Bible in canonical order, as part of an intricate categorical arrangement.[1] Today, those entries are filed alphabetically.

Some libraries adopt published filing codes, e.g., the *ALA Filing Rules*.[2] Others develop sets of rules tailored to their own preferences. In almost every case questions arise that cannot be answered by a simple appeal to the alphabet.

FAMILIAR FILING DILEMMAS

In the first place, there is a significant difference between alphabetizing straight through to the end of a phrase entry and observing the breaks in the string that occur at the end of each word. Most filers know the admonition "nothing before something," or "blank to Z." It means that library catalogs are generally arranged letter-by-letter to the end of each word and then word-by-word to the end of the heading. However, not all files in libraries are based on this premise. Reference librarians have to remember that the *American Peoples Encyclopedia*, the *Americana*, and the *World Book* are arranged word-by-word, while *Britannica*, *Collier's*, and *Compton's* prefer uninterrupted letter-by-letter filing to the close of the entry phrase. The differences are in some areas important, e.g.:

Word-by-word	**Letter-by-letter**
New Hampshire	Newark (N.J.)
New Haven (Conn.)	Newcastle (N.S.W.)
New York (N.Y.)	Newfoundland
New York (State)	New Hampshire
New Zealand	New Haven (Conn.)
Newark (N.J.)	Newman, Arthur
Newcastle (N.S.W.)	Newport (Isle of Wight)
Newfoundland	NEWSPAPERS
Newman, Arthur	New York (N.Y.)
Newport (Isle of Wight)	New York (State)
NEWSPAPERS	New Zealand

In entries containing dates, early historical periods usually precede later ones. However, codes differ on whether longer periods should precede or follow shorter ones starting with the same year. The *ALA Filing Rules* and the *Library of Congress Filing Rules*[3] both say to arrange periods of time beginning with the same year in chronological order. They give examples from which the following selection was made:

UNITED STATES – HISTORY – CONFEDERATION, 1783-1789
UNITED STATES – HISTORY – 1783-1865
UNITED STATES – HISTORY – CONSTITUTIONAL PERIOD,
    1789-1809
UNITED STATES – HISTORY – 1865-
UNITED STATES – HISTORY – 1865-1898
UNITED STATES – HISTORY – WAR OF 1898
UNITED STATES – HISTORY – 1898-
UNITED STATES – HISTORY – 20TH CENTURY

The *ALA Rules for Filing Catalog Cards*, 2nd edition,[4] called for arranging periods of time beginning with the same year so that the longest period would file first, e.g.,

UNITED STATES – HISTORY – 1783-1865
UNITED STATES – HISTORY – CONFEDERATION, 1783-1789
UNITED STATES – HISTORY – 1898-
UNITED STATES – HISTORY – WAR OF 1898

If there are two or more editions or impressions of a work, edition dates or numbers may be added to the entry line, solely as filing elements. Again, codes differ on whether the earliest or latest should file first. The *ALA Filing Rules* say to arrange editions in straight chronological order, with earliest date first, e.g.,

Schwartz, Seymour I.
    Principles of surgery. 1969.
    Principles of surgery. 2nd ed. 1974.
    Principles of surgery. 3rd ed. 1979.
    Principles of surgery. 4th ed. 1984.
    Principles of surgery. 5th ed. 1989.

In the list below, the latest ones come first, on the assumption that they are the ones the user is most likely to want.

Sackheim, George I.
    Introduction to chemistry for biology students. 3rd ed. 1983.
    Introduction to chemistry for biology students. 2nd ed. 1977.
    Introduction to chemistry for biology students. 1966.

Numbers or digits in catalog entries give further challenges. Under current sets of rules, character strings beginning with numerals (whether arabic or non-arabic) are arranged before character strings beginning with letters, e.g.,

The 24th Congress of the CPSU and its contribution to Marxism-Leninism.

XXIVth International Congress of Pure and Applied Chemistry, main
    section lectures presented at ....

Twenty-four dramatic cases of the International Academy of Trial Lawyers.

The twenty-fourth session of the International Labour Conference ....

According to the *ALA Filing Rules*, numerals precede character strings, and all such character string/numeral combinations are interfiled regardless of the type of entry, e.g.,

HENRY I, KING OF ENGLAND, 1068-1135
HENRY V, KING OF ENGLAND, 1367-1413
Henry VIII and his wives.
HENRY VIII, KING OF ENGLAND, 1491-1547
Henry VIII's fifth wife.
Henry the Eighth and his court.
Henry the Fifth of England.

However, under *LC Filing Rules* fields with identical leading elements are subgrouped in the order of person, place, thing, title. Thus, while numerals precede character strings, the person entries are all grouped before the title entries, e.g.,

HENRY I, KING OF ENGLAND, 1068-1135
HENRY V, KING OF ENGLAND, 1367-1413
HENRY VIII, KING OF ENGLAND, 1491-1547
Henry VIII and his wives.
Henry VIII's fifth wife.
Henry the Eighth and his court.
Henry the Fifth of England.

In prior rules, however, numerals were most often filed as spelled, and spelled "as spoken," in whatever language the entry appeared. Many catalogs and other sources still file numerals in this way. Interpretation becomes most critical when the primary filing element of a title is expressed on the chief source of information in numerals. In a catalog where numerals are filed as spoken, it is possible that the two books (one by Walter Sellar, the other by Reginald Arkell) entitled *1066 and All That* are lost forever to the patron who cannot pronounce "1066" appropriately. However, filing numerals first can also cause problems for users. How would a user who has heard a title spoken (e.g., 100 classical studies for flute) know whether to look in the numerical section or the alphabetical section? References and/or added entries are required, regardless of the method of filing.

Extensive use of acronyms and initialisms has in recent years aggravated the familiar problem of how to file abbreviations. Computerized filing throws new light on the difficulties encountered in traditional approaches. In the past, initials were most often treated as one-letter words, regardless of whether spaces or punctuation intervened. For machine-readable databases it is easier to file strings of letters, or letters-and-numbers, lacking spacing or punctuation as multicharacter words. It is immaterial whether they consist entirely of capitals (e.g., FORTRAN) or of a combination of upper- and lowercase (e.g., MeSH or Unesco). Nor does pronounceability affect the filing, as it did under previous sets of filing rules that required that one determine whether or not an acronym or initialism was pronounced as a word in order to decide where to file it.

Abbreviated titles of respect or position (e.g., Mr., Dr., St.) formerly were filed as if spelled out in full. But social pressures, as well as the computer, have effected changes. For example, *Webster's New International Dictionary* (second edition) defined "Mrs." as "the form of Mistress when used as a title."[5] The problems ensuing from that edict were impressive. Fortunately, *Webster's* third edition substitutes a more contemporary (and considerably more round-about) explanation that in effect recognizes the abbreviation at its face value. Meanwhile, many libraries had already decided to file "Mrs." and "Ms." as written. Under both of the 1980 sets of filing rules (ALA and LC) abbreviations are arranged exactly as they are written.

Initial articles are usually suppressed as filing words, especially in titles. The practice extends to all languages using articles, since even in inflected languages the number of articles is relatively limited. They can be tabulated for manual filing or programmed out of machine filing. But homonyms (e.g., the French article *la*, as in *la belle epoque*, and the British interjection, as in "La! she was a lady") must be differentiated. Also, articles that initiate proper names (e.g., "La Crosse, Herman Thomas" and "Los Angeles (Calif.)") are always filed for American or English names, and for other languages as well where usage so dictates.

In dictionary catalogs the order of entries with identical wording, which may or may not be punctuated differently, must be decided. The conventional arrangement is: author, subject, title. In practice, it is highly unusual to find an author entry, a subject entry, and a title entry, all with exactly the same wording; the question bears more often on different kinds of entries that start with the same word. Application of the "authors first" guideline leaves unanswered the ordering of surnames and given name entries that start alike (e.g., "Thomas ..."). The *LC Filing Rules* file given name entries (e.g., "Francis, of Assisi, Saint" and "Francis Xavier, Saint") ahead of the same word used as a surname (e.g., "Francis, Connie"). The *ALA Filing Rules* reverse that preference, interfiling all entries, regardless of type, word-by-word to the end of the character string. However, many card catalogs are still filed according to the 1968 *ALA Rules*, according to which all surname entries come first, followed by all other entries that begin with the same word.

Many libraries, particularly large ones with comprehensive collections by and about certain versatile writers, have separated out main and added entries for those persons into at least two categories. However, the original edition of the *ALA Rules* discouraged the practice:

> Arrange in one file all the entries, both main and secondary, for a person as author, joint author, compiler, editor, illustrator, translator and general added entry. Subarrange alphabetically by the title of the book. *Note:* An earlier practice, still followed in some libraries, is to arrange the secondary author entries in a separate alphabet after the main author entries. This practice is not recommended because users of the catalog overlook entries so filed.[6]

It was observed in chapter 1 that divided catalogs permit a simpler filing scheme than do dictionary catalogs. The simplifications, though, depend on the way in which the division is made. Often, subject entries are alphabetized separately from author and title entries. Persons (e.g., "Shakespeare, William") who are both authors and subjects of books have entries in each catalog, rather than having all the entries about them collocated immediately behind all the entries by them. Titles that happen to be identical with a subject heading (e.g., *Freedom of the Press*) are similarly often located in a separate file. There is perhaps less danger of the title entries' being misfiled or overlooked, but closely related titles and subjects are divorced from each other.

In either type of catalog there is seldom any doubt about where to file a *see* reference, but there are definitely two schools of thought on the location of *see also* references. Most catalogers place them immediately after those entries from which they lead, on the theory that the user will have exhausted a search at that point and be most ready for new suggestions. However, both sets of 1980 filing rules (ALA and LC) say categorically to file *see also* references before the first entry under the same word or words.

THE 1980 FILING RULES

The first edition of the *A.L.A. Rules for Filing Catalog Cards* was published in 1942. A Subcommittee of the American Library Association's Editorial Committee was established twenty years later to prepare a revision that would correlate with the 1967 publication of the *Anglo-American Cataloging Rules*. The second edition of filing rules, like the first, was primarily designed for a dictionary catalog.[7] Except for the surname-first groupings in cases of identical entry words, single-alphabet arrangements were preferred over categorical considerations in nearly all cases. Machine filing experiments undoubtedly influenced the trend toward straight alphabetization. Yet the *ALA Rules* were designed for the manually filed catalogs that would continue to predominate for at least another two decades.

The Filing Committee of the Resources and Technical Services Division was appointed in the early 1970s to look into rules for computer filing. However, contact was maintained with the committee that was developing *AACR2* so that the new rules would be applicable for *AACR2* entries. The new *ALA Filing Rules* were thought to be so different from the earlier two sets of ALA rules that they were considered to be a new work, not another edition.[8] The introduction states that they are applicable to any bibliographic displays, not just card formats, and that they can be used to arrange records formulated according to any cataloging rules.[9]

The brief summary of the *ALA Filing Rules* that follows is designed to show the rules that a filer in a modest collection would be most likely to use. In cases where the *LC Filing Rules* vary significantly, this is brought to the reader's attention.

General Rules

As already mentioned, filing is character by character to the end of each word and word by word to the end of the filing element. This is a result of applying the "nothing files before something" principle, with spaces, dashes, hyphens, diagonal slashes, and periods all considered to be "nothing." Also, as already mentioned, numerals precede letters. In addition, letters of the English alphabet precede letters of nonroman alphabets.

Modified letters (e.g., *Æ*) are filed as if they were the plain English equivalent, and diacritical marks are ignored. Punctuation and nonalphabetic signs and symbols (except those noted above as equivalent to "nothing," ampersands, and certain such marks in numeric character strings) are also ignored.

Examples of the Basic ALA Rules

10 ans de politique social en Pologne
$20 a week
150 science experiments step-by-step
1918, the last act
130,000 kilowatt power station
A.A.
A.B.C. programs
Aabel, Marie
$$$ and sense
Camp-fire and cotton-field
Camp Fire Girls
Campbell, Thomas J.
Campfire adventure stories
LIFE
Life—a bowl of rice

"Life after death"
LIFE (BIOLOGY)
Muellen, Abraham
Mullen, Allen
Müllen, Gustav
New York
Newark
% of gain
One hundred best books
Parenting guidebook
Rolston, Brown
Rølyat, Jane
Zookeeper's handbook
$\pi \Sigma A$: A history

The *LC Filing Rules* differ on the treatment of nonroman alphabet letters: these are to be romanized for filing.

Note that under previous rules, hyphenated prefixes and compound words written both as separate words (or hyphenated) and as single words (e.g., *campfire, camp-fire*) were interfiled as the single word. Under the new rules a hyphen is regarded as a space.

Ampersands

Ampersands may be ignored or, optionally, may be spelled out in their language equivalents, e.g.,

Without option	**With option**
Art and beauty	Art and beauty
ART AND INDUSTRY	Art & commonsense
Art & commonsense	ART AND INDUSTRY

Under *LC Filing Rules* the ampersand has the lowest filing value in alphanumeric order, e.g.,

Art & commonsense
Art and beauty
ART AND INDUSTRY

Treatment of Access Points

If access points are not identical they are filed character by character and word by word according to the general rules. The major exceptions are for initial articles, certain kinds of numerals, and certain additions to names (e.g., relators and terms of honor and address). For explanation of these exceptions, see below.

When access points consist of a name and a title, they are filed as two separate elements. The title portion files with all other titles under the same name heading.

Identical Access Points

When arranging identical access points, first consider the functions of the access point. As mentioned earlier, *see* and *see also* references precede the entries of their type. In addition, main and added entries are interfiled but precede subject references and subject entries, e.g.,

Philadelphia.   Free Library. [corporate name entry]
    Annual report ...

    Philadelphia Free Library [title added entry]
Wagner, Robert L.
    The Philadelphia Free Library ...

(Example continues on page 538.)

> PHILADELPHIA.   FREE LIBRARY   [subject entry]
> Bruns, Suzanne.
>   A history of the Philadelphia Free Public
> Library ...

As mentioned earlier, *LC Filing Rules* call for arranging entries with identical leading elements in the order: person, place, thing, title. "Thing" includes corporate body entries. Thus in the example above the title added entry would follow the subject entry.

Subarrangement of identical access points *with equivalent functions* in the *ALA Filing Rules* is determined by consideration of secondary data elements. For records with author or uniform title main entry, the next element considered is the title, followed by the date of publication, distribution, etc. For records with title main entry (not uniform title) the next element considered is the date. If the access point is a personal or corporate name added entry, the next element considered is the title, followed by the date. If the access point is a title added entry, the next element considered is the author or uniform title main entry, if there is one, followed by the date. If the access point is a series or subject added entry, the next element considered is the author or uniform title main entry, if there is one, followed by the title, followed by the date.

Examples Arranged by ALA Filing Rules

(examples are invented)

> Love.
> James, Samuel.
>   Love ...

> Love and beauty.
> Adams, Harriet.
>   Love and beauty ...

> Love and beauty.
> Hansen, Sigurd.
>   Love and beauty ...

> LØVE (DENMARK)
> Friis Møller, Jens.
>   Life in a Danish town ...

> Love, Harold G., 1878-1926.
>   The chemical industry ...

> Love, Harold G., 1911-
> Symposium on the Social Organization of Anthropoid
>   Apes (1st : 1954 : Berkeley, Calif.)
>   Anthropoid apes and their society ...

> Love, Harold G., 1911-
>   Behavior of nocturnal primates ...

Love, Harold G., 1911-
  The primates of Africa ...

Love, Harold G., 1911-
Atkins, Francis Harrison.
  Psychological studies of the great apes ...

LOVE, HAROLD G., 1911-
Coffin, Lyle Warner.
  Harold Love ...

LOVE, HAROLD G., 1911-
Driscoll, Maynard.
  Cousins, once removed ...

LOVE, HAROLD G., 1911-   –BIBLIOGRAPHY
Hennesey, Judy.
  Books by and about Harold Love ...

LOVE (THEOLOGY)
Adam, Karl.
  Love and belief ...

The above entries would have a somewhat different order under the *LC Filing Rules* because of the arrangement of fields with identical leading elements in the order of person (forename, then surname), place, thing (corporate body, then topical subject heading), title.

Examples Arranged by LC Filing Rules

(examples are invented)

Love, Harold G., 1878-1926.
  The chemical industry ...

Love, Harold G., 1911-
Symposium on the Social Organization of Anthropoid
      Apes (1st : 1954 : Berkeley, Calif.)
  Anthropoid apes and their society ...

Love, Harold G., 1911-
  Behavior of nocturnal primates ...

Love, Harold G., 1911-
  The primates of Africa ...

Love, Harold G., 1911-
Atkins, Francis Harrison.
  Psychological studies of the great apes ...

(Examples continue on page 540.)

    LOVE, HAROLD G., 1911-
Coffin, Lyle Warner.
    Harold Love ...

    LOVE, HAROLD G., 1911-
Driscoll, Maynard.
    Cousins, once removed ...

    LOVE, HAROLD G., 1911-   —BIBLIOGRAPHY
Hennesey, Judy.
    Books by and about Harold Love ...

    LØVE (DENMARK)
Friis Møller, Jens.
    Life in a Danish town ...

    LOVE (THEOLOGY)
Adam, Karl.
    Love and belief ...

    Love.
James, Samuel.
    Love ...

    Love and beauty.
Adams, Harriet.
    Love and beauty ...

    Love and beauty.
Hansen, Sigurd.
    Love and beauty ...

Special Rules

Abbreviations

As mentioned earlier, abbreviations are arranged as written.

Examples

Concord (Mass.)
The Concord saunterer
Concord (Va.)
CONCORD (VT.)

Doctor come quickly
Doktor Brents Wandlung
Dr. Christian's office
Dr. Mabuse der Spieler

Initial Articles

Initial articles that form integral parts of place names and personal names are filed as written. Initial articles at the beginning of corporate names, title, and subject headings are ignored unless they begin with a personal name or place name.

Examples

Las cartas largas.
El chico.
The Club.
Der Club.
Club 21 (New York)
Club accounts.
The Club (London)
El-Abiad, Ahmed H., 1926-
El Campo (Tex.)
The El Dorado Trail.
The John Crerar Library today.
La Fontaine, Jean de, 1621-1695.
Las Hurdes (Spain)
Laš, Michal.
Lasa, Jose Maria de.

Initials, Initialisms, and Acronyms

The filing of initials, initialisms, and acronyms depends upon the spacing and punctuation between the characters. If they are separated by spaces, dashes, hyphens, diagonal slashes, or periods, they are filed as if each character were a separate word. If they are separated by other marks or symbols or are not separated, the group of characters is filed as a single word.

Examples

A.A.
A., A.J.G.
A apple pie
A.B.C. programs
Aabel, Marie
AAUN news
The ABC about collecting
U.N.E.S.C.O.   See UNESCO and Unesco.
Under the old apple tree
Unesco
UNESCO bibliographical handbooks
Unesco fellowship handbook

Names and Prefixes

A prefix that forms part of the name of a person or place is filed as a separate word unless it is joined to the rest of the name without a space or is separated from it only by an apostrophe.

Examples

De Alberti, Amelia
De la Roche, Mazo
De Marco, Clara
De senectute
Defoe, Daniel
Del Mar, Eugene

El Dorado (Ark.)
El-Wakil, Mohamed Mohamed
Elagin, Ivan
Eldorado (Neb.)

MacAlister, James
Mach, Ernst
MACHINERY
MacHugh, Angus
Maclaren, Ian
MacLaren, J.
Maclaren, James
M'Bengue, Mamadou Seyni
McHenry, Lawson
McLaren, Jack
Mead, Edwin Doak
M'Laren, J. Wilson

Under previous ALA filing rules names beginning with the prefixes *M'* and *Mc* were filed as if written *Mac*, and many card catalogs are still filed that way.

Numerals

Numerals are arranged according to their value from lowest to highest, but there are some difficulties in reading numbers with punctuation, decimals, fractions, and nonarabic notation and superscript/subscript numerals. If punctuation is for readability, it is treated as if it did not exist. Other punctuation is treated as a space. Decimals are arranged digit-by-digit, and if they are not combined with a whole integer, they precede the numeral 1. Fractions are arranged as if they are characters in the order numerator, line (treated as space), denominator (e.g., $2\frac{1}{2}$ is filed: 2 space 1 space 2). Nonarabic numerals are interfiled with their arabic equivalents. Superscript/subscript numerals are filed as if on the line and as if preceded by a space.

Examples

.300 Vickers machine gun mechanism
1:0 für Dich
1¾ yards of silk
1.3 acres
1^3 is one
⅓ of an inch
2 x 2 = 5
3.2 beer for all
3:10 to Yuma
3 point 2 and what goes with it
$20 a week
XX Century cyclopaedia and atlas
20 humorous stories
XXth century citizen's atlas of the world
200 years of architectural drawing
2000 A.D., a documentary

Dates

Dates in titles are filed as numerals. Dates in a chronological file, such as subdivisions of subjects or personal names with dates, are arranged chronologically, with B.C. dates preceding A.D. dates. Historic time periods that are generalized or expressed only in words are filed with the full range of dates for the period (e.g., *18th century* is equivalent to 1800-1899). Subject period subdivisions are filed chronologically even when words (e.g., the name of a war) precede the dates. Geologic time periods are arranged alphabetically.

Examples

UNITED STATES – HISTORY
UNITED STATES – HISTORY – COLONIAL PERIOD, CA.1600-1775
UNITED STATES – HISTORY – REVOLUTION, 1775-1783
UNITED STATES – HISTORY – CONFEDERATION, 1783-1789
UNITED STATES – HISTORY – 1783-1865
UNITED STATES – HISTORY – 1865-
UNITED STATES – HISTORY – 1865-1898
UNITED STATES – HISTORY – WAR OF 1898
UNITED STATES – HISTORY – 1898-
UNITED STATES – HISTORY – 20TH CENTURY
UNITED STATES – HISTORY – 1933-1945
UNITED STATES – HISTORY – BIO-BIBLIOGRAPHY
UNITED STATES – HISTORY – DICTIONARIES

Under the *ALA Filing Rules*, subjects with subdivisions and those with qualifiers are interfiled ignoring punctuation (see examples on page 544).

Examples Arranged by *ALA Filing Rules*

COOKERY
COOKERY, AMERICAN
COOKERY, AMERICAN—BIBLIOGRAPHY
COOKERY (APPLES)
COOKERY, CHINESE
COOKERY—DICTIONARIES
COOKERY FOR DIABETICS
COOKERY, INTERNATIONAL
COOKERY—YEARBOOKS

The *LC Filing Rules*, however, are more inclined to categorize entries. Topical subject headings are grouped so that the leading element alone is first, followed by entries in the form leading element—subject subdivision. These are followed by entries in the form leading element, comma, additional word(s). Following these are entries in which the leading element is followed by a parenthetical qualifier. Finally, there come entries in which the word that has been the leading element in the preceding entries is the first word of a phrase.

Examples Arranged by *LC Filing Rules*

COOKERY
COOKERY—DICTIONARIES
COOKERY—YEARBOOKS
COOKERY, AMERICAN
COOKERY, AMERICAN—BIBLIOGRAPHY
COOKERY, CHINESE
COOKERY, INTERNATIONAL
COOKERY (APPLES)
COOKERY FOR DIABETICS

Subordinate elements that follow a dash are also grouped according to the *LC Filing Rules*. The order is period subdivision, form and topical subdivisions, and geographical subdivisions. This is the order in which printed versions of LCSH are arranged, and it is further discussed with examples in chapter 22 of this text.

ALTERNATE FILING RULES

The *ALA Filing Rules* summarized above were a response to a feeling that traditional practices were too complex, too awkward, and too concerned with fine theoretical distinctions. Not everyone agrees, as is evidenced by the fact that many libraries have not fully implemented the changes. There are two major considerations: 1) it would be prohibitively expensive to refile a card catalog for a collection of, say, a million volumes or more; and 2) there is a direct relationship between the size of the collection and the need for a finetuned filing system. John Rather argues the case for meaningful complexity:

> Filing arrangement is the capstone of the system of bibliographic
> control that begins with descriptive cataloging and includes subject

analysis and classification. The entire effort to achieve bibliographic control necessarily reaches its fulfillment in the means of displaying catalog information to users. If the arrangement of the file violates the form or meaning of the headings, users will be hampered in their efforts to use the catalog successfully.[10]

The primary issue is categorical versus alphabetical filing. Research libraries hold that the *ALA Filing Rules* to some extent "violate the form or meaning of the headings." The 1968 *ALA Rules* were also criticized for this even though that set of rules maintained more categorization than do the current *ALA Filing Rules*. The 1968 *ALA Rules* Subcommittee claimed:

> An attempt was made to develop an alternative code of rules based on a consistent regard for punctuation, but that method also proved to be not entirely satisfactory, because of lack of consistency in punctuation.[11]

The Subcommittee's reference was a major 1942 rule requiring that subject entries beginning with the same initial element be arranged by type as signified by differing marks of punctuation in the manner still called for by the *LC Filing Rules* and described above.

The Subcommittee held that many of the disadvantages of alphabetical arrangements could be overcome by adding state or country designations after all city names and using parenthetical explanatory terms after all homonyms or homonymous phrases. Movement was made in this direction with implementation of *AACR2*, which calls for making additions to nearly all local place and jurisdictional names.

The following examples compare the arrangements achieved by applying first one, then the other, of the 1942, 1968, and 1980 versions of the ALA rules to the same group of entries:

1942 *ALA Rules*	1968 *ALA Rules*	1980 *ALA Filing Rules*
Love, David T.	Love, David T.	Love [title]
LOVE, DAVID T.	LOVE, DAVID T.	LOVE [subject]
Love, Zachary	Love, Zachary	Love and beauty
The Love Corp.	LOVE [subject]	The Love Corp.
Love County (Okla.)	Love [title]	Love County (Okla.)
LOVE [subject]	Love and beauty	Love, David T.
LOVE – LETTERS	The Love Corp.	LOVE, DAVID T.
LOVE – QUOTATIONS	Love County (Okla.)	LOVE – LETTERS
LOVE, MATERIAL	LOVE – LETTERS	LOVE, MATERIAL
LOVE (THEOLOGY)	LOVE, MATERIAL	LOVE POETRY
Love [title]	LOVE POETRY	LOVE – QUOTATIONS
Love and beauty	LOVE – QUOTATIONS	Love songs, old and new
LOVE POETRY	Love songs, old and new	LOVE (THEOLOGY)
Love songs, old and new	LOVE (THEOLOGY)	Love your neighbor
Love your neighbor	Love your neighbor	Love, Zachary

The 1942 *ALA Rules* responded to the wide diversity of filing practices by including alternatives or variants for 60 percent of the rules. The 1968 Subcommittee opted for simplicity in this respect, developing a consistent code derived from one basic principle, with as few exceptions as possible. The 1980 Committee made the rules simpler still by eliminating the exceptions. However, those who want more categorization have a choice. The *LC Filing Rules* provide for this option, even with computerization in mind. The field tags, indicators, and subfield codes of the MARC format allow adequate identification of elements in headings so that a computer program has been written and is in use at LC that sorts using the *LC Filing Rules*.[12]

SHELFLIST FILING

The notation of most modern classifications, whether pure or mixed, includes arabic numerals (both integers and decimals) that are filed in normal mathematical sequence. A typical series of class numbers from the DDC schedules, which use a pure decimal notation, could appear as follows:

DDC Class Number Order

001	- Knowledge
010	- Bibliography
016	- Subject bibliographies
070.01	- Theory of journalism
070.1	- News media
070.17	- Print media
070.172	- Newspapers
070.19	- Broadcast media
070.4	- Journalism
070.41	- Editing
070.509	- History of publishing
070.59	- Kinds of publishers
078	- Journalism in Scandinavia
	[etc.]

Class number notation for the Library of Congress system is mixed. In its simplest form it consists of one to three roman alphabet letters followed by one to four integers. However, decimals both in pure numeric form and in alphanumeric form may be introduced at various points. A typical sequence might be:

LC Class Number Order

T20	- History of technology in the 20th century
T26.G3	- History of technology in Germany
T26.G5B5	- History of technology in Berlin
TP572	- Directories of brewing and malting
TP573.A1	- General histories of brewing and malting
TP573.5	- Biography of brewers and malters
TP573.5A1	- Collective biography of brewers and malters
TP574	- Schools of brewing and malting
TP1107	- Exhibitions of plastics and plastics manufacture
TP1130	- Handbooks, manuals, tables, etc., of plastics
TP1135	- Plastics plants and equipment
	[etc.]

Cutter number notation also varies with the system. Libraries that use DDC may use cutter numbers assigned through use of the Cutter two- or three-figure alphanumeric tables or the Cutter-Sanborn tables. Two-figure Cutter and Cutter-Sanborn numbers can be filed in straight integer sequence, but those from the three-figure Cutter table must be arranged decimally, as shown:

DDC Call Numbers with Three-Figure Cutter Book Numbers

333 F189 - A work on land economics by an author surnamed Falkinson
333 F19 - A similar work by an author surnamed Fallaby
333 F191 - A similar work by an author surnamed Fallentz
333 F21 - A similar work by an author surnamed Famareus
333 F218 - A similar work by an author surnamed Fantine

Workmarks consisting of lowercase letters, and most often corresponding to the first significant word of the item's title, may be added to the cutter number as follows:

DDC Call Numbers with Workmarks

515.33 R4li - Introduction to Differential Calculus, by an author surnamed Richmond
515.33 R41m- Mean Value Theorems, by the same author
515.33 R4lt - Total and Directional Derivatives, by the same author

Many smaller libraries using DDC bypass the Cutter tables in favor of adding one to three or more capital letters from the main entry word of the item to the DDC class number. These book symbols are, of course, arranged alphabetically as follows. In such libraries congested files are rare, so that lowercase workmarks are not often needed:

(Example is on page 548.)

DDC Call Numbers with Alphabetic Book Numbers

799.1 ROB - A book on fishing by an author surnamed Robb
799.1 ROBE - A similar book by an author surnamed Robertson
799.1 ROBI - A similar book by an author surnamed Robinson

The Library of Congress assigns its own unique cutter numbers to materials, as discussed in chapter 24—Library of Congress Classification. Many LC call numbers include two cutter numbers, of which only the final one is, or incorporates, the number for the particular item. A typical sequence might be:

HC59.7.B7   - Broekmeijer, M. W. J. M. *Fiction and truth about the decade of development.*
HC59.7.C28 - Caiden, Naomi. *Planning and budgeting in poor countries.*
HC59.7.C6   - Committee for Economic Development. *How low income countries can advance their growth.*
HN438.C5G2 - Galpern, A. N. *The religions of the people in sixteenth-century Champagne.*
HN438.P3R8 - Rudé, George F. E. *Paris and London in the eighteenth century.*
HN438.P6H52 - Higonnet, Patrice L. R. *Pont-de-Montvert; social structure and politics in a French village, 1700-1914.*

What needs to be remembered when filing LC call numbers is that the classification part of the notation up to the period files as integers, but any cutter numbers after the period file as decimals.

HN4	*but* HN438.C15
HN5	HN438.C23
HN15	HN438.C4
HN23	HN438.C43
HN43	HN438.C5
HN59	HN438.C59

Dates or edition numbers may be added as a third element to either DDC or LC call numbers to distinguish among different issues of the same title. These might be filed in either chronological or retrospective order, just as in catalog filing, but the majority of libraries prefer chronological shelflist filing. Location symbols of various kinds may also accompany call numbers of some materials. The shelflist filing of such additions is purely a matter of local preference.

CONCLUSION

The final results of the filing debates are by no means settled. Still, progress has been made. Perhaps universal standardization should not be our goal, given the diverse objectives of different libraries and types of libraries.

NOTES

[1] *A Catalog of Books Represented by Library of Congress Printed Cards Issued to July 31, 1942* (Ann Arbor, Mich., Edwards Brothers, 1943); vol. 14, pp. 3-13, gives full explanation of the arrangement.

[2] *ALA Filing Rules* (Chicago, American Library Association, 1980).

[3] *Library of Congress Filing Rules* (Washington, D.C., Library of Congress, 1980).

[4] *ALA Rules for Filing Catalog Cards*, 2nd ed. (Chicago, American Library Association, 1968).

[5] *Webster's New International Dictionary of the English Language*, 2nd ed., unabr. (Springfield, Mass., G. & C. Merriam, 1959), p. 1605.

[6] *A.L.A. Rules for Filing Catalog Cards* (Chicago, American Library Association, 1942), p. 25.

[7] See Pauline Seely, "ALA Filing Rules—New Edition," *Library Resources & Technical Services* 11 (Summer 1967): 377-379; and Pauline Seely, "ALA Rules for Filing Catalog Cards: Differences between 2d and 1st Editions (Arranged by 2d Rule Numbers)," *Library Resources & Technical Services* 13 (Spring 1969): 291-294.

[8] For a critique of the *ALA Filing Rules*, see Hans W. Wellisch,"The *ALA Filing Rules*: Flowcharts Illustrating Their Application, with a Critique and Suggestions for Improvement," *Journal of the American Society for Information Science* 34 (September 1983): 313-330.

[9] *ALA Filing Rules*, pp. 1-2.

[10] John C. Rather, "Filing Arrangement in the Library of Congress Catalogs," *Library Resources & Technical Services* 16 (Spring 1972): 240-261.

[11] *ALA Rules*, 2nd ed., p. vi.

[12] *LC Filing Rules*, pp. 6-7.

SUGGESTED READING

Carothers, Diane Foxhill. *Self-Instruction Manual for Filing Catalog Cards.* Chicago, American Library Association, 1981.

Gorman, Michael. "Fear of Filing: Daunted Librarians Have Ally in New Rules." *American Libraries* 12 (February 1981): 71-72.

Wellisch, Hans H. "The *ALA Filing Rules*: Flowcharts Illustrating Their Application, with a Critique and Suggestions for Improvement." *Journal of the American Society for Information Science* 34 (September 1983): 313-330.

Appendix A
Introduction to the
MARC Formats

The first **MA**chine **R**eadable **C**ataloging (MARC) format was developed at the Library of Congress in 1965. Since then there have been many revisions and refinements and development of several formats for different types of materials. An integrated format combining all current ones is set to be implemented in 1993. All current ones have the same basic structure.

FORMAT

The structure of a machine-readable record is referred to as a format. A format document gives specifications for this structure. There are seven USMARC formats defined by the Library of Congress:

1. Books

2. Serials

3. Visual materials

4. Archives and manuscript control

5. Maps

6. Music

7. Computer files

Records constructed using these formats have the same structural components.

PARTS OF THE RECORD

A record is a collection of fields. A field contains a single unit of information within a record. A field may consist of one or more subfields. Tags, i.e., three-digit numerical codes, identify each field. Every field ends with a field terminator (in OCLC, for example, the field terminator appears as a backwards paragraph sign). Each subfield is preceded by a delimiter sign (often represented by a $ or ‡ or ¦) followed by a single character code (usually alphabetical).

Each record has the same components:

1. Leader

2. Record directory

3. Control fields
   a. Fixed fields

4. Variable fields

Leader – The leader is like the leader on a roll of film. It identifies the beginning of a new record. The leader is fixed in length and contains 24 characters.

Record directory – The record directory contains a series of fixed length entries that identify the tag, length, and starting position of each field in the record.

Control fields – Control fields carry alphanumeric (often encoded) data elements. Control field tags always begin with the digit 0. Many control fields are fixed in length (see also "Fixed fields" below). Common control fields are:

007 Fixed length field – Physical description

008 Fixed length field – General information (see below)

010 LCCN (i.e., LC control [card] number)

020 International standard book number (ISBN)

022 International standard serial number (ISSN)

040 Cataloging source

041 Languages

043 Geographic area code

045 Chronological coverage code

050 Library of Congress call number

082 Dewey Decimal Classification number assigned by LC

090 Call number based on LC Classification assigned by a library other than LC

092 Call number based on Dewey Decimal Classification assigned by a library other than LC

Fixed fields – There are two fixed length control fields that are commonly referred to as fixed fields. Field 007 carries encoded data about the physical description of bibliographic items and is used predominantly for nonbook materials.

Field 008 carries general information about the content of the bibliographic record. This field is usually displayed in a single paragraph at the top of the screen and is usually displayed with mnemonic tags. The field has 40 character positions. The data stored in this field are used to manipulate records for retrieval, filing, indexing, etc. It is this field that is commonly referred to as "the fixed field." It is usually displayed at the top of a record with the character positions preceded by abbreviations indicating for what kind of information the characters are meant to be codes.

A fixed field from the record for a book as it is displayed in OCLC:

Type: a	Bib lvl: m	Source:	Lang: eng
Repr:	Enc lvl:	Conf pub: 0	Ctry: nyu
Indx: 1	Mod rec:	Govt pub:	Cont: b
Desc: a	Int lvl:	Festschr: 0	Illus: a
	F/B: 0c	Dat tp: s	Dates: 1990,

Sometimes fill characters (displayed as ■ or __ or |) are used to indicate elements of the fixed field that were not in use when the record was created or were not provided by the inputting library. A blank space (when written represented as ƀ) is meaningful. That is, a blank is input to represent a coded value. In "Source:" above, the blank means "Library of Congress."

Variable fields — Variable fields carry alphanumeric data of variable length. The variable fields carry traditional cataloging data elements. Three-digit numeric tags (100-999) identify variable fields. In order to talk about these tags in groups, a convention is followed in which all fields beginning with "1" are identified as 1xx fields; those beginning with "2," as 2xx fields; etc. Variable fields consist of heading fields and descriptive fields.

Heading Fields

100   Main entry, Personal name

110   Main entry, Corporate name

111   Main entry, Conference name

130   Main entry, Uniform title

240   Uniform title under personal or corporate name

600   Subject access point, Personal name

610   Subject access point, Corporate name

611   Subject access point, Conference name

630   Subject access point, Uniform title

650   Subject access point, Topical subject heading

651   Subject access point, Geographic subject heading

700   Additional access point, Personal name

etc.

800   Series access point, Personal name
      (Used in conjunction with field 490)

etc.

Descriptive Fields

245 Title, Statement of responsibility
(subfield "a," the title proper, is also used as an access point)

250 Edition statement

260 Publication, distribution, etc.

300 Physical description

4xx Series statement
(These may also be used in place of an 8xx field to show that an additional access point is needed.)

5xx Notes. The most common ones are:

    500 General

    502 Dissertation

    504 Bibliography

    505 Contents

Subfields—All subfields are distinct elements within fields. Subfield definitions vary from field to field. Some of the most commonly encountered ones are:

050 LC call number

    $a classification number

    $b cutter number and date

x00 Personal name
(x00 means that these subfields apply in fields 100, 600, 700, and 800.)

    $a name

    $q qualification of name [e.g., Lewis, C. S. $q (Clive Staples)]

    $b numeration

    $c titles (e.g., Mrs., Sir, Bishop)

    $d dates

    $e relator (e.g., ill. [for illustrator])

x10 Corporate name

    $a name

    $b subordinate unit

    $e relator

    $k form subheading

x11 Conference name

    $a name

    $n number

    $c place

    $d date

245 Title and statement of responsibility

$a title proper

$b other title information

$c statement of responsibility or remainder of area

260 Publication, distribution, etc.

$a place

$b publisher, distributor, etc.

$c date

300 Physical description

$a extent of item

$b other physical details

$c dimensions

4xx and 8xx Series

$a name of series

$x ISSN (4xx fields only)

$v numbering of series

6xx Subject access point

$a main subject (name, topic, etc.)

$x subject subdivision

$y time period subdivision

$z geographic subdivision

Indicators — The one- or two-digit codes that appear after the tags are called indicators. Indicators provide computer instructions for processing the data contained in the field. For example, in the OCLC-formatted 245 field shown below, the first indicator, "1," tells the system that there should be an access point for the title, and the second indicator, "4," tells the system that four nonfiling characters (i.e., T, h, e, and [space]) precede the first significant word of the title:

245 14 The dictionary of misinformation / $c Tom Burnam.

DISPLAY OF MARC RECORDS

MARC records are distributed in the MARC Communications Format. Each record consists of one long character string beginning with the leader, followed by the record directory, followed by the fields one after another, with no breaks, to the end of the record (at which point there is a character to represent a record terminator). Such a record is practically unreadable if printed as transmitted, and so each system has a program that will display the record in a form that is more easily read. Figures A.1, A.2 (see page 556), A.3, and A.4 (see page 557) show the same MARC record as it is displayed in four different systems.

Fig. A.1. MARC record as displayed in OCLC.

```
OCLC:       19124014      Rec stat:    p
Entered:    19890119      Replaced:    19900317      Used:     19910416
Type: a         Bib lvl: m     Source:              Lang:    eng
Repr:           Enc lvl:       Conf pub: 0          Ctry:    cou
Indx: 1         Mod rec:       Govt pub:            Cont:    b
Desc: a         Int lvl:       Festschr: 0          Illus:
                F/B:      0    Dat tp:   s          Dates: 1989,
 1   010    89-2835
 2   040    DLC $c DLC
 3   020    0872876217 : $c $45.00
 4   050 00 Z674 $b .R4 no. 20 $a Z7837 $a BX1751.2
 5   082 00 020 s $a 016.282 $2 19
 6   092    $b
 7   049    YCLM
 8   100 1  McCabe, James Patrick.
 9   245 10 Critical guide to Catholic reference books / $c James Patrick
McCabe ; with an introduction by Russell E. Bidlack.
10   250    3rd ed.
11   260    Englewood, Colo. : $b Libraries Unlimited, $c 1989.
12   300    xiv, 323 p. ; $c 25 cm.
13   440  0 Research studies in library science ; $v no. 20
14   500    Includes indexes.
15   610 20 Catholic Church $x Bibliography.
16   650  0 Reference books $x Catholic Church.
```

Fig. A.2. MARC record as displayed in RLIN.

```
ID:DCLC892835-B    RTYP:c    ST:p   FRN:     MS:p    EL:       AD:01-19-89
CC:9110  BLT:am    DCF:a     CSC:   MOD:     SNR:    ATC:      UD:03-18-90
CP:cou     L:eng   INT:      GPC:   BIO:     FIC:0   CON:b
PC:s       PD:1989/          REP:   CPI:0    FSI:0   ILC:      II:1
MMD:       OR:     POL:  DM:    RR:          COL:    EML:      GEN:    BSE:
010      892835
020      0872876217 :$c$45.00
040      DLC$cDLC$dDLC
050 00   Z674$b.R4 no. 20$aZ7837$aBX1751.2
082 00   020 s$a016.282$219
100 1    McCabe, James Patrick.
245 10   Critical guide to Catholic reference books /$cJames Patrick McCabe ; w
         ith an introduction by Russell E. Bidlack.
250      3rd ed.
260      Englewood, Colo. :$bLibraries Unlimited, $c1989.
300      xiv, 323 p. ;$c25 cm.
440  0   Research studies in library science ;$vno. 20
500      Includes index.
610 20   Catholic Church$xBibliography.
650  0   Reference books$xCatholic Church.
```

Fig. A.3. MARC record as displayed in the NOTIS system at Columbia University.

```
                                     NOTIS CATALOGING              3T22
CU# AEC7406 FMT B RT a BL m DT 11/15/89 R/DT none     STAT mn E/L   DCF i D/S D
SRC    PLACE cou LANG eng MOD   T/AUD   REPRO   D/CODE s DT/1 1989 DT/2
CONT       ILLUS       GOVT   BIOG   FEST 0 CONF 0 FICT 0 INDX 1

019:   : |a BNA
020/1:  : |a 0872876217
035/1:  : |a (CStRLIN)NYCG89-B81315
040:   : |a DLC |c DLC |d DLC
100:1 : |a McCabe, James Patrick.
245:10: |a Critical guide to Catholic reference books / |c James Patrick
McCabe ; with an introduction by Russell E. Bidlack.
250:   : |a 3rd ed.
260:   : |a Englewood, Colo. : |b Libraries Unlimited, |c 1989.
300/1:  : |a xiv, 323 p. ; |c 25 cm.
440/1: 0: |a Research studies in library science ; |v no. 20
500/1:  : |a Includes index.
610/1:20: |a Catholic Church |x Bibliography.
650/2: 0: |a Reference books |x Catholic Chruch.
950/1:  : |1 SLS |a Z674 |b .R4 no. 20
```

Fig. A.4. MARC record as displayed in the MUMS system at LC.

```
--010  001 |a|89-2835
--015  955|a|CIP ver.
--020  05000|abaa|Z674|.R4 no. 20|Z7837|BX1751.2
--030  1001|a|McCabe, James Patrick.
--040  24510|ac|Critical guide to Catholic reference books /|James Patrick McCa
be ; with an introduction by Russell E. Bidlack.
--050  250|a|3rd ed.
--060  260|abc|Englewood, Colo. :|Libraries Unlimited, |1989.
--070  300|ac|xiv, 323 p. ;|25 cm.
--090  440-0|av|Research studies in library science ;|no. 20
--110  500|a|Includes index.
--120  020|ac|0872876217 :|$45.00
--130  61020|ax|Catholic Church|Bibliography.
--140  650-0|ax|Reference books|Catholic Church.
--150  08200|aa2|020 s|016.282|19
--155  952|a|Online
--160  005|a|19900227083313.4
--179  040|acd|DLC|DLC|DLC
--170  FFD  01.     02.      03.      04.x     05.x     06.     07.
             08.     09.      10.      11.      12.      13.     14.
             15.eng  16.      17.      18.      19.      20.s    21.1989
             22.     23.cou   24.      25.      26.b     27.m    28.
             29.     30.y     31.1     32.      33.7     34.     35.7
             36.a    37.      38.p     39.m     40.      41.a
```

Appendix B
Standards for Spacing, Punctuation, Capitalization, Abbreviations, and Numerals in Bibliographic Records— with Special Instructions for Typed Cards

There are still many libraries that find it necessary to type at least some catalog cards locally. For these libraries, the following instructions illustrate a simple and generally effective method for doing so. The sections on punctuation, spacing, capitalization, abbreviations, and numerals are useful in creating original bibliographic records, whether they are input online in MARC format or are to be hand-typed.

The following formalized rules are arbitrary. In any particular setting, different spacing may be set for indentions. The important thing is to be consistent — especially concerning which information starts at the different indentions. Otherwise, users may find it difficult to read and understand the cards. In the following sections indention rules are given first. These are followed by detailed explanations of the typing rules (spacing, punctuation, capitalization, etc.) using International Standard Bibliographic Description (ISBD) format.

TYPED CARDS

Indentions

Standard printed cards from the Library of Congress have the great advantage of more than one style and size of type to help differentiate between distinct items on the card. Lacking this advantage, typewritten cards must rely upon a standardized system of spacing and punctuation for clarity. The following suggestions for spacing have been used successfully by many libraries.

The main entry heading begins nine spaces from the left margin of the card. This segment of nine spaces is called the first indention.

The second indention begins four typewriter spaces to the right of the main entry — or 13 spaces from the left margin. The second indention is used to align title, collation, notes, and tracing. Any of this information that is too long to be recorded on one line is brought back to the first indention in standard paragraph form. All added entries at the top of the card begin at the second indention.

Occasionally there is need of a third indention (16 spaces from the left margin or seven spaces to the right of the beginning of the main entry). This will occur in three instances:

1. When the author entry is too long to be contained on one line, the overflow is carried to the third indention. (To use the second indention in this case would be confusing because the title begins at the second indention.)

2. When an added entry is too long for one line, the second line will carry over to the third indention.

3. In the cataloging of one volume or piece of a set that is in progress, the succeeding volumes or pieces must be allowed for. In this case the typist will space to the third indention in the collation and type the specific material designation [e.g., "cassettes," "reels," or "v." (for "volumes")]. When the set is complete, it then becomes a simple matter to type the completed number of pieces directly to the left of the designation.

Card Format

The main entry heading begins on the fourth line from the top of the card. A typewritten catalog card is single-spaced throughout, with the following exceptions:

1. Double-space before the beginning of the first note.

2. Place the tracing at the bottom of the card, but above the hole.

Figure B.1 (see page 560) is a sample form showing the location of information on a catalog card, indentions, spacing after punctuation, and vertical spacing between parts of the card. Figure B.2 (see page 560) illustrates the format for the second card, which is to be used when there is too much information to fit onto one card. Detailed instructions for spacing, punctuation, and capitalization in the format are given in the following sections.

The Library of Congress carries the tracing for the card set in paragraph form at the bottom of the card just above the hole (see Fig. B.2). For typed cards the tracings, instead of being placed on the front, may be typed on the back of the main entry card. This is particularly true when the tracings are long. In any case, the form, once established, should not vary. The subject headings are typed first in order of importance. If they are equally important, the order does not matter, except that biographical headings, or others in which the person is the subject, always come first. Each subject heading is preceded by an arabic numeral.

Those entries that bring out descriptive elements of a book rather than its subject are preceded by roman numerals and come after all subject entries. As part of the tracing, they follow a specific order: joint author, editor, translator, or any other individual person who has helped to create the work; corporate entries or sponsoring agencies such as societies, university departments, bureaus, and the like; title; series.

Fig. B.1. Sample form for typed card.

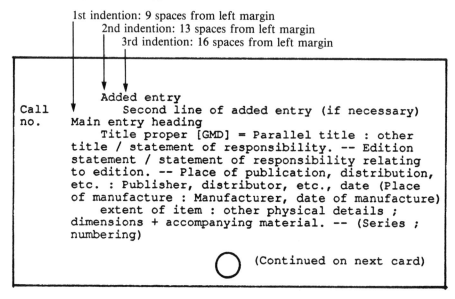

```
1st indention: 9 spaces from left margin
    2nd indention: 13 spaces from left margin
        3rd indention: 16 spaces from left margin
```

```
              Added entry
Call                Second line of added entry (if necessary)
no.       Main entry heading
              Title proper [GMD] = Parallel title : other
          title / statement of responsibility. -- Edition
          statement / statement of responsibility relating
          to edition. -- Place of publication, distribution,
          etc. : Publisher, distributor, etc., date (Place
          of manufacture : Manufacturer, date of manufacture)
              extent of item : other physical details ;
          dimensions + accompanying material. -- (Series ;
          numbering)

                        O    (Continued on next card)
```

Fig. B.2. Sample form for supplementary typed card.

```
              Added entry
Call                Second line of added entry (if necessary)
no.       Main entry heading
              Title proper [GMD] ... date of publication,
          etc.  (Card 2)

              Note 1.
              Note 2.
              ISBN

              1. Subject heading--Subheading.  2. Subject
          heading--Subheading.  I. Added entry.  II. Title.
          III. Series.
                        O
```

Detailed rules and examples pertaining to the elements that make up the bibliographic record are discussed in chapters 3-13, 17-19, and 22-23 of this text.

Works entered under title are typed in the form called the hanging indention. The title begins at the first indention and is continued at the second indention. Physical description and notes are indented as for all other cards. See Fig. B.3.

Fig. B.3. Typed form for hanging indention.

¹Title entry 1st indention

²2nd indention

```
Call      1
no.      An Illustrated dictionary of geography / edited
        by R. Ogilvie Buchanan. -- London : Heinemann
    2    Educational, 1974.
         242 p. : ill. (some col.), col. maps ; 22 cm.

         ISBN 0-435-34390-4

         1. Physical geography--Dictionaries.
         2. Geography--Dictionaries.  I. Buchanan, Robert
         Ogilvie, 1894-

                        O
```

STANDARDS FOR SPACING, PUNCTUATION, CAPITALIZATION, ABBREVIATIONS, AND NUMERALS IN ISBD AND AACR

In 1972 the International Standard Bibliographic Description (ISBD) was adopted as a standard by the International Federation of Library Associations. Its major purpose was to facilitate the international exchange of bibliographic information by standardizing the elements to be used in the bibliographic description, assigning an order to these elements, and specifying a system of symbols to be used in punctuating these elements. In 1974 *AACR1* was revised to incorporate ISBD into its rules for description of monographs, and by the time of publication of *AACR2*, ISBD standards were included for description of all materials. In the following sections, except for the instructions relating specifically only to typed cards, the instructions follow ISBD and *AACR2R* standards.

Spacing

1. The main entry heading begins on the fourth line from the top of the card.

2. Single-space the lines, with the exceptions of double spaces before the first note and before the tracing.

3. The call number begins on the fourth line from the top of the card. Indent the call number one space from the left edge of the card.

4. Leave one space before and one space after

   a. Equals signs
      used to indicate parallel titles or other parallel information:
      La motoneige au Québec = Snowmobiling in Quebec

      used to separate alternative numbering systems in serials:
      Vol. 4, no. 1-   = No. 13-

      used to separate ISSN from key title:
      ISSN 0040-9898 = Toward freedom

   b. Colons
      used before other title information:
      On the contrary : articles of belief, 1946-1961.

      used between place of publication, etc., and publisher, etc.:
      New York : Macmillan

      used between the extent of item and other physical details in the physical description area:
      1 disc (45 min.) : analog, 33 1/3 rpm, stereo.

      used between standard number and terms of availability:
      ISBN 0-87287-153-3 : $15.00

      used between different parts of additions to corporate names:
      Alessandria (Italy : Province)

      used in statements of computer file characteristics:
      Computer data (2 files : 100, 450 records)

   c. Diagonal slashes used to indicate a statement of responsibility:
      Instrument pilot's guide / by L.W. Reithmaier

   d. Dashes used following the periods (full stops) that precede the edition area, the material specific details area, the publication, distribution, etc., area, and the series area. In typescript a dash is made with two hyphens:
      by L.W. Reithmaier. -- 2nd ed. -- Fallbrook, Calif.

      26 cm. -- (Oxford in Asia university readings)

e. Semicolons
used to indicate different functions of subsidiary responsibility:
    by W.W. Hellon ; photography, Woodward C. Helton and James McKinney ; illustrator, Pete Dykes

used to precede dimensions in the physical description area:
    219 p. : ill. ; 24 cm.

    1 score (8 p.) ; 31 cm.

used in the publication, etc., area to separate two places or two places and publishers, etc.:
    Toronto ; New York

    London : Oxford University Press ; Berkeley : University of California Press

used to precede numbering of a series or subseries:
    Studies in Nigerian languages ; no. 1

used to separate projection from statement of scale in cartographic materials:
    Scale 1:50,000 ; Transverse Mercator proj.

used to separate a new sequence of numbering from an old sequence of numbering in serials:
    No. 1 (Winter 1970)-no. 20 (Fall 1974) ; Vol. 1, no. 1 (Jan. 1975)-

f. The plus sign used to separate accompanying materials from the dimensions in the physical description area:
    30 cm. + 1 atlas

g. The mark of omission (...) used to show omission of part of an element:
    by Jack P. Segal ... [et al.]

5. Leave one space after

   a. all commas, closing parentheses, and closing square brackets

   b. periods (full stops) that end each area of the description or that are used after abbreviations

   c. colons that follow the introductory wording in notes:
      Title on spine: Eighteenth century Franklin County deeds

6. Leave two spaces after

   a. the period (full stop) separating the titles and statements of responsibility of works in an item lacking a collective title:
      Henry Esmond : a novel / by Thackeray. Bleak house : a novel / by Dickens

   b. each item in the tracing:
      I. Title. II. Series.

7. Omit the space before all commas, periods (full stops), hyphens, closing parentheses, and closing square brackets.

8. Omit the space after all opening parentheses, opening square brackets, and hyphens that are followed by additional information.

NOTE: The peculiarities of ISBD spacing result from the dual use of punctuation marks: they can be used either as marks of punctuation or as marks of separation. The function of a mark in a particular instance determines the spacing around it. The ISBD rules for punctuation and spacing were designed for international standardization of bibliographic format so that records could be exchanged between countries and would have clearly identifiable parts regardless of language differences or differences in meaning of punctuation marks. The ISBD rules also simplify the conversion of bibliographic records to machine-readable form.

Punctuation

1. Use commas

    a. in the statement of responsibility between names of persons or bodies performing the same function but which are not connected with a conjunction in the chief source of information:
        by Martin L. Bowers, Jon R. Carr, William Knight

    b. between the name of the publisher, etc., and the date of publication, etc., or between name of manufacturer and date of manufacture in the publication, distribution, etc., area:
        American Library Association, 1978

    c. between variations in dates in the publication, etc., area:
        1989, c1986

    d. between different pagination sections of a printed work:
        xxi, 259, 27 p., 15 leaves of plates

    e. between the series or subseries and its ISSN:
        Studies in biology, ISSN 0537-9024

    f. to separate a surname and a forename

    g. following personal names, when additions are made:
        Smith, Paul, 1941-

        John Paul II, Pope

    h. to separate a smaller place from its larger jurisdiction when both are used as an addition to a name:
        Hope Valley (Durham, N.C.)

    i. wherever required by grammar and there is no punctuation prescribed in the rules

2. Use semicolons

   a. to indicate different functions of subsidiary responsibility:
      by John Hinterberger ; illustrated by Jacques Rupp

   b. preceding dimensions in the physical description area:
      ill. (some col.) ; 30 cm.

      1 score (28 p.) ; 28 cm.

   c. preceding the numbering of a series or subseries:
      (Studies in Nigerian languages ; no. 1)

      (Studies in biology, ISSN 0537-9024 ; no. 102)

   d. between a series of titles by the same author from a work lacking a collective title:
      Romeo and Juliet ; King Lear ; Macbeth / by William Shakespeare. --

   e. between two places of publication, etc., in the publication, etc., area:
      London ; New York :

   f. between two separate places of publication, etc., and publishers, etc.:
      London : Oxford University Press ; Berkeley : University of California Press

   g. between two sequences of numbering, dates, etc.:
      Vol. 10, no. 3 (Mar. 1983)-vol. 12, no. 12 (Dec. 1985) ; no. 1 (Jan. 1986)-

   h. between statement of scale and projection in cartographic materials:
      Scale 1:50,000 ; Transverse Mercator proj.

3. Use periods (full stops)

   a. at the end of the publication, distribution, etc., area unless the final mark of punctuation is a square bracket or a right-hand parenthesis:
      Oxford University Press, 1979.

      Aero Publishers, 1979 [c1976]

   b. at the end of each note:
      Includes index.

      Title from container.

   c. at the end of each entry in the tracing:
      1. Sociology.

      I. Title. II. Series.

    d. between a series of separate titles and statements of responsibility from a work lacking a collective title:
> The sorcerer's apprentice / Dukas. Night on bald mountain / Mussorgsky.

    e. preceding the title of a supplement or section:
> Journal of chemical engineering. Supplement

    f. between the title of a series and the title of a subseries:
> Pacific linguistics. Series C

    g. after abbreviations as indicated by the current usage of the language concerned:
> ill.
>
> min.

    h. before subheadings of a corporate body heading:
> United States. Antarctic Projects Office

4. Use parentheses

    a. to enclose the place and name of the manufacturer:
> (London : Wiggs)

    b. to enclose the series area:
> (Books that matter)

    c. to specify the number of components as part of the extent of an item:
> 1 microfiche (140 fr.)
>
> 1 tape (1 hr. 15 min.)
>
> 3 v. (xix, 1269 p.)

    d. in the physical description area to indicate some of the illustrative matter is in color:
> ill. (some col.)

    e. for the physical details of accompanying material in the physical description area:
> 2 v. ; 32 cm. + 1 atlas (159 leaves of plates : 25 col. maps ; 43 cm.)

    f. to enclose statements of coordinates and equinox in cartographic materials:
> (W 126°--W 64°/N 49°--N 23°)

    g. to enclose a date following a numeric and/or alphabetic designation:
> No. 1 (Jan. 1989)

h. for designation of theses:
    Thesis (M.A.)--University of Denver, 1988.

i. to enclose qualifications to the standard number or terms of availability:
    ISBN 0-87287-161-4 (pbk.)

    $10.00 ($8.00 to students)

j. to enclose date, number, place, or other designation added to a corporate or geographic name:
    Franklin County Legal Journal (Corporation)

k. to enclose data giving characteristics of computer files:
    Computer program (1 file : 350 statements)

5. Use colons

a. before other title information:
    Human action : a treatise on economics

    French rooster : [poem]

b. between place of publication, etc., or manufacture and the name of the publisher, etc., or manufacturer:
    New York : Macmillan

c. between the extent of item and other physical details in the physical description area:
    1 globe : col., plastic, mounted on metal stand

d. between standard number and terms of availability:
    ISBN 0-87287-153-3 : $15.00

e. between different additions to corporate names:
    WUNC (Radio station : Chapel Hill, N.C.)

    Symposium on Computer Applications in Medical Care
    (14th : 1990 : Washington, D.C.)

f. between the introductory wording and the main content of notes:
    Bibliography: p. 190-191.

    Summary: A poetical journey into the unconscious of a woman in search of personal power.

    First ed. published with title: Technical topics for the radio amateur.

    Credits: Script, Al DeZutter.

g. in the scale ratio in cartographic materials:
    Scale 1:250,000

Note that in f. there is no space before the colon, and in g. there is no space before or after the colon. In these cases, the colon is used as a mark of punctuation rather than a mark of separation.

6. Use period (full stop) and dash

    a. preceding the edition area, the material specific details area, the publication, distribution, etc., area, and the series area:
        / drawn by Robert Morgan. -- Rev. ed. -- Scale 1:500,000. -- London :

        ; 78 x 80 cm. -- (World climatology series)

        In the cases in a. the format is period-space-hyphen-hyphen-space. The dash is represented by two hyphens on the typewriter.

7. Use dashes

    a. for sequence in a contents note:
        Contents: The ethic of the group / L.C. Eiseley -- Science and human values / G. Seldes -- Law and the limits / W. Hurst.

        In this case, the format is space-hyphen-hyphen-space.

    b. in thesis notes:
        Thesis (Ph.D.)--Yale, 1979.

    c. to precede subdivisions in subject headings:
        Zip code--New York (N.Y.)--Maps

        Note that there is no space before or after the dash in b. or c.

8. Diagonal slashes are used before the statement of responsibility in the title and statement of responsibility area, the edition area, the series area, and the contents note:
    Introduction to sociology / Paul Sites

    (Reports / British Library, Research & Development ; no. 5416)

9. Use equals signs

    a. before parallel titles and other parallel information:
        La nuit : Etüde für Klavier = Night : piano study

    b. before alternative numbering systems in serials:
        Vol. 4, no. 1-   = No. 13-

    c. before a key title in the standard number area:
        ISSN 0190-1427 = AJS update

10. Plus signs are used to separate accompanying materials from the dimensions in the physical description area:
    30 cm. + 1 disc

11. Question marks are used to denote

    a. conjectural additions:
        [Pittsburg? Calif.]

        Pittsburg [Calif.?]

    b. uncertain dates:
        [1892?]
        [189-?]
        [18--?]

12. Use hyphens

    a. to follow the numeric and/or alphabetic designation and/or the date of first issue of a serial:
        No. 1 (Jan. 1978)-

    b. to show time periods of more than one unit of time (e.g., more than one month, more than one year, etc.):
        Goodwin, Emily, 1948-

        United States--History--1961-1969.

13. Use square brackets:

    a. to show that the information enclosed has been supplied from a source other than the prescribed source of information according to *AACR2R*:
        Christiana [Oslo]

        3e [ed.]

        French rooster : [poem]

    (The prescribed sources of information vary according to the specified area of the record and the type of material being cataloged. These are discussed in general in chapter 3 of this textbook, and more specifically in chapters 4-7.)

    b. to enclose the general material designation (GMD):
        The curious campaign of the comma king [filmstrip]

    It should be noted that adjacent elements in one area that require square brackets should be enclosed in the same set, except for the GMD, which is always enclosed in its own square brackets:
        -- [S.l. : s.n., 1974?]

    Elements in different areas that require brackets are each enclosed in their own set of brackets:
        / [Compiler, Dencho Vlaev]. -- [Sofia] :

14. Omissions of parts of elements, such as an unimportant part of a long title, or all but the first responsible party when more than three are named, are indicated by three dots, called "the mark of omission":
        The Dickens concordance, being a compendium of names and characters and principal places in all the works of Charles Dickens ...

(Example continues on page 570.)

/ [edited by] Henry P. David ... [et al.]

It should be noted that omissions of *entire* elements or areas are not indicated by the mark of omission.

Capitalization

The rules for capitalization, in general, follow standard style for the language involved. Rules for capitalization are given extensive coverage in *AACR2R*, appendix A, first covering rules in general and then giving specific rules by language. An important exception to normal usage is that a title is written like an ordinary sentence; the first word is capitalized, e.g.,

The will to live.
Act one.

If, however, the main entry of a work is its title proper, and if the first word of such a title is an article, the next word is also capitalized, e.g.,

The Will to live.
An Introduction to the physical sciences.

A rule revision is in process that will change this capitalization rule in *AACR2R*. The new rule omits this latter exception. When this goes into effect, the word following an article will not be capitalized regardless of choice of main entry, unless, of course, the word is a proper noun. The capitalization of other words in the title is governed by ordinary rules for capitalization; e.g.,

Across five Aprils
The Spirit of St. Louis.

The first word of every title, alternative title, or parallel title is capitalized, e.g.,

Letters from the West, or, A caution to emigrants.
El gato = The cat.

Abbreviations

Acceptable abbreviations are used in the description areas except in the recording of titles and statements of responsibility and in quoted notes. Acceptable abbreviations are those listed in *AACR2R*, appendix B. Some abbreviations may be used only for a heading (see B.2), and single letter abbreviations are not used to begin a note. When in doubt, the cataloger should *not* abbreviate.

Numerals

Rules for numerals are given in *AACR2R*, appendix C. There are rules prescribing when to substitute arabic for roman numerals; when to spell out numerals; when to substitute Western-style numerals for Oriental numerals; and how to record inclusive numbers, alternative dates, and ordinal numerals.

PRE-ISBD CATALOGING FORMAT

Before the introduction of ISBD in the United States in 1974, the cataloging differed from present cataloging in some ways. Less information was recorded, but what was given appeared in basically the same order as that information does now. The punctuation and spacing were simpler, in one sense, because punctuation was used only for punctuating, not also for separating areas and elements of description. In another sense, however, there was more difficulty in judging, for example, whether to use a comma, semicolon, or colon before a subtitle. And because "double punctuation" was strictly avoided, new catalogers often had difficulty learning, for example, not to precede or follow a square bracket with the comma or period called for by rules of grammar (e.g., the correct form was [New York] Macmillan [1961] *not* [New York], Macmillan, [1961]). A side-by-side comparison of ISBD punctuation and pre-ISBD punctuation may be found in the first edition of *Cataloging with Copy*, appendix F, and many examples of pre-ISBD copy appear throughout that edition.

Glossary of Selected Terms and Abbreviations

Defined in this glossary are selected basic terms for students of cataloging, including a number of terms and identifiers used in bibliographic control, descriptive cataloging, classification, subject heading work, filing, document indexing, networking, and other topics treated in this text. Readers may wish to consult *The ALA Glossary of Library and Information Science*, Heartsill Young, editor, with the assistance of Terry Belanger ... [et al.] (Chicago, American Library Association, 1983). Consult the AACR2R Glossary (appendix D) and Abbreviations (appendix B) for additional terms used in the rules.

Aboutness. The subject of a document. *See also* **Subject analysis.**

Abstract. A condensed narrative description of a document, which may serve as a surrogate for the document in a bibliographic retrieval system.

Abstracting. The process of creating abstracts; a form of bibliographic control. *See also* **Cataloging; Indexing.**

Access. That portion of the descriptive cataloging process in which access points are selected and formulated. *See also* **Description; Descriptive cataloging.**

Access point. Any term (word, heading, etc.) in a bibliographic record that may be used to locate that record. *See also* **Choice of access points; Entry; Heading.**

Accession number. A number assigned to each item as it is received in the library. Accession numbers may be assigned through continuous numbering (e.g., 30291, 30292) or a coded system (67-201, 67-202, etc.).

Accompanying materials. Dependent materials, such as answer books, teacher's manuals, atlases, portfolios of plates, slides, and sound recordings.

Add instructions. Notes in classification schedules that specify what digits to add to a base number; they replace divide-like notes in DDC.

Added entry. A secondary access point; i.e., any other than the main entry. In COM, book, or card catalogs an added entry record often duplicates the main entry record except that it has an additional heading to represent in the catalog a subject, joint author, illustrator, editor, compiler, translator, collaborator, series, etc. (Subject entry is excluded from this definition in LC usage.)

Alphabetical catalog. A catalog with entries arranged in alphabetical order, rather than according to the symbolic notation of a classification. *See also* **Dictionary catalog; Divided catalog.**

Alternative title. The second title of a work, which is joined to the first title with *or* or its equivalent (e.g., *Maria, or, The Wrongs of Woman*). Both titles together are considered to constitute the title proper of the work. *See also* **Title proper.**

Analytical entry. An entry for a part of a work or for a whole work contained in a series or a collection for which a comprehensive entry is made. Name-title analytics (i.e., analytical entries) may be made in the form of added entries.

Anonymous work. One in which the author's name does not appear anywhere in the item; a work of unknown authorship.

Area. A major section of a bibliographic description; e.g., edition area or physical description area.

Artifact. *See* **Realia.**

Author. The person chiefly responsible for the intellectual or artistic content of a work; e.g., writer of a book, compiler of a bibliography, composer of a musical work, artist, photographer, etc. *See also* **Compiler; Editor.**

Author number. *See* **Cutter number.**

Authority control. The process of maintaining consistency in the verbal form used to represent an access point and the further process of showing the relationships among names, works, and subjects.

Authority file. A grouping of records of the authorized forms of names, titles, or subjects chosen for use in a catalog.

Authority record. A printed or machine-readable unit that registers the decisions made during the course of authority work.

Authority work. The process of determining the form of a name, title, or subject concept that will be used as a heading on a bibliographic record; of determining references needed to that form; and of determining relationships of the heading to other headings.

Auxiliary table. A generalized subdivision table appended to a classification schedule for use in building specific class numbers where indicated in the schedule proper.

Bibliographic control. The process of creating, arranging, and maintaining systems for bibliographic information retrieval.

Bibliographic data. Information concerning bibliographic entities.

Bibliographic databases. Computerized databases (such as OCLC, RLIN, Utlas International, WLN, etc.) for bibliographic retrieval.

Bibliographic entity. An instance of recorded knowledge. A bibliographic entity has two properties: a) physical (usually called an item); and b) intellectual (usually called a work). *See also* **Item; Work.**

Bibliographic file. A grouping of bibliographic records. In a catalog or bibliographic database, a bibliographic file is distinct from, but might be linked to, one or more authority files and a holdings file.

Bibliographic record. A catalog entry in card, microtext, machine-readable, or other form carrying full cataloging information for a given item in a library.

Bibliographic service center. A regional broker, providing intermediate communication, training, and service for libraries participating in an online bibliographic network.

Bibliographic tools. Devices such as catalogs, indexes, bibliographies, etc., created for use as bibliographic retrieval systems. *See also* **Bibliographic databases; Bibliography; Catalog; Index.**

Bibliographic universe. The concept encompassing all instances of recorded knowledge.

Bibliographic utility. An online processing center based on a machine-readable database of catalog records.

Bibliography. A list of writings on a given subject or by a given author.

Book catalog. A catalog printed and bound in book form.

Book number. *See* **Cutter number.**

Books in sets. *See* **Monographs in collected sets.**

Boolean operators. The terms *and, or,* and *not* as used to construct search topics through post-coordinate indexing.

Broad classification. A scheme that omits detailed subdivision of its main classes or that facilitates the use in smaller libraries of only its main classes and subdivisions.

BSO. Broad System of Ordering, a classification developed for a proposed worldwide information network covering the whole field of knowledge.

Call number. The notation used to identify and locate a particular item on the shelves; it consists of the classification notation and cutter number, and it may also include a workmark and/or a date. *See also* **Cutter number; Workmark.**

CAN/MARC. A machine-readable bibliographic record format compatible with USMARC, developed by the National Library of Canada.

Card catalog. A catalog in which every entry is printed or typed on a card, usually 3"x5".

Catalog. An organized set of bibliographic records that represent the holdings of a particular collection. It may be arranged by alphabet, by number, or by subject. It may be in the form of cards, book, computer output microform (COM), or computer online.

Catalog record. *See* **Bibliographic record.**

Cataloging. The process of describing an item in the collection, conducting subject analysis, and assigning a classification number. *See also* **Copy cataloging; Descriptive cataloging; Original cataloging; Subject cataloging.**

Cataloging in Publication. *See* **CIP.**

Catchword indexing. *See* **Keyword indexing.**

Categorical filing. The preference in some areas of a filing system for partially classified arrangements over a straight alphabetical sequence.

CD-ROM. Compact disk—read only memory.

CD-ROM catalog. *See* **Online catalog.**

Centralized processing. Any cooperative effort that results in the centralization of one or more of the technical processes involved in getting material ready for use in a library.

Chain index. A direct and specific index based on the extracted vocabulary of a classification system. It retains all necessary context but deletes unnecessary context; all subheadings are superordinate terms.

Chief source of information. The source in an item that is prescribed by the rules as the major source of data for use in preparing a bibliographic description. *See also* **Title page.**

Choice of access points. The process of selecting the main entry or heading and any added entries under which an item is to be listed in the catalog.

CIP. Cataloging in Publication, a program sponsored by the Library of Congress and cooperating publishers; a partial bibliographic description is provided on the verso of the title page of a book.

Class. The first order of structure in a hierarchical classification, at which level major disciplines are represented. A class may incorporate one or more divisions, which in turn may incorporate one or more subdivisions. *See also* **Division; Hierarchical classification; Subdivision.**

Classification. A scheme for the systematic organization of knowledge, usually by subject.

Classification notation. The notation assigned to an item of a collection to show the subject area and to indicate its location in the collection.

Classification schedule. The printed scheme of a particular classification system.

Classified catalog. A catalog arranged in the order of symbols, numbers, or other notations that represent the various subjects or aspects of subjects covered by the items owned by the library. *See also* **Shelflist.**

Close classification. The use of minute subdivisions for arranging materials by highly specific topics.

Closed stacks. Library collections not open to public access or limited to a small group of users.

CODEN. A system of unique letters assigned for ready identification of periodicals and serials, now administered by Chemical Abstracts Service (CAS).

Coextensive subject entry. A principle of subject entry, by which a term, phrase, or set of terms defines precisely the complete contents, but no more than the contents, of an item.

Collation. *See* **Physical description area.**

Collection. Three or more works or parts of works by one author published together, or two or more works or parts of works by more than one author published together. Each work in a collection was originally written independently or as part of an independent publication.

Collocating function. The function of bibliographic control that relates bibliographic entities through the process of collocation.

Collocation. The process of bringing together in a catalog records for names, titles, or subjects that are bibliographically related to one another.

COM. Computer Output Microform.

COM catalog. A catalog produced on COM and requiring a microform reader for its use.

COMARC. Cooperative MARC, an experimental program in which LC worked to develop modes of cooperation with outside libraries and network utilities in building high-quality bibliographic databases and authority records.

Compiler. One who brings together written or printed matter from the works of various authors or the works of a single author. *See also* **Author; Editor.**

Computer file. A body of encoded information (either data or program) that can be read only by a computer.

Computer-produced catalog. *See* **COM; Online catalog.**

CONSER. Conversion of Serials project, a shared national database of serial records from selected libraries, now maintained by OCLC.

Content designation. The act of making a bibliographic or authority record machine-readable by encoding its various elements according to a specified scheme. *See also* **MARC.**

Continuation. 1) A work issued as a supplement to an earlier one. 2) A part issued in continuance of a book, a serial, or a series.

Control field. A field in the MARC format (0xx) that includes numeric or other encoded data for retrieval. *See also* **Field; Fixed field; Variable field.**

Controlled vocabulary. Language, usually in the form of a thesaurus or subject heading list, that is carefully systematized for use in retrieval systems. *See also* **Subject heading; Thesaurus.**

Cooperative cataloging. *See* **Copy cataloging.**

Coordinate indexing. Information retrieval through the use of related terms in a catalog or database to identify concepts.

Copy cataloging. Adapting for use in a catalog a copy of the original cataloging created by another library. *See also* **Original cataloging.**

Corporate body. An organization or group of persons who are identified by a name and who act as an entity.

Cross reference. *See* **Reference.**

Cutter number. The symbols, usually a combination of letters and numbers, used to distinguish items with the same classification number in order to maintain the alphabetical order (by author, title, or other entry) of items on the shelves; sometimes called author number or book number. The word *cutter* is derived from the widespread use of the *Tables* first devised by C. A. Cutter for use in such alphabetical arrangement. *See also* **Call number; Workmark.**

Dash. A symbol of punctuation and separation that in printing consists of a single line and in typing is made by striking the hyphen key twice in succession. In descriptive cataloging the dash usually appears with one space on either side; for subject subdivisions no spaces are used.

DDC. Dewey Decimal Classification.

Depth indexing. Assignment of subject terms to represent all of the main concepts represented in a document. *See also* **Exhaustivity; Summarization.**

Description. That portion of the descriptive cataloging process in which elements that identify an item are transcribed into a bibliographic record. Also, the portion of the bibliographic record that results from this process. *See also* **Access; Descriptive cataloging.**

Descriptive cataloging. That phase of the cataloging process that is concerned with the identification and description of an item, the recording of this information in a bibliographic record, and the selection and formation of access points—with the exception of subject access points. *See also* **Access; Description.**

Dictionary catalog. A catalog arranged in alphabetical order with entries for names, titles, and subjects all interfiled.

Direct entry. A principle of formulation of subject headings that stipulates the entry of a concept directly under the term that names it, rather than as a subdivision of a broader concept. *See also* **Specific entry.**

Divide-like note. A place in a classification schedule referring the user to another location where analogous sequencing and notation set a pattern.

Divided catalog. A catalog in which different types of entries are separated into different sections. Usually the subjects are separated from other entries. Order is usually alphabetical in each section, but the subject section may be in classified order.

Division. In hierarchical classification, the second structural level at which major components of a discipline are represented. A division is a subset of a class and may incorporate one or more subdivisions. *See also* **Class; Hierarchical classification; Subdivision.**

Edition. In the case of books, all the impressions of a work printed at any time or times from one setting of type; also, one of the successive forms in which a literary text is issued either by the author or by a subsequent editor. In the case of nonbook materials, all the copies of an item made from one master copy.

Edition area. The second area of a bibliographic description, which includes the following elements: named and/or numbered edition statement and statement of responsibility relating to a particular edition, if any.

Editor. One who prepares for publication or supervises the publication of a work or collection of works or articles that are authored by others. Responsibility may extend to revising, providing commentaries and introductory matter, etc. *See also* **Author; Compiler.**

Element. A subsection of an area in the catalog entry; for example, the alternative title is an element of the title and statement of responsibility area.

Entry. A representation of a bibliographic record at a particular point in a catalog. There can be one or more entries for any one heading. *See also* **Access point; Bibliographic record; Heading.**

Entry word. The word by which the entry is arranged in the catalog, usually the first word (other than an article) of the heading. Also called "filing word."

Enumerative classification. A classification that attempts to assign a designation for every subject concept required in the system.

Evaluating function. The function of bibliographic control that allows a patron to make an informed choice of materials from a bibliographic tool.

Exhaustivity. The number of concepts covered in a document that will be represented in subject analysis. *See also* **Depth indexing; Summarization.**

Expansive classification. A scheme in which a set of coordinated schedules gives successive development possibilities from very simple (broad) to very detailed (close) subdivision.

Explanatory reference. A reference that gives the detailed guidance necessary for effective use of the headings involved.

Faceted classification. A classification constructed from the combination, in prescribed sequence, of clearly defined, mutually exclusive, and collectively exhaustive aspects, properties, or characteristics of a class or specific subject.

FID. Fédération Internationale de Documentation (International Federation for Documentation).

Field. A separately designated element of a MARC record. A field may contain one or more subfields. *See also* **Control field; Fixed field; Subfield; Variable field.**

Figure-ground analysis. A process of subject analysis in which the central or dominant figure that stands out against a stipulated background is identified. *See also* **Subject analysis.**

File characteristics area. The third area of a bibliographic description for a computer file, which identifies whether the file contains data or program information and stipulates the extent of the file. *See also* **Computer file; Material specific details area.**

Filing word. *See* **Entry word.**

Finding function. *See* **Identifying function.**

Fixed field. A field in a MARC record that is of fixed length. There are two major "fixed fields" in a standard USMARC record, 008 (fixed length data elements) and 007 (physical characteristics). *See also* **Control field; Field; Subfield; Variable field.**

Fixed location. The assignment of each item in a collection to a definite position on a certain shelf.

Form divisions. *See* **Standard subdivisions.**

Form heading. A subject list term that refers to the literary or artistic form or the publication format of a work rather than to its topical content.

Form of entry. The specific spelling and wording used to record an access point on a catalog record.

Free-floating subdivision. A subheading that can be added to headings in a published list, as needed, whether or not it is written in the published list following those headings.

Gathering function. *See* **Collocating function.**

Generalia class. That part of a classification system designed to hold materials of a general nature, usually covering many diverse topics.

Geographic name. The place name usually used in reference to a geographic area. It is not necessarily the political name. *See also* **Political name.**

GMD. General Material Designation, a term that is given in the catalog record to indicate the class of material to which an item belongs (e.g., motion picture).

Guide card. A labeled card with a noticeable projection that distinguishes it from other catalog cards. It is inserted in a card catalog to help the user find a desired place or heading in the catalog.

Hanging indention. The form of indention used in traditional bibliographic record format when the main entry is under title; the title begins at the first indention and succeeding lines of the body of the record begin at the second indention.

Heading. The character string provided at the beginning of an entry in a bibliographic tool that provides means for finding that entry. A heading can represent the name of a person, corporate body, geographic area, title of a work, or a subject. Headings are usually provided at the top of each catalog record or at the top of a column, page, or screen on which several entries for the heading may appear. *See also* **Access point; Entry; Form of entry; Term.**

Hierarchical classification. A classification that attempts to arrange subjects according to a "natural" order—proceeding from classes to divisions to subdivisions.

Hierarchical notation. In classification, the use of symbol groups of varying combinations and lengths to reflect a hierarchy of topics and subdivisions.

Holdings. Bibliographic items (volumes, parts, issues, etc.) contained in a library collection.

Holdings file. A group of holdings records. In an OPAC or a bibliographic database, a holdings file is usually distinct from, but might be linked to, a bibliographic file.

Holdings note. One note in the bibliographic record for a serial that tells which parts of the serial are held by the library. *See also* **Numeric and/or alphabetic, chronological, or other designation area.**

Holdings record. An entry in a holdings file that gives complete holdings for a bibliographic entity.

Identifying function. The function of bibliographic control that allows a user to recognize and locate a specific bibliographic entity.

IFLA. International Federation of Library Associations and Institutions; formerly International Federation of Library Associations.

ILL. Interlibrary loan.

Imprint. *See* **Publication, distribution, etc., area.**

Indentions. Designated spaces or margins at which parts of a catalog record begin; used especially in typing cards.

Index. A tool that exhibits the analyzed contents of a bibliographic entity or a group of such entities, as contrasted with a library catalog, which traditionally lists and describes the holdings of a particular collection.

Indexing. The process of analyzing a bibliographic entity and creating entries for it, especially subject entries, in an index.

Information retrieval. The process of gaining access to stored data for the purpose of becoming informed.

INTERMARC. A French-language format for bibliographic exchange for monographs; similar to USMARC formats. *See also* **UNIMARC.**

ISBD. International Standard Bibliographic Description, an internationally accepted format for the representation of descriptive information in bibliographic records. ISBDs developed so far include: **ISBD(A)**, ISBD for Older Monographic Publications (Antiquarian); **ISBD(CF)**, ISBD for Computer Files; **ISBD(CM)**, ISBD for Cartographic Materials; **ISBD(G)**, General; **ISBD(M)**, ISBD for Monographic Materials; **ISBD(NBM)**, ISBD for Nonbook Materials; **ISBD(PM)**, ISBD for Printed Music; **ISBD(S)**, ISBD for Serials.

ISBN. International Standard Book Number, a distinctive and unique number assigned to a book. ISBNs are used internationally; the U.S. agency for ISBNs is R. R. Bowker Company.

ISDS. International Serials Data System, a network of national and international centers sponsored by UNESCO. The centers develop and maintain registers of serial publications; this includes the assignment of ISSNs and key title.

ISSN. International Standard Serial Number, a distinctive number assigned by ISDS.

Item. A physical object, such as a book, a map, or a sound recording, as distinct from its intellectual content (i.e., the work it contains). *See also* **Bibliographic entity; Work.**

Joint author. A person who collaborates with one or more associates to produce a work in which the individual contributions of the authors cannot be distinguished. *See also* **Author; Shared responsibility.**

Key heading. *See* **Pattern heading.**

Keyword indexing. Use of significant words from a title or a text as index entries.

KWIC indexing. Key Word in Context, a format for showing index entries within the context in which they occur.

KWOC indexing. Key Word out of Context, the use of significant words from titles for subject index entries, each followed by the whole title from which the word was taken.

LC. Library of Congress.

LCC. *Library of Congress Classification.*

LC-MARC. *See* **USMARC.**

LCSH. Library of Congress Subject Headings.

Leaf. A single thickness of paper; i.e., two pages.

Linkage. A relationship between or among headings or records that is manifested implicitly or explicitly in a bibliographic retrieval system.

Literary warrant. The selection of concepts for a subject heading list, thesaurus, or classification in response to the concepts represented in a specific set of documents.

Locating function. *See* **Identifying function.**

LSP. Linked Systems Project, a joint project of LC, OCLC, RLIN, and WLN; the goal is to be able to exchange data among systems in an online mode through a standard network interconnection (SNI).

Machine-readable cataloging. *See* **MARC.**

Machine-readable data file. *See* **Computer file.**

Main class. *See* **Class.**

Main entry. 1) The major access point chosen; the other access points are added entries. 2) A full catalog entry headed by the access point chosen as main entry, which gives all the information necessary for the complete identification of a work. This entry also bears the tracing of all the other headings under which the work is entered.

Manufacturer. The agency that has made the item being cataloged (e.g., printer of a book).

Map series. A group of map sheets having the same scale and cartographic specifications, identified collectively by the producing agency, that, when the series is completed, will cover a given geographic area.

MARC. Machine-readable cataloging. *See also* **CAN/MARC; COMARC; INTERMARC; UK/MARC; UNIMARC; USMARC.**

MARC record. A computerized bibliographic record, which has been content designated according to MARC conventions.

Material specific details area. The third area of a bibliographic description for certain special materials. *See also* **File characteristics area; Mathematical data area; Musical presentation statement area; Numeric and/or alphabetic, chronological, or other designation area.**

Mathematical data area. The third area of a bibliographic description for a cartographic item, which includes the following elements: scale, projection, and, optionally, coordinates and equinox.

Microfiche. A flat sheet of photographic film designed for storage of complete texts in multiple micro-images and having an index entry visible to the naked eye displayed at the top.

Microfilm. A length of photographic film containing sequences of micro-images of texts, title pages, bibliographic records, etc.

Microform. Usually a reproduction photographically reduced to a size difficult or impossible to read with the naked eye; some microforms are not reproductions but original editions. Microforms include microfilm, microfiche, microopaques, and aperture cards.

Mixed notation. A notation that combines two or more kinds of symbols, such as a combination of letters and numbers.

Mixed responsibility. The combination of more than one category of intellectual responsibility for a work. *See also* **Author; Shared responsibility.**

Mnemonic devices. Devices intended to aid or assist the memory.

Monograph. A complete bibliographic unit; it may be issued in successive parts at regular or irregular intervals, but it is *not* intended to continue indefinitely. It may be a single work or a collection that is not a serial.

Monographic series. A series of monographs with a collective title.

Monographs in collected sets. Collections or compilations by one or more authors issued in two or more volumes.

MRDF. *See* **Computer file.**

MUMS. Multiple-Use MARC System, the online system at LC.

Musical presentation statement. A statement in a chief source of information for music that indicates its physical form.

Musical presentation statement area. The third area of a bibliographic description for a music item, in which a musical presentation statement (e.g., "playing score") is transcribed. *See also* **Material specific details area.**

NAL. National Agricultural Library, Washington, D.C.

Name authority file. A file of the name headings used in a given catalog and the references made to them from other forms.

Name-title added entry. An added entry that includes the name of a person or corporate body and the title of a work (usually a uniform title). It serves to identify a work that is included in the larger work that is being cataloged, to identify a work that is the subject of the work being cataloged, to identify a larger work of which the work being cataloged is part, or to identify another work to which the work being cataloged is closely related (e.g., an index).

NLA. The National Library of Australia, Canberra.

NLM. The National Library of Medicine, Washington, D.C.

Nonbook materials. Term used to designate collectively maps, globes, motion pictures, filmstrips, videorecordings, sound recordings, etc.

Notation. A system of numbers and/or letters used to represent a classification scheme.

Note area. The seventh area of a bibliographic description, which is reserved for recording catalog data that cannot be incorporated in the preceding parts of the record. Each note is usually recorded in a separate paragraph.

NUC. The *National Union Catalog,* a publication in the Library of Congress Catalogs series.

Numeric and/or alphabetic, chronological, or other designation area. The third area of a bibliographic description for a serial. It indicates volumes or parts of the serial, but not necessarily those held by a particular library. *See also* **Holdings note; Material specific details area.**

Objective analysis. A form of subject analysis in which main concepts are identified by counting textual references to them. *See also* **Subject analysis.**

OCLC Online Computer Library Center. A bibliographic network; formerly Ohio College Library Center. *See also* **Bibliographic utility.**

Online catalog. A catalog based on and giving direct access to machine-readable cataloging records.

Online Computer Library Center. *See* **OCLC Online Computer Library Center.**

Online public access catalog. An online catalog that is available for use by the general public; also referred to as an OPAC. *See also* **Public access catalog.**

Online retrieval. Direct use of a computer to access stored data. *See also* **Information retrieval.**

OPAC. *See* **Online public access catalog.**

Open entry. A part of the descriptive cataloging not completed at the time of cataloging. Used for uncompleted works such as serials, series, etc.

Open stacks. A library collection where all users are admitted directly to the shelves.

Original cataloging. The process of creating a bibliographic record for the first time, especially without reference to other records for the same item. Also, the cataloging created by this process. *See also* **Copy cataloging.**

OSI. Open System Interconnection. An international system for linking computer networks.

Other title information. Words or phrases (e.g., a subtitle) that appear in conjunction with the title of an item other than the title proper, parallel title, or alternative title. *See also* **Alternative title; Parallel title; Title proper.**

Parallel title. The title proper written in another language or in another script. *See also* **Title proper.**

Pattern heading. A representative heading from a category of terms that would normally be excluded from a subject heading list (e.g., names of individuals), included as an example of normal subdivision practice within that category.

Periodical. A publication with a distinctive title, which appears in successive numbers or parts at stated or regular intervals and which is intended to continue indefinitely.

Usually each issue contains articles by several contributors. Newspapers and memoirs, proceedings, journals, etc., of corporate bodies primarily related to their internal affairs are not included in this definition. *See also* **Monograph; Serial.**

Phonograph records. *See* **Sound recordings.**

Physical description area. The fifth area of a bibliographic description, which includes a statement of the extent of an item, dimensions, and other physical details.

Place name. *See* **Geographic name.**

Plate. An illustrative leaf that is not included in the pagination of the text; it is not an integral part of a text gathering; it is often printed on paper different from that used for the text.

Plate number. A number used by a music publisher to identify a set of printing plates used to print a musical work.

Political name. The proper name of a geographical area according to the law. This name often changes with a change in government.

Post-coordinate indexing. The grouping of a large number of entries under simple concepts in such a way that the user can combine them to locate material on the compound subjects in which he or she is interested.

PRECIS. Preserved Context Indexing System, a technique for subject retrieval in which an open-ended vocabulary can be organized according to a scheme of role-indicating operators for either manual or computer manipulation.

Pre-coordinate indexing. The combination of subject terms at the time of indexing for use in the retrieval of materials on complex concepts.

Preliminaries. The title page or title pages, the verso of each title page, the cover, and any pages preceding the title page.

Processing center. A central office where the materials of more than one library are processed and distributed. Such a center may also handle the purchasing of materials for its constituents.

Producer. Person or agency responsible for financial and administrative production of a motion picture or machine-readable data file and for its commercial success.

Program (computer). *See* **Computer file.**

Pseudonym. A false name assumed by an author to conceal identity.

Pseudo-serial. A frequently reissued and revised publication which at first publication is usually treated as a monographic work.

Public access catalog. The part of a catalog that is available for the use of library patrons. *See also* **Online public access catalog.**

Publication, distribution, etc., area. The fourth area of a bibliographic description, which includes the following elements: place of publication, distribution, etc.; name of publisher, distributor, etc.; date of publication, distribution, etc.; and sometimes place of manufacture, name of manufacturer, and date of manufacture.

Publisher. The person, corporate body, or firm responsible for issuing printed matter.

Pure notation. A notation that consistently uses only one kind of symbol (e.g., either letters *or* numbers, but not both).

Purposive analysis. A method of subject analysis in which the author's aim is identified as the subject. *See also* **Subject analysis.**

Realia. Actual objects (artifacts, specimens, etc.) rather than replicas.

RECON. Retrospective Conversion of Library of Congress records to MARC format, an experimental project on the results of which LC determined that it was not economically feasible to make a complete conversion of its existing card catalogs; also, as a general term, it is used to mean any kind of retrospective conversion. *See also* **Retrospective conversion.**

Record. *See* **Bibliographic record.**

Recto. In a book, the page on the right; the side of a leaf intended to be read first. *See also* **Verso.**

Reference. An instruction in a catalog that directs a user to another catalog entry.

Relational design. A form of database architecture in which different kinds of records that contain a common field (e.g., the 100 field in a bibliographic record and an authority record) are related mechanically.

Relative index. An index to a classification scheme that not only provides alphabetical references to the subjects and terms in the classification but also shows some of the relations between subjects and aspects of subjects.

Relative location. A classifactory arrangement of library materials, allowing the insertion of new material in its proper relation to that already on the shelves.

Reprint. A new printing of an item either by photographic methods or by resetting the type for substantially unchanged text.

Retrospective conversion. The process of changing information in eye-readable bibliographic records into machine-readable form; sometimes referred to as RECON. *See also* **RECON.**

RLG. Research Libraries Group, a consortium formed originally by Columbia, Harvard, and Yale universities and the New York Public Library, now consisting of over 100 large research libraries, but minus Harvard.

RLIN. Research Libraries Information Network, a bibliographic network based at Stanford University under the aegis of RLG. *See also* **Bibliographic utility.**

Romanization. The representation of the characters of a nonroman alphabet by roman characters. *See also* **Transliteration.**

Scope note. A statement delimiting the meaning and associative relations of a subject heading or a classification notation.

Score. An arrangement of all of the parts of a piece of music one under another on different staves. A series of staves on which is written music composed originally for one instrument is not considered a score. Thus, "piano score" is used to designate, not music written originally for the piano, but music written originally for instrumental or vocal parts that has been arranged for the piano.

SCORPIO. Subject-Context Oriented Retriever for Processing Information Online, a text retrieval facility in operation at the Library of Congress.

Secondary entry. *See* **Added entry.**

See also **reference.** A reference indicating related entries or headings.

See **reference.** A reference from a heading not used to a heading that is used.

Selecting function. *See* **Evaluating function.**

Serial. A publication issued in successive parts at regular or irregular intervals and intended to continue indefinitely. Included are periodicals, newspapers, proceedings, reports, memoirs, annuals, and numbered monographic series. *See also* **Monograph; Periodical.**

Series. A number of separate works, usually related in subject or form, that are issued successively. They are usually issued by the same publisher, distributor, etc., and in uniform style, with a collective title.

Series area. The sixth area of a bibliographic description, which includes series information.

Series authority file. A file of series entries used in a catalog with the record of references made to them from other forms, and a record of their treatment as to analysis, tracing, and classification.

Series title. The collective title given to volumes or parts issued in a series.

Shared authorship. *See* **Shared responsibility.**

Shared responsibility. More than one person is responsible for the creation of the intellectual content of a work. *See also* **Mixed responsibility.**

Shelflist. A record of the items in a library; entries are arranged in the order of the items on the shelves. *See also* **Classified catalog.**

s.l. Place of publication, distribution, etc., unknown (*sino loco*).

s.n. Name of publisher, distributor, etc., unknown (*sine nomine*).

SNI. Standard Network Interconnection. *See also* **LSP; OSI.**

Software. *See* **Computer file.**

Sound recordings. Aural recordings, including discs (i.e., phonograph records), cartridges, cassettes, cylinders, etc.

Specific entry. A principle observed in most library subject lists, by which material is listed under the most specific term available, rather than under some broader heading. *See also* **Direct entry.**

Standard number and terms of availability area. The eighth area of a bibliographic description, which includes ISBN or ISSN and, optionally, price or other terms on which the item is available.

Standard subdivisions. Divisions used in DDC that apply to the form a work takes. Form may be physical (as in a periodical or a dictionary) or it may be philosophical (such as a philosophy or history of a subject). Formerly called form divisions.

Statement of responsibility. A statement in the item being described that gives persons responsible for intellectual or artistic content, corporate bodies from which the content emanates, or persons or bodies responsible for performance.

Subdivision. The lowest level of structure in a hierarchical classification, at which specific concepts are represented. *See also* **Class; Division; Hierarchical classification.**

Subfield. A separately content-designated segment of a field in a MARC record. *See also* **Field.**

Subject analysis. The process of discerning the concepts addressed in a document as a precursor to assigning subject headings, index terms, or classification. *See also* **Figureground analysis; Objective analysis; Purposive analysis; Unity analysis.**

Subject authority file. A file of the subject headings used in a given catalog, with the record of the references made to them.

Subject cataloging. The assignment of classification numbers and subject headings to the items of a library collection.

Subject entry. The catalog entry for a work under the subject heading.

Subject heading. A word or group of words indicating a subject.

Subject subdivision. A restrictive word or group of words added to a subject heading to limit it to a more specific meaning.

Subtitle. A secondary title, often used to expand or limit the title proper. *See also* **Alternative title; Other title information; Parallel title.**

Summarization. A form of subject analysis in which only the dominant or main theme of a document is recognized. *See also* **Exhaustivity.**

Superimposition. A Library of Congress policy decision that only entries being established for the first time would follow *AACR1* rules for form of entry and that only works new to LC would follow *AACR1* rules for choice of entry. When LC adopted *AACR2*, the policy of superimposition was dropped.

Switching language. A mediating or communication indexing language used to establish subject indication equivalencies among various local indexing languages.

Syndetic structure. An organizational framework in which related names, topics, etc., are linked to each other via connective terms such as *see* and *see also*.

Synthetic classification. A classification that assigns designations to single, unsubdivided concepts and gives the classifier generalized rules for combining these designations for composite subjects.

Tagging. *See* **Content designation.**

Technical reading. The process of getting acquainted with a bibliographic entity prior to cataloging, in which various internal sources of information are identified and examined.

Term. A separately represented concept in a thesaurus. *See also* **Subject heading.**

Thesaurus. A specialized authority list of terms used with automated information retrieval systems; very similar to a list of subject headings.

Title. The name of a work, usually identified from the chief source of information of an item. *See also* **Alternative title; Other title information; Parallel title; Title proper; Uniform title.**

Title and statement of responsibility area. The first area of a bibliographic description, which includes the title of a work and information on its authorship.

Title page. A page that occurs very near the beginning of a book and that contains the most complete bibliographic information about the book, such as the author's name, the fullest form of the book's title, the name and/or number of the book's edition, the name of the publisher, and the place and date of publication. *See also* **Chief source of information.**

Title proper. The title that is the chief name of an item; excludes any parallel title or other title information. *See also* **Alternative title; Other title information; Parallel title.**

Tracing. The record on the main entry record of all the additional entries under which the work is listed in the catalog.

Transliteration. A representation of the characters of one alphabet by those of another. *See also* **Romanization.**

UDC. Universal Decimal Classification.

UK/MARC. A machine-readable bibliographic record format compatible with USMARC, developed by British National Bibliography for use in the United Kingdom.

Uniform title. The title chosen for cataloging purposes when a work has appeared under varying titles. *See also* **Title; Work.**

UNIMARC. Universal MARC format, first developed in 1977 by the Library of Congress to be an international communications format for the exchange of machine-readable cataloging records between national bibliographic agencies; the second edition, published in 1980, is being used for international exchange of bibliographic data.

Union catalog. A catalog that lists, completely or in part, the holdings of more than one library or collection.

Unit record. The basic catalog record, in the form of a main entry, which when duplicated may be used as a unit for all other entries for that work in the catalog by the addition of appropriate headings.

Unity analysis. Method of subject analysis in which concepts that make a work cohesive are identified. *See also* **Subject analysis.**

USMARC. A machine-readable bibliographic record format developed by the Library of Congress and originally called LC-MARC.

Utlas International. A computer-based bibliographic network offering its database and services to a variety of Canadian and northeastern United States libraries; formerly UTLAS, University of Toronto Library Automated Systems. *See also* **Bibliographic utility.**

Variable field. A field in a MARC record (1xx-9xx) of variable length. *See also* **Control field; Field; Fixed field.**

Verification. Determining the existence of an author and the form of name as well as the correct title of a particular work; in short, using bibliographic sources to verify (i.e., prove) the existence of an author and/or work.

Vernacular name. A person's name in the form used in reference sources in his or her own country.

Verso. In a book, the page on the left; the side of a leaf intended to be read second. *See also* **Recto.**

Videorecording. A recording originally generated in the form of electronic impulses and designed primarily for television playback. The term includes videocassettes, video-discs, and videotapes.

Volume. In the bibliographical sense, a major division of a work distinguished from the other major divisions of that work by having its own chief source of information.

WLN. Western Library Network, a regional bibliographic network based at the State Library of Washington, now servicing libraries mainly in Alaska, Idaho, Oregon, and Washington. *See also* **Bibliographic utility.**

Work. An intellectual entity; the informational content of a bibliographic entity. *See also* **Bibliographic entity; Item.**

Work form. A card or other form that often accompanies a book throughout the cataloging and preparation processes. The cataloger notes on the work form any directions and information needed to prepare catalog entries, references, etc.

Workmark. A letter (or letters) placed after the cutter number. A workmark may consist of one or two letters, the first of which is the first letter of the title of a work (exclusive of articles). Also called work letter. *See also* **Call number; Cutter number.**

Worksheet. *See* **Work form.**

Bibliography

GENERAL WORKS IN THE AREA OF BIBLIOGRAPHIC CONTROL

Bloomberg, Marty, and G. Edward Evans. *Introduction to Technical Services for Library Technicians.* 5th ed. Littleton, Colo., Libraries Unlimited, 1985.

Chan, Lois Mai. *Cataloging and Classification: An Introduction.* New York, McGraw-Hill, 1981.

Dunkin, Paul S. *Cataloging U.S.A.* Chicago, American Library Association, 1969.

Foster, Donald L. *Managing the Catalog Department.* 3rd ed. Metuchen, N.J., Scarecrow Press, 1987.

Hagler, Ronald. *The Bibliographic Record and Information Technology.* 2nd ed. Chicago, American Library Association, 1991.

Hunter, Eric J., and K. G. B. Bakewell. *Cataloguing.* 3rd ed., revised and expanded. London, Bingley, 1991.

Intner, Sheila S., and Jean Weihs. *Standard Cataloging for School and Public Libraries.* Englewood, Colo., Libraries Unlimited, 1990.

Library Technical Services: Operations and Management. 2nd ed. Edited by Irene P. Godden. San Diego, Calif., Academic Press, 1991.

Miller, Rosalind E., and Jane C. Terwillegar. *Commonsense Cataloging: A Cataloger's Manual.* 4th ed., rev. New York, H. W. Wilson, 1990.

Reynolds, Dennis. *Library Automation: Issues and Applications.* New York, Bowker, 1985.

Saye, Jerry D. *Manheimer's Cataloging and Classification: A Workbook.* 3rd ed., rev. and expanded. New York, Dekker, 1991.

Studwell, William E., and David V. Loertscher. *Cataloging Books: A Workbook of Examples.* Englewood, Colo., Libraries Unlimited, 1989.

Soergel, Dagobert. *Organizing Information: Principles of Data Base and Retrieval Systems.* Orlando, Fla., Academic Press, 1985.

Taylor, Arlene G. *Cataloging with Copy: A Decision-Maker's Handbook.* 2nd ed., with the assistance of Rosanna M. O'Neil. Englewood, Colo., Libraries Unlimited, 1988.

Technical Services Today and Tomorrow. Edited by Michael Gorman. Englewood, Colo., Libraries Unlimited, 1990.

SPECIALIZED WORKS IN THE AREA OF
BIBLIOGRAPHIC CONTROL

Aluri, Rao, D. A. Kemp, and John J. Boll. *Subject Analysis in Online Catalogs.* Englewood, Colo., Libraries Unlimited, 1991.

Authority Control in Music Libraries: Proceedings of the Music Library Association Preconference, March 5, 1985. Edited by Ruth Tucker. Canton, Mass., Music Library Association, 1989.

Authority Control in the Online Environment: Considerations and Practices. Edited by Barbara B. Tillett. New York, Haworth Press, 1989.

Beyond the Book: Extending MARC for Subject Access. Edited by Toni Petersen and Pat Molholt. Boston, G. K. Hall, 1990.

Brown, A. G., in collaboration with D. W. Langridge and J. Mills. *An Introduction to Subject Indexing.* 2nd ed. London, Bingley, 1982.

Chan, Lois Mai. *Library of Congress Subject Headings: Principles of Structure and Policies for Application.* Annotated version. Washington, D.C., Library of Congress, 1990.

Classification of Library Materials: Current and Future Potential for Providing Access. Edited by Betty G. Bengtson and Janet Swan Hill. New York, Neal-Schuman, 1990.

The Conceptual Foundations of Descriptive Cataloging. Edited by Elaine Svenonius. San Diego, Calif., Academic Press, 1989.

Dykstra, Mary. *PRECIS: A Primer.* London, British Library, 1985.

Format Integration and Its Effect on the USMARC Bibliographic Format. Washington, D.C., Library of Congress, Network Development and MARC Standards Office, 1988.

Foskett, A. C. *The Subject Approach to Information.* 4th ed. London, Bingley; Hamden, Conn., Linnet Books, 1982.

Foundations of Cataloging: A Sourcebook. Edited by Michael Carpenter and Elaine Svenonius. Littleton, Colo., Libraries Unlimited, 1985.

Frost, Carolyn O. *Cataloging Nonbook Materials: Problems in Theory and Practice.* Littleton, Colo., Libraries Unlimited, 1983.

_____. *Media Access and Organization: A Cataloging and Reference Sources Guide for Nonbook Materials.* Englewood, Colo., Libraries Unlimited, 1989.

Hensen, Steven L. *Archives, Personal Papers, and Manuscripts: A Cataloging Manual for Archival Repositories, Historical Societies, and Manuscript Libraries.* 2nd ed. Chicago, Society of American Archivists, 1989.

Hunter, Eric J. *Classification Made Simple.* Aldershot, England; Brookfield, Vt., Gower, 1988.

Langridge, D. W. *Subject Analysis: Principles and Procedures.* London, Bowker-Saur, 1989.

MARC Format Integration: Three Perspectives. Edited by Michael Gorman. Chicago, American Library Association, Library Information and Technology Association, 1990.

Miksa, Francis. *The Subject in the Dictionary Catalog from Cutter to the Present.* Chicago, American Library Association, 1983.

Policy and Practice in Bibliographic Control of Nonbook Media. Edited by Sheila S. Intner and Richard P. Smiraglia. Chicago, American Library Association, 1987.

Smiraglia, Richard P. *Music Cataloging: The Bibliographic Control of Printed and Recorded Music in Libraries.* Englewood, Colo., Libraries Unlimited, 1989.

Subject Authorities in the Online Environment: Papers from a Conference Program Held in San Francisco, June 29, 1987. Edited by Karen Markey Drabenstott. Chicago, American Library Association, 1991.

Theory of Subject Analysis: A Sourcebook. Edited by Lois Mai Chan, Phyllis A. Richmond, and Elaine Svenonius. Littleton, Colo., Libraries Unlimited, 1985.

Weihs, Jean. *The Integrated Library: Encouraging Access to Multimedia Materials.* Phoenix, Ariz., Oryx Press, 1991.

Weihs, Jean, with Shirley Lewis. *Non-book Materials: The Organization of Integrated Collections.* 3rd ed. Ottawa, Canada, Canadian Library Association, 1989.

CODES, SCHEDULES, STANDARDS, AND MANUALS

Description, Entry, and Heading

General

Anglo-American Cataloguing Rules, Second Edition, 1988 Revision. Prepared by the Joint Steering Committee for Revision of AACR; ed. by Michael Gorman and Paul W. Winkler. Chicago, American Library Association, 1988.

CDMARC Names. Washington, D.C., Library of Congress, 1989- . Quarterly, with each issue cumulative.

The Complete Cataloging Reference Set: Collected Manuals of the Minnesota AACR 2 Trainers. Edited by Nancy B. Olson and Edward Swanson. DeKalb, Ill., Minnesota Scholarly Press, 1988.

Gorman, Michael. *The Concise AACR2, 1988 Revision.* Chicago, American Library Association, 1989.

Hunter, Eric J. *Examples Illustrating AACR2, 1988 Revision.* London, Library Association, 1989.

———, *An Introduction to AACR 2: A Programmed Guide to the Second Edition of the Anglo-American Cataloguing Rules 1988 Revision.* Rev. ed. London, Bingley, 1989.

International Federation of Library Associations. *ISBD(G): General International Standard Bibliographic Description: Annotated Text.* London, International Office for UBC, 1977.

Library of Congress Rule Interpretations. 2nd ed. Washington, D.C., Library of Congress, 1989- . Loose-leaf, with updates.

Library of Congress Rule Interpretations for AACR2, 1988 Revision: A Cumulation through Cataloging Service Bulletin.... Compiled by Alan Boyd and Elaine Druesedow. Oberlin, Ohio, Oberlin College Library, 1989- . Loose-leaf, with updates.

Maxwell, Margaret F. *Handbook for AACR2 1988 Revision: Explaining and Illustrating the Anglo-American Cataloguing Rules.* Chicago, American Library Association, 1989.

Piggott, Mary. *The Cataloguer's Way through AACR2: From Document Receipt to Document Retrieval.* London, Library Association, 1990.

Salinger, Florence A., and Eileen Zagon. *Notes for Catalogers: A Sourcebook for Use with AACR 2.* Boston, G. K. Hall, 1988, c1985.

Saye, Jerry D., and Sherry Vellucci. *Notes in the Catalog Record Based on AACR2 and LC Rule Interpretations.* Chicago, American Library Association, 1989.

Swanson, Edward. *Changes to the Anglo-American Cataloguing Rules, Second Edition, as Published in the 1988 Revision.* Lake Crystal, Minn., Soldier Creek Press, 1989.

Weihs, Jean, and Lynne Howarth. *A Brief Guide to AACR2, 1988 Revision, and Implications for Automated Systems.* Ottawa, Canada, Canadian Library Association, 1988.

Specialized by Type of Material

Cartographic Materials: A Manual of Interpretation for AACR 2. Chicago, American Library Association, 1982.

Descriptive Cataloging of Rare Books. 2nd ed. Washington, D.C., Library of Congress, 1991.

Dodd, Sue A., and Ann M. Sandberg-Fox. *Cataloging Microcomputer Files: A Manual of Interpretation for AACR2.* Chicago, American Library Association, 1985.

International Standard Bibliographic Description.
The following ISBDs have been published by the International Federation of Library Associations and Institutions:

ISBD(A): International Standard Bibliographic Description for Older Monographic Publications (Antiquarian). 2nd rev. ed. 1991.

ISBD(CF): International Standard Bibliographic Description for Computer Files. 1990.

ISBD(CM): International Standard Bibliographic Description for Cartographic Materials. Rev. ed. 1987.

ISBD(M): International Standard Bibliographic Description for Monographic Publications. Rev. ed. 1987.

ISBD(NBM): International Standard Bibliographic Description for Non-Book Materials. Rev. ed. 1987.

ISBD(PM): International Standard Bibliographic Description for Printed Music. Rev. ed. 1989.

ISBD(S): International Standard Bibliographic Description for Serials. Rev. ed. 1988.

Leong, Carol L. H. *Serials Cataloging Handbook: An Illustrative Guide to the Use of AACR2 and LC Rule Interpretations.* Chicago, American Library Association, 1989.

Olson, Nancy B. *Cataloging Microcomputer Software: A Manual to Accompany AACR2, Chapter 9, Computer Files.* Englewood, Colo., Libraries Unlimited, 1988.

_____. *Cataloging Motion Pictures and Videorecordings.* Lake Crystal, Minn., Soldier Creek Press, 1991.

_____. *Cataloging of Audiovisual Materials: A Manual Based on AACR2.* 3rd ed., completely rev. and expanded. DeKalb, Ill., Media Marketing Group, 1991.

Rogers, JoAnn V., with Jerry D. Saye. *Nonprint Cataloging for Multimedia Collections: A Guide Based on AACR2.* 2nd ed. Littleton, Colo., Libraries Unlimited, 1987.

Smiraglia, Richard P. *Cataloging Music: A Manual for Use with AACR2.* 2nd ed. Lake Crystal, Minn., Soldier Creek Press, 1986.

Thomas, Nancy G., and Rosanna O'Neil. *Notes for Serials Cataloging.* Littleton, Colo., Libraries Unlimited, 1986.

Subject Headings

Canadian Subject Headings. 2nd ed. Ottawa, National Library of Canada, 1985.

CDMARC Subjects. Washington, D.C., Library of Congress, 1988- . Quarterly, with each issue cumulative.

Chan, Lois. *Library of Congress Subject Headings: Principles and Applications.* 2nd ed. Littleton, Colo., Libraries Unlimited, 1986.

Documentation: Methods for Examining Documents, Determining Their Subjects and Selecting Indexing Terms. Geneva, Switzerland, International Organization for Standardization, 1986.

Free-Floating Subdivisions: An Alphabetical Index. Washington, D.C., Library of Congress, 1989- . Annual.

Guidelines on Subject Access to Individual Works of Fiction, Drama, Etc. Chicago, American Library Association, 1990.

Guidelines on Subject Access to Microcomputer Software. Chicago, American Library Association, 1986.

Haycock, Ken, and Lynne Lighthall, comps. *Sears List of Subject Headings: Canadian Companion.* 3rd ed. New York, H. W. Wilson, 1987.

Haykin, David Judson. *Subject Headings: A Practical Guide.* Washington, D.C., GPO, 1951.

Library of Congress Subject Headings. 13th- eds. Washington, D.C., Library of Congress, Office for Subject Cataloging Policy, 1990- . Annual.

Library of Congress Subject Headings in Microform. Washington, D.C., Library of Congress, Subject Cataloging Division, 1976- . Quarterly, with each issue cumulative.

Library of Congress Subject Headings Weekly Lists. Washington, D.C., Library of Congress, Subject Cataloging Division, January 1984- . Monthly.

Sears List of Subject Headings. 14th ed., edited by Martha T. Mooney. New York, H. W. Wilson, 1991.

Subject Cataloging Manual: Subject Headings. 3rd ed. Washington, D.C., Library of Congress, 1988.

Classification

Abridged Dewey Decimal Classification and Relative Index. 12th ed. Albany, N.Y., Forest Press, 1990.

Chan, Lois M. *Immroth's Guide to the Library of Congress Classification.* 4th ed. Englewood, Colo., Libraries Unlimited, 1990.

Comaromi, John Phillip. *Dewey Decimal Classification, 20th Edition: A Study Manual.* Englewood, Colo., Libraries Unlimited, 1991.

Dewey Decimal Classification and Relative Index. 20th ed. Edited by John P. Comaromi et al. Albany, N.Y., Forest Press, 1989.

Dewey Decimal Classification Additions, Notes and Decisions. Vol. 5, no. 1- . Albany, N.Y., Forest Press, 1990- . Annual.

LC Classification—Additions and Changes. Washington, D.C., Library of Congress, Subject Cataloging Division, 1928- . Quarterly.

LC Classification Outline. 6th ed. Washington, D.C., Library of Congress, Subject Cataloging Division, 1991.

Library of Congress Classification: Classes A-Z. Var. eds. Washington, D.C., Library of Congress, Subject Cataloging Division, 1933- .

Library of Congress Classification Schedules [Classes A-Z]: A Cumulation of Additions and Changes through.... Detroit, Gale Research Co., 1974- .

Library of Congress Classification Schedules Combined with Additions and Changes through ...: Classes A-Z. Edited by Rita Runchock, Kathleen Droste, and Victoria A. Coughlin. Detroit, Gale Research Co., 1988- . Annual.

Olson, Nancy B. *Combined Indexes to the Library of Congress Classification Schedules.* Washington, D.C., United States Historical Documents Institute, 1974.

USMARC Format for Classification Data: Including Guidelines for Content Designation. Washington, D.C., Library of Congress, Network Development and MARC Standards Office, 1991.

Shelflisting

Comaromi, John P. *Book Numbers: A Historical Study and Practical Guide to Their Use.* Littleton, Colo., Libraries Unlimited, 1981.

Cutter, Charles Ammi. *Three-Figure Author Table.* Swanson-Swift revision, 1969. Distributed by Libraries Unlimited, Littleton, Colo.

_____. *Two-Figure Author Table.* Swanson-Swift revision, 1969. Distributed by Libraries Unlimited, Littleton, Colo.

Cutter-Sanborn Three-Figure Author Table. Swanson-Swift revision, 1969. Distributed by Libraries Unlimited, Littleton, Colo.

Lehnus, Donald J. *Book Numbers: History, Principles, and Application.* Chicago, American Library Association, 1980.

Subject Cataloging Manual: Shelflisting. Washington, D.C., Library of Congress, Subject Cataloging Division, 1986.

Authority Control

Burger, Robert H. *Authority Work: The Creation, Use, Maintenance, and Evaluation of Authority Records and Files.* Littleton, Colo., Libraries Unlimited, 1985.

Clack, Doris Hargrett. *Authority Control: Principles, Applications, and Instructions.* Chicago, American Library Association, 1990.

UNIMARC/Authorities: Universal Format for Authorities. London, IFLA Universal Bibliographic Control and International MARC Programme, 1989.

USMARC Format for Authority Data: Including Guidelines for Content Designation. Washington, D.C., Library of Congress, Network Development and MARC Standards Office, 1989- . Loose-leaf, with updates.

MARC Format

Byrne, Deborah J. *MARC Manual: Understanding and Using MARC Records.* Englewood, Colo., Libraries Unlimited, 1991.

Crawford, Walt. *MARC for Library Use: Understanding Integrated USMARC.* 2nd ed. Boston, G. K. Hall, 1989.

UNIMARC Manual. Edited by Brian P. Holt, with the assistance of Sally H. McCallum and A. B. Long. London, IFLA Universal Bibliographic Control and International MARC Programme, 1987.

UNIMARC: Universal MARC Format. 2nd ed. rev. London, IFLA International Office for UBC, 1980.

USMARC CONCISE Formats for Bibliographic, Authority, and Holdings Data: Including Guidelines for Content Designation. Washington, D.C., Library of Congress, Network Development and MARC Standards Office, 1988.

USMARC Format for Bibliographic Data: Including Guidelines for Content Designation. Washington, D.C., Library of Congress, Network Development and MARC Standards Office, 1988- . Loose-leaf, with updates.

USMARC Format for Holdings Data: Including Guidelines for Content Designation. Washington, D.C., Library of Congress, Network Development and MARC Standards Office, 1989- . Loose-leaf, with updates.

USMARC Format: Proposed Changes. Washington, D.C., Library of Congress, Network Development and MARC Standards Office, 1984- . Semiannual.

Filing

ALA Filing Rules. Chicago, American Library Association, 1980.

Carothers, Diane Foxhill. *Self-Instruction Manual for Filing Catalog Cards.* Chicago, American Library Association, 1981.

Library of Congress Filing Rules. Washington, D.C., Library of Congress, 1980.

Current Information and Updating

ALCTS Newsletter, v. 1, no. 1- . Chicago, American Library Association, Association for Library Collections & Technical Services, 1990- . Eight no. a year. [Supersedes *RTSD Newsletter,* v.1, no. 1 – v. 14, no. 6 (1976-1989).]

Cataloging & Classification Quarterly. Binghamton, N.Y., Haworth Press, 1979- . Quarterly.

Cataloging Service Bulletin, no. 1- . Washington, D.C., Library of Congress, 1978- . Quarterly. [Supersedes *Cataloging Service,* bulletins 1-125 (1945-1978).]

Library of Congress Information Bulletin. Washington, D.C., Library of Congress, 1942- . Weekly.

Library Resources & Technical Services. Chicago, American Library Association, 1957- . Quarterly.

Terminology

ALA Glossary of Library and Information Science. Chicago, American Library Association, 1983.

Prytherch, Ray. *Harrod's Librarians' Glossary of Terms Used in Librarianship, Documentation and the Book Crafts, and Reference Book.* 7th ed. Aldershot, England; Brookfield, Vt., Gower, 1990.

Author/Title/Subject Index

Several italicized indicator words appear in this index:

Example means particular index entry (or subentry) is to a sample of a bibliographic record.

Key means index entry (or subentry) is to a list of words aiding in interpretation or identification of a figure or example.

Surrogate means index entry (or subentry) is to a facsimile of a catalogable item.

ISSN, 503
  defined, 581
  for serials, 176
  for series, 71
  standard number and terms of avail-
      ability area, 76-77
  for subseries, 71
Item, defined, 581
Item-level cataloging, 97
Items made up of several types of materials.
  See Materials, items of mixed; Kits

JSC. *See* Joint Steering Committee for
    Revision of AACR
Jefferson, Thomas, 318
Jewett, Charles C., 495
Johnson, Edward William, 318
Joint author, defined, 581
Joint Steering Committee for Revision
    of AACR (JSC), 34
Jurisdictions. *See also* Government bodies
    and officials
  access points for administrative
      regulations, 219-220
  government bodies, 263-264
  place names of, 254
  in subject headings, 410

Kemp, Alasdair, 326
Key headings (*Sears*), 444. *See also*
    Pattern headings
Key-titles, for serials, 76, 176
Key Word In Context. *See* KWIC
Key Word Out of Context. See KWOC
Keyword indexing, defined, 581
Keyword searching, 398, 426, 454, 462
Kits
  GMD for, 53, 54, 115
  rules for describing, 73
KWIC indexing, 458, 461, 464-466, 581
KWOC indexing, 458, 464-466, 581

LaFontaine, Henri, 346
Lancaster, F. W., 467
Langridge, D. W., 309
Language, of item
  notes on
    cartographic materials, 131
    manuscripts, 131
    motion pictures and videorecordings,
      131

    music, 131
    printed monographs, 90
    serials, 173
    sound recordings, 131
Language and form of name
  for corporate bodies, 259-261
  for personal names, 231-234
Language tables (DDC), 340
Large print, added as qualifier to GMD, 54
Laws
  access points for, 218-219
  uniform titles for, 286-287
LC. *See entries beginning with* Library
    of Congress *or* LC
LC Authority File (LCAF), 410, 411, 478,
    479, 503
LC Catalog, Books: Subjects for 1965-
    1969, 357
LC Classification Outline for Alert
    Service, 498
LC Filing Rules. *See* Filing
LC-MARC. *See* MARC; USMARC
L.C. Subject Headings Weekly Lists, 405,
    449
LCAF. *See* LC Authority File
LCC. *See* Library of Congress
    Classification
LCSAF. *See* LC Subject Authority File
LCSH. See Library of Congress Subject
    Headings
Leaf, defined, 582
Legal materials
  access points for, 218-220
  uniform titles for, 286-287
Legislative bodies, form of name for, 274
Library and Information Science Abstracts
    (LISA), 389
Library Association, 30, 33
Library classification. *See* Classification
Library Journal (LJ), 497
Library of Congress. *See also* Cataloging
    Distribution Service; MARC
    Distribution Service
  bibliographic services, 493, 496-501
  cataloging codes, 30, 33, 36
  cataloging publications, 496-501
  CDMARC Subjects, 405
  CDS Alert Service, 496, 498, 526
  Cutter numbers, 375-379
  manuals. *See Subject Cataloging*
    Manual
  MARC tapes, 48, 459, 496, 497, 498,
    501, 502, 507